D0754766

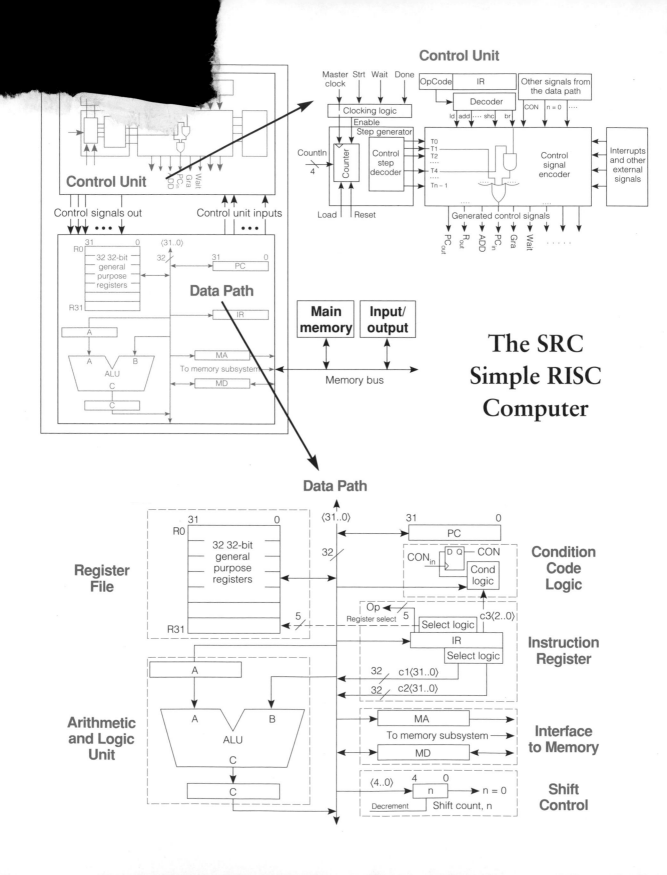

The SRC
Simple RISC
Computer

Register File

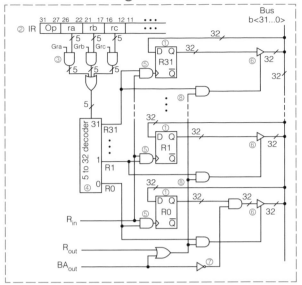

Instruction Register

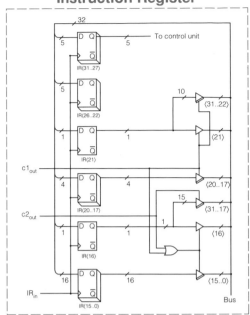

Arithmetic and Logic Unit

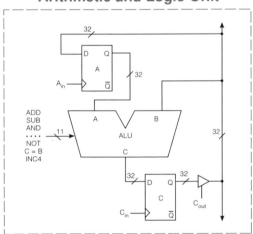

Interface to Memory

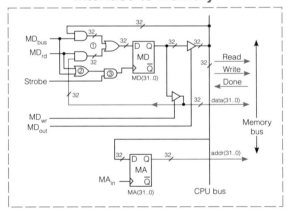

Shift Control

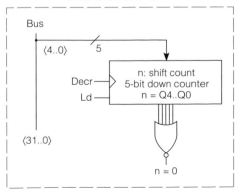

Condition Code Logic

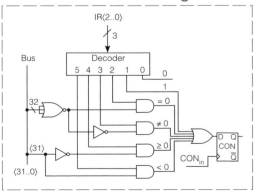

Computer Systems
Design and Architecture
Second Edition

Vincent P. Heuring

UNIVERSITY OF COLORADO, BOULDER

Harry F. Jordan

LATE, OF THE UNIVERSITY OF COLORADO, BOULDER

with a contribution by

Miles Murdocca

INTERNET INSTITUTE USA

PEARSON

Prentice
Hall

Pearson Education International

Vice President and Editorial Director, ECS: *Marcia J. Horton*
Vice President and Director of Production and Manufacturing, ESM: *David W. Riccardi*
Executive Managing Editor: *Vince O'Brien*
Managing Editor: *David A. George*
Production Editor: *Joan Wolk*
Director of Creative Services: *Paul Belfanti*
Art Director: *Jayne Conte*
Cover Manager: *Bruce Kenselaar*
Managing Editor, AV Management and Production: *Patricia Burns*
Art Editor: *Xiaohong Zhu*
Manufacturing Manager: *Trudy Pisciotti*
Manufacturing Buyer: *Lynda Castillo*
Marketing Manager: *Holly Stark*

© 2004, 1997 Pearson Education, Inc.
Pearson Prentice Hall
Pearson Education, Inc.
Upper Saddle River, NJ 07458

All rights reserved. No part of this book may be reproduced in any form or by any means, without permission in writing from the publisher.

If you purchased this book within the United States or Canada you should be aware that it has been wrongfully imported without the approval of the Publisher or the Author.

Pearson Prentice Hall® is a trademark of Pearson Education, Inc.

The author and publisher of this book have used their best efforts in preparing this book. These efforts include the development, research, and testing of the theories and programs to determine their effectiveness. The author and publisher make no warranty of any kind, expressed or implied, with regard to these programs or the documentation contained in this book. The author and publisher shall not be liable in any event for incidental or consequential damages in connection with, or arising out of, the furnishing, performance, or use of these programs.

Printed in the United States of America

10 9 8 7 6 5 4 3 2 1

ISBN 0-13-191156-2

Pearson Education Ltd., *London*
Pearson Education Australia Pty. Ltd., *Sydney*
Pearson Education Singapore, Pte. Ltd.
Pearson Education North Asia Ltd., *Hong Kong*
Pearson Education Canada, Inc., *Toronto*
Pearson Educación de Mexico, S.A. de C.V.
Pearson Education—Japan, *Tokyo*
Pearson Education Malaysia, Pte. Ltd.
Pearson Education, Inc., *Upper Saddle River, New Jersey*

This book is dedicated to the memory of
Harry Jordan,
who died during the preparation of this second edition.

Trademark Acknowledgments

8008, 8080, 8086, Intel, Pentium, and P6 are registered trademarks of the Intel Corporation.

68000, 68010, 68020, 68040, and PPC601 are trademarks of the Motorola Corporation.

Alpha, DECnet, PDP-11, VAX, and VAX11/780 are trademarks of the Digital Equipment Corporation.

AppleTalk, LocalTalk, Macintosh, Macintosh Quadra, FireWire and QuickDraw are registered trademarks of Apple Computer, Inc.

Centronics is a registered trademark of the Centronics Data Computer Corporation.

Espresso is a registered trademark of Berkeley Systems, Inc.

FAST is a registered trademark of National Semiconductor in France, Italy, Canada, the United States, and the Benelux countries.

HPGL and PCL are registered trademarks of the Hewlett-Packard Company.

IBM, 360, and System/360 are trademarks of the International Business Machines Corporation.

Maxtor and LARAMIE are trademarks of the Maxtor Corporation.

MIPS, R3000, and R4000 MIPS are trademarks of MIPS Technology, Inc.

NetWare is a registered trademark of Novell, Inc.

NuBus is a trademark of Texas Instruments, Inc.

PostScript is a registered trademark of Adobe Systems, Inc.

SPARC and UltraSparc are registered trademarks of SPARC, International Inc., licensed to Sun Microsystems, Inc.

Tri-state is a registered trademark of National Semiconductor in member nations of the Madrid Convention.

The UNIX trademark is licensed exclusively through the X/Open Company Ltd.

VITESSE is a registered trademark of the Vitesse Semiconductor Corporation.

Windows is a registered trademark of the Microsoft Corporation.

XNS is a trademark of the Xerox Corporation.

Contents

APPENDIX B

RTN Description of SRC

APPENDIX C

Assembly and Assemblers

APPENDIX D

Selected Problems and Solutions

Index

Preface

To the Instructor

This book is suitable for an introductory course on computer design at the junior, senior, or introductory graduate level. We assume that the student has had at least an introductory course in some high-level programming language such as C or Pascal, and a semester of logic design. However, a comprehensive appendix on digital logic design, written by Professor Miles Murdocca of the Internet Institute USA, provides sufficient background material for teaching the course to students without previous digital design experience.

Appropriate topics for such a book have changed considerably in recent years, as desktop computers have evolved from simple, stand-alone units into complex systems attached to high-speed networks and internetworks. Earlier generations of microprocessors had almost trivial internal structure. Present designs contain multiple pipelined functional units with support for multiple processors and memories. Areas of computer design and architecture that were barely touched upon in the not-so-distant past have become major topics for discussion. Introductory compiler courses now routinely discuss optimization for pipelined processors. Users worry about whether they should add level-2 cache memory to their PCs. Support personnel wearily try to explain to the computer user how to configure the subnet mask for their network slip connection.

The topics of pipelined processor design, the memory hierarchy, and networks and internetworking are moving to center stage in the arena of computer design and architecture. Therefore we devoted the major parts of three chapters to treatment of these subjects.

Given the focus on computer design and computer architecture, we approach the study of the computer from three viewpoints: the view of the assembly/machine language programmer, the view of the logic designer, and the view of the system architect.

In covering the topic of gate-level computer design, we follow a model architecture through the design process, from the instruction set

appendix on digital logic design

pipelined processors

memory hierarchy

networking and the Internet

three views of the general purpose machine

ix

design level to the processor design level. Given the choice of using either a commercial machine with all of the complicating features that are necessary to make such a machine commercially successful, or using a model design that introduces enough practical features to make it both interesting and relevant to the subject, we chose the latter. The model machine, Simple RISC Computer (SRC), is a 32-bit machine with an instruction set architecture that is similar to, but simpler than the current generation of RISCs.

model machine:
Simple RISC
Computer (SRC)

We adopt the view that it is best to use a formal description language in describing machine structure and function. There are many languages from which to choose. We selected a variant of the ISP language, Register Transfer Notation (RTN). We chose this from many alternatives, because most of the languages used by practitioners are aimed more at hardware description and less at machine behavior and function. RTN is simple, easy to learn, and is at the appropriate description level.

formal description
language:
Register Transfer
Notation (RTN)

To the Student

The computer ushers us into the information age. Born a mere fifty years ago, it now exerts a profound influence on almost every facet of our lives. What is the nature of this machine? How does it work inside? How is it programmed internally? What is the nature of each of its connections to the outside world? These are the questions that this book will help you answer, and we hope that when you have mastered it you will be left with no mysteries about how computers work. We feel that one of the best ways to learn how a computer works is to design one, so throughout most of the book we have taken the perspective of the designer rather than that of the observer or the critic.

Computers are arguably the most complex systems humankind has ever built, and like all complex systems they can be appreciated from many viewpoints. A building can be examined for its overall architectural design, and for the way its design affects its overall function. A building also can be examined from the viewpoint of how the size and shape of its rooms and halls relate to the design of its heating and air conditioning systems. Likewise a computer can be examined from the viewpoint of *its* overall structure and function, referred to as its architecture. A computer also can be examined from the viewpoint of one who is using machine or assembly language to program it. And it can be examined from the viewpoint of its lowest abstract logical structure—its design at the logic gate level.

All of these viewpoints are interrelated, and therefore important for mastery of the subject; thus in this book we adopt all three: the viewpoint of the computer architect, the viewpoint of the assembly language programmer, and the viewpoint of the logic designer. We believe that the synthesis of these three views will give you a depth and richness of understanding of the subject that will serve you well, whether your main interest is in computer design, computer science, or computer programming.

We assume that you have had experience with computers as an end-user, and that you have written programs in some high-level language such as Pascal, C, or FORTRAN. We also assume, in the body of the text, that you have had exposure to digital logic circuits. A knowledge of logic circuits is necessary for the understanding of the material in this book. For those who have not had such exposure, or who are uncertain about whether their background in this area is adequate, we have included Appendix A: Digital Logic Circuits, which should provide you with sufficient background for understanding this text.

Preface to the Second Edition

It is a truism that computer design and architecture textbooks are out of date before the printer's ink is dry. Such is always the case in a field as dynamic and growing as ours. While this places more burden on the authors to revise, update, and release new editions, it also presents opportunities to introduce new material, new tools, and new or expanded discussions of old topics. All of these factors contributed to the desire to develop a second edition of *Computer Systems Design and Architecture* (CSDA). We have continued to adhere to the principle of "no mysteries" in this edition, especially as it pertains to the fundamentals of computer design.

no mysteries

This approach has meant sacrificing ancillary or overly descriptive materials relating to modern processors to keep the textbook to a reasonable size. It was, and continues to be our philosoply that a thorough grounding in the fundamental principles of computer design rather than a more superficial discussion of the architectures *du jour* will better meet the needs of students to master the architectures of the future.

New in the second edition:

Tools   Java-based assemblers and simulators with GUI-based interfaces are now available for SRC, the MC68000, and ARC, a SPARC subset. The simulators run on the PC and Macintosh OSX platforms, and all Unix and Linux implementations that run the Java Virtual Machine. VHDL and LogicWorks models of SRC are also available.

The following new or expanded topics have been added:

All chapters have been brought up to date with current information. There are many new and modified Exercises and Examples, including a new feature, Classic Example.

Chapter 2   Expanded discussion of the timing of bus operations during register transfers, including a timing diagram.

Chapter 2   A greatly expanded discussion of performance measurement and estimation. New material on the Pentium 4 architecture.

Chapter 3   New section on calculating performance/speedup.

Chapter 4   Details of the SRC ALU design. New material on SRC control signals.

Chapter 5   Expanded discussion of instruction-level parallelism, including a VLIW design for SRC.

Chapter 7   Discussion and example of temporal and spatial locality. Discussion and examples of SDRAM and DDR RAM.

Chapter 8   Summary of SRC I/O ports. New section using Venn Diagrams to motivate the discussion of Hamming and SECDED encoding.

Chapter 9   New section on Disk System reliability, including RAID and SMART disk drives.

Chapter 10   New section on Gigabit Ethernet. New section on Modern Serial Buses: USB and Firewire. New section on Wasted IP address space: CIDR classless routing, NAT, and DHCP.

Appendix C: Rewritten to target the SRC assembler instead of the 68K assembler. More detailed discussion of the symbol table and the assembly process.

Appendix D: Due to popular student demand, Appendix D, Selected Problems and Solutions, was added. This appendix contains a selection of "classic" problems in computer design and architecture.

Using This Book with Your Curriculum and Syllabus

There are probably almost as many different curricula and syllabi for computer design and architecture as there are schools and instructors in which the subject is taught. As you evaluate the material in this book you may discover the following:

- Some topics may have been covered in a prerequisite course, and so can be omitted.

- Some topics need not be covered because they are covered in a subsequent course or courses.

- Some topics can be omitted or emphasized because of the aims of the course or the instructor. For example, computer science curricula may stress architectural topics and deemphasize the gate-level design material, whereas computer engineering curricula would stress gate-level design.

- Some instructors will choose to emphasize or deemphasize certain topics or change the topic ordering because of their particular philosophy of how the material should be presented.

We have tried to make the topic coverage sufficiently inclusive and self-contained so that you can adapt it to suit your curricula and syllabi. The following figure presents a chart of chapter dependences to aid you in selecting the topics and topic ordering to suit your particular needs. The first two chapters set the stage for the rest of the book, and should be covered first. Chapter 3 treats real machine designs and is essential for any student without a solid background in CISC and RISC instruction sets. Chapters 4 and 5 pursue gate-level design of the CPU. Each of Chapters 6–10 is virtually stand-alone, and can be selected to suit the needs of your particular curriculum and syllabus.

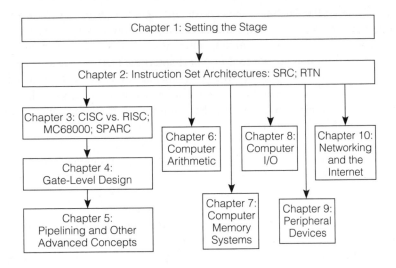

Chapter Descriptions

Chapter 1 takes a brief look at the machine from all three levels, and provides an overview on the subject.

Chapter 2 begins with a discussion of the relationship between machines and machine languages—how the nature of the instruction set influences the rest of the CPU structure. At this point we introduce a language for *formally* describing machine structure and function. That is, we provide a way to unambiguously describe both the machine hardware and how instructions run on it. That language, RTN, is a simple one, and it is at the "just right" level to describe the running of instructions on hardware. We introduce RTN by using it to describe a generic model machine, SRC, that has a 32-bit ISA similar to the current crop of 32-bit commercial machines, but without many of the complicating factors. The chapter concludes by switching to the logic circuit level and putting a computer design spin on conventional logic circuit design by a brief discussion of how RTN operations translate into circuit designs.

The goal of Chapter 3 is to provide the student with a concrete understanding of the difference between CISC and RISC machines. It discusses two commercial machines at the ISA (and RTN) level: the CISC Motorola MC68000 and the RISC SPARC. The chapter provides familiarity with several different machine architectures at the ISA level, so that students develop an appreciation for two philosophically different approaches to machine design. We also discuss some practical issues, such as upward compatibility, and how those issues influence machine design.

Chapter 4 is in many ways the keystone chapter of the book. It describes the interface between the instruction set and the hardware that it runs on, at the gate level. This description unfolds by developing a 1-bus design for the SRC introduced in Chapter 2, with RTN descriptions of machine functioning as a guide. Beginning with the ISA registers, the RTN description adds additional registers that are hidden at the ISA level as it treats how instructions are fetched, decoded, and executed, again at gate level. The discussion proceeds with

CISC versus
RISC machines

CISC: MC68000

RISC: SPARC

Instruction Set
Architectures (ISA)

keystone chapter

design of the "soul of the machine," the control unit, and its heartbeat, the system clocking and timing. This chapter also begins the discussion of how hardware design influences instruction execution speed by examining alternative 2- and 3-bus designs. Two other aspects of processor design are covered in this chapter: the hardware reset, and the exception process. Our goal in Chapter 4 is to leave no mysteries. At the end of the chapter, the student should understand exactly how the central processing unit works at the gate level.

Chapter 5 covers pipelining of the CPU, multiple-instruction-issue machines, and microcoded control unit design. Nearly every current and planned processor design employs pipelining in its CPU, and a thorough understanding of how pipelining works is a necessity for everyone from compiler writers to machine programmers and architects. We first present an overview of the important issues in pipelining and then show the pipeline design process by way of a pipelined design for SRC. A discussion of instruction-level parallelism follows. We treat superscalar operation, where there are multiple functional units in the CPU that are capable of parallel operation, and VLIW, very long instruction word machines, whose instruction words contain a number of processing steps that are executed in parallel. We include an example of a VLIW implementation of SRC. The chapter concludes with a discussion of microcoding. Microcoding is not used much in general purpose microprocessor chips at present, but in addition to its use in fast-turn-around and adaptable special purpose designs, it presents an interesting perspective on computer design.

Chapter 6 covers the design of the arithmetic and logic unit (ALU) of the computer. The design of this very important CPU component has a major impact on overall system performance. Since much of the ALU's performance is based on the underlying algorithms that are implemented in the hardware design, the discussion proceeds from data type (e.g., integer), to algorithm (e.g., addition), to the hardware implementation (e.g., a carry lookahead fast adder). Both integer and floating-point data types are covered. A section is included on how branch instructions use the ALU with a discussion of logic operations and overall ALU design. The chapter concludes with a discussion of floating-point arithmetic.

Chapter 7 presents the design of the memory hierarchy in detail. Beginning with the simplest 1-bit RAM and ROM cells, the chapter builds those cells into chips, chips into boards, and boards into modules. We discuss the general nature of the relationship between two adjacent levels in the hierarchy, and following that, we discuss cache design and the interaction between cache and main memory. This is followed by a discussion of virtual memory, the process of allowing the memory space to spill out from main memory onto the disk. The chapter concludes with a discussion of memory as a system.

Chapter 8 discusses the details of the machine's I/O system. It begins with a treatment of several kinds of buses, treating both bus signals and bus timing, and proceeds with a discussion of the two principal kinds of generic I/O interfaces, serial and parallel. The chapter then covers the relationship between the machine interrupt structure and the I/O system, and between these two and DMA, direct memory access, by which an external device can access main memory without CPU intervention.

Chapter 9 covers the other end of the I/O system: peripheral devices. It treats the structure and functioning of disk drives, video and other interactive display devices, printers, mice, and the interfaces to analog devices. The emphasis is on how these devices actually work, and the nature of the interface between them, the CPU, and the outside world. Peripheral device performance is covered as a main aspect of interest.

Chapter 10 concludes the book with a discussion of computer-to-computer communications. No current treatment of computer systems design and architecture is complete without a fairly in-depth discussion of computer communications and networking. We begin with a discussion of network structure and topology. Following that we present three examples of contemporary machine communications. The first example is the RS-232 serial data communications protocol that permits point-to-point communications between two computers or between a computer and a terminal. The second example is the Ethernet local area network (LAN). We discuss the Ethernet communications protocol at both the physical level and the data link layer, including the Ethernet packet structure, and higher-speed implementations. We also discuss USB and Firewire. The final example of a communications system is the Internet—probably the largest and most important computer communications system on the planet. We discuss the TCP/IP Internet protocol, and Internet addresses and addressing. Also discussed is the wasting of IP addresses by the class A, B, C system, and the use of CIDR, DHCP, and NAT to reclaim them. The chapter, and the book conclude with a very brief discussion of Internet applications and Internet futures.

computers and
networking

RS-232 data
communications

the Ethernet LAN

the Internet

TCP/IP

Internet addresses
and addressing

Instructional Support Materials

For the latest information on these supplements and how to obtain instructional support materials, contact your Prentice-Hall sales representative or visit the Prentice-Hall web site at http://www.prenhall.com.

Solutions Manual   The Solutions Manual contains solutions to virtually all end-of-chapter exercises in *Computer Systems Design and Architecture.*

Electronic Lecture Slides   This set of approximately 600 slides is available in two formats, Adobe Acrobat and Microsoft PowerPoint. The slides include the book's main points presented in a lecture outline format, and nearly all figures and tables from the text. Using the free Acrobat Reader, the transparencies in the Acrobat format can be viewed and printed in various ways from PC, Macintosh, and UNIX platforms. Instructors who have access to PowerPoint can modify the slides in the PowerPoint format. The slides are available at ftp://schof.colorado.edu/pub/CSDA.

Software Support Tools   A growing collection of software support tools are available to adopters by ftp. These tools include Java-based SRC, MC68000, and SPARC subset assemblers and simulators that will run on the PC, Macintosh OSX, and Unix and Linux platforms. VHDL and LogicWorks implementations of SRC are also available. The tools and several other resources are available at ftp://schof.colorado.edu/pub/CSDA.

If You Find an Error

In spite of the good efforts of the authors, editors, reviewers, and class testers, this book undoubtedly contains errors. Please send reports of errors to csdabugs@colorado.edu

Acknowledgments

We also wish to thank our first edition reviewers, who were most helpful in suggesting changes to the original manuscript of this book: George Adams (School of Electrical and Computer Engineering, Purdue University), Dr. Hassan Barada (Computer Engineering Department, King Fahd University of Petroleum and Minerals, Dhahran, Saudi Arabia), Thomas L. Casavant (Electrical and Computer Engineering, University of Iowa), Dr. Peter Drexel (Department of Computer Science, Plymouth State College), Michael A. Driscoll (Department of Electrical Engineering, Portland State University), J. Kelly Flanagan (Computer Science Department, Brigham Young University), Richard Heuring (Cinch Enterprises), William Tsun-yuk Hsu (Computer Science Department, San Francisco State University), Mariusz Jankowski (Department of Engineering, University of Southern Maine), Mike Keenan (Computer Science Department, Virginia Tech), Professor Steven P. Levitan (Department of Electrical Engineering, University of Pittsburgh), Jyh-Charn (Steve) Liu (Computer Science Department, Texas A&M University), Norman Matloff (Department of Computer Science, University of California at Davis), Walid Najjar (Computer Science Department, Colorado State University), Bernhard Weinberg (Computer Science, Michigan State University), D. Scott Wills (Electrical and Computer Engineering, Georgia Institute of Technology), Craig M. Wittenbrink (Board of Computer Engineering, University of California, Santa Cruz), David Wood (Computer Science Department, University of Wisconsin). Also to be thanked are the faculty and students who used the Fall 1995 and Spring 1996 Class Test Editions for their many helpful suggestions and error reports. Faculty were Douglas J. Fouts (Department of Electrical and Computer Engineering, U.S. Naval Postgraduate School), John F. Passafiume (Department of Computer Science, Clemson University). They and their students contributed greatly to the improvement of the book.

We thank Craig Meuller and the Martinique Team at Maxtor for permission to photograph the 1.3 gigabyte Laramie disk drive, and Dr. James Avery for permission to photograph his disk-platter-made-into-a-coffee table (see page 410).

We especially wish to thank Professor Miles Murdocca of the Internet Institute USA for contributing Appendix A: Digital Logic.

Harry Jordan's contributions to CSDA were many and important. He will be greatly missed, both as a colleague and a friend.

Vincent P. Heuring
Boulder, Colorado

heuring@colorado.edu

The General Purpose Machine

Chapter Outline

The goal of this book is to provide you with a clear understanding of the structure and functioning of the digital computer at all levels from the digital logic, or gate level, to the machine language programming level, to the overall system, or architectural level. Throughout the text, we stress the interactions and relationships that exist among these levels.

This introductory chapter describes what we mean by the logic designer's view, the machine/assembly language programmer's view, and the architect's view of a computing system. As we present each view, we describe what part of the machine is "seen" from that particular viewpoint and what the tasks, scope of responsibility, and tools of the trade are for individuals working at that level. We then present a short perspective on the history of computing, both to honor some of those who brought computer design and architecture to its present state and to provide a perspective on how we arrived at the present state. A brief section discussing some of the trends and research activities in the computing field follows, and we conclude by discussing what you will learn in each of the remaining chapters.

1.1 The General Purpose Machine

The digital computer has been called the general purpose machine. Computer science theory tells us that the general purpose digital computer, given enough memory, is equivalent to a *Turing machine* (named after Alan Turing, a British computer scientist of the 1940s). Loosely put, the Turing machine can, given sufficient time, compute all functions that are computable. The key phrases here are *enough memory* and *sufficient time*. The past 50 years have seen the digital computer evolve from having 1,024-bit memories to memories of terabit ($\sim 10^{12}$) capacity, and from executing 1 machine instruction in a millisecond to executing 100,000 or more instructions per millisecond. Even with all this processing power, many tasks remain beyond the capability of the "affordable" computer. These tasks include photorealistic, real-time 3-D animation and image rendering, weather forecasting, and the simulation of complex physical systems, to name just three. Perhaps one day computers will have sufficient processing power to solve all the problems that users care to put to them in a reasonable amount of time, but this is certainly far from true today.

Selecting the appropriate computer for a given application involves many choices. Computers today span the range from controllers for small appliances and toys, through desktop computers for use in the home and office, to the mainframes and supercomputers used in the most demanding applications.

1.1.1 SOME DEFINITIONS AND CONVENTIONS

Some very large and very small numbers are used in studying and describing computers. In normal commercial and engineering usage, the term *kilo* (K) equals 10^3; *mega* (M) equals 10^6; *giga* (G) equals 10^9; and *tera* (T) equals 10^{12}. The powers of 2 are so commonly found in the treatment of computers, because of the binary nature of the machines, that the preceding terms have been co-opted to represent the nearest power of 2. Table 1.1 shows the two usages for these terms. You should find it easy to distinguish the two usages. The powers of 2 are most often used in describing memory capacity, whereas the powers of 10 are used to describe clock frequencies, for example. You also will encounter the terms *milli* (m), 10^{-3}; *micro* (μ), 10^{-6}; *nano* (n), 10^{-9}; and, increasingly, *pico* (p), 10^{-12}. These terms are used frequently throughout the book, and you are encouraged to become familiar with their names and definitions.

The term *byte* is defined as a group of 8 bits. The *nibble*, or *nybble*, less commonly used, is half a byte, or 4 bits. The term *word* is used to mean a group of bits that is processed simultaneously. A word may consist of 8, 16, 32, or some other number of bits. In this book, the size of a word is defined when the term is used in context. Bits in a word can be numbered from left to right or right to left, and manufacturers do it both ways. The leftmost bit, however, is universally called the *most significant bit*, abbreviated msb, and the rightmost bit is called the *least significant bit* (lsb).

In units, seconds are abbreviated as s; bits, b; bytes, B; and words, w. For example, units of gigabits per second are abbreviated Gb/s, nanoseconds are ns, megabytes are MB, and microseconds are μs. Reciprocal seconds are called Hertz, abbreviated Hz, so a clock period of 100ns corresponds to a clock rate of 10MHz.

Table 1.1 Terms for Powers of 10 and Powers of 2

Term	Normal Usage	Usage as a Power of 2
K (kilo)	10^3	$2^{10} = 1{,}024$
M (mega)	10^6	$2^{20} = 1{,}048{,}576$
G (giga)	10^9	$2^{30} = 1{,}073{,}741{,}824$
T (tera)	10^{12}	$2^{40} = 1{,}099{,}511{,}627{,}776$

Where there may be confusion about the number base, binary numbers are generally indicated by a trailing B, as in 0110B, and hexadecimal numbers by the C language prefix, 0x, as in 0x1A2B.

We use standard logic symbols to express digital logic designs. If you are unfamiliar with this symbology, consult Appendix A, "Logic Circuits," for a description of the symbols and meanings used in digital logic circuits.

A `monospaced` font is used to exhibit code, whether the code is a high-level language or assembly language. The equal-sized letters in the monospaced font aid in the readability of listings.

CLASSIC EXAMPLE: The Tolstoy novel *War and Peace* has 696 pages. A CD-ROM can store approximately 600 MB. One character can be stored in one byte. Can the contents of the book be stored on a single CD-ROM? Show your calculations.

ANS: Yes. Assuming 100 char/line and 50 lines per page, the book will require $5{,}000 \times 696 = 3{,}480{,}000$ or 3.32 MB. (Note the difference between Millions and Mega.)

1.1.2 VIEWS OF THE COMPUTER

As with anything complex, there are many views or perspectives of a computer. In the sections that follow we define and illustrate four views: the view of the user, the view of the machine language programmer, the view of the computer architect, and the view of the computer logic designer. In these terms, the user is the person for whom the machine is designed. The machine language programmer is concerned with the behavior and performance of the machine when programmed at the lowest, or machine language, level. The architect is concerned with the design and performance of the machine at the higher system and sub system levels. The logic designer's main focus is on the design of the machine at the digital logic level.

There are many other possible views of the computer and its internal structure and function; these four provide useful illustrations of the various perspectives one might take when viewing a computer. The modern development team may have members skilled in integrated circuit design, logic synthesis tools, applications-level performance measurement, cost analysis, manufacturability, and preferred case color. At a given point in the design cycle, one or another of these individuals may be adopting several different views.

1.2   The User's View

By *user* we mean the person employing the computer *to do useful work.* That person may be using a word processing program, or running a spreadsheet program, or even programming the machine in a high-level language (HLL) such as C, Pascal, or FORTRAN. In any case, the internal structure of the machine is almost entirely obscured by the operating system and application software. Even if the user is programming the computer in some high-level language, the view of the machine becomes the view that is provided by the operating system and the programming language environment. The user's perception of the computer is limited to the speed with which it will run the user's programs, its storage capacity, and the behavior of its peripheral devices. You could say that the user's perception of a computer system is limited to the computer's performance when running the user's programs (Fig. 1.1). We will have little else to say about the user's view.

1.3   The Machine/Assembly Language Programmer's View

The machine/assembly language programmer is concerned with the software required by the machine. To appreciate this perspective, we need some basic definitions.

machine language

- ■ *Machine language:* The collection of all the fundamental instructions that the machine can execute, expressed as a pattern of 1s and 0s.

assembly language

- ■ *Assembly language:* The alphanumeric equivalent of the machine language. Alphanumeric mnemonics are used as an aid to the programmer, instead of the 1s and 0s that the machine interprets.

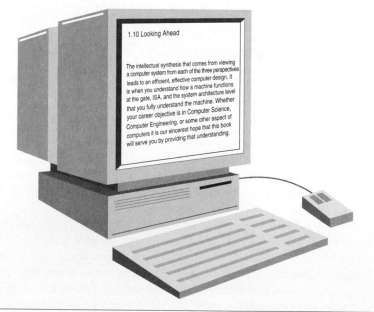

Fig. 1.1 The User's View

■ *Assembler:* A computer program that transliterates[1] the program from assembly language to machine language. Thus the assembly language programmer is programming the machine in its native language. From now on, we use the term *programmer* to mean the machine/assembly language programmer.

assembler

Table 1.2 shows a few Motorola MC68000 assembly language statements and their machine language equivalents. We have broken the encoding into its *fields*, each of which specifies part of the total instruction. Let us examine the nature of those fields. The first instruction, MOVE.W D4, D5, is an instruction to move (actually, copy) a 16-bit word (0011) to the fifth (101), data register (000), from data register (000) number four (100). (A *register* is a storage unit capable of holding a collection of bits.) The second instruction, ADDI.W, is an instruction to the computer to add (00000110) the 16-bit word (01), following, to data register (000), number 2 (010) and store the results in data register D2. The 16-bit integer following is 9 (0000 0000 0000 1001). We will cover the sometimes convoluted mapping between assembly language and machine language in Chapter 3.

instruction fields

register

The first field of the first instruction, 0011, is referred to as the *opcode* field, short for *operation code*. The opcode specifies the particular operation that is to be performed. The last four fields are *operand* fields, which specify where to get the source and destination operands. You would be correct if you guessed that the ADDI.W opcode was 00000110.

opcode

operands

Note that although most high-level programming languages are *portable,* or machine independent, each assembly/machine language is unique to the machine on which its programs run. Machine and assembly languages are discussed in detail in Chapters 2 and 3. Appendix C discusses assemblers and the assembly process in detail. If you are unfamiliar with these concepts, consult Appendix C as needed.

1.3.1 THE STORED PROGRAM CONCEPT

While nearly every class of computer has its own unique machine language, all of today's conventional machines have in common the concept of the stored program and the program counter.

The stored program concept says that the machine language program is stored in the computer along with any relevant data, and the computer is intrinsically able to manipulate that program as if it were data—for example, to load it into memory from disk, move it around in memory, and store it back out on disk.

stored program concept

Table 1.2 Two MC68000 Instructions

MC68000 Assembly Language	Machine Language
MOVE.W D4, D5	0011 101 000 000 100
ADDI.W #9, D2	00000110 01 000 010 0000 0000 0000 1001

1. *Translation* is a one-to-many mapping; *transliteration* implies a one-to-one mapping.

This concept is so much a part of the present-day computer's functioning that, as with the air we breathe, its universality renders it invisible. This was not the case with the first electronic computers developed 50 years ago, however. Those machines were programmed with plug boards, punched paper tape, or some other external mechanical means. Loading a program meant plugging in a patch board or running a paper tape through a reader. The stored program concept originated with Eckert and Mauchley's group in the mid-1940s and was such a good idea that it has been the basis for virtually every general purpose machine architecture devised ever since.

The machine language program that is stored in the machine's memory is executed instruction by instruction. One by one, the machine language instructions are fetched out of the computer's memory, temporarily stored in the *instruction register*, abbreviated IR, and executed by the central processing unit (CPU). This is referred to as the *fetch-execute cycle*. The basic machine operation can be summed up as being one of fetch-execute-fetch-execute-fetch-execute performed repeatedly until the machine is halted. (Today's more advanced machines can have a number of instructions in various stages of execution simultaneously; see Chapters 3 and 5.)

The machine must be provided with information about where to find the next instruction to fetch, and that information is stored in a register known as the *program counter* (PC). This register is sometimes called the *instruction pointer* (IP). We generally use the more common term, *PC*, unless referring to a specific machine whose manufacturer uses the term *IP*.

Figure 1.2 illustrates the instruction fetch process. The figure indicates the sizes of registers and memory by the numbers at the top of each. For example, the general purpose CPU registers shown at the top left are 32 bits wide, the PC is 32 bits wide, and memory contents are shown as 16-bit-wide values. Here's one of the many complications possible in computer addressing: The MC68000 has a byte-addressable memory, meaning that one byte is stored at each address. However, 1-, 2-, and 4-byte values can be fetched from memory as "units." The instruction is 16 bits, or 2 bytes long, and it is fetched as a unit, so the PC must be incremented by 2 to move to the next instruction.

The PC contains the address of, or "points to," the instruction at address 4000 in main memory. The control unit manages the fetching of the instruction located at memory address 4000 into the IR and then decodes the instruction and executes it. Notice that the instruction is the MOVE.W instruction shown in the MC68000 examples in Table 1.2. While fetching the instruction, the control unit is incrementing the PC to point to the next instruction, which is at address 4002. After executing the instruction at memory address 4000, it fetches the instruction pointed to by the PC, which contains 4002, and the process repeats.

(margin notes) instruction register · fetch-execute cycle · program counter

1.3.2   THE PROGRAMMER'S MODEL: INSTRUCTION SET ARCHITECTURE

The collection of all the operations possible in a machine's language is its *instruction set*. The programmer's view is composed of the machine/assembly language instruction set of the machine, along with the machine resources that can be managed with those instructions. This collection of instructions and resources is sometimes referred to as the *instruction set architecture* (ISA). The ISA includes the instruction set, the machine's memory, and all of the programmer-accessible registers in the CPU and elsewhere in the machine. The machine may contain additional registers for temporary or scratch-pad storage that are not programmer-accessible, and are hence not part of the ISA.

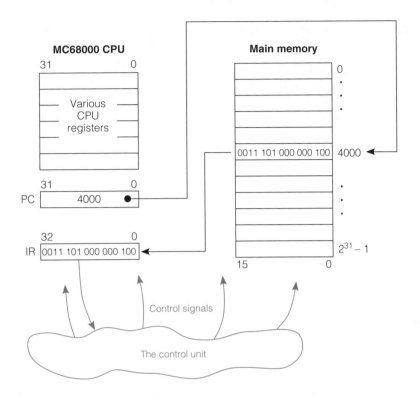

Fig. 1.2 The Fetch-Execute Process

Three Generations of Microprocessors.   Figure 1.3 compares the programmer's models of several generations of microprocessors. The 1970s-vintage Motorola M6800, the late 1970s Intel 8086 and its 2000 successor, the Intel Pentium 4, depicted in dashed gray, the 1980s-vintage Digital Equipment Corporation VAX11, and the 1999-vintage PowerPC G4, originally developed by an IBM-Motorola-Apple consortium. The register names and numbers are noted along the right side, and the word size is indicated by numbers at the top left and right of the registers. Pentium register names are shown inside their respective boxes. The dividing lines down the center of the registers and memory signify that there are instructions that can operate on fractional words. You may wonder why the PPC601 bit ordering is backwards from the others. It is because that processor's convention is to number the most significant bit of the word as bit 0, whereas the other processors number the least significant bit as 0. Notice the progression from a limited number of small registers, small memory capacity, and few instructions to a large number of large registers, large memory capacity, and many instructions. This increase in capacity is due to the increasing size and speed of the very large-scale integrated (VLSI) circuits that are used to implement the microprocessors.

The number of instructions actually declined in the progression from VAX11 to PPC601. This reflects part of the *reduced instruction set computer* (RISC) philosophy. This "less is more" concept saw its beginnings in the work of John Cocke's design of the

Motorola M6800
Intel 8086
DEC VAX11
Motorola PPC G4

reduced instruction
set computer (RISC)

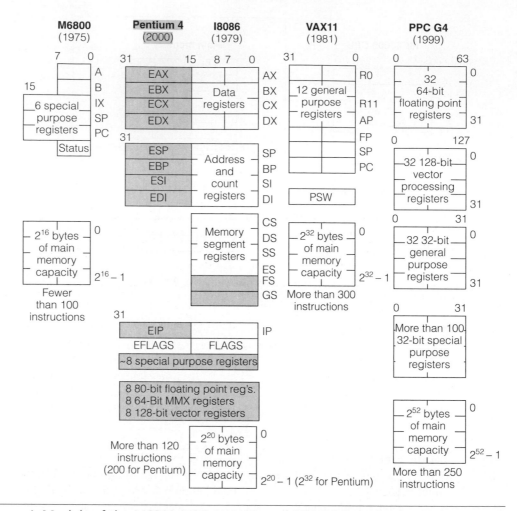

Fig. 1.3 Programmer's Models of the M6800, X86, VAX11, and PPC G4 Computers

IBM 801 in the 1970s. The term *RISC*, and much of the systematic research that established the RISC paradigm, originated with David Patterson of the University of California at Berkeley. It is the basis for many modern machine architectures, and we discuss it and its relationship to the *complex instruction set computer* (CISC) throughout this text.

complex instruction
set computer (CISC)

The Programmer's Manual.   Additional details of the programmer's model are discussed in the manufacturer's literature: instruction execution time and details of the results of arithmetic computation, for example. In effect, the manual discusses the processor and memory state changes that occur upon execution of the instructions in the instruction set. The manufacturer's programmer's manual is the *urtext*, the original definition, in questions of instruction meaning. Though often terse to the point of being incomprehensible upon a first reading, this manual should contain the most precise definition of the machine, and you should examine it prior to any serious assembly language programming effort.

Table 1.3 Instruction Classes

Instruction Class	C	VAX Assembly Language
Data movement	`a = b`	`MOV b, a`
Arithmetic/logic	`b = c + d*e`	`MPY d, e, b` `ADD c, b, b`
Control flow	`goto LBL`	`BR LBL`

Machine Instruction Classes.   Regardless of whether a given machine has 50 instructions or 300 instructions, its instruction set can be broken up into three classes: (1) data movement, (2) arithmetic and logic, and (3) control flow. Table 1.3 shows examples of the three classes in both C and VAX assembly language. In the second example in the table, a single C statement maps to two VAX instructions. This mapping of one HLL statement to several assembly language statements is usually the case, as you will discover in the next chapter. The ratio of HLL statements to machine instructions is often 1:4 or more. The compiler's task is to map the higher-level language construct to the most efficient equivalent sequence of machine language instructions.

The Machine, Processor, and Memory States.   The *machine state* consists of the contents of all registers and machine memory, both programmer-accessible and non–programmer-accessible, that are present in the machine. The *processor state* and *memory state* consist of the contents of all registers internal and external to the CPU, respectively. We use the term *state* here in the formal, state-machine sense as described in Appendix A and in logic design texts. These concepts of machine and processor state will assume importance when we cover procedure calls and machine interrupts, and when we discuss formal machine definitions.

machine state

processor state

memory state

Procedure Calls and Machine Interrupts.   *Procedure calls* are the mechanism used to implement C functions, Pascal functions and procedures, and the like. The machine language support for procedure calls is an important part of the machine's instruction set, and is discussed in Chapter 2. *Machine interrupts* are unexpected interruptions of normal program execution. They may be caused by external events such as the press of a keyboard key or by internal *exceptions*, such as an attempt to divide by 0. Interrupts are also an integral part of the modern digital computer, and they are discussed throughout the book. Their effect on the processor is similar to that of a procedure call, causing execution to begin at a new place, with provision for returning to the spot where the interrupt occurred.

procedure calls

machine interrupts

exceptions

1.3.3   MACHINE INSTRUCTIONS AND DATA TYPING

The rich data type structure built into higher-level programming languages is missing from most assembly and machine languages. At the machine level, it's all "bits-n-bytes."

Data Typing in Higher-Level Languages.   The HLL programmer is familiar with the primitive data types that are part of the language definition: integers; reals, often of several precisions; characters; and Booleans, among others. In addition, the Pascal `type` and C `typedef` statements allow the programmer to define complex types by composition of the primitive types of the language. Data typing helps prevent the programmer from making errors due to misuse of language constructs, and also provides guidance to the compiler about the meaning of the program. Correct type usage is usually enforced by the compiler during syntactic and semantic check phases.

Data Typing and Type Checking at the Machine Level.   HLL data types are designed for ease of representing objects that are of interest to the programmer: integers, reals, characters, Booleans, and so on. The data types at the machine level are designed so that they can be manipulated by a single machine instruction. There is often a considerable difference between the types at the two levels. For example, the only data type recognized by early microprocessors, such as the MC6800 shown in Figure 1.3, was the 8-bit byte taken as an integer. Larger integers had to be manipulated by sequences of machine instructions. There was no type representing real numbers. Most modern machines have integer operations that will operate on 8-, 16-, or 32-bit integers, and some can perform operations on 64-bit integers. Most also have instructions that operate on real numbers. One of the tasks of the compiler writer is to develop a "mapping specification" that describes how the HLL types will be mapped to the types available in the machine.

The representations of signed and unsigned integers as binary numbers have a basis in number theory, but the representation of reals and characters is entirely arbitrary. Until the IEEE standard floating-point format for real numbers came into common usage in the mid-1980s, each machine vendor had its own proprietary floating-point format. The IEEE standard formats are now supported by virtually all machine vendors.

The alphanumeric characters have also had several arbitrary standard representations, from the early CDC "display codes," to IBM's EBCDIC standard. The almost universal standard today is the *ASCII* (American Standard Code for Information Interchange) *code*, which represents 128 common alphanumeric and control functions in a 7-bit code. Recently there has been movement to create a 16-bit code to accommodate languages such as Chinese and Japanese that have many more characters than can be represented using 7 bits.

The representations of integers and real numbers are covered in more detail in Chapter 6, "Computer Arithmetic and the Arithmetic Unit." Character representations are discussed in Chapter 10.

Unfortunately, almost no data type checking is available to the assembly language programmer except for some machine-level typing in the Burroughs series of computers. No safety net prevents the programmer from trying to operate on a real value as if it were an integer, or even from trying to execute a block of data as if it were a program. For example, a given 32-bit value found in the memory of a VAX computer might be representing a 32-bit integer, two 16-bit integers, four ASCII characters, an instruction, a real number, or an array of thirty-two 1-bit Boolean values, depending on the context in which it is taken.

The Mapping between High-Level Languages and Assembly Languages.   The compiler writer has the task of determining the mapping between the high-level language and the machine language; thus, the compiler writer takes the programmer's view of the machine. Much of the effort in instruction set design has been directed toward satisfying the perceived needs of the compiler writer.[2] The compiler writer has the task of specifying

---

2.   Historically, compiler writers have often rejected the offerings of machine architects, eschewing single complex instructions in favor of sequences of simpler instructions.

the relationship between a given HLL construct and the equivalent machine language construct that preserves the meaning of the high-level one. The mapping, or correspondence, between HLL constructs and the equivalent assembly language constructs is generally many-to-many. That is, a single HLL construct can usually be represented by many different, equivalent assembly language constructs, and a single assembly language construct may represent many different HLL constructs. We use the term *mapping* to describe the relationship between the two, whether from high-level language to machine language, or from machine language to high-level language.

This many-to-many mapping makes the life of the compiler writer an interesting one. Although we do not describe the compilation process at all in this text, we often use high-level language to describe machine language constructs, often as comments in the assembly language listing. Because the mapping function "maps both ways," loosely speaking, the high-level language describes the machine language, while the machine language simultaneously describes the high-level language.

Table 1.3 shows three simple examples of such mappings. There is a type mapping between C integers and the 32-bit 2's complement VAX integers, a mapping between the C integer assignment and the VAX MOV instruction, and mappings between C integer multiplication and addition and VAX MPY and ADD instructions. Chapters 2 and 3 present several examples of mapping from HLL constructs to machine language constructs.

1.3.4   TOOLS OF THE TRADE

The assembly language programmer's tools allow the programmer to generate machine language programs from assembly language programs (the assembler), and to link small modules together into a single program (the linker). They also include facilities that allow the programmer to observe the details of program execution (the debugger). We examine each of these tools briefly.

The *assembler* translates assembly language statements to their binary equivalents. It also allows the programmer to specify the addresses where the program and data values should be located in memory when the program runs. The assembler translates symbolic addresses such as LBL, a, b, c, d, and e in Table 1.3 to their equivalent memory addresses. It also does syntax checking on the program and may notify the programmer of what it perceives to be inconsistent uses of variables.

assembler

The *linker* links separately assembled modules together into a single module suitable for loading and execution. This process is exactly analogous to the linkage of modules in high-level languages, and it is done for exactly the same reasons: abstraction and separation of concerns. Once a given module has been assembled and tested, it no longer needs the programmer's attention. It is available for use by any other module that requires its services. The linker also has the responsibility for resolving cross-references to different modules, and for determining the starting point for program execution.

linker

The incidence of errors in assembly language programs is higher than in programs written in high-level language because of the absence of type checking and type composition, the less intuitive nature of the language, and the larger number of statements. In addition, the assembly language programmer is usually working much closer to the hardware, often without the safety net of operating system protections. Run-time errors may crash the system instead of aborting and smoothly returning the user to the operating system

debugger, monitor

with a message such as "bus error." Because of the propensity for such errors, low-level *debugger* or *monitor* programs are commonly used. These tools allow the user to display and alter the contents of memory and registers; allow "disassembly" of machine code back to assembly language; permit the user to run, halt, and single-step the program; and permit the insertion of breakpoints that, if encountered during program execution, immediately halt the program, allowing examination of "the scene of the crime."

development system

The machine programmer may also have a *development system* at his or her disposal. The development system is a collection of hardware and software that is used to support system development. Development systems can be obtained from the processor vendor or from third parties, or they can be developed in-house. They allow the designer to develop software and hardware separately, and they allow the user to observe low-level machine functioning during hardware and software development. They consist of compilers, assemblers, linkers, loaders, emulators, hardware-level debuggers, logic analyzers, and other specialized tools to assist the system developer.

1.3.5   WHY ASSEMBLY LANGUAGE PROGRAMMING?

Assembly language programming is an alive and thriving art, and reports of its death are greatly exaggerated, as the saying goes. The following list describes some of the users of assembly language:

- First and foremost, machine designers need to know and understand the instruction sets of various machines. It is only with such an understanding that the machine designer can view the trade-offs implicit in a new machine design. The designer gains that understanding by writing assembly language programs; thus the presence of Chapter 3, "Some Real Machines," and various exercises in this text.

- Compiler writers need to be intimately familiar with all the details and nuances of the machine language. It is only with such an understanding that they can implement language translators that produce programs that are not only correct but can also be optimized to the greatest extent possible. The ever increasing complexity of modern processors, with more sophisticated cache memory, instruction pipelining, and superscalar operation,[3] places an increasing burden on the compiler writer to use these resources in the most efficient way.

- Compilers do not always generate optimum code. The implementer of time- or space-critical sections of code may need to resort to assembly language to meet performance targets.

- Microprocessor vendors often enhance their products by adding additional capabilities and new instructions that exploit them. Examples include the Intel MMX and SSE extensions, and the Motorola Altivec instructions, which allow programmers to process multiple data items with single instructions. When these new processor features are introduced, there is usually no compiler

---

3.   In pipelining, an instruction is begun, or *issued*, before the previous one has completed. In superscalar operation, several instructions are issued simultaneously.

support for them, and programmers must "escape" into assembly language to exploit them.

- Small controllers are being embedded in more products than ever before. The manufacturers of toys, appliances, cameras, binoculars, and even fever thermometers are employing small special purpose processors in their products to add features and value, or to simplify product operation. The code for these processors is often so specialized in function, or relies so heavily on input and output functionality, that HLLs are inappropriate or even useless for product development. Many software and hardware engineers earn their living writing assembly language programs.

We urge you to approach the study of machine and assembly languages as one would approach the study of a living language such as Spanish or French, not as the study of Latin or Sanskrit.

Key Concepts: Assembly Language Programming

It has been said that without language there can be no thought. While we may reserve that philosophical question for a coffeehouse debate, there is no question that without the machine's instruction set there would be no machine functionality. Here are some key points to remember from this section:

- The instruction set provides the means for expressing the application programs at the hardware level, where the work actually gets done.

- The programmer's model of the machine is an instruction set, memory, and a collection of registers for temporary storage. This collection is sometimes referred to as the instruction set architecture (ISA).

- The instruction set provides the means to manipulate the machine's data types. Instructions can be classified according to whether they perform data movement, arithmetic and logic, or control flow.

- The machine's data types are usually limited to integers of various sizes, floating-point numbers, and sometimes characters and Boolean values.

- It is the task of the compiler writer to provide the mapping between HLL constructs and the ISA. The compiler translates HLL programs to machine language by mapping high-level data types to machine level data types and high-level operations and control constructs to machine operations.

1.4   The Computer Architect's View

The computer architect is concerned with the design and performance of the computer system as a whole. The architect's task is to design a system that will provide optimum performance in the context of the uses to which it will be put. This is in effect a constrained optimization problem. The constraints may include cost, system size, thermal or mechanical durability, timely availability of components, immunity to static discharge, and so on, and may be imposed by outside forces as diverse as Corporate Marketing, the FDA, or the Department of Defense. In the "real world" there will be many constraints, and they may be conflicting. Often the biggest constraint of all is time to completion.

The constraints are made concrete by a set of performance specifications. These may include processing speed, networkability, computer graphics resolution or speed, or any other of a myriad of possibilities, but to be useful, they must be quantifiable. That is, they must be of such a form that when the design and construction work is complete, all will agree on whether the finished system meets its specifications.

The architect employs a set of performance measurement tools to determine whether the subsystems and the completed system meet the specifications set. These include a set of benchmark programs that measure various aspects of performance.

The computer architect designs the system from building blocks that include the basic processor, memories of various performance levels, input and output devices, and interconnection buses. The architect's job is to select the optimum set of building blocks and devices to meet the system's price and performance goals. In doing so, the architect may well become involved in some of the lowest-level details of the design of those building blocks, such as the design of an addition unit that will allow faster integer addition, but he or she must at all times be aware of overall system performance.

1.4.1   THE BIG PICTURE

At the highest level of abstraction, the architect views the machine as a collection of functional units and their interconnections. The functional units include subsystems such as keyboards and printers that provide means to input and output information; the system memory, which might include both high-speed semiconductor *random access memory* (RAM), as well as disk and tape drives; and, of course, the CPU. Provision may have to be made for multiple processors. For example, many microprocessors do not include an integral floating-point math unit, relying instead on a separate coprocessor that can be attached to the system bus.

random access memory (RAM)

The ISA as a Bridge.   The architect also is concerned with the instruction set architecture, for the very reasons cited in the summary of the last section: It forms the interface between the program and the functional units of the computer. It is through the ISA that the machine's resources are accessed and controlled. Thus the architect will be concerned with designing an ISA that best serves that role.

The CPU and Memory.   Machine instructions execute in the CPU and must be fetched along with data that are stored in the main memory of the machine. Those instructions and data may well originate on a disk drive or other peripheral storage device. The speed with which machine instructions execute may depend not only on the speed of internal CPU operations, but also on the speed with which the instructions and operands can be accessed in main memory, the speed with which programs and data can be accessed when stored on a disk drive, and perhaps the speed with which information can be put on a video display unit. All of these functional units—CPU, memory, and peripheral devices—are interconnected by buses, which are data pathways over which information passes. The bus provides yet another arena of concern for the architect.

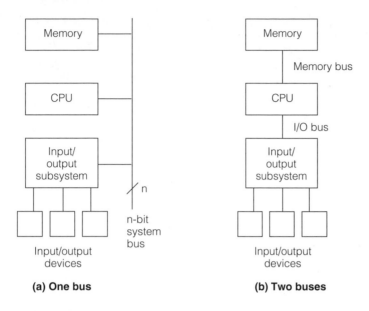

Fig. 1.4 Simple One- and Two-Bus Architectures

Buses.   Multiple devices are interconnected on a bus by timesharing the bus. The bus serves as a multiplexer, allowing multiple devices to use it for communication. Because the bus is shared by multiple devices, it must provide both a data path and a signaling or control path. Buses may be *serial* or *parallel*. Serial buses transmit information serially, one bit at a time. Parallel buses transmit a number of bits simultaneously.

serial and parallel buses

   Figures 1.4a and 1.4b show several ways of interconnecting a computer's functional units using buses. The figure shows a one-bus and a two-bus system, containing a CPU, memory, and an input/output (I/O) subsystem. The slant *n* on the bus line means that the bus contains *n* lines. Input devices connected to the I/O subsystem might include keyboard, mouse, or an incoming communications line. Output devices could include a video monitor, printer, telephone modem, and so on. In the one-bus arrangement, all traffic between the CPU and both memory and the input/output subsystem travels over a single bus. This arrangement has the advantage of simplicity, but the disadvantage that there can be only one bus activity at a time; while the bus is being used for I/O activity, memory accesses must wait. In the two-bus system, the CPU can manage I/O traffic separately from memory traffic. Because I/O operations are often much slower than memory operations, this can result in considerable speedup.

GETTING SPECIFIC: THE APPLE POWERMACINTOSH G4 BUS STRUCTURE

Actual systems are much more complicated than Figure 1.4 indicates. Most general purpose computing systems have many bus systems, some entirely internal to the computing system, and others that provide an interface to the outside world. Figure 1.5 shows a simplified view of the buses in one of the computers that the authors used in the preparation of

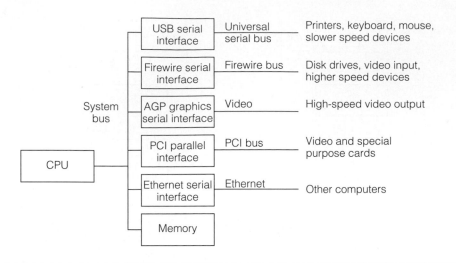

Fig. 1.5 The Apple PowerMac G4 Bus System (Simplified)

this edition, the Apple Power Macintosh G4. The CPU bus was designed for high-speed operation by the CPU vendor, Motorola. (The CPU is a Motorola G4.) The USB, Universal Serial Bus, is a hot-pluggable[4] serial bus with a maximum speed of 12Mbps. It is used for relatively slow communication between the computer and printers or other devices with modest data transmission requirements. The FireWire bus, originally developed by Apple Computer, is also a hot-pluggable serial bus that has a maximum speed of 400Mbps. The name "FireWire" is a copyrighted term of Apple Computer. The bus is also known by its generic name, IEEE1394. Both USB and IEEE 1394 buses will be discussed further in Chapter 8, "Input and Output." The AGP graphics provides a high-speed interface between the processor and video monitor. The PCI bus is a parallel "backplane" bus, with connectors on the Apple motherboard into which memory, graphics processors, or other special purpose cards can be plugged. It provides high-speed access between the processor and devices requiring high-speed processor access. It also has a published standard. The commercial Ethernet interface provides a 10/100/1000 Mb/s communication link between a network of computers over a 1000-ft. distance. Buses play a central role in machine design at all levels and are discussed and elaborated upon throughout the book.

The Memory System. The architect views the memory system as a hierarchy containing faster, more expensive members and slower, less expensive members. Figure 1.6 shows a block-level view of the memory hierarchy. Components toward the left side of Figure 1.6, which are nearer to the CPU, need faster access times, and thus are more expensive. Components on the right provide slower access times, but cost less. Information must flow back and forth in the hierarchy. The architect is concerned with balancing that flow to provide a specified level of service for a specified price. The memory hierarchy is treated in detail in Chapter 7, "Memory System Design."

---

4.   Devices can be plugged and unplugged at will without damage to the system.

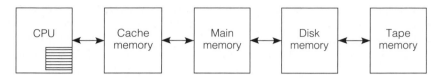

Fig. 1.6 The Memory Hierarchy

Peripheral Devices.   The devices selected to provide the input and output capabilities of the computer system and the buses chosen as interfaces have a major impact on overall system cost and performance. Choices of disk drives, tape drives, interface types, coprocessor chips, and memory speed all interact with one another and must be considered in detail. The computer architect must study many complex issues during system design, and must consider many trade-offs between system cost and system performance. Some of the more common peripheral devices are discussed in the chapters on peripherals and networking.

1.4.2 TOOLS OF THE TRADE

The computer architect does not work in a vacuum. As mentioned earlier in this chapter, system performance depends not only on the kinds of components and subsystems selected, but also on the workload of the computer. The architect typically uses *benchmark* programs to measure various aspects of system performance. For example, the performance of the cache memory shown in Figure 1.6 can be estimated by a model based on the details of its logic circuitry and bus interface. Its performance can then be measured using benchmarks specifically designed to exercise it under certain carefully specified conditions, and these performance measurements can be compared with the calculated values. Cache performance can also be measured under more realistic conditions using a suite of benchmark programs that allow comparisons with other computer systems. The architect may need to design benchmark programs to measure specific performance aspects.

    During the preliminary design phase, before any hardware has actually been built, the architect often uses *simulators* and *emulators* to estimate system performance. Simulators are software tools that mimic aspects of the system's behavior and allow a certain amount of performance estimation in the early stages of the design process. Because simulators mimic hardware performance in software, they are usually slower in operation by orders of magnitude. Emulators can be thought of as hardware-assisted simulators that provide operation speed closer to the speed of the hardware being emulated. Simulation and emulation are used at all design levels, from the simulation of transistor performance in integrated circuits to the simulation of memory hierarchy behavior. Apple Computer uses Cray computers to emulate proposed advanced user interfaces for which no hardware exists.

Communication among Architect, Programmer, and Logic Designer.   As might be imagined, there must be considerable communication between the architect and the programmers who must write software for the machine, and also between the architect and the logic designer. Formal description languages are often used to augment natural language in this communication process. Formal description languages, which are similar in

benchmarks

simulators
emulators

register transfer
languages

Register Transfer
Notation (RTN)

many ways to programming languages, allow a degree of precision of description that is lacking in natural language. These languages are referred to as *register transfer languages*, because they are specifically designed to describe information transfer between registers, a feature that is central to the operation of the computer. In fact, we use a simple language, *Register Transfer Notation* (RTN), to facilitate our communication with you about details of machine structure and function.

Key Concepts: The Architect's View

There is an analogy between the computer architect and the building architect. The building architect must have knowledge of all phases of building design and construction, but the main concern of the architect is that the building's subsystems contribute to a harmonious whole.

The computer architect needs familiarity with and a basic understanding of the ISA and logic design of the machine, and the behavior and function of the individual subsystems of the machine, but the main concern is that the computer system have *balance*: that there be a sense of proportion in the design. Key concepts follow:

- The architect is responsible for the overall system design and performance.
- Performance must be measured against quantifiable specifications.
- The architect uses various performance measurement tools to determine the performance of systems and subsystems. These tools often take the form of benchmark programs that are designed to measure a particular aspect of performance.
- The architect is likely to become involved in low-level details of the computer design. In other words, the architect may wear many hats during system design.
- The architect often uses formal description languages to convey details of the design to other members of the design team.
- The architect strives for harmony and balance in system design.

1.5   The Computer System Logic Designer's View

The computer logic designer is responsible for designing the machine at the logic gate level. We hasten to add that the role of system architect and logic designer is often taken by the same person or project team, and a given project may have dozens of logic designers. The difference between the architect and the logic designer is a subtle one and mainly reflects only a slight difference in perspective. In fact, separation of the two roles can lead to the architect specifying a requirement that cannot be met at reasonable cost or failing to take advantage of a feature well within the designer's capability. As mentioned, some form of register transfer language is generally used to facilitate communication of the design among team members.

1.5.1   THE IMPLEMENTATION DOMAIN

implementation
domain

The *implementation domain* is the collection of hardware devices with which the logic designer works. For example, the logic gate implementation domain may be VLSI on silicon, or it may be transistor-transistor logic (TTL) chips, emitter-coupled logic (ECL) chips, programmable logic arrays (PLAs) or sea-of-gates gate arrays, or it may be fluidic logic gates or optical switches. The implementation domain for gate, board, and module interconnection may be polysilicon lines in an integrated circuit (IC), conductive traces on a printed circuit board, electrical cable, optical fiber, or even free space.

At the lower levels of logic design, the designer may not consider the implementation domain at all, but may consider logic gates and interconnections in their abstract, symbolic form. At the higher and more practical levels of design, however, the implementation domain must be considered. Figure 1.7a shows a 2-1 multiplexer implemented in the abstract domain of Boolean logic. At this abstract logic level the designer is more concerned with the nature of the Boolean logic functions, and less concerned with practical matters such as gate fan-in and fan-out, propagation delays, and so on. Figure 1.7b shows the same multiplexer implemented in the domain of National Semiconductor's FAST Advanced Schottky TTL logic interconnected using printed circuit board traces, and Figure 1.7c shows it implemented with a fiber optic directional coupler switch interconnected with optical fiber. Of course, as a practical matter, logic designers always have implementation issues in the backs of their minds, even when working at the Boolean logic level.

1.5.2   IMPORTANCE OF THE IMPLEMENTATION DOMAIN

The implementation domain becomes important when the user considers the translation from the abstract level of logic gates to some concrete domain. For example, if the designer is implementing a system using VLSI on silicon, the number and size of the processor's registers may be influenced by the amount of silicon "real estate" available on the chip. A designer who is using PLAs will be influenced by the number and size of the product terms available. We normally adopt the more abstract, implementation-domain-independent view, but we mention implementation-domain-specific issues as they occur. For example, in the chapter on memory, we discuss the impact of allowable gate fan-in on decoder design.

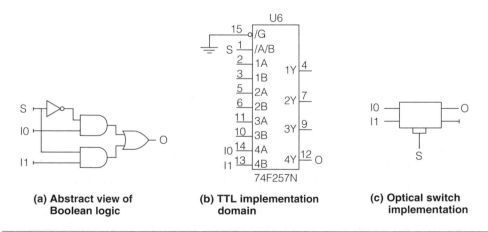

(a) Abstract view of Boolean logic

(b) TTL implementation domain

(c) Optical switch implementation

Fig. 1.7 Three Implementation Domains for the 2-1 Multiplexer

Implementation domains may be distinguished by the organization of the logic gates contained within them. These organizational features include the regularity, modularity, restrictions on interconnection, and circuit granularity. For example, in PLAs, both gates and interconnections are laid out in regular patterns. A specific function is realized by deleting a subset of the possible connections. In the sea-of-gates implementation domain, on the other hand, gates are laid out in a regular pattern, but connections can be made randomly, constrained only by the space available for routing.

Modularity appears in the implementation domain when the designer can incorporate standard subunits such as registers, adders, multiplexers, and so on from a library of subunits that have been previously laid out and tested. This is often the case in standard VLSI design using commercial VLSI design tools, and it is always the case when laying out a printed circuit board using standard TTL ICs.

1.5.3 The Distinction between Classical Logic Design and Computer Logic Design

This text presumes that you are familiar with digital logic design techniques; however, you will find that many of the traditional techniques are of limited use in computer logic design. For example, even though the digital computer is obviously a finite state machine, it is not useful to try to design an entire digital computer using state-machine design techniques. First, there is a combinatorial explosion in the number of states in a machine as complex as a general purpose digital computer. This puts the design problem far beyond the capacity of logic design and minimization tools such as Espresso, MIS, and the like. Second, the principle of abstraction, which is fundamental to the success of computer science in designing programming languages that support million-line programs, also operates at the hardware design level. For example, the design of the CPU register file can proceed with little or no concern for the design of the main memory.

data path
control path

More important, there is a natural separation or partitioning of concerns between the *data path* and the *control path*. By the data path, we mean the design of the storage cells and interconnections between them. By control path, we mean the management of the flow of information along the data path.

Whereas the logic designer sees NAND gates, NOR gates, and D flip-flops, the computer designer sees multiplexers, decoders, and register files. This has the salutary effect of reducing complexity by abstracting away the gates and flip-flops and replacing them with black boxes that have only input constraints and output behavior. The architect of the previous section may abstract the entire central processing unit as a black box that has a defined interface behavior.

1.5.4 The CPU: A Close-Up View

The programmer's models in Figure 1.3 expose some of the details in the CPU. The view of the logic designer goes beyond that to show additional detail that is unimportant to the programmer, but of great importance to the designer. There will be storage registers that are used to hold temporary or intermediate results, an arithmetic and logic unit (ALU) that can perform arithmetic and logic operations, and internal buses. Most important, the designer will be concerned with the mechanism used to control the machine. That mechanism begins with the PC, which contains the address of the next instruction to be fetched

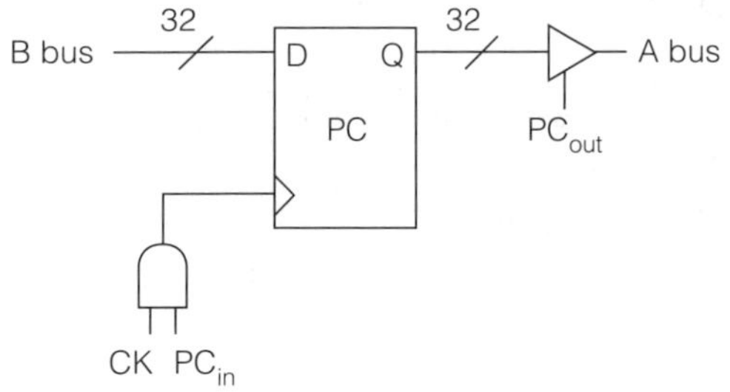

Fig. 1.8 Designer's View of the PC Register

from memory, and the IR, where that instruction is stored after fetching. Figure 1.8 shows how the designer views the PC of a certain 32-bit computer. The register is implemented by an array of 32 D flip-flops. The contents of the register can be gated out onto a bus named the A Bus by asserting the control signal PC_{out}. The contents of the B Bus can be stored in the register by asserting PC_{in} during the leading edge of signal CK. This is actually a portion of the data path of a simple machine that we will elaborate on in Chapter 4, "Processor Design." The interface between the data path and the control path is also indicated in the figure by the two gates and associated control signal names. We also delve into the details of the implementation of the CPU in Chapter 4.

The logic designer also has a similarly "magnified" view of memory and the I/O subsystem, and these topics are discussed at the logic design level in their respective chapters. The logic designer is responsible for the design and possibly the implementation of the machine. Consequently the tools are the tools of the hardware designer—*CAD* (computer-aided design) tools such as logic design and simulation packages, printed circuit layout tools, and *IC* (integrated circuit) design tools—and the tools of the implementer: tools such as logic analyzers, oscilloscopes, and the previously described development system.

CAD tools

IC design tools

Key Concepts: The Logic Designer

The logic designer is responsible for implementation of the computer at the logic gate and interconnection bus level. Key points follow:

- The logic designer works in both the domain of abstract Boolean logic and the selected implementation domain.
- At the abstract logic level, the logic designer is concerned with the correctness of the design. Register transfer languages are used as a means of communication to help ensure correctness.
- At the selected implementation domain level, the logic designer is concerned with fan-in and fan-out constraints, logic minimization techniques, power required, heat dissipation, propagation delay, number of components, and so on.
- The logic designer must bounce between the abstract logic level and the implementation domain level to get an optimum design.
- The logic designer works with logic design and minimization tools, board layout tools, IC design tools, and hardware design tools such as logic analyzers, oscilloscopes, and development systems.

1.6   Historical Perspective

We can fully understand where we are and where we are going only by knowing whence we came. In this very brief historical survey we will try to show in a qualitative way the impact of technology on machine capability and performance.

1.6.1   EARLY WORK

Charles Babbage (1792–1871) designed the first computational machine, the analytical engine, in 1823. Its design contained many of the elements of the twentieth-century computer: an ALU, known as the *mill*; a memory, known as the *store*; output by means of a printer; and input by punched cards of a kind similar to those used to program the looms of that day. Because of its complexity and the primitive nature of the technology of the time, it was never built, although Babbage spent his life trying to implement it.

We owe to George Boole (1815–1864) the development of the algebra named after him, Boolean algebra. This revolutionary algebra, based on 1 and 0 representing "universe" and "nothingness," postulates that everything can be reduced to computations involving these two values. Boolean algebra was to greatly simplify computer design, as it allowed formal description of logic circuits.

Claude Shannon, who moved from MIT to Bell Laboratories in the late 1930s, is considered the father of information and switching theory. In the former area, his research still stands today as the foundation of communications theory. In the latter area, switching theory forms the bridge between Boolean algebra and machine design.

1.6.2   THE RELAY COMPUTER: THE 1930s

While there were several special purpose processors built in the years after Babbage's effort, it wasn't until the 1930s that significant strides were made in the progress toward the general purpose machine. One of the first of these strides was made on the kitchen table of George Stibitz, a Bell Telephone Laboratories mathematician. It was there that Stibitz conceived of a relay-based binary full adder, and immediately tested the concept. The implementation domain was relays scrounged from a Bell Labs scrap heap, input switches made from strips cut from a coffee can, and output using flashlight bulbs. Stibitz worked with the Bell Labs team, headed by S. B. Williams, in the development of four special purpose and six general purpose computers. The Model I could perform complex arithmetic in response to keyboard input. In one of the first demonstrations of digital telecommunications, the Mark I, in New York City, was operated remotely by a teletype terminal in Dartmouth, New Hampshire, during a meeting of the American Mathematical Society.[5] Others at Bell Labs contributed to later efforts.

The German Konrad Zuse independently built several relay computers, apparently without knowledge of the previous work of Babbage. Like the Bell machine, his machine had memory capacity and was programmable. Unlike the Bell machine, it was

---

5.   It was said that the famous cybernetician Norbert Weiner was mildly irritated that the Model I trapped his attempt to divide by zero. To this day, nearly every machine traps attempts to divide by zero in hardware.

compact, and had tape input. A side effect of Germany's involvement in World War II was that Zuse's work was kept secret and had no influence on the direction of computer design.

1.6.3 GENERATIONS

Progress in computer hardware is often measured in "generations." Each generation was born of some significant advance in the digital logic implementation domain and the resulting order-of-magnitude increase in performance and decrease in size and cost.

The First Generation, 1946–59: Vacuum Tubes, Relays, and Mercury Delay Lines. Many people date the modern computer era from the development of the ENIAC (Electronic Numerical Integrator and Computer), designed by Presper Eckert and John Mauchly at the Moore School of Engineering at the University of Pennsylvania. Although it was not unveiled to the public until 1946, it actually became operational during World War II, and was used for computing ballistic tables. The machine consisted of more than 18,000 vacuum tubes and 1,500 electromagnetic relays. It could perform nearly 5,000 decimal additions per second, and its program was hardwired. Reprogramming the machine took most of a day, as it had to be done physically with plug cords and switches. The concept of the stored program computer was first developed by John von Neumann, with Eckert, Mauchly, and several others. Von Neumann wrote the memo describing this first stored program computer, the EDVAC, standing for Electronic Discrete Variable Automatic Computer. The memo was distributed by Herman Goldstine, who, to the consternation of Eckert and Mauchly, put only von Neumann's name on it. The EDVAC was built at the University of Pennsylvania but did not become operational until 1951. Credit for building the first operational stored program computer, the EDSAC (Electronic Delay Storage Automatic Calculator), goes to Maurice Wilkes, of Cambridge University. Wilkes had attended a series of lectures at the Moore School in the summer of 1946, and returned home to Cambridge determined to build a stored program computer. It became operational on May 6, 1949.

It is to John von Neumann that we attribute the clear partitioning of the computing engine into the components, *input*, *output*, *memory*, *ALU*, and *control*, and the concept that a single instruction should be fetched and executed from a common memory—a "one-thing-at-a-time" approach. Many feel that this clear partitioning and the concept of instruction fetch and execute were von Neumann's most significant contributions to computer architecture. (Less clear was his contribution to the concept of the stored program. Most of the participants agree that the concept was generally known to the entire Eckert and Mauchly research group when von Neumann's working paper describing the stored program was written.)

Machines of this era had no high-level languages or even assemblers. Instructions and data were usually input through an array of plugs and switches or by punched tape, and output was by means of an array of small lightbulbs or primitive teletype machines. This array of lights and switches could be used to load and display memory and registers, and to run, halt, and single-step the program. It was referred to as the *front panel*, a term that is still used occasionally today to refer to the equivalent functionality. Debugging was accomplished by setting switches to single-step through the program and observing the pattern of lights as an indication of the machine's internal state.

The 1950s saw a number of commercial firms enter the newly emerging computer market: IBM, RCA, Honeywell, and UNIVAC were the big names of the time. Commercial research and development resulted in the introduction of many new technologies. The implementation domain of this era was vacuum tubes, relays, and various esoteric memory systems—mercury delay-line memories for example.

Core memories were also invented during this period. These memories employed small toroidal magnetic cores to store bits, and represented the first reliable, cost-effective central memories. Core memories persisted in common use until the 1970s, when they were displaced by semiconductor RAM chips. We still occasionally hear the term *core* used to refer to the central memory, generally by people of middle years. The term also persists in common usage in the form of the phrase, *core dump*, referring to a snapshot copy of memory contents stored in a file, usually in response to some unexpected catastrophic event.

Magnetic tape and magnetic drums, and paper tape and card punches and readers came into common usage during this time as means of providing input, output, and storage. Also invented during this time were computer graphics, and the concept of external interrupts, besides many other innovations. It was during this period that Maurice Wilkes invented the concept of the microcoded control unit. Microcoding, in effect, applies software design techniques to the design of machine control units, and was a mainstay in CPU design until the early 1980s. We discuss microcoding in Chapter 5. In 1955, John von Neumann, normally the most prescient of men, urged the U.S. government not to waste money on memories greater than 10K words, as that amount was more than sufficient to handle the computational needs of present and future applications.

The Second Generation, 1959–64: Discrete Transistors.   The invention of the transistor in 1948 by John Bardeen, Walter Brattain, and William Shockley of Bell Labs ushered in the second generation of computers. The discrete transistor was one-tenth the size of the vacuum tube, had three terminals instead of six or more, dissipated as little as a few hundred milliwatts instead of the watts dissipated by the tube, and had a mean time between failures many times greater, due in no small part to the lower temperature at which the transistor operated. The transistor was in large-scale production by 1958, and was used extensively until ICs became available in 1964. During this heyday of computing, cycle times were reduced from 10 μs to 1 μs, memory sizes increased from 10K to 64K, and the number of machine instructions increased from 80 or so to near 200. It was during this time that IBM, through a combination of technical and marketing prowess, attained a dominant position in the computer industry. Machines of this period began to take on the architectural appearance that we see to the present day.

The Third Generation, 1964–75: Small- and Medium-Scale Integrated Circuits.   It is said that computer scientists admit to only three numbers: 0, 1, and as many as you need. This was the case with the development of electronic integrated circuits. First came the transistor, with only one device per component. Then, in 1958, Kilby of Texas Instruments and Noyce of Fairchild Semiconductor, and now chairman of the board of Intel, both independently conceived the concept of building not just devices, but entire circuits on a single piece of semiconducting material. By 1962 both companies were fabricating ICs for sale. The revolution brought about by the IC was caused not just by the fact that it could contain many components, but also by the fact that the components could be fabricated in a number of steps independent of the number of components. The number of components was and is limited by the size and properties of the semiconductor wafer and the particular manufacturing process used. In this sense, the IC became like the printed page: Its cost is related to the printing process itself rather than the number of words that happen to be printed on the page. As technology advanced, manufacturers were able to integrate more and more circuits onto a given IC chip:

1962   small-scale integration: 10–100 components per chip
1966   medium-scale integration: 100–1,000 components per chip
1969   large-scale integration: 1,000–10,000 components per chip
1975   very large-scale integration: greater than 10,000 components per chip

The number of components per chip has doubled about every year since 1962. Industry pundits talk of the billion-transistor chip by the year 2007.

Third-generation "mainframe" machines brought additional increases in machine capabilities and decreases in size. IBM introduced its System/360 in 1965. The 360 had a 32-bit word size and memory capacity from 64K to 16M bytes. The 360 and 370 series comprised a family of machines that provided upward compatibility: The machine code written for a less capable member of the family would run unchanged on all the more advanced members of the family. Multiprogramming, time-sharing multiuser operating systems, the magnetic drum, and later the disk drive were introduced during the third generation. The drum and disk drive, with latencies of a few dozen ms[6] replaced punched cards and magnetic tape, both of which had latencies of seconds in changing from one job to another. The advent of the disk drive made multiprogramming and timesharing possible. Multiprogramming is the running of more than one program simultaneously; timesharing allows more than one user to interact with the machine simultaneously.

As IBM and others were introducing ever larger and more capable machines with prices from $100,000 to several million dollars, upstart firms such as Digital Equipment Corporation (DEC) were building machines that were known as "minicomputers." The "minis" were 8- and 16-bit-word machines, often with as little as 4K of RAM, selling for prices that started at under $20,000. The minis were eagerly embraced by laboratory and industrial firms, and later by small businesses looking for sources of inexpensive computational power. It took IBM and the other mainframe manufacturers years to acknowledge and enter this new "low-end" market. By the middle 1970s, there were dozens of minicomputer manufacturers selling nearly fifty different models.

Fourth Generation, 1975 to the Present: The Microcomputer.   Intel and Texas Instruments had been designing and selling small quantities of limited-capability 4- and 8-bit ICs that contained entire CPUs on a single chip since 1973, but it was the Intel 8080 and the Motorola 6800, both of which had 8-bit accumulators and 16-bit addressing that fueled the microprocessor revolution. Ironically, that revolution started not with products introduced by IBM or DEC, but by companies with names like Apple Computer, Microsoft, and Lotus. It was from the garage and the hobby shop that the first generation of microcomputers emerged. The mainframe and minicomputer manufacturers were leery of entering this hobbyist market, because of the perception that products based on the 8-bit

---

6.   Latency is the time interval between the request for information and the delivery of that information.

microprocessor were toys that admitted of no important application. This timidity on the one hand, and later fear of diminished sales on the other hand, by the mainframe and mini-computer manufacturers allowed companies such as Apple and Microsoft to become household words.

There has been a steady progression in microprocessor capabilities from these 8-bit machines to the 64-bit, 1-ns machines being sold today, and that progression continues unabated.

1.7   Trends and Research

Research in computer design continues. Much current research is aimed at faster, smaller, and cheaper machines. Feature sizes in ICs continue to drop, and we approach the billion-transistor IC. As more components are packed into the same area, heat dissipation becomes a serious concern. Current and planned ICs may dissipate over 100 watts. This is in conflict with the trend toward portable computers, and we can expect much research into lower power devices and systems.

At the CPU architecture level we are seeing radical departures from the fetch-execute paradigm discussed in this chapter. Such techniques as pipelining multiple instructions, so that each simultaneously uses a different part of the CPU hardware, and multiple instruction issue, where the CPU can begin execution of a number of instructions simultaneously, are becoming part of mainstream machine architectures. All of these efforts aim at executing as many instructions as possible in parallel. This has spawned much research into the development of compilers and, to a lesser extent, languages that can exploit these techniques as fully as possible. We will cover pipelining and briefly discuss multiple instruction issue in Chapter 5.

Peripheral devices such as disk drives and video display systems are becoming faster and more intelligent. Many peripheral devices contain advanced special purpose processors, allowing the main system processor to off-load much of the overhead processing to them. These and other aspects of peripheral device design are covered in Chapter 9, "Peripheral Devices."

The networking of computers into larger systems that allow the sharing of files and other data is receiving much attention at the present time. Computer communications and networking are active areas of research and development. We can expect to see faster and more transparent networking, perhaps leading to the day when virtually every computer will be part of a transparent computer network, allowing almost instantaneous access to worldwide computing and data resources.

More upstream research aims to utilize single molecules or small collections of atoms for logic gates and interconnections. Another interesting, if "far out," research area uses DNA recombination techniques to create collections of perhaps 10^{18} molecules to solve particular problems. Each molecule would have a slightly different shape or configuration and would contribute its share to the total computational effort. This may well become the fifth generation of computing hardware (or should we say "wetware"?).

The authors' research group has developed a stored program optical computer, SPOC, that explores computing in the implementation domain of optical switches interconnected by optical fiber, using infrared optical pulses to encode information. The computer does not use any flip-flops for synchronization or data storage. Signals are synchronized by adjusting the time of flight between active circuit elements to ensure that signals arrive at the right place at the right time. Information is stored by using a fiber optic delay line similar to the mercury delay line used by Maurice Wilkes, but with information circulating at the speed of light instead of the speed of sound. One could say that information is being stored in spacetime. The main purpose for this research is to understand the new and different factors facing the computer designer when the speed of light is the limiting factor in information processing. The latest generation of VLSI designs is beginning to use a very limited version of this synchronization technique in so-called *wave pipelining,* where, for a short distance in the chip, groups of signals are purposely designed to propagate in lockstep, assuring their near simultaneous arrival at some destination on the chip.

1.8   Approach of the Text

The intellectual synthesis that comes from viewing a computer system from each of these three perspectives leads to an efficient, effective computer design. It is when you understand how a machine functions at the gate, ISA, and system architecture level that you fully understand the machine. Whether your career objective is in computer science, computer engineering, or some other aspect of computers, it is our sincerest hope that this book will serve you by providing that understanding.

As we introduce the various subjects that are covered in this book, we provide multiple views of each one, to explain its structure and function and, equally important, to describe the relationship between that subject and others that relate to it.

Summary

- The study of computer design and architecture can be approached by examining the machine's structure and function from the three perspectives of the assembly language/machine language programmer, the computer architect, and the digital logic designer.

- The machine/assembly language programmer views the machine as having an instruction set architecture consisting of a collection of registers and memory cells, along with a set of instructions that allows the manipulation of data. A sound understanding of assembly language programming is needed for compiler writing and in the writing of low-level, specialized code for which high-level languages are inadequate or unavailable. Another reason to learn assembly language is that it forms the interface between the hardware and the software. Nobody can claim to understand a machine's architecture until they can program it in its own language.

- The basic computational paradigm of the machine, employed by the machine programmer, is that of the fetch-execute cycle of machine operation. A register in the CPU, the PC, holds the address of, or points to, the next instruction. At the beginning of the fetch-execute cycle, the instruction is fetched into the CPU, decoded, and executed. Meanwhile the PC is advanced to point to the next instruction, which is fetched and executed, and so on. Methods for speeding up and overlapping this process are discussed in Chapter 5.

- In the general purpose computer, programs can be manipulated as data. This stored program concept is at the heart of computer design. It is what allows the operating system to load programs from disk to memory.

- Unlike high-level languages that provide data typing, machine languages have almost no data typing except for the data types that the machine deals with at the instruction set level. Those are usually limited to integers and floating-point numbers of various sizes, and Boolean variables. There is little or no type checking at the assembler level.

- The computer architect is at the center of computer system design and development. The architect has the job of designing a system that meets the performance specifications set for it. This requires the architect to become involved with all aspects of the machine's design. The architect must also select and in some cases design a collection of performance benchmark programs that permit the measurement of each important aspect of performance.

- The digital logic designer does the logic level design work. The designer is involved in design at the level of Boolean logic, to design circuits that provide correct behavior. The designer also needs to consider the implementation domain. The implementation domain is the collection of hardware that the logic designer has at his or her disposal for implementation of the logic design. Selection of the implementation domain may be driven by cost, speed, power, size, or other constraints. The logic designer maps the abstract Boolean logic circuits to the implementation domain. Here such practical concerns as gate fan-in and fan-out, number of gates per package, power consumption, and device delay must be resolved. CAD tools are widely available to assist in this mapping.

- Some form of RTN is usually used to facilitate communication among the team members. RTNs allow information to be communicated precisely and unambiguously.

Bibliography

Additional information on assemblers and assembly language programming can be found in the following texts:

Peter Abel, *IBM PC Assembly Language and Programming,* Prentice Hall, Upper Saddle River, NJ, 2000.

Ambrose Barry, *68000 Assembly Language, Programming And Interfacing: A Unique Approach for the Beginner,* Prentice Hall, Upper Saddle River, NJ, 1997.

A basic introduction to computer design and architecture is given in

M. Morris Mano, *Computer Systems Architecture,* Prentice-Hall, Upper Saddle River, NJ, 1993.

Additional references to various aspects of computer architecture appear in the "Bibliography" sections of Chapters 2–5.

For a particularly good treatment of practical digital logic design, see

Randy H. Katz, *Contemporary Logic Design,* Benjamin/Cummings, Menlo Park, CA, 1992.

A more mathematical treatment of digital design can be found in

Zvi Kohavi, *Switching and Finite Automata Theory,* McGraw-Hill, New York, 1978.

Additional references to digital design texts will be found at the end of Appendix A, "Digital Logic."

Several of the pioneers who built the early machines have written first-person accounts, including the following:

Herman. H. Goldstine, *The Computer from Pascal to von Neumann*, Princeton University Press, Princeton, NJ, 1972.

Maurice V. Wilkes, *Memoirs of a Computer Pioneer,* MIT Press, Cambridge, MA, 1985.

A description of the original stored program computer design principles can be found in

William Aspray, *John von Neumann and the Origins of Modern Computing*, MIT Press, Los Angeles, 1990.

The people who built the early computers are described in the following text:

J. A. N. Lee, *Computer Pioneers*, IEEE Computer Society Press, Los Alamitos, CA, 1995.

There are several monthly publications that cover the computer field, most notably the journal of the IEEE Computer Society. Student membership in the society entitles the member to a monthly copy.

IEEE Computer, IEEE Computer Society, IEEE Headquarters, 345 East 47th St., New York, 10017.

Exercises

1.1 The PowerPC 601 processor addresses a maximum of 2^{32} bytes of memory. What is the maximum number of 64-bit words that can be stored in this memory?   **(§1.1)**[7]

1.2 A certain IBM 970 processor has a system clock frequency of 1.2 GHz, what is the clock period?   **(§1.1)**

1.3 If the cost of RAM is \$95 for a 4MB module, what will it cost to install 32 MW in an originally empty machine if the word size is 32 bits?   **(§1.1)**

1.4 How many 500MB tapes will be required to back up a 120GB hard drive? How long will the backup process require if one tape can be filled in 5 minutes? (No coffee breaks allowed.)   **(§1.1)**

1.5 a. A certain machine requires 1.5 μs to process each 64-byte data record in a database. How long will it take to process a database containing 100×10^8 records?

   b. How many 700MB-capacity CD-ROMs will be required to store the data- base?   **(§1.1)**

1.6 a. What is the percentage relative error in using 2^{10} as an approximation for 10^3?

   b. What is the percentage relative error in using 2^{30} as an approximation for 10^9?

   c. What is the general formula for the relative error in using 2^{10k} as an approximation for 10^{3k}?   **(§1.1)**

1.7 If one printed character can be stored in 1 byte, approximately how many bytes will be required to store the text of this textbook? Do not include the graphics, and do not count the characters one by one. Show your work and state your assumptions.   **(§1.1)**

1.8 Consider computing the electric field in a box 1.5 cm on a side. The spatial resolution in each dimension is to be 50 μm. Assume that it takes 150 instructions for every point in the 3-D grid to do the calculation. How long does the computation take on a computer that can execute at a rate of 100 MFOPS (millions of floating point instructions per second)?   **(§1.1)**

1.9 Describe the tools used by the assembly language programmer.   **(§1.3)**

1.10 Describe the differences between assembly language and high-level languages as regards type checking. What is the source of these differences?   **(§1.3)**

1.11 What is the difference between a programmable calculator and a personal computer?   **(§1.4)**

1.12 How would computers be operated if there were no stored programs?   **(§1.4)**

1.13 What is an ISA, and what are its components?   **(§1.3)**

---

7.   Parenthetical section numbers refer back to the section in the chapter covered by the exercise. For example, Exercise 1.1 covers Section 1.1 (§1.1).

1.14 Using only the instructions in Table 1.3, compile by hand the following C statements into VAX11 assembly language. Assume all variables are integers.   (§1.3)

    a. `V = (W + X)*(Y + Z);`

    b. `A = B*C*D + E;`

    c. `z = x*y`^{2}`;`

    d. `U = V; W = U + Y;`

1.15 Using only the information in Table 1.2, encode the following MC68000 assembly language instructions into machine language. Express your results in binary.   (§1.3)

    a. `MOVE.W D3, D4`

    b. `ADDI.W #65535, D4`

1.16 Describe the advantages of data typing in high-level language programming. (§1.3)

1.17 If assembly language is mostly free of data typing, how are data types expressed in assembly languages?   (§1.3)

1.18 Define the difference between a simulator and an emulator. Which would you prefer to work with, and why?   (§1.4)

1.19 a. Define the term *bus*.

    b. Why are buses used in computers?

    c. Describe the similarities and differences between the computer bus and the electric power grid.

    d. Describe the differences between the computer bus and the water system in your home.   (§1.4)

1.20 Provide a diagram similar to Figure 1.5 for the computer you work at most frequently.   (§1.5)

1.21 How does the computer architect communicate machine specifications to the logic designer?   (§1.5)

1.22 What natural separation distinguishes computer logic design from classical logic design?   (§1.5)

1.23 Estimate the costs of the components in Figure 1.6 for the computer you work at most frequently. State where you got the component costs.   (§1.5)

1.24 Describe as accurately as you can the implementation domain of the computer proposed by Charles Babbage.   (§1.5, 1.6)

1.25 Describe as accurately as you can the implementation domains of the first through the fourth generation of computers.   (§1.5, 1.6)

CHAPTER 2

Machines, Machine Languages, and Digital Logic

Chapter Outline

In Chapter 1 you probably got the sense that there are many different kinds of ISAs. This is indeed the case. This chapter explores the classes of machines and machine languages from the ISA, or the programmer's point of view. Those classes can be differentiated in the following ways:

- The kinds and sizes of registers within the CPU
- The way main memory is structured
- The way instructions access their operands, both from registers and from memory

We will continue to classify instructions by the three classes mentioned in Chapter 1: data movement, arithmetic and logic, and control flow, or branch. We first present the various kinds of registers, memory organization, and operand access methods by reference to pure or abstract machine models, to give a sense of the kinds of ideal machine types.

We then describe a model machine, the *simple RISC computer (SRC)*, at the ISA level. The SRC has many features of a modern RISC without the complicating factors that must be present in a modern commercial computer. This simplicity allows us to completely describe SRC in the text, a task that would require a several-hundred-page machine manual for a real machine. This simplicity also allows us to do a detailed logic design of the machine in later chapters. This would not be possible for a machine as complex as a commercial processor. The SRC is first described informally using words and pictures, and then formally using the simple *register transfer notation* (RTN). The SRC will provide a machine model to illustrate important facets of machine design and architecture in future chapters. The purpose of introducing a formal description language is so that machine features can be described simply and unambiguously. This capability will prove invaluable as you begin exploring hardware design alternatives in Chapter 4 and as advanced features are introduced in Chapter 5.

After taking the programmer's view in discussing the various kinds of ISAs, we conclude the chapter by taking the logic designer's view as we consider some of the logic design techniques used in computer design. The logic designer's view focuses on register transfers—moving data from register to register, perhaps transforming it on the way by passage through an ALU. The concluding section describes how register transfers are accomplished at the gate level, including a first discussion of the timing of those transfers. Registers are interconnected by buses, so we discuss the use of buses as the media by which register transfers occur. You will see that many of these design methods differ from those taught in most logic design courses.

2.1 Classification of Computers and Their Instructions

We first take up the structure of main memory and the CPU registers in various machine classes. Main memory is usually taken to be an array of data units having the smallest size that is accessible using the machine's instruction set. This is now almost always the 8-bit byte, so, for example, a 64-bit floating point number is stored in main memory as a string of eight consecutive bytes, and there will be instructions that manipulate the string as a unit.

Processor state (CPU) registers, on the other hand, are characterized by both their size and the type of data they can contain. You could say they have "personality." They often are referred to, less colorfully, as *special purpose registers.* Early machines had separate registers for holding addresses and data, for example. The M6800 processor shown in Figure 1.3 (reproduced as Figure 2.1) has three 16-bit address registers, PC, SP, and IX, each with a special purpose, and two 8-bit data registers, named A and B. The A and B registers are referred to as *accumulators* or *arithmetic registers* and are used for the temporary storage of operands and results of arithmetic or logic operations. The other 8-bit register, Status, is actually an array of eight 1-bit machine status indicators that indicate such things as whether the previous arithmetic operation resulted in a carry-out from the msb, the most significant bit of the word. As you may imagine, registers that can only be used for a special purpose tend to cramp the programmer's style. In general, computers can be classified according to the structure and function of the registers in the CPU.

We speak of accumulator-based machines, stack machines, and general register machines as though there were actually "pure" machines of each class. In reality, a given machine will have characteristics of several of the classes, with perhaps one kind of machine behavior dominating. Examining the machines in Figure 2.1, we would probably classify the Motorola M6800 and the Intel I8086 as accumulator machines and the Digital VAX and Motorola PPC601 as general register machines, even though all of them have

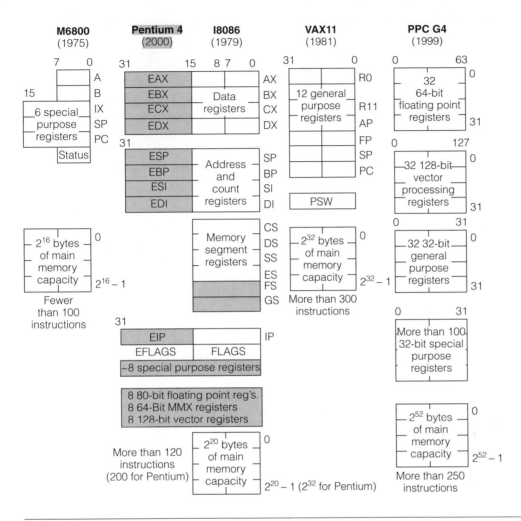

Fig. 2.1 Programmer's Models of the M6800, X86, VAX11, and PPC G4 Computers

machine instructions belonging to other machine classes. For example, the 8086 and the VAX both have PUSH and POP instructions, which are characteristic of stack machines. With that understanding, in the following discussion we refer to hypothetical machines as belonging to a certain classification.

Accumulator machines have a sharply limited number of data accumulators, often just one, in addition to the address registers within the CPU. They are called accumulators because they serve both as the source of one operand and as the destination for arithmetic instructions, and thus they serve to accumulate data. In the days when memory was expensive, accumulator machines were popular, because only one operand address had to be specified; the other operand was located in the accumulator, and the result was stored in the accumulator. Thus machines with accumulators are referred to as 1-address machines. This was an advantage when memory was expensive, but it is now viewed as a severe restriction with memory being comparatively cheap. Because there can be only one or a

accumulator machines

very limited number of accumulators in the CPU, an accumulator machine is quite limited when evaluating arithmetic expressions with many terms and factors.

stack machines
stack

Stack machines do away with register names or numbers altogether. Their CPU registers are organized as a last-in-first-out *stack,* the stack being analogous to the plate dispenser found in cafeterias. Operands are "pushed" onto the stack from memory as plates are pushed onto the dispenser and "popped" off the stack in reverse order: last-in-first-out. Arithmetic operations remove operands from the top of the stack, and the result is placed on the stack, replacing the operands. When expression evaluation is complete, the result is "popped" into a memory location to complete the process. This means that no operand addresses need to be specified during an arithmetic operation, and thus this class of machine is known as a 0-address machine.

general register
machines

General register machines have a set of numbered registers within the CPU. Unlike accumulator and stack machines, the registers in general register machines can be used for almost any purpose. Nearly all modern machines have a set of general purpose registers like those in the VAX and PPC processors shown in Figure 2.1. Such registers can hold both addresses and data, although a popular variation is to have one set of floating-point data registers that is separate from the general purpose integer register set. The integer registers can be used to hold both addresses and data; the floating-point registers hold only floating-point data values. The cost of having a number of general purpose registers within the CPU is the cost of naming them when specifying operand or result location. This is not a big cost: Specifying 1 of 32 general purpose registers only takes 5 bits, which is not a large cost when instructions are 32 bits wide, as most are in today's processors.

We should reemphasize that in a practical system one will see a mixture of the register types within a single CPU. For the reasons we cited earlier, most of today's machines have a mostly general register structure, but there are still special purpose registers of one kind or another within most CPUs. Figure 2.1 shows that the Motorola PPC G4 has more than 50 special purpose registers, for example.

2.2 Computer Instruction Sets

instruction classes:
  arithmetic (ALU)
  data movement
  control, or branch

The instruction set of a computer is nothing more or less than its repertoire: the entire collection of instructions it can interpret and the actions it thereby effects. You might argue that the most important are the *arithmetic,* or *ALU,* instructions, as they "get the job done." Instructions of this class accept one or more operands and produce a result, and they may also generate some side effect such as setting a flag to indicate that the result of the operation was a negative number. The *data movement* instructions move data within the machine and to or from input/output devices. *Control,* or *branch,* instructions affect the order in which instructions are performed, or control the flow of the executing program, much as `goto`, `for`, and function calls do in C.

What must an instruction set specify? Regardless of the kind of machine, or the CPU register structure, or the particular nature of the instruction, every instruction must contain encodings within it to specify the following four things, either explicitly or implicitly:

opcode

1. *Which operation to perform.* This is specified by the operation code, or *opcode.* Some examples are add, load, and branch.

2. *Where to find the operand or operands, if there are operands.* The operand or operands may be contained in CPU registers, in main memory, or in an I/O port. The operand location may be explicitly specified, as in a memory address or general register number, or it may be implicit within the opcode and thus not explicitly mentioned, as when it is in the single accumulator of an accumulator machine or on the stack of a stack machine.

    operands

3. *Where to put the result, if there is a result.* As with operand locations, the result location may need to be explicitly mentioned or it may be implicit in the opcode.

    result

4. *Where to find the next instruction.* In inline code—that is, a sequence of instructions without any explicit branches—the next instruction to execute is the next instruction in the sequence, and thus need not be explicitly mentioned in the current instruction. In instructions that alter the flow of program statement execution, the branch or jump address must be given as part of the current instruction. (The skip instruction is an exception. The address to skip to is implicit—the instruction *after* the next instruction.)

    next instruction

For example, the MC68000 instruction MOVE.W D4, D5, which was described in Table 1.2 in Chapter 1, answers the four questions in the following way:

1. *Which operation:* move an integer word.
2. *Where to find the operand:* in data register D4.
3. *Where to put the result:* in data register D5.
4. *Where to find the next instruction:* (implicitly) in the word following this instruction.

Notice how this instruction "saves space" by specifying the address of the next instruction implicitly. The main point behind accumulator and stack machines was to make the specification of many of these items implicit, thus reducing the size of the instruction and the instruction fetch time.

Each CPU designer has approached the question of how to specify the preceding four items with a unique view of the optimum mix of operation kinds, the nature of operand and result specification, and the kind of control-flow constructs that should be part of the instruction set. The result is that the syntax and meaning of assembly and machine languages are reminiscent of the biblical tower of Babel, where each person spoke his or her own language and could be understood by no one else. Unlike high-level languages, which have standard syntax and semantics regardless of the machine on which they are implemented, the machine language of each machine type is unique. Not only do the languages differ widely in the way they specify these four items, but also they disagree on the mnemonics to be used for the opcodes, on whether upper- or lowercase should be used, and even on whether the source operand should precede or follow the destination operand. In this book we follow the conventions that were established for the particular machine. Either operand order will be explicitly specified, or it can be inferred from context.

2.2.1   ACCESSING MEMORY

Before discussing instruction classes let us consider some additional details of the process by which the computer accesses memory. This goes directly to the last three questions above:

where to get the operands, where to put the result, and where to get the next instruction, since the operands and result may be in memory, and the next instruction certainly will be.

Virtually all memory systems are "dumb," in that they respond to only two commands: **read** the value stored in memory at the address specified by the CPU and return it to the CPU, or **write** into memory a value specified by the CPU, at the address specified by the CPU.

In nearly all memory systems the smallest addressable object is a byte, and all addresses are *byte addresses*. Even though the object referenced by the CPU may be a multiple-byte object, its given address is still the address of its first byte. For example, the 2-byte integer word 0xABCD located in memory at the address 1000 will occupy the two, byte addresses 1000 and 1001, but the CPU will access it by requesting the *word* stored at address 1000. For the present discussion, we will ignore the issue of how the CPU accesses multibyte values.

Transactions between the CPU and memory take place over the CPU bus. Figure 2.2 shows a simplified view of the CPU interconnected with the memory by the system bus. The bus signals include the address lines, A_0–A_{n-1}, the data lines, D_0–D_{b-1}, and three control lines, read, R, write, W, and the "memory function complete" line, COMPLETE. This latter signal provides a means for the memory system to inform the CPU that the read or write action has completed. It is needed when memory access time is longer than the CPU clock period.

The process of memory access proceeds as follows:

For a Memory Read:

1. The CPU issues an address to the memory unit on the address lines, A_0–A_{n-1}, a request to read, R, and possibly the size of the object to be read.
2. The memory system decodes the address, accesses the value stored at that address.

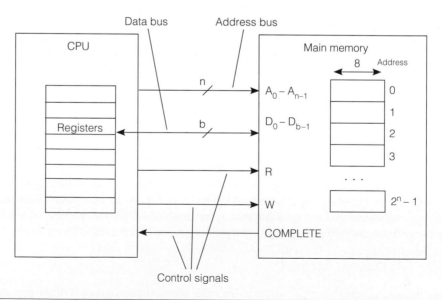

Fig. 2.2 Simplified view of the CPU-Memory Interface

3. The memory system returns the value to the CPU on the data lines, D_0-D_{b-1}.

4. Simultaneous with placing the value on the data lines, the memory system asserts the COMPLETE signal, notifying the CPU that the value on the data lines is valid.

For a Memory Write:

1. The CPU places the address of the value to be written on the address lines, A_0-A_{n-1}, the value to be written on the data lines, D_0-D_{b-1}, and issues a write request, W.

2. After the value has been written to memory at the specified address, the memory system asserts the COMPLETE signal, notifying the CPU that the data has been written to memory.

The memory system will be discussed in greater detail in Chapter 7, Memory System Design.

We now give examples of the three classes of instructions: data movement, ALU, and branch. Following that, we provide a discussion that classifies machines according to how they encode items 2, 3, and 4 of the preceding list in their instruction set. As you shall see, items 2 and 3, specifying the operand and result addresses, are the most complex in practice, and we devote the final discussion in this section on instruction sets to operand access paths and addressing modes.

2.2.2   DATA MOVEMENT INSTRUCTIONS

Where does the data reside in the computer? The primary repository for both data and program is the main memory of the computer. From that staging point, information is moved into the CPU, where it becomes part of the *processor state,* residing in one or another CPU register. The data is processed and then moved back into main memory. Of course, input devices represent the ultimate source of data, and output devices represent the ultimate destination. The processor state also usually includes temporary storage locations for intermediate results. Table 2.1 shows several examples of data movement from various machines.

processor state

Table 2.1 Examples of Data Movement Instructions

Instruction	Meaning	Machine
MOV A, B	Move 16-bit data from memory loc. A to loc. B	VAX11
LDA A, Addr	Load accumulator A with the byte at mem. loc. Addr	M6800
lwz R3, A	Move 32-bit data from memory loc. A to register R3	PPC G4
li $3, 455	Load the 32-bit integer 455 into register $3	MIPS R3000
mov R4, dout	Move 16-bit data from register R4 to output port dout	DEC PDP11
IN AL, KBD	Load a byte from port KBD to accumulator	Intel Pentium
LEA.L (A0), A2	Load the address pointed to by A0 into A2	MC68000

Observe the wide variety of data movements in the table: memory-to-memory, memory-to-CPU, constant-to-CPU, CPU-to-output, and input-to-CPU are all represented. To generalize, the source of data may be an input port (such as the keyboard), memory, a register within the CPU, or a constant that is part of the instruction. The destination may be an output port, memory, or a CPU register. The size of the data item may range from a single byte to a 128-bit, double-precision, floating-point number or, for that matter, a 1MB block of data. Furthermore, more than one instruction may be required to move even one data item from source to destination. For example, the M6800 is restricted to moving at most 1 byte of data from memory to one of the two accumulators, from one of the two accumulators to memory, or from accumulator to accumulator.

In Chapter 1 we mentioned that many machines had instructions that manipulate various sizes of integers and floating-point numbers. An additional data type that some *address data type* machines distinguish is the *address data type*. The LEA instruction in Table 2.1 is an example of an instruction that computes an address and loads it into an address register, where the address presumably will be used to access a data item.

2.2.3   ALU INSTRUCTIONS

In a real sense the arithmetic and logic unit is the heart of the machine. All arithmetic operations, such as addition, subtraction, multiplication, and division, are performed there. It is also there that all logical operations such as AND, OR, and NOT take place.

With the ALU instructions comes the question of what kinds of operand access modes should be allowed. Should the programmer be allowed to specify operands that are in memory locations, or should the programmer be forced to have one or all of the operands in registers before the ALU operation is performed? Should the ALU instruction allow the result to be stored in a memory location, or should it force result storage in a register? The earliest accumulator machines had almost no flexibility in specifying operand and result locations, because there were no general purpose registers in the CPU. In subsequent machines, operands and results of ALU operations could be located in registers or in memory. The VAX11 allowed both operands and the result to be in registers or memory. The newer RISC machines sacrifice that flexibility for a gain in execution speed. We shall see in Chapter 5 that pipeline operation is interfered with by allowing ALU operations to access memory. ALU operands in RISC machines must nearly always be located in registers, placed there by previous data movement instructions, and the final results must be moved to memory by subsequent data movement instructions.

Table 2.2 shows some example ALU instructions from a number of machines. Notice again the lack of any sort of syntactic standardization among the various machine types. The instructions range from one that accomplishes the multiplication of two 32-bit floating-point numbers to one that simply decrements a general register.

2.2.4   BRANCH INSTRUCTIONS

In Chapter 1 we mentioned the program counter (PC) as pointing to the next instruction to be executed. Thus, the PC controls program flow. During normal program execution, the PC is incremented during the instruction fetch to point to the next instruction. A *branch target address* transfer of control, or a branch, to an instruction other than the next one in sequence requires computation of a *target address*, which is the address to which control is to be

Table 2.2 Examples of ALU Instructions

Instruction	Meaning	Machine
MULF A,B,C	Multiply the 32-bit floating point values at memory locations A and B, and store the result in location C	VAX11
nabs r3,r1	Store the negative absolute value of r1 in r3	PPC G4
ori $2,$1,255	Store the logical OR of register $1 with 255 into register $2	MIPS R3000
DEC R2	Decrement the 16-bit integer in register R2	DEC PDP11
SHL AX,CL	Shift the 16-bit value in register AX left by 4 bits	Intel 80186

transferred. A target address is specified in a branch or jump instruction. The target address is loaded into the PC, replacing the address stored there.

There may be special branch target registers within the CPU. If a branch target register is preloaded with the target address prior to the execution of the branch instruction, the CPU will prefetch the instruction located at the branch target address, so that instruction will be ready for execution when the branch instruction finishes execution. Branch target registers are examples of registers that have "personality," as discussed at the beginning of Section 2.1.

A branch may be unconditional, as is the C goto statement, or it may be conditional, which means it depends on whether some condition within the processor state is true or false. The conditional branch is used to implement the condition part of C statements such as

if (X<0) X = –X;

There is no machine instruction that corresponds directly to the conditional statement above. The approach most machines take is to set various status flags within the CPU as a result of ALU operations. The instruction set contains a number of conditional branch instructions that test various of these flags and then branch or not according to their settings. The bit or bits that describe the condition are stored in a register variously called the processor status word (PSW), the *condition code* (*CC*) register, or the status register. Some of the status bits record the results of arithmetic operations. The VAX11 code to implement the preceding statement is

condition code (CC)

```
CMP  X, 0
BGE   OVER
MNEG X, X
OVER:        . . .
```

The most common condition-code bits are zero (Z), overflow (V), carry (C), and negative (N), which are set to indicate that the last arithmetic operation resulted in a zero result, an arithmetic overflow, a carry-out of the most significant bit (msb), or a negative result, respectively.

An alternative approach is to compute the difference of two values and store the result in a register. A conditional branch instruction is then used to test the computed value to see whether the condition is met. This is the method used in the SRC machine to be described in Section 2.3 and 2.4. We discuss conditional branching and the merits of these and other approaches in Chapter 6, "Computer Arithmetic and the Arithmetic Unit."

Table 2.3 Example Branch Instructions

Instruction	Meaning	Machine
BLBS A, Tgt	Branch to address Tgt if the least significant bit at location A is set.	VAX11
bun r2	Branch to location in r2 if the previous floating point comparison signaled that one or more of the values was not a number.	PPC G4
beq $2,$1,32	Branch to location PC+4+32 if contents of $1 and $2 are equal.	MIPS R3000
SOB R4 Loop	Decrement R4 and branch to address Loop if result π 0.	DEC PDP11
JCXZ Addr	Jump to Addr if contents of register CX = 0.	Intel 8086

Table 2.3 shows several examples of branch instructions. Notice that the SOB (subtract one and branch) and JCXZ instructions are specifically designed to control loops; they test the value of a register and branch if the result is zero. The SOB instruction even handles decrementing the register prior to the test. These instructions are used to implement higher-level language constructs such as for, while, and repeat.

2.2.5   4-, 3-, 2-, 1-, AND 0-ADDRESS AND GENERAL REGISTER MACHINE CLASSES

Machine instructions must be encoded into a bit pattern that somehow specifies all of the four items discussed on page 34. Two examples of such encodings were shown in Table 1.2 for the MC68000 processor. The instruction set designer would like to minimize the number of bits devoted to the specification, while at the same time allowing maximum flexibility in how these items can be specified. All things being equal, the designer would like the entire encoding for the instruction to fit into one machine word, and in fact this has become a hallmark of the RISC approach. For a two-operand arithmetic instruction, five items need to be specified:

1. Operation to be performed
2. Location of first operand
3. Location of second operand
4. Place to store the result
5. Location of next instruction to be executed

In this section we consider a number of abstract or hypothetical machines that vary in how many of these five items are explicitly specified, from five down to one. In each hypothetical machine, we study the encoding of an ALU instruction.

As we consider each machine, we quantify the number of bits required to encode one of its instructions. To make the encodings explicit, we assume that the hypothetical machine has 24-bit memory addresses and has 128 instructions. This means 3 bytes will be required to encode each address, and 7 bits to specify one of the 128 instructions. The 7 bits will be rounded up to 1 byte.

The 4-Address Machines and Operations.   The 4-address machine specifies all of the last four items in the list above, so it will require an address for each operand, one for the

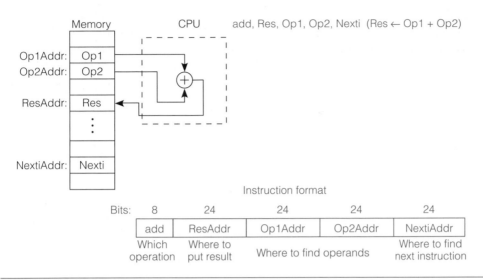

Fig. 2.3 The 4-Address Machine and Instruction Format

result, and one for the next instruction. Figure 2.3 shows schematically the programmer's model of the machine operation and instruction format. Notice that there are no programmer-accessible registers in the CPU, as none are needed. The operands are both fetched from memory, and the result is returned to memory. The address of the next instruction is also specified as an explicit value.

Each address requires 3 bytes, so it will require $4 \times 3 + 1 = 13$ bytes to encode a 4-address ALU instruction. If the normal path between memory and the CPU is 24-bit word "chunks," then the instruction will occupy five words in memory, and five words will need to be transferred to the CPU just to specify the instruction. A layout of the instruction in memory might appear as shown on the next page.

```
23 _ _ _ _ _ _ _ _ 6       0
 ┌──────────────┬──────────┐
 │    Wasted    │    Op     │
 ├──────────────┴──────────┤
 │    Operand 1 address     │
 ├─────────────────────────┤
 │    Operand 2 address     │
 ├─────────────────────────┤
 │     Result address       │
 ├─────────────────────────┤
 │ Address of next instruction │
 └─────────────────────────┘
```

Let us now count the number of *memory accesses* required when the instruction executes. Five words will be transferred to the CPU when the instruction itself is fetched, as shown in the preceding figure. Then the two words representing the operands themselves need to be fetched into the CPU, and after the addition has been performed, the result needs to be written back to memory. This means that $5 + 2 + 1 = 8$ words must be transferred to add the two words and store the result.

Because of the large instruction word size and number of memory accesses, the 4-address machine and instruction format is not normally seen in machine design,

memory accesses per instruction

although the 4-address structure is used internally in some implementations of computer control units. This kind of controller implementation is known as *microcoded control*. In a microcoded design, the steps required to execute an instruction are themselves stored as a sequence of microcode instructions that are executed to effect instruction execution. We discuss the design of microcoded machines in Chapter 5. Time and space costs make the 4-address format uncompetitive for other uses. In fact, much of the effort designers put into instruction set organization goes toward reducing the number of instruction bits needed to specify the preceding five items. In some hypothetical implementation domain where memory costs and access times were small compared to ALU execution time, however, the 4-address machine could be considered as a design alternative.

The 3-Address Machines and Operations. The inclusion within the CPU of a *program counter* that always points to the next instruction eliminates the need to specify the address of the next instruction in all but the class of branch instructions. It is now the responsibility of the control unit to know the size of the currently executing instruction, so the control unit can advance the PC to point to the next address beyond. Machines with a program counter but no operand storage in the CPU are known as 3-address machines. Figure 2.4 shows the operation of a 3-address machine and the corresponding instruction format. Note the inclusion of a program counter that points to the next instruction.

program counter

Figure 2.4 also shows that instructions and data may be stored in different parts of memory. The instruction format now includes only four fields: one that specifies which operation is to be performed, two that specify operand memory addresses, and one that specifies the result address.

There is neither the need nor the ability to specify the address of the next instruction. In our example above, the number of bytes would be reduced from 13 to $3 \times 3 + 1 = 10$ bytes, or four 24-bit words in a machine that accessed 24-bit words instead of bytes.

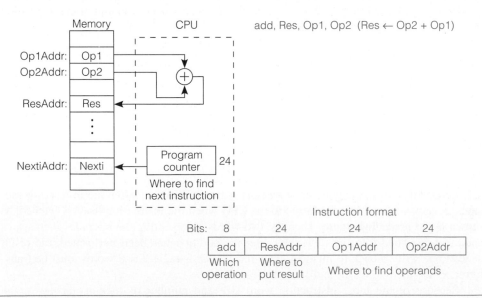

Fig. 2.4 The 3-Address Machine and Instruction Format

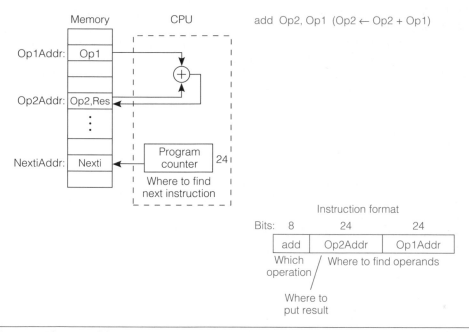

Fig. 2.5 The 2-Address, Machine and Instruction Format

The 2-Address Machines and Operations.   A reduction to two addresses can be obtained by storing the result into the memory address of one of the operands. Figure 2.5 shows the machine structure and instruction format for the 2-address machine. The change from a 3-address machine to a 2-address machine does not require any change in the register structure of the CPU, but only in the instruction meaning and format. Now our example instruction is reduced from 10 bytes to $2 \times 3 + 1 = 7$ bytes, or three 24-bit words in a word-oriented machine.

The 1-Address (Accumulator) Machines and Instructions.   Let us now add a single accumulator, Acc, to the CPU and use it both for the source of one operand and as the result destination. Figure 2.6 shows the programmer's model and instruction format for such a machine. Now the result is kept in the accumulator in the CPU and may be used for further computations. The Acc serves both as the source of one operand and as the storage location for the result. Notice that because there is only a single accumulator, it need not be mentioned in the machine instruction.

The 1-address instruction requires additional operations to *load* and *store* the accumulator's contents, however. These instructions are also 1-address instructions. The instruction `lda Addr` loads the accumulator from address `Addr`, and `sta Addr` stores the accumulator's contents into address `Addr`:

load and store

```
Acc = OpAddr;  ⇒ lda OpAddr
OpAddr = Acc;  ⇒ sta OpAddr
```

Our example addition now requires only $1 \times 3 + 1 = 4$ bytes, or two 24-bit words for the addition, although if one operand were not in memory, or if the final result needed to be written back to memory, additional load or store instructions would be required.

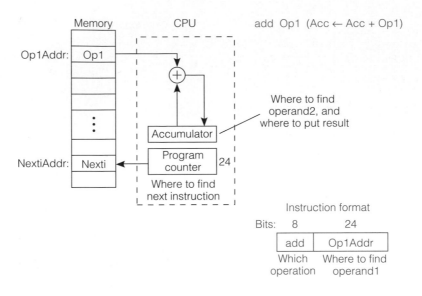

Fig. 2.6 The 1-Address Machine and Instruction Format

The 1-address machines generally provide a minimum in the size of both program and CPU memory required, and the architecture was quite popular in very early mainframes and early microcomputers. The Intel 8080, Motorola 6800, and MOS Technology 6502 were examples of machines that contained accumulators.

The 0-Address (Stack) Computers and Address Formats. The inclusion of a push-down stack in the CPU allows ALU instructions with no addresses. Operands are pushed onto the stack from memory, and ALU operations implicitly operate on the top members of the stack. Figure 2.7 shows the add operation performed on the two operands in the top and second positions on the stack. The operation removes both operands from the stack and replaces them with the result. The push operation from memory to stack is also shown. The code to add two memory operands is a bit more complex:

```
Op3 = Op1 + Op2;  ⇒  push Op1
                      push Op2
                      add
                      pop Op3
```

stack, push, and pop

Notice that the push and pop operations still require a memory address, and the word count for the code above is $3 + 1 = 4$ bytes for each push and pop, and an additional byte for expression evaluation, for a total of $4 \times 3 + 1 = 13$ bytes. The drawback of a 0-address computer is that operands must always be in the top two stack locations, and extra instructions may be required to get them there. Stack machines, like stack calculators, have their adherents. General register machines have achieved more popularity in recent times, however, probably because they are more amenable to machine hardware speedup techniques, such as pipelining, that run instructions in parallel. We cover pipeline techniques in Chapter 5.

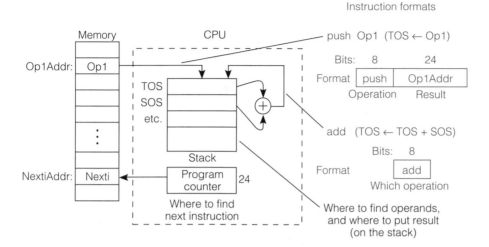

Fig. 2.7 The 0-Address, or Stack, Machine and Instruction Formats

Example 2.1   Expression Evaluation with 3-, 2-, 1-, and 0-Address Machines   Evaluate the expression a = (b + c)* (d − e) in 3-, 2-, 1-, and 0-address machines. For these machines, minimal code to evaluate this expression is shown in the following table:

3-Address	2-Address	Accumulator	Stack
add a,b,c	load a,b	lda b	push b
mpy a,a,d	add a,c	add c	push c
sub a,a,e	mpy a,d	mpy d	add
	sub a,e	sub e	push d
		sta a	mpy
			push e
			sub
			pop a

General Register Machines and 1-1/2 Address Instructions.   Accumulator and stack machines offer the advantage that an intermediate result can be retained in the CPU. Complex operations make it worthwhile to store more than one temporary result in the CPU. Supplying more than one register to the CPU requires the use of instruction bits to encode which register is to be used, but specifying one of n registers requires only $\log_2(n)$ bits, *register selection* and temporary registers can make instruction execution much more efficient. A common type of ALU instruction in the general register machine is the analog of the 3-address instruction, but it uses CPU registers instead of memory addresses. These "small" addresses that specify registers instead of memory addresses are sometimes referred to as

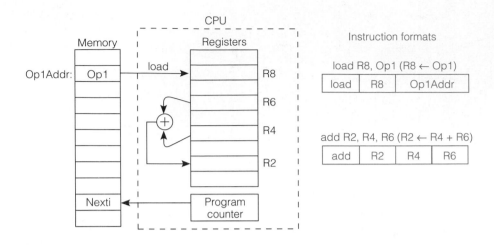

Fig. 2.8 General Register Machine and Instruction Formats

half addresses

half addresses. An instruction that specifies one operand in memory and one operand in a register would be known as a 1-1/2 address instruction. Figure 2.8 shows the structure and formats of a general register machine. The figure shows both a load from memory to register R8 and an add of registers R6 and R4 with the result stored in R2.

Our encoding example is now a bit more complex. Assume that there are 32 general-purpose registers. Each register reference thus requires 5 bits to specify 1 of the 32 registers, and our 3-register add instruction now requires $5 \times 3 + 7 = 22$ bits, which means we can encode the instruction in one 24-bit word. The load instruction will require $7 + 5 + 24$ bits, or two 24-bit words.

General register machines provide the greatest flexibility to the programmer, and virtually every new architecture since 1980 has been of this class. You may wonder at the seeming progression from accumulator machines to general register machines. This is due in large part to the reduction in the cost of machine memory. When RAM is $15 per megabyte, having many general purpose registers is a fine idea. It was not so fine in the heyday of the accumulator, during the early days of computing, when a single *bit* cost $25.

Classifying Machines by Operand and Result Location. Bear in mind that the preceding classes are hypothetical. First of all, there are no 4-address machines. Second, nearly all real machines provide some combination of the above instruction classes. The VAX11 is probably the champion in this category, as it includes instructions from all classes. Real machines are usually classed as being in the load-store, register-memory, or memory-memory classes.

load/store machines

Many modern computers, including RISCs, are of the *load/store*, sometimes called *register-to-register,* variety. These are 1-1/2-address machines in which memory access instructions are limited to two instructions: load and store. The load instruction moves data from memory to a processor register, and the store instruction moves data from the processor to memory. ALU and branch operations in load-store machines can accept only operands located in processor registers, and they must store the result in a processor register. Load/store machines are sometimes called register-to-register machines because ALU operations must have operands and results in registers. The philosophy is that moving data values back and forth between memory and the processor is an expensive operation, and that the instruction set design should discourage this operation by limiting its usage to just a few explicit load and store instructions.

Register-memory machines locate operands and result in a combination of memory and registers. They are classed as 1- or 1-1/2-address machines, in which one operand or the result must be an accumulator or general register. *Memory-to-memory machines* allow both the operands and the result to reside in memory. They are classed as either 2- or 3-address machines, depending on whether one of the operand locations also serves as a result location.

register-memory machines

memory-to-memory machines

Key Concepts: Trade-Offs in Instruction Set and Processor Registers

The range of choices of processor-state structure and instruction types trade off flexibility in the placement of operands and results against the amount of information that must be specified by an instruction.

- The 3-address machines have the shortest code sequences but require an unreasonably large number of bits per instruction.
- The 0-address machines have the longest code sequences and the shortest individual instructions.
- Even in 0-address machines there are 1-address instructions, push and pop.
- General register machines modify the addressing rules by specifying one of a small set of registers, such as 32, by a short address, such as 5 bits. A general register counterpart to a 3-address instruction could specify 2 registers and 1 memory address.
- Load-store machines only include full memory addresses in instructions that move data between memory and registers: load and store.
- Current technology makes register access much faster than memory access and places a premium on short instructions. Both favor the general register organization.

2.2.6   ACCESS PATHS TO OPERANDS: ADDRESSING MODES

The computation process involves the continuous shuffling of program and data into and out of the CPU. The many different kinds of data structures and program variable references possible in modern high-level languages have driven machine architects to develop many sophisticated ways of providing access paths to operands in memory and CPU registers: *addressing modes*. Below we provide an informal description of some of the more common ones. After we discuss the SRC computer and the RTN description language, we use RTN to formally describe these and other less common addressing modes. Be aware that the terms used to describe addressing modes are not standardized in any way, and different machine and assembly language designers have their own terminology for addressing modes.

addressing modes

To access an operand in memory, the CPU must first generate an address, which it then issues to the memory subsystem. That address is referred to as an *effective address*.

effective address

The address may be computed in various ways, and the results of that computation may be interpreted in various ways. The process may involve computing an address in memory where the operand address is stored. Some of the more common addressing modes are shown in Figure 2.9.

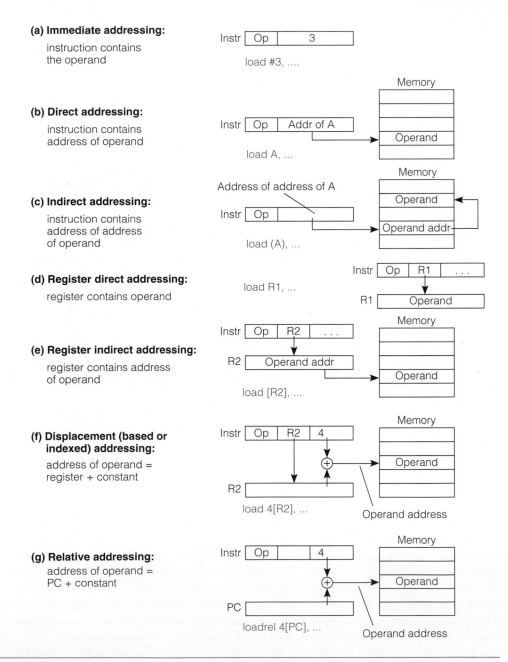

(a) Immediate addressing:
instruction contains the operand

(b) Direct addressing:
instruction contains address of operand

(c) Indirect addressing:
instruction contains address of address of operand

(d) Register direct addressing:
register contains operand

(e) Register indirect addressing:
register contains address of operand

(f) Displacement (based or indexed) addressing:
address of operand = register + constant

(g) Relative addressing:
address of operand = PC + constant

Fig. 2.9 Common Addressing Modes

The *immediate addressing mode,* shown in Figure 2.9a, is used to access constants stored in the instruction. It supplies an operand without computing an address, so it is not used for result addressing. Immediate addressing provides one of the two means of introducing constants into a program. (The other way is by storing the constants as data items in memory and retrieving them by direct addressing.)

immediate addressing mode

The previous code examples have used the *direct addressing mode,* shown in Figure 2.9b. The address of the operand is specified as a constant contained in the instruction.

direct addressing mode

In *indirect addressing,* shown in Figure 2.9c, a constant in the instruction specifies not the address of the value, but the address of the address of the value. An example of the use of indirect addressing is in implementing pointers, where the pointer, which is an address, is stored in memory at the pointer address. Thus, two memory references are required to access the value. The CPU must first fetch the pointer, which is stored in memory; then, having that address, the CPU accesses the value stored at that address.

indirect addressing mode

In the *register direct mode,* shown in Figure 2.9d, the operand is contained in the specified register.

register direct mode

When the address of the operand is in a register, the mode is referred to as the *register indirect mode,* shown in Figure 2.9e. This addressing mode is used to sequentially access the elements of an array stored in memory. The starting address of the array is stored in a register, an access made, and the register incremented to point to the next element.

register indirect mode

To access arrays, or components of the C struct, or the Pascal record (which by definition are stored at a fixed offset from the start address of the structure), the *indexed mode,* sometimes called *displacement* or *based* addressing, is used, as shown in Figure 2.9f. The memory address is formed by adding a fixed constant, usually contained within the instruction, to the address value contained in a register. The term *indexed* is normally used when the constant value is the base of an array in memory, added to the "index" stored in a register. The term *displacement* is used when the base of a struct is held in a register and added to the constant offset, or displacement, of the field in the struct.

indexed, or displacement, or based mode

The *relative addressing mode,* shown in Figure 2.9g, is similar to indexed, but the base address is held in the PC rather than in another register. This allows the storage of memory operands at a fixed offset from the current instruction.

relative addressing mode

The previous discussion is only to provide a flavor for the complexity of addressing modes. A formal description of addressing modes is given in Section 2.5.

2.3   Informal Description of the Simple RISC Computer, SRC

In this section we provide an informal description of SRC, and in the next section we provide a formal description. This example machine is sufficiently simple and lacking in the complications necessary in real machines that in Chapters 4 and 5 it will serve as an example of detailed machine hardware design.

2.3.1   REGISTER AND MEMORY STRUCTURE

Figure 2.10 shows the programmer's model of the SRC machine. It is a general register machine, with 32 general purpose, 32-bit registers, plus a program counter (PC) and an instruction register (IR). Although the main memory is organized as an array of bytes, only 32-bit words can be fetched from or stored into main memory. Its memory operand access follows the load-store model described previously. A word at address A is defined as the 4 bytes at that address and the succeeding three addresses. The byte at the lowest address contains the most significant 8 bits, the byte at the next address contains the next most significant 8 bits, and so on.

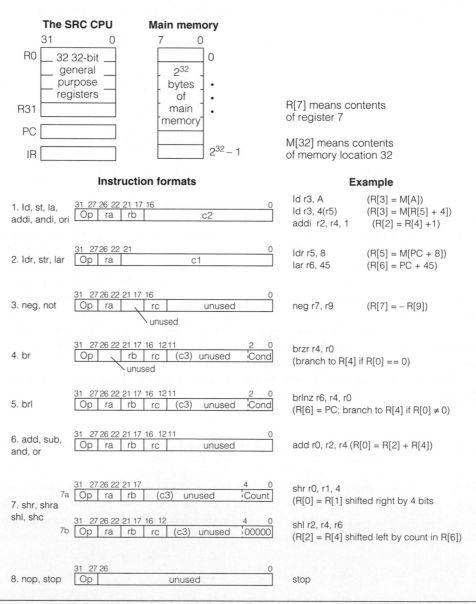

Fig. 2.10 Programmer's Model of the SRC

2.3.2 INSTRUCTION FORMATS

Figure 2.10 shows 23 instructions in 8 different formats:

- Load and store instructions: There are four load instructions—ld, ldr, la, and lar—and two store instructions—st and str.
- Branch instructions: There are two branch instructions, br and brl, that allow unconditional and conditional branches to an address contained in a specified register. The conditional branches test a register's contents and branch when the register contents are $= 0, \neq 0, \geq 0$, or < 0. The instruction brl stores the PC in a specified register.
- Arithmetic instructions: There are four arithmetic instructions: add, addi, sub, and neg. All except addi take two register operands and place the result in a register. The instruction addi adds an immediate constant contained in the c2 field to a register and places the result in a register.
- Logical and shift instructions: There are nine logical and shift instructions: and, andi, or, ori, not, shr, sha, shl, and shc. The shift instructions can shift by a count contained as a constant in the instruction or by a count in a register.
- Miscellaneous instructions: There are two zero-operand instructions: nop and stop.

All instructions are 32 bits long. Because the SRC is of the load-store class of machine, operands in memory can be accessed only through load and store instructions. All instructions have a 5-bit opcode field, allowing 32 different instructions. Here we define only 23 of these instructions. The ra, rb, and rc fields are 5-bit fields that specify one of the 32 general purpose registers. Constants c1, c2, c3, Cond, and Count are used in various ways that we will describe as we discuss the individual instructions. We first discuss the memory addressing modes and then each of the 23 instructions. As we describe each instruction, we include a comment field beginning with a semicolon that describes the operation of the instruction in pseudo C code. The notation M[x] means the value stored at word x in memory.

Notice that there are many unused "holes" in the instructions that waste memory space. This willingness to trade off less efficient use of memory for having all instructions be exactly one word long is a feature of most modern RISC machines. This issue is discussed in more detail in Chapter 3.

2.3.3 ACCESSING MEMORY: THE LOAD AND STORE INSTRUCTIONS

The load and store instructions are the only SRC instructions to access operands in memory.

Load and Store Instructions

```
ld  ra, c2       ;Direct addressing: R[ra] = M[c2]
ld  ra, c2(rb)   ;Indexed addressing(rb ≠ 0); R[ra] = M[c2 + R[rb]]
st  ra, c2       ;Direct addressing: M[c2] = R[ra]
st  ra, c2(rb)   ;Indexed addressing(rb ≠ 0); M[c2 + R[rb]] = R[ra]
la  ra, c2       ;Load displacement address: R[ra] = c2
la  ra, c2(rb)   ;Load displacement address: R[ra] = c2 + R[rb]
```

These instructions use format 1 from Figure 2.10. The register to be loaded or stored is specified in the 5-bit field ra, and the address is specified as the 17-bit value in the c2 field. The rb field serves double duty. If rb = 0 (that is, if the value of the 5-bit field is zero, specifying r0), this serves as a signal to the machine control unit that the memory address is just the value of c2 as a sign-extended 2's complement number. If any of the other 31 registers are specified—that is, if rb ≠ 0—then the memory address is formed by adding R[rb] + c2, resulting in the based, or displacement, addressing mode. Be aware that the addition of c2 to R[rb] takes place when the instruction is executing, that is, at run time. Notice that when c2 is set to 0, the addressing mode becomes register indirect.

Thus the ld instruction loads into register R[ra] the operand stored at address c2 (direct addressing) if rb = 0, or at address c2 + R[rb] if rb ≠ 0 (indexed or displacement addressing); the st instruction does the reverse, storing the operand in R[ra] at address c2 when rb = 0, or at address c2 + R[rb] when rb ≠ 0.

The la (load address) instruction calculates the operand address as above, but then, rather than fetching the operand, it stores the calculated value in R[ra]. Operationally, it loads the value of c2 or c2 + R[rb] itself into a register. This allows complex address calculations to be performed explicitly. In this way, addressing modes not available in the instruction set can be simulated by a series of explicit arithmetic steps.

Several points should be made about these instructions. First, because c2 is a 17-bit value, only operands stored in the first or last 2^{16} bytes of memory can be accessed using the direct addressing mode, or, in the case of the la instruction, only positive or negative constants with magnitudes smaller than 2^{16} can be loaded. To access operands stored elsewhere in memory, the displacement or register indirect addressing modes must be used, with the value in R[rb] serving as the base and the value of c2 serving as an offset. (Recall that the register indirect addressing mode can be achieved by setting c2 equal to 0.) Note also that the address addition is 2's complement, so the 17-bit displacement must be sign-extended to 32 bits before the address addition. See Chapter 6 for a more thorough discussion of 2's complement arithmetic.

Relative addressing computes the operand address as an address *relative to the PC*.

Load and Store Relative

```
ldr  ra,  c1   ;Load register relative: R[ra] = M[PC + c1]
str  ra,  c1   ;Store register relative: M[PC + c1] = R[ra]
lar  ra,  c1   ;Load relative address: R[ra] = PC + c1
```

The effective address is formed by the run-time addition, c1+PC. These relative addressing modes make the instructions *relocatable*. Because the address of the data is specified as a value that is a constant offset from the PC, and hence from the current instruction, the entire module of program and data can be moved, or relocated, anywhere in the machine memory without changing the values of the displacements. This is in contrast to the direct addressing mode, which specifies addresses as absolute memory locations. Because the displacement constant c1 has 22 bits, addresses within $\pm 2^{21}$ of the current instruction can be specified.

Table 2.4 provides examples of the assembly language and resulting machine encoding of several load and store instructions. You should study it until you understand each entry. The operation codes for each instruction are given in the op column.

Table 2.4 Example SRC Load and Store Instructions

Instruction	op	ra	rb	c1	Meaning	Addressing Mode
ld r1, 32	1	1	0	32	R[1] ← M[32]	Direct
ld r22, 24(r4)	1	22	4	24	R[22] ← M[24 + R[4]]	Displacement
st r4, 0(r9)	3	4	9	0	M[R[9]] ← R[4]	Register indirect
la r7, 32	5	7	0	32	R[7] ← 32	Immediate
ldr r12, −48	2	12	–	−48	R[12] ← M[PC −48]	Relative
lar r3, 0	6	3	–	0	R[3] ← PC	Register (!)

Example 2.2   Binary Encoding of an SRC Instruction

As an example of SRC instruction encoding, let us encode the second instruction in Table 2.4, which is `ld r22, 24(r4)`. Working from the msb, the encoding will be

```
op=1    ra=22    rb=4              c1=24
00001   10110    00100   00000000000011000  = 0x0D880018
```
∎

You should verify this encoding and try several examples for yourself.

2.3.4   ARITHMETIC AND LOGIC INSTRUCTIONS

This class of instructions uses the ALU of the SRC machine to do arithmetic, logical, and shift operations. We first cover the "1-operand" instructions `not` and `neg`.

1-Operand ALU Instructions

```
neg  ra,  rc  ;Negate: R[ra] = –R[rc]
not  ra,  rc  ;Not: R[ra] = R[rc]
```

These format 3 instructions take one register operand and provide one register result. The instruction `neg` (op = 15) takes the 2's complement of the contents of register R[rc] and stores it in register R[ra]. The `not` (op = 24) instruction takes the logical (1's) complement of the contents of register R[rc] and stores it in register R[ra]. All other fields in the instruction are unused.

The instructions `add` (op = 12), `sub` (op = 14), `and` (op = 20), and `or` (op = 22) are 2-operand, 1-result instructions. All must be in the general purpose registers. They are specified using format 6. Notice that the least significant 12 bits are unused, because the first 4 fields are sufficient to describe the entire operation.

2-Operand ALU Instructions

```
add  ra, rb, rc  ;2's complement addition: R[ra] = R[rb] + R[rc]
sub  ra, rb, rc  ;2's complement subtraction: R[ra] = R[rb] – R[rc]
and  ra, rb, rc  ;Logical AND: R[ra] = R[rb]∧R[rc]
or   ra, rb, rc  ;Logical OR: R[ra] = R[rb]∨R[rc]
```

There are three ALU instructions that use the immediate addressing mode: addi (op = 13), andi (op = 21), and ori (op = 23). The constant is contained in the 17-bit c2 field and is sign-extended to a 32-bit value before the arithmetic operation is performed. All of these instructions use format 1.

Immediate Addressing ALU Instructions

```
addi ra, rb, c2   ;Immediate 2's compl. addition: R[ra] = R[rb] + c2
andi ra, rb, c2   ;Immediate logical and: R[ra] = R[rb]∧c2
ori  ra, rb, c2   ;Immediate logical or: R[ra] = R[rb]∨c2
```

The shift instructions shift the operand in R[rb] right, left, or "circularly," from 1 to 32 bits, and place the result in R[ra]; the amount of the shift is governed by an encoded 5-bit unsigned integer, so shifts from 0 to 31 bits are possible. The integer representing the shift count is stored either as an immediate value in the 5 least significant bits in the instruction (format 7a), or, if that value is 0, then the shift count is taken from the least significant 5 bits of register R[rc] (format 7b).

There are two forms of right shift, shr and shra (op = 26 and 27, respectively). The first form shifts zeros in from the left as the value is shifted right, and the second form, the so-called arithmetic shift, continually shifts copies of the msb into the word on the left as the contents are shifted right. This arithmetic form of the shift preserves the arithmetic sign of 2's complement numbers during the shift operation.

The left shift, shl (op = 28), shifts zeros in on the right as the value in the register is shifted left. The circular shift, shc (op = 29), shifts the value left by *count* bits, but the value shifted out of the register on the left is placed back into the register on the right. The assembly language forms are shown below.

Shift Instructions

```
shr  ra, rb, rc       ;Shift R[rb] right into R[ra] by count in R[rc]
shr  ra, rb, count    ;Shift R[rb] right into R[ra] by count in c3
shra ra, rb, rc       ;AShift R[rb]right into R[ra] by count in R[rc]
shra ra, rb, count    ;AShift R[rb] right into R[ra] by count in c3
shl  ra, rb, rc       ;Shift R[rb] left into R[ra] by count in R[rc]
shl  ra, rb, count    ;Shift R[rb] left into R[ra] by count in c3
shc  ra, rb, rc       ;Shift R[rb] circ. into R[ra] by count in R[rc]
shc  ra, rb, count    ;Shift R[rb] circ. into R[ra] by count in c3
```

All of these instructions are encoded using format 7 from Figure 2.10. If the count field ≠ 0 (format 7a), then the shift count is taken to be the 5 least significant bits (lsbs), of the c3 field, called "count" in the figure. If the count field = 0 (format 7b), then the shift count is taken from the register encoded in bits 12–16 of the instruction, called rc in format 7 of Figure 2.10.

2.3.5   BRANCH INSTRUCTIONS

The branch instructions br (op = 8) and brl (op = 9) are encoded using formats 4 and 5. Format 4, br, is used to specify a branch instruction that replaces the PC with the target address of the branch. Format 5, brl, is used for the branch and link instruction, which copies the PC into a so-called linkage register prior to the branch. This *link* register allows return from subroutine calls and is used to implement high-level language procedures and functions. Notice that the PC is copied into the linkage register regardless of whether the branch is taken. These two instructions allow branching under five different branch conditions. We mentioned in the previous discussion of branch instructions that many machines maintain a set of condition codes in a status register within the CPU that can be tested as part of a conditional branch. SRC does not use this approach. Rather, it allows any of the 32 general purpose registers to hold a value to be tested for conditional branching. The branch condition to be tested is specified by the least significant 3 bits of field c3, c3$\langle 2..0 \rangle$, as shown in Table 2.5. A two-letter code, nv, zr, nz, pl, or mi, appended to the mnemonic, is converted by the assembler to the branch condition code in c3. The meaning of the ra, rb, and rc fields in the branch instructions is shown on the next page.

subroutine return link

Branch Instructions

```
br   rb,  rc,  c3       ;Branch to R[rb] if R[rc] meets condition in c3
brl  ra,  rb,  rc,  c3  ;R[ra] ← PC; branch as above
```

Table 2.6 shows examples of the forms and encoding of all the branch instructions. The assembler is responsible for converting the branch mnemonic and appended two-letter code of column 1 of the table to operation codes 8 and 9 of br and brl instructions, respectively, as well as the correct c3$\langle 2..0 \rangle$ field value selecting the branch condition. The fields that the assembler will assemble into the 32-bit instruction are given in the table: op, ra, rb, rc, and c3$\langle 2..0 \rangle$. The form in the first column will fix the op and c3$\langle 2..0 \rangle$ fields, and the remaining operands will fix the ra, rb, and rc fields. Note that in some cases one or more of these fields are unused, indicated by a long dash in the corresponding table entry.

2.3.6 MISCELLANEOUS INSTRUCTIONS

In addition to the instructions mentioned above, there are two instructions: nop (op = 0), whose purpose is to do nothing, and stop (op = 31), whose purpose is to halt the machine. The nop instruction is used as a placeholder or as a time waster and is very important in pipelined implementations (see Chapter 5). The stop instruction is used to halt the machine at a specified point in program execution. It is useful in debugging, as it can be inserted at problematical points in the program, and if the stop instruction is reached, the person doing the debugging can examine the machine state at his or her leisure.

Table 2.5 Branch Conditions and Encoding

Assembly Language	c3$\langle 2..0 \rangle$	Branch Condition
brnv, brlnv	0	Never
br, brl	1	Always (unconditional)
brzr, brlzr	2	If R[rc] = 0
brnz, brlnz	3	If R[rc] ≠ 0
brpl, brlpl	4	If R[rc]$\langle 31 \rangle$ = 0 (R[rc] ≥ 0)
brmi, brlmi	5	If R[rc]$\langle 31 \rangle$ = 1 (R[rc] negative)

Table 2.6 Forms and Formats of the br and brl Instructions

Assembly Language	Example Instruction	Meaning	op	ra	rb	rc	c3⟨2..0⟩	Condition
brlnv	brlnv r6	R[6] ← PC	9	6	—	—	000	never
br	br r4	PC ← R[4]	8	—	4	—	001	always
brl	brl r6,r4	R[6] ← PC; PC ← R[4]	9	6	4	—	001	always
brzr	brzr r5,r1	if (R[1]=0) PC ← R[5]	8	—	5	1	010	zero
brlzr	brlzr r7,r5,r1	R[7] ← PC; if (R[1]=0) PC← R[5]	9	7	5	1	010	zero
brnz	brnz r1, r0	if (R[0]≠0) PC ← R[1]	8	—	1	0	011	nonzero
brlnz	brlnz r2,r1,r0	R[2] ← PC; if (R[0]≠0) PC← R[1]	9	2	1	0	011	nonzero
brpl	brpl r3, r2	if (R[2]≥0) PC← R[3]	8	—	3	2	100	plus
brlpl	brlpl r4,r3,r2	R[4] ← PC; if (R[2]≥0) PC← R[3]	9	4	3	2	100	plus
brmi	brmi r0, r1	if (R[1]<0) PC← R[0]	8	—	0	1	101	minus
brlmi	brlmi r3,r0,r1	R[3] ← PC; if (r1<0) PC← R[0]	9	3	0	1	101	minus

You may feel confused about the precise meaning of the instructions after reading the preceding informal description. The English language, or any natural language, is ill suited to describing precise, complicated processes such as machine language interpretation. In the next section we introduce a formal description language much more suited to describing machines and their behaviors.

Example 2.3 SRC Assembly Code for a C Conditional Statement
In presenting SRC code, we will assume some assembly language conventions that are summarized in Appendix C. Let us encode the C conditional statement,

```
#define Cost 125
if (X<0) X = -X;
```

originally discussed on page 39, using SRC assembly language:

```
Cost:  .equ  125        ;Define symbolic constant
       .org  1000       ;Next word will be loaded at address 1000₁₀
X:     .dw   1          ;Reserve 1 word for variable X
       .org  5000       ;Program will be loaded at location 5000₁₀
       lar   r0, Over   ;Load address of jump location if expression is false
       ld    r1, X      ;Get value of X into r1
       brpl  r0, r1     ;Branch to Over if r1 ≥ 0
       neg   r1, r1     ;Negate value
Over:  ...
```

The three "pseudo ops," `.equ`, `.org`, and `.dw`, are instructions to the assembler and program loader, and do not result in any executable code. The pseudo op `.equ` allows the programmer to specify constants symbolically, in almost exact analogy to the `#define` operation of C; `.org` specifies the locations of data and program in memory; and `.dw` reserves space for program variables. Notice also that the assembler allows the use of symbolic labels such as `Over` to represent locations in the program. The assembler will pass over the program text, converting the symbolic values to the actual constants they represent before encoding the program into the binary machine language. ∎

CLASSIC EXAMPLE: COMPUTING MEMBERS OF THE FIBONACCI SERIES

Computation of the Fibonacci number series is often used as an example of a simple number series calculation. The Fibonacci sequence is defined as follows: fib(1) = 1, fib(2) = 1, fib(n) = fib(n–1) + fib(n–2) n > 2. The program below begins by initializing the first two members of the series as memory locations seq and next. Storage for cnt additional members of the series is reserved at memory location ans. After initialization of loop, cnt, and seq, the loop calculates each member of the series from the previous two members, stores the newly calculated member, increments the address of the next member and the count, and branches back to loop if there are more members to count.

```
; fib.asm. Compute Fibonacci numbers.

cnt:    .equ 8              ; # to compute after first two
        .org 0              ; Store sequence at addr. 0
seq:    .dc  1              ; Init. the first Fib. #
next:   .dc  1              ; Init. the second Fib. #
ans:    .dw  cnt            ; Storage for the next 8 Fib. #
        .org 0x1000         ; Begin ass'y. at hex. addr. 1000
        lar  r31, loop      ; Branch address
        la   r0,  cnt       ; Init. count
        la   r1,  seq       ; Init r1 to index of seq[0]
loop:   ld   r2,  seq(r1)   ; Get fib(n-2)
        ld   r3,  next(r1)  ; Get fib(n-1)
        add  r2,  r2,    r3 ; compute fib(n)
        st   r2,  ans(r1)   ; Store fib(n)
        addi r1,  r1,     4 ; Increment index
        addi r0,  r0,    -1 ; Decrement count
        brnz r31, r0        ; loop until done
        stop
```

2.4 Formal Description of SRC Using Register Transfer Notation, RTN

English-language descriptions of a computer's hardware and instruction set are useful to convey general features of a machine design and to describe its general capabilities, but to build a computer, we need a precise specification of its function. Such a specification requires mathematical notation as well as natural language. The importance of moving

register transfer
(RT) language

data among registers and memory cells in a computer, sometimes transforming that data in the process, makes notation schemes known as *register transfer* (RT) *languages* a good method for incorporating the right level of precision into a computer specification. We develop and use a fairly generic RT notation, RTN. It is based on the ISP (Instruction Set Processor) language developed by Gordon Bell and Alan Newell and is similar in basic capabilities to RT languages in current use.

2.4.1 AN RTN DESCRIPTION OF THE SIMPLE RISC COMPUTER, SRC

We introduce the RTN by using it to describe the components and operation of SRC. First we describe the various registers and memories that can hold data values and can be set or used by some instruction. Different aspects of the notation are introduced as they are needed, and a summary of the notation is given in Table 2.7 and in Appendix B.

processor-state
registers

Memory.   The most significant memories are the *processor-state* items, which are used by many instructions.

Processor State

$PC\langle 31..0 \rangle$:	32-bit register named PC (program counter)
$IR\langle 31..0 \rangle$:	32-bit register named IR (instruction register)
Run:	1-bit run/halt indicator, named Run
Strt:	Start signal
$R[0..31]\langle 31..0 \rangle$:	32 32-bit general purpose registers

Memory registers are denoted by alphanumeric names. Bit numbers of a register are contained in angle brackets, $\langle \ \rangle$, after it. Either a single number or a .. separated range may be used. The number to the left of the .. numbers the high-order bit and that to the right the low-order bit. The absence of angle brackets in a definition denotes a single bit. A group of identical registers can have the same name and be distinguished by the index within square brackets, [ ]. The use of a register declared to have multiple words and/or bits, which leaves out the corresponding brackets, is assumed to refer to the entire range. Colons separate statements, in this case definitions, that have no particular ordering.

A RISC machine is characterized by a processor state with a large set of general registers and few other registers. In a real machine there are additional processor-state registers used in connection with interrupts, arithmetic exception conditions, I/O, and other machine activity. We will discuss these at the appropriate points.

The processor-state definitions tell us that the SRC is a general register machine with a program counter. The instruction register (IR) is the place where the individual instructions will be put for decoding of the various fields that specify operations, addresses, register numbers, and so on. Two single bits, Run and Strt, are defined. Run can be considered to be a flip-flop that is set to start the machine running. Strt is somewhat different. It is probably a signal coming from an external source such as a switch and is used to set Run.

The next most important memory elements are those of the large set of identical storage cells known as the *main memory*. The same memory may be addressed as bytes or words in this machine. An examination of the machine instructions of this section will show, however, that there are no instructions that can access or manipulate values smaller than 32-bit words.

Main Memory State

Mem[0..2^{32} – 1]$\langle 7..0 \rangle$: 2^{32} addressable bytes of memory

M[x]$\langle 31..0 \rangle$:= Mem[x]#Mem[x + 1]#Mem[x + 2]#Mem[x + 3]:

The word version of the memory is defined in terms of the byte version using the :=
operator. This "naming" operator defines the object on the left to be the expression on the
right. Whenever the left side appears in another expression, it is interpreted by substituting
the right-side text for it and interpreting the result recursively, if necessary.

The symbol # denotes concatenation of the storage or value on the left with that on the
right. This definition includes a dummy variable, *x*, which would be replaced by an actual
parameter in a use of the left-side name. For example, the meaning of M[40]$\langle 31..0 \rangle$ is
Mem[40]$\langle 7..0 \rangle$#Mem[41]$\langle 7..0 \rangle$#Mem[42]$\langle 7..0 \rangle$#Mem[43]$\langle 7..0 \rangle$.

From the memory definitions for the SRC, it is evident that a memory address will
require 32 bits. Because the instruction register has only 32 bits, it will not be possible for
an instruction to contain a full memory address along with an operation code. Registers,
and the program counter, are long enough to contain a memory address.

Formats.   Different parts of registers may have special purposes for which a separate
name is useful. These *register formats* give alternate names to parts of registers or expressions combining parts of registers. Distinguishing different parts of the instruction register
is particularly important in interpreting the meaning of an instruction.

register formats

Instruction Formats

op$\langle 4..0 \rangle$:= IR$\langle 31..27 \rangle$:   Operation code field
ra$\langle 4..0 \rangle$:= IR$\langle 26..22 \rangle$:   Target register field
rb$\langle 4..0 \rangle$:= IR$\langle 21..17 \rangle$:   Operand, address index, or branch target register
rc$\langle 4..0 \rangle$:= IR$\langle 16..12 \rangle$:   Second operand, conditional test, or shift count register
c1$\langle 21..0 \rangle$:= IR$\langle 21..0 \rangle$:   Long displacement field
c2$\langle 16..0 \rangle$:= IR$\langle 16..0 \rangle$:   Short displacement or immediate field
c3$\langle 11..0 \rangle$:= IR$\langle 11..0 \rangle$:   Count or modifier field

Because different fields overlap, a given bit might have several names and corresponding meanings, depending on the instruction. For example, some instructions use the op, ra,
and c1 fields, while others use op, ra, rb, rc, and c3, as shown previously in Figure 2.10.

Effective Address Calculations.   Some of the most important formats that name expressions using register fields instead of just renaming bits are those used to compute the *effective address* for a memory load or store. Effective addresses can be absolute (disp) or
relative to the PC (rel).

*SRC displacement
address*

Effective Address (Displacement)

disp$\langle 31..0 \rangle$:= ((rb = 0) → c2$\langle 16..0 \rangle$ {sign extend}:Displacement mode
          (rb ≠ 0) → R[rb] + c2$\langle 16..0 \rangle$ {sign extend, 2's complement}):

Note that this definition does not say that R[0] is identically zero. It only says that
when R[0] is chosen as the register accompanying a disp calculation that the c2 field alone
should be taken as the displacement.

The symbol → is an infix form of *if-then*. It has no concept of *else* included. If two conditions on the left of different → signs are true, both right-hand sides are evaluated. In the case above, the two conditions are disjoint, so only one will be true. Note that the right-hand sides of → are values and not operations, so the expression is a conditional definition of the value disp. The → symbol is used instead of the *if-then* notation because of this difference. Although some programming languages use the idea of conditional values, it is more often seen in mathematics. For example, the absolute value can be defined as

$$|x| := ((x{<}0) \to -x: (x \geq 0) \to x):$$

In defining a longer left-hand side in terms of a short right hand side, or in adding two fields of different length, it is necessary to specify how short operands are extended and what to do with a sum that might be too long. This is accomplished by the modifiers contained in brackets, { }, after the operation.

register number versus register contents

The English-language interpretation of this displacement mode address in SRC is that it is formed by adding the contents of a selected register to the displacement field of the instruction unless the register specified is R[0], in which case zero is added to the displacement field. We again emphasize the distinction between (rb = 0) and (R[rb] = 0). The first is a comparison of the *register number* to zero. The second is a comparison of *register contents* to zero. Thus, although R[0] is an ordinary register, it is not used in calculating addresses. Instead, its number allows an address to be based only on the displacement constant in the instruction. This saves having to have a special addressing mode or a permanently zero register for the direct address mode, in which an address is specified directly by the constant in the instruction.

SRC relative address

A second form of effective address in SRC is an address *relative* to the program counter.

Effective Address (Relative)

$\text{rel}\langle 31..0 \rangle := \text{PC}\langle 31..0 \rangle + c1\langle 21..0 \rangle$ {sign extend, 2's comp.}:   Relative addressing mode

It is particularly important for branch instructions. Since a register field is not needed, a longer displacement constant can be used. Since programs are written in a modular way, referring to things in the module that is currently executing can conveniently be done by using the program counter, which points to the next instruction to be executed.

Instruction Interpretation and the Fetch-Execute Cycle.   So far we have dealt with static definitions of storage elements and formats. We now reach the action part of the machine. The actions that occur for every instruction before the specific instruction is ever decoded are known as *instruction interpretation*. More complex things occur in real machines having interrupts and other independent processor activity, but here we only describe starting the machine and the normal fetch-execute cycle of reading the next instruction into the instruction register and advancing the program counter. The instruction interpretation executes repeatedly as long as the machine is turned on. In the following RTN description, the fetch cycle is defined as the time interval during which the instruction is fetched and the PC incremented. It is followed by instruction execution, which will end by invoking instruction interpretation again.

Instruction Interpretation

> instruction_interpretation := (
> ¬Run∧Strt → Run ← 1; instruction_interpretation):
> Run → (IR ← M[PC]: PC ← PC + 4; instruction_execution));

Register transfers are denoted by the assignment arrow ←. The left side of this operator must represent a storage element into which the value obtained from the expression on the right can be placed.

Two or more register transfers separated by a colon are assumed to occur simulta-neously. In the language of logic design (see Appendix A), *simultaneously* means the transfers occur on the same clock pulse. This implies the use of master-slave or edge-triggered flip-flops. The values of all colon-separated right-hand sides are evaluated using the original values of the registers, and then the new values are stored into the left sides. A semicolon separates operations that must occur in sequence. Thus, in the expression above, the value of PC used to evaluate the expressions M[PC] and PC + 4 is the original value, taken before PC has been incremented by 4. After M[PC] and PC + 4 have been computed, the IR is assigned M[PC], and PC is replaced by PC + 4. The oper-ation named instruction_execution, which is defined in the next section, must take place after the new values of IR and PC have been established. It is this sort of detail in more complex cases that is hard to describe concisely in natural language and makes it so important to have a formal notation. The symbol ¬ is logical complement on 1 or more bits, and ∧ and ∨ are used for logical AND and OR, respectively. The two conditions on the left side of → are disjoint, but they do not exhaust all the possibilities. If ¬Run∧¬Strt is true, no action takes place.

The instruction interpretation of SRC does nothing when Run is not set, unless the Strt signal is also present, in which case Run is set. When Run is set, the computer loads the instruction pointed to by the PC into the IR register, advances the program counter, and executes the instruction in IR. Describing the instruction interpretation, which happens for all instructions, before specifying the execution of individual instructions puts their execu-tion in the proper context. For example, when an instruction in the instruction register is executed, the program counter already points to the next instruction, 4 bytes further on in memory.

Instruction Execution.   We now come to the description of what each individual instruction in the machine does. Once the instruction has been fetched and the PC incre-mented, the instruction is executed. The following RTN describes the execution of SRC instructions. It takes the form of a long list of conditional operations. Each condition is a particular value of the operation code field of the IR register. The values are all distinct, so only the action appropriate to one instruction will occur. It is useful to name the condition that the operation field equals a particular value with the assembly code mnemonic corre-sponding to that value, and this is done "in-line," using the parenthesized definition to save a long separate list.

At the end of this large conditional statement, found on page 64, instruction_ interpre-tation is invoked, resulting in recursion: instruction_interpretation invokes instruc-tion_execution, which invokes instruction_interpretation.

Memory Reference Instructions.   Instructions can be divided into different classes based on what kind of action they perform. SRC, like other RISC computers, is distinguished by having a separate set of instructions that load registers from and store them into memory. The following instructions use a memory address, so their description includes the names defined in the effective address section.

Load and Store Instructions

instruction_execution := (
ld (:= op= 1) → R[ra] ← M[disp]:	Load register
ldr (:= op= 2) → R[ra] ← M[rel]:	Load register relative
st (:= op= 3) → M[disp] ← R[ra]:	Store register
str (:= op= 4) → M[rel] ← R[ra]:	Store register relative
la (:= op= 5) → R[ra] ← disp:	Load displacement address
lar (:= op= 6) → R[ra] ← rel:	Load relative address

Different instructions allow memory cells to be addressed either by displacement or relative mode. The ability to load the value of an address directly into a register, supplied by la and lar, has several uses in this machine. It is a way to place a short constant included in an instruction into a register. It can put a simple address into a register where arithmetic can be done on it for more complex addressing. It is also a way to put the target of a transfer of control, or branch, instruction into a register.

Branch Instructions.   Some special formatting on the constant field of the instruction is used only with branches.

Branch Instructions

cond := ($c3\langle 2..0\rangle$=0 → 0:	Never
$c3\langle 2..0\rangle$=1 → 1:	Always
$c3\langle 2..0\rangle$=2 → R[rc]=0:	If register is zero
$c3\langle 2..0\rangle$=3 → R[rc]≠0:	If register is nonzero
$c3\langle 2..0\rangle$=4 → R[rc]$\langle 31\rangle$=0:	If positive or zero
$c3\langle 2..0\rangle$=5 → R[rc]$\langle 31\rangle$=1):	If negative
br (:= op= 8) → (cond → PC ← R[rb]):	Conditional branch
brl (:= op= 9) → (R[ra] ← PC: cond → (PC ← R[rb])):	Branch and link

In SRC, transfer of control to a different point in the instruction stream is accomplished by a branch instruction, br, which changes the address of the next instruction in PC if a selected condition is true. The branch and link instruction, brl, first stores the address of the next instruction into a selected link register, so that control can be returned to the next instruction in sequence, and then branches if cond is true, behaving exactly like the br instruction. Notice that brl will store the link in R[ra] regardless of whether the branch is taken. In addition to being useful for subroutine call and return, the linkage register can be used for PC-relative addressing. The condition cond is defined to be one of six true (= 1) or false (= 0) values. One of the conditions is always true (or 1), so these instructions include unconditional branches, called *jumps* in many machines. Branch targets in SRC must be contained in a register, whereas branch and jump instructions in other machines often use an addressing mode like relative or displacement, as in the load and store instructions of SRC. There are good reasons to have an address with the branch, but the condition also uses up instruction bits, and there are some things that can be done to improve performance if a branch target is explicitly set up before the branch is executed.

ALU Instructions.   We next come to the arithmetic instructions. For the time being we will limit this simple SRC computer to add, subtract, and negate on 32-bit 2's complement numbers. We will see how to extend this when we discuss computer arithmetic.

Arithmetic Instructions

add (:= op = 12) $\rightarrow$ R[ra] $\leftarrow$ R[rb] + R[rc]:
addi (:= op = 13) $\rightarrow$ R[ra] $\leftarrow$ R[rb] + c2$\langle 16..0 \rangle$ {2's complement, sign extend}:
sub (:= op = 14) $\rightarrow$ R[ra] $\leftarrow$ R[rb] $-$ R[rc]:
neg (:= op = 15) $\rightarrow$ R[ra] $\leftarrow$ $-$R[rc]:

The add instruction has two forms: one that adds two registers and an *immediate* form that allows a small signed constant to be added to a register. The immediate form is useful for incrementing or decrementing counters and dealing with address offsets into arrays or records. Since all the arithmetic is 2's complement, it will only be mentioned when it is necessary to specify how to extend an operand to match the length of the other. The subtract instruction does not need an immediate form because a negative constant can be used with addi.

Nonnumeric data in a computer is manipulated mostly by logical operations, limited in this machine to *and*, *or*, and *not*. The and $\wedge$, or $\vee$, and not $\neg$ operators operate bitwise on multiple bit quantities, extending the shorter to match the length of the longer when necessary.

Logical Operations

and (:= op= 20) $\rightarrow$ R[ra] $\leftarrow$ R[rb] $\wedge$ R[rc]:
andi (:= op= 21) $\rightarrow$ R[ra] $\leftarrow$ R[rb] $\wedge$ c2$\langle 16..0 \rangle$ {sign extend}:
or (:= op= 22) $\rightarrow$ R[ra] $\leftarrow$ R[rb] $\vee$ R[rc]:
ori (:= op= 23) $\rightarrow$ R[ra] $\leftarrow$ R[rb] $\vee$ c2$\langle 16..0 \rangle$ {sign extend}:
not (:= op= 24) $\rightarrow$ R[ra] $\leftarrow$ $\neg$R[rc]:

The immediate forms are useful with *and* for clearing, or *masking*, fields of bits and with *or* for setting constants into fields.

The shift operations are needed to manipulate characters and other data shorter than a word. Shifts are also used with the arithmetic operations and have both logical and arithmetic versions. An immediate value for the shift count is very often desirable, but using a register for a computed count is also important. The count is the lower 5 bits of the constant field, because a shift count of more than 31 is not useful, but if these bits are 0, also not a useful shift count, the lower 5 bits of the register specified by rc is used instead.

bit-field masking

Shift Operations

n := ((c3⟨4..0⟩ = 0) → R[rc]⟨4..0⟩:   Shift count can be in a register or the
        (c3⟨4..0⟩ ≠ 0) → c3⟨4..0⟩):   constant field of the instruction
shr (:= op = 26) → R[ra]⟨31..0⟩ ← (n @ 0) # R[rb]⟨31..n⟩:
shra (:= op = 27) → R[ra]⟨31..0⟩ ← (n @ R[rb]⟨31⟩) # R[rb]⟨31..n⟩:
shl (:= op = 28) → R[ra]⟨31..0⟩ ← R[rb]⟨31 − n..0⟩ # (n @ 0):
shc (:= op = 29) → R[ra]⟨31..0⟩ ← R[rb]⟨31 − n..0⟩ # R[rb]⟨31..32 − n⟩:

Arithmetic right shift extends the sign, while a zero-fill right shift is useful for packing characters or other short fields into a word.

A new piece of notation here is the operator @, which takes an integer left side and concatenates the right side with itself that number of times. For example, 5@0 is 00000. The shifts in SRC are a logical right shift; an arithmetic right shift, which extends the sign bit; a left shift that fills with zeros on the right; and a circular shift that can be thought of as left or right depending on the shift count. All of them can be described by concatenating selected fields of the shifted quantity and repetitions of zero or the sign bit in various ways.

Miscellaneous Instructions.   The nop instruction causes no action to take place, and the stop instruction halts the computer until the next start signal is received.

Miscellaneous Instructions and End of Instruction Execution

nop (:= op = 0) → :   No operation
stop (:= op = 31) → Run ← 0   Stop instruction
);   instruction_interpretation):   End of instruction_execution; invoke
                                              instruction_interpretation.

Stop is the last in the long list of conditional actions that define the name, instruction_execution. Thus it is followed by the right parenthesis that matches the left parenthesis at the beginning of the conditional expression. Immediately following instruction_execution is instruction_interpretation, which will increment the PC and fetch the next instruction, *ad infinitum*. We will discuss the complications of reset and exception processing in Chapter 4.

This completes the specification of the very simple SRC computer. We will consider both the implementation of this computer and the extension of its specification as the book progresses. It is a complete machine in the sense that a compiler could be written for it that would generate code for modern high-level languages. Indeed, compilers have been written for simpler machines. Extensions that we will see later include interrupts, enhanced arithmetic, and input/output, or I/O.

I/O is actually allowed for with the instruction set presented. Many computers associate memory addresses with I/O devices and communicate data using only the load and store instructions. We will use this *memory-mapped* I/O technique with SRC also.

memory-mapped I/O

Table 2.7 summarizes the RTN notation used to describe SRC. The entire RTN description of the SRC can be found, without the explanatory notes, in Appendix B.

Table 2.7 Register Transfer Notation (RTN)

$\leftarrow$	Register transfer: register on LHS stores value from RHS
[ ]	Word index: selects word or range from a named memory
$\langle\rangle$	Bit index: selects bit or bit range from named register
n..m	Index range: from left index n to right index m; can be decreasing
$\rightarrow$	If-then: true condition on left yields value and/or action on right
:=	Definition: text substitution with dummy variables
#	Concatenation: bits on right appended to bits on left
:	Parallel separator: actions or evaluations carried out simultaneously
;	Sequential separator: RHS evaluated and/or performed after LHS
@	Replication: LHS repetitions of RHS are concatenated
{ }	Operation modifier: information about preceding operation, e.g., arithmetic type
( )	Operation or value grouping: arbitrary nesting; used with operators or separators
$= \neq < \leq > \geq$	Comparison operators: produce 1 or 0 (true or false) logical value
$+ - \times \div$	Arithmetic operators: also $\lceil \rceil, \lfloor \rfloor$, and mod
$\wedge \vee \neg \oplus \equiv$	Logical operators: and, or, not, exclusive or, equivalence

Notes: Expressions can be values and/or actions. Actions can be considered side effects if a value is present. A list of conditional expressions need not have disjoint conditions. Right-hand sides (RHS) of conditionals are evaluated for all conditions that are true. No sequencing is implied unless there are sequential separators between conditional expressions. There is no *else* equivalent. LHS means left-hand side.

Key Concepts: Describing a Computer Instruction Set

■ The many things that must be covered in describing a complete computer can be organized into four categories.

1. Processor and memory state: Sizes and numbers of storage registers in the CPU, memory structure, and I/O state if applicable. This is often called the programmer's model of the machine.
2. Formats and interpretation of data in registers: Data types, instruction formats, and effective address interpretation. Arithmetic data types are often simple in comparison to the interpretation of instructions.
3. The instruction interpretation sequence: This fetch-execute cycle is the heartbeat of the machine and underlies the execution of all instructions.
4. Description of individual instructions: Instruction classes include data movement (load and store), branch, ALU operations, and miscellaneous.

■ Data movement instructions determine the flexibility available in transferring data from one part of the processor state to another.

■ Branch instructions are closely related to the fetch-execute cycle because they determine what instruction is executed next.

■ Although assemblers can transform mnemonic and symbolic information into numeric form, each assembly language instruction corresponds to one binary machine instruction.

2.4.2 FORMAL VERSUS INFORMAL DESCRIPTIONS

Both formal and informal machine and machine language descriptions have their place. Informal descriptions tend to provide a more intuitive "feel" for the meaning of a construct, but can be confusing, imprecise, or incomplete in their descriptive power. Formal descriptions provide the means to be precise and exact, but can be dry and difficult to understand. We use both in this book, as appropriate to what is being described, and urge you not to gloss over the RTN descriptions, regardless of the tendency to do so. You may even find that, as you progress in your knowledge of computer design, you will tend to gloss over the informal descriptions and concentrate on the RTN.

You may have some confusion about RTN's use as a description language, in contrast with the machine language of the machine that it describes. RTN should be considered a *metalanguage*, a language that is used to describe languages.

metalanguage

Figure 2.11 shows a way to view this situation: SRC's machine language is interpreted by some particular machine language interpreter (hardware) or a simulator (software) that recognizes the SRC language. For example, in Chapters 4 and 5 we will play the role of RTN compiler and design four such SRC interpreters consisting of hardware. The software that accompanies this textbook includes such a simulator, written in ANSI C, which you can compile and run. The resulting simulator will accept SRC machine language as input. In addition to being a way to unambiguously communicate a machine's structure and functioning, RTN can be used to automate the production of interpreters for the machine.

RTN can also help reduce the possibility of error in design and implementation. RTN helps prevent two kinds of errors that can arise during design and implementation:

1. Errors caused by a misinterpretation of the machine description
2. Errors of design and implementation

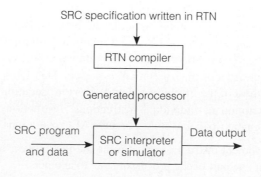

Fig. 2.11 The Relationship of RTN to the SRC

In the first case, RTN provides the ability to describe machine structure and function unambiguously. In the second case, compilers and interpreters can be written for RTN that would automatically generate simulators or even machine hardware. An RTN compiler could be designed to output an ANSI C simulator. Alternatively, the RTN compiler could be designed to output a description of the machine suitable for input to IC mask-making machinery. The resulting integrated circuit would be a microprocessor that accepted the SRC machine language.

It is true that there could be errors in the RTN compiler, but experience has shown that formal description languages and automatic generators provide superior results, and they are in nearly universal use in modern computer design. VHDL, Very high-speed integrated circuit Hardware Description Language, is one industry standard that is based on the Ada programming language. There are other special purpose description languages that allow the specification of machine components at the gate, logic block, and subsystem levels.

2.5 Describing Addressing Modes with RTN

The ways in which operands and results are accessed by a computer are very important to its usefulness. Here, too, the precision of a formal notation can help make clear what actually happens. In Section 2.2.6 we provided an informal description of several common addressing modes. If you were approaching this material for the first time, you may have found these informal definitions unclear and confusing. The use of RTN provides a way of formally describing the addressing modes discussed in Section 2.2.6 as well as several other less common addressing modes.

The need for different addressing modes is based on common ways of structuring data in computer programs. A simple variable in memory can be addressed by a constant whose value is known when the instruction is generated. Instructions are conveniently located by offsets relative to the location of the current instruction, which is contained in the PC. The address of an array element requires an index that is not known until execution time. For linked lists, part of the list data in memory is the address of another list element. Stack access requires both computing an address using a pointer and changing the pointer to select the next element. Operands and results can be in registers as well as memory, so register numbers may replace memory addresses for locating them. Finally, for operands, only the value is needed, and if this is known when the instruction is generated, no address is needed at all. The operand value is moved immediately from its field within the instruction word to where it will be used.

The RTN description of common addressing modes in Table 2.8 describes loading a value into a target general register. The program counter, general registers, and memory of an n-bit computer with m-bit memory addresses are assumed to be defined by the following:

$PC\langle m-1..0\rangle$:	Program counter
$R[0..2^q-1]\langle n-1..0\rangle$:	General registers
$M[0..2^m-1]\langle n-1..0\rangle$:	Memory

It can be seen from this RTN that q bits are needed to select a register and m bits to address a memory location. The letters a, t, and x represent fields of the instruction register.

Table 2.8 Some Common Addressing Modes

Common Name	Common Assembler Syntax	Meaning	Typical Usage
Register	Ra	$R[t] \leftarrow R[a]$	Temporary variable
Register indirect	(Ra)	$R[t] \leftarrow M[R[a]]$	Pointers to structures
Immediate	#x	$R[t] \leftarrow x$	Constant operand
Direct, absolute	x	$R[t] \leftarrow M[x]$	Global variable
Indirect	(x)	$R[t] \leftarrow M[M[x]]$	Accessing a value through its pointer
Indexed, based, or displacement	x(Ra)	$R[t] \leftarrow M[x + R[a]]$	Arrays and structures
Relative	x(PC)	$R[t] \leftarrow M[x + PC]$	Instructions or values stored within the program
Autoincrement	(Ra)+	$R[t] \leftarrow M[R[a]]$; $R[a] \leftarrow R[a] + 1$	Sequential access or stack pop
Autodecrement	–(Ra)	$R[a] \leftarrow R[a] - 1$; $R[t] \leftarrow M[R[a]]$	Sequential access or stack push

Fields a and t select registers, and are thus q-bit fields. Field x is used to produce a memory address, so it must either be m bits long, or it must be extended to m bits, usually by sign extension. For immediate mode, x is extended to n bits. Notice that the first "addressing" mode does not produce a memory address, since the operand is in a CPU register.

There are many variations on the addressing modes in Table 2.8, especially in CISC machines. Some machines provide an extension to the index mode by allowing a second register to be added. In this case, the effective address becomes $x + R[a] + R[b]$, so-called based indexed addressing. Others provide for the values of the increment and decrement to be k, rather than just 1, where k is a small integer. This allows easy access to k-byte operands stored sequentially in memory. Some old machines distinguished preindexed indirect from postindexed indirect. The former referenced the memory cell $M[M[x + R[a]]]$, while the latter referenced $M[M[x] + R[a]]$. A formal notation really helps here.

Example 2.4   Addressing Modes
Let us exercise our knowledge of addressing modes by considering how each of them would behave when executing the instruction move R1, 1000. Assume that the instruction syntax is such that operand flow is right to left; that is, the destination operand is R1. Also assume that each instruction executes independently from the same given machine state. We will use the addressing mode syntax given in Table 2.8. Table 2.9 shows the effect of the various addressing modes on the contents of R1, with the indicated machine state.

Notice that the autoincrement and autodecrement instructions are missing from this table. They would operate exactly as the register indirect case, but R2 would be incremented after, or decremented before, the value was fetched from memory.

Table 2.9 Addressing mode example

Machine State			
Registers		Memory	
PC	4000	Addr	Data
R2	3000	1000	2000
		2000	3000
		3000	4000
		4000	5000
		5000	6000

Addressing Mode	Instruction	Contents of R1
Immediate	MOV R1, #1000	1000
Direct	MOV R1, 1000	2000
Indirect	MOV R1, (1000)	3000
Register Indirect	MOV R1, (R2)	4000
Indexed	MOV R1, 1000(R2)	5000
Relative	MOV R1, 1000	6000

2.6 Register Transfers and Logic Circuits: From Behavior to Hardware

The previous sections in this chapter used register transfers to describe how computers execute instructions. This section provides a bridge between the software and the hardware by describing how register transfers are implemented at the hardware level.

In logic circuits courses, AND, OR, and NOT gates are thought of as components of Boolean expressions and flip-flops as state variables in sequential circuits. In computer design, a view of these circuit components as supporting data transmission and storage is at least as important. The register transfer notation, RTN, that we have introduced and used to describe machines supports this view of computer design. You should not take this section to be a review, but rather as an alternate view of logic circuit design that is often not presented in logic circuits texts. If you are unfamiliar with logic circuits, now would be a good time to refer to Appendix A, which contains some tutorial material on the subject.

2.6.1 LOGIC CIRCUITS TO IMPLEMENT REGISTER TRANSFERS

We now relate data transfer operations to the logic circuits that implement them. If A and B are 1-bit registers, the register transfer A←B can be implemented by the two-flip-flop circuit of Figure 2.12.

It is important to consider not only where the data move but when. The data bit "moves" (is copied) into A when the *Strobe* signal is activated. Figure 2.12b shows Strobe as a short pulse to avoid distinguishing different clocking schemes: latch, edge-triggered, and so on. The Strobe signal connects to the "clock" input of A. Strobe signals are seldom directly connected to the machine clock, so the term *strobe input* may be less confusing. In summary, the connection determines where data are transmitted, and the timing of the strobe determines when.

strobe

flip-flop strobe input

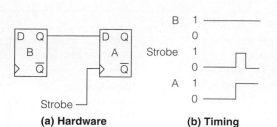

(a) Hardware   (b) Timing

Fig. 2.12 Register Transfer Hardware and Timing for a Single-Bit Register Transfer: A ← B

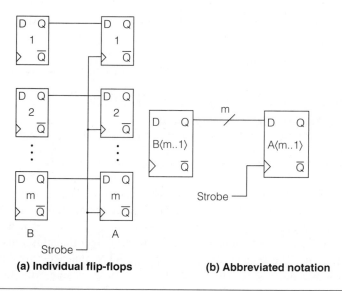

(a) Individual flip-flops   (b) Abbreviated notation

Fig. 2.13 Multiple-Bit Register Transfer: A<m..1> ← B<m..1>

Multiple-Bit Register Transfers.   We are seldom interested in 1-bit data items, so we need convenient ways of representing multiple-bit data paths and registers. The conventions we will use are shown in Figure 2.12. The slash on the B to A connection in the abbreviated notation on the right denotes a bundle of m wires. Since each wire connects to a different Q output and D input, there must be m different flip-flop sources and m destinations. The fact that Strobe is only one wire implies a parallel connection to the corresponding inputs of all m flip-flops in the A register.

Data Transmission in the Computer.   Logic gates and flip-flops can be viewed in terms of their data transmission behavior. If one input of an AND gate is called a *gate* signal and the other a *data* signal, then one way to view the AND operation is that the output of the AND gate will be equal to the data input if the gate input is 1 and will be 0 if the gate is 0. An OR gate can be viewed as merging two data inputs onto its output in the following sense. If one data input is guaranteed to be 0 at a particular time, the output will be equal

gate signal

to the other input at that time. An exclusive OR gate does the same thing, provided the "guaranteed 0" condition holds. Another useful data transmission view of the exclusive OR gate is that it implements a controlled complement. With one input labeled data and the other control, the output will be equal to the data if the control is 0 and will be equal to the complement of the data if the control is 1. Figure 2.14 summarizes these interpretations of logic gate behavior.

Merging and Extracting Data.   The real utility of this viewpoint comes when we adopt the multidevice and multiwire conventions used in Figure 2.13. If two multibit data items are separately gated and the gated signals merged, as shown in Figure 2.15, we obtain a two-way multiplexer. The temporal behavior is crucial. Only if the gate signals G_x and G_y are never 1 at the same time does the output represent a copy of the data at either x or y. It is important to be able to read the number of gates from the figure. There are 2m two-input AND gates and m two-input OR gates. Two sets of m AND gate inputs are connected in parallel to the G_x and G_y signals, respectively.

A general n-way gated merge is shown in Figure 2.15. It multiplexes n sets of m-bit data under the control of n gating signals G_0 through G_{n-1}. The rule for correct operation of the circuit as a multiplexer is that $G_i \land G_j = 0$ for all $i \neq j$ and at all times. This allows either all $G_i = 0$, in which case the output is 0, or one and only one $G_i = 1$, in which case

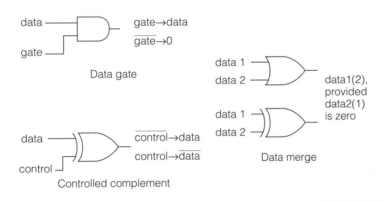

Fig. 2.14 Data Transmission View of Logic Gates

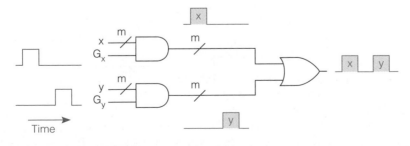

Fig. 2.15 Two-way Gated Merge, or Multiplexer

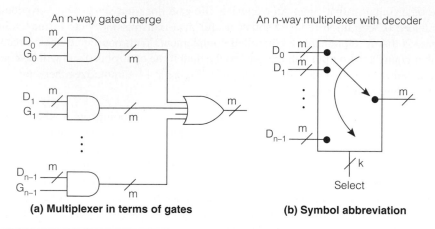

(a) Multiplexer in terms of gates

(b) Symbol abbreviation

Fig. 2.16 Basic Multiplexer and Symbol Abbreviation

the output is D_i. A standard way of producing a set of signals such that one and only one of them is 1 is with a k-bit binary to one-out-of-n=2^k decoder. This decoder has k inputs and 2^k outputs, and the simplest design for it contains k inverters and 2^k AND gates of k inputs each. Attaching the outputs of such a decoder to the gate inputs of the n-way gated merge gives the standard form of a multiplexer, which we will sometimes abbreviate with the symbol at the right of Figure 2.16. Whether a multiplexer includes a decoder depends on the form in which the gating or select signals are available in the system. Both binary and decoded forms are useful in different circumstances.

Controlled Extraction of Data.   If we have m wires on which the data x and y are multiplexed, x can be separated from y by a set of m AND gates gated by G_x, as shown in Figure 2.17. This is only one way to extract a particular set of data from a multiplexed signal. The other way uses strobing. If you know when x appears, a set of flip-flops with their D inputs attached to the multiplexed signals and strobed at that time will record x. The data y could be recorded by strobing the same or a different set of m flip-flops at the time y appears in the multiplexed signal.

Multiple Register Transfers.   Multiplexers and timing are the key to transferring data from one of several source registers to one of several destinations. Consider the register connection in Figure 2.17. To do the register transfer B←C using this hardware, the signals

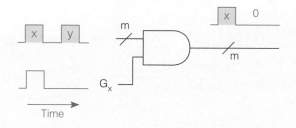

Fig. 2.17 Separating Merged Data

G_C and S_B are activated at the same time. Since the OR gate outputs can only equal one source data item at a time, only one value can be transferred per step. Actually, the timing needs a more detailed discussion. When the *gate* signal G_C goes from 0 to 1, the data from register C propagates through the m AND gates, then through the m OR gates, arriving at the D inputs to the B register flip-flops. The time at which the strobe S_B acts to record the data in B must be after the arrival of the data at B plus a flip-flop setup time. The *setup*   setup time
time is the time interval during which flip-flop inputs must be held constant before the clocking event. The data may also have to be held constant for a certain period of time after the clocking event—the *hold time*. This hold time for the data after the strobe point is   hold time
usually much smaller than the *propagation time* and may even be zero. Refer to the manu-   propagation time
facturer's data sheets for specifications of setup and hold times. The logical timing relation between gate and strobe is shown at the right of Figure 2.18.

In practice, the form of the control signals, especially the strobes, depends on the implementation domain. Different triggering modes of latches, master-slave flip-flops, and positive and negative edge-triggered flip-flops place the logical strobe point at different places on the actual strobe signal. The logical picture shown in Figure 2.18 is closest to the actual timing for a positive gated latch.

2.6.2   THE BUS AS DATA HIGHWAY

A shared data path such as the output of the OR gate in Figure 2.18 is known as a *bus*. Informally, the term *bus* is used to describe any connection over which data move. More precisely, it is a multiplexed connection of the type described in the following discussion. The difficulty in attaching a large number of registers to a shared line with the hardware of Figure 2.16 is the large number of inputs to the m OR gates. If registers are widely distributed throughout the machine, connecting n inputs to a common OR gate presents a wiring problem. Wiring the output of the OR is less difficult because only one wire for each bit needs to go to all destination registers in parallel. Fortunately, electronics offers an alternative to connecting $m \times n$ inputs to OR gates.

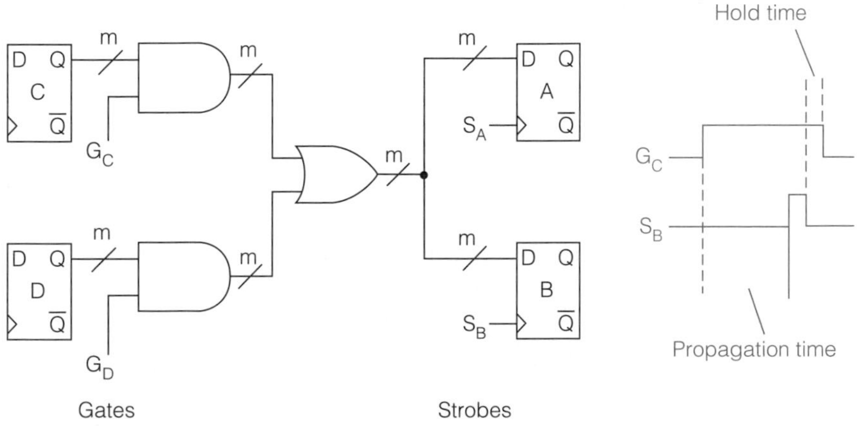

Gates   Strobes

Fig. 2.18 Multiplexed Register Transfers Using Gates and Strobes

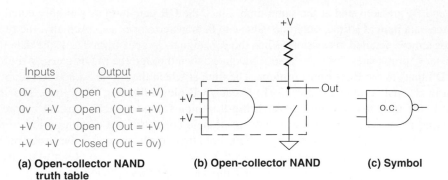

Inputs		Output	
0v	0v	Open	(Out = +V)
0v	+V	Open	(Out = +V)
+V	0v	Open	(Out = +V)
+V	+V	Closed	(Out = 0v)

(a) Open-collector NAND truth table

(b) Open-collector NAND

(c) Symbol

Fig. 2.19 NAND Gate Output Circuit

Eliminating the Multiplexer by Open-Collector Gates. To simplify a brief excursion into electronics, we will talk only about the output circuits of logic gates and idealize their behavior. Transistors in an output circuit can be viewed as controlled switches. Suppose, for example, an AND gate controls the simple output circuit sketched in Figure 2.19, where the output transistor is shown as a switch that connects the out terminal to ground for a logic 0 and to +V (through a resistor) for a logic 1. The output transistor complements the AND logic, making the overall gate a NAND.

If the outputs of two such gates are directly connected as shown in Figure 2.20 (an illegal connection for most logic gates), the logic value at the common terminal no longer equals the output of either gate individually. It will be +V only if both switches are open

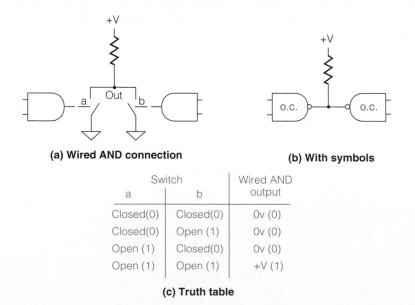

(a) Wired AND connection

(b) With symbols

Switch		Wired AND
a	b	output
Closed(0)	Closed(0)	0v (0)
Closed(0)	Open (1)	0v (0)
Open (1)	Closed(0)	0v (0)
Open (1)	Open (1)	+V (1)

(c) Truth table

Fig. 2.20 Wired AND Connection of Open-Collector Gates

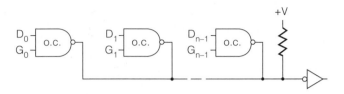

Fig. 2.21 Open-Collector Wired OR Bus

(both gate outputs are 1) and will be 0 for all other cases because it is connected to ground by one or both switches. The connected point thus becomes the AND function of what the values of the unconnected outputs would have been. The *pull-up resistors* of the two out- pull-up resistors puts are connected in parallel, and thus conduct more current through a closed switch than intended. Removing the resistors from each gate output makes the gates *open-collector* type. The *collector* is the name for the transistor terminal corresponding to the stationary collector switch contact. The symbols for the open-collector NANDs are shown in Figure 2.20b. One external pull-up resistor then serves both gate outputs.

The *wired AND* connection can be extended to more than two gates if a single exter- wired AND nal pull-up resistor is then supplied for each wired AND, regardless of how many gate outputs are connected. The important thing is that the AND function of the connection is distributed over all the gates whose outputs are connected and does not require a separate wire for each AND input. This is the characteristic we would like to have for the OR gates of a bus multiplexer. DeMorgan's laws tell us that an AND is also the complement of the OR of complemented inputs, so for negative true logic the wired AND becomes a *wired* wired OR *OR*. A multiplexer can then be formed from a set of NAND gates with open-collector outputs, a pull-up resistor, and an inverter, as shown in Figure 2.21. This distributed multiplexer is the reason for our brief excursion into electronics. The ability to accomplish the OR function of a multiplexer by connecting to a single wire has a major impact on the architecture of computers, and it cannot be represented by combinations of simple AND, OR, and NOT gates.

This standard wired OR bus can simply be repeated m times for m-bit data, with each of the n gate signals wired in parallel to n inputs of a set of n NAND gates. Simply adding a slash m to the correct wires in Figure 2.21 gives a diagram for an m-wire bus, as shown in Figure 2.23. This style of distributed OR function will be seen later to be important for interrupt requests from multiple I/O devices to a processor.

Eliminating Multiplexers By Using Tri-State Gates. A slightly different form is more commonly used for the present purpose of multiplexed register transfers. A *tri-state* or three-state gate output consists of two transistors in series between +V and ground, controlled so that both are never conducting at the same time. Figure 2.22 shows this arrangement using our representation of transistors as controlled switches. The figure shows the truth table for the gate: It is in the high-impedance (Hi-Z) state when the enable input is low, thus in effect disconnecting its output. Many different kinds of gates are available in tri-state configurations.

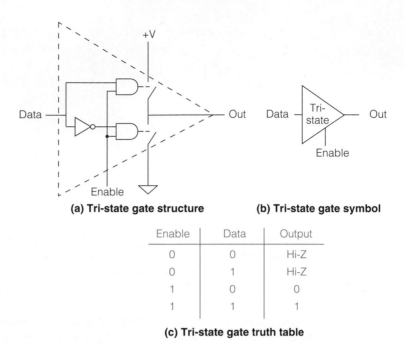

(a) Tri-state gate structure

(b) Tri-state gate symbol

Enable	Data	Output
0	0	Hi-Z
0	1	Hi-Z
1	0	0
1	1	1

(c) Tri-state gate truth table

Fig. 2.22 Tri-State Gate Internal Structure and Symbol

Connecting the outputs of several tri-state gates together does not form an AND function. In fact, if all enables are low, the logic value of the common output is not even defined. However, if n tri-state gates have their enables connected to G_0 through G_{n-1} of Figure 2.16 and their data inputs connected to D_0 through D_{n-1}, then connecting the outputs together performs the same function as one of the OR gates in the important case when one and only one $G_i = 1$. Having two gating signals equal to 1 simultaneously is not only bad from the logic function point of view, it can damage the circuit. If the data inputs are such that one enabled output is connected to +V while another is connected to ground, there will be a strongly conducting path between the power supply and ground. This will cause a large current to flow with possible heating and burnout results.

Register Transfers Using a Tri-State Bus.   An m-wire tri-state bus can be used to connect n registers together as in Figure 2.23, so that the contents of any one of them can be

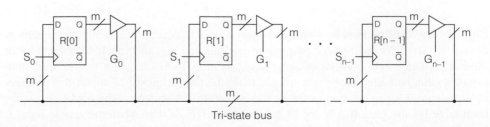

Fig. 2.23 Registers Interconnected by a Tri-State Bus

copied into any other. As was the case in Figure 2.18, the register transfer is done by applying a gate signal for the source and a strobe signal at the destination. There are only m data wires, so only a single m-bit register value can be gated onto the bus at one time. It is possible to copy the source value into more than one destination by applying two or more strobes simultaneously, but if two different values are to be transferred at the same time, more than one bus is needed.

2.6.3   A REGISTER TRANSFER BUS WITH ARITHMETIC CAPABILITY

Although a single bus can interconnect registers so that the register transfer Dst←Src can be done for any source and destination registers, if the data is to be transformed by arithmetic, more structure is needed. To allow 1 to be added to a register value using an increment circuit, the input and output of the incrementer must be connected to different places because they have different data values. The scheme shown in Figure 2.24 allocates a temporary storage register W to the output of the incrementer. The operation R[j]← R[k] + 1 is obtained by the two-step sequence (W←R[k] + 1; R[j]←W). The sequence of control signals to effect this operation is (R[k]$_{out}$, W$_{in}$; W$_{out}$, R[j]$_{in}$). Figure 2.24 also shows how a two-operand addition can be done using registers connected by one bus by having a temporary register Y for one operand, taking the other operand from the bus, and putting the result in a special register Z. Adding two registers and placing the result in a third, R[3]←R[1] + R[2], must be done in three steps using the special registers, (Y←R[2]; Z←R[1] + Y; R[3]←Z). The control sequence for this operation is (R[2]$_{out}$, Y$_{in}$; R[1]$_{out}$,Z$_{in}$; Z$_{out}$, R[3]$_{in}$).

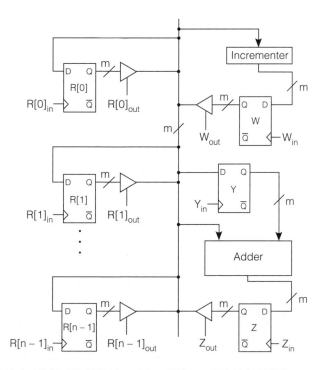

Fig. 2.24 Registers and Arithmetic Units Connected by One Bus

Control SignalTiming. The timing of these control signals is of critical importance to the proper operation of the circuit. Figure 2.25 shows the three steps required to perform the operation. Pacing the operation is the clock signal, Clk. Although circuits can be designed to operate without a clock signal, the presence of a clock makes the synchronizing, or pacing, of the operation much less dependent on the propagation time of specific circuit elements. Notice the difference in shape between the gating signals, $R[1]_{out}$, $R[2]_{out}$, and Z_{out}, and the strobe signals, Y_{in}, Z_{in}, and $R[3]_{in}$. The gating signals become active at the start of the clock period, and stay active throughout the clock period, to allow time for the signals to propagate through the circuit. The strobe signals do not become active until near the end of the clock period, when signals have propagated to their destination. Upon reflection one will conclude that there is a minimum clock period below which the circuit will not operate correctly, because signals have not had sufficient time to propagate from all outputs to all inputs. We will show how to estimate what this minimum clock period is in Chapter 4.

Rules of Buses

The Rules of Buses. Clocked data transfer on buses can be a bit confusing when it is first encountered. The beginning student may wonder about exactly how and when information is transferred on a bus. Here are two simple rules referred to by the authors as the Rules of Buses:

__The First Rule of Buses:__ Only one item can be on the bus during a given clock cycle.

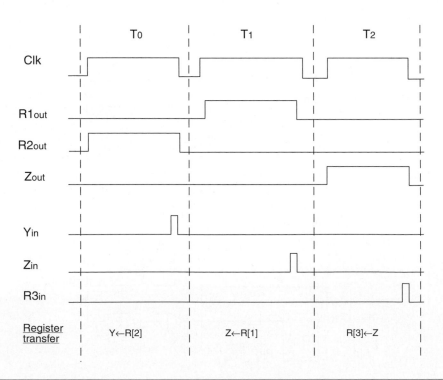

Fig. 2.25 Timing of the Register Transfer Y←R[2]; Z←R[1] + Y; R[3]←Z

This rule arises as a direct result of the gate-and-strobe paradigm discussed above: When a value is gated onto the bus, the gating signal remains active for the duration of the active part of the clock signal. Only one value is on the bus during a given clock cycle. (In certain advanced designs a technique known as *wave pipelining* is used to overcome this limitation. In wave pipelined designs the signal propagation time and shape on the bus are precisely controlled so that several different values can be "pipelined" one after the other onto the bus during a given clock cycle.)

wave pipelining

> *The Second Rule of Buses*: *The contents of the bus disappear at the end of the clock cycle. No information is "stored" on the bus from cycle to cycle; any value to be saved must be strobed into a register at the end of the clock cycle.*

This rule is a corollary of the first rule. Since the gating signal is made inactive at the end of the clock cycle, no signal remains after that time.

Abstract RTN, Concrete RTN, and Control Signals. Let us now examine the two kinds of RTN descriptions described above in more detail. The first is in terms of *what* the transfer accomplishes:

$R[3] \leftarrow R[1] + R[2];$ (Abstract RTN)

The second describes *how* it is accomplished:

$Y \leftarrow R[2]; \ Z \leftarrow R[1] + Y; \ R[3] \leftarrow Z;$ (Concrete RTN)

Finally, we describe it by a series of control signal assertions, or *control sequence*:

$R[2]_{out}, Y_{in}; \ R[1]_{out}, Z_{in}; \ Z_{out}, R[3]_{in}$ (Control sequence)

control sequence

The first description is an *abstract* RTN description because it describes the register transfer in terms of its effects only. The second description is a *concrete* RTN—it refers to how the register transfer happens in a particular hardware implementation. The control sequence is a translation of the concrete RTN to the sequence of control signals needed to accomplish the concrete RTN. Notice further that what was accomplished in one step in the abstract description actually took three steps in the particular hardware implementation. We will use concrete RTN and control sequences extensively in Chapter 4 when we describe and design the SRC computer hardware.

abstract RTN
concrete RTN

2.6.4 REGISTER TRANSFER OPERATIONS AND DATA PATH

Hardware structures that interconnect registers, including arithmetic units and other data transformers, constitute the *data path* of a computer. Several connections between the behavior of a machine specified in RTN and the structure of the data path have been illustrated previously. A register transfer A←B implies the existence of a connection, either unique or shared, from B to A. A collection of register transfers between different sources and destinations may be implemented by a shared bus connection, provided that two source values do not need to be moved at the same time. With the proper control signals, a simultaneous transfer of one source to two or more destinations, as in (A←B: C←B), can be done using one bus.

RTN statements involving data transformation imply the existence of arithmetic units in the data path. Examples would include A←B + 1 and A←B + C. The +1 operation can be represented by an increment circuit, while B + C implies a full m-bit adder for two variable data values. We can also see from the examples above that an operation like R[3]←R[1] + R[2] can be broken down into several steps whose result is the same as that of the original statement, provided that the changed values of Y and Z are not important. This shows that RTN can be used at several levels. An abstract RTN statement describes the overall effect of the steps on the *visible* registers, ignoring other temporary registers. The concrete RTN statements describe the details of the register transfer on specified hardware, including the registers and buses used in the data path.

Key Concepts: RTN, Behavior, and Implementation

Register transfer notation both specifies the behavior of computer operations and describes hardware to implement that behavior.

- Computer design largely separates data operations from control operations, although both are implemented with logic circuits.
- Abstract RTN describes the overall result of one or more data transfers and transformations, such as the execution of a complete instruction.
- Concrete RTN describes operations done by specific hardware on a single cycle of a system clock.
- Concrete register transfers are implemented by simple combinations of logic gates and flip-flops.
- Transfers from multiple sources to one destination are based on multiplexers.
- A very important distributed form of multiplexer, the bus, uses special electronics to allow a simple wire connection to replace the OR logic of a multiplexer, so that distributed registers are easily connected.
- Control signals gate multiplexers and strobe registers to cause data transfers.

Summary

- From the programmer's and architect's perspective, computers and their instructions are often classified by the way operands are accessed by the CPU. The number of explicit operand addresses mentioned in an instruction has varied from three to zero. The accumulator class was most common in the early days of computing, and the general register, load-store machine/instruction is most popular today.

- The instruction set—the entire collection of instructions that a machine can interpret and execute—can be grouped into three categories: data movement, arithmetic and logic, and branching (control flow).

- Most machines include a number of different addressing modes to accommodate the many different kinds of memory operand references required to access data structures in modern programming languages. The most common addressing modes in use today are immediate, direct, register indirect, relative, and based (also known as indexed or displacement). Less common today are the various memory indirect addressing modes and the autoincrement and autodecrement modes.

■   We introduced a simple example machine, the SRC, to begin illustrating computer architecture principles. The SRC is classed as a general register, load-store machine with RISC (reduced instruction set computer) characteristics. In this chapter we concentrated on the ISA of the SRC. The SRC's ISA was described using both informal notation and RTN. RTN was also used to describe general machine addressing modes. RTN provides a tool for the formal and unambiguous description of machines and operations.

■   RTN statements can be mapped into the hardware used to implement them. AND, OR, and NOT gates and flip-flops support data transmission and storage. Multiplexers are used to route a value from one of several sources to a destination. Open-collector and tri-state gates form an important distributed type of multiplexer for use in bus implementations.

Bibliography

The number of addresses per instruction and addressing modes are treated in almost all computer design texts. See, for example, the following:

V. C. Hamacher, Z. G. Vranesic, and S. G. Zaky, *Computer Organization*, 3rd ed., New York: McGraw-Hill, 1990.

W. Stallings, *Computer Organization and Architecture*, 5th ed., Upper Saddle River, NJ: Prentice-Hall, 2000.

Register transfer notations are treated more or less formally in computer design texts. The following text uses a programming-language-style pseudocode to describe register transfer behavior:

A. S. Tanenbaum, *Structured Computer Organization*, 4th ed., Upper Saddle River, NJ: Prentice-Hall, 1999.

The following text has a chapter on register transfers and their implementation in hardware:

M. M. Mano, *Computer System Architecture*, 3rd ed., Englewood Cliffs, NJ: Prentice-Hall, 1993.

These authors base the organization of their text on the register transfer language AHPL:

F. J. Hill and G. R. Peterson, *Digital Systems: Hardware Organization and Design*, 3rd ed., New York: John Wiley, 1987.

Our RTN is similar to the ISP language introduced in the following text. This ISP is a register transfer language oriented primarily toward communicating with humans. A version of the language slanted more toward automated processing, called ISPS, is also described in this text:

C. G. Bell and A. Newell, *Computer Structures: Readings and Examples*, New York: McGraw-Hill, 1971.

D. Siewiorek, C. G. Bell, and A. Newell, *Computer Structures: Principles and Examples*, New York: McGraw-Hill, 1982.

The following is a more recent text based on the commercially used VHDL (Very high-speed integrated circuit Hardware Design Language). This language mirrors many details of the VLSI circuits for which it is intended:

M. R. Zargham, *Computer Architecture: Single and Parallel Systems,* Upper Saddle River, NJ: Prentice-Hall, 1996.

Texts that use a hypothetical RISC-style machine as a vehicle for presentation include the following. The RISC machine on which the second of the two is based is very similar to the commercial MIPS processor:

J. M. Feldman and C. T. Retter, *Computer Architecture: A Designer's Text Based on a Generic RISC,* New York: McGraw-Hill, 1994.

D. A. Patterson and J. L. Hennessy, *Computer Organization and Design: The Hardware/ Software Interface,* 2nd ed., San Mateo, CA: Morgan Kaufmann, 1997.

The following text treats wave pipelining in detail:

C. Thomas Gray, Wentai Liu, and Ralph K. Cavin III, *Wave Pipelining: Theory and CMOS Implementation,* Norwell, MA: Kluwer Academic Publishing, 1994.

Exercises

2.1 Refer to the four items on page 35 that an instruction must specify. What would need to be specified by the MC68000 instruction ADDI.W #9, D4 described in Table 1.2?   **(§2.1)**

2.2 Repeat Exercise 2.1 for the JCXZ instruction in Table 2.3.   **(§2.1)**

2.3 According to the discussion in Section 2.2.1, how many instructions would the MC6800 have to execute to move a 128-bit floating point-number from one memory location to another?   **(§2.1)**

2.4 Write the code to implement the expression A = (B - C)*D on 3-, 2-, 1-, and 0-address machines. Do not rearrange the expression. In accordance with programming language practice, computing the expression should not change the values of its operands.   **(§2.2)**

2.5 Compute the total memory traffic in bytes for both instruction fetch and instruction execution for the code that implements the expression evaluation the four machines in Exercise 2.4 above. Assume opcodes occupy one byte, addresses occupy two bytes, and data values also occupy two bytes.   **(§2.2)**

2.6 Do problems 2.4 and 2.5 above, but for the expression A= B*C + D*E. (Feel free to use a temporary variable, called, say, T, if you feel you need one.) Assuming that addresses are 16 bits, data values are 16 bits, and opcodes are 8 bits, compute the size of your program, in bytes, and the amount of memory traffic the program would generate, in bytes, when it executes. When you compute the amount of memory traffic generated by the program, compute separately the amount of traffic due to instruction fetch and instruction execution.   **(§2.2)**

2.7 Write SRC code to implement the expression in Exercise 2.4. Assume SRC has a multiply instruction.   **(§2.3)**

2.8 Compute the total memory traffic in bytes for both instruction fetch and instruction execution for the code in Exercise 2.7.   **(§2.3)**

2.9 Repeat Exercise 2.6 for a general register machine. Assume 8-bit opcodes, 5-bit register numbers, and 24-bit addresses.   **(§2.2)**

2.10 Suppose the instruction word in a general register machine has space for an opcode and either three register numbers or one register number and an address. What different instruction formats might be used for an ADD instruction, and how would they work?   **(§2.2)**

2.11 There are reasons for machine designers to want all instructions to be the same length. Why is this not a good idea in a stack machine?   **(§2.2)**

2.12 In the last two instructions of Table 2.3, which of the five items on page 40 are explicitly specified and which are implicit?   **(§2.2)**

2.13 Tell which addressing modes are used by each of the instructions in Table 2.2. **(§2.2)**

2.14 Suppose that SRC instruction formats are considered different only when field boundaries in the instruction word change and not when some fields or parts of fields are unused. How many different formats should appear in Figure 2.10 in this case?   **(§2.3)**

2.15 Encode the program on page 56 in hexadecimal.   **(§2.3)**

2.16 Write SRC code to implement the following C statements, assuming all variables are 32-bit integers:

a. `if (a < 0) a = -a; else a = 0;`

b. `for ( i = 0; i < 10; i++ )`
   `ndigit[i] = i+1;` assuming a declaration of ndigit[10].   **(§2.3)**

2.17 Testing a difference against zero is not the same as comparing two numbers in finite precision arithmetic. Propose an encoding for an SRC branch instruction that specifies two registers to be compared, rather than one register to be compared against zero.

a. What potential problems might there be with implementing the modified instruction?

b. How would condition codes improve the situation?

c. Can you suggest a restructuring of the SRC branch that would help without using condition codes?   **(§2.3)**

2.18 Procedure-calling sequences are standard groups of instructions that transfer control from the main program to a procedure, supplying it with input arguments if necessary. Return sequences finish the procedure by setting up any output arguments and transferring control back to the point following the call. Write a call and return sequence for an SRC procedure that computes the absolute value of an integer passed and returned in r0. Assume r31 is the linkage register.   **(§2.3)**

2.19 Examine the RTN descriptions for `la` and `addi`.

a. How do the instructions differ?

b. Give the pros and cons of eliminating one or the other.   **(§2.4)**

2.20 Modify the SRC RTN to include a SingleStep button. SingleStep functions in the following way: when Run is true, SingleStep has no effect. When Run is false, that is, when the machine is halted, pressing SingleStep causes the machine to execute a single instruction and then return to the halted state.   **(§2.4)**

2.21 Modify the SRC to include the swap (op = 7) instruction that exchanges the contents of two registers, ra and rb, by writing abstract RTN for the new instruction.   **(§2.4)**

2.22 a. Modify the SRC RTN to include a conditional jump instruction, `jpr` (op = 25). It should use format 2 in Figure 2.10. The jpr instruction uses relative addressing, rel, instead of a branch target register. The jump should be taken only if ra = 0.

b. Change the meaning of `jpr` so that the jump is taken only if the register specified by the ra field has a nonzero value.   **(§2.4)**

2.23 Describe in words the difference between the two addressing modes described in RTN as follows:

a. M[M[X + R[a]]]

b. M[M[X] + R[a]].   **(§2.5)**

2.24 Write SRC instructions to load a value into a register using each of the addressing modes of Table 2.8. Use multiple SRC instructions for a mode only when necessary.   **(§2.5)**

2.25 Assume that in a certain byte-addressed machine all instructions are 32 bits long. Assume the following state of affairs for the machine:

Address	Value
PC	100
r0	200
r1	300
100	200
104	300
108	400
200	500
300	600
500	700

Fill in the following table, assuming that each statement executes from the initial state defined above. The lea, load effective address, instruction is similar to the LEA instruction shown in Table 2.1. **(§2.5)**

Instruction	Addressing Mode	Value of r0 after Execution
`load r0, #200`	Immediate	
`load r0, 200`	Direct	
`load r0, (200)`	Indirect	
`load r0, r1`	Register	
`load r0, [r1]`	Reg. Ind.	
`load r0, -100[r1]`	Based	
`lea r0 -100[r1]`	Based	
`load r0, 200[PC]`	Relative	

2.26 Consider the C `int` array variable V[2]. Assume that C ints are 32 bits in size and that the base address of V is in r3.

a. Write a single SRC instruction similar to those in Exercise 2.25 that will store V[2] in r4. **(§2.5)**

2.27 Using the hardware in Figure 2.24, write the RTN description and the control sequence that implements the following:

a. R[0] ← R[1] + R[2] + 2

b. R[3] ← R[4] + R[5] + R[6].   **(§2.6)**

Draw timing diagrams similar to Figure 2.25 for the control sequences developed above. **(§2.6)**

2.28 Design a circuit similar to Figure 2.24, but without the incrementer, so that any register can be added to any register and the result stored in any register *in one clock cycle*. **(§2.5)**

2.29 Design data path logic that will allow any two of the following register transfers that do not have the same destination to be done in one step.   **(§2.5)**

   $A \leftarrow B$:
   $A \leftarrow C$:
   $C \leftarrow B$:
   $B \leftarrow C$:

2.30 It is a widespread practice to develop simulators for computers that are under development. The simulators run on other available machines, and they allow designers and programmers to evaluate machine hardware and software in advance of the availability of the machine. A simulator may simulate only the abstract behavior of the machine, without any pretense of performing the operations the way an actual machine would perform them, or it may simulate the structure and function of the machine down to the gate level and below. If a compiler were available for RTN, the compiled code could be thought of as being a simulator for SRC at the most abstract level.

   Begin the process of writing a behavior-level simulator for SRC by declaring the memory, formats, and effective address parts of the machine in ANSI C. Assume that only the first 4,096 32-bit words are implemented, and assume that integers on your machine are 32-bits long.   **(§2.4)**

Some Real Machines

Chapter Outline

The purpose of this chapter is to provide an understanding of commercial CPUs and to give a perspective on why commercial CPUs are designed the way they are. An understanding of the trade-offs involved in the design of real machines is necessary for the appreciation of the design techniques covered in the rest of the book. After seeing concrete examples of real machines, you should be better able to judge which features of real machines are reflected in discussions that are abstract or SRC-based and which are glossed over.

We begin with a discussion of machine economics and performance measurement. We devote the three main sections in the chapter to a discussion of the characteristics that differentiate complex instruction set (CISC) computers from reduced instruction set (RISC) computers. First we describe some of the characteristics of the RISC approach to machine design as contrasted with the CISC. We then describe the ISA of the CISC Motorola MC68000 informally, using figures and verbal descriptions, and at the same time we provide a formal RTN description for key features. This will serve both to aid in the description of the processor, and to provide additional opportunity for you to become familiar with RTN. We conclude with a description of the SPARC ISA as an example of the RISC concept.

3.1   Machine Characteristics and Performance

The computer market has grown from zero size to its multi-hundred-billion dollar size by providing capabilities that were unattainable by any other means. Computers have become commonplace because of the performance they deliver *and* the price at which they deliver it. This section provides a perspective on the price and performance characteristics of computers. First we discuss the importance of price, and the issue of upward compatibility and then introduce computer performance measurement.

3.1.1   ECONOMICS IS THE DRIVING FORCE

Computer engineering and computer design are very much concerned with cost and cost/performance trade-offs. It is the cost and performance of components in the implementation domain that determine the performance of a given system developed to sell at a given price. Prices of the individual circuit building blocks diminish at an accelerating rate. Vacuum tubes used in the computers of the 1940s and 1950s cost several dollars apiece. Discrete transistors cost less than a dollar in the 1960s, but the real revolution in electronic component cost began with the invention of the IC.

The same small chip of silicon contains ever increasing numbers of components. The cost of the IC is dominated not by the number of components on it, but by the research and development costs that must be amortized over the early lifetime of the chip, by the yield of good chips per wafer, and by the cost of the package containing the chip. Today, it is not uncommon for the socket to cost more than the IC in it. The keyboard and monitor may well cost more than the motherboard.

The economics of the previous generations has been turned on its side. In a sense, the chip is free; it is the information on it and the means of conveying and protecting the chip that must be paid for. The same rule holds for applications software. A $1 CD ROM costs $500 when Microsoft Office is encoded on it. These trends can be expected to continue for at least the next decade. Some day, we may pay for the operating system and receive the hardware to run it for free. Until that day, however, computer designers will face trade-offs as they try to satisfy system specifications. The engineer is concerned with performance, and that performance is usually measured or estimated by running a series of selected programs.

3.1.2   UPWARD COMPATIBILITY

Since the IBM 360 family, which advertised upward compatibility (the ability to run software developed on earlier, less capable family members on later, more advanced members), customers have been much more likely to upgrade their hardware if their present software will run on it. This is a natural tendency, since many users have as much or more money invested in their software as in their hardware, and are very reluctant to buy or rewrite their entire software base just to get the claimed advantages of a new generation. When the hardware vendor announces a new architecture, the vendor also announces planned upgrade paths that provide increasing price/performance while maintaining the ability to run software written for an earlier model. This upward compatibility may take many forms:

- Binary compatibility. Binary files compiled for earlier versions will run on the new family member. Sometimes the source code must be recompiled to take advantage of some new feature of the new machine.

- Binary compatibility with certain exceptions. Binary files compiled for earlier versions will run on the new member, provided that certain "rules" that were announced or specified as being required for upward compatibility were followed when the software was first written.

- Source code compatibility. Source code written for the earlier version will run on the newer family member when it is recompiled.

- Emulation capability. The vendor provides a binary interpreter that runs on the new machine, interpreting the old binary code at run time, instruction by instruction. This has the advantage of requiring no effort to run old software on the new machine, but generally results in a considerable performance penalty. Often software running under emulation actually runs slower on the new machine than on the old, but the penalty may be accepted by the user as a compromise that allows the old software to run until it can be ported to native form, either by the user or by the software vendor.

3.1.3 PERFORMANCE MEASUREMENT

There are several ways of making quantitative performance comparisons. Consider the comparison of two different ways of driving a car between two points. It can be made in terms of speed ("I averaged 34 miles per hour going the old route, and 46 miles per hour going the new route."), or in terms of time ("it took me 96 minutes taking the old route, and only 71 minutes taking the new route.").

Calculating Speedup.   When comparing speeds, or *rates*, the old speed is compared with the new speed by dividing new by old. In the example above:

$$\text{Speedup} = \frac{\text{Speed going the new route}}{\text{Speed going the old route}} = \frac{S_{new}}{S_{old}} = \frac{46}{34} = 1.35 \qquad \text{[Eq. 3.1]}$$

for an improvement of 0.35 or 35% to two significant digits. One can calculate the % improvement, or speedup, directly by using the equation

$$\%\text{Speedup} = \frac{S_{new} - S_{old}}{S_{old}} \times 100 = \frac{46 - 34}{34} \times 100 = \frac{12}{34} \times 100 = 35\% \qquad \text{[Eq. 3.2]}$$

For comparisons in terms of time rather than speed, or rate, recall that time is the reciprocal of speed:

$$\frac{\text{Miles}}{\text{Hour}} = \frac{1}{\dfrac{\text{Hours}}{\text{Mile}}}; \ \text{ or } S = \frac{1}{T} \qquad \text{[Eq. 3.3]}$$

Thus

$$\%\text{Speedup} = \frac{S_{new} - S_{old}}{S_{old}} \times 100$$

$$= \frac{\dfrac{1}{T_{new}} - \dfrac{1}{T_{old}}}{\dfrac{1}{T_{old}}} \times 100 \qquad \text{[Eq. 3.4]}$$

$$= \frac{T_{old} - T_{new}}{T_{new}} \times 100$$

In the present case,

$$\boxed{\%\text{Speedup} = \frac{T_{old} - T_{new}}{T_{new}} \times 100 = \frac{96 - 71}{71} \times 100 = 35\%} \qquad \text{[Eq. 3.5]}$$

We box this equation because it will be used frequently throughout the text.

Estimating Computing System Performance. Estimates of machine performance vary from the qualitative ("It takes 16 seconds to load Microsoft Word 6.0") to fairly careful tests using software suites designed specifically to measure a particular aspect of system performance. Generally, the performance testing is begun by defining a *workload,* that is, a suite of programs that can be run and whose execution time can be measured. Ideally, the workload should consist of exactly those programs that customers will want to run on their machines. The impracticality of satisfying the ideal for all users and all time leads to the selection of a set of *benchmark* programs that are intended to approximate the real workload. These benchmark programs are generally chosen so as to provide a program mix that exercises a system feature that the tester wishes to evaluate.

workload

benchmark

CLASSIC EXAMPLE: ESTIMATING PERFORMANCE A certain computer system takes 125 ms to render a certain graphic image, and this time is reduced to 100 ms when a graphics processor card is added to the system. What is the speedup?

$$\text{Speedup} = \frac{T_{old}}{T_{new}} = \frac{125}{100} = 1.25, \text{ or a 25\% speedup} \qquad \blacksquare$$

Execution Time, Clock Speed, and Clocks per Instruction (CPI). Computer system performance is usually measured by the time to execute a program or program mix, rather than the speed with which it executes programs. A computer system that completes a given program faster than another computer performs better on that workload. The *program execution time,* or *wall clock time,* is made up of many factors. We ignore factors such as waits for I/O that do not depend on processor speed for the moment. The processor-related time is given by

program execution, or wall clock time

$$\boxed{\text{Execution time} = T = IC \times CPI \times \tau} \qquad \text{[Eq. 3.6]}$$

where IC is the instruction count, CPI is the average number of system clock periods to execute an instruction, and τ is the duration of a clock period. Once again we box this equation because of the importance it will assume during later chapters. A computer with a faster system clock, with fewer clocks per instruction, or taking fewer instructions to do the job will better performance.

Example 3.1 Speedup Due to a Clock Frequency Increase The master clock in a certain computer system is increased in frequency from 700 MHz to 1.2 GHz. What is the speedup due to this improvement if no other factors such as memory access time interfere with the improvement?

Since, according to the problem definition, neither IC nor CPI changed, and since the clock period, τ, is proportional to the reciprocal of clock frequency,

$$\text{Speedup} = \frac{(\text{IC} \times \text{CPI} \times \tau)_{\text{old}}}{(\text{IC} \times \text{CPI} \times \tau)_{\text{new}}} = \frac{1/700}{1/1200} = \frac{1200}{700} = 1.71, \text{ or } 71\% \text{ speedup}$$

■

MIPS. One of the most general and least useful performance metrics is MIPS, millions of instructions per second. This value is measured for a given program or set of programs by counting the number of instructions, measured in millions, and dividing by the time to execute them. There are a number of problems with MIPS as a measure of machine performance. Perhaps the most serious is that instructions vary so much in their capability from machine to machine. The instruction count for a program compiled for a RISC machine may be 20% greater than the count for a CISC machine, for example, and yet RISC computers can generally run at clock speeds several times faster than CISC clock rates. MIPS figures were widely quoted in the late 1970s and early 1980s. There was a period when the VAX 11/780 was treated as a common yardstick of MIPS performance, and machine performance was quoted in terms of MIPS relative to a VAX.

millions of instructions per second, MIPS

FLOPS and MFLOPS. The supercomputing community was generally interested more in the number of floating-point operations that a machine could perform per second, and began to measure performance in MFLOPS, millions of floating-point operations per second. This measure was an improvement on MIPS, since at least the unit of measure was the user-oriented floating-point operation. Even so, the measurement depended upon which floating-point operation was performed and what program was used in making the measurement. MFLOPS differs from MIPS in two ways. Floating-point operations are complex, and without hardware support for them, floating-point programs will run slowly, even on a machine with a high MIPS rate. Second, when using MFLOPS, the overhead instructions required to get operands, store results, implement loops, and so on, are effectively lumped with the floating-point operations they support.

millions of floating-point operations per second, MFLOPS

Whetstones and Dhrystones. The Whetstone benchmark was the first major "synthetic" benchmark program—that is, a program specifically designed for performance testing. Developed in the mid-1970s, it is named after the Whetstone Algol compiler, which was developed in the small town of Whetstone, outside Leicester, England. Statistics gathered using the Whetstone compiler were used to design a small program specifically for benchmark use. The program was designed primarily to measure floating-point performance, and performance is

Whetstones

Dhrystones

SPEC benchmarks

quoted in MWIPS, millions of Whetstone instructions per second. Its original publication language was ALGOL 60, but it has since been ported to FORTRAN, Pascal, and C.

The Dhrystone program, its name a play on the word Whetstone, was developed in 1984 as an integer performance benchmark, versus the Whetstone benchmark's emphasis on floating-point performance. It is a small program, less than 100 high-level language statements, compiling to 1–1.5 KB of code.

Both the Whetstone and Dhrystone benchmarks are small programs whose forms encourage "overoptimization" by optimizing compilers, with a resulting distortion of the test results.

SPEC—System Performance Evaluation Cooperative.   There has been a trend away from synthetic performance measures toward programs that are in general use. The SPEC consortium, consisting of representatives from many computer companies, was formed in 1987 with the purpose of establishing a standard set of such benchmarks. The standard *SPEC benchmark* suite includes a compiler, a Boolean minimization program, a spreadsheet program, and a number of other programs that stress arithmetic processing speed. According to the SPEC bylaws,

> SPEC, the Standard Performance Evaluation Corporation, is a non-profit corporation formed to . . . establish, maintain and endorse a standardized set of relevant benchmarks that can be applied to the newest generation of high-performance computers. . . . SPEC develops suites of benchmarks intended to measure computer performance. These suites are packaged with source code and tools and are extensively tested for portability before release. They are available to the public for a fee covering development and administration costs. By license agreement, SPEC members and customers agree to run and report results as specified in each benchmark suite's documentation.

The current SPEC benchmarks were updated in 1992 to include separate integer and floating-point suites, SPECint92 and SPECfp92. SPEC performance was eagerly embraced by computer manufacturers, and some manufacturers went so far as to optimize their compilers to do well on SPEC benchmarks, even putting special flags in the compiler whose specific purpose was to optimize SPEC performance. The current SPEC agreement tries to circumvent this practice by specifying additional rules about compiler behavior. SPEC is also introducing a series of new benchmarks to measure the performance of client-server systems and several other broader aspects of computer performance.

All of the performance measurement efforts are attempts to achieve the ideal goal of telling users how well a computer will perform on their workloads. Useful information can be obtained by prospective customers who know the relationship of the measured programs to their own, and who understand what the manufacturer has done to make the computer perform better on the benchmarks and whether these improvements will affect the user's programs too.

3.2   RISC versus CISC

Before we discuss the CISC MC68000 and the RISC SPARC microprocessor, we describe some of the factors that differentiate RISC machines from CISC machines. You should understand at the outset that the RISC is a concept or a philosophy of machine design rather than a specific set of architectural features. The term itself is somewhat of a misnomer, in the sense that the new generation of RISC machines have hundreds of instructions, some of which may be quite complex by any definition.

3.2.1   CISC DESIGNS

The CISC machine is *not* the result of a particular philosophy of machine design. Rather, it is the result of the efforts of designers to incorporate more features such as addressing modes and instruction types in an environment where memory costs and access times were high, and a premium was placed on compact instruction codes.

General Characteristics of CISC Machines.   If there is an overriding characteristic of the CISC machine, it is an approach to ISA design that emphasizes doing more with each instruction. As a result, CISC machines have a wide variety of addressing modes, 14 in the case of the MC68000, and 25 in its more capable descendent, the MC68020. Furthermore, CISC machines take a "have-it-your-way" approach to the location and number of operands in its various instruction. The VAX has 0- through 3-address instructions, for example. The VAX ADD instruction can have 2 or 3 operands, and any one of them can be in a register or in memory. The result is instructions that are of widely varying lengths and execution times.

CISC: complex instruction set computer

Historical Factors.   These capabilities were welcomed by users, since they allowed more operations to be compressed into the same program size. When the M6800 was introduced, 16 K RAM chips cost $500, and 40 MB hard disk drives cost $55,000. When the MC68000 was introduced, 64 K RAM chips still cost several hundred dollars, and 10 MB hard drives cost $5,000. Program and data storage were at a premium.

As succeeding generations of computers were developed, manufacturers continued to offer upward compatibility from simpler models to faster and more capable models, and it was only natural that the added capability would involve more complexity. Upward compatibility virtually demanded the introduction of complexity.

Furthermore, machine architects were aware of the "semantic gap," that is, the gap that existed between machine instruction sets and high-level language constructs. It was felt that narrowing the gap with complicated instructions and addressing modes would lead to performance increases. The compiler writers rejected most of these "improvements," finding that they did not fit well with language requirements or that they were of only limited usefulness. Research conducted in 1971 by Donald Knuth and in 1982 by David Patterson showed that 85% of a program's statements were assignment, conditional, or procedure calls. Nearly 80% of the assignment statements were MOVE instructions, without arithmetic operations. As the manufacturers added capabilities to their processors, they found that it was increasingly difficult to support higher clock speeds that would have otherwise been possible. Complex instructions and addressing modes worked against faster clock speeds, because of the greater number of microscopic actions that had to be performed per instruction.

Until recently RAM memory had been dropping in price approximately 40% per year. At a certain point, RAM prices had dropped sufficiently so that the pressure on system designers was less to design instructions that "did more" than it was to design systems that were faster. It was also becoming cost-effective to employ small amounts of higher-speed

memory latency

cache memory to reduce *memory latency*—the waiting time between when a memory request is made and when it has been satisfied.

3.2.2   THE BRIDGE FROM CISC TO RISC

From the earliest days of computing, architects have attempted to increase instruction execution rates by overlapping the execution of more than one instruction. The most common ways of overlapping instructions are prefetching, pipelining, and superscalar operation. We briefly define them here and provide more in-depth discussion in Chapter 5.

In the instruction execution model presented in Chapters 1 and 2, an instruction is fetched, then executed, and then the next instruction is fetched. In many current machines, these operations are overlapped. It is possible to speed up execution considerably by

prefetching

prefetching, that is, fetching the next instruction or instructions into an instruction queue before the current instruction is complete. The earliest 16-bit microprocessor, the Intel 8086/8, prefetches into an on-board queue up to six bytes following the byte currently being executed, so they are immediately available for decoding and execution, without latency. Prefetching can be considered a primitive form of pipelining.

pipelining

Some of the earliest machines employed primitive forms of *pipelining.* Put simply, pipelining instructions means starting, or issuing the next instruction prior to the completion of the currently executing one. The current generation of machines carries this to considerable lengths. The PowerPC 601 has 20 separate pipeline stages in which various portions of various instructions are executing simultaneously. We will discuss pipelining of the SPARC RISC in Section 3.4.6.

superscalar
operation

Superscalar operation refers to a processor that can issue more than one instruction simultaneously. The PPC601 has independent integer, floating-point, and branch units, each of which can be executing an instruction simultaneously. If superscalar operation is to be used to its fullest extent, then some instructions will be executed out of order. For example, if two instructions issue simultaneously, the one with the shortest execution time will finish ahead of the other.

Designers of CISC machines incorporated prefetching, pipelining, and superscalar operation in their designs, but with instructions that were long and complex, and with operand access being dependent on complex address arithmetic, it was difficult to make efficient use of these new speedup techniques. Furthermore, complex instructions and addressing calculations hold down clock speed compared to simple instructions. RISC machines were designed to efficiently exploit the caching, prefetching, pipelining, and superscalar methods that were invented in the days of the CISC machines.

3.2.3   RISC DESIGN PHILOSOPHY

RISC: reduced
instruction set
computer

The name RISC, reduced instruction set computer, focuses on reducing the number and complexity of instructions in the machine. Actually, there are a number of strategies that are employed by RISC designers to exploit caching, pipelining, superscalarity, and so on. You should be aware, however, that a given RISC design may not use all the techniques described in the following paragraphs.

One Instruction per Cycle.   This seemingly simple concept is possibly the most important in RISC design. Early definitions of RISC asked that every instruction complete in a single clock cycle. With the common use of pipelining, the current goal is that (at least) one instruction will issue per clock cycle. Since program execution time depends on throughput, and not on individual instruction execution times, issuing (and thus completing) instructions at an average rate of one per cycle is the correct goal. The key is to do this by making instructions simple, not by making clock periods longer, thus reducing CPI in Equation 3.6 without changing τ.

Fixed Instruction Length.   If one instruction is to issue per clock cycle, it is natural that RISC designers would limit all instructions to a fixed length, usually 1 word. That word specifies everything there is to know about the instruction: what the operation is; where to get the operands, if there are operands; where to put the result, if there is a result; and where to find the next instruction.

Only Load and Store Instructions Access Memory.   With word sizes of 32 bits in common usage, and given the time penalty to access operands in memory, RISC designs require that all operands be in registers when they are operated upon. Access to operands in memory is limited to two operations, load and store. This clean partitioning of processor activities between operand access and operations minimizes traffic between the processor and memory, and assures that all operands will be in registers when they are needed. This in turn minimizes pipeline delays due to absence of an operand.

Simplified Addressing Modes.   Complicated addressing modes mean longer clock periods, since there is more address arithmetic to perform. RISC machines usually limit themselves to only two addressing modes: register indirect and indexed, where the index may be in a register or may be an immediate constant that is contained within the instruction. The latter carries no penalties with it, since the preceding principle of fixed instruction length assures that the constant is in the processor when it is needed, as it is part of the instruction word.

Fewer, Simpler Operations.   Simpler operations imply shorter clock cycles, since less has to be done in a given clock cycle. There is no room in the RISC instruction set for perhaps the most characteristic CISC VAX instruction, POLY, which evaluates a polynomial by Horner's method. Any given complex instruction can be decomposed into a sequence of simpler instructions. If the cache is able to keep up with the execution of these instructions, then the only penalty is increased use of RAM storage. The question to be asked when considering whether to add a given instruction is, "Will adding this instruction be worth the increased complexity in the control unit, and possible increase in clock period?" Only if the answer to this question is a clear yes should it be added.

Delayed Loads and Branches.   "If you can't win, change the rules." In certain RISC architectures, loads, stores, and branch instructions require more than a single clock cycle to execute. In the case of loads and stores, this delay occurs because of the time required to access memory, and in the latter case it occurs because of the delay in accessing the instruction stored at the branch address. The concept of delayed loads and branches acknowledges that since they are bound to take more than a single clock cycle to execute, the processor is allowed to execute the instruction following the load or branch while it completes. This means that the programmer or compiler should strive to place an instruction after the delayed instruction that does not depend on its result. Failing that, a NOP instruction must be located in this position, which is called a *delay slot*. Compiler help is

delay slot

useful here because it is often difficult for an assembly language programmer to remember that the instruction following a branch will be executed whether the branch is taken or not.

Prefetch and Speculative Execution.   The advantages of prefetching become even greater in RISC designs. When all instructions are one word long, it becomes more feasible to examine instructions as they enter the pipeline to see if they involve operand access or branching. If they do, the operand or branch target can be prefetched, resulting effectively in zero execution time for the branch instruction or operand access. Having the branch target address available, and having several functional units that can execute multiple instructions in parallel, some processors begin execution at the target address in advance of knowing whether the condition has been met, and discard the results if it has not. This is known as *speculative execution.*

speculative execution

Let the Compiler Do It.   RISCs have shorter, smaller instructions, each of which does less. This "tearing apart" of single complex instructions into more and simpler instructions creates more dependences between instructions. To utilize the machine's resources to the fullest, execution must be allowed to proceed out of order whenever possible. This places a great burden on the machine programmer, because he or she must consider not only whether a given program is correct, but also whether it has been optimized to the particular machine it will run on with respect to pipeline utilization and out-of-order and delayed execution. Most compilers for RISCs have been developed with special care and attention to optimization for the special RISC characteristics. Because of the complexity required to write optimum code for machines that have pipelining, delayed loads and branches, and so on, code written for these machines is usually written in a high-level language rather than assembly language.

GETTING SPECIFIC: THE POWERPC   The PowerPC architecture is an example of the degree to which a real machine exhibits the above techniques. The PowerPC G4 has over 200 instructions, and some are complex. For example, its instruction, fctiwz, floating-point convert to integer word with round toward zero, is not simple in anyone's book. It is a load/store machine with fixed instruction length and few addressing modes. It has 11 independent execution units, and can have 16 instructions in various stages of execution simultaneously. It does not have delayed loads or branches, but does extensive prefetch and speculative execution. Thus the PowerPC exhibits some RISC hallmarks but not others. ■

3.3   A CISC Microprocessor: The Motorola MC68000

Having discussed the principal differences between CISC and RISC processors, we now examine in detail the ISA of a CISC microprocessor, the Motorola MC68000.

Motorola achieved a good degree of success with their 8-bit M6800, introduced in 1975, and the more capable descendent, the M6809, introduced several years later. The first member of the 32-bit Motorola MC68000 family, the MC68000, was introduced in 1979. It was one of the first generation of 32-bit microprocessors, and would definitely be classed as a CISC machine, having 14 addressing modes and many instructions. Since the introduction of the original MC68000, Motorola has introduced many other family members ranging from the MC68008, which has the same internal architecture as the

Table 3.1 Order of Presenting or Developing a Computer ISA

Memories: structure of data storage in the computer	
	Processor-state registers
	Main memory organization
Formats and their interpretation: meanings of register fields	
	Data types
	Instruction format
	Instruction address interpretation
Instruction interpretation: things done for all instructions	
	The fetch-execute cycle
	Exception handling (sometimes deferred)
Instruction execution: behavior of individual instructions	
	Grouping of instructions into classes
	Actions performed by individual instructions

MC68000, but with a cost-saving 8-bit external data bus instead of the 16-bit data bus of the MC68000, to the MC68040, which has, among other advanced features, a 32-bit data path to main memory.

There is no universal naming convention for expressing the word size of a given processor architecture. We will adhere to the common convention of calling the machine an *n-bit machine* if the majority of its internal data operations employ n-bit operands. All members of the MC68000 family are 32-bit processors by this definition, since the majority of their operations are on 32-bit quantities, even though internal and external data paths may vary from 8 to 32 bits from family member to family member.

n-bit processor

It is helpful to manage the description, or development, of a computer by considering its many details in a well-defined order. We followed such a plan implicitly when presenting SRC in Chapter 2. Table 3.1 makes this presentation order explicit. First, the memory cells in the machine state are described, then the interpretation of values stored in those cells, and finally the actions that transform the state by moving values or changing them with operations. The actions are broken down into those that occur for all instructions and those that apply only to specific instructions.

ISA presentation order

3.3.1   CPU AND MEMORY ARCHITECTURE

Figure 3.1 shows the processor-state registers of the MC68000. Inspection of the figure shows the architecture to be a variation on the general register machine, the variation being that there are two banks of registers: D0–D7, used primarily for arithmetic operands, and A0–A7, used primarily for addresses. During this discussion of the MC68000, we will interleave the informal, textual description of the processor with its RTN description. This will help you to become more familiar with the more formal RTN description technique, as well as providing additional detail.

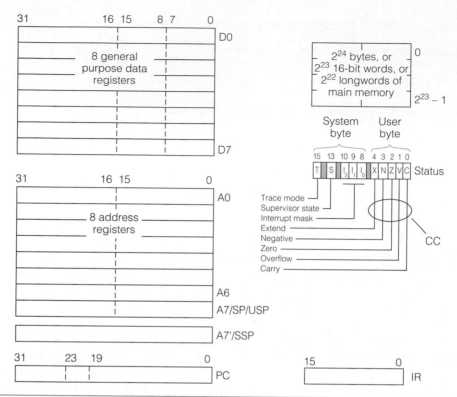

Fig. 3.1 The MC68000 Processor State

CPU Registers.   Referring to Figure 3.1, we find several types of processor-state registers in the MC68000:

- There is a 32-bit PC, but in the MC68000 only the least significant 24 bits are used, because there are only 24 address pins to minimize pin count.
- The IR is a 16-bit register that holds the first 16-bit word of the instruction. Upon the start of instruction execution, that word is fetched, and the PC is incremented by 2 to point to the next instruction word. Certain instructions may be longer than 16 bits, and in that case these 16-bit "extra words" are fetched sequentially as required and the PC incremented to point to the next unfetched word. When the final word of the instruction has been fetched, the PC will point to the first word of the *next* instruction.
- General data and address registers, D0–D7, A0–A7 and A7′ hold the data and addresses used by the executing program. Register A7 is the user stack pointer, and register A7′ is the supervisor stack pointer, whose use is described later in the section on exception processing.
- CC, the status register, composed of a system byte and a user byte, is a set of 1-bit flags that indicate certain processor conditions:

T: trace mode select
S: supervisor mode select
I_2–I_0: interrupt mask
C: carry
V: overflow
Z: zero
N: negative
X: extend

The last 5 bits are known as the condition codes, CC.

With RTN, the same information is described by declaring registers and by giving names to fields that have special uses. The 8-word D and A register sets appear as small memories—a common feature of general register machines.

RTN for the Processor State

$D[0..7]\langle 31..0\rangle$:	General purpose data registers
$A[0..7]\langle 31..0\rangle$:	Address registers
$A7'\langle 31..0\rangle$:	System stack pointer
$PC\langle 31..0\rangle$:	Program counter
$IR\langle 15..0\rangle$:	Instruction register
$Status\langle 15..0\rangle$:	System and user status bytes
$SP := A[7]$:	User stack pointer, also called USP
$SSP := A7'$:	System stack pointer
$C := Status\langle 0\rangle$: $V := Status\langle 1\rangle$:	Carry and overflow flags
$Z := Status\langle 2\rangle$: $N := Status\langle 3\rangle$:	Zero and Negative flags
$X := Status\langle 4\rangle$:	Extend flag
$INT\langle 2..0\rangle := Status\langle 10..8\rangle$:	Interrupt mask in system status byte
$S := Status\langle 13\rangle$: $T := Status\langle 15\rangle$:	Supervisor state and trace flags

The first six lines of the description declare physical registers. The rest of the lines introduce formats that associate mnemonic names with individual registers or subfields. This is done in the pictorial description of Figure 3.1 by careful labeling. Much of the formatting is associated with bits of the status register. The detailed function of these bits depends on how they are used in specific arithmetic instructions and in the interrupt system, and will be described in connection with them.

Main Memory.   Main memory is limited to 2^{24} bytes in the MC68000, by design: There are only 24 address pins, to minimize costs. The processor can access bytes, 16-bit *words*, or 32-bit *longwords*. The latter two must be stored on word and longword boundaries that are multiples of the accessed object's size in bytes; that is, word and longword addresses must be multiples of 2 and 4 respectively. This means that the lsb of a word address must be 0, and the 2 lsbs of a longword address must be 0. If this constraint is violated, the processor signals a bus error to the operating system and terminates program execution. This kind of *alignment constraint* is referred to as *hard alignment*. Some other machines, such as the Intel 8086 family have *soft alignment* constraints. A soft alignment constraint means that a word can be stored aligned or unaligned, but the latter may result in a performance

MC68000 words and longwords

alignment constraint

hard alignment

soft alignment

penalty, because the two aligned words containing the desired, unaligned word may have to be fetched and the desired word assembled from byte fragments of the two fetched words.

big-endian

The machine is *big-endian* in the way it organizes the bytes and other fractional words into words. This means that byte 0 contains the msb (big end), and byte 1 contains the lsb in the case of 16-bit words. The "endian-ness" of memory storage will be covered in more detail in Chapter 7.

In the RTN description of main memory, only the byte memory is physically present. Word- and longword-oriented memories are merely a reformatting of the underlying byte-oriented memory.

RTN for Main Memory

$Mb[0..2^{24} - 1]\langle 7..0\rangle$:	Main memory as bytes
$Mw[ad]\langle 15..0\rangle := Mb[ad]\#Mb[ad + 1]$:	Main memory as words
$Ml[ad]\langle 31..0\rangle := Mw[ad]\#Mw[ad + 2]$:	Main memory as longwords

The big-endian organization is reflected in the order in which bytes are concatenated into words and words concatenated into longwords. The RTN could describe the hard alignment constraints in the MC68000 by adding bit indices to the dummy parameter, ad, that specifies the byte address. This has been suppressed here in the interests of simplicity, but it can also be left out in the early stages of a new design to leave some flexibility in the implementation decisions.

3.3.2   OPERAND AND INSTRUCTION FORMATS AND THEIR INTERPRETATION

The processor can perform operations on bytes, words, and longwords. The operand type is signalled to the assembler by .B, .W, and .L for byte, word, and longword operands, respectively. For example a byte move would be expressed as MOVE.B, and a word move as MOVE.W. If the extension is omitted, word is assumed as the default. Most instructions, but not all, can operate on any of the three operand types. As the dashed lines in Figure 3.1 indicate, bytes are stored in the least significant 8 bits and words in the least significant 16 bits of the register.

Arithmetic operations interpret bytes, words, and longwords as unsigned or 2's complement binary numbers. These should be familiar to you, but if not, Chapter 6 provides a general coverage of this material. We do not discuss floating point operations in connection with the MC68000, so we also leave out floating point formats. This leaves the instruction as the item with the most complex format.

As we saw in Chapter 2, instructions specify registers or memory addresses for operands, results, or the target of a branch. Interpreting these specifications is one of the more logically intricate parts of presenting a machine design for several reasons. First the number of bits in an instruction is limited, so there is a tendency to use complicated encoding tricks to save bits. Second, no standard formats are specified for instructions like those discussed in Chapter 6 for floating-point numbers. Finally, there is the desire in CISC machines to supply all possibly useful variants of instructions, making their descriptions naturally longer than those for RISCs.

Operand Access Paths–Addressing Modes of the MC68000.   Access paths to memory and register operands (addressing modes) are usually specified by a 6-bit field within the instruction, as shown in Table 3.2. The figure at the top of the table shows the 6-bit effective address (EA) specifier. The meanings of the mode and register fields are described in the table footnotes. Since this is our first detailed excursion into complex addressing modes for a commercial computer, we will cover them in some detail before describing some of the common MC68000 instructions.

All instructions start with a 16-bit word that is in the instruction register (IR) when the instruction starts. This word contains one or two address specifiers consisting of mode and register fields, as shown at the top of Table 3.2. Some addressing modes require additional 16-bit words. These words are usually just 8-, 16-, or 32-bit constants, but in the case of indexed addressing, there is a lot of structure in the second instruction word. Both D and A registers can be used as index registers, so a 4-bit field specifies one of 16 index registers. Figure 3.2 shows some possible instruction formats, and the following RTN describes various fields of the instruction.

MC68000 instruction formats

RTN for the MC68000 Instruction Address Format

$op\langle 3..0\rangle := IR\langle 15..12\rangle$:   Operation code
$rg2\langle 2..0\rangle := IR\langle 11..9\rangle$:   Second register field for move
$md2\langle 2..0\rangle := IR\langle 8..6\rangle$:   Second mode field for move
$md1\langle 2..0\rangle := IR\langle 5..3\rangle$:   First address mode field
$rg1\langle 2..0\rangle := IR\langle 2..0\rangle$:   First address register field
$XR[0..15]\langle 31..0\rangle :=$
      $D[0..7]\langle 31..0\rangle \# A[0..7]\langle 31..0\rangle$:   Index register can be D or A
$xr\langle 3..0\rangle := Mw[PC]\langle 15..12\rangle$:   Index specifier field
$wl := Mw[PC]\langle 11\rangle$:   Short or long index flag
$disp8\langle 7..0\rangle := Mw[PC]\langle 7..0\rangle$:   Displacement for index mode
$index := ((wl = 0) \rightarrow XR[xr]\langle 15..0\rangle$:   Short or long index value
      $(wl = 1) \rightarrow XR[xr]\langle 31..0\rangle))$:

We group addressing modes into those that calculate a memory address using a general register, those that do not use a general register but still calculate an address, and modes that do not access main memory.

Addressing Modes Using a Register to Calculate a Memory Address.   Addressing modes in the MC68000 that use a processor register to calculate a memory address are summarized in the following RTN. The summary contains information from Table 3.2 in a more precise form. Most information about addressing modes comes from mode and register fields in the instruction, so the effective address is a function of these fields. The fields are made dummy parameters, md and rg, of the effective address calculation because they come from different places in the instruction register for source and destination addresses.

The length of the operand, B, W, or L, is encoded differently in different instructions, which we will not describe here. Since two addressing modes require the data length, we assume a function, datalen(IR), which returns the value 1, 2, or 4 when the instruction specifies an operation on bytes, words, or longwords, respectively.

$d := datalen(IR)$:   Number of bytes in accessed value

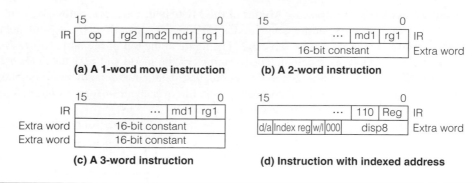

Fig. 3.2 Some MC68000 Instruction Formats

Table 3.2 Motorola MC68000 Addressing Modes

	5 4 3 2 1 0[†]				
	Mode	Reg			

Addressing Mode Name	Mode #	Reg #	Notation[‡]	Extra Word	Operand Location
Data register direct	0	0–7	Dn	0	Dn
Address register direct	1	0–7	An	0	An
Address register indirect	2	0–7	(An)	0	Mem[An]
Autoincrement	3	0–7	(An)+	0	Mem[An]; An ← An + WS
Autodecrement	4	0–7	-(An)	0	An ← An-WS; Mem[An]
Based	5	0–7	disp16(An)	1	Mem[An + disp16]
Based indexed short	6	0–7	disp8(An, XnLo)	1	Mem[An + XnLo + disp8]
Based indexed long	6	0–7	disp8(An, Xn)	1	Mem[An + Xn + disp8]
Absolute short	7	0	addr16	1	Mem[addr16]
Absolute long	7	1	addr32	2	Mem[addr32]
Relative	7	2	disp16(PC)	1	Mem[PC + disp16]
Relative indexed short	7	3	disp8(PC, XnLo)	1	Mem[PC + XnLo + disp8]
Relative indexed long	7	3	disp8(PC, Xn)	1	Mem[PC + Xn + disp8]
Immediate	7	4	#data	1–2	No location, data is value

[†]When the 6-bit field specifies the dst (destination) operand of a MOVE instruction, the mode and reg fields are reversed.

[‡]An and Dn denote one of the eight address or data registers, respectively.

WS = word size in bytes: 1, 2, or 4.

disp8 and disp16 are 8- and 16-bit displacements.

Xn is one of D0–D7, or A0–A7.

XnLo is the low-order 16 bits of register Xn, sign-extended to 32 bits.

All values smaller than 32 bits are sign-extended to 32 bits before addition.

data is an 8-, 16-, or 32-bit value as indicated by .B, .W, or .L in the instruction.

RTN for Addressing Modes That Calculate Main Memory Operand Addresses

ea(md, rg) := (
   (md = 2) → A[rg⟨2..0⟩]:   Mode 2 is A register indirect
   (md = 3) → (A[rg⟨2..0⟩];   Mode 3 is autoincrement
      A[rg⟨2..0⟩] ← A[rg⟨2..0⟩] + d):
   (md = 4) → (A[rg⟨2..0⟩] ← A[rg⟨2..0⟩] – d;   Mode 4 is autodecrement
      A[rg⟨2..0⟩]):
   (md = 5) → (A[rg⟨2..0⟩] + Mw[PC];   Mode 5 is based or offset
    PC ← PC + 2):   addressing
   (md = 6) → (A[rg⟨2..0⟩] + index + disp8; Mode 6 is based indexed
    PC ← PC + 2):   addressing

In mode 2, *address register indirect addressing*, the effective address is the contents of an A register, but the operand (or result) is in memory, as shown in Figure 3.3 below. There is no data register indirect mode in the MC68000.   *address register indirect addressing*

Modes 3 and 4, *autoincrement* and *autodecrement* addressing, are exactly like mode 2, register indirect, except that the register containing the address is incremented by 1, 2, or 4 after (autoincrement) or before (autodecrement) the address is used. Again, only address registers may be specified. The RTN expressions for autoincrement and autodecrement use the semicolon to specify the sequence of operations and depend on the data length, d. Examples of move instructions using these modes follow: *autoincrement addressing*   *autodecrement addressing*

```
MOVE.L  (A5)+,  ...   ;A5 is incremented by 4 after the move.
MOVE.W  -(A4),  ...   ;A4 is decremented by 2 before the move.
```

The combination of a postincrement and a predecrement is useful in accessing push-down stacks.

In mode 5, *based addressing*, the address in an A register serves as a base to which is added a 16-bit displacement contained in the word following the instruction. This mode requires a 2-word instruction, as noted in the "Extra word" column in Table 3.2. In multi-word instructions, the program counter must be advanced past the extra words before fetching the next instruction. The advance appears as a side effect of the address calculation, PC ← PC + 2, in the RTN.   *based addressing*

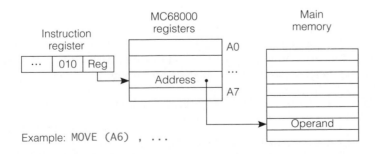

Example: MOVE (A6) , ...

Fig. 3.3 Mode 2: Address Register Indirect Addressing

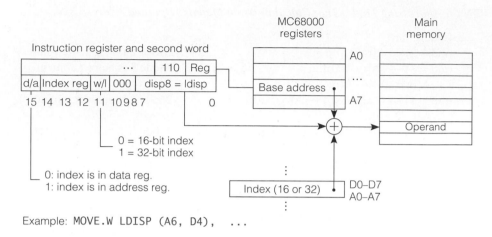

Example: MOVE.W LDISP (A6, D4), ...

Fig. 3.4 Mode 6: Based Indexed Addressing

As noted in the last chapter, there is little to distinguish based from indexed address-ing save the intent of the programmer, provided the displacement is large enough to satisfy that intent. The MC68000 has no simple indexed addressing mode, but since the displace-ment is a 16-bit value, based addressing is an adequate substitute. Based addressing is often used to access a field in a `struct` stored in memory, where the offset to the desired field in the `struct` is known at the time the program is assembled and can be inserted into the displacement. Based addressing is also used to access items in a stack frame or parameter-passing area whose base is known.

based indexed addressing

Mode 6, *based indexed addressing* specifies a three-component addressing mode that computes the address as

(contents of base register + contents of index register + 8-bit constant)

as shown by the RTN. The definition, disp8 := Mw[PC]⟨7..0⟩, shows that the constant is contained in the extra word following the instruction word. The base is in an A register, but the index can be in either a data or address register, as shown by the RTN definition of XR. The computation can involve the entire 32 bits of the index register, or just the low-order 16 bits, as indicated in the RTN definition of index. The based indexed addressing mode is diagrammed in Figure 3.4.

Addressing Modes Not Using a Register Number.   Mode 7 is used for addressing modes that do not need a register number. These include relative addressing, where the PC plays the role of a base register, and absolute addressing, where no base register at all is used. The register field selects a specific mode in this group.

RTN for Addressing Modes That Do Not Specify a Register:

(md = 7 ∧ rg = 0) →   Mode 7, register 0: short absolute
(Mw[PC]{sign extend to 32 bits}; PC ← PC + 2):
(md = 7 ∧ rg = 1) →   Mode 7, register 1: long absolute
(Ml[PC]; PC ← PC + 4):

$(\text{md} = 7 \wedge \text{rg} = 2) \rightarrow$	Mode 7, register 2: PC relative
$(\text{PC} + \text{Mw[PC]}\{\text{sign-extend to 32 bits}\};$	
$\quad \text{PC} \leftarrow \text{PC} + 2):$	
$(\text{md} = 7 \wedge \text{rg} = 3) \rightarrow$	Mode 7, register 3: relative indexed
$\quad (\text{PC} + \text{index} + \text{disp8}; \text{PC} \leftarrow \text{PC} + 2) \qquad):$	

Note that md = 7, rg = 4 is missing here because it specifies the immediate mode, which does not calculate an address. It is described on page 106.

Mode 7, reg = 0 or 1, specifies *absolute short* and *absolute long addressing*. Absolute addressing is also called *direct addressing*. Absolute addresses do not change as the program is relocated in memory, and are thus used to specify addresses that are independent of program location. Examples would include I/O ports in memory mapped I/O, and special purpose addresses, fixed by the operating system, for example. The existence of two forms, absolute short and absolute long, reflects upward compatibility concerns in moving from a processor with a short address to a new model with a longer one. The first, or first two extra words after the instruction word specify a 16- or 32-bit address. The former is sign-extended to a 32-bit address. Assembly language instructions using absolute short and absolute long addressing can have several word-length specifiers, as in the following examples.

absolute short and absolute long addressing

direct addressing

```
MOVE.B PRINTERPORT.W, ...
MOVE.W INTVECT.L, ...
```

In the first example, the `MOVE.B` specifies that a byte is being moved, whereas the `PRINTERPORT.W` specifies absolute short addressing with a 16-bit word.

Mode 7, reg 2, *relative addressing* specifies the address as a signed 2's complement offset relative to the program counter, PC. This means that if the program is moved or relocated to run at a different location, the operand address will move with it.

relative addressing

The MC68000 instruction set does not allow relative addressing to be used to specify a destination operand; this addressing mode could be used to modify the program, and so-called self-modifying code is frowned upon because of the extreme difficulty of debugging it.

Mode 7 reg 3, *relative indexed addressing*, is exactly analogous to the based indexed addressing of mode 6, except that the PC is used instead of the A register base address. The diagram of Figure 3.4 serves for this mode also if PC is substituted for the A register input to the adder. Relative indexed addressing can be used to access a table of data values or jump targets stored with the program. An assembly language example of this mode follows:

relative indexed addressing

```
MOVE.W LDISP(PC, D4), ...
```

Addressing Modes That Use No Memory Address.   Not all operands or results have a memory address. They may be contained in A or D registers, where register numbers instead of memory addresses serve to locate them. There are also immediate operands contained in one or more extra instruction words. Specifications for such operands or results are still called addressing modes, even though they do not calculate memory addresses.

Given the ability of the MC68000 to operate on bytes, words, or longwords, different parts of a register are used for an operand, and a different number of additional instruction words are used for immediate operands. An RTN description must detail these distinctions based on d := datalen(IR). We shorten the description below by leaving the RTN for the word operand, opndw, for you to fill in.

RTN Description of Operand Value

memval(md, rg) :=	A memory address
$((md\langle 2..1\rangle = 1) \vee (md\langle 2..1\rangle = 2) \vee (md\langle 2..0\rangle = 6) \vee$	is used with
$((md\langle 2..0\rangle = 7) \wedge (rg\langle 2\rangle = 0)))$:	these modes only.
opndl(md, rg)$\langle 31..0\rangle$:= (	A long operand can be
memval(md, rg) $\rightarrow$ Ml[ea(md, rg)]$\langle 31..0\rangle$:	in memory,
md = 0 $\rightarrow$ D[rg]$\langle 31..0\rangle$:	in a D register,
md = 1 $\rightarrow$ A[rg]$\langle 31..0\rangle$:	in an A register,
(md = 7 $\wedge$ rg = 4) $\rightarrow$ (Ml[PC]$\langle 31..0\rangle$: PC $\leftarrow$ PC + 4)):	or an immediate.
opndw(md, rg)$\langle 15..0\rangle$:= (. . .):	Word operand
opndb(md, rg)$\langle 7..0\rangle$:= (	byte operands use the
memval(md, rg) $\rightarrow$ Mb[ea(md, rg)]$\langle 7..0\rangle$:	low-order 8 bits of
md = 0 $\rightarrow$ D[rg]$\langle 7..0\rangle$:	registers and of
md = 1 $\rightarrow$ A[rg]$\langle 7..0\rangle$:	the second 16-bit
(md = 7 $\wedge$ rg = 4) $\rightarrow$ (Mw[PC]$\langle 7..0\rangle$: PC $\leftarrow$ PC + 2)):	instruction word.
opnd(md, rg) := (	The operand length in the
(d = 1) $\rightarrow$ opndb(md, rg): (d = 2) $\rightarrow$ opndw(md, rg):	instruction tells
(d = 4) $\rightarrow$ opndl(md, rg)):	which to use.

data register
direct, address
register direct

Both modes 0 and 1, *data register direct* and *address register direct* addressing, locate the operand or result in a general purpose register. The RTN, opnd(0,rg) := D[rg] and opnd(1,rg) := A[rg], make the memory address conspicuous by its absence. Assembly language examples follow:

```
MOVE D6, ...
MOVE A6, ...
```

immediate
addressing

Mode 7 reg 4, *immediate addressing,* is used to access constants that are stored as part of the program. Byte, word, and longword constants can be accessed by this addressing mode. Notice that the constant is stored immediately after the first instruction word, as shown by the RTN and in Figure 3.5.

The figure and the last line of the RTN definition of byte operand, opndb, show that only the low-order 8 bits of a second 16-bit instruction word are used for the immediate byte value. This is a result of an implementation decision to process long instructions in 16-bit parcels using the 16-bit IR register. It is an example of an implementation decision influencing the instruction set architecture. Processing 8-bit instruction parcels would surely be possible, but the implementation domain determines whether it is efficient.

Result Storage. Results do not necessarily need a memory address to locate them either, but they do need a storage register of some kind. Therefore, the immediate mode is not useful when a result is to be stored. The only place it could be put is into part of the instruction word, again leading to programs that modify their own instructions during execution. The MC68000 designers decided to disallow not only the use of immediate result addressing, but also the use of instructions that store results into relative addresses.

A complete RTN description for the MC68000 would include a definition of a result, rslt(md, rg), that excluded immediate and relative addressing modes and handled the byte, word, and longword distinction contained in the instruction code. We leave this as an exercise and assume it in the RTN for the MC68000 instructions that follow.

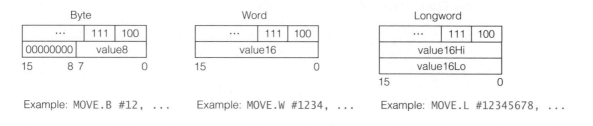

Fig. 3.5 Mode 7, Reg 4: Immediate Addressing

One final addressing mode is the modified form of relative addressing used by branch instructions. It allows using an 8-bit constant in the branch instruction word as an offset in place of the extra word used by mode 7, reg 4. Since it is used only by the branch instructions, it will be discussed with them.

Key Concepts: CISC Addressing Modes and the MC68000

- The existence of a large number of addressing modes and the ability to use them in many different instructions is a hallmark of a CISC architecture.

- The basic elements used in all the addressing modes are CPU registers, the PC, and constants contained in one or more instruction words.

- The requirement for a variable amount of constant data for calculating addresses causes the instruction length to vary from one to three words. Actually, a MOVE instruction might require two extra words for both source and destination addresses for a total of five instruction words.

- Note that the A registers are favored over the D registers in computing addresses. Only A registers can be used in register indirect, autoincrement, and autodecrement addressing. Although both A and D registers can be used as index registers, only an A can be a base register.

- Some addressing modes have side effects on the processor-state registers. Autoincrement and autodecrement change the address register, and modes that use extra instruction words have the side effect of advancing the program counter past these extra 16-bit parcels.

3.3.3   THE MC68000 INSTRUCTION SET

Here we introduce a subset of the MC68000 microprocessor instruction set. First, we discuss operations performed independently of the particular instruction being executed. This instruction interpretation is abbreviated here to include only the fetch-execute cycle. Exception handling is properly part of instruction interpretation, but we postpone its discussion until after the instruction set has been discussed.

The instruction set is structured by dividing it into classes of related instructions. We cover the most commonly used data movement, arithmetic and logic, and program control instructions. We omit the less common instructions in those classes, as well as a number of special purpose instructions. Refer to the manufacturer's literature for a complete description of the instruction set.

The Fetch-Execute Cycle.   Some activity occurs in the same way for all instructions of the MC68000. This basic heartbeat of the machine is the fetch-execute cycle. At the minimum, it consists of fetching the first 16-bit instruction word, advancing the program counter, and then executing the specific instruction given by the IR contents. During instruction execution, the program counter may need to be advanced again if the instruction has extra 16-bit parcels specifying data or addresses. The Run bit, usually an external signal, just serves to halt instruction interpretation.

RTN for Instruction Interpretation

Instruction_interpretation := (	When running, fetch and
Run $\rightarrow$ ((IR$\langle 15..0 \rangle$ $\leftarrow$ Mw[PC]$\langle 15..0 \rangle$:	execute an instruction.
PC $\leftarrow$ PC + 2); instruction_execution);	

We will see when we discuss exceptions later that there is more to instruction interpretation than just fetch and execute. In addition to exception processing, there is also status information that affects the overall interpretation of instructions.

Processor Control and Privilege Level.   The upper byte of the status word (Figure 3.1) is devoted to system status and control. The MC68000 has two privilege levels, supervisor and user. When the S bit, Supervisor state, is 1, the machine is in supervisor mode. In supervisor mode, all the machine instructions can be executed, including *privileged instructions* that allow manipulation of the status word and the system stack pointer, A7′. When S = 0, these privileged instructions cannot be executed. Information about the processor privilege level also appears on certain external signal pins, thus allowing an external memory management unit to enforce access limitations on memory. Thus access to system resources is enforced at the lowest levels of the machine's hardware.

privileged
instructions

Data Movement Instructions.   Table 3.3 shows some of the common data movement instructions, along with their encodings. Refer to the notes at the bottom of the table for a description of the abbreviations and field names used in the table.

data movement
instructions

The first three MOVE instructions include the only memory-to-memory operations in the MC68000 instruction set. Examining the other 2-operand instructions will show that one or both of the operands must be in a register. The instruction format is that of Figure 3.2a. These fields are named in Table 3.3 according to their different uses in the particular instruction. A simplified RTN description of the move instruction, omitting the setting of condition codes, follows:

move := (op := 0) $\rightarrow$ rslt(md2, rg2) $\leftarrow$ opnd(md1, rg1):

Table 3.3 shows that the N and Z condition-code bits are affected by the MOVE operation. If the operand is negative or 0, then the respective condition-code bits are set. This allows the use of a conditional branch operation that tests the N or Z bits immediately after an operand is moved, without performing an explicit arithmetic operation to set the bits. The V and C bits are reset to 0 in all cases. This is the "logical" action, since obviously there can be no arithmetic overflow or carry in the absence of any arithmetic operation. A more complete RTN description makes use of a temporary register, tmp$\langle 31..0 \rangle$, which is used as a mechanism for describing what actually happens, but which may not be present

Table 3.3 MC68000 Data Movement Instructions

Mnemonic	Operands	Opcode Word	XNZVC	Operation	Operand Size
MOVE.B	EAs,EAd	0001ddddddssssss	−xx00	dst ← src	byte
MOVE.W	EAs,EAd	0011ddddddssssss	−xx00	dst ← src	word
MOVE.L	EAs,EAd	0010ddddddssssss	−xx00	dst ← src	longword
MOVEA.W	EAs,An	0011rrr001ssssss	-----	An ← src	word
MOVEA.L	EAs,An	0010rrr001ssssss	-----	An ← src	longword
LEA.L	EAc,An	0100aaa111ssssss	-----	An ← EAc	address
EXG	Dx, Dy	1100xxx1mmmmmyyy	-----	Dx ↔ Dy	longword

Notes:

EAs: Source EA—any addressing mode, except cannot move byte to address register.

EAd: Destination EA—any addressing mode except immediate or relative.

EAc: Control EA—all modes except register, autoincrement, autodecrement, or immediate.

ssssss, dddddd: src and dst addressing mode specifiers. See Table 3.2, top.

rrr, yyy: One of eight registers.

aaa: one of the eight address registers

An, Dn: one of the eight address or data registers, respectively.

mmmmm: mode field. 01000—exchange data registers; 01001—exchange address registers; 10001—exchange data and address registers, where xxx specifies the data register, and yyy specifies the address register

Condition codes: − = unchanged from previous value; x = changed by the operation; 0, 1 = value.

in a particular implementation. The register, tmp, is needed because each use of opnd(...) results in another operand fetch.

$$\text{move } (:= op\langle 3..2\rangle = 0) \rightarrow ($$
$$\text{tmp} \leftarrow \text{opnd(md1, rg1)}; (Z \leftarrow (\text{tmp} = 0): N \leftarrow (\text{tmp} < 0): V \leftarrow 0: C \leftarrow 0):$$
$$\text{rslt(md2, rg2)} \leftarrow \text{tmp}):$$

Programmers debate the usefulness of setting flags on a move instruction, since a programmer may not wish the flags disturbed by a move instruction that follows some arithmetic operation.

MOVEA allows the movement of a value, usually an address, to one of the address registers without affecting the condition codes. This is a sensible decision on the part of the designers, since presumably if an address is being moved, the programmer is unlikely to be interested in its arithmetic value. Examination of the operation code shows that MOVEA is just a normal MOVE with mode 1 addressing. The extra complexity of checking the mode to determine how to set the condition codes adds to the RTN needed to describe the move instruction, and to the hardware a designer must build to implement it.

LEA (load effective address) allows the programmer to perform address computations, and then to store the address in an address register without any operand fetch. This permits complex, multipart address arithmetic to be performed prior to operand fetch. The RTN definition

$$\text{lea } (:= (op\langle 3..0\rangle = 0100_2) \wedge (\text{md2} = 7)) \rightarrow A[\text{rg2}] \leftarrow \text{ea(md1, rg1)}:$$

shows that the address, and not the contents of the memory cell it points to, is loaded into the destination register. Thus not all source addressing-modes will be legal with this instruction, since register and immediate modes do not calculate an address.

EXG (exchange registers) exchanges the contents of two registers. Besides the form shown in Table 3.3, which allows the exchange of two data registers, there are two additional forms that allow exchange of address registers, and of address registers with data registers. Condition codes are not affected.

There are a number of other special purpose data movement instructions that allow movement of a small immediate value to a register (MOVEQ), exchanging of the upper and lower words of a register (SWAP), and others.

Even a cursory examination of Table 3.3 reveals a lack of regularity. There are many special cases and exceptions to the rules, which reflected Motorola's desire to pack as many instructions and addressing modes into as few bits as possible. This trade-off is always tempting to instruction set designers, especially if the instruction word size is small.

Arithmetic and Logical Instructions.   Table 3.4 shows a subset of the arithmetic and logic operations that are available in the MC68000. ADD, SUB, and CMP all have the same encoding except for the first 4 bits, which are used to specify which operation is to be performed. All three operations can be performed on bytes, words, and longwords, depending on the value of the op-mode field mmm. One of the operands must be in a data register Dn; the other is specified by the 6-bit EA field. The mmm field, which is in place of the destination mode field in the move instructions, also specifies whether the destination is Dn or is specified by EA, as described in the table notes. CMPI, compare immediate, allows the comparison of an immediate value with a value stored at EA.

Subtract is a typical arithmetic instruction. As with most of the arithmetic operations, it has the feature of the two address instructions described in Chapter 2, in that one of the operands is replaced by the result. We give its RTN description without the condition-code setting.

RTN for a Typical Arithmetic Instruction:

$$\text{sub} (:= \text{op} = 9) \rightarrow ($$
$$(\text{md2}\langle 2\rangle = 0) \rightarrow D[\text{rg2}] \leftarrow D[\text{rg2}] - \text{opnd}(\text{md1}, \text{rg1}):$$
$$(\text{md2}\langle 2\rangle = 1) \rightarrow (\text{memval}(\text{md1}, \text{rg1}) \rightarrow (\text{tmp} \leftarrow \text{ea}(\text{md1}, \text{rg1});$$
$$M[\text{tmp}] \leftarrow M[\text{tmp}] - D[\text{rg2}]):$$
$$\neg\text{memval}(\text{md1}, \text{rg1}) \rightarrow \text{rslt}(\text{md1}, \text{rg1}) \leftarrow \text{rslt}(\text{md1}, \text{rg1}) - D[\text{rg2}])):$$

The CMP and CMPI operations differ from the other arithmetic and logic operations in that no result is stored after the operation is performed. CMP and CMPI are used to set the condition codes without altering any of the operands.

MULS performs signed multiplication on two words. The result is stored as a longword in one of the eight data registers, Dn. Likewise, DIVS performs signed division of a longword contained in a data register, Dn, by a word located at EA. The quotient of the division is stored in the lower word of Dn, and the remainder is stored in the upper word of Dn. There are also unsigned multiply and divide instructions.

Table 3.4 MC68000 Integer Arithmetic and Logic Instructions

Mnemonic	Operands	Opcode word	XNZVC	Operation	Oprnd size
ADD	EA,Dn	1101rrrmmmaaaaaa	xxxxx	dst ← dst + src	b,w,l
SUB	EA,Dn	1001rrrmmmaaaaaa	xxxxx	dst ← dst – src	b,w,l
CMP	EA,Dn	1011rrr0wwaaaaaa	-xxxx	dst – src	b,w,l
CMPI	#dat,EA	00001100wwaaaaaa	-xxxx	dst – immed.data	b,w,l
MULS	EA,Dn	1100rrr111aaaaaa	-xx00	Dn ← Dn*src	l ← w*w
DIVS	EA,Dn	1000rrr111aaaaaa	-xxx0	Dn ← Dn/src	l ← l/w
AND	EA,Dn	1100rrrmmmaaaaaa	-xx00	dst ← dst∧src	b,w,l
OR	EA,Dn	1000rrrmmmaaaaaa	-xx00	dst ← dst∨src	b,w,l
EOR	EA,Dn	1011rrr1wwaaaaaa	-xx00	dst ← dst⊕src	b,w,l
CLR	EAs	01000010wwaaaaaa	-0100	dst ← 0	b,w,l
NEG	EAs	01000100wwaaaaaa	xxxxx	dst ← 0 – dst	b,w,l
TST	EAs	01001010wwaaaaaa	-xx00	dst – 0	b,w,l
NOT	EA	01000110wwaaaaaa	-xx00	dst ← ¬dst	b,w,l

Notes:

rrr is a D register number.

mmm is a 3-bit mode field specifying the dst as EA or Dn, and operands as b, w, or l:

Byte	Word	Long	Destination
000	001	010	Dn
100	101	110	EA

EA is an effective address.

aaaaaa is a 6-bit address specifier. Not all modes are available to all instructions.
 See the manufacturer's literature for details.

ww is a word-size specifier field: 00—byte; 01—word; 10—long.

CMPI is followed by 1 or 2 words containing the immediate data to compare.

The logical operations AND, OR, and EOR (exclusive or) are encoded exactly like ADD, except for the left 4 instruction bits, which specify the operation. The logical operations can be used for "masking" operations: AND is used to clear portions of a word, OR to set portions of a word, and EOR to complement portions of a word.

The four unary operations CLR, NEG, TST, and NOT are also similar to one another. The first 8 bits specify the operation, the next 2 bits, ww, specify whether the operand is a byte, word, or longword, and the last 6 bits specify the EA of the operand. CLR clears (zeros) the operand, NEG performs the arithmetic negation (2's complement) of the operand, TST sets the Z and N flags according to whether the operand is zero or negative, and NOT performs the logical (1's) complement of the operand.

There are additional instructions that allow the operations ADD, SUB, CMP, AND, OR, and EOR with immediate data.

While the logical operations AND, OR, NOT, and TST in Table 3.4 can be used to clear, set, complement, or test single bits, the MC68000 instruction set also has a separate group of bit operations that allow clearing, setting, complementing, and testing single bits:

BCLR, BSET, BCHG, and BTST. These instructions can operate on bytes or longwords. The bit number to be operated on can be specified in immediate mode, or it can be in a data register. The bit number of a byte is specified in the low-order 3 bits, and that of a longword in the low-order 5 bits. Again, refer to the Motorola manual for more details.

The MC68000 shift and rotate instructions can be used to shift or rotate bytes, words, or longwords left or right a specified number of bit positions. The bit that "falls off the end" of the operand is stored in either the C or X flag of the condition code register, and rotates can be "through" the X flag. Table 3.5 shows the shift and rotate instructions that are available. The table has only one entry for both left and right directions because the d bit determines the direction of shifting or rotation.

The shift and rotate instructions are used for "bit picking," that is, the ability to isolate a portion of a word, when used with the logical operations AND, OR, and NOT.

MC68000
program control

Program Control Instructions. Table 3.7 shows the class of program control instructions. The MC68000 allows conditional branching on the basis of the state of one or more of the condition-code bits, C, N, V, and Z. The possible branch conditions are shown in Table 3.7.

Table 3.6 borrows some assembly language notation to shorten the register transfer description in the Operation column. For example, $-(SP)\leftarrow$ means the SP register is decremented and then used as a memory address in which to store the value, the normal stack push operation. Similarly (SP)+ represents a stack pop with postincrement.

The Bcc conditional branch instruction is used to control program flow based on the state of one or more condition-code bits. We will describe the derivation and meaning of the branch conditions that test multiple flags, such as GT, in Chapter 6, "Computer Arithmetic and the Arithmetic Unit." An example of using the Bcc instruction would be to test a variable, say X, and branch to another program location, say LOC, if X = 0. This fragment would represent a mapping from the following C statement:

```
if ( X = 0 ) goto LOC[1]:
TST    X                        ;sets N and Z.
BEQ    LOC                      ;branch to LOC if X=0.
```

The DBcc (decrement and branch if condition, sometimes called *don't* branch if condition) is a powerful primitive used in loop control. It has three parameters: a count register, Dn; a branch target, disp; and a termination condition, one of the condition-code tests, cc. As the pseudocode in the last column of Table 3.6 shows, the instruction operates as follows when used for loop control:

1. The condition cc is tested. If it is true, the instruction terminates after advancing the PC to the next instruction.
2. If the condition is false, Dn is decremented. If the result is -1 (indicating that it previously was 0) then the instruction terminates, and control falls through to the next instruction, thus terminating the loop.
3. If the result of decrementing Dn was not -1, then the relative branch is taken back up to the top of the loop.

---

1.   You will notice the presence of what Brian Kernighan and Dennis Ritchie, authors of the C language, refer to as "the infinitely abusable goto statement." Unfortunately, the machine language branch and jump instructions implement the goto, and there are almost no alternatives to its use.

Table 3.5 MC68000 Shift and Rotate Instructions

Mnemonic	Operands	Opcode Word	XV	Operation
ASd	EA	1110000d11aaaaaa	xx	ASL / ASR (C, X, Dn)
ASd	#cnt,Dn	1110cccdww000rrr	xx	
ASd	Dm,Dn	1110RRRdww100rrr	xx	
ROd	EA	1110011d11aaaaaa	-0	ROL / ROR (C, Dn)
ROd	#cnt,Dn	1110cccdww011rrr	-0	
ROd	Dm,Dn	1110RRRdww111rrr	-0	
LSd	EA	1110001d11aaaaaa	x0	LSL / LSR (C, X, Dn)
LSd	#cnt,Dn	1110cccdww001rrr	x0	
LSd	Dm,Dn	1110RRRdww101rrr	x0	
ROXd	EA	1110010d11aaaaaa	x0	ROXL / ROXR (X, C, Dn)
ROXd	#cnt,Dn	1110cccdww010rrr	x0	
ROXd	Dm,Dn	1110RRRdww110rrr	x0	

Notes:

d is a direction bit: 0 = shift/rotate right, 1 = shift/rotate left. d is specified as R or L in the instruction; e.g., ROL specifies rotate left.

rrr is one of Dn.

ccc is cnt field; 0 = 8, 1 – 7 = count.

RRR is D register where count is located.

EA is an effective address, specified by aaaaaa.

aaaaaa is a 6-bit effective address specifier. All addressing modes are available except address register direct, relative, relative indexed, and immediate.

ww is a word-size field: 00—byte; 01—word; 10—long.

Condition-code bits N, Z, and C are affected by all instructions:

   N = msb of result.

   Z =1 if result = 0; otherwise set to 0.

   C = last bit shifted out of operand; cleared if count = 0.

   This means that the DBcc instruction can be used to control a loop that terminates either when the loop count equals 0 or when another specified termination condition, cond, occurs. If no condition is to be tested, and DBcc is just used for its decrement-and-branch-if-not-zero capability, the DBF (DB False) form is used.

   Scc tests the same condition codes as DBcc, but sets the result byte to 0xFF if the condition is true, and to 0x00 if it is false. (The definition of true as 0xFF and false as 0x00 is an arbitrary choice of the designer.) The ability to set a Boolean variable to true or false depending on the condition cc is useful in evaluating complex Boolean expressions.

Table 3.6 MC68000 Program Control Instructions

Mnemonic	Operands	Opcode Word	Operation
		Conditional Instructions	
Bcc	disp	0110ccccdddddddd DDDDDDDDDDDDDDDD	**if** (cond) **then** PC ← PC + disp
DBcc	Dn,disp	0101cccc11001rrr DDDDDDDDDDDDDDDD	**if** ¬(cond) **then** (Dn ← Dn − 1 **if** Dn ≠ −1 **then** PC ← PC + disp) **else** PC ← PC+ 2
Scc	EA	0101cccc11aaaaaa	**if** (cond) **then** (EA) ← 0xFF **else** (EA) ← 0x00
		Unconditional Instructions	
BRA	disp	01100000dddddddd DDDDDDDDDDDDDDDD	PC ← PC + disp
BSR	disp	01100001dddddddd DDDDDDDDDDDDDDDD	−(SP) ← PC; PC ← PC + disp
JMP	EA	0100111011aaaaaa	PC ← EA
JSR	EA	0100111010aaaaaa	−(SP) ← PC; PC ← EA
		Subroutine Return Instructions	
RTR		0100111001110111	CC ← (SP) +; PC ← (SP) +
RTS		0100111001110101	PC ← (SP) +

Notes:

rrr is one of Dn.

If 8-bit displacement dddddddd is zero, then displacement is DDDDDDDDDDDDDDDD.

EA is an effective address.

aaaaaa is a 6-bit effective address specifier. Not all addressing modes are available to all instructions. See the manufacturer's literature for details.

ww is a word-size field: 00—byte; 01—word; 10—long.

cccc is defined in Table 3.7.

Table 3.7 MC68000 Conditions

Name	Meaning	Code	Logic	Name	Meaning	Code	Logic
T	true	0000	1	F	false	0001	0
CC	carry clear	0100	$\overline{C}$	LS	low or same	0011	C + Z
CS	carry set	0101	C	LT	less than	1101	$N \cdot \overline{V} + \overline{N} \cdot V$
EQ	equal	0111	Z	MI	minus	1011	N
GE	greater or equal	1100	$\overline{N} \cdot \overline{V} + N \cdot V$	NE	not equal	0110	Z
GT	greater than	1110	$\overline{N} \cdot \overline{V} \cdot \overline{Z} + N \cdot V \cdot \overline{Z}$	PL	plus	1010	$\overline{N}$
HI	high	0010	$\overline{C} \cdot \overline{Z}$	VC	overflow clear	1000	$\overline{V}$
LE	less or equal	1111	$N \cdot \overline{V} + \overline{N} \cdot V + Z$	VS	overflow set	1001	V

BRA and JMP both map to the C goto statement. BRA branches to an 8- or 16-bit immediate displacement relative to the PC. The 8-bit displacement dddddddd is used if it is not equal to 0. If it is, then the next word is taken as a 16-bit displacement. Note that no other encoding in the instruction indicates this property, so the comparison of ddddddd to 0 must be made when the instruction word is being interpreted. JMP differs from BRA in causing a jump to a standard effective address rather than an immediate value. This address may be absolute rather than relative.

BSR, JSR, RTS, and RTR are used to implement procedure calls and returns. BSR and JSR both begin by pushing the current value of the PC, which points to the next instruction in sequence, onto the stack. BSR then executes a branch as does BRA, and JSR executes jump, as does JMP. Pushing PC onto the stack is like Hansel and Gretel leaving a trail of cookie crumbs so they could find their way back to grandma's house: executing RTS at the end of the procedure pops the top of stack into PC, causing execution to resume at the instruction after the BSR/JSR. If the programmer wishes to restore the status register to its state prior to the call, the status register can be pushed onto the stack, or saved in An with the MOVE USP (move user stack pointer) instruction, which we do not further describe. RTR pops the top of stack into status, and then pops the top of stack into the PC.

3.3.4   PROGRAM EXAMPLES AND THE MC68000 ASSEMBLER

Although there are many more instructions in the MC68000 repertoire, we have given examples of the three major classes: data movement, arithmetic, and program control. Simple program fragments show how these instructions are used together and introduce some aspects of the MC68000 assembler. For more information on MC68000 assembly language, see Appendix C. The program of Figure 3.6 searches an array of 132 bytes, representing a line of text, for the return character, ^M (control-M), which has the decimal ASCII value of 13.

This example introduces a number of Motorola pseudo-operations; that is, operations that are instructions to the assembler, linker, or loader rather than opcodes:

MC68000 assembler pseudo-operations

- ■ EQU, equate, defines the value of a constant symbolically, so that it can be referred to throughout the program by its symbolic value. Notice the use of #LEN as an operand of the MOVE.B instruction. The # is needed to indicate to the assembler to use immediate mode. EQU can also be used to define an address rather than a simple constant, so this distinction is needed.

- ■ DS.B/W/L is used to define storage, DS (reserve storage would perhaps be a better term), for an array of bytes, words, or longwords that will be loaded along with the program before execution.

- ■ #LINE, the immediate mode, is used to indicate the *value* of an address as opposed to its contents. Note that LEA LINE could have been used instead of #LINE.

- ■ ORG, origin, is used to indicate where the program fragment that follows it should be placed in memory when the program module is loaded prior to execution. In the fragment above, the first byte of array LINE will be located at 0x1000. (The Motorola assembler takes digit sequences prefixed by $ to be hexadecimal integers, and those without prefixes as decimal integers. Character constants are enclosed in single quotes: 'X'.)

```
CR     EQU      13              ;Define the return character.
LEN    EQU      132             ;Define line length.
       ORG      $1000           ;Locate LINE at 0x1000.
LINE   DS.B     LEN             ;Reserve storage for LEN bytes.
       MOVE.B   #LEN-1, D0      ;Initialize count -1 in D0.
       MOVEA.L  #LINE, A0       ;Starting address of array into A0.
LOOP   CMPI.B   #CR, (A0)+      ;Make the comparison.
       DBEQ     D0, LOOP        ;Double test: if LINE[131 - D0] ≠ 13
                                ;then decr D0; if D0 ≠ -1 branch to LOOP
       ...                      ;else fall through to next instruction.
```

Fig. 3.6 Example Program to Search an Array

You should note the difference between EQU and DS. The former merely provides a shorthand notation for a constant used in the program. It makes the program easier to read, and if the constant needs to be changed, only one change needs to be made. The latter, DS, reserves the specified amount of storage in memory at load time.

assembly-time actions

We take this opportunity to remind you of the distinction between actions that take place at assembly time versus those that happen at load or run time. This distinction can be confusing to the beginning assembly language programmer. Consider, for example, the subtraction, #LEN-1 that is indicated as the first operand of MOVE.B. When does this subtraction take place? It takes place at assembly time. Why? There are two clues: first, it is in the operand field of the instruction rather than the opcode field (not that just placing a subtract operator in the opcode field would indicate subtraction!); and second, operators such as "−" are high-level language concepts, not assembly language concepts. The assembly language symbol for subtraction is SUB. The subtraction #LEN-1 takes place *once,* at the time the program is assembled.

A second example program, shown in Figure 3.7, is a subroutine named CLEARW that clears a block of words. This example illustrates the use of JSR and RTS for procedure call and return, respectively. CLEARW expects the base address of the block in A0, and the count of words to be cleared, ≥0, in D0. The calling program is named MAIN. It is the responsibility of MAIN to establish the procedure-entry conditions prior to executing the JSR instruction. These include placing the address of the base of the array in A0 and the number of words to clear in D0.

Notice that the initial instruction in the subroutine is a branch to the DBF to decrement the count, since the count actually runs from count −1 down to 0, and to handle the case where the call was made with D0 = 0; in that case the loop must not be entered.

```
MAIN     ...
         MOVE.L   #ARRAY, A0     ;Base of array
         MOVE.W   #COUNT, D0     ;Number of words to clear
         JSR      CLEARW         ;Make the call.
         ...
CLEARW   BRA      LOOPE          ;Branch for initial decrement
LOOPS    CLR.W    (A0)+          ;Autoincrement by 2.
LOOPE    DBF      D0, LOOPS      ;Decrement Do;fall through if -1
         RTS                     ;Finished.
```

Fig. 3.7 A Subroutine to Clear a Block of Words

Key Concepts: Motorola MC68000 Instructions

- ■ Instructions can be divided into the classes of data movement, arithmetic and logic, and program control.
- ■ Both data movement and ALU instructions in the MC68000 can access registers or memory locations for operands or results.
- ■ Branch instructions interpret logical combinations of the condition-code bits specifying a relation between numbers compared by a previous instruction.
- ■ Branch instructions specify a relative address near to the current instruction as a branch target.

3.3.5   EXCEPTION PROCESSING

Exceptions are unexpected events that occur during normal processing that call for special intervention by the processor. The three kinds of exceptions in the MC68000 microprocessors are interrupts, traps, and traces. *Interrupts* are externally generated events that require processor intervention, such as a key being pressed on a keyboard, incipient power failure, bus error, and so on. *Traps* are internally generated exceptions, such as arithmetic overflow, attempts to divide by 0, and failure of a bounds check imposed on a register. A *trace* is essentially a high-priority trap generated after every instruction, and is used to single-step a program during debugging. The trace mode is entered by setting the T bit of the status register, shown in Figure 3.1.

The Exception Processing Sequence.   There are four steps to the handling of exceptions in the MC68000 series of machines:

1. Record and adjust processor status.
2. Determine address of exception handler.
3. Save previous state on stack.
4. Jump to exception handler.

In the first step a temporary copy is made of the status register, and then the S-bit is set, placing the processor in supervisor mode; the T (trace) bit is reset, disabling the trace mode for the duration of the exception handling. (It would be awkward if the T bit were set during trace handling, since there would be a trace exception generated after every instruction of the trace-handling routine.)

Every exception must have a software routine to process it, called an *exception handler*. The exception handler is very much like an ordinary subroutine. The address of the handler is specified by an *exception vector number*. In step 2, the address of the exception handler is determined by the acquisition of a vector number. In the case of interrupts, the external interrupting device is responsible for providing the vector number immediately after the processor has acknowledged the interrupt: that is, when it has informed the device that its request has been granted. For internally generated exceptions, the vector number is provided internally. The vector number is an 8-bit value used to generate the exception vector by shifting it left by 2 bits. The vector itself is the 4 bytes beginning at the 10-bit address generated by shifting the vector number left by 2 bits. These 4 bytes comprise a 32-bit address that is loaded into the PC. Thus the *exception vector* is the value of the new PC, and represents the address at which the exception handler will be found. When the exception is an interrupt, the handler is also called an *interrupt service routine*.

exceptions

interrupts

traps

trace

exception
handler

exception vector

interrupt service
routine

In the third step, the old PC and saved status register are pushed onto the supervisor stack A7′, and in the fourth step the PC is loaded with the exception vector, beginning execution of the exception handler. Return from the handler is by means of the RTE instruction, return from exception. The RTE instruction works the same as the RTR instruction in Table 3.6, except that both the system and user bytes of the status register are restored instead of just the condition codes.

Interrupt Priorities.   The MC68000 family allows the prioritization of interrupts into seven levels of priority. The current priority is indicated by bits 8–10 of the status word. The processor has three external pins on which the priority of the interrupting process is signaled. Priorities less than or equal to the current priority are ignored, unless the incoming priority is 111, 7 decimal, the so-called non-maskable interrupt, NMI. The NMI is used to signal events that must be serviced in all cases, and is discussed further in Section 4.8.2. The interrupt handler is free to set the priority of the current process to a new value by manipulating the priority bits in the status word. The processor examines the external interrupt lines only after the execution of each instruction; instructions cannot be interrupted in the middle of their execution.

interrupt
priorities

Exception processing appears in the RTN description of a computer as a modification to the instruction interpretation sequence. Its description requires some additions to the processor-state declarations. The revised RTN that follows covers both exception handling and the machine reset operation.

RTN for Exception Processing

Reset:	Reset input
exc_req:	Single-bit exception request
exc_lev$\langle 2..0 \rangle$:	Exception level
vect$\langle 7..0 \rangle$:	Vector number for this exception
exc := exc_req $\wedge$ (exc_lev > INT):	There is a request with level > current mask in status register
tmp$\langle 15..0 \rangle$:	Temporary storage for status register

Instruction_interpretation := (
Run $\wedge \neg$(Reset $\vee$ exc) $\rightarrow$
    (IR $\leftarrow$ Mw[PC]: PC $\leftarrow$ PC + 2;   Normal execution state
        instruction_execution):
Reset $\rightarrow$ (INT$\langle 2..0 \rangle \leftarrow$ 7: S $\leftarrow$ 1: T $\leftarrow$ 0:   Machine reset
    SSP $\leftarrow$ Ml[0]: PC $\leftarrow$ Ml[4] :
    Reset $\leftarrow$ 0: Run $\leftarrow$ 1):
Run $\wedge \neg$Reset $\wedge$ exc $\rightarrow$ Exception handling
(Tmp $\leftarrow$ Status: S $\leftarrow$ 1: T $\leftarrow$ 0 ;   Record and change status
    SSP $\leftarrow$ SSP - 4; Ml[SSP] $\leftarrow$ PC: Push PC and status onto
    SSP $\leftarrow$ SSP - 2; Mw[SSP] $\leftarrow$ Tmp;   stack
    PC $\leftarrow$ Ml[vect$\langle 7..0 \rangle$#00$_2$]);   Jump to handler
instruction_interpretation):

3.3.6   Input/Output in the MC68000

There are two ways to perform input and output activities in a computer system: by memory-mapped I/O and by isolated I/O. Figure 1.4 shows schematically how the two methods differ in their employment of processor buses. *Memory-mapped I/O*, used by the MC68000 family, and for that matter by most new processor designs, employs just one bus, the system memory bus. Some of the memory space is devoted to input and output instead of being populated entirely with memory. Performing input and output becomes a matter of reading or writing to particular memory addresses reserved for I/O.

Isolated I/O, on the other hand, uses separate input and output machine instructions that read or write bytes or words from an I/O space that is similar to the memory space. I/O commands use the I/O bus, and memory commands use the memory bus. There are I/O addresses, usually referred to as I/O ports, just as there are memory addresses. This method has the advantage that the memory space can be devoted entirely to system memory, and it was popular when memory space was limited to 16- or 20-bit addresses. It is less popular now that most processors have address lengths of 24, 32, or more bits, thus having room for I/O ports mapped to the memory space without limiting the amount of RAM or ROM that the system designer and user can use. In addition, having a separate I/O bus means another set of pins on the IC package, and packaging engineers are already struggling to provide enough pins to support the larger address and data buses that are the norm with modern processors. The original Motorola MC68000 has 64 pins. The Motorola PowerPC 601 has 64 pins devoted to its data bus alone, and a total of 304 pins.

Illustrative Example: Reading Characters from the Keyboard.   We limit our treatment here to the example memory-mapped keyboard interface of Figure 3.8 and will take up I/O programming in more detail in Chapter 8, "Input and Output." This example assumes a system with a 24-bit address bus, as the MC68000 has, so only six hexadecimal digits are used to specify addresses. The figure shows that the system is populated with RAM memory from 0x000000 to 0xFF7FFF. The keyboard interface is mapped above that: The keyboard status byte, KBSTATUS, is located at 0xFF8006, and the byte representing the ASCII value of the key that was pressed, KBDATA, is located 2 bytes above it, at 0xFF8008. The msb of KBSTATUS is 1 if a key has been pressed since KBDATA was last read; otherwise it is 0. Reading KBDATA clears the msb of KBSTATUS.

```
KBSTATUS   EQU      0xFF8006
KBDATA     EQU      0xFF8008
           . . .
RDCHAR     TST.B    KBSTATUS      ;Set flags.
           BPL      RDCHAR        ;Spin in busy-wait loop until msb = 1.
           MOVE.B   KBDATA, D0    ;Store character in D0.
           RTS                    ;Return to caller.
```

This general-purpose subroutine can be used by any process that needs to get a character from the keyboard. Notice that the absolute addressing mode is used in reading KBSTATUS and KBDATA. If the program is relocated in memory, we definitely wish to continue reading from the absolute addresses of the two keyboard interface ports. Also notice that the character read from the keyboard is returned in register D0. This is a common programming convention for subroutines that return a scalar value such as a character, an integer, or a floating-point number: It is returned in the accumulator or in the lowest-numbered general register.

memory-mapped I/O

isolated I/O

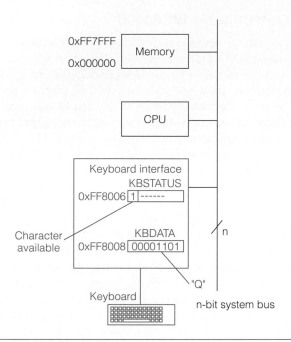

Fig. 3.8 A Memory Mapped Keyboard Interface

Also notice the so-called busy-wait loop formed by the instructions TST.B and BPL. Given that clock speeds are likely to be >1 MHz, and typing speeds are generally in the 10s of Hz, the example subroutine will spend more than 99% of its time busy-waiting. This is unacceptable in practice. Most likely a key press would trigger an interrupt, and the subroutine on page 119 would be replaced by an interrupt service routine. The interrupt service routine would look very much like the subroutine, except that the busy-wait loop would be dispensed with.

3.4   A RISC Architecture: The SPARC

The SPARC (scalable processor architecture) was introduced by Sun Microsystems in 1987, not as a microprocessor but as an architectural family. The SPARC is an open architecture in the sense that a number of semiconductor vendors have been licensed by SPARC International to produce SPARC chips using various implementation domains: CMOS, ECL, and GaAs, for example. SPARC International is a consortium of computer manufacturers, and membership is open to any company. The SPARC specification defines the general purpose integer, floating-point, and coprocessor registers and others that are part of the processor state, and 69 basic machine instructions. The original memory model assumed a linear, 32-bit virtual address space, and is essentially a byte-oriented, 32-bit design. (Virtual addressing allows a single memory space to spill onto the disk. It is discussed in detail in Chapter 7.) All SPARC binaries are upwardly compatible.

original SPARC

We will describe the original SPARC architecture in detail in the discussion that follows. SPARC International designates this as Version 7. When implementation details are important, we will use information from the first implementation, the Fujitsu MB86900, which had a 16.6 MHz clock and an average performance of 10 MIPS. The average CPI was thus 1.66. We will conclude with a brief description of the newer additions to the SPARC family.

The original SPARC CPU architecture defines three processing units: the integer unit, IU; the floating-point unit, FPU; and a coprocessor, CP. The IU is the heart of the machine. It does all address and integer computations and handles program control. The FPU, which we will not treat in detail, is defined by the architecture specification so that it can be implemented as a separate coprocessor chip or integrated with the IU. The CP is user-supplied and has user-defined operations. The SPARC architecture specification only defines its interface to the SPARC system.

Research in the early 1980s showed that a high percentage of memory traffic was taken up with saving and restoring registers during procedure calls and returns. A clever means of overcoming this overhead, employed by the SPARC, is the use of overlapping *register windows*. The concept behind register windows is to have a large number of CPU registers, but to make only a subset of them visible to the programmer at any one time. The register set is divided into groups: some registers are dedicated to global variables, some to incoming procedure parameters, some to local variables of the procedure, and some to outgoing parameters. When a procedure call is made, a new overlapping window is created. The overlap is designed so that the registers containing the outgoing parameters of the calling procedure become the registers containing the incoming parameters of the called procedure. This mechanism passes parameters from procedure to procedure at essentially zero cost.

register windows

Simply supplying a larger register set would require more bits for each register number field in an instruction and would burden the user or compiler with the management of more registers. With the register window mechanism, an adequate number of parameters can be passed in registers, and reading and writing to a stack in memory can be confined to procedures that have many parameters or use large structures. If the window set is full, the registers of an occupied window must be spilled, or written into memory, to free them for use by the called procedure.

Although the SPARC architecture definition is separate from any implementation, concession was made to an anticipated pipelined implementation. The architecture specifies a *branch delay,* which we will discuss briefly in connection with the branch instructions. The mystery behind its utility will probably not be removed, however, until the discussion of pipelined design in Chapter 5. The SPARC does not have a load delay, as do some other RISC machines. We will briefly discuss the four-stage pipeline of the MB86900 later in this section.

branch delay

3.4.1 SPARC PROCESSOR AND MEMORY ARCHITECTURE

When the register windows are suppressed, the SPARC programmer's model is fairly typical of RISC machines. It has a general register organization with separate integer and floating-point register sets. The branch delay requires two program counters: PC, which points to the currently executing instruction, and nPC, which holds the next value of PC. The processor state, including only the 32 immediately visible general registers, is shown in Figure 3.9 As usual in RISC machines, all SPARC instructions are the same length, 32 bits, matching the size of IR. The processor-status register, PSR, contains the condition-code bits: negative (n),

SPARC programmer's model

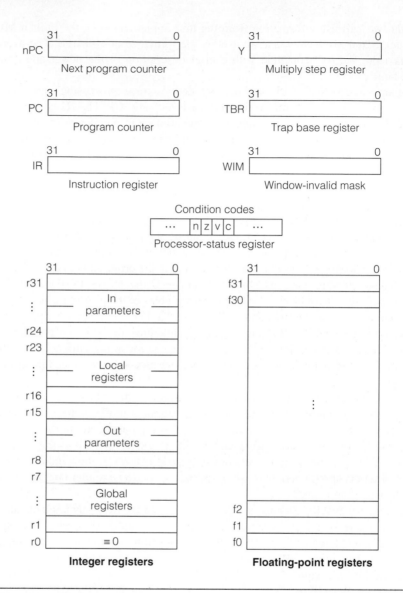

Fig. 3.9 Simplified SPARC Processor State

zero (z), overflow (v), and carry (c). Also contained in the PSR is the current window pointer, bits used by traps and interrupts, and a few others. The window-invalid mask (WIM) is used by the register window mechanism, the trap base register (TBR) by trap and interrupt response, and the Y register by the multiply step instruction. The 32 floating-point registers can hold 32 single-precision (32 bits), 16 double-precision (64 bits), or 8 extended-precision (128 bits) floating-point numbers.

The principal registers in the SPARC can be described by the following RTN, which suppresses register windows and parts of the status register.

RTN for SPARC without Register Windows

SPARC processor-
state RTN

PC⟨31..0⟩:	Currently executing instruction
nPC⟨31..0⟩:	Next program counter value
IR⟨31..0⟩:	Instruction register
r[1..31]⟨31..0⟩:	General registers (current window only)
r[0]⟨31..0⟩: = 0	
f[0..31]⟨31..0⟩:	Floating-point registers
WIM⟨31..0⟩:	Window-invalid mask
TBR⟨31..0⟩:	Trap base register
Y⟨31..0⟩:	Multiply step register
PSR⟨..⟩:	Processor-status register
CCR⟨3..0⟩ := PSR⟨..⟩:	Condition-code register in PSR
n := CCR⟨3⟩: z := CCR⟨2⟩:	Negative and zero bits
v := CCR⟨1⟩: c := CCR⟨0⟩:	Overflow and carry bits

Register Windows.   The concept of register windows is central to the SPARC programmer's model. Figure 3.10 shows schematically how they work in the SPARC system. The total number of registers is implementation-dependent, but the original SPARC has 120 total registers. Of these, the first 8, g0..g7, also referred to as r0..r7, are devoted to global variables and are available to all procedures. Register r0 is identically = 0; that is, reads from this register always return 0, and writes to it have no effect.

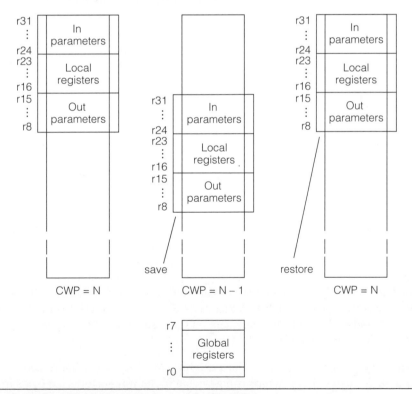

Fig. 3.10 SPARC Register Windows Mechanism

The remaining 112 registers are devoted to the register window system. The last 8 in a given window are used for input parameters to this procedure. The second 8 are devoted to local variables, and the first 8 are used to pass parameters to a procedure to be called. There is a *current window pointer, CWP,* that is invisible to the nonsystem programmer. CWP is decremented by the `save` instruction, making the next window active, and making the *outs* of the old window the *ins* of the new window. Invoking the `restore` instruction reverses the process. The return address is placed in register r15 by a procedure call and is available in r31 after a `save`.

current window
pointer, CWP

An attempt to invoke a `save` when all windows have been used causes a trap exception, resulting in a *spill* of the first window register set. This means that the registers of the set are stored on a memory stack prior to returning control to the invoking program. The register windows "wrap around" when all windows are full, acting like a circular buffer. When the last window is full, the contents of the first window are spilled, making it available to the calling routine. A `restore` when executing with the first window register set also causes a trap that pops the saved registers from the stack and restores them.

register window
spill

The following RTN supplies some details of the workings of the window register mechanism. It defines the registers r[0..31] in terms of 8 global registers and up to 512 window registers and shows how `save` and `restore` alter the definitions.

RTN Description of Register Windows

$WR[0..511]\langle31..0\rangle$:	Window registers (maximum allowable)
$WIM\langle31..0\rangle$:	Window-invalid mask
$CWP\langle4..0\rangle$:	Current window pointer (part of PSR)
$wrb\langle8..0\rangle := CWP\#0000_2$:	Window register base
$g[0]\langle31..0\rangle := 0$:	Global register 0 is identically zero
$g[1..7]\langle31..0\rangle$:	Global registers
$r[0..7] := g[0..7]$:	First 8 registers are global
$r[8..31] := WR[wrb..wrb + 23]$:	Last 24 registers change with CWP

$save \rightarrow ((WIM\langle CWP - 2\rangle = 1) \rightarrow window\_ov:$
$\qquad (WIM\langle CWP - 2\rangle = 0) \rightarrow (WIM\langle CWP\rangle \leftarrow 1: CWP \leftarrow CWP - 1)):$
$restore \rightarrow ((WIM\langle CWP + 2\rangle = 1) \rightarrow window\_un:$
$\qquad (WIM\langle CWP + 2\rangle = 0) \rightarrow (WIM\langle CWP\rangle \leftarrow 0: CWP \leftarrow CWP + 1)):$

The `save` and `restore` instructions use the window-invalid mask WIM to determine an overflow (window_ov) or underflow (window_un) trap. In the absence of a trap, they update WIM and CWP to change the window and keep a record of occupied ones. Actually, `save` and `restore` do more than this, but these are all the operations connected with changing the window. Since the out parameters of a new window will overlap the window after it, it is window CWP–2 that must be tested for invalid (in use). Although shown as +1 and –1 in the RTN, increment and decrement of CWP is done modulo the number of implemented windows.

Main Memory.   Memory addresses have 32 bits. Memory has a linear address space, consisting of 2^{32} bytes. The machine is big-endian in the way it stores the bytes in longer halfwords, words, and so on. Byte 0 contains the msb, and byte 3 contains the lsb in the case of 32-bit words. Note that SPARC words are 32 bits, whereas an MC68000 word was 16 bits. The big-endian order is reflected in the RTN declaration of the memory, but memory alignment constraints are not included.

RTN for the SPARC Memory

Mb[0..2^{32}-1]$\langle 7..0 \rangle$:	Byte memory
Mh[a]$\langle 15..0 \rangle$:= Mb[a]$\langle 7..0 \rangle$#Mb[a + 1]$\langle 7..0 \rangle$:	Halfword memory
M[a]$\langle 31..0 \rangle$:= Mh[a]$\langle 15..0 \rangle$#Mh[a + 2]$\langle 15..0 \rangle$:	Word memory

memory mapping unit

The SPARC architecture defines a *memory mapping unit* (MMU) that allows for multiple address spaces. Only one at a time is available to user code, but supervisor programs may access several for different users, system tables, or I/O registers. Access to these alternate address spaces makes use of an 8-bit address space indicator (asi). Besides expanding the size of the available memory space, the MMU supplies the important function of protecting sensitive memory areas from unauthorized access. The MMU will be left out of our discussion of the SPARC instructions, but we will treat memory mapping in Chapter 7.

3.4.2 OPERAND AND INSTRUCTION FORMATS AND INTERPRETATION

Integer instructions can access bytes, 16-bit halfwords, 32-bit words, and 64-bit double-words. Words and larger-sized memory objects must be aligned on even word boundaries. That is, the least significant 2 bits of their addresses must be 0. The machine instructions can operate on 8-, 16-, 32-, and 64-bit unsigned and 2's complement signed integers, and 32-, 64-, and 128-bit floating-point numbers.

SPARC halfwords, words, and doublewords

The SPARC also supports limited data typing in hardware by the inclusion of a *tagged data* type. The least significant 2 bits of tagged data are reserved for user-defined data type information. The instruction set contains instructions that inspect the tag field and set the overflow bit, and optionally cause an overflow trap if either one of them is set. This feature can be quite useful in supporting languages such as Lisp, Smalltalk, and Prolog, in which data typing must be done at run time.

tagged data

Instruction Formats.   Again, it is the instruction format that involves the most complexity in interpretation, though it is less complicated than in the CISC MC68000. The SPARC has 55 basic integer instructions and 14 floating-point instructions. There are several additional coprocessor formats that we will not cover in this text. Most SPARC instructions use one of the three different formats shown in Figure 3.11, two of which have variants. Further information about the field names can be read from the comments in the following RTN version of Figure 3.11. The use of the asi field is not discussed.

RTN for SPARC Instruction Format

op$\langle 1..0 \rangle$:= IR$\langle 31..30 \rangle$:	Instruction class, opcode for format 1
disp30$\langle 29..0 \rangle$:= IR$\langle 29..0 \rangle$:	Word displacement for call, format 1
a := IR$\langle 29 \rangle$:	Annul bit for branches, format 2a
cond$\langle 3..0 \rangle$:= IR$\langle 28..25 \rangle$:	Branch condition select, format 2a
rd$\langle 4..0 \rangle$:= IR$\langle 29..25 \rangle$:	Destination register for formats 2b & 3
op2$\langle 2..0 \rangle$:= IR$\langle 24..22 \rangle$:	Opcode for format 2

disp22$\langle 21..0 \rangle$:= IR$\langle 21..0 \rangle$:   Constant for branch displacement or sethi
op3$\langle 5..0 \rangle$:= IR$\langle 24..19 \rangle$:   Opcode for format 3
rs1$\langle 4..0 \rangle$:= IR$\langle 18..14 \rangle$:   Source register 1 for format 3
opf$\langle 8..0 \rangle$:= IR$\langle 13..5 \rangle$:   Sub-opcode for floating-point, format 3a
i := IR$\langle 13 \rangle$:   Immediate operand indicator, formats 3b & c
simm13$\langle 12..0 \rangle$:= IR$\langle 12..0 \rangle$:   Signed immediate operand for format 3c
rs2$\langle 4..0 \rangle$:= IR$\langle 4..0 \rangle$:   Source register 2 for format 3b

Addressing Modes.   True to its RISC nature, the SPARC allows memory access only through loads and stores. The number of addressing modes is very limited compared to the CISC MC68000. Load and store only allow two modes:

register plus register address

1. register + register

register plus immediate address

2. register + sign-extended, immediate 13-bit constant.

Two more addressing modes are used for branches and `call`.

Since any one of the 8 global and 24 window registers can be used in address computation, direct, displacement, register indirect, and indexed addressing can be synthesized from the two forms allowed by load and store. If the identically 0 register g0 is used as the first register, form 1 becomes register indirect, and form 2 becomes direct addressing. Direct addressing can only address the bottom or top 4K of memory. To see why, sign-extend a positive or negative 13-bit constant to make an absolute 32-bit address. Load and store can only do PC relative addressing with the aid of an instruction, such as jump and link, that stores the PC in a register.

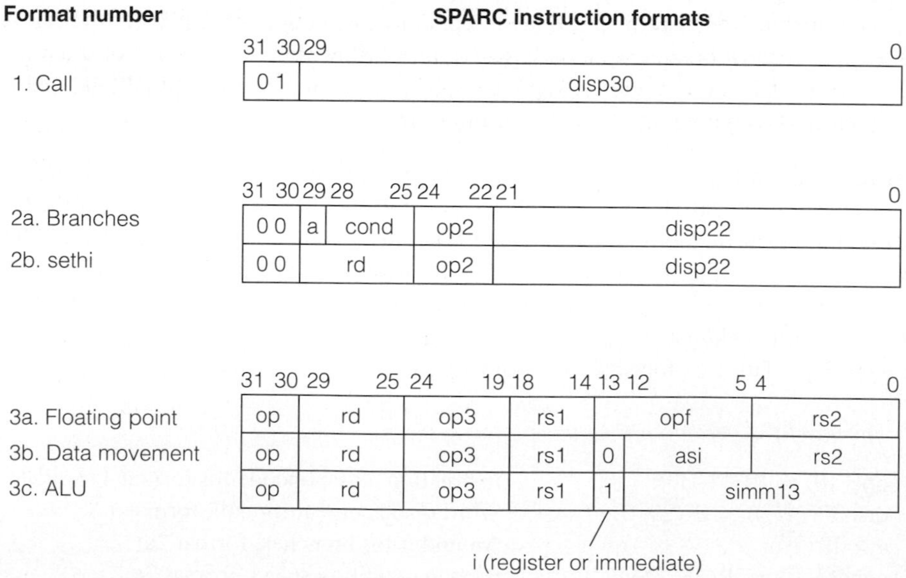

Fig. 3.11 SPARC Instruction Formats

branch address

Branches and `call` use addressing relative to the program counter. Since instructions are always 32 bits and aligned on word boundaries, the relative displacement is a word off-set. This allows the 30-bit displacement in `call` to reach all of the 32-bit address space, and the 22-bit displacement used in branches to extend ±8M bytes from the current instruction. The following RTN summarizes all the addressing modes in the SPARC.

RTN for SPARC Addressing Modes

$$\text{adr}\langle 31..0 \rangle := (i = 0 \rightarrow r[rs1] + r[rs2]:$$

Address for load, store,

$$i = 1 \rightarrow r[rs1] + simm13\langle 12..0 \rangle \text{ \{sign ext.\}}):$$

and jump

$$\text{calladr}\langle 31..0 \rangle := PC\langle 31..0 \rangle + disp30\langle 29..0 \rangle \#00_2:$$

Call relative address

$$\text{bradr}\langle 31..0 \rangle := PC\langle 31..0 \rangle + disp22\langle 21..0 \rangle \#00_2 \text{\{sign ext.\}}:$$

Branch address

3.4.3 THE SPARC INSTRUCTION SET

The instruction interpretation in the SPARC is complicated both by trap and interrupt response and by the two program counters necessitated by delayed branches. We will again defer the discussion of traps until after the instruction set has been presented. The branch delay behavior will be considered in more detail with the discussion of branch and call instructions. A skeleton outline of instruction interpretation without interrupts is given by the following RTN.

RTN Description of SPARC Instruction Interpretation

SPARC instruction interpretation

instruction_interpretation := (IR ← M[PC]; instruction_execution;
    update_PC_and_nPC; instruction_interpretation):

The major classes of SPARC instructions are data movement, arithmetic and logical, and control and branch. We will not treat floating-point instructions. They are similar in character to register-to-register integer arithmetic instructions but act on the separate set of floating-point registers, for which separate load and store instructions are also needed. We also do not discuss coprocessor instructions. The only ones defined in the architecture specification are those that move data to and from the coprocessor. Nor do we discuss privileged instructions executed only by the operating system when the processor is in supervisor mode. The SPARC does have a rich set of these; see the SPARC literature for more details.

Data Movement Instructions. The SPARC is a load-store architecture, so the only instructions that access memory are load and store instructions, except for the `swap` instruction and some privileged instructions for managing interlocked processes. Table 3.8 shows the load, store, and data movement instructions and encoding. Notice that SPARC supports byte, halfword, word, and doubleword data moves. Addresses are of the form rs1 + simm13, or of the form rs1 + rs2, depending on the value of the i bit, bit 13. The data is loaded into rd, and stored from rd. The data is loaded into the least significant bits of the register. The remainder of the register is either cleared or sign-extended, depending on whether it is an unsigned or signed load, respectively. The `ldd` instruction must specify an even register for rd, and the doubleword is loaded into rd and rd + 1. The `swap` instruction swaps the word in rd with the memory word.

Table 3.8 SPARC Data Movement Instructions

Mnemonic	op	op3	Meaning
ldsb	11	00 1001	Load signed byte from address.
ldsh	11	00 1010	Load signed halfword from address.
ld	11	00 1000	Load signed word from address.
ldub	11	00 0001	Load unsigned byte from address.
lduh	11	00 0010	Load unsigned halfword from address.
ldd	11	00 0011	Load doubleword from address.
stb	11	00 0101	Store byte to address.
sth	11	00 0110	Store halfword to address.
st	11	00 0100	Store word to address.
std	11	00 0111	Store doubleword to address.
swap	11	00 1111	Swap register with memory word at address.
or	10	00 0010	r[rd] ← r[rs1] OR (r[rs2] or immediate)
sethi	00	(op2 = 100)	Sets high-order 22 bits of rd (Format 2).

Note:
Except for or and sethi, adr = r[rs1] + r[rs2] if i = 0, or r[rs1] + simm13 if i = 1.

partial word loads and stores

Providing load and store support for partial words adds six load and store instructions. It also may complicate the CPU-to-memory interface. If the unit of data transfer between processor and memory is 32 bits, then implementing stb could require reading an entire 32-bit word, replacing the correct byte, and rewriting the word into memory. Some RISC machines choose to avoid the extra instructions and the added memory interface complexity by not providing partial word loads and stores. In these machines, partial word operations must be synthesized using shift and logical operations on full words moved to and from memory. The Hewlett-Packard Corporation's Alpha architecture is an example of such a RISC.

The reader may wonder at the inclusion of a logical operation, or, with the data movement instructions. It is used as a move instruction, where rs2 = g0, effectively or-ing rs1 with the identically 0 register, g0, and moving the result to rd. There are a number of these synthetic instructions in the SPARC instruction set.

The sethi instruction is a special case of a data movement instruction. The instruction uses format 2b, with op2 = 100, and is used to load immediate values into the high-order 22 bits of a register. It sets bits 9–0 of rd to 0, and the 22 bits contained in disp22 are loaded into bits 31–10 of rd. The sethi instruction does not set the condition codes. The nop instruction can be synthesized from the sethi instruction by letting rd = 0 and disp22 = 0.

Arithmetic Instructions.   Table 3.9 shows the SPARC arithmetic instructions. The second operand for integer arithmetic instructions is determined in the same way that is used to compute the address for load and store. If the format 3 bit named i is 0, the second operand is r[rs2], and if i = 1, it is the sign-extended 13-bit constant simm13. The determination of the second operand and a typical arithmetic instruction, sub, are described by the following RTN.

Table 3.9 SPARC Arithmetic Instructions

Mnemonic	op	op3	Meaning
add	10	0S 0000	Add; add and set CCs.
addx	10	0S 1000	Add with carry; add with carry and set CCs.
sub	10	0S 0100	Subtract; subtract and set CCs.
subx	10	0S 1100	Subtract with borrow; subtract with borrow and set CCs.
mulscc	10	10 1100	Do one step of a multiplication.

Notes:

Set CCs if S = 1. Mnemonics: addcc, addxcc, subcc, and subxcc.

Instructions use format 3: r[rd] ← r[rs1] op (r[rs2] or immediate).

RTN for the Subtract Instruction

$$opnd2\langle 31..0\rangle := ((i = 0) \rightarrow r[rs2]: (i = 1) \rightarrow simm13\langle 12..0\rangle \{sign\ ext.\}):$$
$$sub\ (:= op = 10_2 \wedge op3 = 000100_2) \rightarrow r[rd] \leftarrow r[rs1] - opnd2:$$

The SPARC adopts a "have-it-your-way" approach with regard to setting the condition-code bits in arithmetic and logical instructions. If the S bit is 0, then the codes are undisturbed; if the S bit is 1, then the four condition-code bits are set as a result of the instruction. The addx and subx instructions are used to implement multiple-precision arithmetic. The addx instruction performs the addition rs1 + opnd2 + Carry. The subx instruction performs the operation rs1 − opnd2 − Carry.

SPARC condition-code setting

There are no multiply and divide instructions in the original SPARC hardware. Multiply and divide instructions are either done using floating-point instructions, or done in software. There is some support for integer multiplication using the mulscc instruction, which does one step of the multiplication by the shift-and-add technique, discussed in Chapter 6.

RISC machines tend to confine multistep arithmetic operations to their floating-point units, where such instructions are unavoidable. This accounts for the lack of integer multiply and divide in the original SPARC. A one-step multiply would require a lot of logic, and hence much area on the processor chip. As integration densities improved, more RISC machines have provided integer multiply instructions, including later versions of the SPARC.

The SPARC logical and shift operations are shown in Table 3.10. The shift instructions shift the value in r[rs1] by a shift count given by opnd2 and put the result in r[rd]. Only the low-order 5 bits of the shift count are used. Unlike the arithmetic instructions, the shift instructions do not have any provision for setting the condition codes. There are no rotate instructions (see Exercise 3.17).

SPARC logical and shift operations

The number of logical operations could be reduced with no loss of capability, but the only thing gained would be fewer opcodes. Implementation of a new logical operation is practically free and has no impact on processor speed. The NOT operation is only left out because it is synthesized using orn with g0 as its first operand.

Table 3.10 SPARC Logical and Shift Instructions

Mnemonic	op	op3	Meaning
and	10	0S 0001	AND; AND and set CCs if S = 1.
andn	10	0S 0101	NAND; NAND and set CCs if S = 1.
or	10	0S 0010	OR; OR and set CCs if S = 1.
orn	10	0S 0110	NOR; NOR and set CCs if S = 1.
xor	10	0S 0011	XOR; XOR and set CCs if S = 1.
xnor	10	0S 0111	XNOR; XNOR and set CCs if S = 1.
sll	10	10 0101	Shift rs1 left logical by opnd2 bits into rd.
srl	10	10 0110	Shift rs1 right logical by opnd2 bits into rd.
sra	10	10 0111	Shift rs1 right arithmetic by opnd2 bits into rd.

Notes: All instructions use format 3; r[rd] ← r[rs1] op (r[rs2] or immediate).

Append cc to mnemonic for S = 1 instructions that set the condition codes.

Branch and Control Transfer Instructions.   The SPARC has a rich set of branch instructions, as well as several instructions that implement procedure calls, as shown in Table 3.11. In the conditional branch instruction, the condition is specified by the 4-bit cond field in format 2. Unconditional branch, ba, is just one of the conditional branch instructions, with the condition, cond, set to 1000. The branch target address is computed as a word offset relative to the PC, as described in the RTN for the branch effective address, bradr⟨31..0⟩, on page 127.

SPARC program control

The SPARC architecture uses delayed branching, but with a twist. Usually when a processor has delayed branching, the instruction after the branch instruction is executed prior to completing the branch instruction. If an instruction that would otherwise precede the branch can be moved there without affecting program correctness, well and good. If not, a nop instruction is located in the branch delay slot.

Table 3.11 SPARC Branch and Control Transfer Instructions

Mnemonic	Format	op	op2 or op3	Meaning
bcc	2	00	010	Conditional branch to bradr.
ba	2	00	010	Unconditional branch (branch always).
call	1	01		Jump to calladr and link PC into r[15] (o[7]).
jmpl	3	10	11 1000	Jump to adr. Link PC to rd.
save	3	10	11 1100	Provide new register window. Perform ADD.
restore	3	10	11 1101	Restore old register window. Perform ADD.

Notes: Some cond fields for bcc follow: always, ba, 1000; not equal, bne, 1001; equal, be, 0001; less or equal, ble, 0010; carry clear, bcc, 1101; carry set, bcs, 0101; negative, bneg, 0110; overflow clear, bvc, 1111; and overflow set, bvs, 0111. See the SPARC manual for additional conditions.

The twist is that SPARC branch instructions have an *annul bit*, a, shown in format 2a of Figure 3.11, which allows programmer control over the execution of the instruction in the branch-delay slot. If the conditional branch is taken, the delay instruction is always executed. If the branch is not taken and the a bit is 1, then the instruction is annulled—that is, not executed. If the branch is not taken and the a bit is 0, then the delay-slot instruction is executed.

branch-delay annul bit

By setting the a bit to 1, the programmer or compiler can move the first instruction of the code at the jump target to the delay slot; it will be executed if the branch is taken, and not if the branch is not taken. If the a bit is 0, then the programmer or compiler can move one of the instructions in the code prior to the branch instruction to the delay slot, where it will always be executed. The ba instruction is an exception. If the annul bit is 1, the delay instruction will be annulled, and if it is 0 the delay instruction will be executed. The programmer sets the a bit to 1 by inserting an a in the instruction: bcc, a, disp.

There are two instructions that implement traditional procedure calls: call and jmpl. The instruction call uses the 30-bit displacement of format 1 as a jump address, but shifts it left 2 bits first. This allows the call instruction to reach the entire address space; call leaves the return address in r15 of the current window. The procedure call instruction jmpl uses format 3. This instruction allows a nonrelative target address to be computed at run time using the register indirect or indexed addressing modes. The return address is placed in rd. The jmpl instruction is also used to return from a call. The return instruction retl is actually synthesized as jmpl %r15 + 8, %r0.

Procedure call

Return from procedure

The instructions save and restore manipulate the register windows as described on page 123. The save instruction provides a new window, and restore restores the old window. If a register spill is not generated, these instructions also do an add of rs1 + rs2 into rd, with rs1 and rs2 being read from the old window, and the result being written into rd in the new window. The add instruction provides a convenient way to adjust the stack pointer to allow space for parameters to be passed on the stack.

3.4.4 THE SPARC ASSEMBLER AND EXAMPLE PROGRAMS

A line of SPARC assembly language has the following form:

```
label:    instruction        !comments
```

The label and its colon are optional, and the comments, preceded by !, are essential only to the reader, not the assembler. The instruction consists of a mnemonic followed by any operands and destination it requires. The destination is always rightmost. A %r (%g, %o, %l, or %i) followed by a number specifies a register (global, output, local, or input). Referring to Figure 3.10, the output registers %r8–%r15 are also called %o0–%o7; the local registers %r16–%r23 are also called %l0–%l7; and the input registers %r24–%r31 have alternate names %i0–%i7. For example, the add instruction

```
add    %l2, %g1, %o3
```

places the sum of r[18] and r[1] into r[11], using the alternate register names.

Memory addresses enclosed in square brackets [] denote a memory access, as in

```
ld      [%r4 + %r5], %r6
st      %r2, [%r3 - 28]
```

Addresses for branch, jump, and call are not enclosed in brackets. The address for branch and call is usually a label, whose relative offset from the PC is computed by the assembler and put in the displacement field. The instruction mnemonic specifies the opcode fields, and possibly other information. For example, branch mnemonics specify the condition, and jmp specifies a jmpl with destination register %r0.

Pseudo-operations of the SPARC assembler begin with a period. A few of them are .begin, start assembly; .org, locate code in memory; .equ, equate a symbol to a constant; and .end, end of assembly.

Figure 3.12 shows a simple example of a program to add two integers. It illustrates a nop placed in a branch-delay slot after the return instruction. In this case, the st instruction could be moved into the delay slot to eliminate the nop. The example also assumes that the assembler will be able to generate direct addresses for x, y, and z. The assembler includes functions %hi and %lo that extract the high-order 22 and low-order 10 bits, respectively, of their arguments, so a memory cell w that is not directly addressable can be loaded into %r2 by the following instructions:

```
sethi     %hi(w), %r1
ld        [%r1+%lo(w)], %r2
```

Figure 3.13 shows a program with a subroutine that adds x, y, and the constant −17 to illustrate subroutine linkage. Note that mov is constructed from or with %g0, and %sp (stack pointer) is another name for %o6. Also recall that the destination register for save and restore is in a different window than the operands. The stack pointer is advanced by 16 words on entry to the subroutine to give space to store the 16 new window registers if necessary.

```
          .begin
          .org
prog:     ld        [x],     %r1             ! Load a word from M[x] into register %r1.
          ld        [y],     %r2             ! Load a word from M[y] into register %r2.
          addcc     %r1,     %r2,     %r3    !%r3 ← %r1+%r2; set CCs.
          st        %r3,     [z]             ! Store sum into M[z].
          jmpl      %r15,    +8,      %r0    ! Return to caller.
          nop                               ! Branch-delay slot.
x:        15                                ! Reserve storage for x, y and z.
y:        9
z:        0
          .end
```

Fig. 3.12 Example SPARC Assembly Program

```
              .begin
              .org
      prog:   ld      [x],    %o0     ! Pass parameters in
              ld      [y],    %o1     !   first 3 output registers.
              call    add3            ! Call subroutine to put result in %o0.
              mov     -17,    %o2     ! Set last parameter in delay slot.
              st      %o0,    [z]     ! Store returned result.
              ...
      x:      15
      y:      9
      z:      0
      add3:   save    %sp,-(16*4),%sp  !Get new window and adjust stack pointer.
              add     %i0, %i1, %l0    ! Add parameters that now appear in
              add     %l0, %i2, %l0    !   input registers using a local.
              ret                      !Return. Short for jmp %i7+8.
              restore %l0, 0, %i0      ! Result moved to caller's %o0.
              .end
```

Fig. 3.13 Example of Subroutine Linkage in the SPARC

3.4.5   INTERRUPTS AND TRAPS IN SPARC

Exceptions in the SPARC are called *traps* if they are generated internally and *interrupts* if they have an outside source. There is a trap-enable bit in the processor-status register, PSR, as well as a 4-bit processor interrupt level, PIL. Interrupts are only accepted if their level is greater than the current level. Traps use the window mechanism in such a way that traps should never be enabled unless the next register window is free.

SPARC traps

SPARC interrupts

The following steps take place when a trap occurs:

SPARC trap response

1. Advance the register window, as in `save`.
2. Store PC, nPC, and PSR in local registers of the new window.
3. Disable traps.
4. Transfer control to the trap handler.

The trap handler address is determined from the trap base register, TBR, and an 8-bit trap type generated internally or supplied by an external interrupting device. The handler address is obtained by using the trap type as an offset into a table of handler addresses, whose base is given by TBR. The trap handler cannot change in or out registers of the new window because the ins overlap the window of the program executing when the trap occurred, and the outs overlap the next window, which is not known to be free. At the end of the handler, a return from trap instruction, `rett`, reverses the preceding four steps to restore the processor to its original state.

3.4.6   PIPELINING IN THE SPARC MB86900

Various implementations of the SPARC architecture use varying degrees of pipelining and multiple instruction issue. The MB86900 was the first SPARC chip to be implemented, and was designed using Fujitsu's CMOS gate-array technology. Maximum clock speed is 16.6 MHz. The MB86900 has four pipelined stages, one each for instruction fetch, instruction decode, instruction execution, and result write-back.

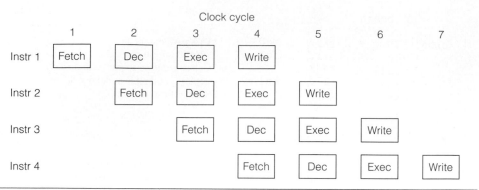

Fig. 3.14 The SPARC MB86900 Pipeline

Figure 3.14 shows the pipelining of four instructions. During the first pipeline step, the instruction is fetched from memory. During the second step, that instruction is decoded, and the source operands are read from the register file and passed to the execution unit. During the third step, the execution unit performs the arithmetic or logical operations, and the result is saved in a temporary register. During the fourth step, the result is written back to the register file.

The existence of a branch delay allows branches to progress normally through the pipeline if they can determine the branch target early enough to fetch the second instruction entering the pipeline after a branch. The branch target instruction is speculatively fetched before the condition codes have been updated. If it turns out that the condition is met, then execution of the target instruction can continue without interruption; otherwise the next instruction in sequence is fetched. We discuss the details of pipeline implementation in Chapter 5.

3.4.7   ADVANCED SPARC IMPLEMENTATIONS

SPARC International has recently released the specification for SPARC V9, a 64-bit implementation of the SPARC architecture. The specification spells out how traditional SPARC instructions deal with the additional 32 bits in the 64-bit registers, and also introduces some new instructions. Examination of the instructions and formats reveals that there are a number of unimplemented instructions. Some of these have been used to introduce additional capabilities to the new 64-bit SPARC architecture: 64-bit multiply and divide; load, store, and floating-point operations on 128-bit quadwords; software-settable branch prediction; branch-on-register-value (which sometimes eliminates a compare instruction) and conditional move instructions that may eliminate certain branch instructions entirely.

The register window concept is not without its detractors, who say that it slows down the chip compared with a single, small set of registers, and that the windows rapidly fill up and require spilling, thus obviating the advantage. SPARC's answer in V9 has been to decouple traps from the window mechanism by including additional registers for servicing traps, and to increase the number of registers available to the window system. The window pointer mechanism and method of determining window overflow and underflow has also been significantly changed.

The UltraSPARC is an implementation of SPARC V9 produced by a joint venture between Sun Microsystems and Texas Instruments. This implementation is superscalar, with two integer units, five floating-point units, a branch unit, and a load/store unit. It also contains a special purpose unit for high-speed graphics and image processing.

Key Concepts: The SPARC as a Typical RISC

- While a RISC machine may have fewer instructions than a CISC, the instructions are always simpler. Multistep arithmetic operations are confined to special units.
- Like all RISCs, the SPARC is a load/store machine. Arithmetic operates only on values in registers.
- A few regular instruction formats and limited addressing modes make instruction decoding and operand determination fast.
- Branch delays are quite typical of RISC machines and arise from the way a pipeline processes branch instructions.
- The SPARC does not have a load delay, which some RISCs do, and does have register windows, which many RISCs do not.

Summary

- Machine price and performance are the driving forces in the growth of the computer industry. Machine performance can be measured in many ways, from simple wall clock measurements or MIPS rates to more sophisticated measures that attempt to mimic real-world performance, such as Whetstone or Dhrystone counts. More recently the SPEC benchmarks have used real-world programs in suites that allow a more focused and realistic approach to performance measurement.

- CISC machines are characterized by instructions and addressing modes that emphasize economy of encoding. The result is instructions that vary widely in word length, number of memory accesses, and instruction execution time, and addressing modes that encourage memory traffic. These ISAs were appreciated at a time of higher memory costs. However, when CISC designers tried to apply hardware techniques to speed up execution, such as pipelined operation and superscalar designs, they found that complicated instructions and addressing modes interfered.

- RISC machines place much emphasis on single-word instructions and a load/store type of memory access. Architects find that simpler instructions with fixed word size and limited-memory operand access fit better with architectural speedup methods such as pipelining and superscalar operation. Simpler instructions and addressing modes also allow faster clock frequencies. Simpler instructions do require more memory and more memory access, but faster memory and instruction prefetch techniques have eliminated or greatly reduced the penalty, and are more than compensated for by simpler CPU design, faster clock frequencies, and pipelining and superscalar operation.

Bibliography

Several journal articles have cast the comparison between RISC and CISC in the form of a debate; some examples follow:

R. P. Colwell, C. Y. Hitchcock III, E. D. Jensen, H. M. B. Sprunt, and C. P. Kollar, "Computers complexity and controversy," *IEEE Computer Magazine*, vol. 18 (Sept. 1985), pp. 8–19.

R. P. Colwell, C. Y. Hitchcock III, E. D. Jensen, and H. M. B. Sprunt, "More controversy about 'Computers complexity and controversy,'" *IEEE Computer Magazine*, vol. 18 (Dec. 1985), p. 93.

M. J. Flynn, C. L. Mitchell, and J. M. Mulder, "And now a case for more complex instruction sets," *IEEE Computer Magazine*, vol. 20 (Sept. 1987), pp. 71–83.

Several textbooks use the Motorola MC68000 as an example machine. More detailed information about the MC68000 can be obtained from Motorola product literature and the following texts:

J. Bacon, *The Motorola 68000*, Prentice-Hall, Englewood Cliffs, NJ, 1986.

J. Wakerly, *Microcomputer Architecture and Programming: The 68000 Family*, John Wiley & Sons, New York, 1989.

The architecture specification of the original SPARC can be found in:

Sun Microsystems, *The SPARC Architecture Manual*, Sun Microsystems, Mountain View, CA, 1987.

The specifications for SPARC V8 and SPARC V9 are to be found in:

SPARC International, *The SPARC Architecture Manual*, Version 8, Prentice-Hall, 1992.

Measurements of instruction set usage by real programs that led to the idea that many CISC instructions are infrequently used are reported in the following articles:

D. E. Knuth, "An empirical study of FORTRAN programs," *Software Practice and Experience*, vol. 1 (1971), pp. 105–133.

D. A. Patterson and C. H. Sequin, "A VLSI RISC," *IEEE Computer*, vol. 15, no. 9 (Sept. 1982), pp. 8–21.

Kernighan and Ritchie's criticism of the `goto` statement is found in:

B. W. Kernighan and D. M. Ritchie, *The C Programming Language*, 2nd ed., p. 65, Prentice-Hall, Englewood Cliffs, NJ, 1988.

Exercises

3.1 A program contains the following instruction mix:
   - 20% load/store instructions with execution time of 3 ns each
   - 70% ALU instructions with execution time of 2.1 ns each
   - 10% branch instructions with execution time of 2.3 ns each

   a. If the clock period is 500 ps, calculate the average CPI for the program.

   b. What is the average MIPS rate of the program? (**§3.1**)

3.2 In each of the following lines of MC68000 code, what value will be in the destination after execution of each instruction? Also what addressing modes were used? The following conditions apply:
   A0 = 0x1000, M[0x1000] = 0xABCD, M[0xFFE] = 0xDCBA.

   a. `MOVE.L    #'AZB', D0`

   b. `MOVE.L    #0xABCDEF1, (A0)`

   c. `MOVE.W    A0, D0`

   d. `MOVE.W    -(A0), D0`   (**§3.3**)

3.3 Consider the short section of MC68000 code below, which is executed with the initial conditions given. What values would PC, D0, D1, and D2 have after execution? (**§3.3**)

Initial conditions: D0 = 0x1   D2 = 0x10
                       D1 = 0x2

Code:

```
        ORG         $2000
        ADD         D0, D1
        DBLE        D2, $2000
```

3.4 Consider the following MC68000 assembly language program. (The pseudo-operation, DC.W N, Define Constant Word, reserves space for *one* word in memory, and initializes it to the specified value, N in the example above, at load time.)   (§3.3)

```
X  EQU    1000
   ORG    2000
Y  DC.W   X
Z  DC.W   Y
   ORG    3000
   ① MOVE.W       #X, D0
     MOVE.W       Y, D1
     MOVE.W       Z, A0
     MOVE.W       (A0)+,   D2
```

a) What are the contents of the following registers after this fragment has executed? Numerical values are decimal. Provide answers in decimal.
   D0_____ D1_____D2_____
   A0_____

b) At what address is the last instruction located?_____

c) How many memory traffic, in words, will the indicated instruction, ①, generate, including instruction fetch and instruction execution? _____

3.5 Complete the RTN description of the MC68000 word operand, opndw, on page 106.   (§3.3)

3.6 Using the RTN definition of operand, opnd, for the MC68000 on page 106 as an example, write an RTN definition for the result, rslt(md,rg), as suggested on page 106. Take into account the restrictions on where results may be stored.   (§3.3)

3.7 Write an RTN description of the MC68000 DBcc instruction.   (§3.3)

3.8 Generate hexadecimal machine code for the following MC68000 instructions.   (§3.3)
   a. MOVE.W   (A3), (A4)
   b. MOVE.W   0xFF(A4, D5), 0x1000
   c. ADD.L   #1, D3
   d. ROL   #3, D4
   e. BLE   -255

3.9 a. At what address is LOOP located in the example in Figure 3.6?

   b. What is the size of the program in bytes?

   c. Encode the program in hexadecimal notation.   (§3.3)

3.10 a. Derive equations for the total number of instructions executed and the number of memory references made in the program fragment shown in Figure 3.7, as a function of the size of COUNT.

   b. Encode the subroutine in hexadecimal notation.   (§3.3)

3.11 The text states that most processors do not allow interrupts in the middle of instructions.

　　a. Discuss possible reasons for this prohibition.

　　b. Discuss possible reasons why some instructions must be interruptable.   **(§3.3)**

3.12 How many possible I/O addresses are there in the system shown in Figure 3.8?   **(§3.3)**

3.13 Recode the two example MC68000 programs, (1) the array search in Figure 3.6 and (2) the CLEARW in Figure 3.7 in SPARC assembly language. Compare and contrast the instruction counts, and the data and program memory accesses in the CISC and RISC processors.   **(§3.3)**

3.14 Repeat Exercise 3.13 but code for SRC.   **(§3.3)**

3.15 Translate the following SPARC instructions into hexadecimal.   **(§3.4)**

　　a. `addcc      %r3, %r5, %o7`

　　b. `sethi      0x1250FFF, %i1`

　　c. `ldub       [%i7 + 0x6EE], %r22`

3.16 Write RTN descriptions of the SPARC shift instructions, `sll`, `srl`, and `sra`, using the RTN definitions and formats given for the SPARC.   **(§3.4)**

3.17 Synthesize ROL, ROR, ROLC, and RORC from the SPARC shift instructions and any other SPARC instructions needed. (ROLC and RORC refer to rotate left through carry and rotate right through carry, respectively.) Assume a shift count of n defined with a `.equ`.   **(§3.3, 3.4)**

3.18 Write a SPARC assembly language routine that stores the sequence of integers 1, 3, 5, 7, 9, 11, 13 into memory as bytes, beginning at address 0x1000.   **(§3.4)**

3.19 Recode the SPARC integer addition program in Figure 3.12 in SRC assembly language, and assess the differences in instruction counts. What recommendations would you make, if any, for changes in the SRC ISA to make it more effective?   **(§3.4)**

3.20 Write SPARC instructions or instruction sequences to simulate the 14 MC68000 addressing modes found in Figure 3.2. Your instructions should load one of the registers using each of the addressing modes.   **(§3.3, 3.4)**

3.21 Write RTN descriptions of the SPARC load and store instructions in Table 3.8. Incorporate the memory alignment restrictions that halfwords must be located at even byte addresses and word addresses must be divisible by 4.   **(§3.4)**

3.22 Because so many instructions in the MC68000 reference memory, it is not possible to handle alignment constraints by just defining load and store correctly. Define word and longword memories in the MC68000 to include the hard alignment constraints by modifying the RTN on page 100. Assume that there is an operation bus_error that causes an exception to signal the operating system when it is invoked.   **(§3.3)**

3.23 Suppose the SPARC only allowed loads and stores of full words. Use SPARC shift and logical instructions, along with full word loads and stores to store a byte that is right-justified in `%r1` into a byte address given in `%r2`.   **(§3.3)**

3.24 Discuss the differences between a CISC processor and a RISC processor.   **(§3.2)**

3.25 Describe what purpose a user mode and a supervisor mode might serve in the MC68000.   **(§3.3)**

CHAPTER 4

Processor Design

Chapter Outline

In prior chapters you examined machines from the assembly and machine language programmer's view, and to a lesser extent from the architect's view. You have developed the ability to read and understand RTN machine descriptions. With an understanding of the instruction set architecture of contemporary computers, and with a tool to precisely define those architectures (RTN), we move to the heart of the subject of computer system design: the design of the central processing unit, from the logic designer's view. The logic design tools and RTN language presented in Chapter 2 will be used extensively in this chapter, so if any of those concepts have grown hazy in your memory, you may wish to revisit them before proceeding.

In discussing processor design, we will return to the example machine, SRC, presented in Chapter 2. To illustrate the complete design process, we move steadily through a design of SRC based on a 1-bus interconnection architecture, spending little time on the many alternatives possible at each stage. The chapter moves from the microarchitecture through data path design to logic design of the data path and finally the control unit. After completing the process with one set of design choices, we will consider alternative designs based on 2- and 3- bus microarchitectures. To simplify the presentation, we defer discussion of reset and exception processing to the end of the chapter, first discussing the topic in general and then applying it to the SRC.

4.1   The Design Process

The goal of the chapter is not simply to present a design of SRC, but to *do* the design in the way a designer would approach it. This design process has already begun in Chapter 2, where the informal description of SRC was formalized by means of an RTN description. Some of the machine hardware was clearly specified in doing this: the so-called programmer-visible registers. The next step is to specify the *data path*—the set of interconnections and auxiliary registers needed to accomplish the overall changes an instruction makes in the programmer-visible objects. RTN will also be useful in describing the actions that take place in the data path. In the process of describing the data path, we must make assumptions about how its hardware components behave. This set of assumptions becomes a specification for the logic design of the data path hardware. The next step is to design this hardware. In doing so, the designer contemplates the *control signals* that must be generated to cause actions to take place, such as strobes to load registers and gates to apply outputs to a bus. The last part of the design process is to devise a *control unit* that will generate the control signals in the correct order to effect the correct data path activity.

The steps of the design process can be more easily related after you have been exposed to more of them, so we will return to this subject later in the chapter. An important idea to keep in mind, however, is that each step produces specifications for what must be done in the next step. The answer to the question, "How do you know the hardware works so that this step makes sense?" is often, "This step specifies that the hardware to be designed must work this way." One result of a design step is thus a set of specifications, or design notes, that place demands on subsequent steps. An example of this is the design of the ALU, which will not be treated in detail until Chapter 6. At the completion of processor design, we will have collected a set of functions that the ALU must perform in order for our processor design to be correct. Unfortunately, a step may occasionally require a change in a previous one. Such circularity is inevitable, but the steps are ordered so as to make it rare.

An important initial concept is the distinction between abstract and concrete RTN descriptions of an instruction set architecture (ISA). This distinction was introduced in the discussion on page 79 in connection with designing hardware to implement RTN state-
abstract RTN   ments. The *abstract RTN* describes the overall effect of instructions on the programmer-visible registers. The abstract description is entirely implementation independent: It describes only those static (registers) and dynamic parts (operations) of a machine that are necessary to understand its operation. Thus the RTN descriptions in Chapters 2 and 3
concrete RTN   are abstract. The *concrete RTN* describes detailed register transfer steps in the data path that produce the overall effect. The unit of activity in the abstract RTN is an instruction execution, while the steps of the concrete RTN correspond to processor clock pulses. There may be many concrete RTN descriptions of an ISA, corresponding to particular implementations.

Different architectures can support the same ISA. Consider the SPARC architecture described in the previous chapter. The SPARC International specification defines an abstract machine, with an abstract instruction set architecture. Many companies have created concrete implementations of that abstract instruction set architecture that differ from one another in all sorts of practical details such as bus structure, execution times, degree of pipelining, and extent of multiple instruction issue. All execute the same instructions, however, and (we hope) all provide the same results, although they each differ significantly in architectural details and other practical ways. In our terms, all would have the same abstract RTN, but different concrete RTNs.

In the following section we discuss the concrete RTN specification of a 1-bus design of SRC.

4.2   A 1-Bus Microarchitecture for the SRC

To construct a concrete RTN description corresponding to the abstract RTN, we must first define the microarchitecture for the implementation. We use the term *microarchitecture* to refer to a view of the machine that exposes the registers, buses, and all other important functional units such as ALUs and counters. Before launching into the microscopic structure of SRC, we will consider its overall structure. Figure 4.1 shows how the subsystems of SRC interact with one another. The figure includes keys to the more detailed figures that describe the components of the data path and control unit. The principal subsystems shown in the figure are the CPU, main memory, and input/output. The data path, shown at the bottom of the figure, interacts with the control unit, shown at the top of the figure. The control unit *receives* signals that describe the state of the data path and the control unit *sends* control signals to the data path. These signals control the data flow within the CPU, and between the CPU and main memory and input/output (I/O). Main memory and I/O will be described in detail in Chapters 7 and 8 respectively. This chapter focuses on the design of the data path and the control unit, in that order.

microarchitecture

Figure 4.2 shows a portion of a 1-bus SRC microarchitecture. For clarity, the figure suppresses the details of gate and bus structure and the control signals. Those will be added later. Notice the addition of four registers not found in the abstract RTN specification: A, C, MA, and MD. The first two are needed in this particular microarchitecture to temporarily store one operand and the result when doing ALU operations. To understand why the A and C registers are needed, remember the "rule of buses": *only one item on the bus per step.* MA and MD are used as interface registers to the memory system. MA contains the address of the memory operand, and MD is used as a buffer for outgoing and incoming values.

"rule of buses"

4.2.1   THE ABSTRACT AND CONCRETE RTN FOR THE SRC
ADD INSTRUCTION

As examples of abstract and concrete RTN descriptions, consider the RTN for the complete SRC add instruction, including the instruction fetch:

Abstract RTN: (IR ← M[PC]: PC ← PC + 4; instruction_execution);
                instruction_execution := (• • •
                add (:= op = 12) → R[ra] ← R[rb] + R[rc]:

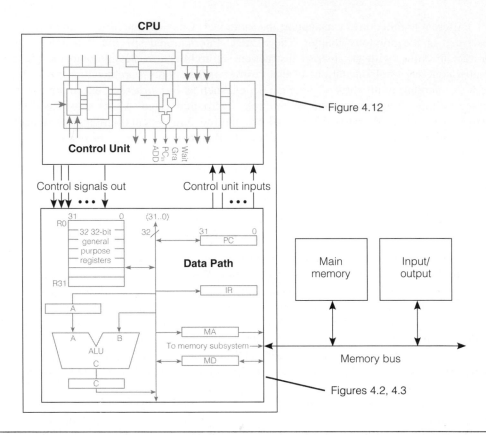

Fig. 4.1 Block Diagram of SRC

This abstract specification says that the instruction pointed to by the PC is fetched into the instruction register, IR; the PC is incremented by 4, so it points to the next instruction, which is 4 bytes away; and the instruction is executed. If that instruction is an add, then after execution, register ra contains the sum of registers rb and rc. It says nothing of how the machine goes about performing the addition. That description will depend on the particular data path design.

The concrete RTN description of the add instruction in a machine that employs the microarchitecture of Figure 4.2 is presented in Table 4.1. The abstract operations of fetching and executing the add instruction took only two steps; in this particular concrete implementation, the operation takes six steps—three for instruction fetch and three to execute the add:

1. Copy the PC into the MA register, increment the PC, and store the result in register C.

2. Read from memory into MD the value stored in the address pointed to by MA, and copy C into the PC.

3. Copy the contents of MD into the IR. (The hardware decodes the instruction. It turns out to be an add).

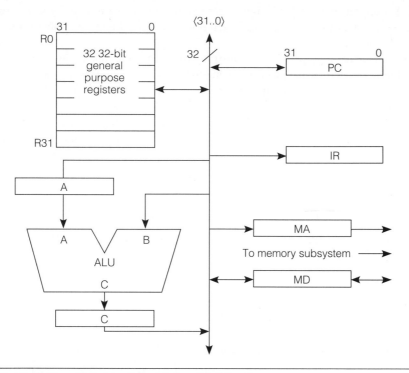

Fig. 4.2 High-Level View of the 1-Bus SRC Design

Table 4.1 Concrete RTN for the add Instruction

Step	RTN
T0	MA ← PC: C ← PC + 4;
T1	MD ← M[MA]: PC ← C;
T2	IR ← MD;
T3	A ← R[rb];
T4	C ← A + R[rc];
T5	R[ra] ← C;

  4. Copy register rb out onto the bus and store into register A.
  5. Copy register rc out onto the bus (and thereby into the B input of the ALU), perform an ADD,[1] and store the result into register C.
  6. Copy the contents of register C onto the bus and store into register ra.

Notice that in each of the first two steps there are two operations going on in parallel. This
is signified by a colon ":" separating the operations that are happening simultaneously.

---

1.   We use all uppercase (ADD) for ALU operations, and lowercase (add) for operation codes.

The PC + 4 appearing in step T0 implies hardware to do the increment by 4. This is a reasonable requirement for an integer ALU and is an example of a design note for the specification of the ALU.

The first three steps perform the instruction fetch. Since every instruction must be fetched before it can be decoded, and since obviously the processor can know nothing about the next instruction until it is fetched, *every* instruction in this 1-bus design will begin with the same three steps.

Note that we equate steps with clock cycles, so in this particular microarchitecture the add instruction will take 6 clock cycles: 3 for the instruction fetch and 3 to perform the addition and store the result. In this chapter and the next we will demonstrate alternative microarchitectures that can perform the add instruction in fewer steps.

4.2.2 THE CONCRETE RTN FOR SOME TYPICAL SRC INSTRUCTIONS

In this section we examine one from each class of SRC instructions. We begin with the addi instruction, in which a constant that is contained in the c2 field of the instruction is added to a register. We then cover the ld and st instructions, which load a 32-bit value stored in memory to one of the general registers (ld), or store a 32-bit value from one of the general registers into memory (st). Then we cover the branch instruction, br, and we conclude with a representative shift instruction, shr.

Arithmetic Operations: The addi Instruction. The addi instruction,

addi

$$\text{addi } (:= op= 13) \rightarrow R[ra] \leftarrow R[rb] + c2\langle 16..0 \rangle \text{ \{two's comp., sign-extend\}}:$$

adds a constant stored in the sign-extended c2 field of the instruction to the contents of one of the general registers, as shown in Table 4.2. From now on we will omit the details of the instruction fetch in T0–T2, since they are the same in all cases. Notice the similarity of this instruction to the add instruction already discussed. They differ only in step T4, where the second operand is fetched from the instruction register and sign-extended instead of being fetched from one of the general registers. Implicit in step T4 is that sign extension happens in the hardware. We shall show how this sign extension is accomplished in Section 4.4.2.

Data Move Instructions: Load Register from and Store Register to Memory. The abstract RTN for the load and store instructions follows:

ld and st

$$\text{ld } (:= op = 1) \rightarrow R[ra] \leftarrow M[disp]: \quad \text{Load register}$$
$$\text{st } (:= op = 3) \rightarrow M[disp] \leftarrow R[ra]: \quad \text{Store register}$$

Table 4.2 The addi (add immediate) Instruction

Step	RTN
T0–T2	Instruction fetch
T3	$A \leftarrow R[rb]$;
T4	$C \leftarrow A + c2\{\text{sign extend}\}$;
T5	$R[ra] \leftarrow C$;

Table 4.3 The ld and st (load/store register from memory) Instructions

Step	RTN for ld	RTN for st
T0–T2	Instruction fetch	Instruction fetch
T3	A ←((rb = 0) →0: (rb ≠ 0) →R[rb]);	A ←((rb = 0) →0: (rb ≠ 0) →R[rb]);
T4	C ← A + (16@IR⟨16⟩#IR⟨15..0⟩);	C ← A + (16@IR⟨16⟩#IR⟨15..0⟩);
T5	MA ← C;	MA ← C;
T6	MD ← M[MA];	MD← R[ra];
T7	R[ra] ← MD;	M[MA] ← MD;

To repeat the definition of disp:

disp⟨31..0⟩ := ((rb = 0) → c2⟨16..0⟩ {sign-extend} :   Displacement   disp
          (rb ≠ 0) → R[rb] + c2⟨16..0⟩ {sign-extend, 2's comp.}) :   address

The concrete RTN for these instructions is given in Table 4.3. You should examine this table carefully, step by step. Notice that disp is implemented at step T3 by loading register A with 0 if rb is R0, or with the contents of R[rb] if rb is any other register. As with the sign extension described on page 150, this is also accomplished by the hardware. We discuss how it is accomplished in Section 4.4.2. Notice also that the two instructions are identical through step T5. Steps T3–T5 compute the operand memory address in both cases. Then, in steps T6 and T7 the operand is read from memory into MD and then into R[ra] in the case of ld, and R[ra] is loaded into MD and written to memory in the case of st. In step T6 the MD register receives its operand from the memory bus in the case of a load, and from the data bus in the case of a store. MD is unusual in that it can transmit and receive data from two buses: the processor bus and the memory bus.

Branch Instructions.   The br instruction uses the cond field, c3⟨2..0⟩, to specify the branch condition, and if that condition is met, the branch is taken:

br (:= op= 8) → (cond → PC ← R[rb]):   Conditional branch   br

where cond is given by:

cond :=(c3⟨2..0⟩=0 → 0:   Never
          c3⟨2..0⟩=1 → 1:   Always
          c3⟨2..0⟩=2 → R[rc]=0:   If register is zero
          c3⟨2..0⟩=3 → R[rc]≠0:   If register is nonzero
          c3⟨2..0⟩=4 → R[rc]⟨31⟩=0:   If positive or zero
          c3⟨2..0⟩=5 → R[rc]⟨31⟩=1):   If negative

Note that c3⟨2..0⟩ is IR⟨2..0⟩.

Table 4.4 shows the rather simple form that the concrete RTN takes in the branch instruction. The computations in T3 and T4 must seem a bit mysterious at this point: cond is computed by the hardware by using c3⟨2..0⟩ and R[rc], and stored from step T3 to T4 in a 1-bit register, CON. The particular hardware design will be covered in the section on branch instruction hardware, on page 157.

Table 4.4 The Branch Instruction, br

Step	RTN
T0–T2	•••
T3	CON ← cond(R[rc]);
T4	CON → PC ← R[rb];

Table 4.5 The shr Instruction

Step	RTN
T0–T2	Instruction fetch
T3	$n \leftarrow IR\langle 4..0 \rangle$;
T4	$(n = 0) \rightarrow (n \leftarrow R[rc]\langle 4..0 \rangle)$;
T5	$C \leftarrow R[rb]$;
T6	Shr $(:= n \neq 0 \rightarrow (C\langle 31..0 \rangle \leftarrow 0\#C\langle 31..1 \rangle: n \leftarrow n-1; Shr))$;
T7	$R[ra] \leftarrow C$;

shr

Shift Instructions: The shr Instruction. The SRC allows multiple-bit shifts, specified by the value of n, the shift count, but our ALU can perform only single-bit shifts. Thus the data must be repeatedly cycled through the ALU until the operand has been shifted the specified number of places. Consider the shr instruction:

$$shr \ (:= op = 26) \rightarrow R[ra]\langle 31..0 \rangle \leftarrow (n @ 0) \# R[rb]\langle 31..n \rangle :$$
$$n := (\quad (c3\langle 4..0 \rangle = 0) \rightarrow R[rc]\langle 4..0 \rangle : \qquad \text{Shift count is in register or}$$
$$(c3\langle 4..0 \rangle \neq 0) \rightarrow c3\langle 4..0 \rangle): \qquad \text{constant field of instruction}$$

Table 4.5 shows how this is accomplished. Once again, how the hardware actually computes the value of n at step T4, and how the multiple-bit shift is actually accomplished at step T6 must remain somewhat of a mystery until we discuss the details of the shift-control hardware design in the sections describing the shift hardware, on page 156, but we can infer that step T6 will have to be repeated n times.

The abstract RTN defines the shift count n as a name for a conditional expression, but the concrete RTN introduces a physical register $n\langle 4..0 \rangle$ to hold the initial count and serve as a down counter in the implementation of the detailed steps. The introduction of physical implementation hardware in place of abstract RTN names is fairly common in writing concrete RTN. Using the same name for the register and the abstraction connects the hardware with its purpose, but might lead to confusion.

4.3 Data Path Implementation

As the designers are developing the concrete RTN, they are also contemplating the details of the data path design needed to support that RTN. We will now develop the SRC data path in detail, beginning with some general issues to be considered during data path design.

The design of the data path involves decisions at several levels of abstraction. The highest level is that of the microarchitecture, where the basic registers and interconnections of an implementation are laid out. There are also design decisions to be made about the type of flip-flop used to implement registers and the type of interconnecting bus to use. In general, the high-level decisions affect the register transfers that can be performed and how many of them can be performed simultaneously. The low-level decisions affect the speed at which each register transfer can be done, and thus the overall clock rate of the machine. There is a limited influence of the flip-flop type on the kind of register transfer that can be done.

Key high-level decisions that must be made when implementing the data path include more than just selecting the number and kind of interconnection buses, though this important choice gives an overall character to the design. As in this chapter, the terms *1-bus, 2-bus*, and *3-bus* are often used to recall the overall character of a microarchitecture. Other decisions include the design of the ALU and the CPU-to-memory interface, whether a separate incrementer for the program counter is included, and so on. These decisions influence the extent to which pipelining and other overlapping processing can be implemented.

Low-level decisions relate to the selection of an implementation domain for the registers and buses. These decisions determine what signals must be applied to the data path hardware to cause it to carry out its actions. These *control signals* gate data onto buses, strobe values into flip-flops, specify the ALU function, control memory activity, and so on. *The control signals form the interface between the data path and the control unit,* and are thus an important part of data path design.   control signals

To keep the first presentation of the design process simple, we focus our discussion of data path implementation domains on flip-flops interconnected with tri-state buses. The many possible on- and off-chip implementation possibilities are not considered in any detail.

Register Implementation Domain.   In designing the registers, the main choice is between edge-triggered and level-sensitive flip-flops. Level-sensitive devices occupy less space than edge-triggered devices in an IC, but TTL packages usually contain the same number of components regardless of which type they are. The principal advantage of edge-triggered devices is their clocking behavior. Edge-triggering simplifies clocking, since the trailing edge of the gating clock pulse can be used to strobe data into the flip-flop.

The choice of flip-flops actually has some influence on the concrete RTN steps that can be written for a data path. Level-sensitive flip-flops, often called *latches,* do not normally allow new inputs from another such latch that may change on the same clock pulse. In particular, the new value may not depend on the latch's own current value. Thus a register transfer of the form $C \leftarrow A + C$; implies that the C register is implemented with edge-triggered flip-flops. Master-slave flip-flops can also be used in this situation. The subtle distinction between edge-triggering and master-slave operation is unimportant in the case of D-type flip-flops, which is the type we will primarily use in the data path.   latch

4.4   Logic Design for the 1-Bus SRC

The previous section provided a general overview of the design of a general register machine such as SRC. With that general view in mind, this section will develop the design down to the gate level. First, we present an overview of the design, and then we develop each of the blocks at the gate level. We begin with the design of the data path hardware, including the memory interface, and then design the IR hardware, from which most of the control signals are developed. Following this, we design the control unit.

4.4.1   OVERVIEW OF THE DESIGN OF THE 1-BUS SRC

Figure 4.3 shows a slightly more detailed view of the proposed 1-bus data path in the SRC machine. The figure shows the registers and ALU of Figure 4.2 with some additional components, along with "road map" information indicating which figures describe the gate-level design. The PC and IR we are already familiar with: The PC points to the next instruction to be executed, and the IR holds the current instruction. There are three control signals associated with the PC and IR: PC_{out}, PC_{in}, and IR_{in}. We show the IR hardware producing a 5-bit register select and the c1, c2, and c3 constant fields. Registers MA and MD, memory address and memory data, and their associated control signals provide the interface to the memory system. Notice that MA only receives data from the bus and passes it on to the memory subsystem, whereas MD is bidirectional: It sends data to the memory subsystem upon a "write" and receives data from the memory system upon a "read." The 5-bit register, n, stores the shift count, and in this design n is a counter that can be decremented. The Cond logic employs the least significant 3 bits of the c3 field in the IR, which specify the

PC_{out}
PC_{in}
IR_{in}

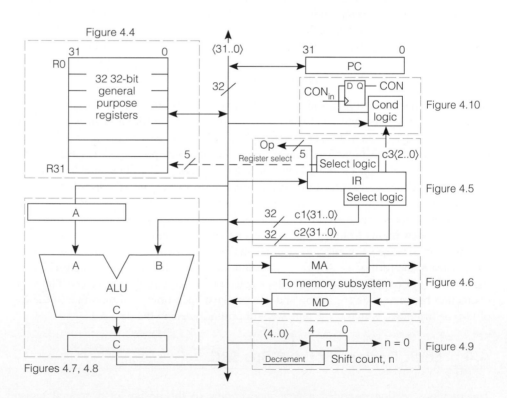

Fig. 4.3 More Complete View of Registers and Buses in the 1-Bus SRC Design, Including Some Control Signals

condition to be tested in conditional branch instruction, as well as the bus contents to compute whether a given condition is true. The result of that computation, a 1-bit value, is stored in the flip-flop named CON.

4.4.2 GATE-LEVEL DESIGN OF SRC

In this section we fill in the blocks shown in Figure 4.3, and describe the control signals that implement the RTN of the instructions in the preceding discussion. We begin with the register file, then cover the extraction of the c1 and c2 constant fields and the opcode field from the instruction register. Next, we show the design of the memory interface. With that hardware background, we will describe the instruction fetch and the add, addi, ld, and st instructions' control sequences. We then cover the design of n, the shift count register, and the shr instruction, and conclude with the description of the condition register and the br instruction.

The Register File. Figure 4.4 shows the gate-level design of the general register file, $R[0..31]\langle31..0\rangle$, ①. The ra, rb, and rc fields in the IR, ②, specify source and destination registers. The control signals Gra, Grb, and Grc, ③, gate one of the three register fields into the 5–32 decoder, ④, which decodes the register field to 1 of 32 select lines. These decoder outputs can be used to either strobe, ⑤, or gate, ⑥, the bus into or out of the selected register, when they are asserted along with control signals R_{in} or R_{out} respectively.

Gra
Grb
Grc
R_{in}
BA_{out}
R_{out}

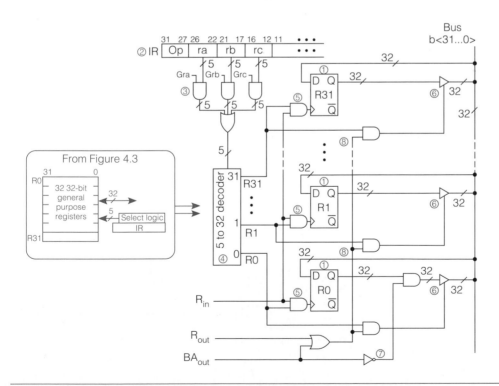

Fig. 4.4 The Register File, $R[0...31]\langle31...0\rangle$, and Its Control Signals

The control signal BA_{out} (BA for base address) is used to accommodate the calculation of the base address from which the displacement address is calculated:

$$\text{disp}\langle 31..0 \rangle := ((rb=0) \rightarrow c2\langle 16..0 \rangle \{\text{sign-extend}\}; \quad\quad \text{Displacement}$$
$$(rb \neq 0) \rightarrow R[rb] + c2\langle 16..0 \rangle \{\text{sign-extend, 2's comp.}\}); \quad\quad \text{address}$$

The BA_{out} signal gates 0's onto the bus if R0 is selected, ⑦, or the selected register's contents if one of R1..R31 is selected, ⑧.

extracting c1 and c2

Extracting Constants c1 and c2, and OP from the Instruction Register. Figure 4.5 shows the method of extracting fields c1, c2, and the opcode field, $IR\langle 31..27 \rangle$, from the instruction register. Notice that some of the flip-flop symbols in the figure represent one device, while others represent multiple devices. In this figure we depart from convention and show multiple-bit flip-flops and bus drivers as 3-D objects as an aid to distinguishing them from their single-bit counterparts. This nonstandard notation is used here to give a visual cue to the mixture of single- and multiple-bit parts of the IR.

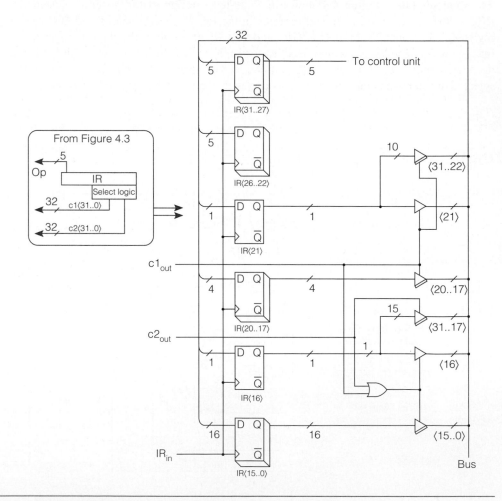

Fig. 4.5 Extracting c1, c2, and OP from the Instruction Register, $IR\langle 31..0 \rangle$

Recall the definitions of c1 and c2:

$c1\langle 21..0\rangle := IR\langle 21..0\rangle$:　　　　Long displacement field
$c2\langle 16..0\rangle := IR\langle 16..0\rangle$:　　　　Short displacement or immediate field

A scan of the RTN from Chapter 2 will also show that in all usages of these two fields they must be sign-extended to 32 bits. In 2's complement notation, this means copying the msb of the field to all higher-order bits. The circuit in the figure accomplishes this by fanning out the msb of the appropriate field to all the higher-order bits. The opcode field, $IR\langle 31..27\rangle$, is directly connected to the control unit, as shown in the figure. The control signals to access the sign-extended values of c1 and c2 are $c1_{out}$ and $c2_{out}$.

$c1_{out}$

$c2_{out}$

The Memory Interface: Memory Address and Memory Data Registers. Figure 4.6 shows the gate-level details of the processor-memory interface, including two buffer registers, MA and MD. MA receives an address from the processor bus, which is strobed into the MA register with an MA_{in} control signal. The figure shows the output of MA being continuously connected to the memory address bus, $addr\langle 31..0\rangle$. If other devices can drive the memory address bus, then the contents of MA will have to be gated onto addr.

memory interface, MA and MD

MA_{in}

The MD (memory data) register is a bit more complex. It can receive data from two different sources: the *processor* bus, prior to a memory write, and the *memory* bus, after a memory read. The MD_{bus} and MD_{rd} signals select between these two sources, serving as multiplexer select lines, ①. In this role, they act as gate signals. They also serve as strobes, strobing the selected data into the MD register, after being ORed together, ②, and ANDed with a strobe-shaped pulse, Strobe, ③. As we pointed out earlier in the chapter, data in MD can be gated to two destinations: the processor bus, via the MD_{out} signal, and the memory bus, via the MD_{wr} signal.

MD_{bus}

MD_{rd}

MD_{wr}

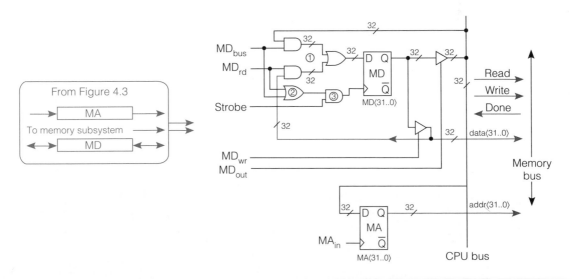

Fig. 4.6 The CPU-Memory Interface: Memory Address and Memory Data Registers, MA$\langle 31..0\rangle$ and MD$\langle 31..0\rangle$

Three additional control signals are associated with the memory bus : Read, Write, and Done. They do not originate or terminate in this figure, but are rather control signals that originate (Read, Write) or terminate (Done) in the control unit, to be described later. Read tells the memory system to read the word from the address in MA, with the read data appearing in MD. Write tells the memory system to write the word in MD to the memory address in MA. Done is a signal generated by the memory system, asserted when the memory system has completed the read or write operation. In systems with sufficiently fast memory, or with predictable response times for memory operations, the Done signal is not needed. In this design we assume the signal is needed, for completeness' sake.

The ALU and Its Associated Registers.   Figure 4.7 shows the detail of the interface between ALU and the A and C registers. The A register is loaded from the bus by the A_{in} control signal. For the complete 1-bus SRC design, the ALU will require 12 control signals: ADD, SUB, AND, OR, SHR, SHRA, SHL, SHC, NOT, NEG, C = B, and INC4. The C = B function copies the B input of the ALU through the ALU to the inputs of the C register. C_{in} allows the C register to be loaded from the output of the ALU, which we will find useful when we implement the shift instructions. C_{out} gates C onto the CPU bus. It is also useful in the 2-bus design. INC4 causes the ALU to increment its B input by 4; it is used to increment the PC to point to the next instruction. The ALU is a combinational circuit that continuously computes its outputs as a function of its inputs. A change in its inputs will produce valid outputs by the strobe time of the current clock cycle. Figure 4.8 shows a possible logic-level design for the 1-bus SRC. To show gate-level detail, only one bit of

ALU

A_{in}
MA_{in}

ADD, SUB,
AND, OR,
SHR, SHRA,
SHL, SHC,
NOT, NEG,
C=B, INC4
C_{in}

C_{out}

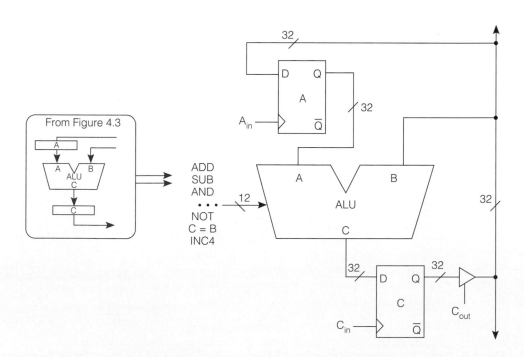

Fig. 4.7 The ALU and Its Associated Registers

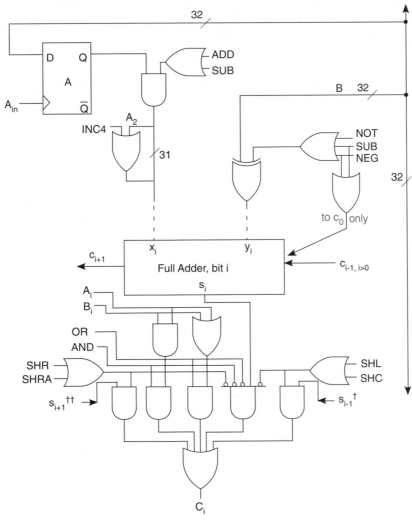

Fig. 4.8 A Logic-Level Design for One Bit of the 1-Bus SRC ALU

the 32-bit ALU is shown. Its operation is described below. We use SMALL CAPS to distinguish the gates used in the ALU from the actual ALU control signals.

■ The AND gates at the output from the A register serve to control whether the output of the register appears at the x inputs of the full adder. Only ADD and SUB gate the contents of the A register into the x inputs of the adder. In all other cases the x input to the full adder is zero, except when INC4 is asserted, in which case bit A2 is set to "1," representing a binary value of 4 at the x inputs.

- The XOR gate at the "y" input acts as a controlled complement, as described in Figure 2.14. The SUB, NEG, and NOT signals complement the value appearing at the y inputs. In addition, the SUB and NEG signals are input to c_0, the carry-in to the LSB. Note that this serves to form the 2's complement of the B input to the ALU.

- AND and OR bypass the full adder completely, taking their inputs directly from the A register.

- The shift, AND, and OR signals inhibit the output from the full adder, gating their respective signals to the C output of the ALU instead.

- The SHR and SHRA signals gate the output of the full-adder of the next most-significant bit to the output; the SHL and SHC signals gate the output of the full adder of the next least-significant bit to the output. There are exceptions to this behavior at the lsb and msb, as described in the footnotes of the figure. At the lsb, SHL gates a "0," and SHC gates s_{31} to the output. At the msb, SHR gates a "0," and SHRA gates a copy of s_{31} to the output.

- Note the C=B does not require any control signals to be asserted.

The general design of ALUs is discussed in Chapter 6.

4.4.3 THE SRC 1-BUS CONTROL SEQUENCES

control sequences

With the 1-bus hardware described above, we are in a position to describe the *control sequences* that implement instruction fetch and execution. Control sequences are just lists of control signals appearing in the data path logic. A control signal is true in steps where it appears and false where it does not appear. The control signals for a step are just those strobes and gates that cause the data path hardware to perform the register transfers of the concrete RTN for that step. We will repeat the concrete RTN to guide us in forming control sequences. The hardware descriptions of the previous sections will provide guidance in translating the concrete RTN to control sequences. We first describe the instruction fetch, and then cover the add, addi, ld, shift, and branch instructions.

The Instruction Fetch. Table 4.6 shows the RTN and control sequence for the instruction fetch. The presence of the Wait control signal at step T1 means that there is potentially a gap of 1 or more clock cycles between T1 and T2, to allow for memory system access.

Register-to-Register add. We now describe the control sequence of the complete add operation,

add

$$\text{add } (:= \text{op= } 12) \rightarrow R[ra] \leftarrow R[rb] + R[rc]:$$

Table 4.6 The Instruction Fetch

Step	RTN	Control Sequence
T0	MA ← PC : C ← PC + 4;	PC_{out}, MA_{in}, INC4, C_{in}
T1	MD ← M[MA] : PC ← C;	Read, C_{out}, PC_{in}, Wait
T2	IR ← MD;	MD_{out}, IR_{in}
T3	Instruction_execution	

Table 4.7 The add Instruction

Step	RTN	Control Sequence
T0	MA ← PC: C ← PC + 4;	PC_{out}, MA_{in}, INC4, C_{in}
T1	MD ← M[MA]: PC ← C;	C_{out}, PC_{in}, Read, Wait
T2	IR ← MD;	MD_{out}, IR_{in}
T3	A ← R[rb];	Grb, R_{out}, A_{in}
T4	C ← A + R[rc];	Grc, R_{out}, ADD, C_{in}
T5	R[ra] ← C;	C_{out}, Gra, R_{in}, End

Notice the use of the Grb, R_{out} combination in T3 of Table 4.7, as a means of gating a register onto the bus, and the complementary pair in T5, Gra, R_{in}, to strobe data into a register. All of the arithmetic and logic instructions use control sequences similar to those described in this section and the one below.

By convention we use "out" signals to select the bus transmitter (there can be only one in a 1-bus system), and "in" signals to select the bus receiver or rceivers. An additional control signal, End, is used to signal the control unit that the instruction execution is complete, and the next instruction should be fetched.

The reader should avoid the temptation of assigning meaning to the particular ordering of the control signals within a given step. The sequence "PC_{out}, MA_{in}" is equivalent to "MA_{in}, PC_{out}." Notice once again that the absence of an A_{out} signal implies that the A register is continuously providing input to the A ALU input, and the bus is continuously providing its contents to the B ALU input.

Add Immediate to a Register.   Table 4.8 shows the addi instruction,

addi (:= op= 13) → R[ra] ← R[rb] + c2$\langle 16..0 \rangle$ {2's comp., sign-extend};

including its control sequence. From now on we will omit the details of the instruction fetch in T0–T2, since they are the same in all cases. Notice that in step T4 the second operand is fetched from the instruction register and sign-extended instead of being fetched from one of the general registers. The $c2_{out}$ instruction sign-extends the operand as it extracts it from the instruction register.

End

addi

Table 4.8 The addi (add immediate) Instruction

Step	RTN	Control Sequence
T0–T2	Instruction fetch	Instruction fetch
T3	A ← R[rb];	Grb, R_{out}, A_{in}
T4	C ← A + c2{sign-extended};	$c2_{out}$, ADD, C_{in}
T5	R[ra] ← C;	C_{out}, Gra, R_{in}, End

Table 4.9 The ld (load register from memory) Instruction

Step	RTN	Control Sequence
T0–T2	Instruction fetch	Instruction fetch
T3	$A \leftarrow ((rb = 0) \rightarrow 0: (rb \neq 0) \rightarrow R[rb]);$	Grb, BA_{out}, A_{in}
T4	$C \leftarrow A + c2\{sign\text{-}extended\};$	$c2_{out}$, ADD, C_{in}
T5	$MA \leftarrow C;$	C_{out}, MA_{in}
T6	$MD \leftarrow M[MA];$	Read, Wait
T7	$R[ra] \leftarrow MD;$	MD_{out}, Gra, R_{in}, End

ld

Load Register from Memory.   The Abstract RTN for this instruction is $R[ra] \leftarrow M[disp]$. The concrete RTN for disp is shown on page 144. The concrete RTN and control sequences for the ld instruction are given in Table 4.9. You should examine this table carefully, step by step. Refer to the design of the CPU-memory interface in Figure 4.6. Notice that the selection of a register or 0 described in the RTN of T3 is effected by the BA_{out} control signal. Likewise, the sign extension described in the RTN of step T4 is accomplished by the $c2_{out}$ control signal. Figure 4.6 shows control signals MD_{rd} and Strobe as being used to strobe data from the memory bus into MD. These are not shown in the table, because it is assumed that the memory system is responsible for asserting these signals. The store instruction is identical except for steps T6 and T7, where the general register value is copied into MD, and the write signal asserted.

shifts

Shift Instructions.   Steps T3 and T4 of Table 4.5 show that the shift count, n, is extracted from $IR\langle 4..0\rangle$ or from $R[rc]$, depending on whether n is nonzero. The RTN for this is

$$n := ((c3\langle 4..0\rangle = 0) \rightarrow R[rc]\langle 4..0\rangle:$$
$$\quad (c3\langle 4..0\rangle \neq 0) \rightarrow c3\langle 4..0\rangle \,);$$

Shift count can be in a register or
the constant field of the instruction.

In this design, the ALU can do only a single-bit shift per cycle. (The ALU operations SHR, SHRA, SHL, and SHC discussed previously are 1-bit shifts.) This means that the shift count must be stored in a register and decremented as the shifting proceeds.

Figure 4.9 shows the design of the shift counter. It relies on a down counter that can be loaded with the count field, which can be gated from the IR or from one of the general registers. Figure 4.5 shows that both $c1_{out}$ and $c2_{out}$ will gate the count field out of the IR, and R_{out} will gate the count field from a register. The control sequence shown below for the shr instruction will show that the count field out of the IR, and R_{out} will gate the count field from a register. The control sequence shown below for the shr instruction will show that the count field, $IR\langle 4..0\rangle$ is strobed into the down counter shown in Figure 4.8 above using the Ld signal, and this value tested for n = 0 with the n=0 control signal. If the test succeeds, then $R[rc]\langle 4..0\rangle$ is gated into the counter. The shifting is then begun. The counter is decremented by the Decr control signal, and the n = 0 signal is computed as the NOR of the count bits. The n = 0 signal will become true when the count reaches zero.

Ld
n=0
Decr

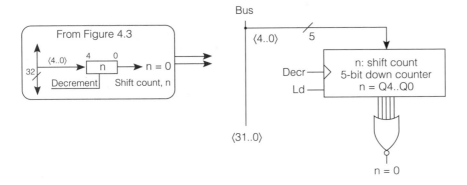

Fig. 4.9 Shift Counter

The Shift Right, shr Instruction.   The abstract RTN of the shr instruction is shown on page 146. The shift instructions use the shift hardware shown in Figure 4.9. Since our ALU can perform only single-bit shifts, the data must be repeatedly cycled through the ALU and the count decremented until it reaches zero. Table 4.10 shows how this is accomplished. Step T6 is somewhat complicated. If $n \neq 0$, then the contents of register C are shifted and returned to the register. In addition, the down counter is decremented, and the Goto6 signal causes the step to repeat.

shr

Goto6

There is a potential timing problem with this one-step approach, where T6 branches to itself to accomplish multiple-bit shifts. First, the Decr signal should have a strobelike shape, appearing late in the clock cycle, because the value of the $n = 0$ output established in the previous cycle must remain valid for the duration of the active part of the cycle before being decremented. Furthermore, the Goto6 signal must be carefully timed, since it effects the "looping" of the control unit. This is discussed in more detail in Section 4.5.

An obvious improvement could be made in this design by modifying the ALU so that multiple-bit shifts could be made in one cycle, by one pass through the ALU. We discuss this kind of shifter, known as a *barrel shifter,* in Chapter 6.

barrel shifter

Table 4.10 The shr Instruction

Step	RTN	Control Sequence
T0–T2	Instruction fetch	Instruction fetch
T3	$n \leftarrow IR\langle 4..0 \rangle$;	$c1_{out}$, Ld
T4	$n = 0 \rightarrow (n \leftarrow R[rc]\langle 4..0 \rangle)$;	$n = 0 \rightarrow (Grc, R_{out}, Ld)$
T5	$C \leftarrow R[rb]$;	$Grb, R_{out}, C = B, C_{in}$
T6	Shr (:= $n \neq 0 \rightarrow (C\langle 31..0 \rangle \leftarrow 0\#C\langle 31..1 \rangle$: $n \leftarrow n - 1$; Shr));	$n \neq 0 \rightarrow (C_{out}, SHR, C_{in}, Decr, Goto6)$
T7	$R[ra] \leftarrow C$;	$C_{out}, Gra, R_{in}, End$

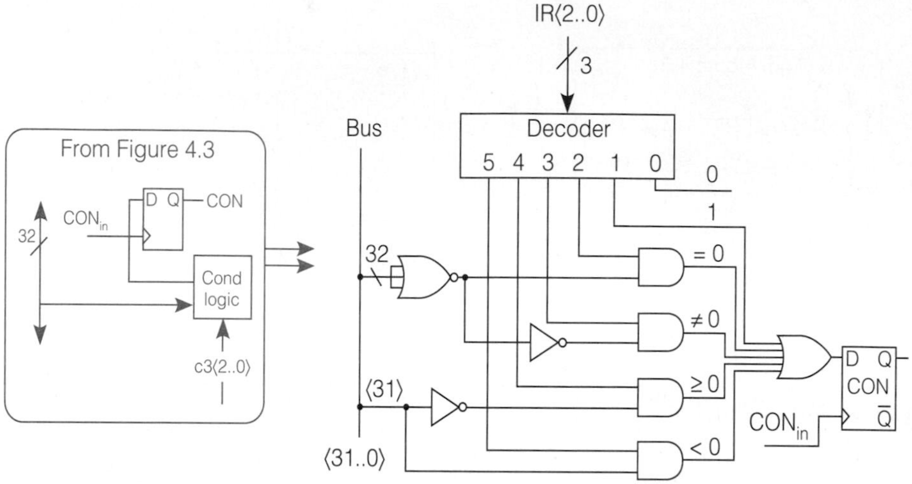

Fig. 4.10 Computation of the Conditional Value CON

branches

Branching. Branch conditions are dependent on the cond field, $c3\langle2..0\rangle$, and conditional branches are dependent on the value of a general register rather than the value of a flag or flags register:

$$\text{cond} := (\ c3\langle2..0\rangle = 0 \rightarrow 0: \qquad\qquad \text{Never}$$
$$c3\langle2..0\rangle = 1 \rightarrow 1: \qquad\qquad \text{Always}$$
$$c3\langle2..0\rangle = 2 \rightarrow R[rc] = 0: \qquad\quad \text{If register is zero}$$
$$c3\langle2..0\rangle = 3 \rightarrow R[rc] \neq 0: \qquad\quad \text{If register is nonzero}$$
$$c3\langle2..0\rangle = 4 \rightarrow R[rc]\langle31\rangle = 0: \quad\ \ \text{If positive or zero}$$
$$c3\langle2..0\rangle = 5 \rightarrow R[rc]\langle31\rangle = 1\ ); \quad \text{If negative}$$

The computation of cond depends on the values of $c3\langle2..0\rangle$ and in the case of $c3\langle2..0\rangle = 2$ to 5, on the value of register R[rc]. Figure 4.10 shows $IR\langle2..0\rangle$, which is where $c3\langle2..0\rangle$ is located, being decoded and used to select one of the five possible conditions. The D flip-flop named CON is used to store the value computed. It is loaded by the CON_{in} control signal. CON must be stored for 1 cycle because it cannot be used in the same cycle in which it is computed. To see why, consider the use of the bus in steps T3 and T4 of Table 4.11.

CON_{in}

Table 4.11 The Branch Instruction br

Step	RTN	Control Sequence
T0–T2	Instruction fetch	Instruction fetch
T3	CON ← cond(R[rc]);	Grc, R_{out}, CON_{in}
T4	CON → PC ← R[rb];	Grb, R_{out}, CON → PC_{in}, End

The br Instruction.   The br instruction,

br (:= op = 8) → (cond → PC ← R[rb]):   Conditional branch

br

encompasses all of the unconditional and conditional branches of the SRC instruction set
by allowing the specification of the branch condition in $IR\langle 2..0\rangle$, as shown in Figure 4.10.
Table 4.11 shows the rather simple form that the control sequence takes in this case. In the
computation at step T4, the control signal CON is used to control whether PC_{in} is asserted:
$CON \rightarrow PC_{in}$, may seem a bit mysterious, but it is formed simply by an AND gate. We
will show this in more detail as we discuss control unit design in Section 4.5.

CON

4.4.4   REVIEW OF THE DESIGN PROCESS

We have now seen more of the steps in the design process and are in a position to give a
more complete overview. The process begins with an informal description of a computer
and ends with a complete logic design of the computer, including both the data path used
to perform operations on instructions and data, and the control unit that generates signals
to cause the data path operations to happen in the right order. The steps in the design process follow:

1. Develop an informal description of the computer and its instructions.
2. Write a formal description at the programmer's level (abstract RTN).
3. Specify a high-level data path architecture that can accomplish the register trans-
    fers specified in the abstract RTN.
4. Write concrete RTN sequences for each instruction, using only the specific register
    transfers allowed by the data path configuration.
5. Using the capabilities required by the concrete RTN, design logic circuits for the
    data path and expose the control signals that cause activity.
6. Write the control signals for each concrete RTN step, producing a complete set of
    control sequences for all instructions.
7. Design a sequencer and control unit, driven by a master clock, to generate the con-
    trol sequences.

We have seen all but the last step. Steps 1 and 2 were done in Chapter 2. Steps 3 and 4
were the subject of Section 4.2, and steps 5 and 6 were done in Section 4.4.

At each step, decisions are made that affect the following steps. For example, the
decision to use a single bus restricts the number of concrete register transfers that can be
done in one step, and the appearance of a register on the left (right) side of a concrete RT
implies an input (output) connection to the bus. Any decisions made in a step of the design
process should be logged, so that they can be used in following steps.

Sometimes the one-way nature of the process breaks down. The hardware for a particular register might be considerably simplified if the concrete RTN steps in which it
appears are modified slightly. It is even possible that the length of the master clock cycle
might be reduced by redefining the instruction set slightly. Most of the information flow in
the process, however, is forward across the steps, and backward influences can be taken
care of by minor iterative refinement of the design.

4.5   The Control Unit

So far we have seen how to implement the data path and how to define control sequences that implement a machine's instruction set. In this section we show how to design the control unit that generates those control sequences. First, however, we discuss the nature of the timing pulses that pace the CPU in its operations.

4.5.1   CLOCKING AND TIMING

Information is processed by register transfers—the moving of information out of a register, along a bus, possibly through combinational logic, and into another register. These actions take time, and this section discusses how to estimate how much time they take. Being able to estimate the timing of such actions is crucial in determining the maximum clock frequency that a circuit will support.

A Run Through the Data Path.   Figure 4.11 shows an example of the clocking and timing relationships that exist along the data path. In this discussion we use level-sensitive flip-flops, since they better illustrate the critical issues involved in clocking data in and out of registers. We follow the convention that a triangle at the clock input signifies an edge-triggered device, and the absence of a triangle signifies a level-sensitive device. (The use of edge-triggered flip-flops is discussed in the subsequent section "Using edge-triggered flip-flops" on page 163.) The figure shows information being propagated from a level-sensitive, flip-flop-based register R1, the transmitter, through tri-state gates and bus, through a combinational logic block such as an ALU into a second, level-sensitive, flip-flop-based register R2, the receiver. Propagation time through the wires interconnecting the registers and logic gates is assumed negligible in this example. The figure follows the signal as it travels from output register to input register:

1.   The information propagates through the bus gate in time t_g.
2.   The information then travels across the bus in time t_{bp}. The bus contains multiple wires; t_{bp} is the worst-case time—that is, the time taken to propagate through the "slowest" wire of the bus. The difference between propagation times through the slowest and fastest wires of a bus is known as *bus skew*.

bus skew

3.   The information propagates through the ALU or other combinational logic block in time t_{comb}.
4.   The signals arrive at register R2. The propagation time through R2 is t_l.

Estimating the Minimum Clock Period.   The minimum clock period for a given register transfer is the time required to propagate data entirely around the circuit, so that the new value is in the destination register and ready for another cycle. The minimum clock period *for this particular register transfer* is

$$t_{min} = t_g + t_{bp} + t_{comb} + t_l$$

Designing the Minimum Strobe Signal.   Data will be valid at R2 and ready to be strobed after the data signals have propagated to R2, plus a "flip-flop setup time." Therefore R_{in} can be brought high after a time interval $t_{R2valid}$:

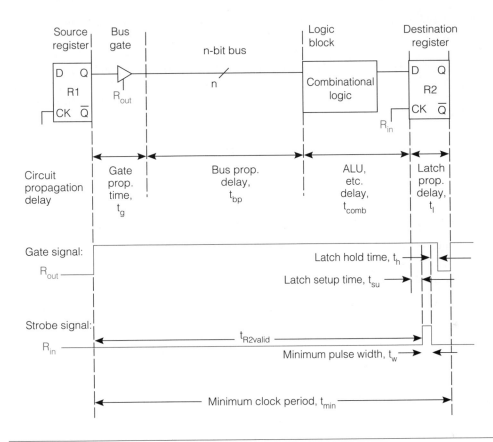

Fig. 4.11 Clocking the Data Path: Register Transfer Timing

$$t_{R2valid} = t_g + t_{bp} + t_{comb} + t_{su}$$

R_{in} must be held high for at least the time interval t_w, the minimum pulse width as defined by the flip-flop vendor. Thus R_{in} can be brought low after a time $t_{R2valid} + t_w$.

Designing the Minimum Gate Signal. The gate signal R_{out} is assumed to go high at the start of the clock cycle. It is assumed that it must be held high until the data signals have been strobed into R2, plus a "flip-flop hold time," t_h. Thus R_{out} can be brought low after a time $t_{R2valid} + t_w + t_h$.

The figure shows the gate signal R_{out} being high for this entire duration. This is a conservative approach. Depending on clock rise and fall times and the amount of signal dispersion,[2] R_{out} may be brought low before the entire time interval has elapsed. The prudent

2. Dispersion refers to the degree to which the signal "spreads" as it propagates through the system. It is caused by impedance mismatches and variations in propagation velocity of the various frequency components of the pulse.

engineer will conduct measurements to ascertain the minimum time R_{out} must be held high if there is a desire to shorten the high interval.

Clock Skew. The preceding discussion is predicated upon being able to deliver the appropriate clocking signal *to the device* at the appropriate time. Since devices are distributed in space, clocking signals originating from a point may arrive at different devices at different times. This distribution of clock arrival times is known as *clock skew*. It can be compensated for to an extent by adjusting path lengths, or by advancing or retarding the clocking signals appropriately. In any case, the designer must take clock skew into account if she or he wishes to run the circuit at maximum speed.

Example Timing Parameters. Example timing parameters for National Semiconductor FAST TTL gates and flip-flops and VITESSE GaAs gate-array components are shown in Table 4.12. The table contains only the "pessimistic" values: the maximum propagation delays and setup and hold times, and minimum strobe width. The prudent engineer will add a 10% or greater "Murphy's law factor" to these values to account for variation in test equipment and power supply voltage, and the possibility (probability? certainty?) that some parts from the vendor will be outside the specification range. The factor of 10 or so in speed improvement of the GaAs devices over the TTL devices is due more to the fact that the TTL devices are discrete components, each of whose outputs must contain a pad- and pin-driver, than to the fact that they are fabricated from silicon.

CLASSIC EXAMPLE: CALCULATE THE MAXIMUM CLOCK FREQUENCY A CIRCUIT CAN SUPPORT

Calculate the maximum clock frequency for the circuit shown in Figure 4.11, using the data from Table 4.12.

Answer: For the FAST TTL parts, the minimum clock period is given by

$$t_{min} = t_g + t_{bp} + t_{comb} + t_l = 5 + 5 + 14 + 6 = 30 \text{ ns}$$

Table 4.12 Timing Parameters for FAST TTL and GaAs Gates and Flip-flops

Name	Parameter	FAST Delays	VITESSE Delays
Gate propagation time	t_g	5 ns	150 ps
Bus propagation time (assumed)	t_b	5 ns	500 ps
Logic delay	t_{comb}	14 ns	~400 ps
Flip-flop propagation time	t_l	6 ns	440 ps
Flip-flop setup time	t_{su}	2 ns	146 ps
Flip-flop hold time	t_h	3 ns	104 ps
Flip-flop strobe width	t_{min}	4 ns	N.A.[†]

†Edge triggered flip-flop.

plus 10% safety margin = 33 ns. Therefore the maximum clock frequency
= $1/(33 \times 10^{-9})$ = 30 MHz.

For the VITESSE gate array the minimum clock period is given by

$$t_{min} = t_g + t_{bp} + t_{comb} + t_l = 150 + 500 + 400 + 440 = 1490 \text{ ps}$$

plus 10% safety margin = 1.6 ns. Therefore, the maximum clock frequency
= $1/(1.6 \times 10^{-9})$ = 625 MHz. ■

Register Transfers Using Level-Sensitive Flip-Flops. Under the clocking conditions we have been describing, it is essentially not possible to gate a signal out of a given register, and back into the same register in the same clock cycle. Unless inordinate care is taken, the new value in the register will "race around" the circuit and cause a second updating of the register. The designer can use edge-triggered or master-slave flip-flops, or employ two-phase clocking to surmount this problem. *Caveat architecte.*

Using Edge-Triggered Flip-Flops. The use of *edge-triggered* instead of level-sensitive flip-flops simplifies the design of the strobe signal, since it is the *edge* of the strobe signal rather than its level that clocks data into the flip-flop. Using edge-triggered flip-flops solves the problem of gating data out of a register and back into the same register in the same clock cycle, as with the C register's use in the shr instruction. If edge-triggered flip-flops are used, the same clock signal can be used for both gate and strobe: Data are gated onto the bus by the active part of the clock cycle (between the leading and trailing edges), and the trailing edge strobes it into the flip-flops. If a single clock is used, then it must remain high for at least $t_{R2valid} = t_g + t_{bp} + t_{comb} + t_{su}$. There is normally no concern about the hold time, since $t_{R2valid}$ will always be greater than t_h.

(margin note) edge-triggered flip-flops

4.5.2 THE 1-BUS SRC HARDWIRED CONTROL UNIT

The *control unit* is in a real sense the heart of the processor. It accepts as input those signals that are needed to operate the processor, and provides as output all the control signals necessary to effect that operation.

(margin note) control unit

Figure 4.12 shows a block-level view of the SRC control unit, with its input and output signals. The outputs of the control unit are the control signals that we have been using to generate the control sequences for the opcodes of the machine. These control signals are derived by the control signal encoder from four principal input sources:

1. The opcode field of the IR. This field is decoded to provide the encoder with information about which instruction is being executed.
2. Other signals in the data path. In SRC, this would include generated signals such as CON and n = 0. In machines with status and condition-code registers, these would be included.
3. Control step information. The step generator generates signals T0, T1, ….
4. External signals such as Strt, the start signal, Done, the asynchronous memory completion signal shown in Figure 4.6, and other external signals such as interrupts.

The Control Signal Encoder. The control signal encoder uses these inputs to generate the control signal sequences. The encoder is just a combinational logic circuit and can be specified most simply by a set of Boolean equations for its outputs in terms of its inputs. A

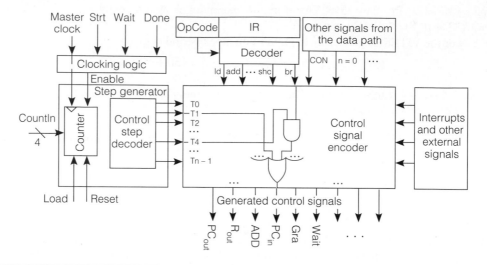

Fig. 4.12 Control Unit Detail with Inputs and Outputs

hardwired
controller

hardwired controller uses combinational logic that corresponds directly to the Boolean equations to produce the control signal outputs. Other controller types, such as the microprogrammed controller described in Chapter 5, generate the same control sequences in other ways.

How are the control signal equations generated? For the answer to this question, we must examine all of the control sequences of the machine. Some of these are contained in Tables 4.6 to 4.11. There will be one control sequence for each opcode, and perhaps additional ones for interrupt and trap handling, and so on. The logic for each control signal is generated by combing through the control sequences looking for every occurrence of that control signal, and writing the Boolean equation for the signal. For example, the C_{out} signal occurs at T1 in all the instructions, and at T5 in the add instruction:

$$C_{out} = T1 + T5 \cdot add + \ldots$$

C_{out} occurs in all the T1 steps because "All T1's are alike," since T0–T2 are the instruction fetch steps. The ellipsis (…) in the equation above implies that there will be other contributions to C_{out} besides those shown. There will be one term for each unique occurrence of the control signal in the set of control sequences that make up the instruction set. Notice that this fragment of the control logic is shown in the first part of Figure 4.13.

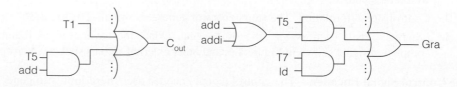

Fig. 4.13 Generation of the Logic for the C_{out} and Gra Signals

As another example, the Gra signal, the signal that gates out the ra register field, has occurrences at T5 in the add and addi instructions, and at T7 in the ld instruction. From these, we can begin to describe how the Gra signal is generated:

$$Gra = T5 \cdot (add + addi) + T7 \cdot ld + \ldots$$

This is shown in the second part of Figure 4.13. For a processor with significant size, the final OR gate will have considerable fan-in, and must be generated using several gate levels, or a wired OR.

The control signals that are generated from information in the data path may require special treatment. The End signal, for example, is input to the Reset line of the control step counter, resetting its value to 0. It must be timed so that its arrival resets the counter at the end of the step in which it occurs.

The CON signal (Figure 4.10), which is used to describe the truth of one of the six conditions, is used to control the loading of the PC at step T4 of the br instruction, shown in Table 4.11. This is accomplished by ANDing it with T4 and br:

$$PC_{in} = \ldots + CON \cdot T4 \cdot br + \ldots$$

Thus if CON is true at step T4 in the br instruction, the PC_{in} signal will be asserted.

In step T4 of the shr instruction, $n = 0 \rightarrow (Grc, R_{out}, Ld)$, the $n = 0$ signal is ANDed with the control signals to the right of the $\rightarrow$ symbol to provide the control signals. In Grc for example, it takes the form

$$Grc = \ldots + (n = 0) \cdot shr \cdot T4 + \ldots$$

R_{out} and Ld take the same form. The timing of these signals will also be critical, because Ld is used to load the counter that generates the $n = 0$ signal.

The Control Step Generator. The *control step generator,* shown in the left part of Figure 4.12, is a synchronous, parallel-load up counter in this design. It accepts an increment signal, the master clock in this case, an enable signal, a Reset signal that causes the counter to restart its step output at T0 at the next clocking event, and the signals Load and CountIn that are used to execute branches in the control step sequence. Load and CountIn are used by the shr instruction, for example, and the Reset signal is generated by the End signal that terminates every control sequence.

The shr instruction uses the $n = 0$ control signal generated from the shift counter (Figure 4.9) in step T6 of the shr control sequence shown in Table 4.10 to control the looping required to provide support for multiple-bit shifts. The value of n is initially set from the c3 field of the instruction or the low-order bits of one of the general registers. If $n \neq 0$ at step T6, the control step counter is loaded with the value 6, 0110, which will cause the counter to output a 6 during the next cycle. Figure 4.14 shows the detail of the hardware (Mck stands for master clock).

The Clocking Logic. The clocking logic is shown in Figure 4.15. As the figure legend shows, signals may come from an external source, for example the Strt signal; they may be generated within the circuit, such as the Run signal; they may originate elsewhere in the control unit, such as the Read, Write, and Stop signals; or they may originate from other internal sources, such as the master clock. The circuit accomplishes four distinct things:

control step
generator

Load

CountIn

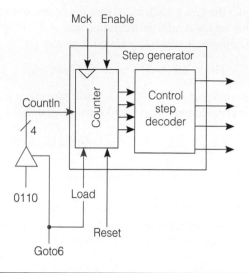

Fig. 4.14 Branching in the Control Unit

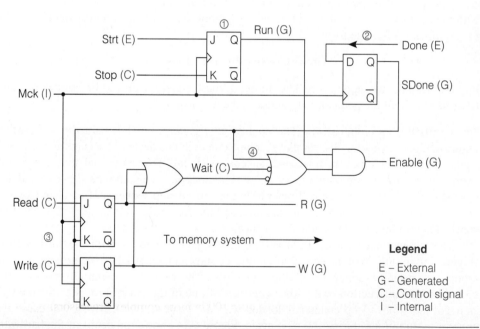

Fig. 4.15 The Clocking Logic

1. Generation of the Run signal from the external Strt signal. The flip-flop at location ① in the figure is used to synchronize changes in Run with the clock. The input logic arises from the RTN logic for the Run signal:

$$\neg Run \wedge Strt \rightarrow Run \leftarrow 1$$

The Stop signal, which resets the JK flip-flop, is generated in response to the *stop* opcode: stop (:= op= 31) → Run ← 0.

2. Generation of the SDone signal, ②, which is a synchronized version of the asynchronous Done signal originating in the memory subsystem and shown in Figure 4.6. Done is asserted by the memory system when a memory operation is complete. If the Done signal is synchronous, then the synchronizer is not needed.

3. Generation of the R and W signals, ③, from the Read and Write control signals. This circuit is required because the memory system expects R or W to be continuously asserted during a read or write operation, respectively, whereas the Read and Write signals are asserted only during the timing cycle in which they occur.

4. Generation of the Enable signal, ④, which enables the control step counter. In the figure, the Enable signal is used to halt the control step counter when the processor must wait for memory actions to complete. The logic to generate it is straightforward: The step counter should be enabled when the Run signal is active, and when a memory operation is Done, or when the Wait signal is not active, or when neither R nor W is true. That is,

$$\text{Enable} = \text{Run}\cdot(\text{SDone} + \overline{\text{Wait}} + \overline{(\text{R} + \text{W})})$$

System Initialization. When a computer is first powered up, or after it is given a reset command, it must be initialized for consistent operation. This includes resetting the mechanism that begins the instruction fetch operation and providing the address of the first instruction to be executed. The specification and circuitry that implement these and any other initialization actions are missing from both the RTN and from this discussion. For example, in the SRC the initialization circuitry must reset the control step counter so that the computer begins execution at step T0, and it could also specify the location of the first instruction to be executed by loading the PC with some initial value, perhaps zero. Implementation of this reset circuitry is relatively straightforward.

Implementing the Control Unit. The control unit implementation domain may be gates in an IC, PALs, PLAs, or other programmable gate arrays. The principal problem to be addressed in selecting the control unit implementation domain is the large number of inputs, outputs, and product terms. It is conceivable that a heavily used control signal in the SRC machine might have fan-in from virtually every opcode. This means a fan-in of up to 32 in the case of SRC, and it can be over 100 in more complex processors.

One area where significant speed improvements can be made is in control step timing. It should be obvious from looking at the concrete RTN of almost any instruction that different control steps will take different amounts of time. For example a simple register transfer will take less time than an ALU operation. One way to exploit these time differences is to generate several clock signals with different periods, and use the appropriate one at each time step. Another approach is to use asynchronous or self-timed circuits that, in effect, compute their own completion times. These advanced techniques are beyond the scope of this book.

4.6 The 2- and 3-Bus Processor Designs

The more interconnections there are between processing elements, the more items of information can move per clock cycle. In a processor data path based on buses, the busing strategy in processor design is probably the single most important factor governing ultimate processor performance. As we will see in the remainder of this chapter, increasing the number of buses increases performance. We should not be surprised at this fact. N buses will permit the movement of N items of information per clock. On the other hand, additional buses incur additional costs regardless of the implementation domain, be it printed circuit board, cable, or IC. We contrast the performance of 1-bus, 2-bus, and 3-bus systems in the remainder of this section, and we sketch designs for a 2-bus and a 3-bus SRC. They will have different concrete RTNs that reflect their unique architectural designs.

4.6.1 A 2-Bus SRC

Figure 4.16 shows a possible 2-bus microarchitecture for the SRC machine. Information travels out of the registers on the B bus, labeled the "Out bus" in the figure, and into the registers on the A, or "In bus." We have also been able to eliminate the C register, as the ALU output can occupy the A bus while one of the operands is on the B bus.

To perform a register transfer in this design, the value must be gated onto the Out bus, and strobed in from the In bus. In Figure 4.16 there is only one possible way to interconnect the B bus with the A bus, and that is through the ALU. The ALU function C = B copies the contents of the B bus to the C output of the ALU, and from there to the A bus. Consider how the add instruction would look in this architecture: Table 4.13 shows that the add can now be performed in five steps instead of six. Step T4 is where the savings are found: since there are 2 buses, the add can be accomplished in one step instead of two, because the result operand can be strobed directly into R[ra].

Additional control hardware is required for this transfer. Examination of Figure 4.4 shows that only one of the Gra, Grb, or Grc control signals can be asserted per cycle, and step T4 requires two, Grc and Gra. The solution is to provide an additional set of "strobing" controls—call them Sra, Srb, and Src—that are used to strobe information into the registers, separate from the gating signals, Gra, Grb, and Grc. This approach will also require two separate 5-to-32 decoders in the register file.

Table 4.14 shows the concrete RTN for the load instruction executing on the 1-bus versus the 2-bus design. Notice that here also there is a 1-clock improvement in number of clock cycles, from 8 to 7 clocks. This is because steps T4 and T5 in the 1-bus design can be accomplished in one step, T4, in the 2-bus design.

Performance and Design. Let us do a rough estimate of the performance improvement to be gained by going from the 1-bus to the 2-bus design. At first glance, it may seem obvious that there will be a performance improvement due to the decrease in the average number of clock cycles required to execute a given program. However, this performance improvement may be offset by an increase in the minimum clock period because of the need for signals to traverse 2 buses instead of just 1 in a given clock period. This can be seen by comparing the signal propagation times for a bus operation in the two designs: Most register transfers in the 2-bus design require the two bus propagation delays instead of the one that is required in the 1-bus design.

Sra
Srb
Src

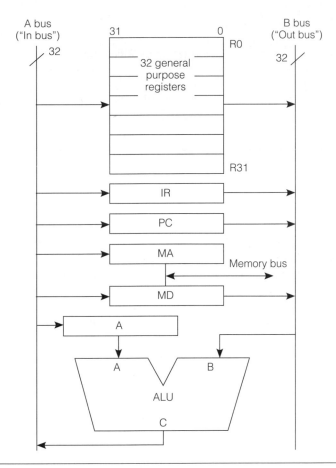

Fig. 4.16 The 2-Bus SRC Microarchitecture

Table 4.13 The 2-Bus add Instruction

Step	RTN	Control Sequence
T0	MA ← PC;	PC_{out}, C = B, MA_{in}
T1	PC ← PC + 4: MD ← M[MA];	PC_{out}, INC4, PC_{in}, Read, Wait
T2	IR ← MD;	MD_{out}, C = B, IR_{in}
T3	A ← R[rb];	Grb, R_{out}, C = B, A_{in}
T4	R[ra] ← A + R[rc];	Grc, R_{out}, ADD, Sra, R_{in}, End

We will first estimate the speedup to be expected from the decrease in CPI (clocks per instruction), ignoring for the moment the possible increase in clock period:

$$\% \text{ Speedup} = \frac{T_{1\text{-bus}} - T_{2\text{-bus}}}{T_{2\text{-bus}}} \times 100 \qquad \text{[Eq. 4.1]}$$

Table 4.14 The 1- and 2-Bus Load Instruction Timing

Step	RTN for 1-bus ld	RTN for 2-bus ld
T0–T2	Instruction fetch	Instruction fetch
T3	A ← ((rb = 0) → 0: (rb ≠ 0) → R[rb]);	A ← ((rb = 0) → 0: (rb ≠ 0) → R[rb]);
T4	C ← A + (16@IR⟨16⟩#IR⟨15..0⟩);	MA ← A + (16@IR⟨16⟩#IR⟨15..0⟩);
T5	MA ← C;	MD ← M[MA]
T6	MD ← M[MA];	R[ra] ← MD;
T7	R[ra] ← MD;	

where, from Equation 3.1,

$$T = \text{Execution time} = \text{IC} \times \text{CPI} \times \tau \qquad \text{[Eq. 4.2]}$$

We can assume that IC, instruction count, will not change when going from the 1-bus to the 2-bus design. In the absence of practical data on the change in CPI when moving from the 1-bus to the 2-bus design, we will make the naive assumption that all instructions behave as does the load instruction discussed previously—that is, all instructions will execute in 7 clock cycles instead of 8. Now substituting the equation for Execution time we get

$$\% \text{ Speedup } = \frac{\text{IC} \times 8 \times \tau - \text{IC} \times 7 \times \tau}{\text{IC} \times 7 \times \tau} \times 100 = \frac{8-7}{7} \times 100 = 14\% \qquad \text{[Eq. 4.3]}$$

If we now assume that the clock period is increased by 10% as a result of increased signal propagation time over the second bus, then $\tau2 = 1.1\tau1$, and our equation for speedup becomes

$$\% \text{ Speedup } = \frac{\text{IC} \times 8 \times \tau_1 - \text{IC} \times 7 \times 1.1 \times \tau_1}{\text{IC} \times 7 \times 1.1 \times \tau_1} \times 100 = \frac{8-7.7}{7.7} \times 100 = 3.\dot{9}\% \qquad \text{[Eq. 4.4]}$$

Thus the point of this example is that much of the performance advantage gained by decreasing CPI may be lost because of an increase in clock period. Exercise 4.12 provides experience in using a more practical means of estimating the influence of adding a second bus on the clock period.

4.6.2   A 3-Bus SRC

Adding a third bus means that all three buses can be used in ALU operations: two for the source operands and one for the result. Figure 4.17 shows the design, with 3 buses, A, B, and C, corresponding to the ALU inputs and outputs. Table 4.15 shows the efficiencies that are achieved in the add instruction by including a third bus. We are down to three control steps, and we have been able to eliminate another register, A. Two things are accomplished in step T0: the initiation of the instruction read, and the incrementing of the PC. The add is now accomplished in one step, T2. All three buses are used in this step, A and B for the operands, and C for the result. Notice that two sets of register gating signals are required to

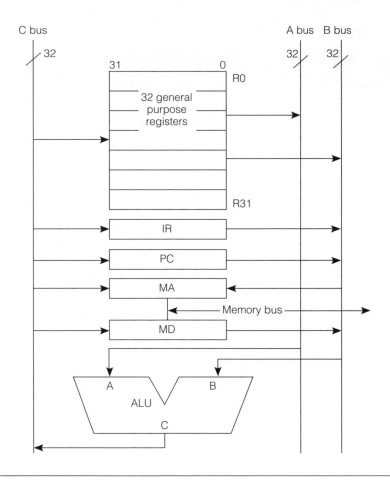

Fig. 4.17 The 3-Bus SRC Design

simultaneously gate two registers onto two buses. This ability to do two simultaneous reads and a write to a register file implies that the register file must have two read ports and a write port, and is referred to as a three-port register file. The register file will require three decoders, two separate sets of gate signals, and still a single strobe. The new control signals required are GA_{rc}, RA_{out}, GB_{rb}, RB_{out}, and S_{ra}.

GA_{rc}
RA_{out}
GB_{rb}
RB_{out}
S_{ra}

For the two-step fetch of Table 4.15 to work, the memory interface must also be changed. The memory address must be sent to memory at the beginning of the cycle, not at the end, as it would be if MA were implemented using edge-triggered flip-flops. This change will permit the Read and Wait signals to be asserted in the same step as the MA_{in} signal. If memory is sufficiently fast, this will allow a complete memory access in a single clock cycle. There are several ways to get MA onto the memory bus at the beginning of the clock cycle, including the use of ordinary latches for MA, or devising a structure to bypass MA and gate the value onto the memory bus at the beginning of the clock cycle.

As the number of buses increases, the ways in which the various components can be interconnected also increases, and finding the optimum configuration can require much study and simulation.

Table 4.15 The 3-Bus add Instruction

Step	RTN	Control Sequence
T0	MA ← PC: MD ← M[MA]: PC ← PC + 4;	PC_{out}, MAB_{in}, INC4, PC_{in}, Read, Wait
T1	IR ← MD;	MD_{out}, C = B, IR_{in}
T2	R[ra] ← R[rb] + R[rc];	GArc, RA_{out}, GBrb, RB_{out}, ADD, Sra, R_{in}, End

Performance and Design.   We can now estimate the impact of going from 1 bus to 3. Again consider the load instruction, this time executing on the 3-bus design. As Table 4.16 shows, load can now be accomplished in just 4 clock cycles instead of the 7 clocks required in the 2-bus design, once again assuming transparent MA latches and sufficiently fast memory. Assuming that the 3-bus design also increases the clock cycle by 10%, as does the 2-bus design, and with the naive assumption that all instructions now take 4 clocks instead of 7, the speedup versus the 1-bus design is

$$\% \text{ Speedup} = \frac{IC \times 8 \times \tau_1 - IC \times 4 \times 1.1 \times \tau_1}{IC \times 4 \times 1.1 \times \tau_1} \times 100 = \frac{8 - 4.4}{4.4} \times 100 = 82\% \qquad \text{[Eq. 4.5]}$$

a considerable improvement.

Suppose memory access takes 3 cycles to complete instead of being complete in 1 cycle. Also assume that 20% of the instructions are loads, and that the processor does not wait on stores. Then, since every instruction has an instruction fetch, and 20% of the instructions have an additional load, the CPI for the 1-bus design is

$$CPI_{1\text{-bus}} = 8 + 2(\text{instruction fetch}) + 0.2 \times 2(\text{data fetch}) = 10.4$$

The CPI for the 3-bus design becomes

$$CPI_{3\text{-bus}} = 4 + 2(\text{instruction fetch}) + 0.2 \times 2(\text{data fetch}) = 6.4$$

Table 4.16 The 3-Bus Load Instruction

Step	RTN	Control Sequence
T0	MA ← PC: MD ← M[MA]: PC ← PC + 4;	PC_{out}, MAB_{in}, INC4, PC_{in}, Read, Wait
T1	IR ← MD;	MD_{out}, C = B, IR_{in}
T2	MA ← ((rb = 0) → 0: (rb ≠ 0) → R[rb]) + (16@IR⟨16⟩#IR⟨15..0⟩): MD ← M[MA];	GArb, $BA^{\dagger}_{out}$, $c2_{out}$, ADD, MAC_{in}, Read, Wait
T3	R[ra] ← MD;	MD_{out}, C = B, S_{ra}, R_{in}, End

†Assumes that the BA_{out} signal gates the base address onto the A bus.

Now the speedup including the increased clock period is:

$$\% \text{ Speedup} = \frac{IC \times 10.4 \times \tau_1 - IC \times 6.4 \times 1.1 \times \tau_1}{IC \times 6.4 \times 1.1 \times \tau_1} \times 100 = \frac{10.4 - 6.4 \times 1.1}{6.4 \times 1.1} \times 100 = 48\%$$

which is still a considerable amount. At this point, the designer might well construct a simulator to get a more realistic estimate of speedup by running benchmark programs.

Key Concepts: The Processor Design Technique

Processor design is an exceedingly complex undertaking. At this point we have covered only a small part of this process. Nevertheless, we can summarize the main components of the design process:

- The designer begins with an abstract RTN definition of the target machine. This definition includes the programmer-visible registers.
- The designer then begins the design of the microarchitecture of the machine, beginning with the data path. This will include not only the programmer-visible registers previously described, but also any other temporary registers that the design might require.
- The bus structure of the data path will have a significant impact on performance. An increased number of buses will mean a lower CPI, but may also increase the clock period.
- As the data path is being designed, the designer is developing the concrete RTN. This step defines the operations to be accomplished on each clock cycle and fixes the CPI of each instruction.
- The data path will need to generate signals that convey its state whenever that state information is required to control some operation. It will also require control signals to effect operations defined by the concrete RTN. The signals generated by the data path are input to the control unit, which in turn provides the control signals to the data path.
- The control unit is designed as a combinational logic circuit that implements the functions described in the concrete RTN.
- In reality, the designer will iterate this process a number of times, refining the design as performance and cost become more evident. The impact of a contemplated design decision can be assessed in a quantitative way by simple calculations and verified by more exact calculations or simulations.

4.7   The Machine Reset

In this section we discuss the reset process in general, and then add a reset capability to the SRC. There are several reasons why a machine requires a reset capability, but they all stem from the need to initialize the processor to a known, defined state. At a minimum, the control step counter must be set to zero, so the machine controller begins operation at the start of the instruction fetch, and the PC must be set to a known value, so machine operation begins at a known instruction.

4.7.1   POSSIBLE RESET OPERATIONS

In addition to resetting the control step counter and initializing the PC, the "well-mannered" reset operation must also clear any interrupt enable flags, lest an incoming interrupt upset the normal system initialization operation. It may also clear the condition codes, or at least set them to a known value, if there is a condition-code register. The reset operation may also set other processor-state registers and perhaps external flags to known values. Upon receiving the reset signal, most processors cease internal operations immediately, or within a few clock cycles. During hardware debugging the external reset pin may be asserted in response to some logical condition, and if the reset action "freezes" the processor state, it can be examined by a diagnostic program in a state very close to the state that caused the reset. In addition, very complex instructions may take an arbitrary amount of time to execute, during which time they may further modify the processor and memory state from its condition when the reset signal was asserted, an action which is undesired.

Some processors have two reset actions: a "soft" reset and a "hard" reset. The soft reset often only initializes the PC and interrupt flags, while the hard reset continues on to initialize other registers in the processor state, and perhaps external devices also.

Initializing the PC.   It is the responsibility of the processor control unit to initialize the PC. The PC may be initialized with the starting address of the routine that is responsible for further machine startup activities, the direct approach, or it may be initialized with the *address* where the address of the routine is stored, the indirect approach. For example, the Intel 8086 processor essentially initializes the PC to 0xFFFF0 upon a reset.[3] The instruction memory at that address would normally contain a JMP (jump) instruction, with the jump target being a location in ROM where the so-called *bootstrap program* is located. The bootstrap program, known as the "boot" program for short, continues the system initialization process.

bootstrap

GETTING SPECIFIC: THE MC68000 RESET PROCESS   The MC68000 series, on the other hand, loads an exception vector into the SSP register from address 0x0 and into the PC from location 0x4. The system memory must be programmed with the appropriate addresses at these two locations, and of course the boot code must be found at the location pointed to by the vector above, prior to the onset of a reset operation. Here we repeat the fragment of RTN describing the MC68000 reset process from page 132:

instruction_interpretation := (
Run $\land \neg$(Reset $\lor$ exc) $\rightarrow$ (IR $\leftarrow$ Mw[PC] :
    PC $\leftarrow$ PC + 2; instruction_execution);   Normal execution state
Reset $\rightarrow$ (INT$\langle 2..0 \rangle \leftarrow$ 7 : S $\leftarrow$ 1 : T $\leftarrow$ 0:   Machine reset
    SSP $\leftarrow$ Ml[0] : PC $\leftarrow$ Ml[4] :
    Reset $\leftarrow$ 0 : Run $\leftarrow$ 1;
    instruction_interpretation);

---

3.   We say "essentially" because the 8086 memory address is computed from the value in two registers, the IP, Intel's name for the program counter, and the CS (code segment) register. See Chapter 7 for details.

We see that the 68000's reset action first prevents its own interruption by setting the interrupt priority to 7, the highest value, clearing the trace bit, setting the supervisor bit, initializing the SSP to the address stored at memory location 0 and the PC to the value stored at memory location 4, clearing the reset bit, and setting the run bit. It then invokes instruction_interpretation, which begins an instruction fetch.

Sources of the Reset Signal. The processor will invariably have an external input pin devoted to the reset signal. There may be several reset pins, devoted to a hard and a soft reset. Being external, these signals are asynchronous, and must be synchronized to the processor clock. While most users are all too familiar with the action of resetting the machine by a press of the thumb, the reset pin also serves an important purpose during the hardware and software development phase, at which time it may be connected to diagnostic hardware programmed to reset the machine upon detecting some abnormal condition. Some processors include a RESET operation in their instruction set. Often the only action of this operation code is to assert the external reset signal.

4.7.2 ADDING AN INITIALIZATION AND RESET CAPABILITY TO THE SRC

We will now modify the SRC behavior to perform a hard reset upon receiving the start signal, Strt, and a soft reset upon receiving a Rst signal after it is running. The hard reset will initialize the PC and the general registers, and the soft reset will initialize only the PC. We will assume that the reset signal is external and asynchronous.

Abstract RTN of the SRC Reset Operation. The original RTN of the SRC machine must be modified to incorporate the hard and soft resets. The processor state must include the reset signal:

Rst: External reset signal

The instruction interpretation must be modified in two places: at the original starting action, and during instruction execution. The original RTN was

instruction_interpretation := ($\neg$Run$\land$Strt $\rightarrow$ (Run $\leftarrow$ 1; instruction_interpretation):
Run $\rightarrow$ (IR $\leftarrow$ M[PC]: PC $\leftarrow$ PC + 4; instruction_execution)):
instruction_execution := (ld (:= op = 1 ...);

On machine start it must be modified to initialize the PC and general registers, and upon reset it must clear the reset flag and initialize only the PC:

instruction_interpretation := ($\neg$Run$\land$Strt $\rightarrow$ (Run $\leftarrow$ 1: PC, R[0..31] $\leftarrow$ 0);
Run$\land\neg$Rst $\rightarrow$ (IR $\leftarrow$ M[PC]: PC $\leftarrow$ PC + 4; instruction_execution):
Run$\land$Rst $\rightarrow$ (Rst $\leftarrow$ 0: PC $\leftarrow$ 0); instruction_interpretation):

Recall that the recursion in this definition assures that instruction_interpretation executes repeatedly. This abstract RTN definition is deficient in implying that instructions will execute to completion before testing the reset condition, and this is not the desired action in the practical case. There is no cure for this at the abstract specification level, since its "granularity" is at the whole instruction level. If we wish to describe the immediate termination of instruction execution, we must move to the concrete RTN level, where the "atomic" actions occur.

Table 4.17 The add Instruction with Reset Processing

Step	RTN	Control Sequence
T0	$\neg Rst \rightarrow (MA \leftarrow PC: C \leftarrow PC+4)$: $Rst \rightarrow (Rst \leftarrow 0: PC \leftarrow 0: T \leftarrow 0^\dagger)$	$\neg Rst \rightarrow (PC_{out}, MA_{in}, INC4, C_{in},$ Read): $Rst \rightarrow (ClrPC, Goto0)$;
T1	$\neg Rst \rightarrow (MD \leftarrow M[MA]: PC \leftarrow C)$: $Rst \rightarrow (Rst \leftarrow 0: PC \leftarrow 0: T \leftarrow 0)$	$\neg Rst \rightarrow (C_{out}, PC_{in}, Wait)$: $Rst \rightarrow (ClrPC, Goto0)$;
T2	$\neg Rst \rightarrow (IR \leftarrow MD)$: $Rst \rightarrow (Rst \leftarrow 0: PC \leftarrow 0: T \leftarrow 0)$	$\neg Rst \rightarrow (MD_{out}, IR_{in})$: $Rst \rightarrow (ClrPC, Goto0)$;
T3	$\neg Rst \rightarrow (A \leftarrow R[rb])$: $Rst \rightarrow (Rst \leftarrow 0: PC \leftarrow 0: T \leftarrow 0)$	$\neg Rst \rightarrow (Grb, R_{out}, A_{in})$: $Rst \rightarrow (ClrPC, Goto0)$;
T4	$\neg Rst \rightarrow (C \leftarrow A + R[rc])$: $Rst \rightarrow (Rst \leftarrow 0: PC \leftarrow 0: T \leftarrow 0)$	$\neg Rst \rightarrow (Grc, R_{out}, ADD, C_{in})$: $Rst \rightarrow (ClrPC, Goto0)$;
T5	$\neg Rst \rightarrow (R[ra] \leftarrow C)$: $Rst \rightarrow (Rst \leftarrow 0: PC \leftarrow 0: T \leftarrow 0)$	$\neg Rst \rightarrow (C_{out}, Gra, R_{in}, End)$: $Rst \rightarrow (ClrPC, Goto0)$;

†Resets time step counter to start instruction_interpretation.

Concrete RTN of the SRC Reset Operation.   We will now add the reset operation to the 1-bus SRC design. If the processor is to cease operation immediately upon receiving the reset signal, then a check must be made for its presence at each clock cycle. The concrete RTN for the add instruction with reset included is shown in Table 4.17.

The ClrPC signal clears the PC, perhaps by loading the bus with all zeros and asserting the PC_{in} signal. The Goto0 signal resets the control step counter to zero, in a manner analogous to the Goto6 signal described on page 165. The hard reset is performed in a similar fashion.

The actual hardware design is left as an exercise, but note that in normal practice the leading edge of the (synchronized) reset signal halts processing and the trailing edge initiates the resumption of processing. Thus pressing the reset button causes a cessation of operation during the time it is pressed. Notice that the two conditions, Rst and ¬Rst, are mutually exclusive, and that Rst automatically places the control sequence counter into the running state. This obviates the need to generate and use the ¬Rst signal.

4.8   Machine Exceptions

In this section we cover exceptions from the processor's point of view. We discuss the need for various kinds of exceptions, and the processor's handling of them. In Chapter 8, "Input and Output," we revisit external exceptions, or interrupts, from the viewpoint of the I/O device and subsystem. Exceptions can be classed as internal and external, synchronous and asynchronous. The former distinction is based on whether the exception arises from within or outside of the processor itself. Generally, internal exceptions are synchronous, as they occur in response to events that are paced by the internal processor clock. External exceptions may be synchronous, but are more often asynchronous, as they are triggered by events that occur in response to external events that bear no relationship to the processor clock. For example, an internal exception would be generated upon an attempt to divide by zero; this is clearly synchronous with the clock. On the other hand, an external exception generated upon a mouse click will be asynchronous with the system clock.

4.8.1   THE EXCEPTION PROCESS

The exception process allows the modification of instruction flow based on internal or external events such as an attempt to divide by zero, or a signal from an external device. Exceptions interrupt the normal sequence of instruction execution, giving rise to their alternate name of interrupts. Notation is not standard among authors, but exception tends to denote anything that changes the normal instruction sequence, including hardware faults, while interrupts often refer to an externally generated exception, such as an I/O request. Exception recognition and processing are fundamental to processor design. In this section we describe the exception process in general and conclude by adding exception processing to the SRC.

We discussed in Chapter 3 how the MC68000 handles exceptions at the abstract RTN level. While other machines may have different ways of processing exceptions, all exception handling mechanisms have the common threads described in the following paragraphs.

Processor Must Be Able to Control Exception Handling.   Some processors such as the MC68000 devote several bits to describing the exception priority level, and only exceptions whose priorities are greater than the current priority are acknowledged. Another approach is to replace the interrupt priority level with a single enable/disable flag. The management of internal exception priorities and request conflicts is then the responsibility of the processor's control unit in the case of internal exceptions—that is, the priorities are "hard wired" into the processor control. In the case of an external interrupt, it is the responsibility of the external interrupt controller to manage interrupt priority and request conflicts.

Processor Must Identify Interrupting Device.   The interrupting device must communicate its type and/or the address of its exception handler. There are two basic approaches to managing this communication: exception vectors, and the use of a "cause" or "information" register. An exception vector points to the exception handler. The vector is defined as the address of the handler and may also contain an additional word specifying other information about the exception. In the vectored approach, the interrupting process has the responsibility to communicate the address of the handler to the processor as soon as the interrupt has been acknowledged. This approach has the advantage that each exception has its own vector, pointing to its handler. The disadvantage is that considerable address space can be taken up storing the vectors and fragments of the handlers' code.

The alternate approach uses just one "general purpose" exception handler. The current PC is stored in an alternate register, and the address of the general purpose handler is copied into the PC. It is the responsibility of the process raising the exception to load the "cause" register with sufficient information so that the exception handler knows which exception has been raised and can take the appropriate action. (That action may indeed be to invoke a procedure that handles the exception.) This is the approach taken by the MIPS processor.

Processor State Must Be Saved.   The processor must have a way of saving information about its state or context so that it can be restored upon return from the exception. This usually means saving the PC and any registers containing interrupt priority information. This is accomplished by saving these registers on the stack, or by copying them to special purpose "storage" registers in the processor. The PC and also usually the interrupt status of the interrupting process are then loaded with the address and interrupt status of the interrupting process.

Exceptions Must Be Disabled During Critical Operations.   The processor must disable interrupts during the time when it is engaged in switching contexts from the one currently executing to the one raising the exception, lest another incoming interrupt disturb the context switch.

Exception Handler Must Save Registers It Uses.   It is the responsibility of the interrupting process to save any registers it wishes to use that were not saved automatically during context switch. This is because the entire context of the interrupted process, including all the registers that it was using when it was interrupted, must be restored when exception processing is complete.

A detailed description of the exception process might be:

1.   An interrupt signal is asserted, internally or externally.

2.   If there is a priority word, the processor compares the current interrupt priority with the priority of the incoming process to determine whether the interrupt should be serviced. A timer interrupt might have a higher priority than a keyboard input, for example. Otherwise it checks the interrupt enable flag.

3.   Simultaneously, the processor finishes the current instruction, if possible. Some exceptions must halt the current instruction mid-stream, as, for example, an attempt to divide by zero.

4.   If the interrupt request is to be granted, then the processor saves some part of the current context, at least the PC and interrupt priority, on the processor stack or in an internal register. It disables interrupts during this period.

5.   The interrupting device or process (printer, memory, ALU, etc.) provides a type code, or vector, or the address where the vector can be found to the processor. This information is usually put on the processor's data lines by the interrupting device in the case of an external interrupt, and stored in a register by the processor. In the case of internal exceptions, the type code or vector may be placed directly in a processor register by the same hardware that detected the exception.

6.   If necessary, the processor converts the type code into a vector address, usually by shifting the type code left some number of bits.

7.   The processor loads the PC and possibly a status register with the vector or vector address and the status information respectively. Processing then continues from this address, which is the address of the exception handler. The exception handler has the responsibility to save any other registers that it intends to use prior to overwriting them. They are normally saved on the processor stack.

8.   The exception handler processes the exception.

9.   When exception processing is complete, the handler restores any registers it had saved and executes a "return from interrupt" instruction. That instruction finishes restoring the context of the interrupted process by reloading the PC and any other saved status information.

4.8.2   KINDS OF EXCEPTIONS

The modern processor has a number of exceptions hardwired into its exception process-ing capability. This represents a trend toward processor vendors subsuming more of the responsibility for trapping unusual conditions that may occur during system operation. Here we describe a number of different exceptions that are generated or accepted by the current generation of machines.

System Reset.   Some systems treat the reset function as an exception, to be processed as any other exception would be processed. The MC68000, described previously, takes that approach. The SPARC architecture takes the approach a step further, having several reset operation codes and allowing several kinds of software reset.

Machine Check Exceptions.   Both the PPC601 and the Intel Pentium processors have a "machine check" exception. The machine check exception is raised by the memory sub-system, through an external pin on the processor, to indicate a memory failure such as an error in the memory error checking and correction (ECC) circuitry.

Data Access Exceptions.   This class of exception is raised when an attempt is made to access data in a region of memory that is either not physically present, or is outside the region allocated to the program or process. These exceptions are normally raised by the memory management unit. In the former case, the exception is a normal effect of the vir-tual memory system, where blocks of data may be kept on disk rather than in physical memory. The effect of the exception in this case is to suspend the program or process gen-erating the exception until the block of memory has been brought in from disk to main memory. In the latter case, it is an attempt to access memory beyond that allocated to the process or program that raises the exception. This is the usual cause of the "bus error" message encountered by the programmer when his or her program attempts to access memory not allocated to it. In this case, the exception handler aborts the program and prints the dreaded message on the user's terminal. The behavior of the virtual memory sys-tem is discussed in more detail in Chapter 7, "Memory System Design."

Instruction Access Exceptions.   Instruction access exceptions are similar to the data access exceptions discussed above, but they occur in response to instruction accesses rather than data accesses. (Many modern machines provide for separate storage of instruc-tions and data. Instructions and data, although stored in the same physical memory, may be stored in separate cache memories, and thus may call for separate exception handlers.)

Alignment Exceptions.   In machines with hard alignment constraints, attempts to access improperly aligned data may result in an alignment exception. The alignment exception may also be raised if an attempt is made to access a data type that is stored across a page boundary. (A *page* is a block of memory that is handled by the virtual memory system as a unit. It is usually from 512 bytes to 2 K bytes in size. Pages may be located in secondary storage, that is, on disk, and brought in as needed.)

memory page

Program Exceptions.   There are several program-generated exceptions in common usage. The *illegal instruction* exception is raised in response to an attempt to execute an instruction that is not in the machine's instruction set. It is usually detected by the control unit, which is unable to decode it to a legal instruction. The *unimplemented*

illegal instruction

unimplemented
instruction

instruction is similar; it reflects an attempt to execute an instruction that is legal, but is not part of the particular processor's instruction set. An example would be an attempt to execute a floating-point instruction on a processor family member that does not include the floating-point instructions. In this case, the exception handler may contain software routines to perform the particular floating-point computation in software rather than hardware. This provides a convenient mechanism for handling an extended instruction set, where some processor family members can interpret the extended instructions in hardware, while others cannot. The *privileged instruction* exception is raised when a nonprivileged program attempts to execute instructions that violate the privilege level under which the program or process is executing. For example, certain instructions are reserved for use by the operating system because they allow access to the programs and data of all users, and their use by other users would violate system security. Certain *arithmetic errors* also raise exceptions. We have mentioned that attempts to divide by zero raise exceptions on most machines, as do certain floating-point computations that result in overflow (a number too large to represent accurately) or underflow (a number too small to represent accurately).

privileged
instructions

arithmetic errors

Miscellaneous Hardware Exceptions.   There are a number of hardware-based exceptions. For example some processors contain programmable countdown timers that raise an exception when they have counted down to zero. They can be used as "watchdog timers" to raise an exception if a certain event has not occurred in a given time interval. Consider an attempt to print to a printer that is not turned on. The attempt to contact the printer can "time out" and raise an exception if the printer does not respond within the set time interval.

Trace and Debugging Exceptions.   Debugging system programs and system hardware can be a difficult endeavor. One way to ease the effort is to allow single-stepping of the program; that is, putting the processor in a mode where an exception is raised after the execution of every instruction. The single-stepping exception is usually turned on by setting a trace or trap bit in the processor status word. The exception handler allows examination and modification of the processor and memory states, permits the programmer to execute another single step, or controls program execution in other helpful ways.

nonmaskable
interrupt, NMI

Nonmaskable Exceptions.   Many processors have a "nonmaskable" exception or interrupt—*NMI*. This kind of exception cannot be ignored by the processor under any condition, and if there is a priority mechanism internal to the processor, the NMI is invariably assigned a priority at the highest level. As might be surmised, it is reserved for exceptions of the most grave nature, such as power failure or some other potentially catastrophic event. In data-critical applications, when an NMI is received, the interrupt handler may attempt to save the machine's entire processor and memory state to disk while sufficient energy exists in the power supply capacitors to operate the system, or it may issue a "dying gasp" communication to an external device.

External Exceptions—Interrupts.   The interrupt mechanism permits the system designer to use exception processing to handle external events such as sending characters to a printer. This mechanism has replaced device polling, in which the processor must take the time to periodically check the status of external devices to see if they require service. We will revisit the subject of polling versus interrupts in Chapter 8.

4.8.3   EXCEPTION PROCESSING IN SRC

The version of the SRC that we introduced in Chapter 2 did not contain any exception processing mechanism. Here we remedy that, and use it as an example of implementing exception processing. The example below contains all the important features that are required in exception processing while still being simple enough to use as an example. For clarity we have omitted the reset capability described in Section 4.7.2. As we proceed with the example, you will observe that the interrupt mechanism is a blending of the two approaches to identifying the exception that we have discussed: The SRC processor has both vectored interrupts and a register into which the process causing the exception can write information. The RTN of the process follows:

Processor Interrupt Mechanism

ireq:	Interrupt request signal
iack:	Interrupt acknowledge signal
IE:	1-bit interrupt enable flag
IPC$\langle 31..0\rangle$:	Storage for program counter saved upon interrupt
II$\langle 31..0\rangle$:	Interrupt information: information on source of last interrupt
Isrc_info$\langle 15..0\rangle$:	Information from interrupt source
Isrc_vect$\langle 7..0\rangle$:	Type code from interrupt source
Ivect$\langle 31..0\rangle$:= 20@0#Isrc_vect$\langle 7..0\rangle$#4@0:	

Interrupt requests are signaled by the external asynchronous ireq signal. There is only a single interrupt flag, so interrupts are either enabled or disabled: there is no priority mechanism within the processor. Rather than saving the PC on a stack, the SRC saves it in the IPC register, from which software can save it on a stack if desired. II is the interrupt information register, visible to the programmer. Isrc_info is the information returned by the device when the interrupt is acknowledged by the processor. It is loaded into II by the control unit.

The interrupting process is also responsible for supplying the 8-bit register Isrc_vect with a type code specifying the location of the handler. The vector is generated from the type code by shifting it left by 4 bits, preappending 20 zeros, and storing the resulting address in the 32-bit register Ivect. (Ivect is used in the RTN specification to make the conversion of the type code into the vector explicit. It may not be represented by a register in the physical implementation.)

The modified instruction interpretation sequence is

instruction_interpretation :=	
($\neg$Run$\wedge$Strt $\rightarrow$ Run $\leftarrow$ 1:	Start
Run$\wedge\neg$(ireq$\wedge$IE) $\rightarrow$ (IR $\leftarrow$ M[PC]:	Normal fetch
PC $\leftarrow$ PC + 4; instruction_execution):	
Run$\wedge$(ireq$\wedge$IE) $\rightarrow$ (IPC $\leftarrow$ PC$\langle 31..0\rangle$:	Interrupt
II$\langle 15..0\rangle$ $\leftarrow$ Isrc_info$\langle 15..0\rangle$:	
IE $\leftarrow$ 0: PC $\leftarrow$ Ivect$\langle 31..0\rangle$:	
iack $\leftarrow$ 1; iack $\leftarrow$ 0):	
instruction_interpretation);	

If there is an interrupt request, and if interrupts are enabled, then

- The PC is copied to the IPC.
- Isrc_info is loaded into II.
- The iack bit is set. (The processor may not acknowledge a given request for an arbitrarily long time, so it is the responsibility of the requesting device to hold ireq high until the processor signals that it has "caught" the interrupt request by asserting iack for one clock period. The interrupting device must then deassert ireq within one clock period.)
- Interrupts are disabled by clearing the IE bit.
- The PC is loaded with the exception vector.

Thus begins the exception handler routine. As we mentioned before, it is the responsibility of the exception handler to save any registers it intends to use. In addition, since IPC and II contain the information needed to return to the interrupted process, the handler *must* store the IPC and II registers in another location before it enables interrupts. If this is not done, then when interrupts are enabled the first exception will overwrite IPC and II. The svi and ri instructions provide a convenient way of performing this action: svi saves II and IPC to general registers ra and rb respectively, and ri reverses the process, restoring II and IPC from registers ra and rb:

Additional Instructions to Support Interrupts

svi (:= op = 16) → (R[ra]⟨15..0⟩ ← II⟨15..0⟩:   Save II and IPC.
          R[rb] ← IPC⟨31..0⟩):
ri (:= op = 17) → (II⟨15..0⟩ ← R[ra]⟨15..0⟩ :   Restore II and IPC.
          IPC⟨31..0⟩ ← R[rb]):

The programmer must have a way of explicitly controlling whether interrupts are recognized by the processor. This need is served by two instructions, een and edi, exception enable and exception disable:

een (:= op = 10) → (IE ← 1):   Exception enable
edi (:= op = 11) → (IE ← 0):   Exception disable

The rfi, return from interrupt, instruction returns control to the interrupted process by copying IPC to PC and setting the interrupt enable flag.

rfi (:= op = 30) → (PC ← IPC: IE ← 1):

It is important that these two register transfers be done as one atomic action, because no combination of branch and een instructions can accomplish the same result.

Table 4.18 shows the RTN for the concrete, 1-bus SRC design. Notice that, in keeping with the abstract RTN, the interrupt recognition occurs only at step T0. Thereafter, execution proceeds without heed for the value of ireq. The pair of RTN statements, iack ← 1; iack ← 0, signifies that the interrupt acknowledge signal is pulsed in step T0. The ; separator does not imply another clock. In order for all of the register transfers specified for exception processing to happen during 1 clock cycle, some further data paths must be added; not all can use the bus. The II and IPC registers must be added to the data path.

Table 4.18 RTN of the SRC Instruction Fetch with Interrupts

Step	Concrete RTN	
T0	$(\neg(\text{ireq} \wedge \text{IE}) \to (\text{MA} \leftarrow \text{PC}:$ $\text{C} \leftarrow \text{PC} + 4)$;	$(\text{ireq} \wedge \text{IE}) \to (\text{IPC} \leftarrow \text{PC}: \text{II} \leftarrow \text{Isrc\_info}:$ $\text{IE} \leftarrow 0: \text{PC} \leftarrow 20@0\#\text{Isrc\_vect}\langle 7..0 \rangle\#00:$ $\text{iack} \leftarrow 1; \text{iack} \leftarrow 0: \text{End})$;
T1	$\text{MD} \leftarrow \text{M[MA]} : \text{PC} \leftarrow \text{C}$;	
T2	$\text{IR} \leftarrow \text{MD}$;	
T3	Instruction_execution;	

Since the information supplied by the interrupting device only has one possible destination, it might bypass the bus and use separate data paths to II and IPC.

We mentioned in connection with the general discussion of reset that exceptions should be prevented immediately following a reset. Thus the reset and exception modifications to the instruction interpretation of SRC interact. A complete instruction interpretation definition, including hard and soft reset, exceptions, and normal instruction fetch appears as follows:

instruction_interpretation :=
$(\neg \text{Run} \wedge \text{Strt} \to (\text{Run} \leftarrow 1: \text{PC}, \text{R[0..31]} \leftarrow 0$;   Hard reset
                instruction_interpretation):
$\text{Run} \wedge \text{Rst} \to (\text{Rst} \leftarrow 0: \text{PC} \leftarrow 0$;   Soft reset
                instruction_interpretation):
$\text{Run} \wedge \neg \text{Rst} \wedge (\text{ireq} \wedge \text{IE}) \to (\text{IPC} \leftarrow \text{PC}\langle 31..0 \rangle$:   Interrupt
                $\text{II}\langle 15..0 \rangle \leftarrow \text{Isrc\_info}\langle 15..0 \rangle$:
                $\text{IE} \leftarrow 0: \text{PC} \leftarrow \text{Ivect}\langle 31..0 \rangle$:
                $\text{iack} \leftarrow 1; \text{iack} \leftarrow 0$;
                instruction_interpretation):
$\text{Run} \wedge \neg \text{Rst} \wedge \neg(\text{ireq} \wedge \text{IE}) \to (\text{IR} \leftarrow \text{M[PC]}$:   Normal fetch
        $\text{PC} \leftarrow \text{PC} + 4$; instruction_execution):

4.8.4 FURTHER COMPLICATIONS

There are several facets of the processor design that complicate exception processing. They have to do with how to handle exceptions that occur in the middle of instructions. While we have designed our SRC exception processing mechanism to wait until the currently executing instruction has finished, this may not be possible in the practical case for two reasons. The first is that in some cases it may be advantageous to allow exceptions to halt instructions in the midst of execution to detect the exact cause of the exception or to prevent an erroneous value from being written to a register or memory. The second is that, in the case of pipelined and multiple-instruction-issue processor design, there may literally be no time at which all instructions have simultaneously finished executing.

Exceptions That Halt Instructions. There are several reasons why it may be advantageous to stop execution in the middle of an instruction to service the exception. Some complex instructions can take arbitrarily long to execute. The Intel 80×86 processor family's string instructions can operate on strings of up to 2^{32} words. Other processors have similarly complex instructions. In addition, an exception may be generated upon an attempt to access one of the operands of a multi-operand instruction, if that operand happens to be located in a page that is not presently in main memory. This kind of exception is often referred to as a *page fault*. The instruction cannot complete until the exception has been serviced, and the operand paged in. Complex arithmetic instructions may also generate an exception in the midst of execution, and the exception must be processed in order for execution to proceed.

page fault

In all these cases the instruction must be halted in mid-execution. If execution is to continue after the exception, then the exception handler must "fix up" the instruction. It may be appropriate to roll back the instruction to its starting point, returning the processor and memory to the exact state they were in before the execution started, or it may be appropriate for the handler to store the *microstate* of the processor—that is, the state at the instant the exception occurred—and then restore the processor and memory to that state, thus continuing execution in the middle of the instruction where the exception occurred. This microstate would include the state of temporary registers that are not normally thought of as being part of the processor state, such as the A and C registers of SRC, and the value of the control step counter. In any case, allowing exceptions to halt instructions before they have completed complicates processor design considerably.

microstate

Exceptions in Pipelined and Multiple-Instruction-Issue Machines.   In the case of pipelined and multiple-instruction-issue machines, it is the responsibility of the system designer to set a policy for exception handling that the programmer can live with. We consider this subject in more detail in Chapter 5.

Summary

- In this chapter we have covered processor design at the gate level, and also discussed reset and exception processing. The design process we used was based on the abstract RTN as a starting point.

- The design process began with a design for the processor data path. Having at least a preliminary design for the data path, the designer writes a concrete RTN specification for the instruction set of the machine. With that specification, the designer can return to the data path to fill in the details of register design, control signals, and bus and memory interfaces. Once the hardware design is more or less complete, the designer can return to the concrete RTN, and fill in the control sequences corresponding to the RTN. This exercise often exposes weaknesses in the design, so the process may need to be iterated several times.

- Having completed the control sequences, the designer can begin to design the timing and control unit of the processor. This again is an iterative process, as unforeseen problems often force a reconsideration of some aspect of the design. We covered hardwired control unit design in this chapter. The microcoded control unit is an alternative to the hardwired control unit. We will discuss microcoded control unit design in the next chapter.

- The CPU may contain one or several buses. The CPU bus structure is dictated by performance and cost issues. More buses usually produce better performance, but at a cost of increased clock period and increased area occupied by buses.

■ Rough estimates of performance can be useful by helping the designer to understand the performance impact of various design alternatives. These estimates are usually quantified by simulation or more accurate calculations.

■ The processor needs a reset capability to initialize it to a known state. Some processors have two kinds of reset, referred to as hard reset and soft reset. The hard reset initializes more of the processor than the soft reset.

■ Exception processing is part of virtually every processor. Exceptions allow the processor to be interrupted by unplanned events. Such events may occur internally, such as an attempt to divide by zero, or an event may be external, such as the press of a key. We discussed the main classes of exceptions and developed an RTN description for exception handling by SRC.

Bibliography

Textbooks differ in the degree to which they describe the hardware details of computer design. Some that take a hardware view similar to the one in this text follow:

F. J. Hill and G. R. Peterson, *Digital Systems: Hardware Organization and Design,* 3rd ed., Wiley, New York, 1987.

D. A. Patterson and J. L. Hennessy, *Computer Organization and Design: The Hardware/Software Interface,* 2nd ed. Morgan Kaufmann, San Francisco, CA, 1997.

V. Carl Hamacher, Zvonko G. Vranesic, and Safwat G. Zaky, *Computer Organization,* 5th ed., McGraw-Hill, New York, 2001.

I. Englander, *The Architecture of Computer Hardware and System Software: An Information Technology Approach*, 2nd ed, John Wiley and Sons, New York, 2000.

John Hayes, *Computer Architecture and Organization*, 3rd ed. McGraw-Hill, 1997.

Books taking a more high-level, block diagram approach to processor design include:

Andrew S. Tanenbaum, *Structured Computer Organization*, 4th ed., Prentice-Hall, Englewood Cliffs, NJ, 1998.

M. Morris Mano, *Computer Systems Architecture*, 3rd ed., Prentice-Hall, Englewood Cliffs, NJ, 1993.

William Stallings, *Computer Organization and Architecture*, 6rd ed., Macmillan, New York, 2002.

A number of real architectures have been compared and classified in the following texts. The classifications are well done, but the machines are dated.

C. Gordon Bell and Allen Newell, *Computer Structures: Readings and Examples*, McGraw-Hill, New York, 1971.

Daniel P. Siewiorek, C. Gordon Bell, and Allen Newell, *Computer Structures: Principles and Examples*, McGraw-Hill, New York, 1982.

To study current machines it is usually necessary to rely on periodicals or manufacturers' literature. IEEE's *Computer* magazine often has articles on specific new architectures. *Communications of the ACM* is more software-oriented, but sometimes contains articles on new architectures of note, such as the group of articles on the DEC Alpha chip in the February 1993 issue.

Exercises

4.1   Write concrete RTN steps for the SRC instructions la and str using the 1-bus SRC microarchitecture of Section 4.2.   **(§4.2)**

4.2   Extend the SRC instruction set by adding the instruction swap ra, rb, (op = 7), that exchanges the contents of the two specified registers.

   a.   Define a plausible abstract RTN for this instruction.

   b.   Develop the concrete RTN for it, assuming the 1-bus SRC microarchitecture.   **(§4.4)**

4.3   Extend the SRC instruction set by adding an instruction, sethi ra, c2 (op = 18), that is the equivalent to the SPARC sethi instruction. Sethi sets the high-order 16 bits of R[ra] with the least significant 16 bits of the c2 constant field, without disturbing the least significant 16 bits of ra. Unfortunately the SRC ALU does not have a SETHI operation, so the operation must be synthesized from the existing ALU operations.

   a.   Define a plausible abstract RTN for this instruction.

   b.   Develop the concrete RTN for it, assuming the 1-bus SRC microarchitecture.   **(§4.4)**

4.4   Extend the SRC instruction set by adding the xor command, (op = 19), which is similar to the and command, but performs the XOR operation instead of AND.

   a.   Develop the abstract RTN for the xor command.

   b.   Write the concrete RTN and control signals for the xor instruction for the 1-bus SRC microarchitecture. (Unfortunately, the SRC ALU does not have the XOR operation as one of its primitives, but only the operations ADD, SUB, AND, OR, SHR, SHL, NEG, NOT, C = B, and INC4.)   **(§4.4)**

4.5   Write concrete RTN steps and control sequences for the not instruction implemented in the 1-bus microarchitecture.   **(§4.4)**

4.6   Why, in Figure 4.8, does the C = B signal not have to be asserted when that operation is to be performed?   **(§4.4)**

4.7   The SRC instruction set includes the neg instruction, which computes the arithmetic 2's complement negation of a register operand. Assume that the NEG operation is not in the set of operations the ALU can perform. (See page 152.) Develop the concrete RTN and the control sequence to implement the neg instruction for the 1-bus design.   **(§4.4)**

4.8   Using Table 4.6 to 4.11, develop as much as you can of the control signals MD_{out}, C_{in}, and LD. Show both the Boolean equations and the gate-level designs.   **(§4.5)**

4.9   Repeat Exercise 4.8, but develop the equations for *all* the SRC instructions excluding those related to exceptions. It may help to use the control signals in Figure 5.3.   **(§4.5)**

4.10   The number of SRC opcodes seems constrained to 32 by the 5-bit opcode field. However, there are a number of instructions that have unused fields or portions of fields that can be used to extend the number of opcodes. There are, for example, the 0-operand instructions that do not require any additional information from other fields in the instruction. Design a scheme for encoding all of the 0-operand instructions by using some of the bits outside the opcode field. Do not change any of the other opcodes in the process; they and their instructions should remain unchanged. Exactly how does this affect the control unit in Figure 4.12?   **(§4.5)**

4.11   For this problem, assume gate delays of 1 ns, bus propagation delays of 2 ns, latch propagation delays of 3 ns, and no other delays. Also assume unlimited gate fan-in and fan-out. You should also assume that latch propagation delays include setup, hold, and minimum pulse width times, as shown in Figure 4.11.

   a.   Consider the control unit shown in Figure 4.12. How long does it take for the control signals to become valid at the output of the control unit from the time of the rising edge of the

T control step signal? Assume that the decoded opcode signals are valid at the rising edge of the clock.

    b. Assume that the delay of the control unit in Figure 4.12 is 6 ns. What is the minimum clock period for step T6 of Figure 4.10?   **(§4.5)**

4.12 In the section on performance estimation on page 168 it was arbitrarily assumed that the minimum clock period of the 2-bus design would be 1.1 times the clock period of the 1-bus design. Given the delays in Exercise 4.11, revisit this problem.

    a. Calculate the minimum clock period for the 1-bus and 2-bus designs, assuming a 25% increase in clock periods as a safety factor.

    b. Using the clock periods you calculated, compute the speedup to be expected for the 2-bus design.   **(§4.6)**

4.13 The 2-bus SRC design shown in Figure 4.16 allows savings in the number of control steps to perform an add instruction, but at the expense of additional control hardware. The text describes the need to provide additional gate and strobe hardware so that data can be gated from and strobed to the general registers on the same cycle. Redesign the hardware shown in Figure 4.4 to accommodate this change.   **(§4.6)**

4.14 Repeat Exercise 4.12 for the 3-bus design. Use the figures on instruction count for the 3-bus design that are given on page 172.   **(§4.6)**

4.15 Repeat Exercise 4.5 for the 2- and 3-bus microarchitectures.   **(§4.6)**

4.16 Repeat Exercise 4.7 for the 2- and 3-bus microarchitectures.   **(§4.6)**

4.17 Estimate the number of gates required in the control signal encoder in Figure 4.12 to implement the following for the SRC.

    a. 1-bus design

    b. 2-bus design

    c. 3-bus design

In each case also estimate the fan-in and fan-out of the AND and OR gates, and then the numbers of gates and number of levels of gates if a more realistic fan-in and fan-out of 8 is assumed. Do not count each and every gate; instead make projections based on the concrete RTN descriptions in this chapter.   **(§4.6)**

4.18 Modify the hardwired control unit design shown in Figure 4.12 and Figure 4.15 to support the Rst and modified Run signals described in Section 4.7.2. You will also need to modify the register file, shown in Figure 4.4. Assume that the Rst signal is asynchronous.   **(§4.7)**

4.19 Design a new opcode for SRC, reset, (op = 18), that does a hard reset or a soft reset, depending on the value of $c1\langle 0 \rangle$.   **(§4.7)**

4.20 Examine the concrete RTN steps in the chapter to see if it is possible to implement register C of Figure 4.2 using latches instead of edge-triggered or master-slave flip-flops.   **(§4.3)**

4.21 Section 4.8.2 describes the kinds of exceptions that are likely to be encountered in the modern processor. Pick one of the 32-bit commercial RISC processors, and describe briefly each of the exceptions it accepts.   **(§4.8)**

4.22 In most cases, an interrupted program must be resumed after the exception that interrupted it has been handled. In some cases, however, the nature of the exception precludes resuming the program. Identify the two different kinds of exceptions of those discussed in Section 4.8.2.

4.23 Add a control signal column to Table 4.18.   **(§4.8)**

CHAPTER 5

Processor Design—Advanced Topics

Chapter Outline

This chapter begins with a discussion of several techniques that are used to speed the processor's operation.

Pipelining, as first described in Chapter 1, is the process of issuing a new instruction before the previous one has completed execution. It is a technique used heavily in RISC processors, and represents a way to hide the latency of instruction execution. Pipelining is an important topic, and we devote considerable attention to it, including developing a pipelined design for SRC.

Superscalar (multiple-instruction-issue) and VLIW designs are additional means of increasing processor throughput. *Superscalar*, sometimes called *multiple-instruction-issue* architectures, have several complete functional units within the processor, allowing several instructions to be issued per clock cycle instead of just one. Vector instructions, usually seen in supercomputers, allow operations on multiple operands simultaneously. *VLIW* (very long instruction word) machines also contain multiple functional units per CPU, but their instruction words are longer than those of conventional machines and allow the specification of multiple operations per instruction.

We conclude with a discussion of microcoded control unit design. In the previous chapter we discussed the hardwired approach to control unit design. At present this is the most popular method of implementing the control unit, but the alternative design method, microcoding, has been popular in the past, and is still used to implement special purpose processors.

Microcoding is a software like approach to control unit design, wherein the control signals are stored as words in a microcode memory instead of being generated from random logic. Section 5.4 includes a more complete discussion of microcoding and a demonstration of its use.

5.1   Pipelining

We discussed pipelining briefly in Chapter 3 in connection with the SPARC architecture. In this section we treat the subject in detail. After a short overview, we discuss the philosophy and basic assumptions that underlie the pipelined approach. Pipelined designs can be confusing at first. To alleviate some of that confusion, we discuss the technique of pipeline design before doing the design. SRC is used to illustrate the principles.

5.1.1   Overview

There is an analogy between pipelining instructions in a computer and manufacturing parts on an assembly line. In both instances the goal is to keep the equipment busy as much of the time as possible, and in both instances total throughput may be increased by decreasing the amount of work done at a given stage and increasing the number of stages, even though the time for a given instruction or part to go through the process may increase.

This overlapping comes at a price. In the fetch-execute-fetch-execute . . . model that we have used so far, the results of a given operation can be freely used by the next operation, since the previous operation is guaranteed to have completed before the next operation begins. This is not true in pipelining, where the operation that produces a result may not have written the result before the next operation tries to use it. There are several approaches to solving this problem, and we cover them in detail.

The Pipeline and the Assembly Line.   We can use the similarity between a pipeline and an assembly line to describe the structure and behavior of the pipeline. Consider a plant that manufactures several kinds of similar small parts that may require drilling, cutting, polishing, and packaging. Assume that each different part must be handled differently at each stage in the process, and that not all parts require work at each stage. Without the assembly line process, a worker would obtain a given piece of raw material and, using the directions for how to manufacture the finished part, would take the part from station to station, drilling at the first, cutting at the second, polishing at the third, and finally packaging the product. Then the worker would repeat the process with the next piece of raw material. Figure 5.1a shows the process similarity between the steps that must be taken to add two registers and store the result in a third register, and manufacturing an end plate (whatever that is). The figure indicates that without pipelining in the first instance and without an assembly line procedure in the second instance, all of the functional units are idle except the ALU in the case of the add instruction and the part-drilling station in the case of the part manufacture.

Keep the Functional Units Busy.   Pipelining and the assembly line both have the objective of keeping the functional units busy by starting on a new object as soon as the previous one has exited the first functional unit rather than waiting for the object to emerge from the process. Figure 5.1b shows how the situation changes with pipelining and the analogous situation with an assembly line. Now five different instructions are in various stages of execution, and five different parts are in various stages of manufacture. The worker at each assembly line station must know what to do for each different part that might arrive, and the pipeline stage must do the right thing for its particular instruction. The program fragment being executed follows:

```
shr    r3, r3, 2    ;Storing result into r3
sub    r2, r5,r1    ;Idle—no memory access needed
add    r4, r3,r2    ;Performing addition in ALU
st     r4, addr1    ;Accessing r4 and addr1
ld     r2, addr2    ;Fetching instruction
```

Notice that if pipeline stages are numbered top to bottom, the instructions are "backwards" in the pipeline from the usual program sequence as shown in the preceding code.

■   The shr instruction was the first to enter the pipeline, and is in the process of writing its result into register r3.

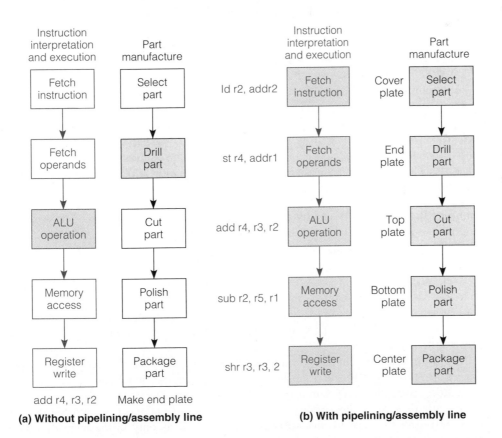

(a) Without pipelining/assembly line   **(b) With pipelining/assembly line**

Fig. 5.1 Executing Machine Instructions versus Manufacturing Small Parts

- The sub instruction is in the memory access stage, and since this instruction has no memory access associated with it, no action is occurring. (Just as the equivalent assembly line stage would be inactive if the bottom plate did not require polishing.)
- The add instruction is in the third stage, where its operands have been fetched, and they are being added in the ALU.
- The st instruction in the second stage is having its operands—addr1, contained in the c2 field of the instruction, and r4, contained in the register file—extracted and readied for their use in stage 4, the memory access stage.
- The ld instruction is being fetched from memory.

All the functional units are busy, or at least have instructions in them in various stages of execution. This example thus meets the ideal of one instruction issued into the pipeline on each clock cycle.

Bandwidth versus Latency.   The 3-bus machine that we studied in the last chapter takes 3 clock cycles to perform an add instruction. If all instructions executing on that machine took the same 3 clocks, then the *bandwidth* of the machine in instructions per second would be one-third of the clock frequency. For example, if the clock frequency is 100 MHz, then the bandwidth would be 33 MIPS. The *latency*, or time interval to process each instruction, would be 3 clock cycles, or $3/(100 \times 10^6) = 30$ ns. If we assume that our pipelined machine runs at the same clock frequency, then its bandwidth would be equal to the clock frequency, or 100 MIPS, but the latency would be increased to 5 clock cycles, or 50 ns.

To summarize, pipelining increases bandwidth, or throughput, at the expense of latency, the amount of time required for each instruction to execute. This bandwidth/latency trade-off is frequently found in situations such as the preceding, where items are queued for processing. Since many instructions must be executed to run a program, program completion time depends directly on the number of instructions executed per second, or the bandwidth. The latency of an individual instruction only affects the completion time of a sequence with very few instructions.

Complicating Factors—Dependence among Instructions.   In the simple fetch-execute designs we studied in Chapter 4, each instruction completes before the next begins. Thus there is assurance that any register or memory value that is modified by a given instruction will be available to instructions following it. This may not be the case in pipelined designs, however, since several instructions may be in the pipeline together. An instruction that modifies a value may not have updated the register or memory location before an instruction following it attempts to read the value. This relationship between two instructions, where a value produced by one instruction is not available to a following instruction, is known as *dependence*.

The program fragment shown on page 191 exhibits data dependence: The first two instructions, shr and sub, are responsible for storing operands in r2 and r3 that are used by the add instruction. An examination of the pipeline shows that this value has not been stored yet in the case of the shr instruction, since it is just in the register write stage, and it certainly isn't the case for the sub instruction, which is only in the memory access stage. In this case there are two possible ways out: detect the dependence and *stall* the pipeline—that is, don't allow an instruction to enter the pipeline—until its operands are

bandwidth

latency

dependence

pipeline stalls

available for it, or detect the dependence and *forward* the operand to the dependent instruction when it reaches the ALU stage.

A similar problem exists when loading values from memory into a register, since the load may not be complete when the value is needed. In this case, it may not be possible to forward the value to the instruction that needs it. The processor may have to detect the dependence and stall the pipeline until the value is ready for access. Software solutions are possible also. The compiler can detect the dependence and rearrange instructions to remove it, or failing that, it can insert nop instructions, which are really just software-initiated pipeline stalls.

The most frequent solution to the "delayed load" problem is to issue a decree to those programming the machine: *Values loaded from memory into the register file cannot be accessed until two (or some other set number of) instructions later.* This doesn't really violate the concept that pipelining shouldn't change the instruction set (see Section 5.1.2). The instruction set is unchanged, but there has been a restriction placed on when operands can be accessed after a load instruction.

Likewise, branch targets cannot usually be computed before the instruction following the branch instruction has entered the pipeline. Here again the hardware can detect the dependence and stall the pipeline, or the condition can be accepted and a *branch delay* instituted by decree: *The instruction following a branch will be executed whether the branch is taken or not. If the branch is taken, the instruction following it will be executed before the branch is taken.* The location of the instruction following a branch instruction is known as a *branch delay slot*.

Both of these new rules place additional constraints on the compiler—it must recognize and respect them. If it cannot find an appropriate instruction to place after the load or branch instruction, it must insert a nop. Both of these decrees will be assumed in the design of the pipelined SRC machine. This entire class of pipeline-induced instruction dependences is discussed later in Section 5.2, "Pipeline Hazards."

Margin notes: data forwarding; delayed load; branch delay; branch delay slot

5.1.2   BASIC ASSUMPTIONS IN PIPELINE DESIGN

Pipelining has been used since the 1960s to increase instruction throughput. Since that time a number of common hardware and software characteristics have been found to enhance the effectiveness and efficiency of pipelining. Not all pipelined designs have all of these characteristics, and some pipeline designs employ other hardware and software features. Nevertheless, those we discuss in the following paragraphs seem to be most prevalent.

The Instruction Set Is Unchanged.   Most processor instruction sets are implemented on a variety of architectures, some optimized for speed, others for low cost. Various family members may have no pipelining at all, and others may be highly pipelined. The basic ground rule in designing a new pipeline architecture for an existing instruction set is that instructions should execute and provide the same results on all architectures regardless of pipeline structure, with the possible exception of imposing rules about instruction dependence such as those already noted.

Formally, the abstract RTN must remain unchanged regardless of the concrete RTN of a particular pipelined design. This rule follows from the concept of upward compatibility, which allows processor manufacturers to create new generations of machines to which users can easily upgrade without making major changes in their software.

Modifications to Memory.   If instructions are to be issued into the pipeline at a rate of one per clock cycle, and if all cycles must take the same time to complete, then the memory access model developed in the previous chapter needs significant modification. There are two problems with that model: having to wait for memory accesses to complete, and having to fetch both instructions and data from the same memory space. The problem of having to wait for memory accesses to complete can be addressed by employing faster (and more expensive) main memory, or by using slower main memory plus a cache memory. The cache memory is a small amount of high-speed memory that is kept filled with what the caching hardware "predicts" will be the next memory locations accessed. The latter problem arises because the pipeline model above relies on being able to simultaneously access instructions in stage 1 and data in stage 4. This is not possible with the simple memory model developed in Chapter 4. Two separate memories are needed, or at least the appearance of two separate memories, so that instructions and data can be accessed simultaneously. This separation of memory spaces into program space and data space is referred to as the Harvard architecture, harkening all the way back to Howard Aiken's design of the Mark III computer, developed at Harvard University in the 1940s, which had separate program and data memories.

Harvard
architecture

The Register File.   We found it convenient to employ a 3-port register file for the 3-bus design in Chapter 4. In that design two operands were fetched from the register file, passed through the ALU, and the result written back into the register file all in the same cycle. Virtually all pipelined designs also require a 3-port register file, for the same reasons that the 3-bus design requires it: to allow the reading of two operands and the writing of a third in a single clock cycle.

Modifications to Buses and the Data Path.   Pipelined designs replace the buses used in Chapter 4 with direct connections between registers. This point-to-point approach allows many register transfers to take place simultaneously in each stage, which indeed they must if the goal of allowing many activities to proceed simultaneously is to be achieved. This actually makes the data path easier to visualize, since each interconnection is used for a specific purpose rather than having functionality that changes from clock cycle to clock cycle.

A corollary to the "rule of buses," that the bus can only have a single item on it during any one clock cycle, is that the value stays on the bus only for the duration of the clock cycle. This means that extra registers, called *pipeline registers*, are needed to convey information from stage to stage, even if it is not modified by a given stage. Thus both the data and at least portions of the instruction must travel in tandem from stage to stage. Each instruction must "carry its own bags," so to speak. That is, whatever the instruction must "know" about itself at each stage must be carried along until that stage is reached. This is accomplished by pipelining a portion of the instruction register along with any data items. Instructions and data are clocked from stage to stage in the pipeline registers.

pipeline registers

We will also need to make changes to the ALU of Chapter 4. The shift operations in particular must complete in a single clock cycle regardless of the size of the shift. We will postulate an ALU that can do such multibit shifts, and will discuss how multibit shifts are actually accomplished (with the aid of the "barrel shifter") in Chapter 6.

Additional Hardware.   Pipeline designs usually need additional hardware to provide the extra speed. A likely candidate is a separate incrementer to increment the PC, freeing the ALU to be used for arithmetic operations. There will also be a number of multiplexers used to route information where it is desired in the data path.

5.1.3 DESIGN TECHNIQUE

The SRC instruction set will be used to demonstrate the process of actually designing a pipelined architecture. We will implement the instruction set described by the abstract RTN developed in Chapter 2. We do not employ the reset or exception handling features developed in Chapter 4, as they introduce complications best avoided in an initial design. We do, however, discuss the impact that exceptions have on the pipeline design later in this section.

The instruction set is of primary importance in governing the structure and function of the pipeline. Therefore the pipeline design effort begins by examining how various classes of machine instructions map to a pipeline structure. Having developed a sense for how the various instruction classes "fit" into a pipeline, the details of the pipeline's data path are refined so that all instructions are accommodated within it. Having the details of the pipeline data path, control signals are added to manage the flow of instructions through the pipe. The design is finalized by developing the hardware to handle data dependences in the pipeline: hazard control. We follow this design process in developing the pipelined design for SRC.

Classifying Instructions. We can classify or partition the SRC instructions by their overall register transfer behavior, that is, by how and where data flows during instruction execution. (The classes will turn out to be three: load/store, ALU, and branch.) In order to better show the behavior of the instruction classes, we will depict their operations graphically as a function of the step of the instruction in which the operation occurs. We use the same five steps summarized in Figure 5.1: (1) instruction fetch, (2) decode and operand access, (3) ALU operations, (4) data memory access, and (5) register write. These five steps of register transfer activity will become five pipeline stages when the appropriate pipeline registers and data path control have been added.

Progressing Stage by Stage. Figure 5.2 shows the five stages of activity for an ALU operation. The details of the operation of the various components of Figure 5.2 will emerge in the discussion that follows. Note again that these are not pipeline stages at this point, since only one instruction can be executing at one time. The step labels in this figure partition the instruction into its behavior at each clock cycle of fetch and execution. Stages are delimited by the dashed lines in the figure.

In interpreting Figure 5.2, note that data are clocked from stage to stage, 1 clock cycle per stage. The registers on the dotted lines form the interface between stages. Registers are numbered according to the stage to which they provide input. All registers are assumed to consist of edge-triggered or master-slave flip-flops. The registers at the top of a given stage are input registers to the stage, and are read at the beginning of the clock cycle. The registers at the bottom of a given stage are the stage's output registers, and are written at the trailing edge of the clock pulse.

Opcode-Based Control Signals. Before presenting the hardware design, we need to specify some control signals that will be needed to control the flow through the pipeline. The gathering of opcodes into groups with similar properties continues to be useful in generating

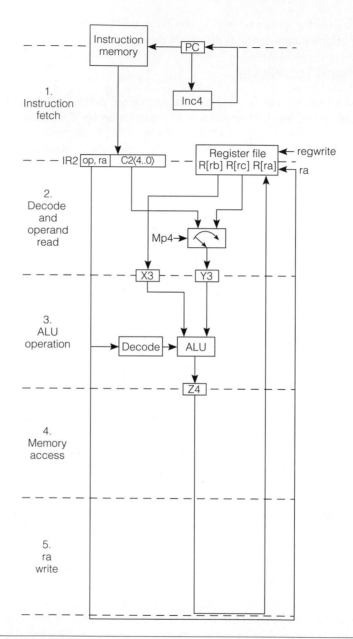

Fig. 5.2 ALU Operations Including Shifts

the signals that control the register transfers through the pipeline. The control signals shown in Figure 5.3 will be needed.

Some notes about Figure 5.3 are in order: cond and imm are used only in step 2, so IR2, the instruction register for stage 2, is used as the register from which their signals are generated. The other signals in the figure will be required in several different stages. In this

branch := br ∨ brl :
cond := (IR2⟨2..0⟩=1) ∨ ((IR2⟨2..1⟩=1) ∧ (IR2⟨0⟩⊕R[rc]=0)) ∨
           ((IR2⟨2..1⟩=2)∧(¬IR2⟨0⟩⊕R[rc]⟨31⟩)):
sh := shr ∨ shra ∨ shl ∨ shc :   Shifts
alu := add ∨ addi ∨ sub ∨ neg ∨ and ∨ andi ∨ or ∨ ori ∨ not ∨ sh :
imm := addi ∨ andi ∨ ori ∨ (sh ∧ (IR⟨4..0⟩ ≠ 0)):   Immediate operand
load := ld ∨ ldr :   Load instructions
ladr := la ∨ lar :   Load address instructions
store := st ∨ str :   Store instructions
l-s := load ∨ ladr ∨ store :   Memory address instructions
regwrite := load ∨ ladr ∨ brl ∨ alu: Instructions that write to the register file
dsp := ld ∨ st ∨ la :   Instructions that use disp addressing
rl := ldr ∨ str ∨ lar :   Instructions that use rel addressing

Fig. 5.3 Control Signals Needed to Describe Pipeline Stage Activity

latter case a number is appended to the signal name to show which stage generates it. For example, branch2 is generated in stage 2 from IR2 by testing the opcode field in IR2.

ALU Instructions. All the ALU operations, including shifts, are described by Figure 5.2. We have made good on our promise to add separate instruction memory and data memory. We have also added a PC incrementer separate from the ALU, a 3-port register file, and several registers used for temporary operand and result storage. In this figure and those that follow we indicate the register file address inputs by the lowercase specifiers ra, rb, and rc, and register file data inputs and outputs as R[ra], R[rb], R[rc]. Let us follow the progression of the fetch and execution of the ALU instructions stage by stage as illustrated in Figure 5.2.

Stage 1. The instruction pointed to by the PC is fetched from instruction memory, and the PC is incremented. At the end of the cycle, IR2 and the PC are updated with their new contents.

Stage 2. The instruction is read from IR2 and decoded. It is an ALU instruction. Recall that all ALU and shift operations are of the following forms:

R[ra] ← R[rb] op R[rc]; Register form
R[ra] ← R[rb] op c2⟨16..0⟩; Immediate form

with the exception that the shift operations contain the shift count in c2⟨4..0⟩ if it is ≠0, or in R[rc] if c2⟨4..0⟩ = 0. Therefore, stage 2 fetches either R[rb] and R[rc] or R[rb] and c2. R[rb] is stored in temporary register X3. The little "switch box" is a set of 32 2–1 multiplexers, with the control labeled Mp4. The control selects either c2 or R[rc] for input to Y3 depending on whether the instruction is immediate or register:

Y3 ← (imm → c2: ¬imm → R[rc]): Second ALU operand

The signal imm is derived from the op field of IR2 according to the equation for imm in Figure 5.3 and is used to control Mp4.

Stage 3. The instruction is decoded to select the proper ALU operation, and the result is stored in temporary register Z4.

Stage 4. Since there is no memory access in ALU instructions, nothing happens in this stage.

Stage 5. In this stage the result in register Z4 is stored in R[ra]. Notice that both the value stored in Z4 and the register number stored in the ra field of IR2 are needed at this stage. The regwrite signal, defined previously will be true, enabling the write into the register file.

The temporary registers between stages, such as X3, Y3, and Z4, become very important when we combine the step-by-step operation of the several instruction classes into one pipeline design.

Load and Store Instructions.   Figure 5.4 shows the family of memory access instructions, ld, ldr, st, and str. The load and store instructions have identical memory address computations, and differ only in stage 4, the memory access stage. Once again, we discuss the instruction fetch and execute stage by stage. Here is the RTN for this class of instruction:

ld (:= op = 1) → R[ra] ← M[disp]:Load register
ldr (:= op = 2) → R[ra] ← M[rel]:Load register relative
st (:= op = 3) → M[disp] ← R[ra]:Store register
str (:= op = 4) → M[rel] ← R[ra]:Store register relative
la (:= op = 5) → R[ra] ← disp:Load displacement address
lar (:= op = 6) → R[ra] ← rel:Load relative address
disp⟨31..0⟩ := ((rb = 0) → c2⟨16..0⟩ {sign ext.}:Displacement
        (rb ≠ 0) → R[rb] + c2⟨16..0⟩ {sign ext., 2's comp.}):address
rel⟨31..0⟩ := PC⟨31..0⟩ + c1⟨21..0⟩ {sign ext., 2's comp.}:Relative address

Stage 1. Instruction fetch and PC increment, as before, with incremented value of PC recorded in PC2.

Stage 2. Operand fetch. If the addressing mode is relative, then PC2 and c1 are routed into X3 and Y3. If the addressing mode is disp, then R[rb] and c2 are routed into X3 and Y3. If the instruction is a store instruction, then R[ra] is copied from the register file into MD3. The logic to control Mp3 and Mp4 is derived from the following equations:

$$X3 ← (rl → PC2: dsp → R[rb]): \text{1st address component}$$
$$Y3 ← (rl → c1: dsp → c2): \text{2nd address component}$$

where once again rl and dsp are derived from the op field of IR2 as defined in Figure 5.3.

Stage 3. The relative or displacement address is computed by adding X3 and Y3. The results are stored in Z4.

Stage 4. If the instruction is a load from data memory, either ld or ldr, then the value in data memory at the address in Z4 is copied into Z5. If the instruction is a la or lar, then the address in Z4 is copied directly into Z5. If the instruction is a store, then the value in MD3 is written into data memory at the address stored in Z4.

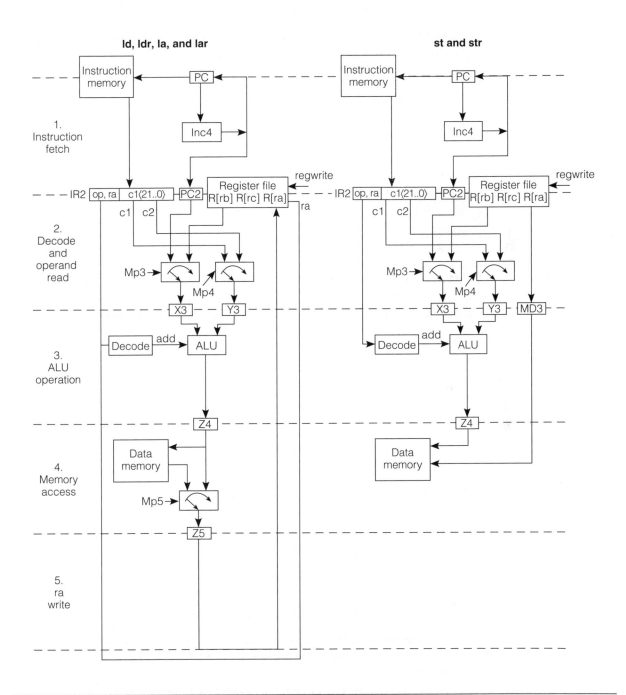

Fig. 5.4 The Memory Access Instructions: ld, ldr, st, and str

Stage 5. If the instruction is a load of any kind, then once again regwrite will be true, and the value stored in Z5 will be written into the register file at the register address stored in the ra field of IR2.

Branch Instructions. The branch instructions form a different class of instructions, as they must change the value of the PC by essentially feeding back a new value into the PC. The RTN for the branch instructions follows:

$$
\begin{array}{lll}
\text{cond} := (c3\langle 2..0\rangle = 0 \rightarrow 0: & & \text{Never} \\
\quad c3\langle 2..0\rangle = 1 \rightarrow 1: & & \text{Always} \\
\quad c3\langle 2..0\rangle = 2 \rightarrow R[rc] = 0: & & \text{If register is zero} \\
\quad c3\langle 2..0\rangle = 3 \rightarrow R[rc] \neq 0: & & \text{If register is nonzero} \\
\quad c3\langle 2..0\rangle = 4 \rightarrow R[rc]\langle 31\rangle = 0: & & \text{If positive or zero} \\
\quad c3\langle 2..0\rangle = 5 \rightarrow R[rc]\langle 31\rangle = 1): & & \text{If negative} \\
\text{br } (:= op = 8) \rightarrow (\text{cond} \rightarrow PC \leftarrow R[rb]): & & \text{Conditional branch} \\
\text{brl } (:= op = 9) \rightarrow (R[ra] \leftarrow PC: \text{cond} \rightarrow (PC \leftarrow R[rb])): & & \text{Branch and link}
\end{array}
$$

The condition calculated from $c3\langle 2..0\rangle$ and R[rc] is used to decide whether the PC should be replaced with R[rb]. Figure 5.5 shows how the two instructions behave. In the previous instruction classes, the values of PC and PC2 were the same. In the branch instructions, if the branch is taken, then the PC receives the new branch address, stored in R[rb]. If the instruction is brl, the value of the old PC is incremented and then stored in PC2, to be written into R[ra], the link register, in stage 5, regardless of whether the branch is taken or not. Mp1 is controlled according to the following equation:

$$\text{cond(IR2, R[rc])} \rightarrow PC \leftarrow R[rb]: X3 \leftarrow PC2: \text{Conditional new PC}$$

A Word About the Global State. The registers at each pipeline stage shown in Figures 5.2, 5.4, and 5.5 contain information about the state of the instruction executing at each stage in the pipeline; the register file and data and instruction memories represent the global state of the machine, and do not "belong" to any pipeline stage. For example, values are read from the register file in stage 2, and written into it in stage 5, so even though the register file is shown as being in stage 2, it should not be considered as part of the stage 2 state.

The Instruction Set. We have now rationalized the entire instruction set except for the stop instruction, which is left as an exercise. A study of the three previous figures shows that all the instructions fit the five-stage model, with only minor differences in hardware and control. This model could be used to execute the entire instruction set as long as each instruction is allowed to execute to completion before the next is allowed to be fetched. We now proceed to modify the preceding data paths so that we can issue a new instruction at each clock cycle.

5.1.4 DESIGNING THE PIPELINED DATA PATH

As already discussed, all information pertaining to the instruction that will be used in subsequent stages, both instruction and data, must be propagated through the pipeline in the pipeline registers.

Adding Hardware and Control to Support Pipelining. We begin by adding the pipeline registers and the associated multiplexers. This process is greatly simplified by having compressed the instruction set and control signals into classes. Without this simplifying step, each instruction would need to be considered separately, and there are nearly 30 instructions. This process proceeds by carefully examining Figures 5.2, 5.4, and 5.5 and determining which information needs to be propagated to the next stage, proceeding from top to bottom and left to right.

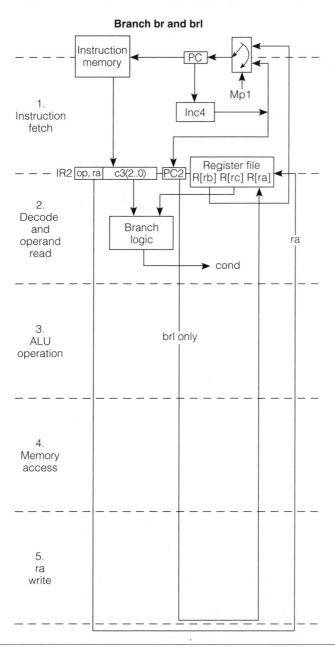

Fig. 5.5 The Branch Instructions

RTN and the Pipeline Design.   We now describe the pipeline registers and the RTN that controls the data flow through the pipeline. Figure 5.6 shows all of the pipeline registers and the RTN descriptions of the flow of all the instructions through the pipeline. This figure captures the essence of a pipelined design for SRC. It combines all the data path (pipeline) registers, and the actions specified for the different instruction classes in Figures 5.2, 5.4, and 5.5. The number of pipeline registers can be minimized by using the same one for several instruction classes, often at the expense of adding a multiplexer at the pipeline register's inputs. Work on a figure of this kind is usually started as the individual instruction classes are being considered, and its details are fleshed out as their treatment proceeds.

Notice that control signals are labeled with the stage from which they are computed. The equation

$$PC \leftarrow (branch2 \rightarrow PC + 4 : branch2 \rightarrow (cond(IR2, R[rc]) \rightarrow R[rb]:$$
$$\neg cond(IR2, R[rc]) \rightarrow PC + 4)):$$

shown in stage 2, describes the loading of the PC. If there is *not* a branch instruction in stage 2, then the PC is incremented by hardware in stage 1. If stage 2 (that is, IR2) does contain a branch instruction and if the branch condition determined by the value of IR2$\langle 2..0 \rangle$ is true, then the PC is replaced by R[rb]. You should study this figure and its relationship to Figures 5.2, 5.4, and 5.5, noting the additional pipeline registers, and verifying that the RTN of Figure 5.6 does allow the instructions to execute as before.

The IR register must be propagated from stage to stage to provide information to its instruction. A number has been added to the register name to indicate in which stage it is used: IR2 in the second stage, IR3 in the third, and so on. The specific fields and where they are used are also indicated. All of the fields in IR2—op, ra, rb, rc, c1, and c2—are used in stage 2. Stages 3, 4, and 5 require only the op field and the ra field. In stage 3 the ALU instructions require the opcode field to determine which ALU operation to perform. Stage 4 requires the same field to supply the load and store instructions with the information they will need to control data memory access, and stage 5 requires ra to tell its instruction which register in the register file to write its value into and op to tell the stage whether a register write is required.

Z4, the ALU output register, will contain a memory address if the instruction is a load or store; it will contain the incremented PC if the instruction is a brl, and it will contain the ALU result if the instruction is an ALU instruction. Z5 will contain

- an address if the instruction is a la or lar,
- a memory value if the instruction is a ld or ldr,
- the old PC if the instruction is a brl, and
- the ALU result if the instruction is an ALU operation.

Lastly, MD3 must be propagated to MD4 for a data memory write.

Figure 5.7 shows the hardware needed to implement the operations defined in Figure 5.6, and now it includes the multiplexers that implement the register transfers shown in Figure 5.6.

The labeling has been changed on the inputs and outputs of the register file. Now the address inputs are labeled a1, a2, and a3, and the corresponding data inputs and outputs labeled R1, R2, and R3. This change is necessary because the store instructions read R[ra]

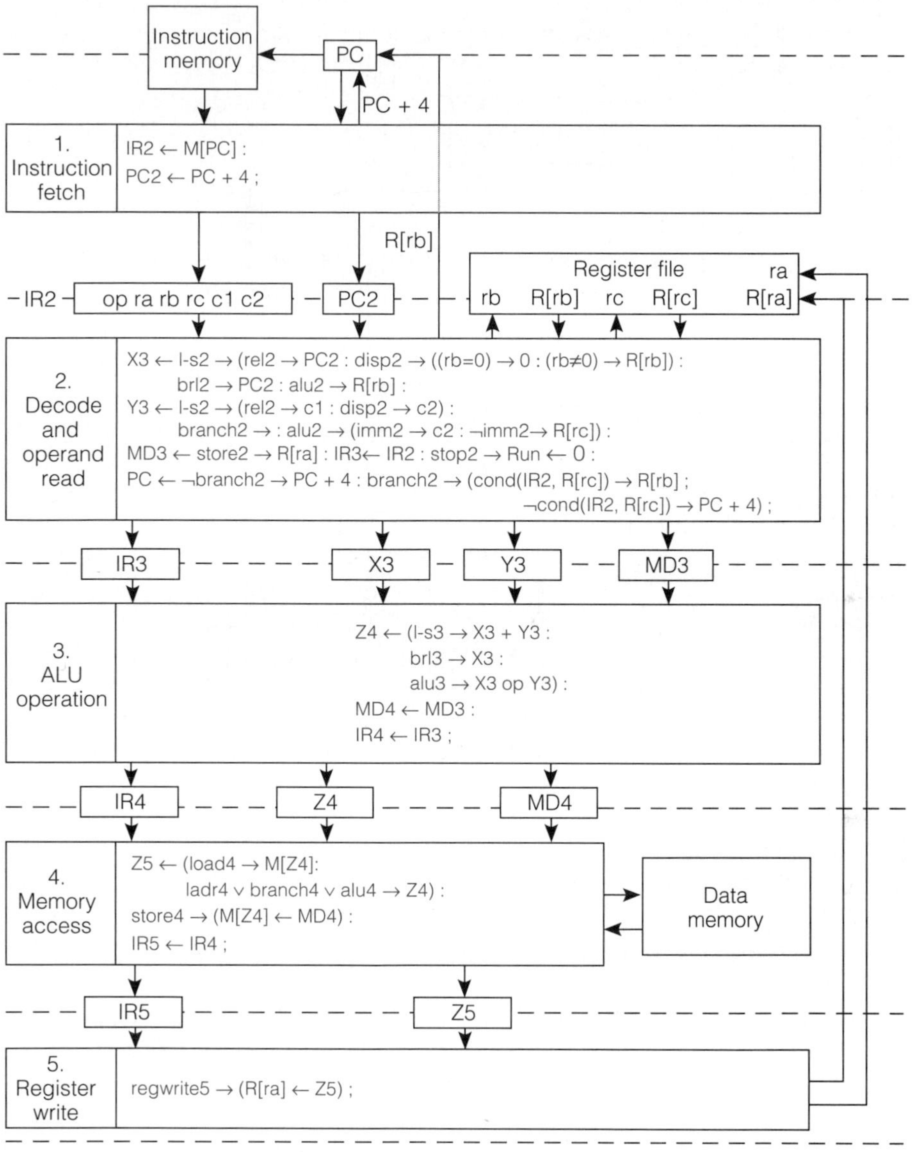

Fig. 5.6 The SRC Pipeline Registers and RTN Specification

in stage 2, instead of using rb or rc as all other instructions do. The figure indicates which register field from the instruction, ra, rb, or rc, is sent to which address input, a1, a2, or a3. The corresponding gate signals are G1, G2, and GA1. The latter serves the same purpose as the BA_{out} signal in Figure 4.4, to gate out all zeros if R0 is selected, as part of the disp calculation. The strobe signal to write into register a3 is W3.

As before, multiplexers, now labeled Mp1 to Mp5, are used to allow the pipeline registers to have multiple input sources. The multiplexer output equations are shown on the side

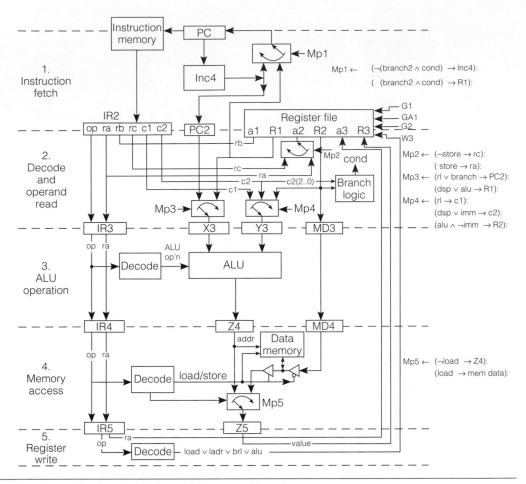

Fig. 5.7 The Pipeline Data Path with Selected Control Signals

of the figure. For example, Mp4 has three inputs, c1, c2, and R2. The c1 input will be selected if the instruction in stage 2 is one of the three rel instructions, ldr, str, and lar. The second multiplexer input, c2, is selected if the instruction in stage 2 is one of the imm instructions defined previously; the three immediate instructions, addi, andi, or ori: if it is one of the three instructions that uses the disp addressing mode, ld, st, or la, or if it is a shift instruction and the shift count in the least significant 5 bits of $c2 \neq 0$. The third multiplexer position, selecting R2, is chosen if the instruction is an ALU instruction and not immediate, or if it is a shift instruction and the shift count in the least significant 5 bits of $c2 = 0$.

There is a complication in the register operand access in stage 2 caused by the store instructions. In all other instructions, rb and rc specify source operands to be accessed in stage 2, and ra specifies the register into which the result is to be stored in stage 5. In the store instructions, R[ra] contains the value of the operand to be fetched out of the register file in stage 2 and stored in data memory in stage 5. Multiplexer Mp2 is used to route ra instead of rc to register read address port a2 in this case. The value fetched, R[ra], is copied into MD3, to be stored in memory in stage 4.

Generating the Control Signals.   Unlike the monolithic control units that generated the control signals for the machines in the last chapter, the generation of control signals is distributed throughout the stages of the pipeline. This should not come as a complete surprise, since each instruction carries along the opcode field for that very purpose. Furthermore, most control signals that are generated in a given stage are also used in that stage, with a few specific exceptions, such as the PC control already described. Figure 5.7 shows the control signals that control the data flow through the multiplexers, and the gate and strobe signals that control reading and writing the register file. Of course, each register must have a strobe signal that controls the writing of data into it as well. Notice, however, that all the paths are point-to-point, so no gating signals are required except at the multiplexers.

The RTN in Figure 5.7 provides sufficient information to generate all of the gate and strobe signals in the data path. However, there are some special cases relating to pipeline hazards that we will cover later.

5.1.5 PROPAGATING AN INSTRUCTION SEQUENCE THROUGH THE PIPELINE

This section will trace the flow of five instructions through the pipeline. The instructions and their memory addresses follow:

```
100:    add r4, r6, r8   ;R[4] ← R[6]+R[8]
104:    ld r7, 128(r5)   ;R[7] ← M[R[5]+128]
108:    brl r9, r11, 001 ;PC ← R[11](=512):R[9] ← PC
112:    str r12, 32      ;M[PC+32] ← R[12]
        ......
512:    sub ...          ;next instr ...
```

Figures 5.8 through 5.12 depict the flow of these instructions through the pipeline, beginning with the fetch of the add instruction, and finishing with the fetch of the sub instruction. Assume that the PC has been initialized to 100, and that the register file contains the values shown in Figures 5.8 through 5.12. The active data and data path are shown in black lines; the remainder of the pipeline has been grayed out. The figures depict the state of affairs after the data have been read from registers and passed through all combinational logic blocks, but before the trailing edge of the clock has clocked it into the next stage's registers.

We urge you to study this sequence of figures carefully. The figures are best understood by focusing on a given stage, input registers first. Examine the IR register first of all, and identify the instruction and its data flow. Follow it from top to bottom and left to right. Ignore all the stages except the one being studied. A key point to understand is that no stage influences any other stage during a given clock cycle!

First Clock Cycle: add Enters the Pipeline.   In Figure 5.8 the PC contains 100, the address of the add instruction being fetched from instruction memory, and the incrementer has incremented the value in the PC to 104, the address of the next instruction. The 104 value "waits at the doors" of PC and PC2 for the trailing edge of the clock to clock them in, and thus begin the next clock cycle. The figure shows the add instruction having been fetched and awaiting clocking into IR2. Notice that stages 2 through 5 are grayed out, as we have no information about what is occurring in them.

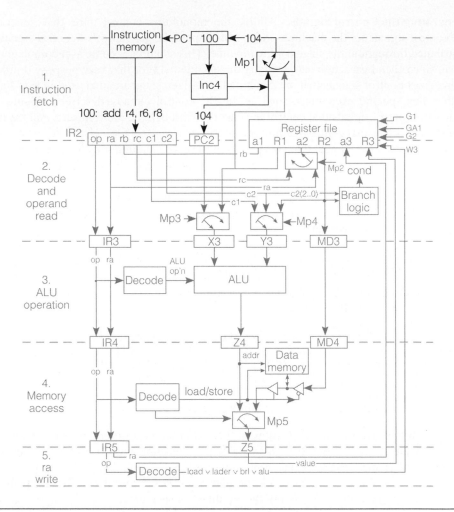

Fig. 5.8 First Clock Cycle: **add** Enters Stage 1 of the Pipeline

Second Clock Cycle: add Moves to Stage 2; ld Enters the Pipeline.   Figure 5.9 shows the state of affairs toward the end of the next clock cycle. The add instruction is now executing in stage 2. Its operands, stored in r6 and r8, having the values 4 and 5, have been fetched from the register file in preparation for being clocked into X3 and Y3, and op and ra are being sent to IR3.

Meanwhile, back at stage 1, the instruction at address 104, a ld instruction, has been fetched and awaits clocking into IR2. The value in the PC, 104, has been incremented and awaits being clocked into PC and PC2.

Third Clock Cycle: add Moves to Stage 3, ld Moves to Stage 2, brl Enters the Pipeline.   In Figure 5.10 the add instruction has moved to stage 3. Its operands reside in X3 and Y3, the op in IR3 has been decoded and has sent the add command to the ALU. The result value, 9, awaits clocking into Z4, and add and ra await clocking into IR4.

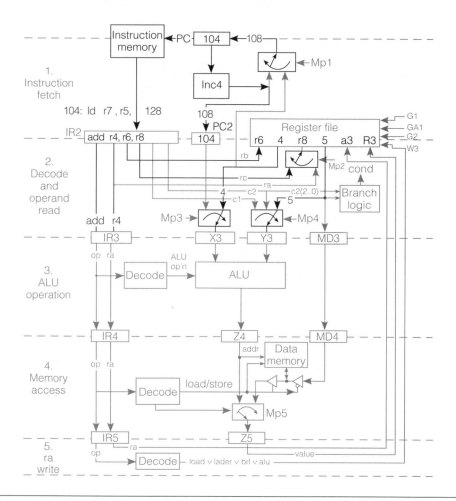

Fig. 5.9 Second Clock Cycle: **add** Enters Stage 2, While **ld** is being Fetched at Stage 1

Meanwhile, in stage 2, the ld instruction has been decoded. The ld uses the disp mode, where the operand memory address is gotten by adding R[rb] to c1. In this specific case, rb is r5, and c1 is 128. Thus the figure depicts the contents of r5, 16, being routed to the inputs of X3, and c1, 128, being routed to the inputs of Y3. The op and ra fields, ld and r7 in this case, await clocking into IR3.

At stage 1, the instruction at 108, brl, has been fetched and awaits clocking into IR2. The PC has been incremented to 112, and that value will be clocked into PC and PC2 at the falling edge.

Fourth Clock Cycle: add Moves to Stage 4, ld to 3, brl to 2, and str Enters the Pipeline. In Figure 5.11 add has moved to stage 4. Since add does not access data memory, the opcode and ra move to IR5, and the ALU result, 9, is gated to the inputs of Z5.

Stage 3 now contains the ld instruction. The memory address is calculated in this stage by adding the contents of X3 and Y3. The result, 144, awaits clocking into Z4.

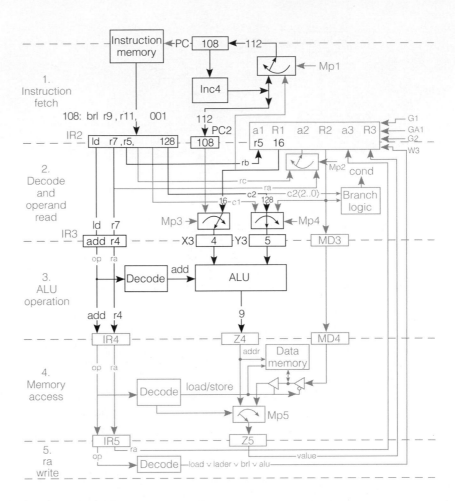

Fig. 5.10 Third Clock Cycle: **brl** Enters the Pipeline

Stage 2 contains the brl instruction. Thus, op and ra, the link register, will be loaded into IR3. The cond field of the instruction, having value 001, branch always, has been gated onto the c2 bus, and into the branch logic, where "always" (=1) is sent to the control input of Mp1 in stage 1. The condition (branch ∧ cond) is thus true, so Mp1 gates the branch target, the contents of rb = r11, 512, to the inputs of PC. Notice that now the input to PC is 512, so at the next clock cycle the instruction at the branch target, 512, will be fetched.

Here we finally see in detail why there is a branch delay slot, as noted on page 193. While the branch target address is being retrieved from the register file in stage 2, the next instruction, str, at location 112, is being fetched from instruction memory in stage 1. Under the decree of branch delay, that str instruction will proceed through the pipeline regardless of whether the branch is taken, thus keeping the pipeline full. If there were no branch delay, a nop instruction would need to be placed after every branch instruction. It also now becomes clear why we need PC and PC2: At the beginning of the next clock cycle

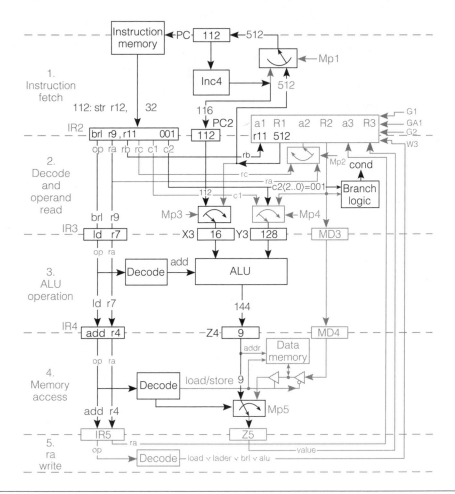

Fig. 5.11 Fourth Clock Cycle: str Enters the Pipeline

PC will contain the branch target address 512, while PC2 will contain 116, which will be used to compute the PC-relative address needed by the str instruction. We will discuss the branch delay problem and other similar instruction dependence issues in Section 5.2, "Pipeline Hazards."

Fifth Clock Cycle: add Completes, ld Loads, brl Propagates, str Gets Its Operands, sub Is Fetched. In the fifth clock cycle, shown in Figure 5.12, our old friend the add instruction completes its execution. The result operand, 9, and the register address, r4, are gated to the inputs of the register file. Notice that the value is not written into the register file until the end of stage 5, and thus is not available as register contents until the next clock cycle. This important fact is discussed in the next section.

In stage 4, the ld instruction's memory address, 144, is conveyed to the data memory along with the read control signal obtained by decoding the op field of IR4. The operand, 55, has been fetched from data memory, and appears at the inputs to Z5; op and ra are gated from IR4 to the inputs of IR5.

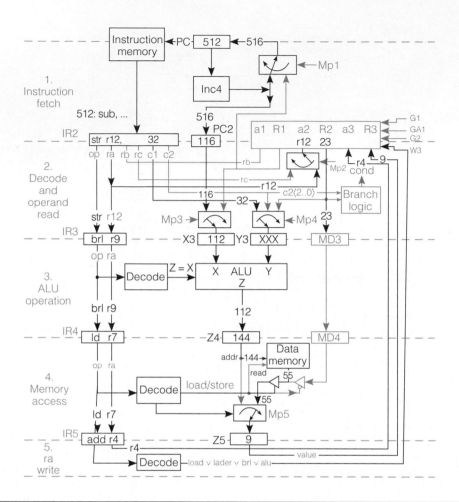

Fig. 5.12 Fifth Clock Cycle: **add** Completes, **sub** Enters the Pipeline

In stage 3 our `brl` instruction has little to do but gate the link value, 112, from X3 to the inputs to Z4. This is accomplished by the stage 3 instruction decoder, which has decoded the op field and sent the appropriate ALU control, Z = X, to the ALU control inputs.

Stage 2 is fetching the operands for the `str` instruction, M[PC + 32] ← R[r12]. The register operand, `r12`, is stored in the ra field, so the ra field is routed to the right input of Mp2, into the a2 address input of the register file. The value in r12, 23, is gated to the inputs of the MD3 register. Meanwhile, the memory address must be computed from PC + c1, so PC is gated to the inputs of X3, and c1 is gated through the leftmost input of Mp4 to the inputs of Y3.

In stage 1, the `sub` instruction has been fetched from the branch target address, 512, and so it goes.

The flow of instructions through a pipeline can be confusing at first. We urge you to go over these figures several times, and then to practice by following a made-up instruction sequence through the pipeline to gain a clear understanding of the process.

5.2 Pipeline Hazards

> **hazard** *n* **1** : a game of chance like craps played with two dice. **2** : a source of danger. **3 a** : CHANCE, RISK **b** : a chance event : ACCIDENT
> – *Merriam-Webster's Collegiate Dictionary*

Pipeline hazards are entirely predictable, deterministic events that occur as side effects of having instructions in the pipeline that depend upon the results of instructions ahead of them that have not exited the pipeline—there is no element of chance. Thus when speaking of pipeline hazards, we should use Merriam and Webster's definition 2. The element of hazard or danger comes only from a rogue compiler or assembly language programmer who has not properly taken the pipeline's behavior into account when compiling or writing the program. On the other hand, the compiler must make a static, compile-time analysis of hazards, which cannot predict the direction that conditional branches will take at run time. Therefore, the compiler's estimate must be the most pessimistic one. The assembly language programmer is more "hazardous" to the correct execution of a program written for a pipelined processor, because of the well-known tendency for human beings to make errors due to carelessness and inattention.

pipeline hazards

Pipeline hazards can be classed by the kind of instruction that causes them. There are several ways of making this classification. We will group the hazards as data hazards and branch hazards.

5.2.1 DATA HAZARDS

Read after write, or RAW Data hazards are hazards in which an instruction modifies a register or memory location, and a succeeding instruction attempts to access the data in that register or memory location before the register or memory location has actually been updated. In the SRC pipeline, instructions that modify the register file and data memory are alu, load, store, and brl. Instruction classes that access the register file and data memory include alu, load, ladr, store, and branch. We discuss two other kinds of hazards, write after write, WAW, and write after read, WAR, on page 219.

data hazards

Example 5.1 Finding and Characterizing a RAW Pipeline Data Hazard Consider the following two instructions:

```
100: add r0, r2, r4
104: sub r3, r0, r1
```

Notice that the add instruction modifies r0, and the sub instruction reads r0. We know from Figure 5.7 that the add instruction will not update r0 until the end of stage 5, while the sub instruction needs that value in stage 2. This is a pipeline data hazard.

In the absence of any special hardware to detect this hazard, by how much must the two instructions be separated to prevent the hazard? Since r0 will not be updated until the end of the clock cycle when add is in stage 5, the value will not be available in the register file until add has left the pipeline. Thus sub can be no closer than stage 1 when add is in stage 5, a separation of four instructions!

To anticipate our subsequent discussion of data forwarding, note that the result operand of the add instruction is actually available in register Z4 when the sub instruction requires it, in stage 3. Forwarding hardware can be designed to detect this particular hazard and to forward the value to register Y3 in time for the sub instruction to use it.   ∎

Data hazards are caused by data dependences.   The task in determining all possible data hazards in a given pipeline structure and instruction set is to consider all possible interactions between all instructions at all stages in the pipeline. This may seem to be a daunting task, but it is made simpler once again by grouping instructions by their classes based on their writing and reading behavior. We will first consider the example of a pair of ALU instructions, and then analyze the entire SRC instruction set. You will probably want to consult Figures 5.6 and 5.7 for reference as we discuss the various combinations of when data is written and read in the pipeline.

The ALU instructions are both writers of data and readers of data. As Example 5.1 showed, there is potential for a data hazard between ALU instructions: They prepare to write data to the register file in stage 5, but the data does not actually enter the register file and become available for reading by subsequent instructions until the instructions have exited the pipeline, to a fictitious "stage 6." On the other hand, ALU instructions read all their data in stage 2. Thus, in the absence of some hardware trick, ALU instructions that access a register that has been written by a previous instruction must be separated from that instruction by at least four instructions.

"stage 6"

While ALU instructions don't write to the register file until "stage 6," the data is actually available in Z4 when the ALU instruction is in stage 4. And although the second ALU instruction normally reads its operands in stage 2, it does not actually use the operands until stage 3, when the ALU operation is performed. We can envision hardware that would detect the hazard between the two instructions, and would forward the data from Z4 to the proper ALU input in the previous stage. This hardware solution to the problem of data hazards is known as *data forwarding*.

data forwarding

Implementing data forwarding for ALU instructions requires further analysis. First, we associate with the ALU instructions a pair of numbers: the stage where the data are Normally Available, and the stage where data are Earliest Available. For the ALU writer, this Normally Available/Earliest Available pair would be 6/4. The ALU reader also has a pair of stages associated with its register-reading requirements: Normally Required and Latest Required. For the ALU reader, this Normally Required/Latest Required pair is 2/3. By taking the pairwise difference, we obtain the Normal/Forwarded minimum spacing for the ALU pair as $(6 - 2)/(4 - 3) = 4/1$. This says that ALU instructions *must* be separated by at least four stages unless there is a forwarding scheme, and then they need be separated by only one stage.

Table 5.1 displays these values for all pairwise combinations. The Normal/Earliest stage values for the writers are shown in the top shaded area of the table, and the Normal/Latest stage values for readers are shown in the left shaded area. The resulting Normal/Forwarded no-hazard requirements for instruction pairs are shown in the boxed rectangle in the lower right of the figure. The Normal no-hazard distance is 4 for all instructions—a dismal result from the standpoint of the goal of issuing one instruction per clock cycle. The Earliest value is more encouraging: It is 1 for most instruction pairs, although the load instruction has a minimum distance of 2 from all instructions except branch, where it is 3. This is the cause of the unavoidable "delayed load" discussed on page 193.

Table 5.1 Data Dependences for the Modifier Instructions

	Instruction Class		alu	load	ladr	brl
			6/4	**6/5**	**6/4**	**6/2**
	alu	2/3	4/1	4/2	4/1	4/1
	load	2/3	4/1	4/2	4/1	4/1
	ladr	2/3	4/1	4/2	4/1	4/1
	store (rb)	2/3	4/1	4/2	4/1	4/1
	store (ra)	2/4	4/1	4/1	4/1	4/1
	branch	2/2	4/2	4/3	4/2	4/1

The top header spans: **Write to Register File** / **Data Available Normal/Earliest, Stage** over the alu, load, ladr, brl columns. The left vertical label reads *Read from Register File Normal/Latest, Stage*. A brace at the right of the alu/load/ladr/brl columns is labeled "Normal/ forwarded no hazard".

Table 5.1 considers only register writes and subsequent register reads, although it does cover hazards due to loads from data memory to the register file. What are the data hazards associated with stores? Fortunately, the only possible hazard after a store is a subsequent load, since only the load instructions access data memory, and since both stores and loads happen in stage 4, there is no hazard.

Branch Hazards.   We have discussed the unavoidable branch delay before, on page 193. Avoiding this problem is difficult because it requires determining the new PC value by the instruction fetch stage. But all that is known at fetch time is the address of the instruction, not the outcome of a branch test, or even whether the instruction is a branch. Reducing branch delay must therefore be based on speculation. By keeping information on whether the instruction previously encountered at a particular address was a branch and what the new PC value turned out to be, a prediction can be made for the new PC value. Delay only occurs if the prediction turns out to be wrong, in which case the incorrect instruction fetch must be corrected and the prediction information associated with the instruction address must be updated.

Despite the difficulties, *branch prediction* schemes can be made very successful. They can succeed 80% to 90% of the time, depending on the code being executed, and make a major improvement in performance. Branch prediction is beyond the scope of this book. It is based on the use of cache memory, not discussed until Chapter 7. It is an important feature of the design of a large majority of modern processors. To mention some terminology associated with the topic, the cache memory used with branch prediction is called the *branch target buffer* (*BTB*). The BTB may occupy a large fraction of the area of a processor chip.

branch prediction

BTB, branch target buffer

5.2.2   HAZARD DETECTION AND RESOLUTION

The potential for hazards to occur will exist in any architecture that has more than one instruction executing simultaneously. The hazards can be detected by hardware at run time, or by software at compile time. When hazards are detected by hardware, they can be resolved by either stalling the pipeline or by forwarding operands as soon as they become available, rather than stalling the pipeline until the register file has been updated.

Hazard Detection in the Compiler, Resolved by the Compiler.   It is possible to place the burden of hazard detection and elimination on the compiler. The compiler can analyze the code sequence and either rearrange the instructions to remove the hazard or, not finding a possible rearrangement, can insert nop instructions as software bubbles in the pipeline. A pipeline *bubble* is a nop instruction placed between instructions that form a hazard. The compiler may need to insert several bubbles between "staller" and "stallee," depending on the nature of the dependence. Likewise, if branch and load delay slots are permitted, that is, if the hardware allows the decrees discussed on page 193, then the compiler can attempt to find candidate instructions and move them to follow the load or branch instruction.

pipeline bubble

This "let George do it" philosophy of off-loading the hazard detection and removal duties to the compiler has a number of disadvantages. It puts an additional burden on the compiler writer, who may be a third party, to develop a compiler that is both correct and efficient. This will result in compilers that are more expensive, bigger, later to market, and possibly buggy, especially when asked to optimize the emitted code. The result is less customer satisfaction with the processor. An even more serious problem is that without hardware detection there can be no data forwarding, and consequently no reduction in the no-hazard distance of four instructions. Furthermore, the compiler must perform a "static" analysis of the code. That is, it must assume the most pessimistic of stances regarding the direction of branches, since at compile time it cannot predict with certainty which direction a conditional branch will take. It must analyze both directions and emit code that is correct in the worst case.

Hazard Detection by Hardware, Resolved by Pipeline Stalls.   Because of the limitations involved with letting the compiler deal with hazard detection, we will focus more attention on the hardware solution of data forwarding. The basis for hardware hazard detection is to test for hazards at each place where they can occur, as described in Table 5.1. We will use the 2-operand ALU-ALU instruction pairs to illustrate the process of detecting a data hazard. We first show how to resolve the hazard by inserting bubbles in the pipeline. The following facts about the pipeline describe the situation:

1. The minimum spacing that must be observed between data-dependent instructions to avoid a data hazard in the absence of data forwarding is four instructions.
2. The dependent instruction, the "stallee," must be paused at stage 2 until the hazard has been resolved, because it cannot complete its operand fetch until the operand has been written to the register file. The instruction behind it in stage 1 must also be held in stage 1 as long as the pipeline is stalled.
3. The two dependent instructions may be one, two, or three instructions apart, so hazard detection hardware must detect all three of these cases.

4. The "staller" must be allowed to continue through the pipeline until it has exited, and any intervening instructions between staller and stallee should also be allowed to complete.

If the instructions are in adjoining stages, then the hazard must be detected in stage 3. We will describe the detection, stall, and bubble insertion process using RTN. The control signals described in Figure 5.3, with the appended digit telling which stage's IR is used to determine them, are what is needed to describe hazard detection.

You may wish to refer to Figure 5.14, which shows graphically the process of pipeline detection, stall, and bubble insertion, as we formally describe that process.

The following RTN expression detects data hazards between stages 2 and 3, stalls stages 1 and 2 for 1 clock cycle, and inserts a bubble in stage 3:

$$\text{alu3} \land \text{alu2} \land ((\text{ra3} = \text{rb2}) \lor ((\text{ra3} = \text{rc2}) \land \neg \text{imm2})) \qquad \textbf{5.1}$$
$$\rightarrow (\text{pause2: pause1: op3} \leftarrow 0) :$$

The expression states that if the opcodes in stages 2 and 3 are both alu, and if ra in stage 3 equals rb or rc in stage 2 (unless it is an immediate instruction, in which case there is no rc), there is a hazard between the instructions in stages 2 and 3. In that case, signals are emitted to pause pipeline stages 1 and 2 (pause1 and pause2), and to insert a bubble in the pipeline between the staller in stage 3 and the stallee in stage 2 (op3 ← 0).

The pause1 and pause2 control signals are used to inhibit the stage 1 and stage 2 clocks, respectively, so that the instructions in those stages remain there, and op3 ← 0 copies the nop opcode (op = 0) into the op field of IR3 at the falling edge of the current clock cycle. Thus, at the beginning of the next clock cycle, the staller has moved on to stage 4, there is a nop in stage 3, and the stallee in stage 2 and the instruction behind it in stage 1 are stalled in their current stages. The nop instruction in stage 3 becomes the bubble in the pipeline, propagating from stage to stage. Now a data dependence must be detected between instructions in stages 2 and 4.

The hazard detection hardware that detects a data hazard between stages 2 and 4 will cover two cases:

1. The hazard detected was originally a hazard between instructions in stages 2 and 3, as in the preceding case, that got a bubble inserted between them.

2. The hazard is between instructions that were originally two stages apart, and is thus detected for the first time when the instructions are in stages 2 and 4.

In both cases, the hazard must be detected, stages 1 and 2 again stalled, and a bubble inserted after the stallee in stage 2. The following RTN expression detects ALU hazards between stages 2 and 4, stalls stages 1 and 2 for 1 cycle, and inserts a bubble in stage 3:

$$\text{alu4} \land \text{alu2} \land ((\text{ra4} = \text{rb2}) \lor ((\text{ra4} = \text{rc2}) \land \neg \text{imm2})) \qquad \textbf{5.2}$$
$$\rightarrow (\text{pause2: pause1: op3} \leftarrow 0) :$$

RTN fragment 5.2 is identical to 5.1 except that IR4 replaces IR3, replacing alu3 and ra3 with alu4 and ra4. Stages 1 and 2 are stalled, and a new bubble is inserted in stage 3. If a bubble *had* been previously inserted in stage 3, then it moves to stage 4, and the staller moves to stage 5.

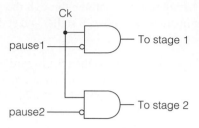

Fig. 5.13 Pipeline Clocking Signals

Data hazards between stages 2 and 5 must be handled in an analogous way:

$$\text{alu5} \wedge \text{alu2} \wedge ((\text{ra5} = \text{rb2}) \vee ((\text{ra5} = \text{rc2}) \wedge \neg\text{imm2}))$$
$$\rightarrow (\text{pause2: pause1: op3} \leftarrow 0) :$$

5.3

At the end of the clock period, the staller in stage 5 will write its data into the register file, and at the start of the next clock there will be no dependence detected with the stallee in stage 2. In the worst possible case, that of a hazard between instructions originally only one instruction apart, three bubbles have been inserted in the pipeline.

Similar hazard detection and control-signal-generation hardware must be designed for all possible combinations of interfering instructions in all phases of the pipeline.

Figure 5.13 shows one possible scheme for pausing stages 1 and 2 using the pause1 and pause2 signals: Use them to inhibit the clocks of stages 1 and 2.

Figure 5.14 shows an example of a pipeline stall due to a data dependence between two ALU instructions. At clock cycle 1 a dependence is detected between the instruction in the ALU stage, which will update r2, and the instruction in the operand fetch stage, which wants to fetch the value in r2. The dependence is shown by a circle around the staller, pointing to the stallee. At each clock tick, bubbles are inserted into the pipeline until the dependence is resolved at clock cycle 5.

Hazard Detection by Hardware, Resolved by Data Forwarding.   Data forwarding solves the problems of data-dependent pipeline hazards by forwarding the dependent data value as soon as it is available. Depending on the dependence, fewer or no bubbles may need to be inserted than were inserted in the preceding nonforwarded case. The basic concepts are simple, even if the implementation details are complex. The data hazard must be detected exactly as before, but bubbles only need to be inserted until the dependent data is available, at which time it is forwarded to the stallee. Forwarding can also be used without stalling if the code generator emits code that is guaranteed to meet the forwarding requirements.

Again we will take the SRC ALU instruction dependence as an example. Examining the Normal/Forwarded no-hazard ALU entries in Table 5.1, we see that ALU instructions that are only one stage apart can have data forwarded from "producer" to "consumer," avoiding any stall at all. We now substitute the terms *producer* for staller and *consumer* for stallee, because, at least in the case of the SRC ALU instructions, no stalls are needed. The hazard doesn't need to be detected nor the data forwarded until the consumer is in stage 3,

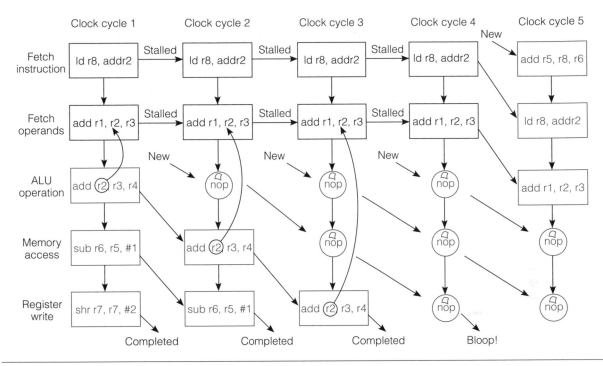

Fig. 5.14 Stall Due to a Data Dependence Between Two ALU Instructions

ready to perform its ALU operation, and the producer is in either stage 4 or stage 5. The hardware detection and forwarding circuit must detect the dependence between stages 3–4 and between stages 3–5. If one exists, then it must forward the operand to the proper ALU input. If that examination is to take place when the consumer instruction is in stage 3 and the producer instruction is in stage 4 or 5, then IR3, IR4, and IR5 must be increased in size to include the rb and rc fields of the instruction. The RTN will appear as follows:

$$\text{alu5} \wedge \text{alu3} \rightarrow (\,(\text{ra5} = \text{rb3}) \rightarrow X \leftarrow Z5 : \quad ;3\text{--}5 \text{ dependence}$$
$$(\text{ra5} = \text{rc3}) \wedge \neg\text{imm3} \rightarrow Y \leftarrow Z5\,) ;$$

$$\text{alu4} \wedge \text{alu3} \rightarrow ((\text{ra4} = \text{rb3}) \rightarrow X \leftarrow Z4 : \quad ;3\text{--}4 \text{ dependence}$$
$$(\text{ra4} = \text{rc3}) \wedge \neg\text{imm3})) \rightarrow Y \leftarrow Z4) :$$

where X and Y are the left and right inputs, respectively, to the ALU. Notice that no pipeline bubbles or stalls are necessary. The hazard detection and forwarding hardware is shown in Figure 5.15. The hardware takes its inputs from the op, rb, and rc fields of IR3 and the op and ra fields of IR4 and IR5. If it detects an ALU-ALU data hazard, it will determine on which ALU input the hazard exists, and whether the hazard exists between stages 3 and 4 or 3 and 5. It will switch the forwarded data from Z4 or Z5, using Mp6 and Mp7 to forward the data to the proper ALU input or inputs.

The dependences can be rather intricate, and can involve all three stages. Consider the following sequence of instructions in stages 3, 4, and 5 of the pipeline:

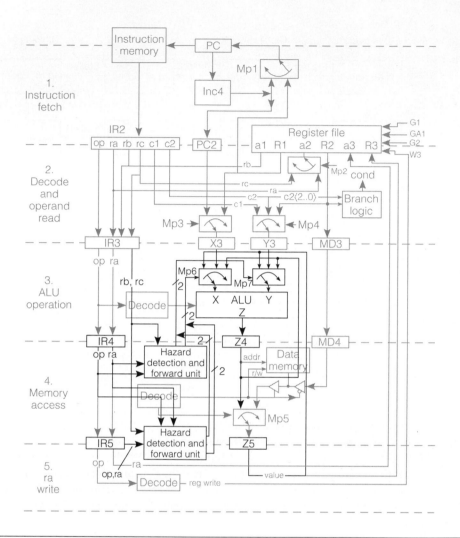

Fig. 5.15 Hazard Detection and Forwarding

```
add r5, r1, r1  ;instr C, issued 3rd, in stage 3
add r1, r4, r1  ;instr B, issued 2nd, in stage 4
add r1, r3, r2  ;instr A, issued 1st, in stage 5
```

When instructions A and B are at stages 3 and 4, the result of instr A is forwarded to instr B. At the next clock, when A is in 5, B is in 4, and C is in 3, the hazard detection units in both stages 4 and 5 will detect hazards. Only the hazard detection unit in stage 4 should forward its result, which is in Z4, to both X3 and Y3; thus the semicolon between the preceding two RTN expressions. The semicolon implies that the dependences between 3 and 4 should take precedence over the dependences between 3 and 5 because the X or Y value set by a 3–5 dependence is replaced by a value from a 3–4 dependence. In reality, X and Y are not registers, but multiplexer outputs. This use of a semicolon is not the ideal way to express precedence in this case. In most instances of RTN the existence of a semicolon implies that the expression on the right hand side of the semicolon is evaluated after the one on the left hand side, generally during the next clock cycle. A more satisfactory way to write the RTN is left for an exercise.

Additional hardware will be required to detect the other data hazards and forward data appropriately. Some hazards may require a combination of pipeline stall and data forwarding.

5.2.3 WRITE AFTER WRITE (WAW) AND WRITE AFTER READ (WAR) HAZARDS

The data hazards we have discussed so far are referred to as "read after write," or RAW hazards. This phrase refers to the notion that a data item can only be *read* by an instruction after it has been *written* by a preceding instruction. In a machine having a single pipeline, where instructions are executed in the order in which they occur in the instruction stream, this is the only kind of data hazard that can occur. In machines where instructions can be executed in parallel or out of order, two additional hazards can occur: write after write hazards, WAW, and write after read hazards, WAR.

Consider the three instruction pairs below, where the original instruction sequence was to execute instruction 1, then execute instruction 2:

RAW	**WAW**	**WAR**
1. add r0, r1, r2	1. add r0, r1, r2	1. add r2, r1, r0
2. sub r4, r3, r0	2. sub r0, r4, r5	2. sub r0, r3, r4

- In the RAW example there is clearly a hazard between instruction 2 reading r0 before instruction 1 has written it, as we have discussed at length in this section.

- In the WAW example, suppose the two instructions were executed on a machine that can reorder instructions so they execute out of order. In this case, the control unit must ensure that the sub instruction writes to r0 *after* the add instruction has written to r0, otherwise r0 will have an incorrect value after the two instructions have executed.

- Likewise in the WAR example, a machine that can execute instructions out of order must ensure that the sub instruction writes to r0 *after* the add instruction has read r0, otherwise the add instruction will read an incorrect value in r0.

Flynn limit

Nothing can be done to "fix" the RAW hazard aside from forwarding the result to the next instruction prior to updating the register file. Since we live in a cause-and-effect universe, the result cannot be used before it has been computed.

The other two hazards, however, are only caused by the two instructions having the same destination register (WAW) or having a destination register that is the same as the source register of the instruction above it (WAR). In both cases the hazard can be avoided by either renaming one of the registers if a spare register is available, or storing the result of the second instruction in a temporary register until after the first instruction has executed.

5.2.4   EXCEPTIONS AND THE PIPELINE

Internal and external exceptions must also be considered when designing the pipeline structure. The exception handling mechanism in heavily pipelined machines, especially those that also have multiple pipelines—the so-called multiple-instruction-issue, or superscalar machines—can become extremely complex. Under some conditions in machines of this type, the designers have abandoned any pretense of being able to sort out the state of affairs during and after the exception so that the machine can continue execution in an orderly way. Exceptions of this type are politely referred to as *imprecise exceptions,* meaning that nobody knows exactly what happened to the pipeline interior during exception handling.

imprecise exceptions

precise exceptions

Under most conditions, however, these machines implement *precise exceptions.* In precise exception handling there are clearly defined rules for what happens to instructions in the pipeline before, during, and after the exception is processed. External exceptions are usually taken to have occurred immediately after the instruction that just entered the pipeline, so the PC must be saved; the new PC reflecting the address of the exception vector must be loaded into the PC, and instructions in the pipeline allowed to complete before the exception is taken. On the other hand, an internal exception may have been raised by an instruction in the midst of execution: For example, a divide-by-zero exception may occur in the ALU stage of the pipeline. In this case the instructions ahead of the one that faulted are allowed to finish execution. How to deal with the instruction that caused the exception is problematical. Ideally the contents of the registers in its stage would be saved for later analysis, and the instruction aborted and replaced with a nop. Instructions in the pipeline behind the one that caused the exception may be restarted after the exception handler has completed.

5.2.5   PERFORMANCE AND DESIGN

Let us now make some quantitative estimates of the performance improvements to be gained in pipelined designs. Assuming that to a first approximation the clock periods are the same for unpipelined and pipelined designs, the equation for speedup without and with a performance improvement, in this case, pipelining is

$$\% \text{ Speedup } = \frac{(IC \times CPI \times \tau)_{w/o} - (IC \times CPI \times \tau)_w}{(IC \times CPI \times \tau)_w} \times 100 = \frac{CPI_{w/o} - CPI_w}{CPI_w} \qquad \text{[Eq. 5.1]}$$

If the average CPI for a 1-bus unpipelined design is 5, and the pipelined design can issue and complete one instruction per clock, then

$$\% \text{ Speedup } = \frac{CPI_{w/o} - CPI_w}{CPI_w} \times 100 = \frac{5-1}{1} \times 100 = 400\% \qquad \text{[Eq. 5.2]}$$

a dramatic speedup.

We can now factor in the loss in performance due to pipeline stalls. Assume that there is one pipeline stall for every four instructions that are issued. This means 5 clocks for four instructions, or 5/4=1.25 CPI. Now the speedup becomes

$$\% \text{ Speedup } = \frac{CPI_{w/o} - CPI_w}{CPI_w} \times 100 = \frac{5-1.25}{1.25} \times 100 = 300\% \qquad \text{[Eq. 5.3]}$$

Key Concepts: The Pipeline Design Process

The pipeline design process involves a number of important steps that begin with analysis of the instruction set and proceed by the stepwise refinement of the proposed pipeline design:

- Partition the instruction set into classes according to how they will utilize the various pipeline stages.
- Map each instruction class onto the pipeline stages.
- Design a unified pipeline data path, including the number and size of pipeline registers that will accommodate all instruction classes.
- Add multiplexers and control signals to operate the pipeline stages.
- Add hardware to handle pipeline hazards.

5.3   Instruction-Level Parallelism

There are two fundamental ways of increasing a processor's instruction execution rate: by increasing clock speed, which decreases the overall execution time per instruction, or by increasing the number of instructions that are executing simultaneously. The former approach involves IC technology and is out of the hands of the computer designer. The latter approach is architectural, and very much the province of the architect and logic designer. We have already encountered one example of the latter approach: instruction-level pipelining. In a pipelined processor, forwarding, branch prediction, and other optimizations target the ideal maximum speed of one instruction issue (or completion) per clock cycle. This maximum rate of one issue per tick is sometimes called the Flynn limit. For a processor to exceed this limiting speed, more than one instruction must be issued simultaneously on the same clock tick. In order for simultaneously issued instructions to execute correctly, there must be no dependence between them. The corresponding program property is called *instruction-level parallelism* (*ILP*).

ILP, instruction-level parallelism

There are two ways of exploiting ILP to speed up processing. Static multi-issue, or *VLIW* (very long instruction word) design has the programmer or compiler identify independent instructions and assemble them into several instruction words that can be fetched from memory in one cycle and the component instructions issued into multiple pipelines on the same clock tick. In dynamic multi-issue, or *superscalar*, architectures, multiple instructions are fetched simultaneously to fill an instruction buffer. Instructions in the buffer are then examined by hardware at each tick to determine which can be issued simultaneously into the available pipelines. The term, superscalar, arises from the earlier use of the distinction between vector and scalar architectures. A vector machine can perform multiple arithmetic operations in parallel on different components of a vector, as opposed to a scalar machine that performs only one instruction at a time.

VLIW

superscalar

5.3.1   GENERAL APPROACHES TO ILP

The multiple pipelines required to execute several instructions in parallel may be identical or specialized for different types of instructions. Typical multi-issue processors divide instructions into three classes: integer, floating point, and branch, and have one or more

IU, integer unit
FPU, floating point unit

BPU, branch
prediction unit
LSU, load-store unit

VPU, vector unit

integer units *(IUs)*, floating point units *(FPUs)*, and branch prediction units *(BPUs)*. Separate load-store units *(LSUs)*, may be devoted to memory operations. Highend processors may even compete with vector processing computers by including vector processing units *(VPUs)*, that can process multiple data words in parallel. Examples of the latter are the Motorola Altivec unit and the Intel MMX unit.

Static and dynamic multi-issue processors represent the two extremes in which all dependence analysis is done, respectively, at compile time by a compiler program or at run time by hardware. Both techniques have advantages and disadvantages, and mixtures of the two are common. An advantage of static multi-issue is that the compiler has the luxury of examining many instructions and possibly transforming the code to extract multiple, independent instructions to be placed into a long instruction word. A disadvantage is that the outcomes of data dependent branches are not known at compile time, and analysis is limited by the fact that either outcome is possible. Dynamic multi-issue has the advantage of access to run time information such as the branch path but the disadvantage that practical hardware implementations can prefetch and analyze only a limited number of instructions at a time.

Dynamic Multi-Issue Machines.   Dynamic multi-issue machines load instructions into an instruction cache and make issue decisions about which instruction can be issued into which pipeline, on the fly, at run time. This places a considerable burden on the processor. There is increased complexity in both logic circuitry to make the decisions about which instruction to issue into which pipeline, in bookkeeping logic to track instruction and operand location and dependences, and in instruction caching. On the other hand, compilers for dynamic multi-issue machines need only arrange instructions so they yield a correct program. This means that different microarchitectures for a given ISA do not require changes in the compiler. Thus programs compiled for the Intel x86 architecture will run on all the members of the Intel x86 family, as well as on AMD and other processors.

Static Multi-Issue Machines.   Static multi-issue machines rely on the compiler to make all instruction scheduling decisions at compile time. The only run time decisions that need to be made are concerned with dependences introduced by stalls and branches. This results in a processor with less complexity and less chip area to deal with instruction issue, and thus more chip area available for caches, etc. In effect, some of the information about the processors microarchitecture is moved back into the compiler. Decisions about instruction issue need be made only once, at compile time. But this raises an important question: What happens when the microarchitecture is modified to include enhancements or when another manufacturer wishes to develop a competitive chip with the same ISA but a different microarchitecture? While it is possible to include flexibility in the compiler to accommodate new or different microarchitectures, and in the new microarchitectures to accommodate programs compiled by "legacy" compilers, neither solution is ideal by any means. New or modified compilers must be developed for each new microarchitecture to take full advantage of new or modified features. Furthermore, adding additional complexity to the compiler increases the possibility that there will be compiler bugs.

5.3.2   STATIC MULTI-ISSUE—VLIW MACHINES

As the name suggests, the VLIW machine relies on a wide instruction word, at least 64 and up to 128 bits. Each word contains fields to control the routing of data to multiple register files and execution units. This allows the compiler much more control over data operations. Whereas the superscalar processor's control unit must make instruction-issue decisions on the basis of a small amount of local information (that contained within the instruction queue), the VLIW machine has the luxury of making these execution-order decisions at compile time, thus permitting optimizations that minimize hazards and the resulting stalls. This can be a major advantage in the execution of straight-line code, but it is a disadvantage in dealing with branch instructions, because there is less advance warning of branch instructions, which results in longer, more frequent stalls. Examples of commercial VLIW machines include the Multiflow, KSR-1, Tera, Intel i860, and Apollo DN10000.

Example 5.2   Design of a Dual-Issue VLIW version of SRC   Our example of a VLIW machine is an SRC with two 32 bit instructions per 64-bit word, statically scheduled by the compiler. The instructions in a word are simultaneously issued into two pipelines. Figure 5.16 shows the two pipelines and the instructions that can be executed by each.

Many choices for the functionality and behavior of the two pipelines are possible, and we will make some arbitrary but reasonable ones:

■   In order not to have multiple data memory operations per cycle, only Pipeline 1 will execute loads and stores. As we will see in Chapter 6, a fast shifter is the most expensive arithmetic circuit in SRC. Coupled with the fact that shifts are infrequent compared to other instructions, this suggests limiting shift operations to Pipeline 2.

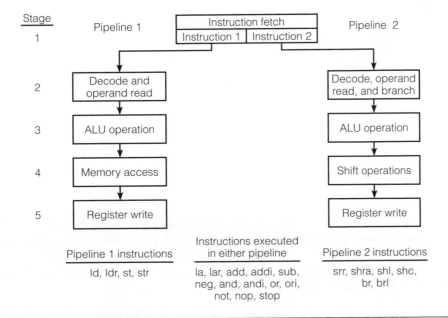

Fig. 5.16 Structure of the Dual Pipeline SRC

- Both pipelines can do integer add, subtract, and logical operations.
- Only one branch per instruction word is allowed, processed in Pipeline 2.
- Operands in the pipelines are forwarded wherever possible.
- *The pipelines work similarly to the pipeline design of Section 5.1* except for the additional stage introduced for the shift instructions and the lack of a branch delay slot,

Register File Usage.   Issuing two instructions can cause up to four reads and two writes on the register file in each cycle, two reads and one write per pipeline. This can increase to five reads and one write if the instruction in Pipeline 1 is a store. To accomplish this, increased register file activity additional read and write ports can be provided, as was done in the register files of the two- and three-bus designs of Chapter 4. Alternatively, one could duplicate the register file, writing both copies of a register simultaneously but reading them independently. The two techniques are easily combined. (It becomes the responsibility of the compiler to avoid scheduling two instructions that write to the same register into the same instruction word.) We make the simplifying assumption that the register file is designed so that a value being written into a result register at stage 5 is immediately available to an instruction being issued from stage 2 to stage 3 without requiring a cycle to pass through the register file.

Dependences and Forwarding.   To average more than one instruction issue per tick, forwarding is to be applied wherever possible. There are simply too many instructions in the two pipelines for simple stalling of instruction issue on a dependence to be a sensible choice. Stalls occur only when the pipeline structure makes forwarding impossible. There is no branch delay slot in this implementation. (Branch delay itself should also be eliminated, but this is done by branch prediction techniques, which are beyond the scope of this text and will not be treated.)

Programming Examples.   Figure 5.17a shows the scalar version of the SRC program to compute elements of the Fibonacci series seen in Chapter 2. Figure 5.17b shows the same program rewritten for the static dual-issue version of SRC. There are several interesting features to this parallelized version.

1. Total program length has been reduced from 11 lines to 7. More important, the loop, where the program will spend most of its time, has been reduced from 7 lines to 4.
2. To minimize the size of the loop a nop was inserted as the second instruction in line 2. This allows both Fib(n-1) and Fib(n-2) to be accessed at the start of the loop at line 3, summed at line 4 in Pipeline 1, and the sum stored as Fib(n) at line 5 in Pipeline 1.
3. The decrement of the count has been moved two instructions above the branch so that the new value will be available to the branch instruction at line 6. (Recall that branch instructions need the branch target value in stage 2, whereas it is not available from the addi instruction until it reaches stage 4. Thus the need to separate the two instructions by two pipeline stages.)

As a more complex example, Figure 5.18 shows the transformation of a sequential SRC code taken from Figure 8.10 in Chapter 8, into two instruction per word code for a

(a) Program for a scalar version of SRC

```
; fib.asm. Compute Fibonacci numbers.
; The Fibonacci sequence is defined as follows:
; fib(1) = 1, fib(2) = 1,
; fib(n) = fib(n-1) + fib(n-2) n > 2.
cnt:   .equ 8                  ; No. to compute after first two
       .org 0                  ; Store sequence at addr. 0
seq:   .dc  1                  ; Init. the first Fib. No.
next:  .dc  1                  ; Init. the second Fib. No.
ans:   .dw  cnt                ; Storage for the next 8 Fib. Nos.
       .org 0x1000             ; Begin ass'y. at hex. addr. 1000
       lar  r31, loop          ; Branch address
       la   r0,  cnt           ; Init. count
       la   r1,  seq           ; Init r1 to index of seq[0]
loop:  ld   r2,  seq(r1)       ; Get fib(n-2)
       ld   r3,  next(r1)      ; Get fib(n-1)
       add  r2,  r2,      r3   ; compute fib(n)
       st   r2,  ans(r1)       ; Store fib(n)
       addi r1,  r1,      4    ; Increment index
       addi r0,  r0,      -1   ; Decrement count
       brnz r31, r0            ; loop until done
       stop
```

(b) Program for a dual-issue version of SRC

```
       Pipeline 1              Pipeline 2            Line #

       lar  r31, loop          la   r0, cnt            1
       la   r1,  seq           nop                     2
loop:  ld   r2,  seq(r1)       ld   r3, next(r1)       3
       add  r2,  r2,r3         addi r0, r0,     -1     4
       st   r2,  ans(r1)       addi r1, r1,     4      5
       brnz r31, r0            nop                     6
       stop                                            7
```

Fig. 5.17 SRC Program to Compute the Fibonacci Series

dual-issue SRC. In studying this example the reader should focus on the dependences induced by register and memory reads and writes rather than on the meaning of the program, which will be discussed in detail in Chapter 8

Two instructions can be packed into the same word if their operand reads and result writes are independent, and if they can be scheduled into separate pipelines. Depending on how clever the compiler is, transformations other than simple dependence analysis can be used to improve code packing. Examples in Figure 5.18 are:

*1   The constant R6 is loaded repeatedly to move its instruction into the outer loop.

*2   The instruction ld   r0, Done(r2) has been duplicated to save a cycle in the inner loop.

*3   Register R0 has been replaced by R7 to get the constant −1 for storing after the conditional branch.

```
          Single Issue                    Pipeline 1                  Pipeline 2
Driver:lar    r4, Next        Driver:lar r4, Next           lar  r5,  Check
       lar    r5, Check                                     
       lar    r6, Start       Start:lar r6, Start           la   r2,  0           *1
Start: la     r2, 0                                         
       la     r3, 1               ld   r0, Done(r2)         la   r3,  1           *2
Check: ld     r0, Done(r2)    Check:ld   r0, CICTL(r2)      brmi r4,  r0
       brmi   r4, r0                                        
       la     r3, 0               la   r3, 0                brpl r4,  r0
       ld     r0, CICTL(r2)                                 
       brpl   r4, r0                                        
       ld     r0, CIN(r2)         ld   r1, Bufp(r2)         la   r7,  -1          *3
       ld     r1, Bufp(r2)                                  
       st     r0, 0(r1)           ld   r0, CIN(r2)          addi r1,  r1, 4
       addi   r1, r1, 4                                     
       st     r1, Bufp(r2)        st   r0, 0(r1)            addi r0,  r0, -CR
       addi   r0, r0, -CR                                   
       brnz   r4, r0              st   r1, Bufp(r2)         brnz r4,  r0
       la     r0, -1                                        
       st     r0, Done(r2)        st   r7, Done(r2)         nop
Next:  addi   r2, r2, 8       Next: addi r2, r2, 8          addi r0,  r2, -248    *4
       addi   r0, r2, -256                                  
       brnz   r5, r0              ld   r0, Done(r2)         brnz r5,  r0          *2
       brzr   r6, r3              nop                       brzr r6,  r3
```

Fig. 5.18 Compiler Transformation of a SRC Program for a Dual-Issue SRC

*4   Constant propagation combined $R0 \leftarrow R2 + 8 - 256$ into $R0 \leftarrow R2 - 248$ to change two dependent instructions into independent ones.

Forwarding in the Dual-Issue SRC.   Given two instruction per word code, the dual issue SRC hardware must accomplish any required forwarding and stall the issue of a two instruction word if forwarding of one of its operands is impossible. Forwarding may take place within one of the two pipelines or between pipelines. Figure 5.19 shows some details of the two pipeline SRC processor. Multiplexers (Mi, Ni) for each pipeline, stage, and operand allow that operand to be taken from the normal pipeline flow or wherever a forwarded result may be available. Four result buses, A, B, C, and D, correspond to places where new result register values may be produced.

Tables and Data Structures.   The control of forwarding and stalls in the dual-issue SRC is based on four data structures, two static tables of information about instruction dependences and two dynamic tables describing results and operands of instructions that are issued but not complete. The static tables are used by the compiler in scheduling instructions into the dual-issue instruction word. The dynamic tables are used at runtime to control forwarding of operands.

The first static table describes the availability of result values for each instruction as it flows through the pipeline. The information in this table is similar to the "Write to Register File/Data Available /Earliest" entries in the first row of Table 5.1, as modified for the two-pipeline design. For example, referring to that table and to Figure 5.19, the result of

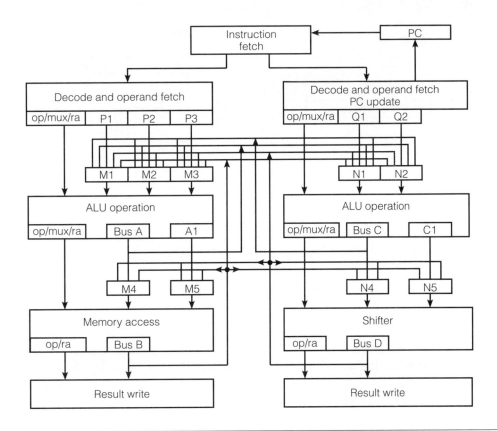

Fig. 5.19 Dual-Issue SRC Pipelines and Forwarding Paths

an add is available first at stage 3 from either bus A or C, depending on whether the instruction is in Pipeline 1 or Pipeline 2. One cycle later the result will be available at stage 4 (bus B or D). Because of the simplifying assumption that operands are available in the register file (RF) as soon as they are written in stage 5, there need be no forwarding from stage 5. Likewise, the result of a ld is not available until stage 4 and is only allowed in pipeline 1 (bus B).

The second static table describes for each operand of each instruction where that operand is required at the latest to take part in instruction execution. The information in this table is similar to the "Read from Register File/Normal, Earliest Stage" entries in the first column of Table 5.1, as modified for the two-pipeline design. For example, the instruction st ra, rb(c2) requires the rb value to be available at the output of the multiplexer M1 in stage 3 but can wait until stage 4 for the value of ra to be available at the output of M5.

The first dynamic table, the register status table, describes the location of each operand for the instructions in stage 2. This location will be in the register file unless the operand is being produced by an instruction that is still "in flight" ahead of the instruction needing it in the pipeline. For these operands the table entry describes the first stage and time at which the operand value is available for forwarding and where it is available on subsequent cycles until the instruction exits its pipeline.

(b) Dynamic Table #1: Register status table for instruction in stage 3

Register	Location†
R4	RF
R5	$(A, t);(B, t+1)$
R6	$(B, t);(RF, t+1)$
R7	$(D, t);(RF, t+1)$
R8	$(C, t);(D, t+1)$
R9	RF

† Bus A, B, C, D, or register file (RF)

(a) Instructions issued

Stage	Issue time	Instruction word	
		Instruction 1	Instruction 2
5	$t-2$	add r6, r4, r4	shc r7, r1, 8
4	$t-1$	addi r5, r3, 16	lar r8, 12
3	t	st r8, 4(r7)	sub r9, r5, r6

(c) Dynamic Table #2: Op codes and multiplexer settings issued at time t

Pipeline 1	Pipeline 2
st M1=D, M2=P2, M3=C, M4=A, M5=A1	sub N1=A, N2=B, N4=C, N5=d

Fig. 5.20 Dynamic Information for Example Instructions in a Dual-Issue SRC

In this simple example machine, instructions are issued into stage 2, the decode stage. On subsequent clock cycles they proceed into stage 3 and then stage 4. Since in stage 5 any values written to the register file are immediately available *in* the register file, forwarding only takes place from stage 3 or stage 4. New register status information is set when an instruction having that register as a result is issued and is updated on each cycle until the instruction is complete. For example, for sub ra, rb, rc issued into pipeline 2, the ra value is available on bus C at the end of the next cycle and on bus D at the end of the following cycle. For shr ra, rb, 5 the ra value is not available in the next cycle after issue but is available on bus D in the following cycle.

The second dynamic table describes, for each incomplete instruction, how each of its operand multiplexers should be set to obtain the correct value from the register file or by forwarding. This information is constructed from the static table describing instruction operands and the register status table. It flows through the pipeline with the instruction. If a result register value is not available for forwarding by the cycle in which it is required as an operand, the multiplexer settings cannot be constructed, and the instruction must be stalled until its operands are available

Figure 5.20 shows the dynamic information for a sequence of three instruction words at the time, t, (Figure 5.20a) when the third instruction pair (st, sub) is issued into stage 3 (the ALU stage) of the two pipelines. The multiplexer settings (Figure 5.20c) for the instructions issued at t are built from the register status table information (Figure 5.20b), constructed from the instructions issued at $t-1$ and $t-2$ and updated on subsequent ticks, and from the static information on the latest stage where the operands are required by different instructions. The flow of operands is shown in Figure 5.21. The first operand of st is R7, and the register status table says it is available on bus D at the clock tick, so multiplexer M1 is set to D. The second operand is the constant field from the decode stage, so M2 = P2. The third operand, the register to be stored, is R8, available on bus C at time t, so M3 = C. The stage 4 multiplexers for pipeline 1 are set for normal pipeline flow, M4 = A

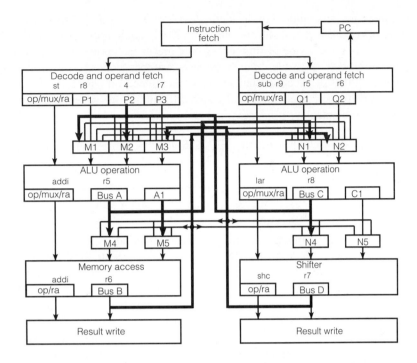

Fig. 5.21 Operand flow into the st r8, r(r7) instruction in Pipeline 1, Stage 2.

and M5 = A1. The first and second operands of the sub instruction issued into pipeline 2 at time t are found from the status table to be available on buses A and B, respectively, so N1 = A and N2 = B.Only one path through stage 4 is used by sub, so N4 = D and N5 = d is a don't care.

5.3.3 DYNAMIC MULTI-ISSUE—SUPERSCALAR ARCHITECTURES

In *superscalar* architectures there are also multiple pipelines, and multiple instructions are issued per clock cycle. The selection of the instructions to issue simultaneously, however, is done by hardware at run time instead of being determined by the compiler. Multiple instructions are fetched in parallel from memory into an instruction buffer. Then, at each clock cycle, issue control hardware examines the dependences among instructions in the buffer and those already issued but incomplete to select as many instructions as possible to issue into the available pipelines. Forwarding can be handled by the same mechanisms as static multi-issue since it was also a run time operation in that case. With an N instruction buffer and M pipelines, up to M instructions could be issued per tick, but dependences might reduce this number.

With dynamic multi-issue, it would be possible to issue a conditional branch from the instruction buffer, and when the test is resolved, perhaps on the next tick, to issue an instruction preceding the branch simultaneously with one following it. This would be impossible with static multi-issue. On the other hand, the N instruction buffer means that sequential instructions separated by more than N are not candidates for simultaneous issue in the dynamic case but could be in the static case. Prefetching the correct instructions in the presence of conditional branches is a problem for dynamic multi-issue. Just as branch prediction is beyond the scope of this text, so are clever techniques such as prefetching instructions from both possible branch targets. Another concern involving program counter change is that of exception handling. As mentioned on page 220, it is especially difficult with multi-issue machines, and most difficult in the superscalar case. Many dynamic multi-issue machines implement imprecise interrupts.

GETTING SPECIFIC: SUPERSCALAR PROCESSORS   Here are some typical superscalar architectures:

- PowerPC G4: Eleven pipelined functional units: 4 IUs, an FPU with a separate floating point register file, a BPU, an LSU, and 4 VPUs. It is capable of executing sixteen instructions simultaneously.

- Intel P6: Five functional units: 14-stage pipeline, 2 IUs, separate load and store units, FPU and BPU. Since the P6 must execute the CISC-like 80×86 instruction set, instructions entering the pipeline are decoded and fragmented into simpler RISC-like micro-ops, as they are called, which are dispatched to one of the five functional units. Instructions may be executed out of order, provided that doing so does not cause hazards.

- HP Alpha 21164: This processor has a 7-stage pipeline, 2 IUs, and 2 FPUs: one for add/subtract, and one for multiply/divide, branch prediction.

The three preceding descriptions are inadequate to express the true capabilities of these processors. Their performance is highly influenced by the size and speed of the cache memories and buses, the way that the processor manages branch prediction and hazards, and of course the quality of the compiler that generates the code.

The trend in advanced processors is to prefetch and decode as many instructions as possible prior to execution, and on the basis of that decoding to speculatively prefetch and begin execution of several branch instruction streams, discarding the results of all but the correct stream. Based on its analysis of the instructions in its prefetch buffers, it may reorder them, possibly fragmenting them into their microoperations for independent execution.   ■

5.4   Microprogramming

We now turn from the discussion of ways to increase machine performance to the presentation of an alternative approach to control unit design: microprogramming, also known as microcoding. The hardwired approach to control unit design that we described in Chapter 4 treats the relationship between control inputs and control outputs as a series of Boolean functions, one for each control signal. In the microcode approach, the relationship between inputs and outputs is treated as a memory system. Control signals are stored as words in a *microcode memory*. At each clock tick during instruction execution, the appropriate (micro)control word is fetched from microprogram memory to supply the control signals. In this section we discuss the general design of the *microcode control unit*, and then design a microcoded control unit for SRC. We conclude the section with a discussion of alternative approaches to microcoding, with several examples from actual machines.

microcode memory

microcode control unit

You should bear in mind that, like the other topics in this chapter, microcoding represents an alternative way to design the control unit. Whether the control unit is hardwired or microcoded should not be visible to the machine programmer, save perhaps through the execution speed. Unlike pipelining, microcoding can be used with any sort of microarchitecture. Exactly the same abstract RTN must be implemented on the microcoded unit as was implemented by the hardwired approach. As we shall see, the control signals emanating from the control unit to the data path will remain unchanged, and there will be only minor changes in the concrete RTN and the control sequence.

As with most of the concepts underlying computer design, the concept of microcoded control units originated early in the history of computing. Maurice Wilkes proposed the concept in 1951, as a way of simplifying the control logic of the computer. Although Wilkes did construct a machine, the EDSAC2, with a microcoded control unit, it was not until the early 1960s that IBM made the concept popular with the entirely microprogrammed 360 line of computers. The technique saw widespread usage from then until the late 1980s, when hardwired control units again came into popular usage, largely because of their faster speed and the greater availability of CAD tools for logic design. Microcoded control units may well again become popular as implementation domains change. In fact, we will see later, in the section entitled "Perspectives on Microcoding" on page 243, that some view RISC instructions as a form of microcode.

5.4.1 GENERAL APPROACH

Let us stress that the microcoded control unit must emit the same control signals in the same sequence as does the hardwired controller if the machine is to execute the same instruction set. It is only the means of generating these signals that differs. The microcode control unit is in itself a small stored program computer. It has a *micro PC,* μPC, a *microprogram memory,* and a *microinstruction word,* which contains the control signals and sequencing information. The action of the microcode control unit is exactly like that of a general purpose computer: fetch a microinstruction, execute it (by applying the control signals in the microcontrol word to the computer's data path), determine the address of the next microinstruction, and fetch that next instruction.

micro PC, μPC

microprogram memory

microinstruction word

You must be careful not to confuse the μPC with the main machine PC, the μIR with the main machine IR, and microinstructions with main machine instructions.

The Microcode Engine. There are many ways to design a microcoded control unit. Figure 5.22 shows a block diagram of a typical design. The μPC contains the address of the next microinstruction to be fetched from the *control store,* a fast local memory that contains the control words. The control word is copied into the μIR, the microinstruction register. The control word contains three kinds of fields:

control store

1. The control signal field, c bits in size, containing the control signals, such as PC_{in}, MA_{out}, and so on, with 1 bit for each control signal
2. The *branch address* field, n bits in size, which contains a microbranch address, where n is the number of bits in the μPC
3. The *branch control* field, containing k bits, which contains various signals to control branching in the microcode control unit

branch address

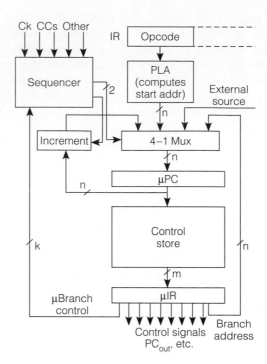

Fig. 5.22 Block Diagram of Microcoded Control Unit

Since the branch address field contains n bits, the same number of bits contained in the µPC, every microinstruction is capable of being a branch instruction and can branch to any location in the control store. The branch control field specifies various branch conditions to the control unit *sequencer,* which controls overall operation.

The µPC can be loaded from four different sources by using the 4–1 multiplexer:

1. The (possibly incremented) µPC. This operation is similar to the operation of the conventional PC. It allows the microprogram to be stepped sequentially from microinstruction to microinstruction. As with the PC, although called a (micro) program counter, in this design it is not a counter, but just an ordinary register. In fact, many texts refer to it as the micro address register to signify the fact that it is not a counter. Here we follow the more normal convention of calling it the µPC. Note that if the incrementer does not increment the value, but passes it on to the multiplexer unchanged, the controller will loop to the same instruction—a valuable property, as we shall see.

2. The output of the PLA. The PLA serves as a lookup table, mapping the opcode field of the IR to the starting address of the microcode routine for the particular opcode.

3. An external source. This input allows the µPC to be initialized to a starting value to begin instruction fetch, interrupt service, or the reset operation, for example.

4. The branch address field from the current microinstruction. This field allows conditional or unconditional microbranches to anywhere in the control store.

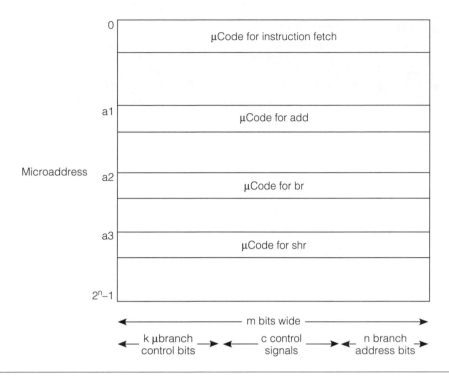

Fig. 5.23 The Control Store

In the microcoded control unit, the machine microstate is encoded in the value of the μPC and in any other registers holding control information. Thus, if machine operation is stopped in the middle of execution of a microcontrol sequence, the values in those registers must be saved just as the machine state must be saved.

The Control Store. The control store contains the microroutines for all instructions in the instruction set, as well as microroutines for the reset and exception processing operations. Figure 5.23 shows a typical layout of the control store. The control store behaves just as normal main memory does: apply an address to it, and it returns the control word stored at that address. Quantitatively it differs from the typical main memory, however. Access times are much faster, since the control store is normally located on board the processor chip. Typical control stores are often 70 bits or more wide, and contain only 2–4 K of control words. It could be said that the control store is wider but not nearly as deep as typical main memories. The control store capacity, B, in bits is given by $B = (k + c + n) \times 2^n$. We will see in the section on horizontal and vertical microcode that is possible to reduce this number by "compressing" the control word.

Example 5.3 Microcode for the add Instruction

Table 4.7 showed the control sequence for the SRC add instruction. Table 5.2 shows the equivalent microcode sequence for that instruction. The table shows the address of each microinstruction, followed by that portion of the microinstruction dealing with micro–branch control, whose detail is suppressed for the time being. Following the branch control information

Table 5.2 Control Signals for the add Instruction

Address	Branch Control	PC$_{out}$	C$_{out}$	MD$_{out}$	R$_{out}$	MA$_{in}$	C$_{in}$	PC$_{in}$	IR$_{in}$	A$_{in}$	R$_{in}$	INC4	Read	Wait	ADD	Gra	Grb	Grc	End
100	•••	1	0	0	0	1	1	0	0	0	0	1	0	0	0	0	0	0	0
101	•••	0	1	0	0	0	0	1	0	0	0	0	1	1	0	0	0	0	0
102	•••	0	0	1	0	0	0	0	1	0	0	0	0	0	0	0	0	0	0
200	•••	0	0	0	1	0	0	0	0	1	0	0	0	0	0	0	1	0	0
201	•••	0	0	0	1	0	1	0	0	0	0	0	0	0	1	0	0	1	0
202	•••	0	1	0	0	0	0	0	0	0	1	0	0	0	0	1	0	0	1

are the fields in the microcontrol word that directly cause the execution of the add instruction. Notice that the first three microinstructions at addresses 100–102 execute the instruction fetch. The instruction at address 100 contains 1s in the fields for PC$_{out}$, MA$_{in}$, INC4, and C$_{in}$. The reader can verify that the control bits in this table correspond to the control signals shown in Table 4.7. In this example the microcode for the add instruction begins at address 200. We have not shown the microbranch instructions that cause the branch to that address, but we cover the microbranching mechanism in detail below. ■

Generating Microcode from the Control Sequence: Branching and Looping. The only real difference between the microinstruction control word and the equivalent control word that emerges from the hardwired control unit is in the signals that control the microcode controller—execution control signals. The two principal types of execution control signals that we encountered in the last chapter were

1. Conditional execution. An example would be a sequence such as CON → PC$_{in}$, which tests the value of CON, and if it is true, causes PC$_{in}$ to be asserted.
2. Conditional and unconditional branches such as (n ≠ 0 → ... Goto6). This is actually an example of a looping construct implemented as a conditional branch.

We shall see that both of these constructs can be implemented by conditional branches that are specified in the microcode word instead of using AND gates to control conditional actions.

Consider a simple microcontrol unit that implements a (macro) instruction set, not SRC, that has conditional branches based on the condition codes N (negative flag) and Z (zero flag). Let us assume that we also want to implement conditional execution and conditional and unconditional branches like the two items in the preceding list. Figure 5.24 shows one possible design that implements conditional and unconditional branching in the microcontroller. The 4–1 multiplexer at the top of the figure allows one of four different values to be loaded into the μPC:

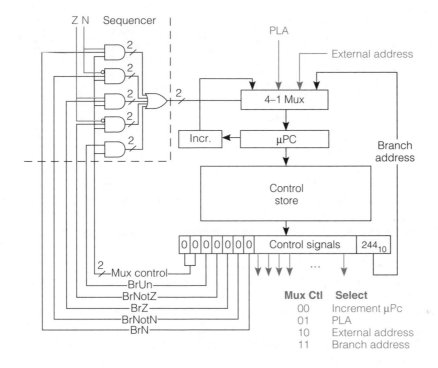

Fig. 5.24 Branching Controls in the Microcoded Control Unit

1. The incremented µPC. This is the "normal" case, allowing the µPC to be stepped from address to address sequentially, as in the first three instructions in Table 5.2.

2. The contents of a PLA. The PLA's function is to decode the opcode of the instruction to the starting address of the microcode routine in the control store. This is the action that caused address 200 to be loaded into the µPC in Table 5.2.

3. An external microaddress, such as the address of microcode to perform the reset function.

4. A branch address that is part of the microcode word.

The first two branch control signals on the far left side of the control word in Figure 5.24 specify which multiplexer input is to be selected, and the next 5 bits select the condition under which that input is to be selected. These 5 bits specify Branch Unconditionally (BrUn), Branch if Not Zero (BrNotZ), Branch if Zero (BrZ), Branch if Not Negative (BrNotN), and Branch if Negative (BrN). Notice that if all of the 5 bits are zero, the output of the logic block in the upper left of the figure will be zero, selecting the Incr. PC multiplexer input. This is the normal, fall-through situation in the execution of the microcode. In the practical design, the sequencer would have more controls to handle.

This scheme provides a considerable amount of flexibility in controlling branches. Branches can be formed by choosing one alternative from each of the following two lists:

$$Br \begin{Bmatrix} NotN \\ N \\ NotZ \\ Z \\ Unconditional \end{Bmatrix} \begin{Bmatrix} PLA \\ ExternalAddr \\ BranchAddr \end{Bmatrix}$$

For example, one could generate a branch on N = 0 to an externally supplied microaddress. This branching capability makes microcode appear more like a conventional programming language than like the concrete RTN we saw in the last chapter. To emphasize that similarity, we will cease using T0, T1, . . . to describe control steps, and instead use control store addresses, with the understanding that there is a new control word fetched every cycle (except when there is a Hold signal stopping the clock until a memory access completes).

We now examine a few ways in which the branching capability can be used. Table 5.3 shows five examples of microcode branching. (The code at 204–205 is an example of implementing a while loop.) In the control word at location 200, the mux control setting of 00 coupled with the presence of zeros in all the other branch control entries means that the μPC input will be selected under all conditions. The next instruction to be executed will be at location 201. The microbranch address is unused in this case. In the second example, the mux control setting of 01 will select the PLA output address unconditionally. Again, the branch address is unused. The microinstruction at address 202 has a mux control setting of 10, and the BrZ bit is set, so the branch will be taken to the address on the external address lines, provided that the Z bit is set; otherwise execution will continue at 203. The microinstruction at address 203 specifies a branch to microaddress 300 if the N bit is set; otherwise execution continues at address 204. The microinstructions at 204 and 205 implement a while loop: The instruction at 204 is a test of the N bit. If it is 0, then a branch is taken to location 206, bypassing instruction 205. If the N bit is 1, then control falls through to 205, which contains the control signals to be executed and an unconditional branch back up to the while test at 204. Notice that all the (macro) control signals

Table 5.3 Microcode Branching Examples

Address*	Mux Ctl	BrUn	BrNotZ	BrZ	BrNotN	BrN	Control Signals	Branch Address†	Branching Action
200	00	0	0	0	0	0	• • •	XXX	None–201 next
201	01	1	0	0	0	0	• • •	XXX	To output of PLA
202	10	0	0	1	0	0	• • •	XXX	To external address if Z
203	11	0	0	0	0	1	• • •	300	To 300 if N (else 204)
204	11	0	0	0	1	0	0• • •0	206	To 206 if N (else 205)
205	11	1	0	0	0	0	• • •	204	Br to 204

*The address fields are specified in decimal. All others are in binary.
†XXX = Don't care, branch address not used.

are zeros at location 204, since the code at this location only implements the test. If several tests were required to determine a branch target, then there might be several sequential microinstructions whose only purpose would be to compute the value of the microbranch. It is sometimes possible to implement a multiway branch by using bit ORing, to be discussed later.

Continuing the theme that microprograms are very similar to ordinary programs, it is possible to implement all sorts of high-level language control constructs using the preceding microcontrol structure. For example, the six instructions in Table 5.3 above can be expressed in C-like notation as follows:

```
{...};
{...}; goto PLA;
{...}; if Z then goto Extern_Addr;
{...}; if N then goto Label1;
while (N) {...};
```

Control constructs such as repeat and if-then-else are also possible (see Exercise 5.18). A number of microcode compilers have been developed that allow the designer to write microcode in a way that is similar to programming in a high-level language—using high-level control statements, symbolic labels, assignment statements, and so on. This greatly eases the chore of developing the control unit: The developer can write the microprogram in a high-level language, compile it to microcode, download the compiled code to microcontrol store RAM, and immediately test the code. This greatly shortens development time.

Horizontal and Vertical Microcode Schemes.   The microcode developed in our discussion thus far is completely *horizontal*. There is 1 bit for each control signal. There are no control signal decoders, so the control signals in the μIR can be immediately routed to their destination. A *mostly horizontal* trade-off is possible that reduces the width of the control word at the expense of an additional level of decoding after the μIR. Consider a 1-bus machine that had, say, 16 ALU operations and seven Register-out control signals that gate signals onto the processor bus. Since there can be only one ALU operation per clock cycle, and since only one signal can be gated onto the bus per clock cycle, it is possible to encode the ALU operations into a single 4-bit field, and the Register-out signals into another 3-bit field, to be decoded into the appropriate control signals.

horizontal microcode
mostly horizontal microcode

Figure 5.25 shows this encoding. The net savings are $(16 + 7) - (4 + 3) = 16$ bits *per word*. If a number of encodings such as this can be performed, considerable savings in control store size are possible. A caution needs to be sounded here, however. This encoding of fields only works when at most one value can be selected from the field under all conditions, since a decoder selects one and only one of 2^n. For example, it would be impossible to encode C_{in} and MA_{in} in the same field in the 1-bus SRC machine discussed in the last chapter, in Table 4.7, since they both occur simultaneously in step T0 of the instruction fetch. Furthermore, it is fortuitous that there are only seven register-out control signals, since one signal in the field must be reserved for "No signal out" otherwise we are slated to be always gating one signal or another out onto the bus. This is acceptable for the ALU controls, since the ALU is always working anyway.

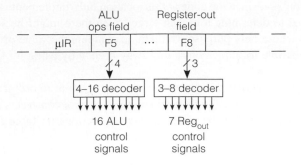

Fig. 5.25 A Somewhat Vertical Encoding

vertical microcode

A completely *vertical* scheme would encode every *distinct* microinstruction as a single signal that is to be fanned out to the control points that are to be asserted. So, for example, if there are 512 distinct and different microinstructions, then the control word could be encoded in 9 bits. A next address field would still be required, costing another 9 bits. Figure 5.26 shows the difference between a completely horizontal encoding, where all the control signals are conveyed to the data path, and a completely vertical scheme, where control signals for a given step are fanned out to the appropriate locations in the data path. The vertical encoding shows the (single) control signal that implements the first step of the instruction fetch in the 1-bus SRC. From this signal, PC_{out}, MA_{in}, INC4, C_{in}, are fanned out to these control points in the data path. This fanning out and ORing of the control signals is not practical because of the high degree of fan-out and fan-in, but it does become practical when the output of the control store is used to select a wide, essentially horizontally encoded microinstruction word in yet another memory: nanocode stored in a nanocode ROM. This approach is especially appealing when the same microinstruction occurs many times in the control store, since all occurrences can be pointed to the same location in the nanostore.

5.4.2   ILLUSTRATIVE EXAMPLE: A MICROCODED, 1-BUS SRC DESIGN

Let us go back to the 1-bus design of Figure 4.3 and redo the control mechanism using the microcode approach. For simplicity's sake, we will use the clocking logic developed in Figure 4.12. We also show how the reset and exception processes are implemented, assuming a synchronized reset signal, and an Exception signal that has been processed through logic that has tested the IE flag, etc. Recall that there are no condition codes in the SRC, but there are two signals that control conditional branching: the CON signal and the n = 0 signal. CON effects a branch only on true, while the n = 0 signal causes a branch on true and on false. These two signals take the place of the N and Z flags in the microcode control unit above and make their appearance in the microcontrol word as branch control signals BrCON, Br(n ≠ 0), and Br(n = 0).

Microcode for the add Instruction.   We will begin as before with the add instruction. Table 5.4 shows the microcode sequence that implements the 1-bus SRC add instruction. Notice that the concrete RTN is the same as it was in the hardwired control unit. The first three microinstructions at addresses 100–102 accomplish the instruction fetch. There is an

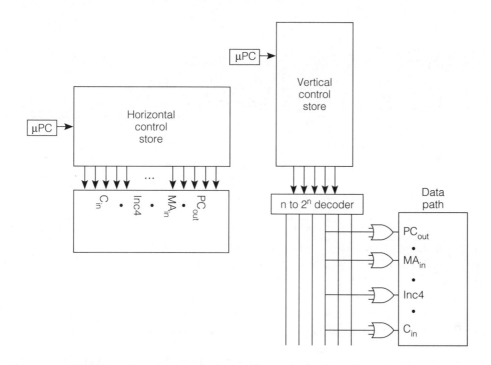

Fig. 5.26 Completely Horizontal and Vertical Microcoding

Table 5.4 The add Instruction

Address	Mux Ctl	BrUn	$\overline{\text{BrCON}}$	Br(n ≠ 0)	Br(n = 0)	End	PC$_{out}$	MA$_{in}$	Control Signals	Branch Address	Actions
100	00	0	0	0	0	0	1	1	•••	XXX	MA ←PC: C ←PC + 4;
101	00	0	0	0	0	0	0	0	•••	XXX	MD ←M[MA]: PC ←C;
102	01	1	0	0	0	0	0	0	•••	XXX	IR, μPC ←PLA ←MD;
200	00	0	0	0	0	0	0	0	•••	XXX	A ←R[rb];
201	00	0	0	0	0	0	0	0	•••	XXX	C ← A + R[rc];
202	11	1	0	0	0	1	0	0	•••	100	R[ra] ←C; μPC ←100

unconditional branch at 102 to the PLA output. The PLA has decoded the add operation code to address 200, so the branch is to address 200. The code at 200–202 performs the addition, and there is an unconditional branch at location 202, to 100, where instruction fetch is located. We have added an additional control signal to the microinstruction word, End. This instruction may seem redundant in light of the unconditional branch to 100, but

Table 5.5 The shr Instruction

Address	Mux Ctl	BrUn	$\overline{\text{BrCON}}$	Br(n $\neq$ 0)	Br(n = 0)	End	PC$_{out}$	MA$_{in}$	Control Signals	Branch Address	Action
100	00	0	0	0	0	0	1	1	•••	XXX	MA ←PC: C ←PC+4;
101	00	0	0	0	0	0	0	0	•••	XXX	MD ←M[MA]: PC ←C;
102	01	1	0	0	0	0	0	0	•••	XXX	IR, μPC ← PLA ←MD;
300	00	0	0	0	0	0	0	0	•••	XXX	n ←IR⟨4..0⟩;
301	11	0	0	1	0	0	0	0	≡0	303	n≠0 → μPC ←303;
302	00	0	0	0	0	0	0	0	•••	XXX	n ←R[rc]⟨4..0⟩ ;
303	00	0	0	0	0	0	0	0	•••	XXX	C ← R[rb];
304	11		0	0	1	0	0	0	≡0	306	n=0 → μPC ←306;
305	11	1	0	0	0	0	0	0	•••	304	C⟨31..0⟩ ← 0#C⟨31..1⟩: n ←n-1: μPC ←304;
306	11	1	0	0	0	1	0	0	•••	100	R[ra] ←C: μPC ←100;

in this design it is needed to signal the sequencer of the end of the instruction, in case an external event such as an exception needs to take control at the end of instruction execution.

Microcode for the shr Instruction. We next consider the shr instruction. It is a bit more interesting than the add instruction because it has two instances of conditional execution and a conditional branch. Table 5.5 shows the microcode for this instruction. In a sense, the instructions at 301 and 304 are "wasted," in that they only implement the conditional branch and perform no useful register transfers. Exercise 5.19 provides an opportunity to compress these branch microinstructions.

The SRC Microcode Control Unit Sequencer. Some changes must be made to adapt the generic sequencer shown in Figure 5.24. We need to substitute the conditional branch control signals discussed previously, and we will add to the control unit detail by including the conditioned reset and exception signals. We presume that these signals have been conditioned in the clocking logic circuitry by synchronizing them to the master clock. The reset signal is also presumed to have been converted to a 1-clock-period pulse. Figure 5.27 shows these modifications. The branch control signals are handled as before. The exception and reset signals both operate by causing an unconditional branch to their microcode addresses, presumed to be 400 and 000, respectively. This is done by using the OR of the two signals to multiplex in a 10 (External address) control signal to the 4–1 microcode address multiplexer. The two signals are also used to generate the branch addresses that are input to the External address input. In keeping with the abstract RTN descriptions of the SRC reset and exception actions described in Chapter 4, the reset signal causes an immediate microbranch to the reset microcode at 000, whereas the exception signal is ANDed with the End signal output by the microcode at the end of each instruction_execution. This means that exception processing waits until the end of instruction execution.

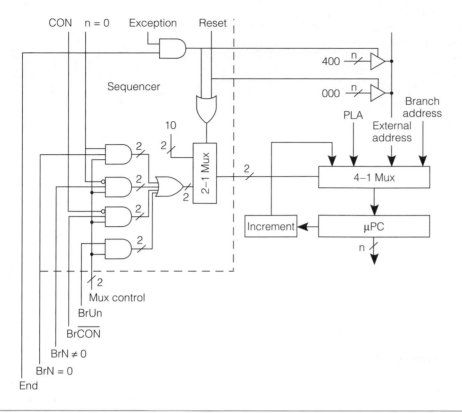

Fig. 5.27 The SRC Microcode Sequencer

A Mostly Horizontal Encoding of the SRC Microinstruction Word. Let us see how much we can compress the SRC microinstruction control word. The first step in the process is to find all the SRC control signals developed in the last two chapters. These signals are then grouped into sets such that each set has at most one member asserted at one time. We may have to add a "No signal" signal to the set if there can be a condition where none of the signals should be asserted. The designer is put on notice here that instruction sets and control signals change with time and circumstance. "Creeping featurism" is an unavoidable part of all system design enterprises, and can cause great embarrassment to the designer who has been so zealous in packing bits into a vertical encoding that the design cannot be modified to include additional instructions without extensive redesign. The wise designer leaves room for expansion, just as the wise tailor does.

Table 5.6 shows a possible encoding. The two mux control bits in field F1 were already encoded. The five branch control signals in F2 are obvious candidates for encoding, since at most one can be asserted at any one time. F3 contains the End signal. It is left unencoded because it can occur in so many contexts. The seven Out signals are also obvious candidates for encoding, since the "rule of buses" guarantees that at most one can be asserted at a given time. In the "plan ahead" mode, notice that the None signal could be used to gate all zeros onto the bus, which may be useful at a future time in initializing a register. The F6 field contains all the other control signals that can be grouped together. C_{in}

Table 5.6 Somewhat Vertical Encoding of the SRC Microinstruction

F1	F2	F3	F4	F5	F6	F7	F8	F9
Mux Ctl	Branch Control	End	Out Signals	In Signals	Misc.	Gate Registers	ALU	Branch Address
00 01 10 11	000 Un 001 $\overline{\text{CON}}$ 010 CON 011 n = 0 100 n ≠ 0 101 None	0 Cont. 1 End	000 PC_{out} 001 C_{out} 010 MD_{out} 011 R_{out} 100 BA_{out} 101 $c1_{out}$ 110 $c2_{out}$ 111 None	000 MA_{in} 001 PC_{in} 010 IR_{in} 011 A_{in} 100 R_{in} 101 MD_{in} 110 Ld 111 None	000 Read 001 Write 010 Wait 011 Decr 100 CON_{in} 101 C_{in} 110 Stop 111 None	00 Gra 01 Grb 10 Grc 11 None	0000 ADD 0001 C = B 0010 SHR 0011 INC4 • • • 1111 NOT	10 bits
2 bits	3 bits	1 bit	3 bits	3 bits	3 bits	2 bits	4 bits	10 bits

was bumped out of F5 and into F6 because it occurs together with MA_{in} in the first step of the instruction fetch. CON_{in} was placed in F6 because it differs from the other "in" signals, in that it gates a value into a single flip-flop. While F6 satisfies the criterion of having at most one signal asserted in the current instruction set, it is more likely that several of its members might be asserted simultaneously in some future extension because of the variegated nature of the signals it contains. F7 contains the register field gate signals, only one of which can be asserted at a time. F8 contains the ALU instructions, of which we assume there are 16 in the complete SRC design. Finally, F9 can also be viewed as an encoded field, encoding the branch address.

A count of the control signals shows that the purely horizontal encoding requires 58 bits, whereas the new encoding results in 31 bits, a savings of almost 50% in bit count. This represents a considerable savings in space, at a cost of the time to decode the signals and the cost of five decoders.

5.4.3   ALTERNATIVE APPROACHES TO MICROCODING

There have been many different microcoding schemes developed since the technique became popular in the 1960s. "Bit ORing" was used to achieve a multiway branch in a single instruction. Another technique, nanocoding, was used by the VAX designers to save bits. Several techniques for speeding up the fetching of the microcontrol word have achieved popularity in more recent years. Many of these techniques are modifications of those that have been used to speed up macro instruction fetch and execution: Prefetching and pipelining, in particular, have been used as speedup methods.

Bit ORing.   The bit ORing technique can be used to compute multiway branches in a single step. In these designs there are control fields within the microinstruction word that OR bits into the microinstruction address, causing a branch to one of several addresses, depending on the bits ORed. ORing a bit or bits into the least significant part of the microinstruction address can be used to skip over one or a few addresses, and ORing a bit or a few bits into the most significant bits of the microinstruction word can be used to branch over large distances in the control store.

Nanocoding.   The MC68000 employed a nanocode approach to save control store memory bits. The microprogram consisted of 550 17-bit words, of which 10 bits were used to point into a nanoprogram memory of 340 68-bit words. This consumes $(550 \times 17) + (340 \times 68) = 32,470$ bits, compared with $(550 \times 68) = 37,400$ bits if a single-level control store had been used, for a savings of nearly 5,000 bits. In the late 1970s, when the MC68000 was being designed, 5,000 bits were a lot of bits. In addition, at the time it was more fashionable to have a more sophisticated instruction set and to plan on increasing execution speed in future product releases than it was to introduce a faster product and to plan on adding more instructions and features at a later time.

Writable Control Stores.   The designers of the first VAX machines in the middle-to-late 1970s were caught between the cost of memory and the desire to implement as many instructions as possible. The VAX 11/780 had a ROM-based microcode control store, and a block of RAM, the "writable control store" (WCS) devoted to additional microinstructions. The WCS was used to add additional instructions, patch buggy microcode, and provide code to emulate the older 16-bit PDP11, providing upward compatibility to those who wanted an upgrade path for their old PDP11 software. The presence of the WCS, which was loaded from disk, meant that the DEC field service engineer could show up with a disk containing bug fixes or microcode updates. The VAX microinstruction word was 96 bits wide, with a 13-bit next address field, and 4,096 addresses. The next address field was used as the next address for all instructions, thus dispensing with the need to provide an incrementer or counting function on the μPC. Branches were accomplished by using the bit ORing technique.

Subroutines in Microprogramming.   Advanced Micro Devices, AMD, developed a so-called bit-slice architecture in which one could string together 4- or 16-bit slices of the data path to form data paths of arbitrary width. Each "slice" had 16 general purpose registers and a slice of the ALU. The control was by means of a microprogrammable control unit. This control unit had a great deal of flexibility, allowing users to develop their own microprograms using an AMD development system. This meant the user could develop custom, special purpose microprocessors to perform particular functions without having to have expertise in VLSI design and access to an IC fabrication facility. One interesting feature of the microcode control unit was that it was capable of performing microcode subroutines. The control unit had a stack pointer into a 5-word stack, so subroutines could be nested five-deep. It also had a counter that could be loaded, decremented, and tested, so `for` loops could be implemented in microcode.

Perspectives on Microcoding.   When microcoding was first used, the access times of the ROM memories used as control stores were shorter than the access times of RAM memories, so microcoding offered a potential advantage in execution speed. At this point in the history of computer development, the microcode approach has been eclipsed by the hardwired approach. The main reason is that in the implementation domain of VLSI circuitry, RAM memory is as fast or faster than ROM memory. RISC processors place an emphasis on speed, and having to access the microcode memory seems to put it at a disadvantage. On the other hand, the same techniques used to speed up the operation of the main processor—pipelining, prefetching, and so on—can be used to speed up microinstruction access. Another reason for the increasing popularity of hardwiring is the advent of advanced software tools for PLA and PAL design. The PLA is, after all, at the heart of the hardwired controller.

It is risky to predict the total demise of microcoding, however. Some observers see RISC instructions as coarse-grained microcode. It is coarse-grained in the sense that one CISC instruction can be broken up into several RISC instructions, just as a single macroinstruction is broken up into several microinstructions. One current difference is that RISC instructions are still highly encoded—vertically encoded, you could say. The reason for this encoding is the cost of memory. Perhaps in the future, as memory prices continue to fall, architectures will emerge in which microinstructions are stored in main memory, to be fetched and immediately executed without any decoding being required. This would do away with instruction sets as we know them today, replacing them with microinstruction sets. The compiler will then convert the high-level language program directly into register transfers, in effect designing custom microinstruction sequences tailored to the particular problem.

Key Concepts: Hardwired versus Microcoded Control Units

The hardwired and microcode methods form two radically different approaches to control unit design. Each has advantages and disadvantages when performance and cost are compared:

- Speed: Hardwired control units win hands down in the speed category. They have a latency of just a few gate delays, considerably less than microcoded control units, which must perform a memory fetch for each control step. This can be improved somewhat by pipelining memory requests.

- Ease of prototyping: The microcode design approach wins here, since it is generally easier to reprogram a memory chip than to reprogram random logic.

- Flexibility of use: Once again, microcoding is superior when the designer wishes to change instruction sets. This might be desirable for instruction set upgrades or when several instruction sets are to be emulated.

The characteristics of the two approaches as summarized in the preceding list tend to favor hardwired units when a processor is to be put into high-volume production, and to favor microcoding when developing prototypes or when manufacturing small quantities.

Summary

Having shown how to design a computer with unified data paths and a hardwired control unit in Chapter 4, we show in this chapter several alternate techniques of machine design.

- Pipelining is a way to make a machine faster by executing multiple instructions simultaneously. The method requires a bit more hardware because each pipeline stage must be able to operate independently, but it has the potential of issuing a new instruction every clock cycle.

■ Pipeline hazards are an impediment to reaching the potential of a fully utilized pipeline. Hazards can be addressed by stalling the pipeline, by forwarding results to instructions that need them, by having the compiler insert nops, or by a combination of these techniques.

■ To take fuller advantage of the pipeline, the rules of instruction set usage are usually modified to include the effect of delayed loads, stores, and branches.

■ Multiple-instruction-issue machines remove the limitation, inherent in pipelining, that only a single instruction can be issued per clock cycle. Dynamic multi-issue, or superscalar, machines, and static multi-issue, or VLIW machines, have multiple functional units, and can start more than one instruction at a time. Their scheduling methods and hazard management are quite complex. Consult the bibliography section for more details.

■ Microprogramming is a softwarelike method for control unit design. It treats the control sequence generator as a simple computer. Microprogramming can be used for rapid prototyping of new designs, or for the design of small controllers where the speed demand is moderate.

Bibliography

Other computer design texts that present pipelining as a design alternative include the following:

M. Morris Mano, *Computer System Architecture,* 3rd ed., Prentice-Hall, Englewood Cliffs, NJ, 1993.

Arthur B. Maccabe, *Computer Systems: Architecture, Organization, and Programming,* Richard D. Irwin, Boston, MA, 1993.

Extensive treatments of pipelining can be found in:

David A. Patterson and John L. Hennessy, *Computer Organization and Design: The Hardware/Software Interface*, Morgan Kaufman, San Francisco, CA, 1994.

Advanced treatments of pipelining and superscalar machine design can be found in:

Michael J. Flynn, *Computer Architecture: Pipelined and Parallel Processor Design,* Jones and Bartlett, Boston, MA, 1995.

John L. Hennessy and David A. Patterson, *Computer Architecture: A Quantitative Approach,* 2nd ed., Morgan Kaufman, San Francisco, CA, 1995.

Microprogramming is well treated at the level of this textbook in:

V. Carl Hamacher, Zvonko G. Vranesic, and Safwat G. Zaki, *Computer Organization,* 4th ed., McGraw-Hill, New York, 1996.

A good treatment of microprogramming in connection with the VAX architecture can be found in:

H. M. Levy and R. H. Eckhouse, Jr., *Computer Programming and Architecture: The VAX,* 2nd ed., Digital Press, Bedford, MA, 1989.

The use of microprogramming to build a family of compatible computers is exemplified in connection with the IBM 360 family by an extensive treatment in:

Samir S. Husson, *Microprogramming: Principles and Practices,* Prentice-Hall, Englewood Cliffs, NJ, 1970.

Exercises

5.1 Some of the registers in Figure 5.6 represent programmer-visible state, and some are implementation-dependent parts of the pipeline. Both must be represented in the processor-state declarations of a concrete RTN for the pipeline.

Write RTN declarations for all the registers and memory needed in a pure RTN description of Figure 5.6, distinguishing programmer-visible from implementation items by grouping and comments. Declare only the number of bits needed by the instruction register in the various stages.   (**§5.1**)

5.2 The concrete RTN of Figure 5.6 defines the pipelined implementation of the SRC. In the figure, the statements in each block are terminated by a semicolon to indicate that all RTs for a stage occur in 1 clock. Actually, the RTs for all stages occur at every clock. If the concrete RTN is separated from the figure, it must be changed to show this.

Write instruction fetch-and-execute RTN to go with the pipelined processor state developed in Exercise 5.1. Except for some important details like start, stop, interrupts, and so on, the results of Exercises 5.1 and 5.2 will give a complete RTN for a pipelined implementation of the SRC.   (**§5.1**)

5.3 Use a sheet similar to Figure 5.7 of the text to trace the code fragment given on page 191 through the pipeline. Assume the following decimal register and memory values: r2 = –4, r3 = 32, r5 = 8, addr1 = 1000, addr2 = 2000, PC = 100, M[2000] = 100. Insert nop bubbles into the pipeline as needed to resolve any dependences.   (**§5.1**)

5.4 The following code fragment is executed in a pipelined SRC with forwarding hardware. If variables correspond to memory locations, a:200, b:204, c:208, and x:212, what compiler language assignment statement does the code below seem to correspond to? Trace the execution, taking into account delay slots and forwarding, to see if it executes correctly.   (**§5.1**)

```
        ld r1, 200(r0)
        ld r2, 204(r0)
        lar r4, POS
        sub r0, r1, r2
        brpl r4, r0
        ld r3, 208(r0)
        sub r0, r2, r1
POS:    add r0, r0, r3
        st r0, 212(r0)
```

5.5 In the pipelined version of SRC, the branch instructions have a branch delay slot to avoid stalling the pipeline for a cycle. Assume that the compiler schedules instructions into the branch-delay slot. In this context, consider the implications of the brl instructions storing PC + 4 in the link register.

a. What problem does this pose for subroutine return?

b. How should the compiler handle this problem?   (**§5.1**)

5.6 First, informally define how the SRC stop instruction should behave in the pipelined design. Then extend the concrete RTN in the five stages of Figure 5.6 to include the SRC stop instruction.   (**§5.1**)

5.7 a.–e. Translate the concrete RTN in the five stages of Figure 5.6 to control sequences.

   f.–j. Translate the control sequences to digital logic circuits. You may wish to begin by abstracting the RTN definitions in Figure 5.3 to "black boxes," to be used as needed.   (**§5.1**)

5.8 Use a sheet similar to Figure 5.7 of the text to trace the execution of the following code. Assume the pipeline has hazard detection and forwarding.

```
400    add    r0,   r1, r2
404    brpl   r3,   r0
408    neg    r0,   r0
412    st     r0,   4(r4)
```

Use decimal values in your trace. Specify the opcode field as ascii text, add, for example. Assume the following decimal values in registers and memory: r0 undefined, r1 = 5, r2 = −4, r3 = 412, r4 = 1000. Your trace should include a summary of the pipeline register's contents at each clock cycle, beginning with the fetch of the instruction at 400, in a manner similar to the series of figures beginning with Figure 5.8. If there are pipeline stalls, indicate where they occur and show clearly which operand(s) is/are responsible. If there is forwarding, show clearly which value is forwarded, and to where. **(§5.1)**

5.9 For the following pairs of instructions,

a. indicate how many bubbles must be placed between them in the presence of and in the absence of data forwarding to resolve the dependence.

b. trace each pair through a sheet similar to Figure 5.7. **(§5.1)**

```
1.  la   r2,  (r4)        2.  not r2,  r4          3.  lar r31, −12
    shc  r6,  r4, r2          sub r6,  r2, r0          brl r31, r30

4.  add r2,  r0, r4       5.  add r2,  r2, r4      6.  brl r31, r30
    st  r0,  12(r2)           st  r2,  12(r2)          shl r31, r30, 2
```

5.10 Figure 5.6 forms a good framework for checking the correct pipelined execution of individual instructions. Remove the RTN operations from the five pipeline stage boxes, and insert just the RTN register transfers for each one of the following operations, to verify that the global state is correctly updated by the time the instruction exits stage 5: **(§5.1)**

a. brl;   b. ld;   c. shl;

5.11 If there were no nop instruction in the SRC instruction set, could one be synthesized from the existing SRC instruction set described in Chapter 2 that could be inserted by the compiler and not trigger any hardware hazard detection circuitry? **(§5.1)**

5.12 The RTN fragments 5.1 to 5.3 on page 220 describe the hazard detection with bubble insertion for the 2-operand ALU-ALU instructions.

a. Write analogous equations to detect hazards between an alu instruction followed by a ld instruction.

b. Write equations similar to fragments 5.1 to 5.3 to cover instruction pairs from Table 5.1, as assigned by your instructor. **(§5.1)**

5.13 In the discussion of the RTN expression describing hazard detection and data forwarding on page 216, it was stated that the use of a semicolon to specify precedence was less than ideal. Write an RTN expression to accomplish the same result without using a semicolon. **(§5.1)**

5.14 Design the digital logic circuitry of the 2-operand ALU-ALU portion of the stage 4 hazard detection and forwarding unit shown in Figure 5.15. **(§5.1)**

5.15 Describe in one paragraph the difference between the superscalar architecture and the VLIW architecture. **(§5.2)**

5.16 What is the maximum speedup of the VLIW implementation of SRC in Section 5.3 relative to a) the 1-bus SRC, and b) the pipelined version of SRC? **(§5.2)**

5.17 Write a four-page summary of the principles of operation of the following:

    a. The Motorola PowerPC G4

    b. The Intel P6

    c. The MIPS R4000

    d. A processor assigned by your instructor   **(§5.2)**

5.18 Write control sequences equivalent to those in Table 5.3 that implement the following constructs:

    a. `repeat {•••} until` (Z);[1]

    b. `if` (Z) $\{•••_1\}$ `else` $\{•••_2\}$;

    The subscripts indicate that code blocks 1 and 2 differ from one another.

    c. Is it possible to implement the `for` construct using the microcontroller architecture shown in Figure 5.24? Explain why or why not.   **(§5.3)**

5.19 The pairs of instructions at 301–302 and 304–305 in Table 5.5 implement the `if-then` and `while` statements respectively, and neither branch uses its associated control signals. Suggest alternative approaches that will reduce each pair to one instruction. Minor hardware modifications may be necessary.   **(§5.3)**

5.20 One of the authors, who wishes to remain anonymous,[2] initially encoded fields F6 and F7 of Table 5.6 in a single field.

    a. Give two reasons why this is an error.

    b. Why is he sure that all three operations can be grouped together in F7?   **(§5.3)**

5.21 Examine the control sequences for the 1-bus design in Chapter 4. Are there any cases where control signals that appear in the same step are encoded in the same field of Table 5.6? How could conflicts be resolved by changing either the encoding or the control sequences?   **(§5.3)**

5.22 Design a microcode sequence to implement the 1-bus SRC `br` instruction using the concrete RTN of Table 4.11 as a jumping-off point.[3]   **(§5.3)**

5.23 Design a microcode sequence to implement the 1-bus reset and exception processing routines located at microaddresses 000 and 400, respectively. The routines should implement the abstract RTN for these processes developed for SRC in Chapter 4.   **(§5.3)**

---

1.   The Pascal `repeat` statement is like the C `while` statement, except the test is at the bottom of the loop.
2.   But whose initials are V. P. H.
3.   No pun intended.

Computer Arithmetic
and the Arithmetic Unit

We finally come to the part of a computer that computes. The arithmetic unit is the heart of the machine in the sense that it carries out the operations that give their name to the class of machines we are studying. In control unit design, we saw how to use the RTN notation to add mathematical structure to control unit specification, so that the design task could be better defined. Computer arithmetic also contains a great deal of mathematical structure that is extremely valuable in the practical task of designing an optimal circuit in a given implementation. You have probably seen simple treatments of binary numbers and arithmetic, so we will concentrate on using the mathematics both to describe what needs to be done as well as to carry out transformations in pursuit of a better design. Algebra is sufficient for most discussions, with a little of the notation and ideas of finite mathematics. We will cast the discussion of computer arithmetic in algebraic form, and use numbers for examples or to illustrate ideas for which the mathematical discussion is outside the scope of this book.

6.1 Number Systems and Radix Conversion

Digital number systems are characterized by a *base* or *radix, b*. Humans use base 10, and computers are usually said to use base 2. Actually, computers may use a number of different bases. The most interesting ones are powers of 2, where digits can often be simply treated as groupings of base

2 bits. In concession to humans, some computers use base 10 somewhere in their hardware, although the slow speed of human-oriented I/O often makes software handling of base 10 numbers more cost effective than special hardware. Base 10 hardware is sometimes used in financial calculations requiring both high speed and elimination of number system conversion error. Other interesting bases for computer design are bases 4, 16, 256, and 2^{16}, which group 2, 4, 8, and 16 bits, respectively. Trade-offs in speed, complexity, and packaging can often be understood more easily by interpreting the number system base as one of these instead of as base 2.

6.1.1   DIGITAL NUMBER REPRESENTATION

Using *positional notation*, an m-digit base b number is written as a string of m digits, $x = x_{m-1}x_{m-2} \cdots x_1 x_0$, where the digits x_i are in the range $0 \le x_i \le b - 1$. The value of an unsigned integer is given by

$$\text{value}(x) = \sum_{i=0}^{m-1} x_i b^i \qquad \text{[Eq. 6.1]}$$

Since only a finite number of digits can be used in a practical implementation, the system designer is quite interested in the maximum value that can be represented with a given number of digits. The largest unsigned number $\hat{x}$ that can be represented with m digits in the base b number system is obtained by making all of the digits of the number as large as possible: $x_i = b - 1, i = 0, 1, \ldots, (m-1)$. With a little algebra, we find that this largest number has the following value:

$$x_{max} = \sum_{i=0}^{m-1} (b-1)b^i \qquad \text{[Eq. 6.2]}$$

$$= (b-1) \sum_{i=0}^{m-1} b^i$$

$$= b^m - 1$$

The "little algebra" involves the sum of a geometric series, which comes up quite often in studying digital arithmetic. Its general form is

$$\sum_{i=0}^{m-1} b^i = \frac{b^m - 1}{b - 1} \qquad \text{[Eq. 6.3]}$$

When the variable in the summation is less than 1, it is better to write

$$\sum_{i=0}^{m-1} r^i = \frac{1 - r^m}{1 - r} \qquad \text{[Eq. 6.4]}$$

since this makes both numerator and denominator positive in this case.

As an example of the largest unsigned number that can be represented, three base 5 digits can represent numbers from 0 up to $444_5 = 5^3 - 1 = 124_{10}$. Interesting, but less useful, is the fact that the geometric progression sum formula lets us calculate other numbers having special forms. For example

$$66666_9 = 6 \times \frac{9^5 - 1}{8} = 44286$$

Five bytes can represent unsigned numbers up to $256^5 - 1 = 2^{40} - 1$.

Radix Conversion.   Before moving on to arithmetic operations, we will consider the conversion of numbers from a representation in one base to another. Because humans work with base 10 and computers use a base of 2 or a power of 2, this *radix conversion* operation is of obvious interest. Although this operation is usually more cost effective in software, it is possible to build hardware to do it, and studying the procedure gives us a better insight into the manipulation of digitally represented numbers in general.

The division algorithm is needed for number system conversion. It states that for integers a and d, with $d > 0$, there exist integers q and r such that $a = q \cdot d + r$, with $0 \le r \le b - 1$. Notice that the remainder is in the range of a base b digit. Formal notation for the quotient uses the floor $\lfloor \ \rfloor$ operator, $q = \lfloor a/d \rfloor$. Informally, the floor operator is just the quotient of the division. The remainder uses the mod operator, $r = a \bmod d$.

There are different algorithms for converting between bases, often learned in elementary courses as the "base 2 to base 10 algorithm" and the "base 10 to base 2" algorithm. The difference between the algorithms is not a result of the values of the two bases, but is solely a result of the base of arithmetic in which the computations are carried out. Thus one algorithm is used to convert base 2 numbers to base 10 by a person translating a binary number (a human calculator), and a different one is used in a program written for a computer (an electronic calculator) using base 2 calculations to translate internal base 2 numbers to base 10 for output. The human computes in the target base, while the computer uses the source base for calculations, and this, not the numeric value of the base, determines the algorithm used. We will assume that calculations are performed in the calculator's base, c, and let the other base be b. Then one algorithm converts a number from base b to the calculator's base c, and the other converts numbers in the calculator's base, c, to base b.

An important aspect of conversion is that the first b nonnegative integers, 0 through $b-1$, are represented in base b by b different symbols. The sets of symbols used for different bases may be completely different, or as is more commonly the case, the set of symbols for the smaller base may be a subset of the set used in the larger base, as the binary digits 0 and 1 are a subset of the decimal digits 0 through 9, which are themselves a subset of the hexadecimal digits, commonly represented as the symbols 0 through F. In any case, the numbers represented by single symbols must be converted to the other base by a list of correspondences, which we can think of as a lookup table.

Converting a Base b Integer to the Calculator's Base, c.   We start with the algorithm to convert from base b to the calculator's base, c.

1. Start with base b representation: $x = x_{m-1} x_{m-2} \cdots x_1 x_0$.
2. Initialize the base c value x to 0.

3. Working left to right, get the next symbol x_i.
4. Convert the base b symbol to a base c number D_i by means of a table.
5. Update the base c value by $x = xb + D_i$.
6. If there are more digits, repeat from step 3.

We refer to a table in step 4 because base b digits and base c digits may be represented by different symbols. If $b > c$, some of the base b digit symbols will not be base c digit symbols. Rather, D_i will be a several-digit base c number. If $b < c$, it is possible to use a subset of the symbols of base c for the fewer symbols needed in base b, as we do when we use the base 10 symbols 0 and 1 for the two digits needed in binary. Whatever scheme is used, it is easy to think of a table of digit correspondences with the number of entries equal to the maximum of b and c. The standard convention for base 8 is to use the subset 0 through 7 of the decimal digits for the 8-symbol set, and the convention for base 16 is to extend the decimal digits to 0, 1, . . . , 9, A, B, C, D, E, F.

Example 6.1 Convert the Hexadecimal Number $AC2_{16}$ to Base 10

The calculator's base is assumed to be 10, and we are converting *from* base 16. The successive changes to x are

$$x = 0$$
$$x = x + A(= 10) = 10$$
$$x = 16 \cdot 10 + C(= 12) = 172$$
$$x = 16 \cdot 172 + 2 = 2754$$

∎

Converting an Integer from the Calculator's Base to Base b. The algorithm to convert an integer from the calculator's base to base b is as follows:

1. Start with the base c integer x to be converted.
2. Initialize $i = 0$ and $v = x$, and produce digits right to left.
3. Set $D_i = v \bmod b$ and $v = \lfloor v/b \rfloor$. Convert D_i to base b digit x_i.
4. Set $i = i + 1$, and if $v \neq 0$, repeat from step 3.

Since the base c number D_i is a remainder, it is less than b and must be in the table corresponding to a base b digit. For $b \geq 2$, the only possibility for number system bases, the quotient is always less than the dividend. Thus v decreases at each step, and only a finite number of base b digits can be generated, although it will be more than the number of base c digits if $b < c$.

Example 6.2 Convert 3661_{10} to Base 16

The calculator's base is again assumed to be 10, and we are now converting *to* base 16.

$$3661 \div 16 = 228(\text{rem} = 13) \Rightarrow x_0 = D$$
$$228 \div 16 = 14(\text{rem} = 4) \Rightarrow x_1 = 4$$
$$14 \div 16 = 0(\text{rem} = 14) \Rightarrow x_2 = E$$

Thus, $3661 = E4D_{16}$.

∎

Digital Fractions and Fixed-Point Numbers.   Unsigned fractions are represented as are integers, but with the *radix point* (called the decimal point if the base is 10) at the left end. An m-digit base b fraction $f = .f_{-1}f_{-2}...f_{-m}$ can be considered to be just the integer having the same digits, divided by b^m. Thus one way to convert from base b to base c is to convert the integer and divide by the scale factor at the end. As we described integer conversion to base c, this treats the digits from left to right. A number may have both an integer part to the left of the radix point and a fractional part to its right. The value of such a number

$$x_{n-1}x_{n-2} \cdots x_1 x_0.x_{-1}x_{-2} \cdots x_{-m}$$

can be obtained by dividing b^m into the value of the $(m+n)$-digit integer obtained by removing the radix point.

A number in a fixed length computer register that is understood to have its radix point in a specific position is a *fixed-point* number. The most common types of fixed-point numbers are integers, for which the radix point is at the far right, and fractions, for which it is at the far left. We will see below that the position of the radix point is fairly arbitrary with respect to addition and subtraction, provided both operands have it in the same position, but that specific multiply and divide instructions usually support only one choice of radix point position, far left or far right.

As in decimal notation, moving the radix point one position to the right corresponds to multiplying a number by the base b, and moving it one position to the left corresponds to dividing by b. Both are called *scaling operations* on digital numbers. Since the radix point is normally associated with a fixed position in a word, these operations are usually thought of as shifting the number left one position to multiply by b and shifting right one position to divide by b, with the position of the radix point remaining fixed. A left shift can result in *overflow* if nonzero digits "fall off" the left end of a register, and a right shift can result in loss of accuracy if nonzeros fall off the right end. An arithmetic operation results in overflow if the result does not fit into the number system.

Converting a Base b Fraction to the Calculator's Base, c.   Another way to convert base b fractions to base c treats digits from right to left, dividing rather than multiplying at each step.

1.   The base b representation is $.f_{-1}f_{-2}...f_{-m}$.
2.   Initialize $f = 0.0$ and set $i = -m$.
3.   Find base c equivalent D of digit f_i from table.
4.   Update $f = (f + D)/b$ and $i = i + 1$.
5.   If $i = 0$, the result is f. Otherwise repeat from step 3.

Example 6.3   Convert $.2AD_{16}$ to Calculator's Base, 10   The steps are

$$f = 0$$
$$f = (0 + 13)/16 = 0.8125$$
$$f = (0.8125 + 10)/16 = 0.67578125$$
$$f = (0.67578125 + 2)/16 = 0.16723633$$

Notice that the number of digits in the base 10 result becomes large very quickly. In fact, it is a special relation between 10 and 16 that prevents division by 16 from producing a nonterminating base 10 result. For other bases, as well as for practicality, the base c computation will keep only a limited number of fraction digits. A 1-unit change in the lowest-order digit of the base 16 fraction of the example would amount to $16^{-3} = 0.00024$, so keeping only four base 10 digits is consistent with the accuracy implied by having only three digits in the base 16 fraction.

Converting a Fraction from the Calculator's Base, c to Base b.   The conversion of a fraction from the calculator's base to another does not involve division, but it still suffers from the fact that terminating fractions in one base may not terminate in another:

1.   Start with an exact fraction f in base c.
2.   Initialize $i = 1$ and $v = f$.
3.   Set $D_{-i} = \lfloor bv \rfloor$ and $v = bv - D_{-i}$. Convert D_{-i} to a base b digit f_{-i} by using a table.
4.   Increment $i = i + 1$ and repeat from step 3 unless either $v = 0$ or enough digits have been generated.

The nonterminating fraction problem shows up in step 4. There is no guarantee that v will ever become zero. Thus termination must also consider the number of digits generated.

Example 6.4   Convert 0.31_{10} to Base 2

$$0.31 \times 2 = 0.62 \Rightarrow f_{-1} = 0$$

$$0.62 \times 2 = 1.24 \Rightarrow f_{-2} = 1$$

$$0.24 \times 2 = 0.48 \Rightarrow f_{-3} = 0$$

$$0.48 \times 2 = 0.96 \Rightarrow f_{-4} = 0$$

$$0.96 \times 2 = 1.92 \Rightarrow f_{-5} = 1$$

$$0.92 \times 2 = 1.84 \Rightarrow f_{-6} = 1$$

$$0.84 \times 2 = 1.68 \Rightarrow f_{-7} = 1, \ldots$$

Thus $0.31_{10} = 0.0100111_2$.   ∎

Converting from Base b to Base c, Where $c = b^k$.   The base conversion process is considerably simplified for the special case when base $b = c^k$. In this case, the base c value expression can be manipulated into the following form:

$$\text{value}(x) = \cdots + (x_{ki + (k-1)} c^{k \cdot i + (k-1)} + \cdots + x_{k \cdot i} c^{k \cdot i}) + \cdots$$

$$\cdots + (x_{k-1} c^{k-1} + \ldots + x_0) \qquad \text{[Eq. 6.5]}$$

$$= \cdots + x_{ki + (k-1)} c^{k-1} \cdots + x_{ki}) b^i + \cdots x_{k-1} c^{k-1} + \cdots + x_0$$

This shows that digit i of the base b form is a simple k-digit base c number. Thus conversions from base c to base b can be done by collecting base c digits in groups of k and replacing each group by the base b symbol from the table. Conversions from base b to base c simply amount to replacing each base b symbol by its k-digit base c equivalent.

Example 6.5   Convert from Base 16 to Base 2, and from Base 2 to Base 8

$$E4D_{16} = 1110\ 0100\ 1101_2 = 111001001101_2$$

and

$$010011110_2 = 010\ 011\ 110_2 = 236_8$$ ■

6.1.2   REPRESENTING NEGATIVE INTEGER NUMBERS

There is no single, universal way of representing negative integers in the computer. Four ways are in common usage: sign-magnitude, radix complement, diminished radix complement, and bias, or excess representations. We will discuss the first three methods in this section, and defer a discussion of biased representations until we discuss floating-point numbers in Section 6.4.1.

Perhaps the simplest way of representing both positive and negative numbers is the sign-magnitude representation. This is the method we use in common, pencil-and-paper arithmetic. In *sign-magnitude* representation, a symbol representing the sign is appended to the left side of the number. In everyday usage, we use the "+" and "–" signs. Positive 435 is +435, negative 435 is –435. In the computer we represent negative numbers by appending a "1" as the most significant bit, and we represent positive numbers by appending a "0" as the most significant bit. For example, if numbers are represented as 4-bit values in the computer, we would represent +3 as 0011 and –3 as 1011. The disadvantage of sign-magnitude representation in the computer is that arithmetic operations are rather complicated. Arithmetic operations are performed by examining the sign bit, stripping it off the number, performing the appropriate arithmetic operations, and inserting the appropriate sign bit. As we shall see below, when using the radix complement and diminished radix complement representations, arithmetic operations are as simple as with their unsigned counterparts.

Probably the most common way of representing signed integers in the computer is to use the radix complement. This method is closely connected with the complement operation. There are actually two complement operations, known in general as the radix complement and the diminished radix complement. In addition to being useful in performing arithmetic on negative numbers, these two operations also form the basis for two systems for representing negative numbers. The *radix complement* in base b is called the b's complement, and the *diminished radix complement* is called the $(b-1)$'s complement. In base 2, these number systems, and the corresponding operations, are familiar under the names *2's complement* and *1's complement*. Of course, 2's complement might mean the diminished radix complement in base 3, but this is unlikely, and there will normally be no confusion.

sign-magnitude

radix complement
diminished radix
complement

2's, 1's complement

Complement Operations.   The two forms of the complement operation are defined to act on m-digit, base b numbers.

Definition: Given an m-digit base b number x, the radix complement of x is

$$x^c = (b^m - x) \bmod b^m \qquad\qquad \text{[Eq. 6.6]}$$

Definition: The diminished radix complement of an m-digit base b number x is

$$\hat{x}^c = b^m - 1 - x \qquad\qquad \text{[Eq. 6.7]}$$

Notice that the $\bmod\ b^m$ operation only has an effect for $x = 0$, where it gives $x^c = 0$. Also note the very important relation between the two versions of the complement:

$$x^c = (\hat{x}^c + 1) \bmod b^m \qquad\qquad \text{[Eq. 6.8]}$$

As we will see, the relation is important because one complement is easy to compute, while the other is often easier to use.

Complement Number Systems.   Complement number systems use unsigned base b numbers to represent both positive and negative values. This is an alternative to the *sign-magnitude system* for negative numbers, in which a separate, two-valued *sign* symbol, plus or minus, is added to a base b digit string. In any base except base 2, the two-valued sign symbol carries less information than a base b digit. This also means that we need to provide for two different kinds of digits: the sign digit and the base b digit. The most important reason for using complement representations of negative numbers, however, is that they make signed addition and subtraction easier, as we will see later.

The complement operation is used to define the relationship between the unsigned number representing a negative value and its absolute magnitude. Since an m-digit unsigned number in base b can represent the b^m numbers from 0 to $b^m - 1$, it is natural to use half the range for positive numbers and the other half for negative numbers. Positive numbers are almost universally represented by the unsigned representations of their magnitudes. Thus positive numbers from 0 to $b^m/2$ correspond to the identical unsigned representations. This leaves unsigned numbers from $b^m/2$ through $b^m - 1$ to represent negative numbers. The motivation for complement number systems comes from two facts: the formula for a complement involves the number with a minus sign, and the complements of m-digit base b numbers below $b^m/2$ are above $b^m/2$ and vice versa. A complement number system represents a negative number between -1 and $-b^m/2$ by the unsigned number that is the complement of its absolute value.

Two different number systems arise depending on which complement operation is used on the absolute values of negative numbers. One difference between them is in the number of distinct negative values that are represented. We were deliberately vague in the last paragraph about the unsigned number $b^m/2$ that divides representations of positive and negative numbers. The precise specification is that in the radix complement number system positive nonzero numbers range from 1 to $\lceil b^m/2 \rceil - 1$, and negative nonzero numbers range from -1 to $-\lfloor b^m/2 \rfloor$. In the diminished radix complement number system negative numbers range from -1 to $-(\lfloor b^m/2 \rfloor - 1)$. (Remember that $\lfloor\;\rfloor$ is the floor, or "round down," operator, and $\lceil\;\rceil$ is the ceiling, or "round up," operator.) The reason that there is one more negative nonzero value in the radix complement system is that the diminished radix complement system uses a distinct unsigned number to represent -0, whereas the radix complement of zero returns an unsigned zero. We are almost always interested in even values of b, so the floor and ceiling operations can be eliminated. Table 6.1 summarizes both complement number systems for an even base b, and Table 6.2 gives specifics for 8-bit base 2 representations.

floor operator, $\lfloor\;\rfloor$
ceiling operator, $\lceil\;\rceil$

Using an even base has an additional advantage. The representations of all positive numbers have a leftmost digit in the range $0 \le x_{m-1} < b/2$, but the leftmost digit of negative numbers is in the range $b/2 \le x < b$. For base 2, this means that the leftmost bit of negative numbers is 1, and it is 0 for positive numbers. Thus it is known as the *sign bit*. This way of recognizing positive and negative numbers from their leftmost digit does not change the fact that the complement number systems represent both positive and negative numbers using only the numeric digits of base b. In the sign-magnitude representation, the sign symbol's two possible values make it very similar to a binary digit, but quite different from a base b digit for a large value of b. As we will see in the next section, the strictly numeric character of complement representations of negative numbers has some advantages for computer arithmetic operations.

Table 6.1 Complement Representations of Negative Numbers

Radix Complement		Diminished Radix Complement	
Number	**Representation**	**Number**	**Representation**
0	0	0	0 or $b^m - 1$
$0 < x < b^m/2$	x	$0 < x < b^m/2$	x
$-b^m/2 \le x < 0$	$|x|^c = (b^m - |x|)$	$-b^m/2 + 1 \le x < 0$	$|\hat{x}|^c = b^m - 1 - |x|$

Table 6.2 Base 2 Complement Representations

8-bit 2's Complement		8-bit 1's Complement	
Number	**Representation**	**Number**	**Representation**
0	0	0	0 or 255
$0 < x < 128$	x	$0 < x < 128$	x
$-128 \le x < 0$	$256 - |x|$	$-127 \le x < 0$	$255 - |x|$

The definition of representations of negative numbers in terms of a complement operation leads to the important relationship between arithmetic negation and the complement operation expressed by the following theorem:

Theorem: If $-b^m/2 < x < b^m/2$, then the radix complement (diminished radix complement) of the representation of x in the radix complement (diminished radix complement) number system is the representation of $-x$.

Proof: We give a proof only for the radix complement. It is done most directly by cases.

Case 1. $x = 0$: The radix complement of 0 is $(b^m - 0) \bmod 0 = 0$, which is the representation of -0.

Case 2. $0 < x < b^m/2$: The radix complement of x is $x^c = b^m - x$ and is in the range $b^m/2 < x^c < b^m$, which makes it the representation of a negative number with absolute value x.

Case 3. $-b^m/2 < x < 0$: The representation $|x|^c$ is in the range $b^m/2 < |x|^c < b^m$, so its complement is $b^m - (b^m - |x|) = |x|$, which is in the right range for positive numbers and represents $-x$.

We omitted the number $-b^m/2$ because $-(-b^m/2) = b^m/2$ is outside the range of positive numbers. Nevertheless, the m-digit radix complement number system for an even base has one negative number for which there is no positive number. In the diminished radix complement system, this asymmetry appears as the separate representation for -0.

The computation of the two complements differs in an important way. Applying some algebra to the diminished radix complement, using the formula for the sum of a geometric series, gives the following:

$$\hat{x}^c = b^m - 1 - x = \sum_{i=0}^{m-1} (b-1)b^i - \sum_{i=0}^{m-1} x_i b^i = \sum_{i=0}^{m-1} (b-1-x_i)b^i \qquad \text{[Eq. 6.9]}$$

Now, since x_i is a base b digit, it is in the range $0 \le x_i \le b - 1$, and $b - 1 - x_i$ is in the same range, and hence is represented by a single base b digit. Thus each digit of a diminished radix complement can be computed independently from the corresponding digit of the number being complemented. This is in contrast to the radix complement, whose leftmost digit may depend on the values of all the digits of the original number. The relationship $x^c = (\hat{x}^c + 1) \bmod b^m$ gives an easy way of computing the radix complement given the diminished radix complement, and shows that the interdependence of digits comes from propagating the carry in the add 1 operation.

Table 6.3 shows some examples of numbers in different computer-oriented representations. The accuracy of the computer numbers is adjusted to match that of the decimal representations.

Scaling Complement Numbers. For positive numbers in a radix complement system, scaling by b behaves as described for unsigned numbers, except for overflow. Overflow still occurs if a nonzero digit is shifted left out of the leftmost position. It also occurs, however, if a digit $\ge b/2$ is shifted into the leftmost position of a positive number from the

Table 6.3 Examples of Number Representations

Decimal	2's Complement	1's Complement	Sign-Magnitude	16's Complement	Unsigned
37	0100101	0100101	0100101	25	100101
.87	0.11011110	0.11011110	0.11011110	0.DE	.11011110
−46	1010010	1010001	1101110	D2	—
−0.57	1.01101110	1.01101101	1.10010010	F.6E	—
−2.75	101.01	101.00	110.11	D.4	—

position to its right. This would appear to change a positive number into a negative one—not a possible result of multiplying by $b > 0$. A similar overflow occurs if the leftmost digit changes from $\geq b/2$ to $< b/2$.

For radix complement representations of negative numbers, things are a bit more complex. First consider what kind of a right shift operation would be equivalent to dividing by b. Given an m-digit base b radix complement number $x = x_{m-1}x_{m-2}\cdots x_1 x_0$, with $x_{m-1} \geq b/2$, its value is given by

$$\text{value}(x) = -\left(b^m - \sum_{i=0}^{m-1} x_i b^i\right) \qquad \text{[Eq. 6.10]}$$

The correct right shift operation turns out to insert a $b - 1$ digit into the vacated left position, $\text{rt}(x) = (b-1)x_{m-1}\cdots x_2 x_1$. This gives a negative radix complement number with the value

$$\text{value}(\text{rt}(x)) = -\left(b^{m-1} - \sum_{i=1}^{m-1} x_i b^{i-1}\right) \qquad \text{[Eq. 6.11]}$$

This only differs from

$$\text{value}(x)/b = -\left(b^{m-1} - \sum_{i=1}^{m-1} x_i b^{i-1} - \frac{x_0}{b}\right) \qquad \text{[Eq. 6.12]}$$

by the fraction x_0/b shifted off the right end.

Overflow in left-shifting a negative number can be identified by reversing the above process. Suppose we have a negative m-digit radix complement integer of the form $x = (b-1)x_{m-2}\cdots x_1 x_0$, $x_{m-2} \geq b/2$. Its (negative) value multiplied by b gives

$$b \times \text{value}(x) = -\left(b^{m-1} - \sum_{i=1}^{m-2} x_{i-1} b^i\right) \qquad \text{[Eq. 6.13]}$$

This is just the value of the (negative) radix complement number obtained from the left shift operation $\text{lf}(x) = x_{m-2}x_{m-3}\cdots x_0 0$.

The following rules summarize *arithmetic shifts*, which scale m-digit base b radix complement numbers by b:

> *Right shift*: Insert zero at the left end if the number is positive, but insert $b-1$ at the left if it is negative. No overflow can occur, but any fraction part of division by b is lost.
>
> *Left shift*: Insert zero at the right end. Overflow occurs if either

1. a digit other than zero or $b-1$ shifts off the left end, or
2. the sign of the number changes (the truth value of $x_{m-1} \geq b/2$ changes).

Example 6.6 Multiplying and Dividing by Base b by Using Arithmetic Left and Right Shifts

1. $-5/2$ (4-bit 2's complement representation):
   $1011_2 \div 2_{10} = 1101_2 = -3_{10}$, $+1/2$ has been lost at the right.
2. -6×2 (5-bit 2's complement representation): $11010_2 \times 2_{10} = 10100_2 = -12_{10}$, but using 4 bits, $\text{lf}(1010_2) = 0100_2$ produces overflow.
3. $+122/16$ (2-digit base 16 radix complement representation):
   $7A_{16} \div 16_{10} = 07_{16} = +7_{10}$, where the fraction $+10/16$ has been lost.
4. $-20/16$ (2-digit base 16 radix complement representation):
   $EC_{16} \div 16_{10} = FE_{16} = -2_{10}$, where the fraction $+10/16$ has been lost.
5. -122×16 (3-digit base 16 radix complement representation):
   $F86_{16} \times 16_{10} = 860_{16} = -1952_{10}$. ∎

Key Concepts: Integer Number Representations

- The value of an unsigned integer number x in base b is

$$\text{value}(x) = \sum_{i=0}^{m-1} x_i b^i$$

- The largest unsigned integer number representable by m base b digits is:

$$x_{max} = (b-1)\sum_{i=0}^{m-1} b^i = b^m - 1$$

- There are two different algorithms for number-base conversions: converting from the calculator's base, and converting to the calculator's base. These algorithms work for whole integer numbers and for digital fractions.
- There are several ways to represent signed integers. This section covered sign-magnitude, radix complement, and diminished radix complement representations. Arithmetic operations are considerably simpler in the latter two representations.

- Integers can be scaled by powers of the radix by arithmetic shifts.
- The important number bases in computer usage are 10, 2, and 2^k. Base 2^k digits are just groups of k consecutive bits.

6.2 Fixed-Point Arithmetic

Fixed-point numbers are those which have the radix point in a specific position of a computer word. They include integers, fractions, and numbers that have both integer and fraction parts, provided the same number of digits in a word are devoted to integer and fraction parts in all numbers. This section discusses the operations of add, subtract, multiply, and divide for such numbers.

fixed-point
numbers

6.2.1 FIXED-POINT ADDITION AND SUBTRACTION

The major advantage to using complement number systems is that the addition of signed numbers can be done with little more than an adder for unsigned numbers. We will limit this discussion to the addition of signed numbers in the radix complement system. The extension to the diminished radix complement system is fairly straightforward and is of less use. An adder for m-digit unsigned numbers that ignores any carry from the most significant digit and returns an m-digit result produces $(\tilde{x} + \tilde{y})$ mod b^m, where x and y are unsigned numbers. We introduce the notation rep(.) for the radix complement representation of a signed number and let $x = \text{rep}(x)$ and $y = \text{rep}(y)$ be the representations of signed numbers x and y. The key result is that the unsigned sum of two representations $s = (\tilde{x} + \tilde{y})$ mod b^m is the representation $s = \text{rep}(x + y)$ of the signed sum of x and y, except in the overflow case, where the magnitude of the signed result is too large for an m-digit representation.

> *Theorem*: The m-digit unsigned sum s of the radix complement representations rep(x) and rep(y) of signed numbers x and y is the representation of their signed sum $s = \text{rep}(x + y)$, except when the magnitude of that sum is too large for an m-digit radix complement representation.
>
> *Proof*: It is easiest to separate cases based on the signs of the numbers.
>
> Case 1. Signs are unlike: Without loss of generality, take $x \geq 0$ and $y < 0$. Then
>
> $$s = (x + b^m - |y|) \text{ mod } b^m = (b^m + (x - |y|)) \text{ mod } b^m$$
>
> If $x - |y| \geq 0$, then the mod function discards b^m, corresponding to discarding the carry-out of the left digit, and the result is in range for positive numbers because it is less than x, which is in range. If $x - |y| < 0$, then $s = b^m - |x - |y||$, which is rep($x + y$) when y and the result are negative. Again, it is in range because its absolute value is less than that of y, which is in range.
>
> Case 2. Signs are both plus: Here it is clear that $s = \text{rep}(x + y)$, provided the result is less than $b^m/2$. The overflow case gives an unsigned result

$s \geq b^m/2$, which is clearly wrong because it would represent a negative number.

Case 3. Signs are both minus: With $x < 0$ and $y < 0$,

$$s = (2b^m - |x| - |y|) \bmod b^m$$

which reduces to

$$s = (b^m - |x + y|) \bmod b^m$$

The latter is $\text{rep}(x + y)$, provided the result is in range. Otherwise, the unsigned $s < b^m/2$ appears to be the representation of a positive number.

In addition to showing how to add signed numbers when there is no overflow, the theorem shows how to identify overflow. In both of the overflow cases, the addition of two numbers of the same sign results in the representation of a number of opposite sign. For an even base b, this is signaled by the addition of two representations with their most significant digits less than $b^m/2$, giving a result with a most significant digit greater than or equal to $b^m/2$, or by adding leftmost digits greater than or equal to $b^m/2$ to give a leftmost digit less than $b^m/2$. Thus overflow is strictly a function of the leftmost digits of the addends and the sum.

Unsigned Addition Hardware.   Unsigned base b addition can be partitioned into operations on individual digits. The digitwise procedure for adding m-digit base b numbers x and y is as follows:

1.   Initialize digit number $j = 0$ and carry-in $c_0 = 0$.
2.   Produce digit j sum $s_j = (x_j + y_j + c_j) \bmod b$, and carry
     $c_{j+1} = \lfloor (x_j + y_j + c_j)/b \rfloor$
3.   Increment $j = j + 1$ and repeat from 2 if $j < m$.

Some points about sizes of quantities in the procedure are important. The sum s_j is the correct size for a base b digit since it is a remainder of dividing by b. The size of the carry c_j is determined by the fact that digits of x and y are less than b. If we assume that the carry-in $c_j \leq 1$, which is true initially for c_0, then

$$(x_j + y_j + c_j) \leq ((b-1) + (b-1) + 1) < 2b \qquad \text{[Eq. 6.14]}$$

Thus the integer part of the quotient in step 2 is no more than 1, so $c_j \leq 1$ for all j. The interesting part of this result is that the carry in digitwise addition is either 0 or 1 regardless of the radix. The hardware implications of the above discussion are that we can build an unsigned adder for any base using the architecture shown in Figure 6.1. Lines in the diagram, other than carries, encode base b digits, and would thus require $\lceil \log_2 b \rceil$ bits each. For example, if $b = 16$, digits are represented by 4 binary bits each, except for carries. The digit adders become logic circuits with nine inputs and nine outputs. They could be implemented with two levels of AND/OR logic. Other choices would be to implement each base 16 digit adder with two base 4 digit adders or four base 2 digit adders.

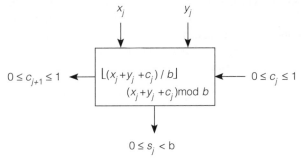

Base b digit adder

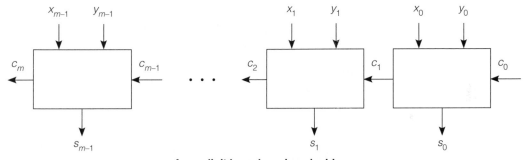

An m-digit base b unsigned adder

Fig. 6.1 Hardware Structure of a Base b Unsigned Adder

Example 6.7   Unsigned Integer Addition in Bases 8, 16, and 2

		2	3	7	4_8			3	F	C	5_{16}			1	0	1	1	0	1_2
	+	6	2	7	6_8		+	7	F	A	E_{16}		+	0	1	1	0	0	1_2
Carry	1	0	1	1			0	1	1	1			1	1	1	0	0	1	
Sum	1	0	6	7	2_8			B	F	7	3_{16}		1	0	0	0	1	1	0_2

Note: In the first and third examples the results need one more digit than the operands. ■

Radix Point Location in Addition. The addition rules for integers also work for numbers with a fractional part, provided the radix points of the two addends are aligned. Common assumptions for *fixed-point* numbers, those having their radix (binary) point at a fixed position of a memory register, are that they are either integers, with the radix point at the far right, or fractions, with the radix point at the far left. These common cases are not important for addition, since adding numbers from registers with any fixed assumption about the radix point position will give a result satisfying the same assumption. We will see later that multiplication gives a reason to assume a pure integer or a pure fraction representation.

No matter where the radix point is assumed to be, it is always possible for the addition of two unsigned m-digit numbers to produce a result with $m + 1$ nonzero digits because there is a carry from the leftmost digit pair. For *single-precision* arithmetic, which assumes all numbers can be stored in a single computer word, this is an exceptional

single precision

multiple precision

situation, or overflow, for m-digit registers. Often, however, this is a normal situation in the addition of *multiple-precision* numbers, which require more than one computer word per number. For this reason, a carry from the left of a fixed-point addition is seldom treated as an exception, but is recorded in a single-bit carry flag, to be tested or used directly in further arithmetic.

Example 6.8   Unsigned, Fixed-Point Addition in Bases 4, 10, and 16

```
          2  1.  3₄  =    9.  7  5₁₀            .A  2  6  C₁₆
       +  1  0.  2₄  =    4.  5  0₁₀         +  .7  9  0  B₁₆     Overflow for
Carry  0  0  1                             1   0  0  1           storage in a
Sum       3  2.  1₄  =  1  4.  2  5₁₀       1  .1  B  7  7₁₆      16-bit word.
```

Choice of Base as an Implementation Alternative.   If we take the smallest possible base $b = 2$, the digit adders become binary full adders with the sum

$$s_j = x_j \overline{y_j} \overline{c_j} + \overline{x_j} y_j \overline{c_j} + \overline{x_j} \overline{y_j} c_j + x_j y_j c_j \qquad \text{[Eq. 6.15]}$$

and carry

$$c_{j+1} = x_j y_j + x_j c_j + y_j c_j \qquad \text{[Eq. 6.16]}$$

ripple carry adders

These equations can be easily implemented in any type of logic: discrete, MSI, or VLSI. For a 64-bit addition, however, the propagation of the carry from digit to digit, called a *ripple carry*, gives 126 levels of logic between the low-order input bits and the high-order output. Adders of this type are called *ripple carry adders*. The maximum number of logic levels between an input and an output is a major determiner of arithmetic speed.

If we treat the 64-bit numbers as having 16 base 16 digits and implement the base 16 digit adders as 2-level AND/OR circuits, there are only 30 levels of logic between low-order inputs and high-order output. Unfortunately, the 2-level implementation of a base 16 digit adder has one output, which is a 60-way OR of 48 six-input ANDs, 8 five-input ANDs, and 4 four-input ANDs. This level of complexity might be possible in a VLSI implementation, but would not be suited for MSI or discrete logic. Taking the 64-bit addition as 32 base 4 digits brings the number of logic levels down to 62, and the most complicated two-level AND/OR expression in a base 4 digit adder has only 12 terms of four literals each. Choosing a small power of 2 base is thus a way to trade off adder speed against logic complexity. There are other ways to trade off logic depth against complexity that we will see when we consider fast carry schemes. There are also ways of using the base b digit formulation with $b = 2^k$ for arithmetic operations other than add.

Complement Adder/Subtracters.   To do subtraction using a radix complement representation of negative numbers, we only need to complement the second input to an unsigned adder and supply overflow detection. Radix complement can be built from the simpler digitwise diminished radix complement, followed by the addition of 1. If the complemented operand is going immediately into an adder, there is a low-order carry input to

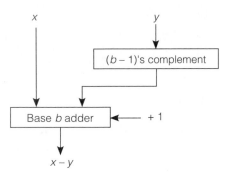

Fig. 6.2 Base *b* Radix Complement Subtracter

the adder that can supply the +1. This allows us to work in the radix complement number system, where signed addition is simple, but use the diminished radix complement operation, which is easier to implement. Figure 6.2 shows a base *b* subtracter.

A combined adder/subtracter can be built by using a multiplexer to select the second operand or its complement as the adder input. The multiplexer control also determines the carry-in to the adder: 0 for addition and 1 for subtraction. Specializing to base 2, let the *j*th bit of the adder input be called q_j and let the subtract control signal be *r*. Then the equation for a multiplexer output is

$$q_j = y_j \overline{r} + \overline{y_j} r$$

This is just the equation for an exclusive OR, so a 2's complement adder/subtracter can be built using only exclusive OR gates and full adders (FA), as shown in Figure 6.3. This circuit is known as a ripple-carry adder-subtractor because the carry bits are computed in a ripple-like fashion beginning at the lsb and proceeding to the msb. This is not an optimum design, as the time to perform an n-bit addition is proportional to n. The overflow detection circuit is not shown, but it is easy to design using x_{m-1}, y_{m-1}, and s_{m-1} as inputs.

Fast Addition by Carry Lookahead. We saw that grouping bits to make digits in a larger base 2^k could reduce the number of levels of logic and thus improve the speed of an adder. The cost is a very high complexity for the two-level AND/OR expressions for bits of the sum. If we relax the requirement for only two levels of logic and examine the carry process, which is the source of the long input-to-output delay, we can reduce the number of logic levels in the delay and also keep the complexity reasonable. The key idea in carry lookahead is to speed up the ripple carry by determining if the addition of digits in a position *j* generates a carry-out, regardless of whether there is a carry-in, or if the addition propagates a carry from input to output in digit *j*.

Let the logical variable G_j be 1 if digit position *j* generates a carry and logical variable P_j be 1 if a carry is propagated from input to output of digit *j*. Then G_j is true if $x_j + y_j \geq b$, and P_j is true if $x_j + y_j = b - 1$. It will be better to take P_j to be the condition $(x_j + y_j) \geq b - 1$, which also agrees with the specification that there will be a carry-out if there is a carry-in. Specializing to binary, G_j and P_j are given by logic functions $G_j = x_j y_j$ and $P_j = x_j + y_j$. With the more restricted definition, P_j would require an

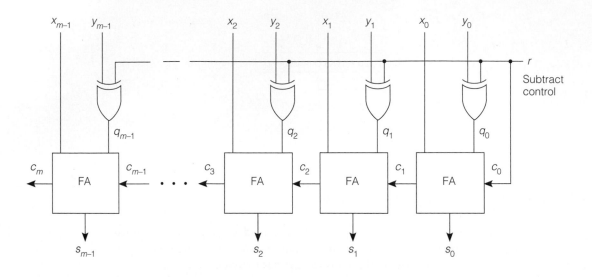

Fig. 6.3 2's Complement Ripple-Carry Adder/Subtracter

exclusive OR gate. The carry-out from bit j can then be expressed by the logic function $c_{j+1} = G_j + P_j c_j$. Using this formula to compute carries for four successive bit positions, we have

$$
\begin{aligned}
c_1 &= G_0 + P_0 c_0 \\
c_2 &= G_1 + P_1 G_0 + P_1 P_0 c_0 \\
c_3 &= G_2 + P_2 G_1 + P_2 P_1 G_0 + P_2 P_1 P_0 c_0 \\
c_4 &= G_3 + P_3 G_2 + P_3 P_2 G_1 + P_3 P_2 P_1 G_0 + P_3 P_2 P_1 P_0 c_0
\end{aligned}
\qquad \text{[Eq. 6.17]}
$$

Since G and P each require one gate, the carry expressions have three gate delays, and the sum bits need two more in the full adders, but the expressions are much less complicated than the 60 terms required for the most significant sum bit of a two-level implementation of a base 16 digit adder. An additional three gate delays are being traded for fewer gates and inputs. In base 16, the largest number of inputs to any gate is five, and in base 64 it is seven, still with only five gate delays. With carry lookahead, the addition problem is broken into three parts: production of the generate and propagate signals, calculation of the carries, and formation of the sum digits, using only the sum circuit from a full adder.

The complexity of the carry lookahead grows with the number of adder bits, and it is probably not feasible to implement, say, a 64-bit adder with the above formulas. Fortunately, the whole idea extends to a multilevel carry computation scheme. For a group of k bits, the whole group generates a carry whenever the high-order bits do, or when the next highest-order bits generate a carry and the high-order bits propagate it, or when the next highest-order bits generate a carry and the two highest-order positions propagate it, and so forth. Similarly, a group of k bits propagates a carry when all bit positions of the group propagate one. For example, consider the equation above for c_4. It can be written as $c_4 = G_0^1 + P_0^1 c_0$, where

$$G_0^1 = G_3 + P_3 G_2 + P_3 P_2 G_1 + P_3 P_2 P_1 G_0 \qquad \text{[Eq. 6.18]}$$

is the carry-generate for the group of four bits and

$$P_0^1 = P_3 P_2 P_1 P_0 \qquad \text{[Eq. 6.19]}$$

is the carry-propagate for the group. We can thus write level 1 generate and propagate functions (taking G_j and P_j as level 0) as follows:

$$G_i^1 = G_{i \cdot k + k - 1} + P_{i \cdot k + k - 1} G_{i \cdot k + k - 2} + \cdots + P_{ik + k - 1} P_{ik + k - 2} \ldots P_{ik + 1} G_{ik}$$
$$P_i^1 = P_{ik + k - 1} P_{ik + k - 2} \ldots P_{ik}. \qquad \text{[Eq. 6.20]}$$

We can then apply carry lookahead to the groups of k digits by using the 269 G^1 and P^1 outputs of the first-level carry lookahead circuits. For the simplest case of $k = 2$, the structure of a multilevel carry lookahead adder is shown in Figure 6.4.

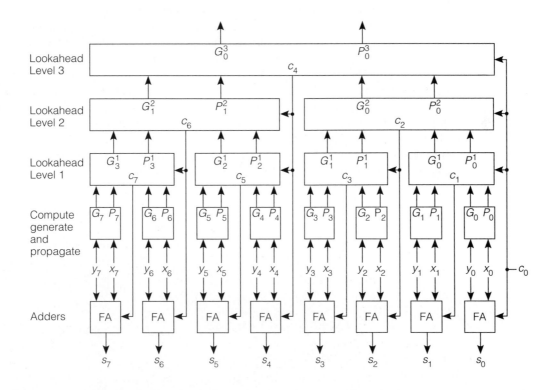

Fig. 6.4 Carry Lookahead Adder for Group Size $k = 2$

For an m-bit adder there are $\log_2 m$ lookahead levels, each with two gate delays. One gate delay is required to produce the original generate and propagate signals, and a final two gate delays are required to produce the sum outputs. Thus the maximum number of gate delays for an m-bit carry lookahead adder with lookahead groups of size 2 is $1 + 4 \log_2 m$. The longest path is obtained by tracing up the tree from the lowest-order bits that can generate a carry and back down to the highest-order bits that can be affected. The key result is that, while the delay in a ripple carry adder is proportional to m, the delay in a carry lookahead adder is proportional to $\log m$. Groups larger than 2 bits are more practical, but it is harder to show this in a diagram. We will pursue larger groups in the exercises.

Carry lookahead is the most popular scheme for speeding up binary addition. It is much less complex than a two-level circuit for a several-bit group and adds only a small amount to the number of circuit levels. Ripple carry and lookahead schemes can be mixed by producing a carry-out at the left end of each lookahead module and using ripple carry to connect modules at any level of the lookahead tree. Another method for dealing with the long delay of ripple carry is *carry completion detection*. It is less useful than carry lookahead and beyond the scope of this book.

6.2.2   MULTIPLICATION ALGORITHMS AND HARDWARE

The process of digital multiplication is based on addition, and many of the techniques useful in addition carry over to multiplication. The general schema for unsigned multiplication in base b is shown in Figure 6.5. Each row, or *partial product*, comes from multiplying one digit of the *multiplier* times the *multiplicand*. The low-order digit of a partial product is determined from just one multiplicand digit, but other digits include the effects of a carry from the digits to the right. In binary, partial products are trivial—either a copy of the multiplicand or zero. The sum of the partial products gives the complete *product*. Various ways of doing the complete multiplication range from treating one pair of digits at a time, as we do in pencil and paper arithmetic, to generating and summing all partial products at once with parallel hardware. Between these extremes are schemes that generate single partial products with parallel hardware and either add them all at the end or add them to a running sum as they are generated. The process of adding to a running sum is called *accumulation* and gives its name to the *accumulator* register in some computers.

partial product
multiplier
multiplicand

product

accumulation
accumulator

					x_3	x_2	x_1	x_0	Multiplicand
					y_3	y_2	y_1	y_0	Multiplier
			$(xy_0)_4$	$(xy_0)_3$	$(xy_0)_2$	$(xy_0)_1$	$(xy_0)_0$		pp_0
		$(xy_1)_4$	$(xy_1)_3$	$(xy_1)_2$	$(xy_1)_1$	$(xy_1)_0$			pp_1
	$(xy_2)_4$	$(xy_2)_3$	$(xy_2)_2$	$(xy_2)_1$	$(xy_2)_0$				pp_2
$(xy_3)_4$	$(xy_3)_3$	$(xy_3)_2$	$(xy_3)_1$	$(xy_3)_0$					pp_3
p_7	p_6	p_5	p_4	p_3	p_2	p_1	p_0		

Fig. 6.5 Digital Multiplication Schema

We start by considering a digitwise multiplication algorithm that differs from pencil and paper arithmetic only because partial products are accumulated as they are generated instead of being added up at the end as a separate process. The digitwise procedure for multiplying two m-digit unsigned integers can be expressed by the following pseudocode.

1.   for $i := 0$ step 1 until $2m - 1$
2. $p_i := 0$;
3.   for $j := 0$ step 1 until $m - 1$
4.   begin
5. $c := 0$;
6.   for $i := 1$ step 1 until $m - 1$
7.   begin
8. $p_{j+i} := (p_{j+i} + x_i\,y_j + c) \bmod b$;
9. $c := \lfloor (p_{j+i} + x_i\,y_j + c)/b \rfloor$;
10.   end;
11. $p_{j+m} := c$;
12.   end;

Lines 1 and 2 initialize the accumulated product to zero. Line 3 treats digits of the multiplier one at a time from low to high order. Line 5 initializes the carry across multiplicand digits, and line 6 steps through multiplicand digits from right to left. Lines 8 and 9 compute an accumulated product digit and a carry digit, respectively. The subscript on p demonstrates that the position of the product digit depends on the positions of both the multiplier and multiplicand digits. Line 11 records the leftmost carry.

If lines 8 and 9 really produce base b digits, the integer values computed must be between 0 and $b - 1$. This is clearly true for p_{j+i} since it is a remainder modulo b. To show that c is a single base b digit, assume that it is at the start and compute an upper bound by assuming that every digit has its maximum value:

$$p_{j+i} + x_i y_j + c \le (b-1) + (b-1)(b-1) + (b-1) = b^2 - 1 \qquad \text{[Eq. 6.21]}$$

Then

$$c \le \lfloor (b^2 - 1)/b \rfloor \le b - 1 \qquad \text{[Eq. 6.22]}$$

so the carry-out is a base b digit if the carry-in is a digit. Since the initial carry is zero, all carries will be base b digits. Note that in digitwise multiplication, the carry is not a single bit regardless of the base, as it is in addition, but a full base b digit. Of course, in base 2 that means only 1 bit, but not in any larger base.

Figure 6.6 shows the structure of a fully parallel *array multiplier* for unsigned base b integers. All signal lines carry base b digits and would require $\log_2 b$ bits if encoded in binary. The computational boxes in the figure are trivial in base 2. Each consists of a full adder, with an AND gate to form the product $x_i y_j$. In binary, this parallel multiplier design requires m^2 full adders, and signals will have to pass through about $4m$ gates on the worst case path from an input to an output.

array multiplier

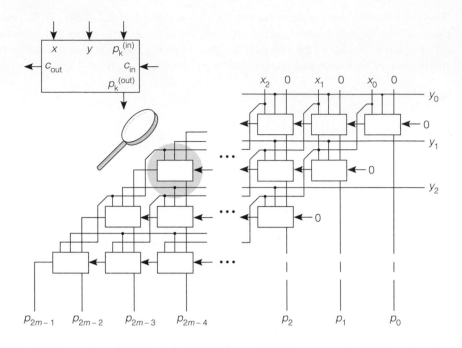

Fig. 6.6 Parallel Array Multiplier for Unsigned Base b Numbers

Sequential-Parallel Multiplier.   To save hardware and still get good speed, multipliers are often built with a combination of parallel hardware and sequential operation. Parallel hardware is supplied for one horizontal row of Figure 6.6, so that the operation $p = p + xy_j b^j$ is done in one step. Multiplication by b^j is accomplished by shifting the partial product j digits to the left with respect to p or, alternatively, shifting p right j digits before adding xy_j. The hardware, which is used in m sequential steps, consists of a partial product generator, an $m + 1$-digit adder, and a $2m$-digit right shift register, as shown in Figure 6.7. In any base except 2, the product xy_j has $m + 1$ digits. Base 2 has a real advantage here because the partial product xy_j is either just x if $y_j = 1$ or 0 if $y_j = 0$. It can be formed bit by bit with no carries and has only m digits instead of the $m + 1$ needed in larger bases. The $(m + 1)$-bit adder can be made fast using any scheme that works for ordinary binary addition, like carry lookahead.

The sequential steps for using the hardware of Figure 6.7 follow:

1. Clear product shift register p.
2. Initialize multiplier digit number $j = 0$.
3. Form the partial product xy_j.
4. Add partial product to upper half of p.
5. Increment $j = j + 1$, and if $j = m$, go to step 8.
6. Shift p right one digit.
7. Repeat from step 3.
8. The $2m$-digit product is in the p register.

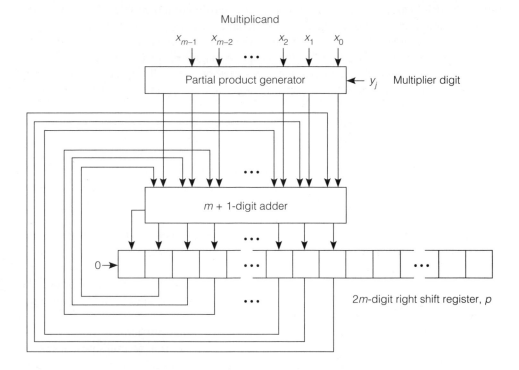

Fig. 6.7 Unsigned Series Parallel Multiplier Hardware

Fixed-point arithmetic assumes a standard position for the radix point in a memory word. If the two m-digit operands come to the multiplier unit from memory, we will want to store the result in memory also. But it is twice as long as a memory word. Even if we are willing to consider only m of the digits as significant, the correct ones must still be selected to preserve the standard position for the radix point that was assumed for the operands. If the radix point is assumed to be at the right of numbers in memory, they are integers, and we would like to store an integer result in the same format. This means storing the low-order m digits of the $2m$-digit p register. If any of the upper m digits is not zero, the multiplication has overflowed the capacity of a memory word. If it is assumed that the radix point in a memory word is at the left, then numbers are fractions, and the product is a $2m$-digit fraction with its most significant part in the high-order m digits of the p register. It is thus correct to store the most significant m digits as the fractional result. Any nonzero digits lost from the low-order part of the p register merely represent a loss of accuracy.

If the radix point in memory words were r digits to the left of the right end, then the radix point in the product would be $2r$ digits to the left of the right end of the p register. Storing a product in the standard fixed-point format would involve taking m digits from somewhere in the middle of the p register, and there would be a possibility of both loss of accuracy and overflow. Machines usually assume a normal memory format of either integer or fraction, and the standard multiply operation returns the corresponding half of the p register. Separate instructions may allow access to the other half of p.

Signed Multiplication.   The sign of a product is easily computed from the signs of the multiplier and multiplicand: positive if they are equal and negative if they differ. If sign-magnitude representation is used for negative numbers, multiplication separates into independent computations of the sign and the unsigned magnitude of the product. If negative numbers are represented by complements, this method can still be applied by complementing any negative operands, multiplying the magnitudes, and recomplementing the product magnitude if its sign is negative.

More direct methods for multiplication with complements are available. Consider the series parallel multiplier of Figure 6.7. If x is a radix complement multiplicand, it can be multiplied by a *positive* multiplier by doing complement addition of the partial products. This means discarding the carry from the adder and doing an *arithmetic* right shift of the p register to scale the partial products correctly. In general, multiplication of an m-digit radix complement number by a single digit gives an $(m + 1)$-digit partial product, so an $(m + 1)$-digit unsigned adder is needed for the summation.

Although the complement addition is not hard in any power of 2 base, the partial product generation is only simple in base 2, where the partial product is either zero or a copy of the multiplicand. The partial product only requires m bits, but it must be sign-extended to $m + 1$ bits and an $m + 1$-bit adder used to prevent overflow in summing the signed partial products. Sign extension must also be done to implement the arithmetic right shift of the running sum of partial products.

The last step in producing complete 2's complement multiply hardware is to handle a negative multiplier as well as multiplicand. For this purpose, it is helpful to use a special property of the 2's complement representation. From Table 6.1 we see that if a 2's complement number x is nonnegative, its value is

$$\text{value}(x) = 0 + \sum_{i=0}^{m-2} x_i \cdot 2^i \qquad \text{[Eq. 6.23]}$$

and if it is negative, its value is

$$\text{value}(x) = -2^m + 2^{m-1} + \sum_{i=0}^{m-2} x_i \cdot 2^i \qquad \text{[Eq. 6.24]}$$

Using the value of the high-order bit, both can be written as follows:

$$\text{value}(x) = -x_{m-1} \cdot 2^{m-1} + \sum_{i=0}^{m-2} x_i \cdot 2^i \qquad \text{[Eq. 6.25]}$$

This allows us to consider a 2's complement number as unsigned, except that the leftmost, or sign, bit has negative weight. If we apply this to the 2's complement multiplier, the last partial product in a signed multiply is just subtracted instead of added.

The diagram of Figure 6.8 shows the hardware for a 2's complement signed multiplier. It includes sign extension, both to prevent overflow in partial product addition and for the arithmetic right shift. The diagram also shows registers for the multiplicand and multiplier. Since bits of the multiplier are used in right to left order, it is useful to put the

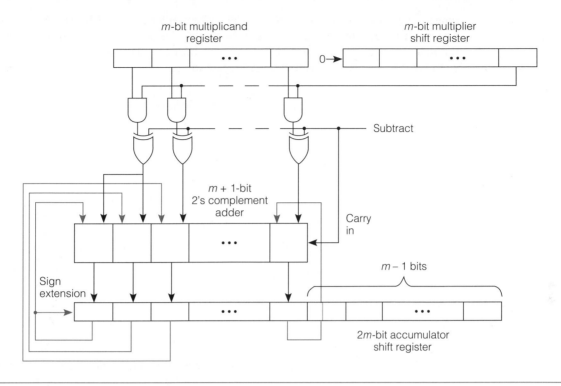

Fig. 6.8 2's Complement Multiplier Hardware

multiplier in a right shift register. The control circuitry, which is not shown, must include a counter to determine when the bits of the multiplier have been exhausted. The procedure for using the hardware of Figure 6.8 to do a 2's complement multiply is as follows:

1. Clear the bit counter and partial product accumulator register.
2. Add the product (AND) of the multiplicand and rightmost multiplier bit.
3. Shift accumulator and multiplier registers right 1 bit.
4. Count the multiplier bit and repeat from 2 if the count is less than $m - 1$.
5. Subtract the product of the multiplicand and bit $m - 1$ of the multiplier.

The product will be left in the $2m$-bit accumulator. It is interesting to note that $2m - 1$ bits are sufficient to represent the product in all but the one case of $(-2^{m-1})(-2^{m-1}) = +2^{2m-2}$, which requires a $2m$-bit 2's complement number to prevent overflow. Multiplier bits are used up from the multiplier shift register at the same rate that product bits are added to the accumulator shift register. Thus the two registers can be combined to save hardware with a little attention to the beginning and ending cases.

The comments about radix point location made in connection with unsigned multiplication also apply in 2's complement, with a slight modification. Since the leftmost bit serves as a sign indicator, the binary point is usually taken to be to the right of the leftmost bit for a fractional representation. The range of positive fractions is $0 \le x < 1$, and the range of negative fractions is $-1 \le x < 0$. The 2's complement of such a fraction x is $1 - x$. The result stored after a 2's complement fraction multiplication is taken from bits $2m - 2$ through $m - 1$ of the p register. Overflow is only possible in the multiplication, $(-1) \times (-1) = +1$. Two's complement integers still have the binary point at the far right.

Example 6.9 Fixed-Point Multiplication with a Negative Operand

```
-5/8 =          1.  0  1  1
× 6/8 =      ×  0.  1  1  0
pp0          0  0.  0  0  0
accum.       0  0.  0  0  0  0              add and shift
pp1          1  1.  0  1  1
accum.       1  1.  1  0  1  1  0           add and shift
pp2          1  1.  0  1  1
accum.       1  1.  1  0  0  0  1  0        add and shift
pp3          0  0.  0  0  0
result       1  1.  1  0  0  0  1  0        add
```

Negative multiplicand

```
6/8 =           0.  1  1  0
× -5/8 =     ×  1.  0  1  1
pp0          0  0.  1  1  0
accum.       0  0.  0  1  1  0
pp1          0  0.  1  1  0
accum.       0  0.  1  0  0  1  0
pp2          0  0.  0  0  0
accum.       0  0.  0  1  0  0  1  0
pp3          1  1.  0  1  0
result       1  1.  1  0  0  0  1  0
```

Negative multiplier

■

Booth Recoding and Similar Methods. The Booth algorithm, named for its originator, A. D. Booth, forms the basis for a number of signed multiplication algorithms that are simple to implement at the hardware level and that have the potential to speed up signed multiplication considerably. Booth's algorithm is based on recoding the multiplier, y, to a recoded, value, z, leaving the multiplicand, x, unchanged. In Booth recoding, each digit of the multiplier can assume negative as well as positive and zero values. There is a special notation, called *signed digit* (SD) encoding, to express these signed digits. In SD encoding +1 and 0 are expressed as 1 and 0, but −1 is expressed as $\overline{1}$.

Booth recoding

signed digit (SD)
encoding

This notion of different signs for different bits should not be completely novel; in Equation 6.24 the value of a 2s complement integer was defined as

$$\text{value}(y) = -y_{m-1}2^{m-1} + \sum_{i=0}^{m-2} y_i 2^i \qquad \text{[Eq. 6.26]}$$

This equation says that to get the value of a signed 2's complement number, multiply the $m - 1$th digit by -2^{m-1}, and multiply each remaining digit i by $+2^i$. For example, −5, which is 1011 in 2's complement notation, would be, in SD notation, $\overline{1}011 = -8 + 0 + 2 + 1 = -5$.

The Booth algorithm is sometimes called "skipping over 1s," since strings of 1s are replaced by 0s, as we explain here. Let us ignore for the time being the negatively weighted msb, and consider the value of the rest of the number. Examination of Equation 6.2 shows that the value of a string of m 1s is 2^m-1. For example the value of a string of four 1s, $1111 = 2^4 - 1 = 100\overline{1} = 16 - 1 = 15$. Furthermore, according to the discussion of scaling on page 258, this string of 1s can be scaled by left shifts, and we can likewise scale the SD notation, so $1111000 = 15 \times 2^3 = 100\overline{1}000 = 128 - 8 = 120$.

If this number were to be used as the multiplier in a multiplication, we could replace four additions by one addition and one subtraction.

The Booth recoding procedure, then, is as follows:

Booth recoding procedure

1. Working from lsb to msb, replace each 0 digit of the original number with a 0 in the recoded number until a 1 is encountered.

2. When a 1 is encountered, insert a $\overline{1}$ at that position in the recoded number, and skip over any succeeding 1s until a 0 is encountered.

3. Replace that 0 with a 1 and continue.

Here is an example:

Example 6.10   Recode the Integer 985

$$0011\ 1101\ 1001 = 512 + 256 + 128 + 64 + 16 + 8 + 1 = 985$$
$$\downarrow$$
$$0100\ 0\overline{1}10\ \overline{1}01\overline{1} = +1024 - 64 + 32 - 8 + 2 - 1 = 985$$

This algorithm is expressed in tabular form in Table 6.4, considering pairs of numbers, y_{i-1} and y_i, and the recoded digit, z_i, as shown:

A trailing 0 is assumed to the right of the lsb. Notice that the recoding operation can proceed in parallel, even though the algorithm above was expressed in serial fashion.   ■

We now consider the msb, or sign bit, of the number. If the sign bit is 0, then the recoding method is unchanged from that given above, because the number is positive. If the sign bit is 1 then we must consider two cases, those being the last two in Table 6.4. In the first of the two cases, where the msbs are 10, the recoding is clearly valid, because the recoded value of the msb, z_i, is −1, in keeping with Equation 6.26. In the second case, we are encountering a string of at least two 1s. Somewhere previous to the most significant 1 we must have encountered a 0, even if it was the assumed 0 to the right of the lsb. When that least significant 1 in the string of 1s was encountered, it was replaced by $\overline{1}$, and then no other additions are performed. This preserves the negative value of the number. Thus Table 6.4 is valid for the entire range of the 2s complement number. Before moving on to extend the Booth recoding method, let us consider an example.

Table 6.4 Booth Recoding Table

y_i	y_{i-1}	z_i	Value	Situation
0	0	0	0	String of 0s
0	1	1	+1	End of string of 1s
1	0	1	−1	Begin string of 1s
1	1	0	0	String of 1s

Example 6.11   Multiplication Using Booth Recoding

Multiply -7 (1001) by -5 (1011). First we must recode -5: $1011 \rightarrow \overline{1}10\overline{1}$. Then we multiply the two numbers in the usual way, but we take into account the sign of each multiplier bit:

x	(-7)						1	0	0	1
$\times z$	$\times (-5)$						$\overline{1}$	1	0	$\overline{1}$
	$-(-7) \times 2^0$	0	0	0	0	0	1	1	1	
	$+(0) \times 2^1$	0	0	0	0	0	0	0		
	$+(-7) \times 2^2$	1	1	1	0	0	1			
	$-(-7) \times 2^3$	0	0	1	1	1				
prod.	$7 - 28 + 56 = 35$	0	0	1	0	0	0	1	1	

■

Booth recoding may result in fewer additions, or it may actually increase the number of additions, depending on the number of isolated 1s. The method we now describe solves this problem by encoding the digits not as binary digits, but as signed radix-4 digits. In practice, this means encoding the bits as pairs, called *bit-pair encoding*. Since we are going to encode pairs of bits, there will be only $n/2$ additions, instead of n. Table 6.5 shows the encoding. The encoding "collapses" pairs of bits y_i, y_{i-1} to a single recoded value z, located at either position i or position $i-1$, depending on whether the absolute value of the multiplier is 1 or 2. This corresponds to the lsb or the msb of each radix 4 digit. In recoding, a trailing 0 is assumed before the lsb, and if there is an odd number of bits in the number being encoded, the number must be sign-extended by 1 bit before recoding. There are no multiplier values whose absolute value is >2 because of the nature of the recoding. Let us recode the number from Example 6.10:

bit-pair encoding

Table 6.5 Radix-4 Booth Encoding (Bit-Pair Encoding)

Original Bit Pair		Digit to Right	Recoded Bit Pair		Multiplier Value	Situation
y_i	y_{i-1}	y_{i-2}	z_i	z_{i-1}		
0	0	0		0	0	String of 0s
0	0	1		1	+1	End string of 1s
0	1	0		1	+1	Single 1
0	1	1	1		+2	End string of 1s
1	0	0	1		-2	Begin string of 1s
1	0	1		1	-1	Single 0
1	1	0		1	-1	Begin string of 1s
1	1	1		0	0	String of 1s

Example 6.12   Encode the Integer 985, Using Bit-Pair Recoding

$$00\ 11\ 11\ 01\ 10\ 01\ [0] = 512 + 256 + 128 + 64 + 16 + 8 + 1 = 985$$
$$\downarrow$$
$$01\ 00\ 0\overline{1}\ 10\ \overline{1}0\ 01 = 1024 - 64 + 32 - 8 + 1 = 985$$

Here we have left the 0s in the recoded number to show the position of the recoded digit. In operation, the 0s merely serve as placeholders and do not participate in the multiplication. ∎

Now let us repeat the multiplication of Example 6.11, but using bit-pair recoding.

Example 6.13   Multiplication Using Bit-Pair Recoding   Multiply –7

(1001) by -5 (1011). First we must bit-pair-recode -5: $1011 \rightarrow 0\overline{1}0\overline{1} = (-4) + (-1)$. Notice that in the example there are only two multiplications, and that the position where the addition occurs depends on the location of the recoded bit. To emphasize this fact, we have omitted the zeros at bits 1 and 3, and put in dashes as placekeepers:

x	(-7)						1 0		0 1	
$\times z$	$\times(-5)$						$-\ \overline{1}$		$-\ \overline{1}$	
	$-(-7)\times 2^0$	0	0	0	0		0 1		1 1	
	$-(-7)\times 2^2$	0	0	0	1		1 1			
$prod.$	$7 + 28 = 35$	0	0	1	0		0 0		1 1	

∎

There are a number of variants on the Booth recoding scheme besides the one shown above, including using radix-8 or even greater, but they are not in common use, as they require lookup tables to store multiples of the multiplicand greater than 2.

6.2.3   DIGITAL DIVISION

Since multiplying two m-digit fixed-point numbers gives a $2m$-digit result, one might expect that dividing a $2m$-digit dividend by an m-digit divisor would give an m-digit quotient. The problem is more complicated than this, however, because in a division that does not come out even, the remainder can always be used to generate more quotient digits. The simplest case to consider is that of dividing an m-digit unsigned integer dividend D by an m-digit unsigned integer divisor d to get an integer quotient q and an integer remainder r. Unless d is very small compared to D, many of the leftmost digits of q will be zero. In fact, if $d > D$, q will be zero and $r = d$. A zero divisor should be checked for at the outset, and no division should be attempted in this case.

If the radix point is assumed to be at the left of unsigned fixed-point values in memory, it would be useful to divide a fraction D by a fraction d to get a fractional quotient q and a remainder scaled down by b^{-m}. However, the quotient is only a fraction if $D < d$. There will be some integer part to q whenever $D \geq d$. In fixed-point fraction arithmetic, this condition is called *divide overflow*.

divide overflow

Sequential Parallel Division.   Operand and result lengths, radix point position, and the character of the remainder can be explained in terms of the hardware of Figure 6.9, which does parallel subtraction of a binary divisor from a shifted binary dividend to produce bits of the quotient from left to right. In decimal division, we subtract a single-digit multiple of the divisor from a dividend, but since we limit our treatment to binary, the only 1-bit multiples are zero and the divisor itself. We can think of the procedure as the reverse of the series parallel binary version of the multiplier in Figure 6.7. The divide hardware contains a $2m$-bit dividend register that can be shifted left with zero fill. A subtracter computes the upper half of the dividend register minus the m-bit divisor. A signal indicating that the difference is positive determines both the current quotient bit and whether to replace the upper half of the dividend register with the difference. The quotient bit is sent into the right end of an m-bit left shift register to yield quotient bits from left to right. In a manner similar to what was described for the shift registers of Figure 6.8, bits of the dividend register are used up at the same rate that quotient bits are produced, so the dividend and quotient could share a single shift register.

integer division

The hardware of Figure 6.9 is used somewhat differently for integer and fraction fixed-point division. The procedure for *integer division* is as follows.

1. Put dividend in lower half of the dividend register and clear upper half. Put divisor in divisor register. Initialize quotient bit counter to zero.
2. Shift dividend register left 1 bit.
3. If difference is positive, shift a 1 into quotient and replace upper half of dividend by the difference. If negative, shift a 0 into the quotient.
4. If fewer than m quotient bits produced, repeat from step 2.
5. The m-bit quotient is an integer, and the m-bit integer remainder is in the upper half of the dividend register.

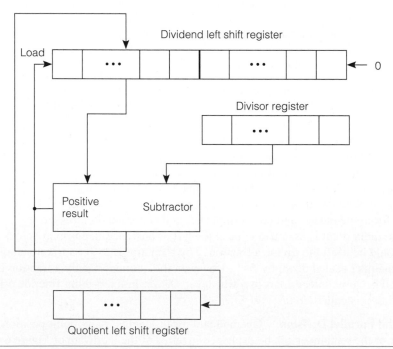

Fig. 6.9 Unsigned Binary Divide Hardware

The only exceptional case in integer division is when the divisor $d = 0$, although the case when $d > D$ performs no useful work since $q = 0$ and $r = D$ at the end.

In fixed-point fraction division, divide overflow of the fractional quotient is possible. When there is no overflow, the m most significant bits of the quotient are produced. *Fraction division* uses the following steps.

fraction division

1. Put dividend in upper half of the dividend register and clear lower half. Put divisor in divisor register. Initialize quotient bit counter to zero.

2. If difference is positive, report divide overflow.

3. Shift dividend register left 1 bit.

4. If difference is positive, shift a 1 into quotient and replace upper part of dividend by the difference. If negative, shift a 0 into the quotient.

5. If fewer than m quotient bits are produced, repeat from 3.

6. The m bit quotient has the binary point at the left end, and the remainder is in the upper part of the dividend register.

The remainder is a fraction scaled by 2^{-m} or an integer scaled by 2^{-2m}. Taking the remainder as a fraction, the relation $D = qd + r2^{-m}$ holds. A few examples make it clear that the subtracter must subtract the m-bit divisor from the upper $m + 1$ bits of the dividend, since it is shifted before the subtraction. Thus the upper part of the dividend register has $m + 1$ bits for fraction division. On the other hand, for single precision fraction division, the lower half of D is not needed, since it starts as zero and is filled with zeros.

Example 6.14 Integer Division   Divide 101101_2 (45_{10}) by 000110_2 (6_{10}), using the algorithm on page 277:

D	0	0	0	0	0	0	1	0	1	1	0	1							
d	0	0	0	1	1	0													
Init.																			
D	0	0	0	0	0	1	0	1	1	0	1	—							
d	0	0	0	1	1	0													
diff.(−)														q					0
D	0	0	0	0	1	0	1	1	0	1	—	—							
d	0	0	0	1	1	0													
diff. (−)														q				0	0
D	0	0	0	1	0	1	1	0	1	—	—	—							
d	0	0	0	1	1	0													
diff.(−)														q			0	0	0
D	0	0	1	0	1	1	0	1	—	—	—	—							
d	0	0	0	1	1	0													
diff.(+)	0	0	0	1	0	1								q		0	0	0	1
D	0	0	1	0	1	0	1	—	—	—	—	—							
d	0	0	0	1	1	0													
diff.(+)	0	0	0	1	0	0								q	0	0	0	1	1
D	0	0	1	0	0	1	—	—	—	—	—	—							
d	0	0	0	1	1	0													
rem.	0	0	0	0	1	1								quotient 0 0	0	1	1	1	

In decimal $D = 45$, $d = 6$, $q = 7$, and $r = 3$, and $dq + r = 6 \times 7 + 3 = 45 = D$. ■

Example 6.15 Fixed-Point Division

Divide $.100101_2$ $(37/64)_{10}$ by $.101100_2$ $(44/64)_{10}$, again using the algorithm on page 277:

D		.1	0	0	1	0	1						
d		.1	0	1	1	0	0						
No ov.													
D	1	.0	0	1	0	1	0						
d		.1	0	1	1	0	0						
diff.(+)		.0	1	1	1	1	0	q					.1
D	0	.1	1	1	1	0	0						
d		.1	0	1	1	0	0						
diff.(+)		.0	1	0	0	0	0	q				.1	1
D	0	.1	0	0	0	0	0						
d		.1	0	1	1	0	0						
diff.(−)								q			.1	1	0
D	1	.0	0	0	0	0	0						
d		.1	0	1	1	0	0						
diff.(+)		.0	1	0	1	0	0	q		.1	1	0	1
D	0	.1	0	1	0	0	0						
d		.1	0	1	1	0	0						
diff.(−)								q	.1	1	0	1	0
D	1	.0	1	0	0	0	0						
d		.1	0	1	1	0	0						
rem.		.1	0	0	1	0	0	quotient .1	1	0	1	0	1

In decimal $D = 37/64$, $d = 44/64$, $q = 53/64$, and $r = 36/4096$. Once again,

$$qd + r = \frac{53}{64} \times \frac{44}{64} + \frac{36}{4096} = \frac{2332 + 36}{4096} = \frac{37}{64} = D$$

Variations on Fixed-Point Divide: Restoring and Nonrestoring Division. There are several alternatives for implementing the divide operation. Two that are often discussed are *restoring* and *nonrestoring* division. Both start with the assumption that the difference is always strobed into the D register, in contrast to the conditional load we discussed in connection with Figure 6.9. In this case, the dividend must be "restored" when the difference is negative by adding the divisor d back into the D register. A trick for not having to restore comes from considering the sequence of three steps coming from two adjacent quotient bits in restoring division: add d back into D; shift D left 1 bit; and subtract d from D. Adding d before the shift is equivalent to adding $2d$ after the shift, so the three steps are equivalent to shifting D left and adding d. Thus instead of restoring, we can remember the last quotient digit, and if it was 1, subtract d after the shift while if it was 0, add d. This nonrestoring division scheme correctly computes all the quotient digits, but may leave a negative remainder. If a positive remainder is needed, adding d to the negative remainder will correct it.

There are also methods for directly performing 2's complement fixed-point divide. These are beyond the scope of this book. The most common alternative in division, however, is to handle signs separately, taking absolute values of operands at the beginning, doing unsigned divide, and complementing negative results when necessary.

restoring and nonrestoring division

Faster operation can be obtained at the expense of considerable hardware with a parallel array divider of the form shown in Figure 6.10. The cells in the diagram are identical and have as inputs 1 bit of the divisor d_j, 1 bit of a modified dividend D_k, a borrow-in bi, and a control signal c. Cell outputs are a borrow-out bo and a partial remainder R_k. The function of a cell is to do 1 bit of the subtraction of d from D for a particular quotient bit. The difference bit is sent to the output R if $c = 0$, but if $c = 1$, $R = D$. An RTN expression for the output R would be

$$R := (c \rightarrow D: \neg c \rightarrow (D - d - bi) \bmod 2):$$

The correct borrow for the subtraction is computed in either case. With the connections shown in Figure 6.10, one row of cells sends on to the next row the difference between D and a shifted version of the divisor d if this difference is positive, or an unmodified copy of the D input to the row if the difference is negative. The leftmost borrow-out supplies both the control signal for the row and the complement of the associated quotient bit.

There is a very large body of knowledge about computer arithmetic and a vast number of possible trade-offs in designing arithmetic hardware. This book can only give a flavor of the range of possibilities that exist in arithmetic design. The interested reader is referred to one of the many good texts on computer arithmetic for further information.

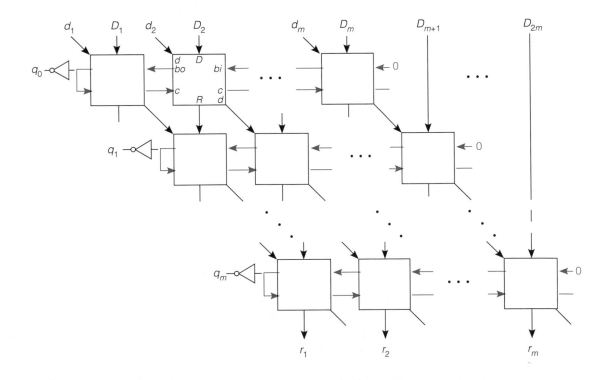

Fig. 6.10 Parallel Array Divider

Key Concepts: Fixed-Point Arithmetic

- Digitwise addition with single-bit carries between digits is the basis for both addition and complement subtraction.

- Speeding up carry propagation with lookahead is the principal technique for achieving fast addition and subtraction.

- Fixed-point multiply and divide are built on repeated additions and subtractions. The repetitions can be done by replicating hardware or by repetitively using a single adder/subtracter, with registers to hold intermediate results.

6.3 Seminumeric Aspects of ALU Design

There are several aspects of ALU design that do not involve arithmetic directly. The behavior of branching after comparison operations and the design of shifters are two of these. Others involve complex character manipulation instructions, which we will not discuss since they are both simple to understand and unpopular in modern designs. The interrupt behavior of an ALU is primarily involved with floating-point operations. The only fixed-point situation considered to be exceptional is overflow.

6.3.1 BRANCHING CONDITIONS

Branching conditions are simply internal states of the machine that can be tested to effect a change in program flow. The conditions to be discussed here arise as side effects of ALU operations, and may be caused by overflow of an arithmetic operation, by an attempt to divide by zero, or by some explicit comparison operation in the ALU, such as comparing two integers for equality. At any rate, the processor design must include the ability to generate and test for a wide range of conditions.

Conditional Branches in HLLs.   The conditional branch is an essential mechanism for controlling program flow. Most modern programming languages provide constructs of the following form:

> `if` (condition) **then** statement;

The semantics of the `if` statement usually specify that if the condition evaluates to true, then `statement` is executed; otherwise, it is skipped. Most programming languages do not specify how true and false are to be represented at the machine level, but compilers generally represent false as 0 and true as either 1, or as any integer $\neq 0$. At the machine level, the expression `condition` is evaluated by performing ALU operations to determine whether the condition is true or false, and then executing a branch around `statement` if the condition is false, and otherwise executing the statement.

Consider a simple comparison, such as "less than" or "greater than or equal." The comparison begins with a subtraction of the operands, followed by an evaluation of the result. The evaluation of the operands and result to decide the outcome of the comparison will differ depending upon the data type. Signed and unsigned integers must be evaluated differently, for example. You may not be too familiar with the unsigned data type, because many programming languages do not define unsigned integers as a data type. C does allow the programmer to specify an integer as unsigned. Unsigned integers have the advantage of providing twice the range if only nonnegative values are to be compared. This is common in system programming, where addresses are to be compared.

For example, in C, if the integers A, B, C, and D are signed 2's complement, the statement:

```
if (A > B ) C = D; ...
```

would translate to the following MC68000 code:

```
      MOVE.W    A, D0
      CMP.W     B, D0
      BLE       Over
      MOVE.W    D, C
Over: ...
```

whereas if the integers are unsigned, then the code to implement the statement would be

```
      MOVE.W    A, D0
      CMP.W     B, D0
      BLS       Over
      MOVE.W    D, C
Over: ...
```

The comparison operation is the same in both cases, subtraction, but the test of the results of the subtraction differs: BLE tests the appropriate flags to evaluate the results of the comparison when the operands are assumed to be signed integers, whereas BLS is designed to test the results when the operands are assumed to be unsigned integers. Notice that the sense of the comparison is reversed, with a branch on A less than or equal to B, since the branch around the assignment statement is to be taken if the "greater than" condition is false.

Branch Conditions and Condition Codes. Condition codes are computed by the ALU and usually stored as part of a processor status register. Not all instructions update all condition codes. The designer specifies which instructions update which flags as part of the instruction set design.

Table 6.6 shows the common ALU flags and algebraic symbols specifying the comparison. It assumes that the subtraction $s \leftarrow x - y$ has taken place, where x, y, and s are m-bit numbers as described earlier in this chapter. It further assumes that s_m is the carry-out from the addition of the most significant bits of the addends. It shows the arithmetic conditions and corresponding Boolean expression for the flag settings that will result if the comparison evaluates to true.

This table deserves some discussion. The Carry flag indicates a carry-out from the most significant bit of the 2's complement adder. The Zero flag indicates that the results of the comparison yielded an all-zeros result. The Overflow and Negative flags have meaning only if the comparison was between signed integers: Overflow in operations involving

Table 6.6 Condition Codes Denoting Various Arithmetic Conditions after a Subtraction, $x-y$, for Signed and Unsigned x and y.

Condition	Unsigned Integers		2's Complement Signed Integers	
	Arithmetic Condition	Flags	Arithmetic Condition	Flags
Carry-out from msb	$s_m = 1$	C	$s_m = 1$	C
Arithmetic overflow	$s_m = 1$	C	$x_{m-1}\bar{y}_{m-1}\bar{s}_{m-1} +$ $\bar{x}_{m-1}y_{m-1}s_{m-1}$	V
Negative	N.A.	N.A.	$s_{m-1} = 1$	N
>	$s_m = 0$ and $s \neq 0$	$\bar{C}\,\bar{Z}$	†	$(NV+\bar{N}\,\bar{V})\,\bar{Z}$
≥	$s_m = 0$	$\bar{C}$	‡	$\bar{N}\,\bar{V}+N\,V$
= (zero)	$s = 0$	Z	$s = 0$	Z
≠	$s \neq 0$	$\bar{Z}$	$s \neq 0$	$\bar{Z}$
≤	$s_m = 1$ or $z = 0$	C+Z	*	$(N\,\bar{V}+\bar{N}\,V)+Z$
<	$s_m = 1$	C	††	$N\,\bar{V}+\bar{N}\,V$

†Result was greater than zero and did not overflow, or result was less than zero, but did overflow.
‡Result was greater than or equal to zero and did not overflow, or was less than zero, but did overflow.
*Result was less than zero and did not overflow, or result was greater than zero, but did overflow, or result was equal to zero.
††Result was less than zero and did not overflow, or result was greater than zero, but did overflow.

unsigned integers is indicated by a carry-out from the msb of the adder into the 1-bit C register, and of course the N flag has no meaning when the operation is on unsigned integers. The rest of the entries in the table indicate the state of the various flags after a comparison that yielded a true result. Notice that a valid comparison can be made between all possible pairs of integers, regardless of whether the result overflows the result register or not.

Alternatives to Condition Codes. Not all machines employ condition codes. The MIPS R2000 RISC processor adopts a "condition codeless" approach. Rather than embodying the result of a previous comparison in the condition codes, the MIPS uses conditional branch instructions that "do it all at once." Each conditional branch instruction does both the comparison and the branch. The instructions include the two operands to be compared, as well as the branch target. An example would be the *bgtu* instruction, *branch if greater than unsigned*:

```
bgtu R1, R2, Lbl      ;Branch to Lbl if the unsigned integer in R1
                       is > the unsigned integer in R2.
```

The advantage of this approach is that the condition is evaluated and the branch taken in a single instruction, saving an instruction and eliminating the need for condition-code register. A disadvantage is that the instruction borders on being "complex," and may cause an increase in the minimum clock period.

There are times when the truth value resulting from an operation must be saved for further computations, as for example in multiple-word arithmetic or in the evaluation of complex Boolean expressions. Since in the MIPS approach these values are not stored in a condition-code register, the MIPS machine has separate "set" instructions that compute the truth of a comparison and save the truth value in a register, 1 for true and 0 for false. An example would be the *sgtu* instruction, *set greater than unsigned*:

```
sgtu R3, R1, R2        ;Set R3 if the unsigned integer in R1 is greater
                        than the unsigned integer in R2.
```

The disadvantage of this approach is that it consumes a general purpose 32-bit register to store a single-bit temporary result.

The reader will have observed that the SRC computer does not use condition codes. It takes a different approach: The comparison is made by a sub instruction, and the condition computed on the value resulting from the subtraction. Consider the previous example C statement:

```
             if (A > B) C=D; ...

    lar    r31, Over
    ld     r1,  A
    ld     r2,  B
    sub    r3,  r2, r1     ; only succeeds if
    brpl   r31, r3         ; there is no overflow
    ld     r3,  D
    st     r3,  C
Over: ...
```

An examination of the entries for "greater than" in Table 6.6 will show that this approach succeeds only if the subtraction of A and B does not result in overflow. Whether the numbers are signed or unsigned, the possibility of overflow exists, and overflow is not tested for by the SRC brpl instruction. A test for overflow after comparison of signed integers requires examination of both the operands and the result, and SRC tests only the result. This is not a serious flaw in a machine designed for instructional purposes, as SRC is. In a commercial machine, however, the design would need to be modified to include more complex tests for branching. Exercise 6.24 will show just how difficult it can be to compute branch conditions in the absence of condition codes.

6.3.2   ALU LOGICAL, SHIFT, AND ROTATE INSTRUCTIONS

The logical, shift, and rotate instructions are used in many ways. Perhaps the most common use is in inserting and extracting fields from words. Examples include accessing the various fields in floating-point numbers, and inserting and retrieving bytes from byte strings. Notice also that shifting an integer has the effect of multiplying it by 2, and a right arithmetic shift has the effect of dividing it by 2. In the latter case, the lsb, being shifted into C, becomes the remainder of the division, with the unwelcome twist that if the number is negative, the remainder in the Carry bit must be viewed as a positive number. Thus, whereas we expect $-3 \div 2 = -1$, R= -1, the shift action results in $-3 \div 2 = -2$, R = +1, an effect that must be accounted for in future uses of the quotient and remainder.

Illustrative Example: Extracting the Exponent from a Floating-Point Number. Floating-point numbers stored in the formats to be discussed in Section 6.4.1 must be unpacked before they can be employed in any calculations. Consider the task of extracting the 8-bit exponent field from bits 30..23 of a 32-bit word. Assume that a floating-point number is in D0 <31..0> of a MC68000 processor, and we wish to extract the exponent as an unsigned integer in D1.

```
MOVE.L   D0,    D1     ;Get copy of FP number into D1.
ROL.L    #9,    D1     ;Exponent now in D1⟨7..0⟩.
ANDI.L   #0xFF,D1      ;Clear bits D1⟨31..8⟩.
```

This code fragment contains a multiple-bit rotate and an AND instruction. Why `ROL.L #9` instead of `SHR.L #23`? According to the Motorola processor user's manual, the MC68000 shift and rotate instructions cost $8 + 2n$ clocks, where n is the shift count, whereas the typical instruction takes only 4–12 clocks. Thus the rotate left through 9 bit positions instead of a shift right of 23 bits saves 28 clock cycles. One obvious way to speed this processor is by the use of a *barrel shifter,* a combinational logic circuit that can shift or rotate a word by any number of bits in constant time. The MC68020 user's manual quotes a worst case for the shift and rotate instructions of 8–12 cycles independent of the shift count. Apparently Motorola introduced a barrel shifter into the MC68020!

Shift Hardware.   The 1-bit shifter such as that used in the SRC or the MC68000 employs multiplexers to route input bits left or right one bit position. The end bits at the msb and lsb positions of the word are treated differently depending on whether the operation is a shift or a rotate or a rotate through another bit position, such as carry.

The Barrel Shifter.   The barrel shifter described previously would be implemented in various ways depending on the implementation domain. If SSI or MSI circuits are used, then n-bit multiplexers can be used to route the correct input to the output. If the implementation domain is CMOS ICs, more interesting switching arrangements, known as *switching fabrics*, become practical. The switching fabric of a barrel shifter can be implemented using a variety of switches to route inputs to outputs.

A first design, an $N \times N$ crossbar, is implemented by tri-state buffers in Figure 6.11 as a 6×6 shifter (actually a 6×6 rotator, as the end bits are routed to the other end of the word). The 3–8 decoder is used to select the shift count. The propagation delay is a constant two levels of gates from input to output, at the cost of $O(N^2)$ gates. If a general purpose shift-rotate unit were desired, additional gating would be required to handle the bits on either end of the word.

An interesting time-space trade-off can be made by designing a *logarithmic barrel shifter*. Figure 6.12 shows a design employing 2–1 multiplexers as 1-bit bypass/shift units. They are arranged in stages, with s_0, the lsb of the shift count, shifting the word 1 bit, s_1 shifting it 2 bits, s_3 shifting it 4 bits, and so on. This design requires only $O(N \log N)$ switches, but the propagation delay is now $O(\log N)$ instead of $O(1)$.

(margin notes) barrel shifter

switching fabrics

logarithmic barrel shifter

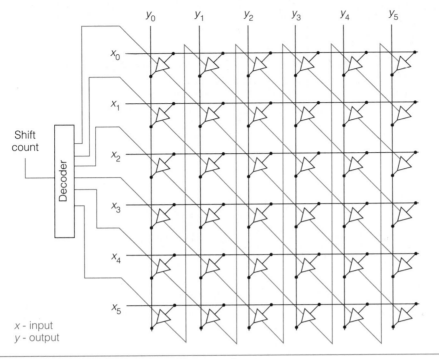

Fig. 6.11 N × N Crossbar Design for Barrel Rotator

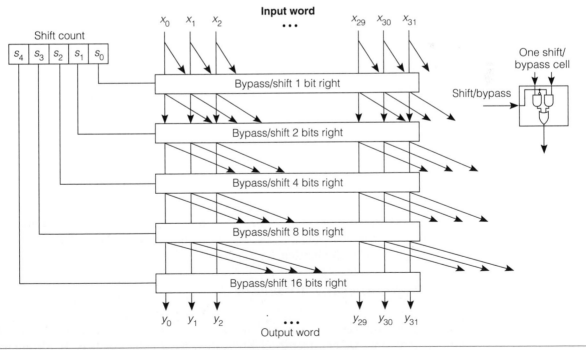

Fig. 6.12 Barrel Shifter with a Logarithmic Number of Stages

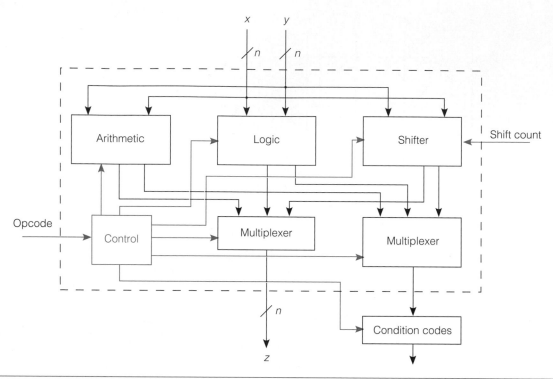

Fig. 6.13 A Possible Design for an ALU

ALU Designs.   There are many trade-offs possible when designing an ALU, depending on implementation domain and cost/performance considerations. They range from designs that employ simple combinational logic units that do ripple carry addition, shift-and-add multiplication, and single-bit shifts, to no-holds-barred units that do fast addition, hardware multiplication, and barrel shifts. The general design employs a multiplexer to select the outputs from various functional units, and to route the correct value to the condition codes. Figure 6.13 shows schematically what must be accomplished: The ALU controller accepts opcodes and perhaps other control information from the system control unit. It uses this information to control the operation of the functional units of the ALU and to route information to the ALU outputs. It also controls the strobing of information into the condition-code register. Although the ALU is usually thought of as a block of pure combinational logic, it may contain state information within its controller, especially if the arithmetic unit or the shift unit require that data pass through it multiple times, as it may in the case of shift-and-add multiplication, for example.

6.4   Floating-Point Arithmetic

Floating-point arithmetic is an automatic way to keep track of the radix point. To start the discussion, we consider explicitly scaling fixed-point numbers. In a computer with a set of fixed-point arithmetic instructions that are standardized, say, for fraction arithmetic, programs can always keep track of a different binary point position as an off-set from its standard left-end position. If the binary point is to be e bits to the right of the left end, the actual value of a number treated by the hardware as a fraction f is $f \times 2^e$. If all numbers have the same scale factor, addition and subtraction are easy, since $f \times 2^e + g \times 2^e = (f + g) \times 2^e$, provided that $f + g$ does not overflow. The scale changes in multiplication and division because, even if both operands are scaled the same,

$$(f \times 2^e) \cdot (g \times 2^e) = (f \cdot g) \times 2^{2e} \text{ and } (f \times 2^e) \div (g \times 2^e) = f/g.$$

If scale factors differ between numbers, addition and subtraction cannot be performed until one of the operands is scaled by shifting right or left to make the scale factors the same. Multiplication and division compute a new scale factor for the result from those of the operands by

$$(f_1 \times 2^{e_1}) \cdot (f_2 \times 2^{e_2}) = f_1 \cdot f_2 \times 2^{e_1 + e_2} \qquad \text{[Eq. 6.27]}$$

and

$$(f_1 \times 2^{e_1}) \div (f_2 \times 2^{e_2}) = (f_1/f_2) \times 2^{e_1 - e_2} \qquad \text{[Eq. 6.28]}$$

Since computation with scaled numbers leads rapidly to different scale factors for each number, it is almost never done in software in the way described above. Instead, a value and its scale factor are both recorded in a single computer word and manipulated by *floating-point* hardware or software.

6.4.1 FLOATING-POINT REPRESENTATIONS

Floating-point numbers correspond to decimal scientific notation of the form -2.72×10^{-2}. The sign of the number is minus, its *significand* is 2.72, and its *exponent* is –2. The *base* is 10 and is fixed for a given type of representation. Some books have called the significand the *mantissa*, but since this term has a related but different definition with respect to logarithms, many modern texts avoid it. A computer's floating-point representation uses binary numbers to encode significand, exponent, and their signs in a single word. With a fixed-length computer word, the first decision that must be made in floating-point arithmetic is how many bits to allocate to each of these numeric values. A larger exponent range means less accuracy for the significand with the remaining bits. The exponent is always a signed integer, but the significand has been treated both as a fraction and an integer, with the choice of fraction most common in modern machines. A common layout for a floating-point number is shown in Figure 6.14. The exponent field must include sign information, because exponents can be positive or negative. The exponent could, of course, be represented by a 2's complement integer, but most often the biased representation, $\hat{e}$, is used. In the *bias*, or *excess*, *representation*, a number, the bias, or excess, is added to the exponent so that the result is always positive. If $-e_{min} \leq e \leq e_{max}$, where $e_{min}, e_{max} > 0$, then $\hat{e} = e_{min} + e$ is a positive quantity, so adding the absolute value of the minimum negative exponent will always work as a bias. The usefulness of employing the biased representation, $\hat{e}$, in the exponent field instead of a signed representation will be made clear after we introduce normalized numbers.

significand

mantissa

bias, or excess representation

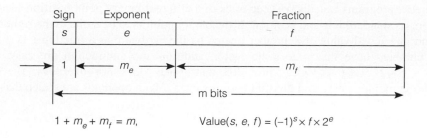

Fig. 6.14 Floating-Point Number Format

Trade-offs between exponent and significand field sizes can take several forms. A 32-bit memory word with 24 bits of accuracy for the significand leaves only 7 bits for the exponent, limiting its range to $-64 \leq e \leq 63$, which allows numbers x in the approximate range $10^{-19} \leq x \leq 10^{19}$ to be represented. This is a rather small range for scientific calculation, but 24 bits is also not very much accuracy. IBM addressed this problem in the floating-point format for its 360/370 series of computers, which used the word and field sizes just described, by taking the exponent to be base 16 instead of base 2. This made the value of a floating-point number $(-1)^s \times f \times 16^e$ and means that the significand is shifted by 4 bits left or right to accommodate a 1-unit change in the exponent. In this way, 24 bits of accuracy are retained in the significand, while the approximate range of numbers is increased to about $10^{-75} \leq x \leq 10^{75}$.

Normalized Floating-Point Numbers.   With the format of Figure 6.14, if f_1 and $2^d f_1$ are both fractions, then the two numbers (s, f_1, e_1) and (s, f_2, e_2), where $f_2 = 2^d f_1$ and $e_2 = e_1 - d$, represent the same numerical value. This corresponds to the fact that in scientific notation

$$(-2.72 \times 10^{-2}) = -0.272 \times 10^{-1} = -0.00272 \times 10^1$$

Scientific notation adopts a standard form that eliminates leading zeros by having exactly one nonzero digit to the left of the decimal point. Thus -2.72×10^{-2} is the standard, or normal, form. Zero cannot fit this rule and is a special case. A *normalized,* nonzero floating-point number in a computer has a significand whose leftmost digit is nonzero. Notice that in the IBM 360/370 format, this is a base 16 digit. In that representation, nonzero numbers are normalized if the leftmost 4 bits of the significand are anything other than 0000_2. The normalized form of zero usually has a significand of zero and an exponent equal to its most negative possible value.

For base 2 floating-point numbers, the only possible nonzero digit is 1. Since the leftmost bit of a normalized significand is always the same, an extra bit of accuracy can be gained by not storing the 1 in a normalized number. The leading 1 becomes a *hidden bit*. A true zero significand is distinguished from one that has all zeros except for the hidden 1 by looking at the exponent. Only the most negative exponent will be associated with a zero significand in a normalized number.

hidden bit

We can now discuss the reasons for placing the exponent field to the left of the significand and for using a biased exponent. If we consider only normalized numbers, any number with a larger exponent is greater in magnitude than one with a smaller exponent. Numbers with the same exponents are ordered by the sizes of their significands. With biased exponents, algebraically larger exponents appear as larger positive integers. If the exponent field is to the left of the significand, a number with a larger exponent will appear as a larger fixed-point number, regardless of its significand bits, because they are less significant than the exponent bits. This allows the sizes of floating-point numbers to be compared using fixed-point comparison operations. Taking the sign as applying to the whole word, fixed-point $=$, $\neq$, $<$, $>$, $\leq$, and $\geq$ on two computer words imply the same relationship between the normalized floating-point numbers that the words represent.

IEEE Floating-Point Standard.   With all the possibilities for field sizes, exponent base, bias, and so on in floating-point numbers, a standard is needed both for communication between computers and for the specification of a common floating-point arithmetic unit for several computers. The ANSI/IEEE Standard 754-1985, "IEEE Standard for Binary Floating-Point Arithmetic," supplies the need. It specifies not only how floating-point numbers are to be represented, but also details how operations on them are to be performed, including rounding, overflow, divide by zero, and so on. Two floating-point formats are specified in the standard: a 32-bit single-precision and a 64-bit double-precision format. Prior to this standard, every company had a different floating-point standard. IBM and DEC, for example, did not even use the same exponent base.

The single-precision format has the form shown in Figure 6.15.[†] The 23-bit fraction field contains the fraction bits of a significand, which also includes a hidden 1 bit for normalized values. The 8-bit exponent field, with positive values between 0 and 255, contains a biased value. The bias is 127, which is actually 1 more than the absolute value of the smallest negative exponent. The biased exponent value is used to distinguish normalized numbers from a special format called *denormalized*, which will be defined momentarily, and from a set of nonnumeric codes used for overflow and other exceptional results of arithmetic operations. Table 6.7 shows how the biased exponent $\hat{e}$ determines the type and value of numbers. The largest, $\hat{e} = 255$, denotes numbers with no numeric value, including $+\infty$, $-\infty$, and values called *Not-a-Number*, or *NaN*. NaNs can record information about exceptional arithmetic conditions. Encoding exceptions in the result is an alternative or supplement to interrupting the processor or setting condition-code bits. Zero divided by zero, $\infty - \infty$, and other such conditions can be distinguished by different values of the fraction field. The sign is ignored for NaNs.

Not-a-Number, NaN

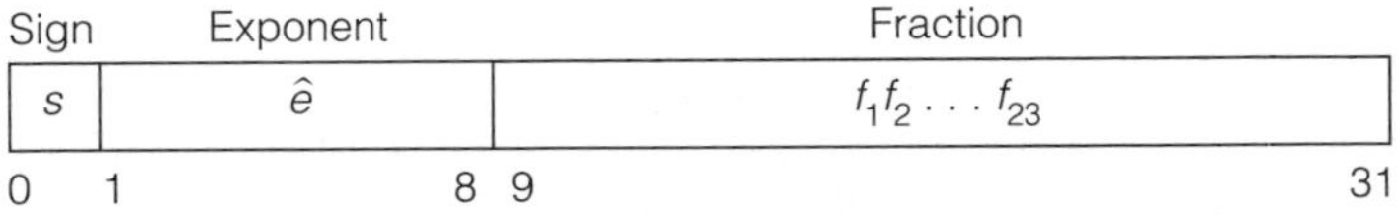

Sign	Exponent	Fraction
s	$\hat{e}$	$f_1 f_2 \cdots f_{23}$

0   1   8 9   31

Fig. 6.15 IEEE Standard Single-Precision, Binary Floating-Point Format

[†]   Note the numbering of the msb as bit 0, and the lsb as bit 31, in contravention to the numbering conventions used else where in this book

Table 6.7 Types and Values Represented by IEEE Single-Precision Format

$\hat{e}$	e	Value	Type
255	none	none	Infinity or NaN
254	127	$(-1)^s \times (1.f_1f_2...) \times 2^{127}$	Normalized
...	...	...	...
2	−125	$(-1)^s \times (1.f_1f_2...) \times 2^{127}$	Normalized
1	−126	$(-1)^s \times (1.f_1f_2...) \times 2^{127}$	Normalized
0	−126	$(-1)^s \times (0.f_1f_2...) \times 2^{127}$	Denormalized

IEEE standard floating-point numbers with numeric values are either normalized or denormalized. The exponent bias in single precision is 127, so for normalized numbers the real exponent is $e = \hat{e} - 127$. An exponent field $\hat{e} = 0$, either specifies a zero, for which the fraction field is also zero, or a denormalized number. As shown in Table 6.7, *denormalized* numbers do not have a hidden 1 bit and have $e = -126$ exponent, instead of the −127 that would result from subtracting the 127 bias from $\hat{e} = 0$. A normalized number x has a magnitude in the approximate range $1.2 \times 10^{-38} \leq |x| \leq 3.4 \times 10^{38}$. *Floating-point overflow* occurs when a result is too large for this range and is accommodated in the standard by the two codes for $+\infty$ and $-\infty$. Results with magnitudes too small for the range could be replaced by a standard zero, but it is sometimes important to distinguish a nearly zero underflowed result from an exact zero. Denormalized numbers allow for gradual underflow by representing smaller and smaller numbers with fewer and fewer bits of accuracy. The smallest denormalized number has a magnitude of about 1.4×10^{-45}, but only 1 bit of accuracy, for a relative error of ±50%.

The IEEE standard double-precision format extends the exponent field to 11 bits and the fraction to 52 bits, as shown in Figure 6.16. The exponent bias for normalized numbers is 1023. A biased exponent $\hat{e} = 2047$ denotes infinities and NaNs, while zero and denormalized numbers have $\hat{e} = 0$ and a value of $0.f_1f_2...f_{52} \times 2^{-1022}$. Although in principle 32-bit floating-point arithmetic could be made faster than for 64 bits, modern machines have a tendency to only implement 64-bit arithmetic internal to the floating-point unit. Conversion instructions manufacture a correctly rounded single-precision result to satisfy the single-precision standard externally. This retains the advantage of single precision in using less memory space and allows extra design effort to be put into making double-precision arithmetic fast.

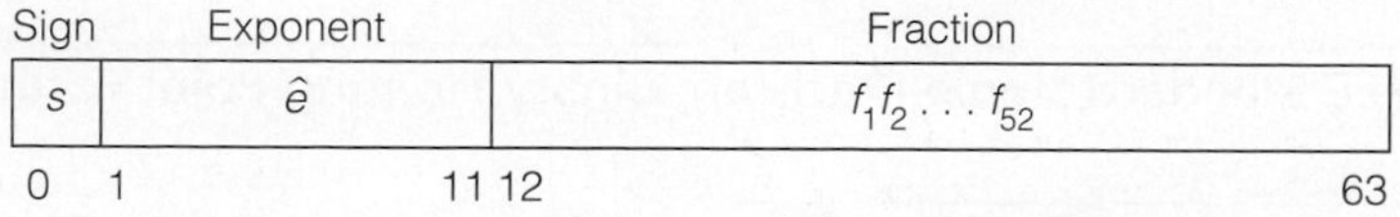

denormalized numbers

floating-point overflow

Sign	Exponent	Fraction
s	$\hat{e}$	$f_1f_2 ... f_{52}$

0   1   11 12   63

Fig. 6.16 IEEE Standard, Double-Precision, Binary Floating-Point Format

6.4.2   FLOATING-POINT ADDITION AND SUBTRACTION

The job of floating-point arithmetic is to implement in hardware the operations described at the beginning of this section for scaled fixed-point numbers. If fixed-point arithmetic hardware is available, floating-point add and subtract are actually more complicated than floating-point multiply or divide. This is because, for multiply and divide, the operations on the significands are quite separate from those on the exponents, while for add and subtract, alignment of operands and normalization of the result involves interaction between exponents and significands. The problems can be illustrated by examples of four-digit scientific notation addition and subtraction:

Operands	Alignment	Normalize and round
6.144×10^2	0.06144×10^4	1.003644×10^5
$+9.975 \times 10^4$	$+9.975 \quad \times 10^4$	$+ .0005 \quad \times 10^5$
	10.03644×10^4	$1.004 \quad \times 10^5$

Operands	Alignment	Normalize and round
1.076×10^{-7}	$1.076 \quad \times 100^{-7}$	7.7300×100^{-9}
$-9.987 \quad \times 100^{-8}$	-0.9987×100^{-7}	$+ .0005 \times 100^{-9}$
	0.0773×100^{-7}	$7.730 \quad \times 100^{-9}$

You can see from these examples that the significand with the smaller exponent is shifted right until the exponents are equal, the addition or subtraction is performed, and then the result must be shifted left or right to put the significand in standard four-digit form. *Rounding* is done by adding a half unit in the lowest-order digit.

rounding

The steps in addition (FA) or subtraction (FS) of floating-point numbers $(s_1, \hat{e}_1, f_1)$ and $(s_2, \hat{e}_2, f_2)$ are as follows.

1. Unpack sign, exponent, and fraction fields. Handle special operands such as zero, infinity, or NaN.

2. Shift the significand of the number with the smaller exponent right by $|e_1 - e_2|$ bits.

3. Set the result exponent e_r to $\max(e_1, e_2)$.

4. If the instruction is FA and $s_1 = s_2$, or if the instruction is FS and $s_1 \neq s_2$, then add the significands; otherwise subtract them.

5. Count the number z of leading zeros. A carry can make $z = -1$. Shift the result significand left z bits or right 1 bit if $z = -1$.

6. Round the result significand, and shift right and adjust z if there is *rounding overflow*, which is a carry-out of the leftmost digit upon rounding.

7. Adjust the result exponent by $e_r = e_r - z$, check for overflow or underflow, and pack the result sign, biased exponent, and fraction bits into the result word.

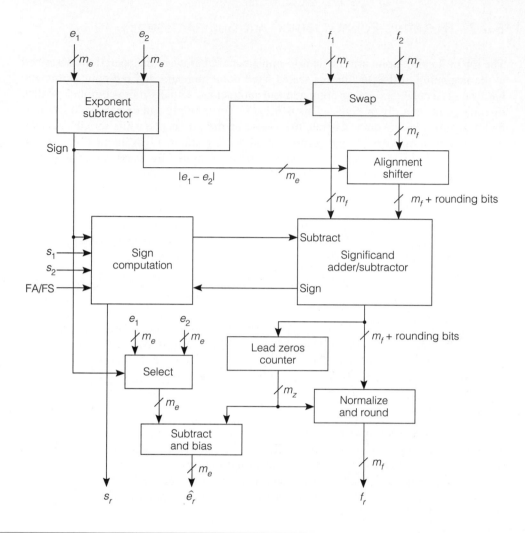

Fig. 6.17 Hardware Structure for Floating-Point Add and Subtract

These steps show that the component operations of floating-point add/subtract are fixed-point add/subtract on both exponent length and significand length numbers, multiple bit shifters, and a leading zero counter. These components must be made as fast as possible to get an acceptable speed for floating-point arithmetic. Figure 6.17 shows the structure of a floating-point add/subtract unit.

Shifters are needed for both significand alignment and normalization. Any amount of right shift may be needed, up to the length of the significand, to align the operands, and cancellation of high-order digits in subtraction may require up to the same amount of left shift to normalize the result. The rounding overflow mentioned in step 6 may require a subsequent right shift of the result, but only by 1 bit. The significand adder/subtracter may use 2's complement internally but returns a sign-magnitude result of either adding or subtracting its positive operands. The exponents can be left in biased form, since $|\hat{e}_1 - \hat{e}_2| = |e_1 - e_2|$.

The lead zeros counter in Figure 6.17 is an example of a circuit called a *priority encoder*. The sign computation involves only a few logic gates.

A floating-point unit controller will supply the gate and strobe signals to implement the sequential steps of FA and FS. Any of the controller design techniques of Chapters 4 and 5 can be used to implement it. Notice that the flow of information in Figure 6.17 is from top to bottom, with no feedback. This makes it possible to introduce registers at appropriate levels and pipeline the design so that a new floating add/subtract instruction can be started before a previous one completes. Hazards must be taken into account, as with any pipeline.

Arithmetic specifications of the IEEE binary floating-point standard, such as its four possible rounding modes and the treatment of denormalized numbers are beyond the scope of this book. Considerable detail is involved in satisfying these specifications, but few new concepts.

6.4.3 FLOATING-POINT MULTIPLICATION AND DIVISION

Allowing only normalized operands has a distinct advantage in floating-point multiply and divide operations, and we will assume that this is the case in what follows. The separateness of sign, exponent, and significand operations only fails to hold when the result is normalized and rounded. A one-place shift is sufficient to normalize the result of a multiply or divide of normalized operands. Another right shift is required in the case of rounding overflow. Here are two examples using four-digit scientific notation with a fraction significand, to help clarify the scaling:

Sign, fraction, and exponent
$$\begin{array}{r} (-0.1403 \quad \times 100^{-4}) \\ \underline{\times(+0.3021 \quad \times 10^5)} \\ -0.04238463 \times 10^{-4+5} \end{array}$$

Normalize and round
$$\begin{array}{r} -0.4238463 \times 10^0 \\ \underline{-0.00005 \quad \times 10^0} \\ -0.4238 \quad \times 10^0 \end{array}$$

Sign, fraction, and exponent
$$\begin{array}{r} (-0.9325 \times 10^2) \\ \underline{\div(-0.1002 \times 10^{-6})} \\ +9.306387 \times 10^{2-(-6)} \end{array}$$

Normalize and round
$$\begin{array}{r} +0.9306387 \times 10^9 \\ \underline{+0.00005 \quad \times 10^9} \\ +0.9306 \quad \times 10^9 \end{array}$$

Floating-Point Multiply Procedure.

1. Unpack signs, exponents, and significands. Handle exceptional operands.
2. Compute result sign, $s_r = s_1 \oplus s_2$, add exponents, $e_r = e_1 + e_2$, and multiply significands, $f_r = f_1 \times f_2$.
3. If necessary, normalize by one left shift and decrement result exponent. Round and shift right if rounding overflow occurs.
4. If the exponent is too positive, handle overflow, and if it is too negative, handle underflow.
5. Pack result, encoding or reporting exceptions.

Floating-Point Divide Procedure.

1. Unpack. Handle exceptions.
2. Compute result sign, $s_r = s_1 \oplus s_2$, subtract exponent of divisor from that of dividend, $e_r = e_1 - e_2$, and divide the significands, $f_r = f_1 \div f_2$.
3. If necessary, normalize by one right shift and increment result exponent. Round and correct for rounding overflow.
4. Handle overflow and underflow on exponent range as in multiply.
5. Pack result and treat exceptions.

As in add and subtract, the detailed treatment of underflow and especially the handling of denormalized operands in multiply and divide are left for other books.

Key Concepts: Floating-Point Representation

- Floating-point numbers are generally represented with the significand having a sign-magnitude representation and the exponent having a biased representation. The exponent base is implicit.

- Floating-point standards must specify the base, the representation, and the number of bits devoted to exponent and significand.

- Normalization eliminates multiple representations for the same value, and simplifies comparisons and arithmetic computations.

- Floating-point arithmetic operations are composed of multiple fixed-point operations on the exponents and significands.

- Floating-point addition and subtraction are more complicated than multiplication and division because they require comparison of exponents and shifting of the significands to "line up the binary points" prior to the actual addition or subtraction operation.

- Floating-point multiplication and division, on the other hand, require only a maximum 1-bit shift of the significand to normalize the numbers.

Summary

- The base b digital positional number systems form the basis for the representation of not only unsigned and signed whole integer numbers, but also fixed-point and floating-point numbers as well. While base 2 is the most commonly used, there are advantages to treating the general case of base 2^n numbers.

- *The b's and to a lesser extent $(b-1)$'s complement number systems are the most commonly used* ways to represent signed integers and fixed-point numbers. They have the advantage of easy conversion to and from the eternally used sign-magnitude number system. Addition and subtraction hardware is simple to design and implement for the complement numbers.

- Fixed-point addition and subtraction form the basis of arithmetic on fractions and floating-point numbers. Fast hardware for fixed-point multiplication and division can be designed with a parallel array of n^2 full adders using purely combinational logic, or it can be designed with just n full adders by cycling the partial results through the hardware n times, with registers to hold intermediate results.

■ Conditional branches require the setting and testing of one or more condition codes. The particular combination of condition codes depends not only on the particular condition, but also on whether the values being tested are signed or unsigned. Some processors dispense with condition codes by having a unified conditional branch instruction that performs the comparison and tests the condition.

■ It is possible to design fast shifters and rotators that can accomplish their operation in a single clock cycle.

■ Floating-point formats represent values using a pair of numbers, significand and exponent. Usually the significand is represented as a sign-magnitude number, and the exponent as a biased number. The IEEE floating-point standard is becoming universally used.

■ Floating-point addition, subtraction, multiplication, and division are, by their nature, complex algorithms. Special purpose floating-point processors are commonly used to speed up the process.

Bibliography

For a simple treatment of computer arithmetic similar to the one in this chapter but confined to binary numbers, see the following:

V. Carl Hamacher, Zvonko G. Vranesic, and Safwat G. Zaki, *Computer Organization,* 4th ed., McGraw-Hill, New York, 1996.

Advanced discussions of the algorithms and mathematics involved in number systems and computer arithmetic are contained in the following texts. The Knuth book expects a good deal of the reader, but can be quite rewarding. Koren's book is intended as a graduate or advanced undergraduate text, and is considerably more accessible.

Donald E. Knuth, *The Art of Computer Programming, vol. 2, Semi-numerical Algorithms*, 2nd ed., Addison-Wesley, Reading, MA, 1981.

Israel Koren, *Computer Arithmetic Algorithms,* Prentice-Hall, Englewood Cliffs, NJ, 1993.

The Booth algorithm was originally described in the following text. It, and several related algorithms are also described in the Koren text above.

A. D. Booth, *"A signed binary multiplication technique,"* Quart. J. Mech. Appl. Math. 4, part 2 (1951).

A broad range of different hardware designs for doing computer arithmetic appears in the following. Parallel designs for fast arithmetic are well treated.

Kai Hwang, *Computer Arithmetic: Principles, Architecture, and Design,* John Wiley & Sons, New York, 1979.

Exercises

6.1 Convert the following decimal values to 8-bit sign-magnitude, 1's complement, 2's complement, and excess 127 representations:

   a. 67

   b. 129

   c. −135

   d. −24

   e. −15

   f. 0   **(§6.1)**

6.2 Convert the following hexadecimal values to 16-bit binary and octal representations:

   a. E0E0

   b. 0B2E

   c. 0432

   d. B0A0

   e. 77EE   **(§6.1)**

6.3 What decimal value does the binary word 1110 1101 0111 0110 have when it represents an

   a. unsigned integer

   b. 1's complement integer

   c. 2's complement integer

   d. sign-magnitude integer   **(§6.1)**

6.4 Repeat problem 6.3 assuming the binary point is

   a. at the far left

   b. in the middle   **(§6.1)**

6.5 Write an ANSI C program to solve problems such as Exercise 6.3. Your program should accept binary or hexadecimal numbers, the latter signified by a leading 0x, and print the corresponding unsigned, 1's and 2's complement and sign-magnitude values as decimal numbers.   **(§6.1)**

6.6 Convert the following decimal numbers to unsigned base 6 numbers:

   a. 119

   b. 343

   c. 96

   d. 43   **(§6.1)**

6.7 Convert the following base 12 numbers to decimal. Assume they are unsigned.

   a. A1B

   b. 12A

   c. B41

   d. AB   **(§6.1)**

6.8 Perform the following 6-bit additions assuming the values are unsigned, 1's complement, 2's complement, and excess 31. In each instance report overflow if it occurs.

a.	b.	c.	d.
101 101	011 110	111 100	101 010
110 100	101 011	011 101	110 111

e.	f.	g.	h.
011 100	110 101	110 001	101 101
100 010	110 010	011 011	110 111 **(§6.2)**

6.9 Write an ANSI C program to perform the additions given in Exercise 6.8. Be careful to limit the word size to 6 bits.   **(§6.2)**

6.10 Design the overflow detector for the 2's complement adder/subtracter of Figure 6.3.   **(§6.2)**

6.11 How long will the carry lookahead adder of Figure 6.4 take to provide a valid result if simple gates have 1-ns delays and XOR gates have 2-ns delays?   **(§6.2)**

6.12 Repeat Exercise 6.8 but perform

   a. Unsigned multiplications

b. 2's complement multiplications

c. Divisions instead of additions   **(§6.2)**

6.13 Repeat Exercise 6.8 but perform multiplications using

a. Booth recoding

b. Bit-pair recoding   **(§6.2)**

6.14 How long will the parallel array multiplier of Figure 6.6 take to provide a valid result if the delay through each computational box is 1.5 ns?   **(§6.2)**

6.15 A binary-encoded, base 4 digit adder has five inputs, x_1, x_0, y_1, y_0, and c_0, and three outputs, s_1, s_0, and c_2. Derive the 12-term Boolean expression for a two-level AND/OR implementation of the sum output bit s_1.   **(§6.2)**

6.16 Design a 3-bit carry lookahead adder and determine the maximum number of gates between any input and each of the four outputs (3 sum bits and a carry).   **(§6.2)**

6.17 Give the set of inputs and outputs for a 4-bit carry lookahead block. Give the number of gates and the number of inputs per gate for a two-level AND/OR implementation of the circuit. The block is to be used in all carry lookahead levels of a circuit like that of Figure 6.4, but for $k = $ 4-bit groups.   **(§6.2)**

6.18 How many gate delays are there in the longest path from some input to some output of a 32-bit adder using 8-bit carry lookahead groups and a multiple level structure? Compare with the longest path for a 32-bit ripple carry adder.   **(§6.2)**

6.19 Design the parallel multiplier of Figure 6.6 for base $b = 2$. Calculate the number of AND, OR, and NOT gates in an implementation using only these gates. Not counting inverters, how many gates are there in the worst-case path from an input to an output?   **(§6.2)**

6.20 Design a binary series parallel unsigned multiplier of the type shown for an arbitrary base in Figure 6.7. Carry all subdesigns to the level of AND, OR, NOT, XOR gates, and D flip-flops. Calculate the number of each logic element needed for multiplying two m-bit unsigned integers.   **(§6.2)**

6.21 Design a controller for the 2's complement multiplier of Figure 6.8. The controller should accept an external start signal, generate all strobes and gates needed to carry out the m steps of the multiply, and return a done signal when complete.   **(§6.2)**

6.22 Design a cell of the divider array of Figure 6.10, using AND, OR, and NOT gates. Compute the gate count for an array to divide a $2m$-bit dividend by an m-bit divisor to get an m-bit quotient. Ignoring inverters, and taking a delay of Δ for any other gate, compute the maximum delay from any input to any output.   **(§6.2)**

6.23 The text asserts that the SRC branch conditions are insufficient to allow some integer comparisons.

a. Discuss the specific reasons for this failing.

b. Describe what you believe to be a minimum set of branch conditions.

c. Modify the SRC abstract RTN described on page 58 and following to include these conditions.

d. Modify the branching hardware described on page 158 to complete your design.   **(§6.3)**

6.24 You are stranded on a desert island with nothing but an SRC computer. Write the code fragment to run on SRC that implements "branch less than" on comparison of two signed 2's complement integers.   **(§6.3)**

6.25 The MC68000 and the SRC take different approaches to implementing conditional branches. The 68000 sets the flags during the comparison and then tests them during a subsequent branch instruction. The SRC requires storage of the result of the computation, and tests it as part of the branch instruction. Discuss the advantages and disadvantages of these two approaches.   (**§6.3**)

6.26 One use of the Carry flag is to implement multiple-word integer arithmetic. Is it possible to implement a 64-bit signed addition in the SRC without a Carry register? If not, why not? If so, describe how this is done, and write an SRC program to add two 64-bit integers stored in r1–r0 and r3–r2, and store the result in r5–r4. Assume the most significant word is stored in the higher-numbered register.   (**§6.3**)

6.27 a. Figure 6.11 shows a 6×6 barrel rotator. Redesign it so that it will perform right or left logical shifts of from 0 to 5 positions according to the value of a 4-bit signed integer, where right shifts are specified by positive numbers and left shifts by negative numbers.

   b. Redesign it further so that it will allow left and right arithmetic and logical shifts and rotates, where the rotates may be direct or through a carry bit. Assume a 3-bit shift/ rotate code: SHR, SAR, SHL, ROR, ROL, RCR, and RCL. The shift count is now taken to be a 3-bit unsigned integer. For the first four codes, the last bit shifted or rotated out should be copied into the carry bit.   (**§6.3**)

6.28 Convert the following decimal numbers to IEEE single-precision floating-point numbers. Report the results as hexadecimal values. You need not extend the calculation of the significand value beyond its most significant 8 bits.

   a. −3

   b. 6.5125

   c. 0.91

   d. 0.000071

   e. 56,000,135

   f. −23.23

   g. 6.02×10^{23} (**§6.4**)

6.29 Convert the following IEEE single-precision floating-point numbers to their decimal values. Report the answers to three significant figures. Use scientific notation if needed to maintain precision: (**§6.4**)

   a. 0x21E0 0000

   b. 0x8906 0000

   c. 0x4B90 0000

   d. 0xf1A6 0000

6.30 What is the smallest, nonzero, positive value that can be represented in the IEEE 754 standard single-precision format, considering the following?

   a. Normalized values

   b. All possible values   (**§6.4**)

6.31 In floating-point addition, can you give an example where $a + b = a$ for some nonzero value of b?   (**§6.4**)

6.32 Show that for floating-point addition, the associative law, $(a + b) + c = a + (b + c)$, does not hold.   (**§6.4**)

6.33 Using a four-digit decimal scientific notation with a fraction significand, compute correctly normalized and rounded results for the following floating-point operations. Report the number and type of shifts required in each case.

   a. $(-0.2873 \times 10^5) + (+0.8851 \times 10^5)$

   b. $(-0.7192 \times 10^{-7}) - (+0.7862 \times 10^{-8})$

c. $(+0.7221 \times 10^{-5}) \times (-0.3442 \times 10^{-9})$

d. $(-0.7723 \times 10^{11}) \div (+0.2060 \times 10^{-8})$ **(§6.4)**

6.34 Design hardware for the swap unit shown in Figure 6.17. Count the number of AND, OR, and NOT gates and inputs needed for a 24-bit fraction field.   **(§6.4)**

6.35 Write an ANSI C program to convert a decimal number to a 32-bit IEEE real. Report the result as a hexadecimal number, and also in scientific notation: $\pm n.nnn \times 10^{nn}$.   **(§6.4)**

6.36 There are reasons other than exponent range that favor the choice of a base 16 exponent for floating-point numbers. In the floating-point add/subtract hardware of Figure 6.17, two fast barrel shifters are needed: one for alignment and one for result normalization. Assume that shifters are implemented as multiplexers, and quantitatively compare the cost and speed of an alignment shifter for a 24-bit fractional significand with exponent base 16 with one for exponent base 2 (no hidden bit).   **(§6.4)**

6.37 Design the lead zeros counter of Figure 6.17 for a 6-bit result. Discuss the trade-offs in speed versus total gate inputs for a length m_f result.   **(§6.4)**

6.38 Assume normalized operands in an arbitrary floating-point number base b. Show algebraically that at most one base b digit left shift is necessary for multiply and at most one base b digit right shift is needed for divide to normalize the result before rounding.   **(§6.4)**

Memory System Design

Chapter Outline

In the chapters on processor design, we treated memory as a monolithic block with storage capacity limited only by the number of address bits, and with the ability to load or store (read or write) an entire register in 1 clock cycle. In the real world, cost, speed, size, power consumption, and other factors complicate the picture. In this chapter, we examine these complications in detail.

We begin by defining some preliminary concepts, including memory capacity and memory performance parameters. We also briefly introduce the memory hierarchy. After this preliminary discussion, we turn to the design of memory hardware, beginning with the single memory cell and moving outward to chip, board, and module design. Much of this discussion will be from the perspective of the logic designer as we consider the gate-level design of the various components.

We turn to the architect's perspective for a more in-depth discussion of the memory hierarchy. The *memory hierarchy* is the combination of storage components that make up the overall physical memory system of a computer. The various components are typically arranged from fastest to slowest in terms of their access times, hence the term *hierarchy*. Cache memory, main memory, and disk memory are discussed as typical components of the hierarchy. We then introduce the concept of virtual memory as a means of allowing the CPU to access information stored anywhere in the hierarchy as if it were in main memory. We conclude by discussing the factors that influence memory system design.

7.1 Introduction: The Components of the Memory System

We begin with a short discussion of the parameters that are used to characterize main memory capacity and organization. Then we briefly discuss the characteristics of the various components that comprise the memory hierarchy.

7.1.1 MAIN MEMORY SIZE AND ORGANIZATION

Figure 7.1 and Table 7.1 show the parameters that characterize the interface between the CPU and main memory. Main memory can be pictured as being composed of a large collection of registers, all the same word size, s bits, which we will refer to as *memory words*. Note that the CPU word size, w, may be different than the main memory word size, s. In general, s-bit words are the smallest units that can be accessed in memory. In many processors, words that are fragments of w can be requested and processed. For example, the PowerPC G4 chip has 32-bit registers, uses byte addresses, but can read or write 8-, 16-, 32-, or 64-bit values from or to main memory. A machine with m-bit addresses has a memory capacity of 2^m s-bit memory words, yielding a memory bit-capacity of $2^m \times s$.

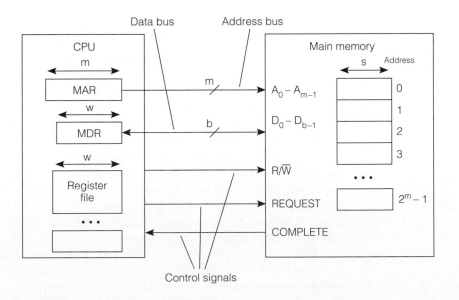

Fig. 7.1 The CPU-Memory Interface

Table 7.1   Some Memory Properties

Symbol	Definition	Intel 8088	Intel 8086	Intel Pentium	PowerPC G4
w	CPU word size	16 bits	16 bits	16/32	64 bits
m	Bits in a logical memory address	20 bits	20 bits	32	32 bits
s	Bits in smallest addressable unit	8 bits	8 bits	8 bits	8 bits
b	Data bus size	8 bits	16 bits	64 bits	64 bits
2^m	Memory capacity, s-sized words	2^{20} words	2^{20} words	2^{32} words	2^{32} words
$2^m \times s$	Memory bit capacity	$2^{20} \times 8$ bits	$2^{20} \times 8$ bits	$2^{32} \times 8$ bits	$2^{32} \times 8$ bits

For cost reasons, a given memory system may not transmit the entire w bits of a word at once. It may transmit portions of the CPU word serially, where they are reassembled by the CPU. We define the size of the largest word actually transmitted as a unit as b. On the other hand, when an s-bit word, $s < w,$ is accessed by the CPU, the memory system may transmit an entire w-bit word, leaving the CPU hardware to extract the desired s-bit fragment. This process is transparent to the machine language program.

The CPU makes a memory access request by asserting REQUEST while indicating a read or write on the $R/\overline{W}$ line. The memory system indicates that its process is complete by asserting COMPLETE. Table 7.1 shows three examples from the Intel 8086 family: the 8088, the 8086, and the Pentium processors. The first two processors have a 16-bit CPU word size, 8-bit memory word size, and 20-bit addresses. The 8086 can transmit an entire 16-bit CPU word in 1 bus cycle over its 16-bit data bus. The 8088 was designed, for cost-saving reasons, with only an 8-bit data bus, and therefore must transmit the word as two separate 8-bit bytes, requiring 2 bus cycles. This is yet another of the time (2 bus cycles versus 1) and space (8-bit bus versus 16-bit bus) trade-offs that are possible in system design. The Pentium processor shown in the table remains binary-compatible with the two former members, but operations can be performed on double (32-bit) words, and the bus size has been extended to 64 bits.

Big-Endian and Little-Endian Word-Ordering Schemes.   Jonathan Swift, in *Gulliver's Travels*, describes a war between those who believed that an egg should be broken from the little end, the Little Endians, and those who believed that the only proper way to break an egg was from the big end, the Big Endians. These terms have become associated with two possible conventions for storing the w/s bytes of a word when $w/s = n > 1$. *Little-endian* organization stores the least significant byte, the little end, at the lower byte address and the most significant byte at the higher byte address. *Big-endian* organization puts the most significant byte, the big end, at the first byte address and the least significant byte after it. Figure 7.2 shows the two conventions illustrated for a 32-bit PowerPC G4 word.

little-endian
big-endian

Both storage strategies have their adherents, but in fact there is little difference between them, and various machines use various byte-ordering conventions. The entire Intel x86 family of processors are little-endian machines, and the 16-bit PDP11 is a big-endian machine. The byte-ordering conventions are important under certain circumstances; for example, when using a debugger, it is important that the user know the byte

	CPU Word			
CPU word bit locations	b31 ... b24	b23 ... b16	b15 ... b8	b7 ... b0
Big-endian byte addresses	0	1	2	3
Little-endian byte addresses	3	2	1	0

Storage of a CPU Word in Memory

Little-endian storage

Memory address	Contents
0	b7 ... b0
1	b15 ... b8
2	b23 ... b16
3	b31 ... b24
...	

Big-endian storage

Memory address	Contents
0	b31 ... b24
1	b23 ... b16
2	b15 ... b8
3	b7 ... b0
...	

Fig. 7.2 Big-Endian and Little-Endian Storage of a PowerPC 32-Bit Word

ordering when examining memory contents by byte. Knowledge of byte ordering is also of obvious importance when multibyte words are communicated between hosts from different vendors. The PowerPC has machine instructions to alter the endian-ness of words being transmitted to its CPU.

random access memory, RAM

RAM and ROM. The abbreviation *RAM* stands for *random access memory*—memory in which all cells can be accessed in equal time. By convention, this term is reserved for semiconductor memory that can be written to as well as read from. Memory that has been preprogrammed and can only be read from is referred to as *ROM, read-only memory*. These terms are somewhat deceiving on the surface, since both RAM and ROM are random access; that is, values can be accessed in the same amount of time regardless of their actual physical location in the memory. This is in contrast to disk memory, for example, where time to access a given value depends on where the read-write head of the disk is located at the precise time an access is requested, and where the particular word is located on the disk. With this *caveat* in mind, we will use the terms RAM and ROM in their generally accepted senses—RAM is semiconductor memory that can be read from and written to; ROM can only be read.

read-only memory, ROM

Memory Operations: READ and WRITE. The memory operations READ and WRITE can be viewed as functions similar to the functions of programming languages, invoked by the CPU, with in and out parameters. The memory functions *as viewed from the standpoint of the memory system* are mirror images, with **in** replacing **out**, and **out** replacing **in**.

READ (**in**: Addr; **out:** Word, Completion_signal)

    On Entry: MAR contains address to be read from.

    On Exit: Completion_signal is true and MDR contains Word stored at Addr, of size w bits.

WRITE (**in**: Addr, Word; **out:** Completion_signal)

    On Entry: MAR contains address to be written to; MDR contains Word of size w bits;

    On Exit: Completion_signal is true; Word as been written to address Addr.

    The CPU reads from the memory by asserting READ and the address from which to read. The memory system responds by loading the data lines with the data stored at Address, and asserts the completion signal. The write cycle is similar, except that the processor loads the data to be written in the MDR and asserts WRITE. The memory asserts the completion function after the value has been stored. The completion signal may be indicated in texts and timing diagrams with signal names such as Done, $\overline{\text{WAIT}}$, ACKNOWLEDGE, READY, or ACCEPT.

7.1.2 MEMORY PERFORMANCE PARAMETERS

The most important memory performance parameters are access time, t_a, the time interval from the start of a read until the assertion of the memory completion signal, and cycle time, t_c, the minimum time interval from the start of a read or write to the start of the next memory operation. The cycle time may be slightly longer than the access time, due to various hardware housekeeping tasks that must be performed by the memory.

    Some memories read or write values not as individual words, but in blocks of k words. In these memories, there will be a *latency, t_l,* in accessing the first word of the block, that differs from the *bandwidth,* ω, the rate at which the words can be transmitted, in words per second, once the first word in the block is available. Thus the access time for the entire block, $t_{bl} = t_l + k/\omega$. These parameters are summarized in Table 7.2.

memory latency

memory bandwidth

Table 7.2 Memory Performance Parameters

Symbol	Definition	Units	Meaning
t_a	Access time	time	Time to access a memory word
t_c	Cycle time	time	Time from start of read to start of next
k	Block size	words	Number of words per block
ω	Bandwidth	words/sec.	Word transmission rate
t_l	Latency	time	Time to access first of a sequence of words
$t_{bl} = t_l + k/\omega$	Block access time	time	Time to access entire block from start of read

7.1.3   THE MEMORY HIERARCHY

Table 7.3 shows how a typical memory hierarchy might be organized, as well as some approximate values for capacity, latency, bandwidth, and cost.

primary,
secondary, and
tertiary memory

The registers, which are internal to the CPU, are the first level of memory. One step outward in the hierarchy comes RAM. Many high-performance systems employ two or three levels of cache memory in addition to the conventional main memory. Beyond the main memory the table shows a disk system, and beyond that a tape system. Conventionally, high-speed memory is referred to as *primary memory,* disk drives as *secondary memory,* and tape, if it exists, as *tertiary memory.* Observe the large differences in capacity, bandwidth, latency, and cost between primary and secondary memory.

Conceptually, each adjacent pair in the hierarchy will have interfaces like those in Figure 7.1, with the exception that the actual physical addresses and data passed between any two interfaces may be of a different form than the format of addresses and data used between CPU and main memory. For example, the disk level of the hierarchy may require addresses specified as track and sector numbers on the disk, and may transmit data in 4–8 K blocks. Considering that block sizes may range from 1 byte to several KB, while access times may range from a few nanoseconds to a few seconds—a factor of 10^9—issues involved in understanding and managing the trade-offs are of considerable interest.

Since the capacity of each level is likely to be smaller than that of the next level farther out in the hierarchy, instructions and data must be continually passed from level to

Table 7.3 The Memory Hierarchy, Cost, and Performance

Component	CPU	1-3 Cache memories	Main memory	Disk memory	Tape memory
Access type	Random access	Random access	Random access	Direct access	Sequential access
Capacity, bytes	64–1024	8 KB–4 MB	64 MB–2 GB	10–200 GB	1 TB
Latency	.4–10 ns	0.4–20 ns	10–50 ns	10 ms	10 ms–10 s
Block size	1 word	16 words	16 words	4 KB	4 KB
Bandwidth	System clock rate	system clock rate - 80 MB/s	10–4000 MB/s	50 MB/s	1 MB/s
Cost/MB	High	$10	$0.25	$0.002	$0.01

level during the course of processing. This transfer of blocks back and forth in the hierarchy takes place transparently to the user's program. Since access times to cache memory are close to the CPU clock period, the cache control mechanism must be implemented in hardware. In contrast, more leisurely disk access times, usually measured in tens of thousands of clock cycles mean that the control mechanism can be implemented partially in software, by routines within the operating system. We discuss these subjects in more detail after we discuss main memory hardware design.

block transfer in memory hierarchy

7.2 RAM Structure: The Logic Designer's Perspective

This section provides an overview of the structure of RAM cells and cell arrays, or chips. We begin with a somewhat idealized view of an individual RAM cell, using logic gates to show functionality. We then show some of the many ways that the cells can be assembled into arrays as integrated circuits, or chips. We discuss the various ways of implementing the RAM cell array. We then discuss the timing of the read and write operations, and descend to the transistor level to describe the actual physical structure of static and dynamic RAM. *Static RAM,* or *SRAM,* retains values stored in it as long as power is applied to the RAM. *Dynamic RAM,* sometimes referred to as *DRAM,* retains its contents for only a few milliseconds, and thus must be periodically *refreshed,* that is, have its value restored to it. We conclude with a discussion of ROM.

static RAM, SRAM

dynamic RAM, DRAM

refresh

7.2.1 MEMORY CELLS AND CELL ARRAYS

Figure 7.3 shows the functional behavior of a static RAM cell. The cell is shown as a clocked D latch with added controls for selecting, reading, and writing to the cell.

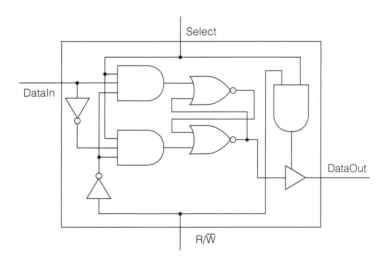

Fig. 7.3 Conceptual Structure of a Memory Cell

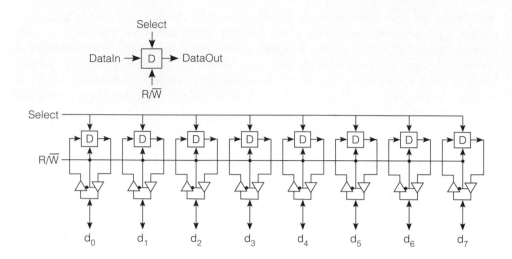

Fig. 7.4 An 8-Bit Register as a 1-D RAM Array

The cell's contents are read by asserting $R/\overline{W}$ and Select, whereupon the value stored in the cell appears at DataOut. In this implementation the output is shown as tri-state. This permits many cells in an array to be connected to a single data-bit line. Data is written to the cell by applying the value to be written to DataIn while asserting W and Select. Notice that in this implementation the actual storage cell requires only two NOR gates, while access control hardware requires five gates—the cost of control exceeds the cost of storage. Sections 7.2.3 and 7.2.5 discuss ways to reduce the cost of the selection hardware and the cost of the individual storage cell.

Figure 7.4 shows an 8-bit register implemented as a one-dimensional array of these cells. The figure shows the data bus being driven by tri-state buffers. Strictly speaking, these buffers would not be required, since the output of each cell is already buffered; they are shown in the figure to indicate buffering of the register from the data bus. This cell structure can be viewed as a one-dimensional, or 1-D, memory, since in terms of cells it has only one dimension, length.

1-D memory

Figure 7.5 shows an implementation of a 2-D array of memory cells. An n-bit to 2^n-bit *address decoder,* a 2–4 decoder in the figure, selects all of the cells in one of the 2^n rows. The $R/\overline{W}$ line selects the given row for reading or writing. The figure also shows the cell array interfaced to a bidirectional data bus, d_0–d_7, through pairs of tri-state buffers that provide access to the data bus for reading or writing as determined by the $R/\overline{W}$ line.

2-D memory
memory address
decoder

Other implementations may use two unidirectional data buses, with a corresponding change to the $R/\overline{W}$ drivers at the bottom of the figure. They may also employ other combinations of control signals. To recapitulate, the row decoder selects one entire row of cells, through the word line. The $R/\overline{W}$ line specifies whether the row will be read or written, and also controls access to the data bus through the buffers at the bottom of the figure. This kind of cell array is referred to as a 2-D array because of the arrangement of cells in rows and columns.

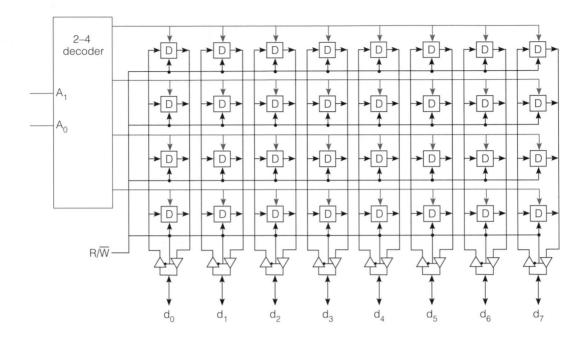

Fig. 7.5 A 4×8 2-D Memory Cell Array

Designs such as those shown in Figure 7.5 are not actually used for RAM chips of any appreciable size, however, because of the impracticability of building large row decoders. For example, a 1 MB $\times$ 8 static RAM employing the design above would require a 20-to-2^{20} line decoder. Such a decoder would require 2^{20} gates, each with a fan-in of 20. Figure 7.6 shows a practical solution to this problem. The figure shows a 64 K $\times$ 1 chip organized as an array of 256×256 1-bit storage cells. RAM chips are most often designed to be only 1 bit wide, because of the savings in pins. A 64 K $\times$ 1 cell array requires 16 address lines, a read/write line, R/$\overline{\text{W}}$, a chip select line, CS, and only a single data line.

Notice how the address lines have been split—the low-order eight address lines select 1 of 256 rows using an 8-to-256 line *row decoder;* thus the selected row contains 256 bits. The high-order eight address lines select one of those 256 bits. The 256 bits in the row selected flow through a 256-to-1 line multiplexer on a read. On a memory write, the incoming bit flows through a 1-to-256 line demultiplexer that selects the correct column of the 256 possible columns. The square 256:256 aspect ratio fits well with IC design and layout, and practical designs do not usually deviate by more than a factor of 2 from this ratio.

The particular row and column configuration shown in Figure 7.6 is only one of many possibilities. For example, the row and column address lines could have been split 9–7 instead of 8–8; the cell array could be composed of 4 64 $\times$ 256 arrays; in the latter case, there would then be four column multiplexers and demultiplexers, each of which would be 1-to-64 line. Figure 7.7 depicts the layout of such a chip. Since there are four independent 2-D arrays in the chip, it is referred to as a $2\frac{1}{2}$-D array.

row decoder

column select

$2\frac{1}{2}$-D memory

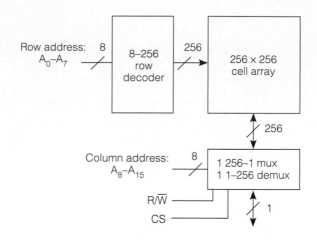

Fig. 7.6 A 64 K × 1 Static RAM Chip

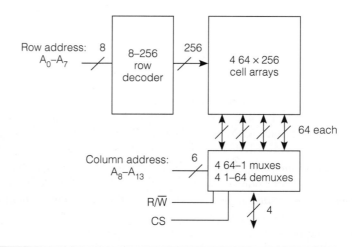

Fig. 7.7 A 16 K × 4 Static RAM Chip

3-D memory

It is also possible to build three-dimensional (3-D) arrays of memory cells. Such an implementation requires an implementation domain that supports an arrangement of memory cells in 3-D space. In the past, small magnetic cores were used as memory elements. These ring-shaped cores naturally supported a 3-D architecture, as select wires could be routed through the cores from all three spatial dimensions. Selection of the third dimension involves splitting the address bits, *m,* into *three* fields, the first selecting the row, the second selecting a column, and the third selecting a particular *plane.* 3-D memory systems may reemerge upon the computing scene. Considerable research effort is being expended on spatially accessed solid state memories implemented in crystals of lithium niobate and other photorefractive materials.

7.2.2   ADVANCED TOPIC: RAM CHIP COSTS AND MATRIX DECODERS

The following sections briefly treat the cost of RAM chips and the design of matrix decoders. They may be omitted without loss of continuity.

Hardware Cost Parameters.   RAM cost has two components: the cost of the memory cells themselves, and the cost of the hardware required to actually select a cell or group of cells within the cell array. In this discussion we express cost in terms of gate count. We begin by calculating the cost of a memory similar to that of Figure 7.5, with an m-bit address and a word size of s bits.

The cost of the memory in Figure 7.5 is composed of the cost of the memory cells themselves plus the cost of the decoders and drivers for columns and rows of the array. We ignore the cost of the word and bit lines inside the cell array itself, as well as costs of pins, package, socket, and bus exterior to the cell array. If these costs are considerable, as they well may be in IC designs, then they can be added in a manner analogous to the terms shown below.

The following equation relates the cost of the memory, C, to the sum of the costs of the cells, plus the cost of the row decoder plus the cost of the column drivers.

$$C = C_{\text{Cells}} + C_{\text{RowDecoder}} + C_{\text{ColDrivers}}$$

$$= C_{\text{C}} \times 2^m \times s + C_{\text{RDG}} \times 2^m + 2 \times s \times C_{\text{CDG}}$$

[Eq. 7.1]

The cost of the cell array, C_{Cells}, is equal to the cost per cell, C_{C}, times the number of cells, $2^m \times s$. The cost of the row decoder is equal to the cost of a row decoder gate, C_{RDG}, times the number of row decoder gates. There will be at least 2^m of these gates, one for each word line. There may be more than that number, because of gate fan-in limitations, as we will see in the following section on tree and matrix decoders. The cost of the column drivers will be equal to the cost of a column driver gate, C_{CDG} times twice the number of bits in an addressable unit, s—twice because two drivers will be required for each bit line, one for read and one for write. This equation is extended to the $2\frac{1}{2}$-D case, shown in Figure 7.7, by observing that there will be s cell arrays, each of size $2^m \times 1$, with decoder and column multiplexer size reduced to $2^{m/2}$. One bit of each addressable unit is then stored in each cell.

Tree and Matrix Decoders.   The address decoders play an important role in memory array design. Recall the previous example, in which a 1 MB memory is implemented as a 2-D array, requiring 2^{20} decoder gates, each with a fan-in of 20. The typical decoder studied in beginning logic circuits classes has m inputs and 2^m AND gates, using one level of gates, each with a fan-in of m. This kind of decoder is called a *one-level* decoder, because there is only one level of gates: Each of the 2^m outputs is computed by an AND gate with m inputs. Gates with fan-ins greater than 8 are generally not available, however, at least in most electronic implementation domains. Most gates are limited to fan-ins of 6 to 8, and thus decoders must often be built using gates that have insufficient fan-in to allow a one-gate-level implementation. In this case, *tree* or *matrix decoders* are used. Figure 7.8a and 7.8b shows tree and matrix decoders implemented

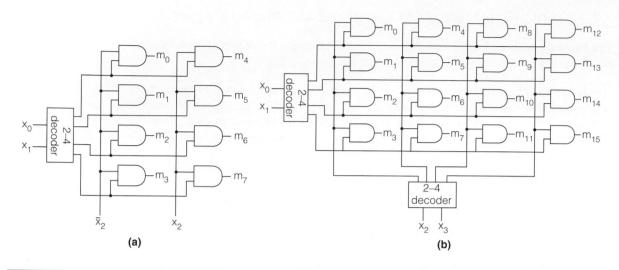

Fig. 7.8 (a) 3-to-8 Line Tree Decoder; (b) 4-to-16 Line Matrix Decoder

tree decoder

from 2-input AND gates, but the concept can be generalized to gates with 3 or more inputs. The 3-to-8 line tree decoder shown in Figure 7.8a shows how a 3-to-8 line decoder that would require three-input AND gates in a one-level implementation can be constructed from 2-input AND gates at a space cost of four additional 2-input AND gates for the 2-to-4 line decoder, and a time cost of one additional gate delay. Notice that the 2-to-4 line decoder produces the four terms $\overline{x}_0\overline{x}_1$, $\overline{x}_0 x_1$, $x_0 \overline{x}_1$, and $x_0 x_1$ at the root of the tree, with x_2 being a "don't care." This first level decoder is sometimes referred to as a "predecoder." At the next level in the tree, each of the four terms is ANDed with x_2 or $\overline{x}_2$, producing the required eight minterms.

matrix decoder

This approach can be extended by ANDing the incomplete minterms with an additional set of incomplete minterms produced by a second 2-to-4 line decoder. Figure 7.8b shows a 4-to-16 line matrix decoder produced from 16 2-input AND gates plus eight additional gates used to form the "incomplete" minterms. Here the space cost is eight additional AND gates, and the time cost is the propagation through the additional layer of AND gates.

7.2.3   STATIC RAM CELL DESIGN

Figure 7.9 shows a practical version of the static RAM cell in Figure 7.3. It uses cross-coupled inverters instead of cross-coupled NOR gates, resulting in considerable savings in chip area. The upper portion of the figure shows one storage cell in a column of storage cells, and the lower portion shows the mechanism for accessing the cell column. This implementation is known as a *six-transistor cell:* one transistor is used to implement each of the two inverters, two transistors are used to control access to the inverters for reading and writing, and two are used as active loads. This is one of the few instances in this text where we must descend below the logic gate level to explain the structure of a circuit.

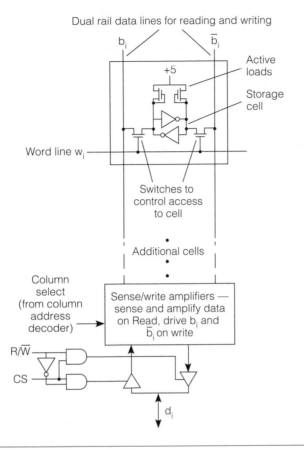

Fig. 7.9 Six-Transistor Static RAM Cell

The following list summarizes the operation of the six-transistor cell:

- The data storage latch is implemented by cross-coupled inverters instead of cross-coupled NOR gates.

- The two access-control transistors enable the cell for both read and write. The cell is selected by the word line as before, but in the six-transistor cell the word line also enables the cell for both reading and writing through the action of the two access-control transistors.

- The DataIn and DataOut lines are replaced by dual rail inputs to the cell. *Dual rail* means that instead of using a single line d to represent a Boolean value, both d and $\overline{d}$ are used. These dual rail inputs, labeled b_i and $\overline{b}_i$ in the figure, are used for both reading and writing values.

  dual rail
  representation

- A value is written into the cell by applying the value to b_i and $\overline{b}_i$ through the sense-write amplifiers while asserting the word line. This causes the new value to be written into the latch.

- A value is read from the cell by *precharging* b_i and $\overline{b}_i$ to a voltage halfway between a 0 and a 1 and then asserting the word line. The value in the latch

  precharge

drives b_i and $\bar{b}_i$ to high and low or low and high. Those values are sensed and amplified by the sense/write amplifier at the base of the column.

■ The control logic at the very bottom of the figure is used to select the column for reading or writing.

7.2.4 STATIC RAM TIMING

We now take up the timing of static RAM operations. Consider the time required to read the contents of a cell in the cell array of Figure 7.6. Assume that the processor issues an address and a Read command simultaneously. The access time for a read will include the time for the address and Read command to propagate through the array to the cell, plus the time for the cell's contents to appear at the internal bus lines, plus the propagation time through the internal bus and through the multiplexer. The read operation timing is summarized in Figure 7.10. The Memory Address, Read, and CS, chip select, signals are presumed to have been applied to the chip simultaneously. The designation t_{AA} stands for the access time from address, the time required for the address and control signals to propagate to the cell and the cell data to propagate to the data line control buffers. After a time period equal to t_{AA}, the data appears at the outputs of the cell, d_0–d_7. The chip retains this data on the data lines until the control signals are deasserted.

Timing for a write operation, shown in Figure 7.11, is similar, except that data to be written to the cell is applied to the data lines simultaneously with the address and control information. The R/$\overline{W}$ line must be held valid for a minimum time interval t_w, the write time, until data, address, and control information have been propagated to the cell and strobed into it. During this period the data lines must be driven with the data to be written.

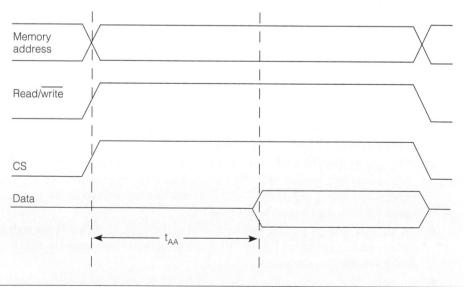

Fig. 7.10 Static RAM Read Operation

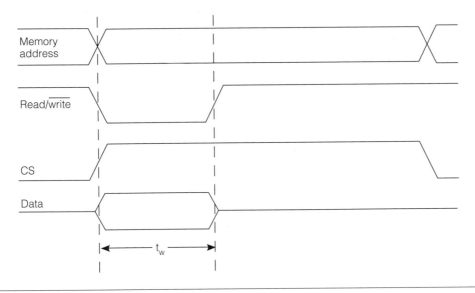

Fig. 7.11 Static RAM Write Operation

There are a number of other practical timing constraints that must be adhered to when implementing a static memory system using RAM chips from a given supplier. The system designer should consult the appropriate data sheets and manuals for details.

7.2.5   DYNAMIC RAM

Information can be stored in a single capacitor instead of a pair of cross-coupled gates, with considerable savings in cell area. Figure 7.12 shows a dynamic RAM cell with its associated control circuitry. Notice that one transistor and a capacitor replace six transistors! Furthermore, there is only one bit line instead of two. The following list summarizes the operation:

- To write a value into the cell, the value, 0 or 1, is placed on the bit line, and the word line asserted. This charges the capacitor if a 1 is being stored, or discharges it if a 0 is being stored.

- To read the value, the bit line is precharged as in the static RAM case and the word line is asserted. The value in the capacitor appears on the bit line, where it is sensed and amplified, discharging the capacitor, and thus destroying its contents. Therefore, the following step occurs.

- The sensed and amplified value is placed back on the bit line as a part of the read process, thus *refreshing* the capacitor.

capacitor refresh

DRAM Refresh Overhead.   If the capacitor is not read, and thus refreshed every 2 to 100 ms or so, its value decays to zero. Therefore it must be refreshed every few ms if it is to retain its value. This requirement that every cell in the chip be refreshed periodically complicates the design of dynamic RAM memories. The square aspect ratio is an aid in this regard, since an entire row can be refreshed at once by doing an internal read operation—that is, reading and refreshing the values of an entire row, without placing the read values

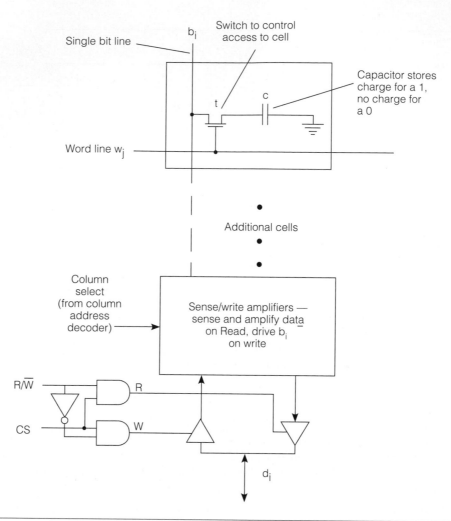

Fig. 7.12 Dynamic RAM Cell Organization

refresh overhead

on the external data bus. This *refresh overhead* is not severe. Consider a 4 MB × 1 DRAM that must be refreshed every 4 ms. If the cells are organized as a 2048 × 2048 array, then there must be 2048 refresh operations every 4 ms. If a refresh takes 80 ns, then the fraction of time devoted to refresh is $2048 \times 80 \times 10^{-9} \times 100 / (4 \times 10^{-3}) \approx 4.1\%$, a not unreasonable overhead in most situations. Furthermore, as we shall discuss in DRAM timing, much or all of this refresh overhead can be hidden in the total cycle time of the memory operation.

Dynamic RAM Chip Organization.   Several factors influence the design of DRAM cell arrays. The most important are the number of I/O pins and the need to refresh the cells. Consider that when an IC has achieved maturity in the marketplace—that is, when its R&D costs have been largely paid off, and when the parts yield is high—that is, few parts have to be discarded because of manufacturing defects, the packaging of the circuit may cost more than the silicon inside. Furthermore, packaging cost is directly related to the number of pins required by the IC, and DRAM parts are among the most cost-competitive of ICs. A 16 MB × 1 DRAM has 24 address pins, 1 or 2 data pins, at least 2 control pins, and 2 pins for power and ground—30 pins in all.

One important scheme for saving pins is to transmit the row address and column address over the same pins, one after the other. This technique, referred to as *time-multiplexing*, cuts the number of pins devoted to the address in half, from 20 to 10 in the case of a 1 M × 1 chip. Two additional control signals must be added, one to inform the chip when the row address is valid on the address lines, and the other to inform the chip when the column address is valid on the address lines. These two are referred to as RAS, row address strobe, and CAS, column address strobe, respectively. An additional pin is saved if the CAS signal also serves as the CS signal, which is usually the case. This is fortuitous, since an entire row can be refreshed by asserting RAS without asserting CAS. These signals are usually active low and appear as $\overline{RAS}$, $\overline{CAS}$, and $\overline{CS}$.

row and column address strobes

Figure 7.13 shows the block diagram of a generic 1 M × 1 dynamic RAM chip. Notice the ten incoming address lines, over which the 20-bit address is time multiplexed, and the

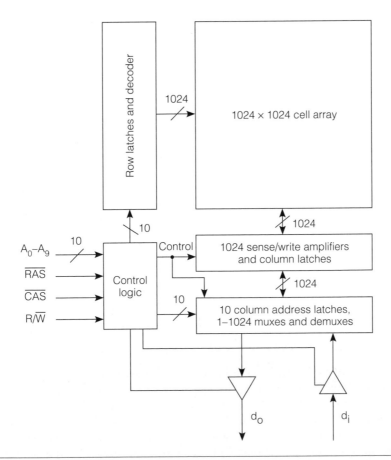

Fig. 7.13 Dynamic RAM Chip Organization

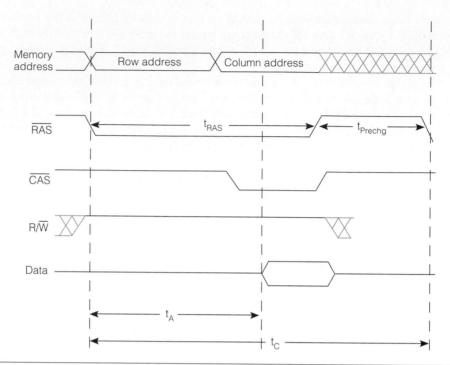

Fig. 7.14 DRAM Read Cycle

control lines, $\overline{\text{RAS}}$ and $\overline{\text{CAS}}$, and R/$\overline{\text{W}}$. The row and column hardware includes address latches for storing the row and column addresses for the duration of a memory cycle and an array of column latches for temporary storage of the column that was read out from the cell array. A memory access consists of a $\overline{\text{RAS}}$ and the row address, RA, followed by a $\overline{\text{CAS}}$ and the column address, CA.

Figure 7.14 shows a typical read cycle for a DRAM chip. The cycle time, t_C, is composed of t_{RAS}, the minimum time RAS must be asserted, and t_{Prechg}, the minimum time RAS must be deasserted to allow the chip to precharge its bit lines. Data are available after the access time, t_A. The assertion of the CAS signal causes the chip to output data, obviating the need for a separate CS signal. The read cycle is terminated when both RAS and CAS are deasserted. Figure 7.15 shows the analogous write cycle for our DRAM. Notice the important timing parameter, t_{DHR}, the time that data must be held after the assertion of RAS initiates a cycle.

Many additional timing constraints must be observed for proper DRAM operation. Consult the original equipment manufacturer's data sheet for timing details.

SDRAM and DDR SDRAM. There is an ever-increasing need for larger amounts of faster RAM to counteract processor memory starvation. This has led to the development of clocked, or synchronous DRAM, SDRAM, and its even faster relative, DDR, or Double Data Rate SDRAM. Unlike proprietary RAM designs, these RAM designs are based on an open JEDEC (Joint Electron Device Engineering Council) standard. The activities of the RAM chip are synchronized with the CPU bus clock, allowing a shorter bus cycle time. SDRAM chips are available in word sizes of 4 to 32 bits per chip.

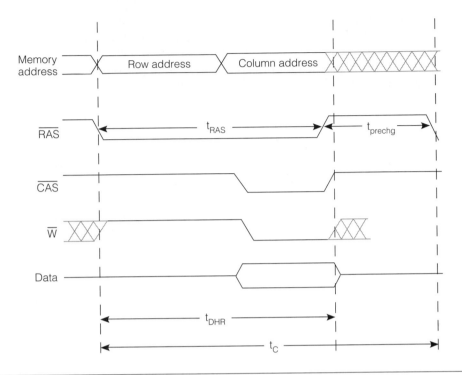

Fig. 7.15 DRAM Write Cycle

They have multiple internal memory "banks," allowing some banks to be read while others are being precharged. They are operated in a programmable "burst" mode. In the burst mode, accesses are started at a given location and continue for a programmable number of locations, typically 2, 4, or 8, in a programmable sequence. SDRAM chips are characterized by their clock speed and initial access latency. Typical clock speeds are in the 100–167 MHz range, with 200 MHz on the horizon. Latency between address and the first data item is 2 or 3 clock periods, and additional words in the burst arrive on succeeding clock pulses. DDR SDRAM doubles the data rate by providing data values at both rising and falling clock edges. Thus 167 MHz DDR SDRAM on a 64-bit bus can provide a burst bandwidth of 167 MHz × 2 × 8 or 2.4 GB/sec.

GETTING SPECIFIC: THE MICRON TECHNOLOGY MT46V32M16TG-xx DDR
SDRAM CHIP   The MT46V32M16TG-xx is a 512 Mb chip organized as 32M × 16 bits. Internally it is organized into 4 banks of $8,192 × 512 × 32$bits. It has a programmable read and write latency of 2 or 2.5 clock cycles, after which it will yield bursts of two 4, 8, or 16 16-bit words per clock cycle. Each of the 4K rows are refreshed once each 64 ms. It also has input mask modes that enable writing of only the low- or high-order byte.   ■

Dynamic RAM Refresh Mechanisms.   The intricacies of DRAM refresh go far beyond what is covered in this section, but the basic approach is to guarantee that every row of the chip gets refreshed according to the manufacturer's specifications. At a minimum,

DRAM chip manufacturers provide the capability to refresh a row by a "RAS-only" refresh cycle. In a RAS-only refresh cycle, the row address is placed on the address lines, and RAS is asserted for a period allowing the row to be read out, refreshed, and written back, without ever asserting CAS. The absence of a CAS phase is a signal to the DRAM chip that a refresh cycle is being requested; consequently, the chip refreshes the specified row without ever placing data on the external data bus.

Many DRAM chips also have a "CAS-before-RAS" cycle. The DRAM chip maintains an r-bit counter, where r is the number of row address bits. Every time the chip encounters a cycle where CAS is asserted before RAS, it initiates a refresh cycle, refreshing the row pointed to by the internal counter, and then increments the counter to point to the next row to be refreshed. It is still the responsibility of an external refresh controller to initiate sufficient refresh cycles to meet refresh time constraints. Most DRAM chip manufacturers also provide DRAM controller ICs that encapsulate the refresh function within the IC. We will revisit the refresh operation during the discussion of memory boards in the next section.

Special Purpose DRAMs.   Several variations on the basic DRAM structure described thus far permit faster than normal access to DRAM contents under certain conditions. The variations all take advantage of the fact that DRAMs read an entire row of data at once, and thus can provide faster access to the data in the row that was read and is present in the column latches.

Page mode DRAMs permit access to the entire row by asserting RAS and the row address, RA, only once, while repeatedly asserting CAS and the appropriate column address, CA. The page mode begins with the usual RAS CAS cycle, but with RAS continually asserted. In subsequent cycles only CAS and the appropriate column address are asserted. (Memory cycles are terminated with semicolons in the following discussion: RAS RA CAS CA_1; CAS CA_2; CAS CA_3; CAS CA_4; and so on.) This results in much faster access time to the values stored in the subsequent columns present in the column latches. Data can be both read and written in page mode.

DRAM fast
access modes

Nibble mode DRAMS provide a variation on page mode access by permitting access to a *nibble*—4 bits—without altering the column address. The signaling convention begins with an ordinary RAS CAS cycle, but with RAS continually asserted, while CAS is asserted three more times: RAS CAS; CAS; CAS; CAS; RAS CAS; CAS; CAS; CAS; and so on. Each additional assertion of CAS causes the next bit in the row to be accessed without incrementing the column address.

Static column mode DRAMs provide yet another variation on the basic approach. The static column mode begins with a normal RAS CAS cycle, after which RAS is continually asserted, with only the column address being changed in each subsequent cycle: RAS CAS CA_1; CA_2; CA_3; CA_4; and so on. Generally, values may only be read using static column mode, unless special write signaling is employed.

video RAM

Video RAM (VRAM) is specifically designed to be used as a video display buffer, where the contents of the VRAM are always read out sequentially to display the contents of a line of video. The VRAM chip clocks the entire row into a shift register for shifting out bit by bit to the display. While this shifting occurs, new values can be stored in the cell array, leading to what is in effect a dual-ported RAM; that is, RAM that can be read from sequentially as it is being updated.

You will have noticed that much of the timing and operation of DRAMs is not obvious from inspection of the timing diagrams. The complexity caused by the need to refresh the chip has forced chip vendors to introduce various special purpose cycles. Rather than add additional pins, special signaling protocols have been introduced that involve the pulsing of the RAS, CAS, and R/$\overline{\text{W}}$ lines. Again, see the vendor's data sheets for details.

7.2.6   READ-ONLY AND READ-MOSTLY MEMORY

There is also a need for memory that has been preprogrammed with information permanently encoded in the chip, read-only memory, abbreviated ROM. ROM is by definition *nonvolatile*. That is, it retains the information in it when power is removed from it. Examples range from low-level operating system routines to the microcode control store discussed earlier, and to video game cartridges. There is also a need for memory in which to store information that is updated infrequently, such as automobile engine control parameters and engine performance history. ROMs are also used to implement combinational logic functions. We briefly discuss the kinds of ROM technologies available and then the various ways in which ROM is used in computer systems.

There is considerable price/performance/capability trade-off possible in read-only memories, depending on user requirements.

Mask-programmed ROMs are the least expensive. The customer specifies the size and encoding pattern of the ROM to the ROM supplier, and receives the programmed ROMs several weeks later, after paying a one-time mask-making charge. The typical ROM structure is similar to 2-D RAM structure, with row decoders and possibly column multiplexers, but without the complications of the write circuitry. Figure 7.16 shows a 4×4 CMOS ROM chip. The chip mask is designed to place transistors at every location where a 1 is to be stored. The word lines are active high, and the bit lines are pulled high by the pull-up resistors located at the top of the figure. Where there is a transistor at the intersection of the bit and word lines, it is turned on by the word line and pulls the line low. This explains the inverters at the outputs.

PROMs, programmable ROMS, have fuses at the intersections of the bit and word lines. By applying the appropriate programming pulses, the fuses can be blown in the desired pattern, resulting in a custom PROM that can be programmed at the user's site. PROMs are usually used for limited-quantity prototyping work.

> types of read-only memory
> PROM

EPROMs, erasable PROMs, can be repeatedly programmed and erased by the user. EPROMs have quartz windows instead of black plastic or ceramic covering their active area. They are programmed by applying special programming pulses, and erased by shining ultraviolet light of the appropriate wavelength and intensity on the window. Erasure time is on the order of 20 minutes when standard EPROM erasers are employed. EPROMs are also generally only used for prototyping or small-quantity, special purpose work, because of their higher relative cost.[1]

> EPROM

Flash EPROMS have recently emerged as contenders for compact, removable, rapid access storage. Flash EPROMS can be erased electrically, although erasure time is on the order of milliseconds to seconds, and information can only be erased by the block.

> Flash EPROM

---

1.   The window should be covered during normal usage, a fact discovered by one of the authors' students, whose proud mother's camera flash, directed at one of the EPROMs in his computer design project, reset the machine. (It rebooted and ran satisfactorily afterward, however.)

EEPROM

EEPROMs, electrically erasable PROMs are at present the costliest alternative, but they allow reading and erasing at the single-byte level.

These properties are summarized in Table 7.4.

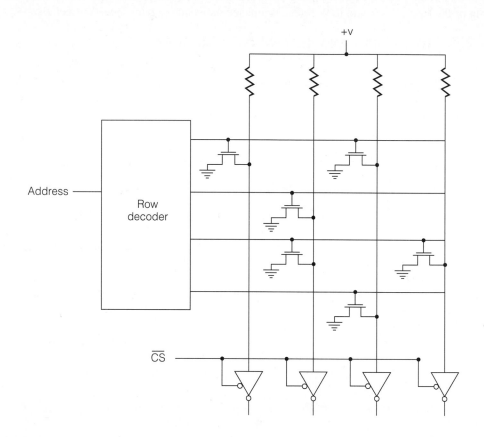

Fig. 7.16 A 2-D CMOS ROM Chip

Table 7.4 ROM Types

ROM Type	Cost	Programmability	Time to Program	Time to Erase
Mask-programmed ROM	Very inexpensive	At factory only	Weeks	N/A
PROM	Inexpensive	Once, by end user	Seconds	N/A
EPROM	Moderate	Many times	Seconds	20 minutes
Flash EPROM	Expensive	Many times	100 µs	1 s, large block
EEPROM	Very expensive	Many times	100 µs	10 ms, byte

Mask-programmed ROMs are used whenever machine code must be available to a processor immediately upon power-up. Applications of ROMs include the "bootstrap loader" inside desktop computers, which contains their startup code, to hand-held calculators and video game cartridges. PROMs and EPROMs are used in prototype development and in applications where product volume does not justify the use of mask-programmed ROMs. Flash EPROMs and EEPROMs are used in applications that require nonvolatility and occasional updating of information. This includes automotive applications, where engine performance data must be collected, and devices such as programmable TV sets and VCRs, which must retain their programming information when they are unplugged or for the duration of power failures.

7.3   Memory Boards and Modules

Large main memories are often more than just memory chip arrays with decoders, multiplexers, and I/O. They can have several levels of structure, and the level described in the previous section may be integrated onto memory chips. Multiple chips may be organized into a memory board providing more bits per word and/or more words than are contained in a single chip. One or more boards can be combined to form a *memory module,* an independent unit satisfying the requirements of the processor interface and often including registers for memory address and data. The complete main memory of a computer may be made up of several memory modules, connected either to expand the memory capacity or to reduce the effective access time by allowing overlapped operation. This section treats the memory structures between the chip and system level.

memory module

7.3.1   Arrays of Memory Chips

We start the discussion of higher-level memory organization by abstracting the structure of an individual memory chip, as shown in Figure 7.17. Data input and output are shown as multiplexed on the same set of pins using tri-state technology, but all the organizations to be described could also be done with separate input and output connections. The figure shows one signal, $R/\overline{W}$, which is high for a read operation and set low for a write. When combined with chip selection, it both enables the tri-state data outputs and generates the strobe for writing data into the selected cell. This technique is commonly applied with the transition of the $R/\overline{W}$ signal timing the strobe. The presence of all select signals and a high $R/\overline{W}$ enables the tri-state data outputs.

Static and Dynamic RAM chips.   Static RAM chips can be assembled into systems without changing the timing characteristics of a memory access by very much. Dynamic RAM chips, however, have enough timing complexity that a memory module built from dynamic RAM chips will have complex control. The causes of timing complexity are the time-multiplexed row and column addresses, and the refresh.

The multiplexed address reduces the number of address pins in the memory chip diagram to $m/2$ and replaces the chip selects by RAS and CAS strobes. It increases access time because two half addresses must be transmitted in sequence. The refresh operation, also discussed in the previous section, requires control circuitry, which could be integrated onto a memory chip. If this is done, the simple chip diagram of Figure 7.17 must have an

DRAM access
time

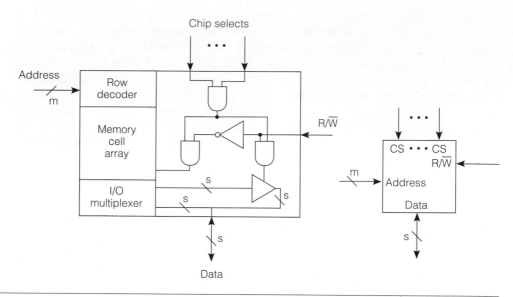

Fig. 7.17 General Structure of a Memory Chip

extra output associated with it to indicate whether the chip has to wait for a refresh cycle before responding or not. This usually takes the form of a Ready signal that can be connected to other chips' ready signals by wired OR, so that the combined signal is low (not ready) if any chip is not ready. Only selected chips will cause Ready to go low, and only when a refresh cycle is in progress.

On-chip refresh control is not common in dynamic RAMs that have only a few bits per chip. If a memory with 32-bit words is made of 32 1-bit dynamic RAM chips, each of which refreshes independently, the probability of finding some chip busy is about 32 times higher than it would be with a single refresh cycle for all bits. The more common approach is to build wide word memories from narrow dynamic RAM chips without internal refresh and to use a separate *memory controller* chip. This chip contains refresh and interface circuitry for all memory chips and refreshes them simultaneously. Therefore, we treat refresh in more detail at the memory module level, where it is usually implemented.

DRAM memory controller

Expanding Memory Word Size. We begin the discussion of multiple-chip memory structures from the point of view of static RAM chips and add comments about things special to dynamic RAM as necessary. Figure 7.18 shows how to combine chips to expand the memory word size while keeping the same number of words. Address, chip selects, and write signals are connected in parallel to all chips. Only the data signals are kept separate, with those from each chip supplying different bits of the wider word. The cost of pins on a chip encourages narrow words for high-capacity memory chips—often only 1 bit. This is because adding a data pin to a chip with 2^m words of s bits increases the number of bits it can store by only a factor of $(s + 1)/s$, while adding an address pin always doubles the capacity. Except for the change from $s = 1$ to $s = 2$, more chip capacity can be accommodated with fewer pins by increasing the address size rather than the word size. Figure 7.18 uses static RAM chips. If dynamic RAM chips are used, the address will be multiplexed on $m/2$ signal lines, and the chip select will be replaced by row address and column address strobes.

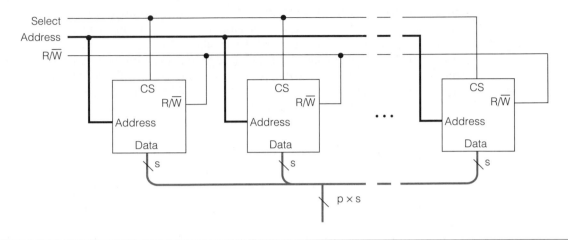

Fig. 7.18 Word Assembly from Narrow Chips

The timing of a multichip memory board is directly related to the timing of the individual chips of which it is made. In the case of static RAM, the only change in timing is that it is necessary to account for the increased fan-out of the signals that drive p chips in parallel. Slightly longer setup times may be required by the p-chip structure because of this fan-out delay. For dynamic RAM chips, RAS, CAS, and R/$\overline{\text{W}}$ may need to be delayed with respect to the multiplexed address signals, but otherwise, the timing is the same. Narrow dynamic RAM chips are even more common than with static RAM, since one extra address pin increases both row and column address sizes by 1 bit and thus can accommodate a fourfold increase in chip capacity. With the parallel connection described, all bits in a word and all words in a row will be refreshed simultaneously.

7.3.2 INCREASING THE NUMBER OF WORDS— ADDRESS SPACE EXPANSION

To increase the number of words in a memory beyond the capacity of a single chip, the chip select lines of several chips are driven by the outputs of a decoder whose inputs are additional address bits. In designing a board, the word capacity is usually increased by a power of 2, so that all outputs of a binary decoder are used, as shown in Figure 7.19. The board may not have all the chips installed with smaller memory configurations. The figure shows 2^k chips of 2^m words per chip being combined to form a 2^{m+k} word memory with the chip size of s bits being the word size of the total system. As in expanding the word size, the R/$\overline{\text{W}}$ and address inputs of all chips are connected in parallel. The m chip address lines are connected to m bits of the $m + k$ bit memory address. The other k bits are inputs to the decoder, which outputs a distinct chip select for each chip. If all decoder outputs go to an installed chip, it really makes no difference which address bits go to the decoder and which to the chips. By convention the high-order address bits select the chip. This becomes necessary to make installed words consecutively numbered when some chips are missing. Each of the s input/output pins on a chip is connected in parallel with the corresponding I/O pin of all other chips, taking advantage of the tri-state nature of the output and the fact that one and only one chip is selected. An enable input to the decoder will provide an enable for the whole memory array.

Both the memory word size and the number of words can be expanded simultaneously. Each chip of Figure 7.19 is replaced by p chips with their address, chip select, and read/write pins all connected in parallel, as in Figure 7.18. Each I/O pin of a chip for a given select signal is wire ORed to an I/O pin of one chip in each group of p chips connected to other select signals. Each of the p sets of 2^k chips corresponding to s wired OR I/O signals supplies s different bits of the $(p \times s)$-bit memory word.

Dynamic RAMs require more connections. The lower m bits of the address are multiplexed onto $m/2$ address lines timed by the RAS and CAS strobes. The RAS pins of all the chips are wired in parallel, but since CAS also acts as a chip select, it must be routed through the k-bit to 2^k decoder driven by the upper k address bits. The decoder enable input then becomes a CAS signal for the whole chip array, and each decoder output is a CAS signal for one chip, or for a set of p chips if words are wider than chips. The timing of the overall CAS signal must match the timing required for the individual chip CAS signals, with allowance made for the propagation time through the decoder. Since column address strobes are often active low, the outputs and enable input of the decoder may need to be inverted. The parallel connection of the RAS pins implies that a refresh cycle, which only requires RAS, will refresh one row of all chips in the array.

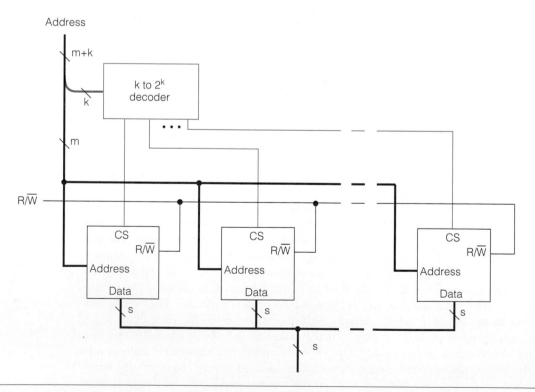

Fig. 7.19 Increasing the Number of Words by a Factor of 2^k

The general diagram of a memory chip in Figure 7.17 shows more than one chip select input per chip. Since all must be true to select the chip, multiple chip selects can simplify the construction of the decoder shown in Figure 7.19 by supplying the last level of AND gates in the decoder. This is particularly useful with the matrix decoder structure shown in Figure 7.20. This structures the memory as a two-dimensional (2-D) array of chips. The q-bit vertical and k-bit horizontal decoders drive two different chip select lines to select one of 2^{k+q} chips. The chip selects are the only connections that are different for each chip. The address, data, and read/write signals are all connected in parallel. An enable input can be added to either the horizontal or vertical decoder if an enable for the whole array is desired. Again, it is simple to expand the word size to $p \times s$ bits by replacing each chip in the array by p chips connected as described with regard to Figure 7.19. Alternatively, one can think of a 2-D matrix of chips for each bit. These matrices are stacked in the third dimension to form a true 3-D memory structure. A physical situation that would correspond directly to a 3-D logical structure would be a daughter board for each 2-D chip array, with daughter boards mounted perpendicularly on a mother board. In current PCs such daughter boards are commonly called *SIMMs,* for single, in-line memory modules.

The combination of chip select with the column address strobe in dynamic RAMs makes it less common for them to have multiple chip selects. A gate external to each chip could combine two or more select lines into a single CAS for the chip. However, the external gates and their packaging and wiring reduce the benefit of the simple horizontal and vertical wiring patterns of the 2-D matrix layout. An alternative is to enable a 2^k-way decoder with the overall CAS signal to produce a CAS for each column. A column CAS signal is then the enable input to a 2^q-way decoder for each column. The column decoders produce individual CAS signals for each chip. A 3-D dynamic RAM array is shown in Figure 7.21.

two-dimensional chip arrays

SIMMs

7.3.3 ADVANCED TOPIC: THE MEMORY MODULE

A memory module presents a specific memory interface to the processor or other unit that references memory. It usually contains buffer registers for the address and data, so that the processor need not hold these values constant for the duration of the memory cycle, or strobe the output data at a precise time in the case of a read. A module operates independently by accepting address, read or write commands, and perhaps data, storing the data on write or returning new data on read. It may be a single array of chips, or it may contain several memory boards. The interface to a memory module is a bus that has signal wires corresponding to

memory bus

- ■ Read and Write—start signals for memory cycles
- ■ Ready—memory is ready for next write or data is available from last read
- ■ Address—must be sent to memory at time of Read or Write signal
- ■ Data—sent with Write or available from memory when Ready becomes true after Read
- ■ Module select—needed when several modules share a bus

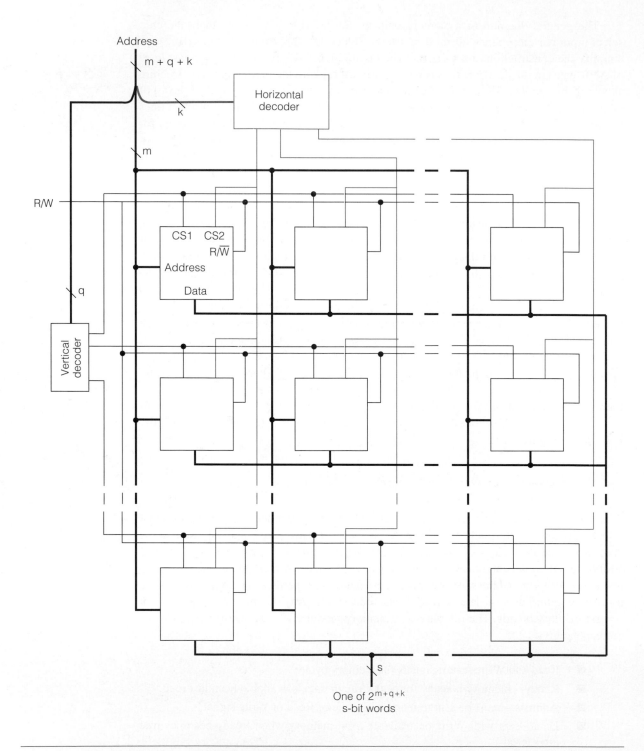

Fig. 7.20 Chip Matrix Using Two Chip Selects

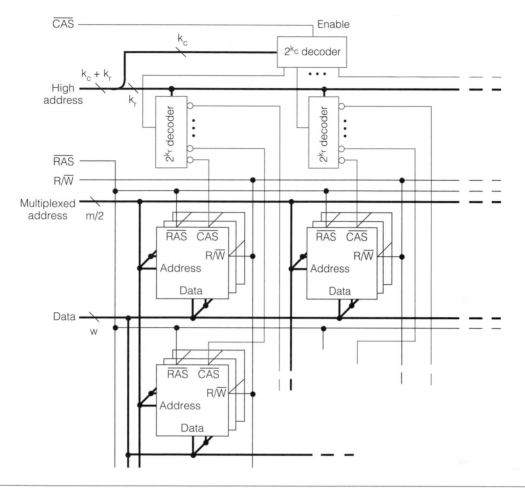

Fig. 7.21 Three-Dimensional Dynamic RAM Array

Figure 7.22 shows a memory module and its bus interface. The bus timing does not have to be bound to the memory access timing. On a read, for example, the memory bus may be used for a short time to send the address and start a read of a slow memory module. That memory module only needs the bus again after the read is complete and the data must be accepted by the processor. The Ready signal tells when this may happen. The control signal generator matches the bus timing to the memory chips, so it depends on the specifics of the processor interface and the memory chips. The general concepts discussed here must be adapted to the details of any real system.

The control signal generator shown in the figure is fairly simple for static RAM. It is limited to strobing the data register after the correct access time delay on a read and generating the Ready signal on completion of a read or write. For dynamic RAM the controller is much more complicated, since it not only generates correctly timed RAS, CAS, and R/$\overline{\text{W}}$ signals and multiplexed address lines, but usually handles refresh for all the chips of the memory too. A dynamic RAM module is shown in Figure 7.23, which also shows the major components of the refresh hardware.

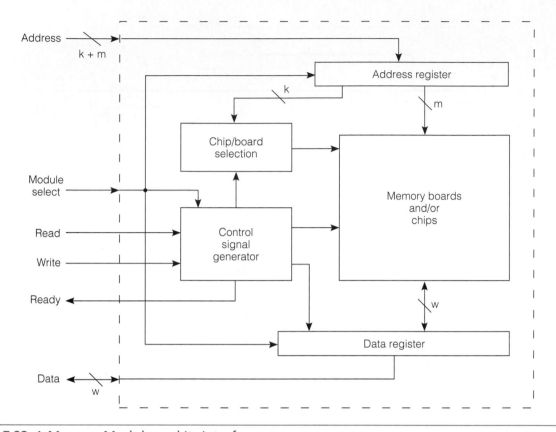

Fig. 7.22 A Memory Module and Its Interface

refresh counter

Refresh is controlled by a clock that generates a refresh request for each row in a chip within the few-millisecond period specified by the manufacturer for refresh. This is independent of the number of chips in the memory, since parallel connection of the address and RAS lines allows a given row of all chips to be refreshed simultaneously. An $m/2$ bit *refresh counter* supplies the row address for refresh. The refresh counter, row address, and column address are inputs to a three-way multiplexer that drives the chip address lines. Row and column addresses are taken from the upper and lower halves of the lower m address register bits, leaving the high-order k bits to select board and chip. The CAS signal and the board and chip selects are independent of refresh, but the RAS signal to the memory array can be generated either by a read or write access or by the refresh control. If a refresh is requested during a read or write, the memory timing generator will not grant the request until the memory access is complete. Similarly, a memory access that arrives during a refresh cycle will not be granted until the refresh cycle is complete. Priority is given to refresh in the case of simultaneous requests. Ready will not be set to true until both the refresh and the access are completed.

Organization of Multiple Memory Modules. There are two ways to organize multiple memory modules in the main memory system that serve two different patterns of

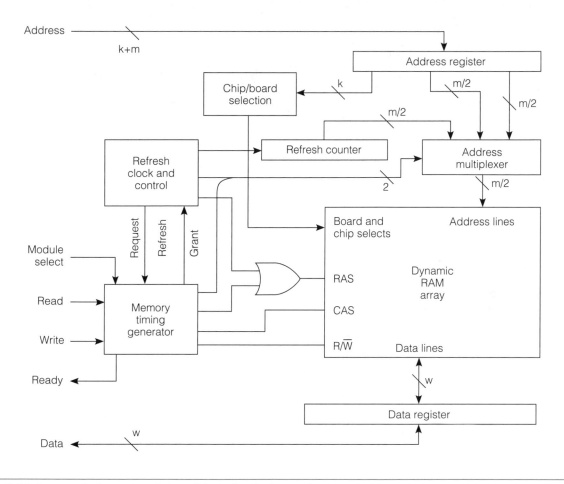

Fig. 7.23 Dynamic RAM Module with Refresh Control

expected memory access. The first pattern occurs when successive memory accesses are to consecutive memory locations, as happens when a block of memory words is to be moved to or from the cache, or when the CPU is accessing consecutive memory locations, as is usually the case when accessing instructions. In this case it would be advantageous to have consecutive memory words in consecutive memory modules, so that memory requests could be pipelined, sending a series of requests in rapid sequence, and receiving the resulting replies in rapid sequence, thus hiding the latency of the memory system. Putting consecutive words in consecutive modules is known as *memory module interleaving*. Since consecutive addresses are in consecutive modules, the module number is selected by the least significant bits of the word, as shown in Figure 7.24a.

memory module interleaving

A second possible memory access pattern occurs when there are multiple entities that can make simultaneous requests for memory access to words in different modules, shown in Figure 7.24b. If the accesses made by the separate entities are to separate memory modules,

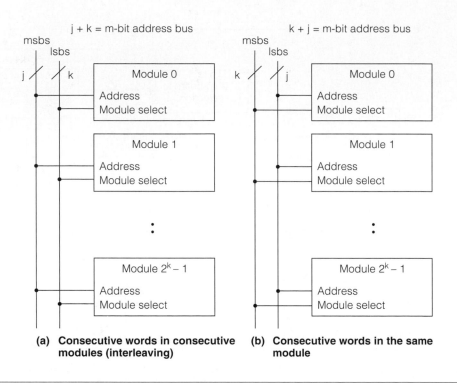

Fig. 7.24 Two Kinds of Memory Module Organization

blocked memory
modules

then several modules can be kept busy simultaneously, even though occupied by large disjoint *blocks* of words. Examples include multiple CPUs sharing a common memory, multiple caches accessing different parts of the memory space, or special purpose controllers that need memory access. Examples of the latter include video display system controllers, discussed in Chapter 9, and DMA, direct memory access controllers. DMA moves blocks of memory into, out of, or within main memory without intervention by the CPU. We shall discuss DMA in detail in Chapter 8.

Multiple Modules and Interleaving. Because the memory module bus interface is separated from the internal workings of the memory system, it may have a separate timing system. Suppose t_b is the time required to transmit information (address, data, or command) over the bus to or from the memory module. Then, if the module cycle time t_c is larger than t_b, it may be useful to attach the bus to several modules and time-multiplex information transmission for all of them. Figure 7.25 shows possible activity timing. There is no benefit to having multiple modules on a bus if successive accesses are to the same module, except for clever tricks like sending the address for the next read while the data from the current one is being returned. The principle of locality says that it is more likely for consecutive addresses to be accessed at nearly the same time than widely separated ones. The probability of accessing different modules successively will thus be higher if successive words are in different modules.

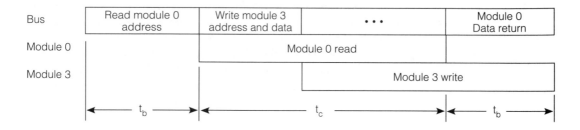

Fig. 7.25 Timing of Multiple Modules on a Bus

Module Interleaving. With module interleaving, the memory address will be of the form:

Word	Module

With 2^k modules and $t_b < t_c/2^k$, it is possible to get up to a 2^k-fold increase in memory bandwidth, provided the device using the memory does not have to wait for completion of one access before starting another. Input/output using DMA usually satisfies this requirement, for example. In practice, if $t_c = q \cdot t_b$, more than q modules are interleaved on a bus. This makes it more likely that successive accesses will be to different modules, even though it does not improve the best-case speed.

Module interleaving is not consistent with the need to furnish machines with different amounts of installed memory. Since the memory module is the largest unit of structure, it is convenient to expand memory by installing more modules. But installing fewer than the maximum number of modules requires that the module be selected by the high-order address bits, so words in installed memory are numbered together. A simple, program-controlled, or even mechanically switched, *address mapping* function can solve this problem. Consider a memory system that can have up to 16 modules, selected by bits m_i, $i = 0, \ldots, 3$. Each module has 2^{28} words, selected by word-address bits w_i, $i = 0, \ldots, 27$. Table 7.5 shows the correspondences to be made between the bits of a 32-bit address presented to the

variable degree of interleaving

Table 7.5 Address Mapping for Multiple Modules

System Address	a_{31}	a_{30}	a_{29}	a_{28}	...	a_3	a_2	a_1	a_0	
1 module installed	m_3	m_2	m_1	m_0	...	w_3	w_2	w_1	w_0	No inter-leave
2 modules installed	m_3	m_2	m_1	w_0	...	w_3	w_2	w_1	m_0	2-way
4 modules installed	m_3	m_2	w_1	w_0	...	w_3	w_2	m_1	m_0	4-way
8 modules installed	m_3	w_2	w_1	w_0	...	w_3	m_2	m_1	m_0	8-way

memory system a_i, the word-address bits in module w_i, and the module selection bits m_i for different amounts of installed memory. The mapping is particularly simple if all of the words of a module are installed, for then the order of the word-address bits does not matter, and only bits at the two ends of the address need to be mapped, as shown in the table. For example, with four modules installed, the low-order 2 bits of the address, a_1 and a_0, are connected to the module address lines, m_1 and m_0; a_3 through a_{29} form the word address in the module, and the upper 2 address bits, which are zero for a four-module system, connect to m_3 and m_2. In the scheme shown, address bits a_4 through a_{27} always connect to w_4 through w_{27} for any configuration. The mapping can be done by a few switches or jumpers on the memory modules. We will see much more elaborate address mapping schemes in connection with the memory hierarchy.

7.3.4   PERFORMANCE TRADE-OFFS IN MEMORY SYSTEM DESIGN

Given the variety of possible implementations, and the several layers of hardware structure that must be analyzed, the design trade-offs in memory system design are considerable. In this section we focus on two design considerations: access-time performance and cost.

Performance and Design: Access Time.   As you can see from the design of memories and modules, several levels of hardware structure must be analyzed to determine system performance. There are also several things taking place during a memory access that must be considered in determining its speed. The number of steps that can be done in parallel also depends on whether the memory is based on static or dynamic RAM. At a high level, the following things happen:

For any access:

- Transmission of address to memory
- Transmission of command (read/write) to memory
- Decoding of address by memory

For read:

- Return of data from memory
- Completion signal

For write:

- Transmission of data to memory
- Storing of data into selected cell
- Completion signal

overlap in memory access

Figure 7.26a and b show how the above operations can fit into the period of the memory cycle, what can overlap, and what must be done in sequence. It includes time for refresh of dynamic RAM and for precharge, which may occur in static RAM also. The worst-case chain of events that must occur in sequence determines access time t_a and cycle time t_c in each case. Two cycle times are possible with dynamic RAM, depending on whether a refresh is pending when the read or write is finished. If the memory module has address and data registers, separate steps to load the registers and read them out will occur at the ends of the access periods.

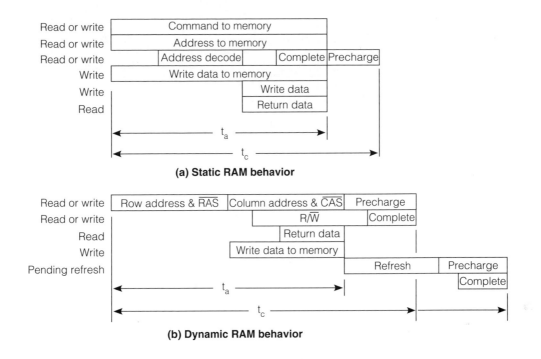

Fig. 7.26 Sequence of Steps in Accessing Memory

To get an accurate idea of the speed of a large memory system, we must look at the steps involved in a memory access in more detail. Each level of organization adds time to the information flow to and from the cells on memory chips. Figure 7.27 shows terms that must be included for a complete access- and cycle-time analysis of a static RAM memory system. It shows which steps can overlap by arranging them in one horizontal row. An optional precharge time is shown after a write. If it is required after a read, it may be overlapped with the return of data.

Illustrative Example: 70 ns SRAMs Do Not Make a 70 ns Memory Module. In this example, we compute the time to perform a read from a hypothetical memory module composed of 70 ns, 4 M static RAM chips. Assume that address bus drivers at the CPU have a 40 ns delay, and assume 10 ns for bus propagation; thus the request arrives at the memory module at 50 ns. With board select decoder chip delay of 20 ns, extra driver time of 30 ns necessary to send the select to another board, and a 20 ns delay of the decoder that selects the memory chip, the request has reached the chip at 120 ns elapsed time.

Let us calculate how the 70 ns chip read access time arises. Assume that our chip is designed as a $2\frac{1}{2}$ D memory with a 6-bit decoder for row selection and a 6-bit multiplexer for bit selection, built with base 4 tree decoders, each with three logic levels. Assuming a 10 ns delay per logic level, the 70 ns access time is composed of 60 ns of gate delays and 10 ns of read time.

All Access	Read	Write
Command and address drivers		Data driver turn-on
Bus propagation time		Data bus delay
Board select decoder		Board data fan-out
Chip select decoder		Chip data fan-out
Cell select decoder		Cell data fan-out
	Chip read delay	Chip write time
	Chip multiplex delay	(Precharge time)
	Board multiplex delay	
	Bus time for data return	

Fig. 7.27 Timing Considerations in a Memory System Timing Analysis

With a 70 ns read access time for the chip, valid data will reach the chip outputs at 190 ns. With a 30 ns chip-to-board-driver delay, data will reach the data bus drivers after an elapsed time of 220 ns. The main memory bus drivers and bus propagation would take the same 50 ns assumed to send the address to memory. Thus the total cycle time for this memory would be 270 ns, considerably greater than the 70 ns RAM chip access time!

Illustrative Example: Improving Memory Bandwidth.   Consider two ways of improving the bandwidth of memories with w-bit words and a cycle time of t_c. One way is to multiplex k modules on a fast bus, and the other is to widen the word to $k \times w$ bits and have the device that is using the memory access a *superword* in time t_c. For the right kind of memory use, say a DMA device doing a block transfer, either technique can increase the bandwidth by a factor of k. The latency is still t_c after a read request before any bits appear.

superword

The performance of the two memory systems will depend on the way they are accessed. For the multiple-module system, the average cycle time $\hat{t}_c$ depends on the probability of an access being a read or a write and on the average wait time $\hat{w}$ for the referenced module to become ready:

$$\hat{t}_c = p(\text{read}) \cdot 2t_b + p(\text{write}) \cdot t_b + \hat{w}$$

The important parameters for the superword memory are the average number of words out of a k-word access that can be used on a read $\hat{k}_r$ or a write $\hat{k}_w$. Using these parameters, the average cycle time is

$$\hat{t}_c = p(\text{read}) \cdot (2t_b + t_c) \cdot \hat{k}_r + p(\text{write}) \cdot (t_b + t_c) \cdot \hat{k}_w$$

If the memory accesses are not as uniform as they are in a block transfer, the multiple-module memory probably has better performance. There is no gain from the superword design unless the next access is to one of three specific words. In the multiple-module approach, a next access to any word of a fraction $(k-1)/k$ of the memory will have a shorter access time.

Let us now estimate the costs of building the two different systems. Of course, an accurate cost calculation requires complete electronic, mechanical, and packaging specifications, identifying suppliers, and so on, but what a designer needs to decide a trade-off is an approximate calculation that treats the two designs consistently. Taking costs as proportional to the number of gates is one way to do this. A VLSI gate is not worth the same amount as a TTL decoder chip gate, so we will estimate separately for each level of structure. Doing levels separately can account for wire cost too. Each gate output is associated with a connection, and within a given level the cost of connection is probably about the same. Treating on-chip connections the same as bus wires would be wrong, but by increasing the cost of a bus driver by its output connections, we can estimate both.

The multiple-module system will have a cost of the form $Cost_1$ in the following equation.

$$\underset{\text{A bus}}{} \quad \underset{\text{A reg.}}{} \quad \underset{\text{Decode}}{} \quad \underset{\text{Cells}}{} \quad \underset{\text{Data I/O}}{} \quad \underset{\text{D bus}}{} \quad \underset{\text{Refresh}}{}$$
$$Cost_1 = C_1 m + kC_2 m + kC_3 2^m + kC_4 w 2^m + kC_5 w + C_6 w + kC_7 m/2$$

The address and data registers, the decoders, the memory cells, and the refresh circuits appear in each module, so their cost is multiplied by k. The address and data buses have m and k bits, respectively. The constants, C_i, are proportional to the costs for the different kinds of hardware required for the different structures. The superword system has only one module, but a wider word, so only the number of cells and the data register and bus costs have a factor of k, as shown in the following equation for $Cost_2$.

$$\underset{\text{A bus}}{} \quad \underset{\text{A reg.}}{} \quad \underset{\text{Decode}}{} \quad \underset{\text{Cells}}{} \quad \underset{\text{Data I/O}}{} \quad \underset{\text{D bus}}{} \quad \underset{\text{Refresh}}{}$$
$$Cost_2 = C_1 m + C_2 m + C_3 2^m + C_4 kw 2^m + C_5 kw + C_6 kw + C_7 m/2$$

Taking the difference between the two cost functions gives the following expression for $Cost_1 - Cost_2$

$$\underset{\text{A reg.}}{} \quad \underset{\text{Decode}}{} \quad \underset{\text{D bus}}{} \quad \underset{\text{Refresh}}{}$$
$$Cost_1 - Cost_2 = (k-1)C_2 m + (k-1)C_3 2^m - (k-1)C_6 w + (k-1)C_7 m/2$$

which will favor the superword memory if it is positive and the multiple-module design if negative.

If constants were all about the same size, the lower decoder cost for the superword memory would dominate, making it the better choice if performance is ignored. But constants are important in practice. Bus wires, connector pins, drivers for long, high-fan-out wires, and bus receivers to reduce errors can make C_6 very large, while VLSI integration can make C_2, C_3, and C_7 very small. Thus the cost of the wider bus alone could make the superword memory more expensive.

We have seen in this section that many layers of structure are possible in assembling RAM chips into the main memory of a computer. The next section shows that the overall memory used by a computer may not be just a complex assembly of many chips of the same type.

7.4 Two-Level Memory Hierarchy

A memory hierarchy combines a fast, small memory matched to the processor speed with one or more slower and larger ones. We will start by discussing the combination of one fast and one slow memory level.

locality

The efficiency of the memory hierarchy depends on moving information into the fast memory infrequently and accessing it many times before replacing it with new information. This is possible as a result of the *principle of locality,* which states that within a given period of time, programs tend to reference a relatively confined area of memory repeatedly. This behavior in programs is not theoretical; it is an observable fact that has been studied by computer scientists and engineers.

spatial locality
temporal locality

working set

The principle of locality has two aspects: spatial locality and temporal locality. *Spatial locality* refers to the fact that when a given address has been referenced, it is likely that addresses near it will be referenced within a short period of time. *Temporal locality* refers to the fact that once a particular memory item has been referenced, it is likely that it will be referenced again within a short period of time. The *working set* is the set of memory locations referenced over a fixed period of time, or window, extending from the current time into the past. In the vast majority of programs, the contents of the working set change slowly with time. That is, many references occur to a fixed working set before the contents of the set change.

Illustrative Example: Temporal and Spatial Locality in a Code Fragment. Both temporal and spatial locality can be found in various combinations in many fragments of code. Consider the following C code that initializes the first n elements of the array A to zero:

```
for (i = 0; i < n; i++)
    A[i] = 0;
```

In this statement, variables i and n exhibit temporal locality, as each one of them is accessed multiple times as the loop is performed. The array A exhibits spatial locality, as each element is accessed in turn. The code body itself exhibits both temporal and spatial locality: it is executed n times (temporal) and the instruction sequence of the code is executed one instruction after the other (spatial). Figure 7.28 shows a memory layout of the loop. Notice how i and n are "hit" n or more (in the case of i) times during execution, while A is scanned once, and the code sequence executed n times. During the execution of the statement the working set is composed of i, n, A, and the code body.

7.4.1 GENERAL PROPERTIES OF A TWO-LEVEL HIERARCHY

primary and
secondary
memory levels

To avoid possible misinterpretation of terms such as *higher* or *lower level,* we will adopt the term *primary level* for the smaller, faster memory and call the larger, slower memory the *secondary level*. These terms were originally applied to a combination of magnetic

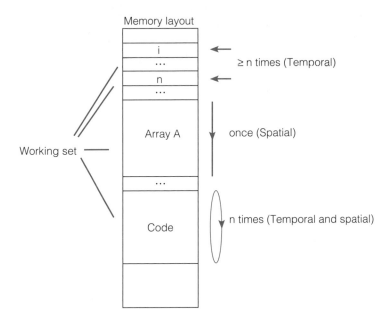

Fig. 7.28 Temporal and Spatial Locality of the **for** Loop

core memory and disk, but we will also allow cache to be a primary level with slower semiconductor memory as the corresponding secondary level. At a different point in the hierarchy, the same semiconductor memory could be the primary level with disk as the secondary level.

To exploit spatial locality, the memory hierarchy is designed so that the primary level contains blocks of consecutive memory words with different starting addresses. These primary-level blocks are a subset of the information in the secondary level. As a program's working set changes, blocks are dynamically moved between levels, bringing new information into the primary level and keeping the secondary-level contents consistent with any changes made to information in the primary level. Requests to the two-level hierarchy start at the primary level and involve the secondary level only when the primary level cannot satisfy a request. Requests can be thought of as being generated by the processor, but they may come from any level in the memory hierarchy.

The speed of a memory level is characterized by its latency, or time to access the first bit of the requested information, and its bandwidth, or bits per second transferred after the access starts. The secondary level usually has a long latency compared to the primary level, but its bandwidth may be fairly high. Disk latency, for example, is very large compared to main memory. This latency makes block transfers the efficient way to move information between levels. The primary-level block size is often determined more by the properties of information transfer than by spatial locality properties. Transferring blocks of a few words to and from disk, for example, is so inefficient that a small block size would not be used with disk. Adjacent levels of the memory hierarchy share a common block size, but blocks at the secondary level may be grouped together for the purpose of communication with a third level.

Primary and Secondary Addresses.   A two-level hierarchy and its addressing are illustrated in Figure 7.29. A *system address* is applied to the memory management unit that handles the mapping function for the particular pair in the hierarchy. If the memory management unit finds the address in the primary level, it provides the *primary address,* which selects the item from the primary memory. This translation must be fast, because every time memory is accessed, the system address must be translated. The translation may fail to produce a primary address because the requested item is not present in the primary level. In this case a *secondary level address* must be formed, so that information can be retrieved from the secondary level and transferred to the primary level. Secondary address translation is allowed to take longer, since it occurs infrequently. A secondary address depends only on the block, but it may be complex. If disk is the secondary level, an address consists of drive number, surface, track, and sector.

The fast primary address translation reflects the blocking of data. A system address is divided into two parts, block and word, as shown in Figure 7.30. The starting address in main memory is obtained by table lookup. In paged systems, high-order bits of the primary memory block starting address are concatenated with the word number from the system address to form the primary address, as shown in Figure 7.30a. Cache memory uses paged addressing. In segmentation, the table lookup gives a base address that is added to the word number to get a primary address, as shown in Figure 7.30b. Segmentation is limited to disk or tape, where blocks can be of variable length and placed anywhere in memory. We discuss segmentation further in Section 7.6.

system address

primary address

secondary address

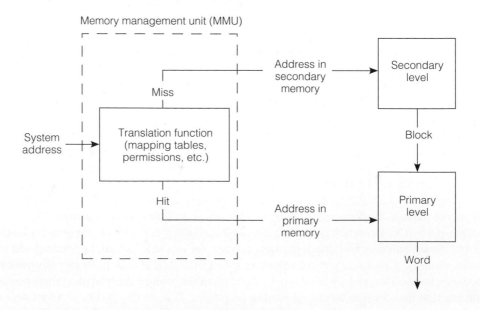

Fig. 7.29 Addressing and Accessing a Two-Level Hierarchy

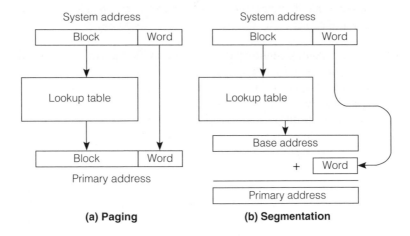

Fig. 7.30 Primary Address Formation

Hits and Misses.   The successful translation of a reference into a primary address is called a *hit,* and failure is a *miss,* or translation fault. The *miss ratio,* sometimes loosely called the *miss rate,* is the number of misses divided by the total number of references in the same program-execution period. Properly, the miss ratio refers to misses per memory reference and the miss rate to misses per unit time. The *hit ratio* is 1 minus the miss ratio. The response to a miss may be slow without reducing the performance very much, provided that the miss ratio is very small. If t_p is the primary memory access time and t_s is the secondary memory access time, the average access time for the two-level hierarchy is

$$t_a = ht_p + (1 - h)t_s \qquad \text{[Eq. 7.2]}$$

The response to a miss involves block transfer between primary and secondary levels and must therefore wait for the long latency of secondary memory. Miss response involves more than just the transfer of information. It must determine where to place the new block in the primary level, and possibly what old information to replace. If the old information has been modified and no longer matches the contents of the corresponding secondary level block, the modified information must be written back to the secondary level before the space in the primary level is used for new information.

Different technologies for secondary-level memory can lead to very different miss response times. Table 7.3 shows how different the sizes and speeds of different levels of the hierarchy may be. Two different regimes, in which miss response time differs by three to four orders of magnitude, lead to very different trade-offs in the determination of things like information placement, replacement, and what to do with the processor during miss response. In the *cache regime,* secondary-level latency is only about 10 times as long as primary-level access time, making it possible for the computer to wait for miss responses if they occur infrequently enough. In the *disk regime,* secondary latency is

miss ratio

hit ratio

cache regime

disk regime

10,000 to 100,000 times as long as primary access, making it essential that the computer system not be kept idle waiting for the miss response.

Disks and Virtual Memory in the Memory Hierarchy.   Historically, the first two-level memory hierarchy was magnetic core memory and magnetic drum, with an access-time difference of about a factor of 10,000. This evolved into today's semiconductor main memory paired with magnetic disk, which has an access-time ratio of about 100,000. A hierarchy consisting of main memory and disk is known as *virtual memory,* which is covered in more detail in Section 7.6.

virtual memory

The most important thing about accessing the disk is that the computer cannot be kept idle for tens of thousands of instruction times waiting for miss response. The processor must be reassigned to programs other than the one causing the miss, if only to run disk driver software. Two types of work are assigned to the processor. The processor assists in miss response, using programs which are guaranteed to be stored at the primary level, and it is used to do *multiprogramming,* which is sharing the processor among several independent programs that simultaneously occupy memory. When a miss occurs for one multiprogrammed job, the processor is given to another one that is ready to run.

multiprogramming

Processor assistance in miss response is not limited to disk I/O. Software can also be used to make placement and replacement decisions and compute disk addresses. As a result, there can be great flexibility in primary memory placement in the disk regime, provided the placement scheme does not interfere with fast translation to a primary address on a hit.

The Cache Regime.   A difference of only about a factor of 10 in access times makes it possible for the computer to wait for the secondary level to respond to a miss, provided the miss ratio is small. A small, fast, semiconductor memory, possibly static RAM, connected to a larger and slower memory of a different semiconductor technology, probably dynamic RAM, fits this regime and is called a *cache.* Cache is usually thought of as the lowest level of the hierarchy, so its access time matches the processor speed. Where there are two cache levels between the processor and main memory, the faster level is called the *primary cache* and the slower level is called the *secondary cache.*

primary cache
secondary cache

Since the processor waits for a cache miss, software cannot be used in miss response, and everything must be done by hardware. This means that placement and replacement decisions and secondary address formation must be kept simple, so that they can be done quickly with limited hardware. For this reason, there is usually less placement flexibility in cache than in the primary level of a virtual memory system. Because cache memory is so fast, it is essential that primary address formation on a hit be extremely fast. Also, because primary- and secondary-level speeds are not very different, it may be feasible for certain types of access to bypass the cache and to go directly between the processor and secondary level.

The Cache Miss versus the Main Memory Miss.   The cache hit time is typically 1–2 clock cycles, and the miss penalty is only a few 10's of clock cycles to bring the desired block into the cache from main memory. A main memory miss penalty typically runs to the hundreds of thousands of clock cycles to bring the block in from disk. As a result, cache miss rates of 1–2% are tolerable, whereas main memory miss rates must be 0.001% or less to avoid serious effects on system performance.

Key Concepts: Design Decisions for a Two-Level Hierarchy

A particular two-level memory hierarchy is characterized by a set of decisions and trade-offs made to maximize performance. These depend both on specific primary and secondary memory technologies and specific patterns of requests to the two-level system. The statistics of memory requests are an important factor in memory hierarchy performance, but a detailed consideration of the influence of program behavior on miss ratio is beyond the scope of this book. The decisions to be made differ strongly between the cache and disk access-time regimes and less strongly for different technologies in a given regime.

The following list summarizes the decisions to be made in designing a two-level memory hierarchy.

- ■ Procedure for translating system address to primary address—This affects both the access time on a hit and the flexibility of information placement in the primary level.

- ■ Block size—Both the efficiency of block transfer and the miss ratio may be influenced by block size.

- ■ Processor dispatch on miss—Does the speed-ratio regime force the processor to wait or be rescheduled?

- ■ Primary-level placement—Placement is *direct* if a given secondary-level block must be placed in one specific spot in the primary level. It is *associative* if a block can be placed anywhere at the primary level with an associative table to keep track of primary and secondary block correspondence. We will discuss direct and associative mapping in more detail in Section 7.5.

- ■ Replacement policy—If there is any flexibility in primary-level placement, a replacement policy determines which current primary-level information to overwrite. It is not needed with direct mapping. Replacement options will also be discussed in more detail in Section 7.5.

- ■ Direct access to secondary level—In the cache regime, it may be possible to move information directly between the processor and secondary level. If so, the following features must be decided upon:

  Write through: A write hit sends information to both primary and secondary levels in parallel. Then write back of replaced blocks becomes unnecessary.

  Read through: A read miss is satisfied directly from the secondary level, and the full block is moved to the primary level in parallel.

  Read or write bypass: Certain infrequent read or write misses access a secondary-level word directly, and no primary memory is allocated for its block.

Summarizing these nine decisions for a particular two-level hierarchy characterizes it very well. The following sections show how these decisions are made for cache and virtual memory.

7.5   The Cache

Cache operations are transparent to the running program. The program issues effective addresses and read or write requests, and these requests are satisfied by memory. Whether it is the cache or main memory that satisfies the request is unknown to the program. Traffic to and from the CPU is in the form of words. Traffic between the cache and main memory is in the form of blocks. These cache blocks are sometimes referred to as *cache lines*.

cache lines

The Mapping Function.   Figure 7.31 shows a schematic view of the cache mapping function. The mapping function is responsible for all cache operations. It is implemented in hardware, because of the required high-speed operation. The mapping function determines the following:

- Placement strategies—where to place an incoming block in the cache.
- Replacement strategies—which block to replace when a cache miss occurs.
- Read and write policies—how to handle reads and writes upon cache hits and misses.

Three different types of mapping functions are in common use: associative, direct-mapped, and block-set-associative. The latter function is actually a combination of the first two, and is sometimes referred to as set-associative. We discuss each mapping method in more detail after first defining memory fields that are used in selecting the cache block and the word within that block.

Memory Fields.   We divide main memory addresses into fields for this discussion. These fields partition the main memory address into blocks and words within the blocks.

Block number	Word within block
26	6

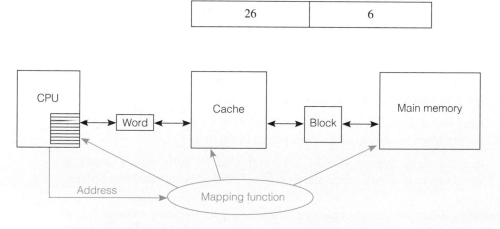

Fig. 7.31 The Cache Mapping Function

In the following example, a 32-bit main memory address is partitioned into two fields, a low-order field specifying the word in a 64-byte block, and a high-order field specifying the block number. Thus there are 2^{26} or 64 M 64-byte blocks in the example. The block number field may be further partitioned for purposes of finding the block in the cache. *In the following discussion of caches, we equate bytes and words, for simplicity's sake.* We also use 16-bit main memory addresses and 8-byte blocks in the following discussions to make the examples easier to comprehend, although such a small main memory address space is unrealistic in practice.

Associative-Mapped Caches. Associative-mapped caches are the simplest to understand, so we discuss them first. In *associative mapping,* any block from main memory can be placed anywhere in the cache. After being placed in the cache, a given block is identified uniquely by its main memory block number, referred to as the *tag,* which is stored inside a separate tag memory in the cache.

associative
mapping

tag

valid bit

Regardless of the kind of cache, a given block in the cache may or may not contain valid information. For example, when the system has just been powered up, and before the cache has had any blocks loaded into it, all the information there is invalid. The cache maintains a *valid bit* for each block, to keep track of whether the information in the corresponding block is valid.

Figure 7.32 shows the various memory structures in an associative cache. There is the cache itself, containing 256 8-byte blocks, or lines, a 256×13-bit tag memory for holding the tags of the blocks currently stored in the cache, and a 256×1-bit memory for storing the valid bits. Main memory contains 8,192 8-byte blocks. The figure indicates that main memory address references are partitioned into two fields, a 3-bit word field describing the location of the desired word in the cache line, and a 13-bit tag field

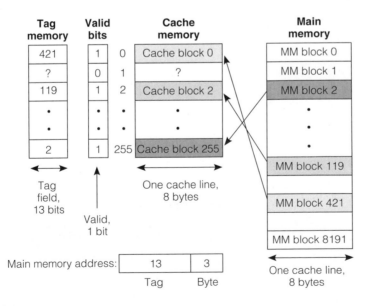

Fig. 7.32 Associative Cache

describing the main memory block number desired. The 3-bit word field becomes essentially a "cache address," specifying where to find the word if indeed it is in the cache. The remaining 13 bits must be compared against every 13-bit tag in the tag memory to see if the desired word is present. In the figure, main memory block 2 has been stored in cache block 255, and so tag entry 255 is 2. Main memory block 119 has been stored in the second cache block, and the corresponding entry in tag memory is 119. Main memory block 421 has been stored in cache block 0, and tag memory location 0 has been set to 421. The three valid bits have also been set, indicating valid information in these locations.

The associative cache makes the most flexible and complete use of its capacity, storing blocks wherever it needs to, but there is a penalty to be paid for this flexibility: The tag memory must be searched in its entirety for each memory reference. Obviously a linear search of the tag memory is impossible, due to time constraints. Instead, tags are stored in an *associative,* or *content-addressable memory.* The entire contents of an associative memory are searched in parallel instead of sequentially.

Figure 7.33 shows the mechanism of operation of the associative cache. The process begins with the main memory address being placed in the argument register of the (associative) tag memory, ①.

If there is a match (hit), ②, *and* if the valid bit for that block is set, ③, then the block is gated out of the cache, ④, and the 3-bit offset field is used to select the byte corresponding to the block offset field of the main memory address, ⑤. That byte is forwarded to the CPU, ⑥.

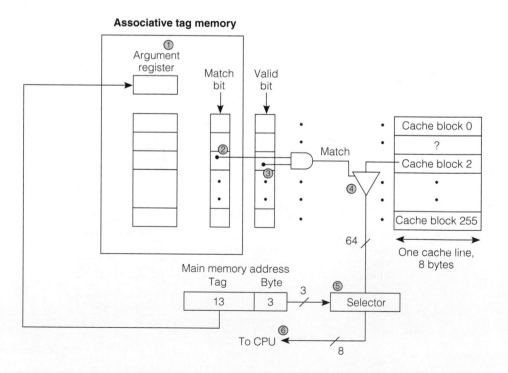

Fig. 7.33 Associative Cache Mechanism

Associative memories are considerably more expensive in terms of gates than ordinary access-by-address memories, because of the need to do simultaneous bit-by-bit comparisons of all bits in the memory. Each bit comparison is made with an XOR gate, whose output will be 0 if there is a match between the two bits. The XORs of all the bits in the word are NORed together, and a 1 output from the NOR gate indicates a word match. This results in a considerable amount of hardware and limits the use of fully associative memories to relatively small systems.

Direct-Mapped Caches. *Direct-mapped* caches form the other extreme, where a given main memory block can be placed in one and only one place in the cache. Figure 7.34 shows an example of a direct-mapped cache. For simplicity, the example again uses a 256 block × 8-byte cache, and a 16-bit main memory address. Main memory has been laid out in a rectangular array in the figure to illustrate block placement in the cache. The main memory in the figure has 256 rows, or groups, by 32 columns, still yielding $256 \times 32 = 8{,}192 = 2^{13}$ total blocks, as before. The cache in the example contains 256 blocks, 1 for each group. The blocks in a given row can be placed *only* in the corresponding (1-block) row of the cache. Notice that the main memory address is partitioned into three fields. The word field still specifies the word in the block. The group field specifies which of the 256 cache locations the block will be in, if it is indeed in the cache. The tag field specifies which of the 32 blocks from main memory is actually present in the cache. Now the cache address is composed of the group field, which specifies the address of the block location in the cache, and the word field, which specifies the address of the word in the block. As before, there is also a valid bit specifying

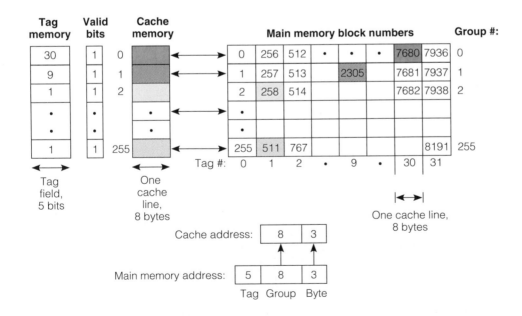

Fig. 7.34 Direct-Mapped Cache

whether the information in the selected block is valid. The figure shows block 7680, from group 0 of main memory placed in block location 0 of the cache (as it must be) and the corresponding tag set to 30. In like manner, main memory block 258 is in main memory group 2, column 1 in main memory, so it is placed in block location 2 of the cache, and the corresponding tag memory entry is 1.

The tasks required of the direct-mapped cache in servicing a memory request are shown in Figure 7.35. The figure shows the group field of the memory address being decoded, ①, and used to select the tag of the one cache block location in which the block must be stored if it is in the cache. If the valid bit for that block location is set, ②, then that tag is gated out, ③, and compared with the tag of the incoming memory address, ④. A cache hit gates the cache block out, ⑤, and the word field selects the specified word from the block, ⑥. Only one tag needs to be compared, resulting in considerably less hardware than in the associative memory case.

The direct-mapped cache imposes a considerable amount of rigidity on the cache organization. It relies on the principle of locality of reference for its success. Examining Figure 7.31, we see that as long as the working set of the executing program consists of not more than 256 contiguous blocks, every reference will be a cache hit. If any program reference strays out of a $256 \times 8 = 2$ K byte cacheful of memory, a cache miss will occur.

The direct-mapped cache has the advantage of simplicity, but the obvious disadvantage that only a single block from a given group can be present in the cache at any given time. If two blocks from the same group are frequently referenced, perhaps by being part

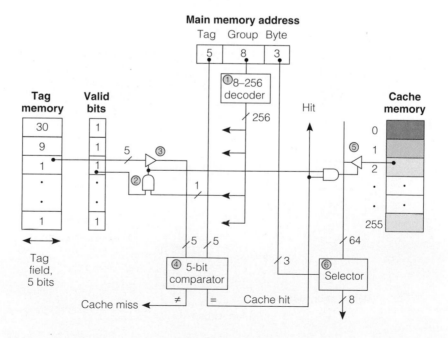

Fig. 7.35 Direct-Mapped Cache Operation

of the same loop, for example, *thrashing*—the repeated moving of the two blocks in and out of the cache—will occur. An obvious improvement in the direct-mapped cache would be to compromise and allow more than one block from a given group to be stored in the cache, in a *block set* of blocks that is associatively searched. This is known as a *block-set-associative cache*.

Block-Set-Associative Caches.   Block-set-associative caches share properties of both of the previous mapping functions. The set-associative cache is similar to the direct-mapped cache, but now more than one block from a given group in main memory can occupy the same group in the cache. Assume the same main memory and block structure as before, but with the cache being twice as large, so that a set of two main memory blocks from the same group can occupy a given cache group.

Figure 7.36 shows a two-way-set-associative cache that is similar to the direct-mapped cache in the previous example, but with twice as many blocks in the cache, arranged so that a set of any two blocks from each main memory group can be stored in the cache. The main memory address is still partitioned into an 8-bit set field and a 5-bit tag field, but now there are two possible places in which a given block can reside, and both must be searched associatively. The cache group address is the same as that of the direct-mapped cache—an 8-bit block location and a 3-bit word address. The figure shows that the cache entries corresponding to the second group contain blocks 513 and 2304, for example. The group field, now called the set field, is again decoded, and directs the search to the correct group, and now only the tags in the selected group must be searched. So instead of 256 compares, the cache only needs to do 2. For simplicity, the valid bits are not shown in the figure, but they must be present, 1 bit for each cache block. The cache hardware would be similar to that shown in Figure 7.34, but there would be two simultaneous comparisons of the two blocks in the set.

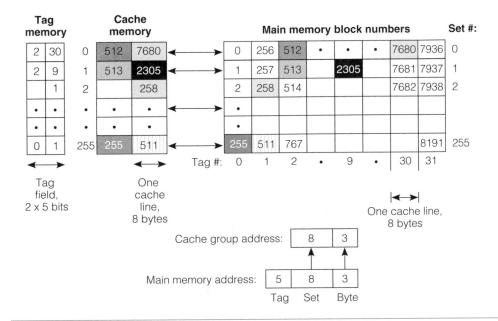

Fig. 7.36 2-Way Set-Associative Cache

GETTING SPECIFIC: THE INTEL PENTIUM CACHE STRUCTURE The Pentium chip has separate instruction and data caches. Each is two-way, block-set-associative, 8 K = 2^{13} bytes in size. Each cache line is 32 bytes, giving a 5-bit byte field. There must be $2^{13}/(2 \times 2^5) = 2^7$ sets, for a 7-bit set field. Addresses are 32 bits. This means the tag field must be $32 - 12$ or 20 bits:

Tag	Set	Byte
20	7	5

∎

Cache Hardware Requirements. The fully associative cache and the direct-mapped cache form the two extremes of a continuum, with the block-set-associative cache being between the two. If there is only a single group, the cache is fully associative. If there is only one block per set, the cache is direct-mapped.

Let us compare the amount of cache hardware required for the three cases. Table 7.6 shows a comparison of tag memory sizes and the amount of comparison hardware, since the remainder of the cache hardware is roughly the same for all three cases. It also shows the Pentium cache and a hypothetical Pentium cache. Define T as the number of bits in a tag, G as the number of bits in the group field, K as the number of lines in a set, B = T + G as the number of bits in the entire block field of a main memory address, and C as the number of lines in the cache.

The Pentium example shows that moving from fully associative to block-set-associative results in a savings of over half in hardware requirements, with the main savings being in the comparison hardware.

Cache Write Policies upon a Cache Hit. There are several policies that the cache designer may employ in handling a write to a block that is present in the cache. The first, termed *write through,* updates both the cache and main memory upon each write. This will be a winning strategy if there are few writes to a given block, but it will be disadvantageous if there are multiple writes, as might be the case in updating a loop counter, for example. The second policy, termed *write back*, writes to the cache only and postpones updating main memory until the block is replaced in the cache. Such a strategy usually employs a *dirty bit* associated with each cache block. The dirty bit is set the first time a value is written to the block. When a block in the cache is to be replaced, its dirty bit is examined, and if it has been set, the block is written back to main memory, otherwise it is simply overwritten.

write through

write back

dirty bit

Table 7.6 Comparison of Cache Structures and Cache Hardware Requirements

Cache Type	No. of Tag Bits	Tag Memory Size, Latches	Compare Hardware, XORs
Associative	$T = B$	$T \times C$	$T \times C$
Direct-mapped	$T = B - G$	$(B - G) \times 2G$	$B - G$
Block-set-associative	$T = B - G$	$(B - G) \times 2G \times K$	$(B - G) \times K$
Intel Pentium—block-set-associative	$20 = 27 - 7$	$20 \times 27 \times 2 = 5120$	$20 \times 2 = 40$
Hypothetical associative Pentium cache	27	$27 \times 256 = 6,912$	$27 \times 256 = 6,912$

Read and Write Miss Policies.   Even if the cache set is not full, there are alternative ways to handle both read and write misses:

- Read miss—In this case the block is brought in from main memory. The desired word may be forwarded immediately, as the block is being updated, or it may be delayed until the entire block has been stored in the cache. The former technique results in faster reads, but introduces additional complexity into the cache hardware.

- Write miss—In this case, the block may be brought into the cache and then updated, termed *write allocate,* or the block may be updated in main memory and not brought into the cache, termed *write-no allocate.* Generally, write through caches use a write-no allocate policy, while write-back caches use a write-allocate policy.

write allocate
write-no allocate

Block Replacement Policy.   So far we have dealt only with block placement policy when the cache is *not* full. We now consider how blocks will be removed and replaced when the cache *is* full. Such a policy must be developed for fully associative and set-associative caches. (The block replacement policy in a direct-mapped cache is trivial: Since there is only one block in each group, it must be replaced.)

Two replacement policies are in common use: *least recently used* (LRU) and random. In the former, block accesses are tracked through the use of counters. The counter associated with a block that is accessed is cleared. The counters that had values less than the value in the counter that was cleared are incremented. The other counters remain unchanged. When a replacement is called for, the block having the highest count is replaced. This requires considerable hardware in a fully associative cache but much less in a set-associative cache. In *random replacement,* a random or pseudorandom technique is used to select a block for replacement. Surprisingly, measurements show that even the random replacement policy is quite effective, given current cache sizes.

least recently used
(LRU)

random
replacement

Performance and Design: Cache.   The direct-mapped and block-set-associative caches may suffer from minor time penalties due to the need to decode the group field. Decoding the group field will result in the same penalties that were discussed in the section on matrix and tree decoders; that is, high fan-in requirements may result in the need to add one or more additional gate layers, with a corresponding increase in delay. This increase will have a direct effect on cycle time. On the other hand, given an equivalent amount of hardware, direct-mapped or set-associative caches will have more capacity because the gates not required for the associative memory can be used to increase the number of cache lines, with a corresponding increase in hit ratio.

A quantitative analysis of cache performance is quite complex and is the subject of ongoing research, but we can get an idea of the factors involved with a simple mathematical analysis. Let h be the hit ratio, the ratio of memory references that hit in the cache to the total number of memory references, and $(1 - h)$ be the corresponding miss ratio. We define T_C as the cache access time upon a cache hit, and T_M as the time to access the value upon a cache miss. Then the average time T_{AV} to access memory during a particular machine execution interval from Equation 7.2 is

$$T_{AV} = h \times T_C + (1 - h) \times T_M$$

[Eq. 7.3]   cache access time

This equation holds for a read-through cache, where the value is forwarded from main memory to the CPU directly as it is received, without waiting for the entire cache line to be loaded before initiating another cache read to forward the value. If this is not the case, T_M is replaced by the cache line fill time. We emphasize that specific values for h will depend not only on the particular cache structure, but also on the access pattern of the particular work load. As an example, let us calculate the *speedup*, S, resulting from changing a direct-mapped cache to a set-associative one:

speedup due to the cache

$$S = \frac{T_{without}}{T_{with}} \qquad \text{[Eq. 7.4]}$$

Example 7.1   Speeding up the Cache
Changing a certain cache from direct mapped to two-way set-associative caused the hit ratio measured for a certain set of benchmarks to improve from 0.91 to 0.96, with $T_C = 20$ ns, and $T_M = 70$ ns. What is the speedup, assuming no change in T_C from the set-associative multiplexer?

Answer: $T_{without} = 0.91 \times 20 + (1 - 0.91) \times 70 = 24.5$ ns;
$T_{with}\quad = 0.96 \times 20 + (1 - 0.96) \times 70 = 22.0$ ns;

so $S = 24.5/22.0 = 1.11$, an 11% improvement in execution time. ∎

GETTING SPECIFIC: THE POWERPC G4 CACHE Figure 7.37 shows the organization of the PowerPC G4 Cache. The on-chip 32 KB cache is 64×8 block-set-associative, with a block size of 16 words of 4 bytes organized as two independent 8-word sectors for convenience in the updating process. A cache block can be updated in two single-cycle operations of 4 words each. Cache requests are buffered so that a cache miss does not block the cache for other uses during the next cycle. Although the cache was designed to adhere

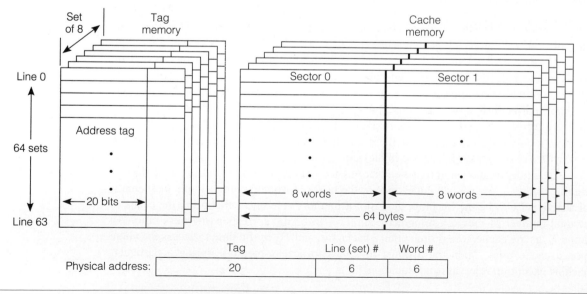

Fig. 7.37 The PowerPC 601 Cache Structure

to a write-back policy, write-through can be implemented on a per-cache-line basis. The cache can also be disabled, thus enforcing a read no-allocate or write no-allocate policy, again on a per-line basis. The cache uses an LRU replacement policy. ■

7.6   Virtual Memory

Virtual memory is the technique of using secondary storage such as disks, to extend the apparent size of physical memory. It permits each process to use the main memory as if it were the only user, and to extend the apparent size of accessible memory beyond its actual physical size. The concept is not new—it was first described by Kilburn et al. in 1962 (see the Bibliography). Virtual memory is implemented by employing a *memory management unit* (MMU) to translate every logical address reference into a physical address reference, as shown in Figure 7.38. The MMU is interposed between the CPU and the physical memory, where it performs these translations under the control of the operating system. Each memory reference issued by the CPU is translated from the logical address space to the physical address space. Mapping tables guide the translation, again under control of the operating system. Since there must be a translation for each memory reference, the translation must be performed by hardware because of the speed required; the operating system is invoked to update the mapping tables.

memory management unit, MMU

Virtual memory usually uses demand paging, which means that a page is moved from disk into main memory only when the processor accesses a word on that page. Virtual memory pages always have a place on the disk once they are created, but are copied to main memory only on a miss, or *page fault,* as a virtual memory miss is most often called.

page fault

Most modern CPUs have a larger logical address space than is populated by physical memory. Using the virtual memory concept, each program may use the entire CPU logical address space as if it were the only user of the machine, at least up to the capacity of the secondary (disk) storage. The operating system assumes the responsibility for dynamically bringing in the portions of the program or data that comprise a reasonable working set without programmer or user intervention. In the past, MMUs tended to be implemented on separate chips or boards, but most of the current generation of processors implement memory management facilities directly on the processor chip.

7.6.1   MEMORY MANAGEMENT AND ADDRESS TRANSLATION

The terms effective address, logical address, virtual address, and physical address are often used without careful definition. An *effective address* refers to an address computed by the processor while executing a program. It is synonymous with the term *logical address,* but the latter term is most often used when referring to addresses as viewed from outside the CPU. The *virtual address* is generated from the logical address by the MMU prior to making a translation. The *physical address* is the address in physical memory. For example, the PowerPC 601 CPU generates 32-bit logical addresses, which the MMU translates to 52-bit virtual addresses before the final translation to physical addresses. Why all this conversion? Because it permits system architects to create processor versions that have varying amounts of logical address space, virtual address space, and physical address space to fit the needs of various members of the processor family. Having said this, we note that often the logical address is equal to the virtual address. Where this is the case, we will use the terms interchangeably.

effective address

logical address

virtual address

physical address

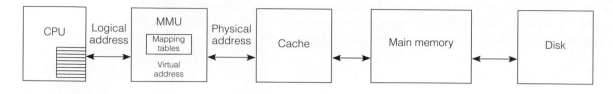

Fig. 7.38 The Memory Management Unit in the Memory Hierarchy

Among the many advantages of using a virtual memory are:

- Simplified addressing—Each program unit can be compiled into its own memory space, beginning at address 0 and extending far beyond the limits of physical memory. Programs and data structures do not require address relocation at load time, nor must they be broken into fragments merely to accommodate memory limitations.

- Cost-effective use of memory—Less expensive disk storage can replace more expensive RAM memory, since the entire program does not need to occupy physical memory at one time.

- Access control—Since each memory reference must be translated, it can be simultaneously checked for read, write, and execute privileges. This allows hardware-level control of access to system resources, and also prevents buggy programs or intruders from causing damage to the resources of other users or the system.

Memory Management by Segmentation. Although less common than paged virtual memory, memory management by segmentation is still used on some machines. Segmentation allows memory to be divided into parcels, or *segments,* of varying sizes depending upon requirements. It provides a good conceptual introduction to the following discussion of paging. Figure 7.39 shows a main memory containing five segments identified by segment numbers. Each segment begins at a virtual address of 0, regardless of where it is located in physical memory.

segments

In pure segmented systems, segments are brought in from secondary memory as needed, and, if they have been modified, stored back to secondary memory when they are no longer needed. This invariably results in gaps between segments, as shown in Figure 7.39. This is referred to as *external fragmentation*. Compaction routines may be run occasionally to recover the blocks of unusable memory.

external
fragmentation

The addressing of segmented memory is shown in Figure 7.40. Each virtual address arriving from the CPU is added to the contents of the segment base register in the MMU to form the physical address. The virtual address may also optionally be compared to a segment limit register to trap references beyond a specified limit. By maintaining a table of segment bases and segment limits, the operating system can switch processes by switching the contents of the base and limit registers.

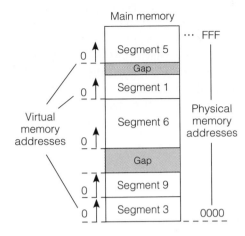

Fig. 7.39 Memory Management by Segmentation

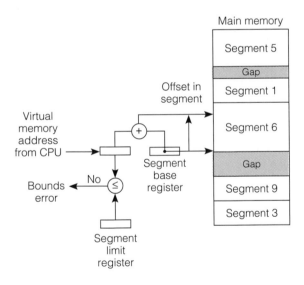

Fig. 7.40 Segmentation Mechanism

GETTING SPECIFIC: INTEL 8086 SEGMENTATION   The 16-bit Intel 8086 employs a form of memory segmentation to increase the amount of memory that can be accessed by the processor as well as to provide separate address spaces for programs and data. In the 8086 scheme, there are four 16-bit segment bases labeled code, data, stack, and extra. The segment bases are initialized by the operating system. During program execution, code references are mapped to the code segment, data references are mapped to the data segment, stack operations are mapped to the stack segment, and a fourth segment, the extra segment, is available for programmer use. The mapping process shifts the segment register left 4 bits before adding the 16-bit logical address, thus forming a 20-bit physical address, as shown in Figure 7.41. Since the segment register has four zeros appended to it in the least significant positions, segments must start on 16-byte boundaries. They are said to have a *granularity* of 16 bytes. Notice that since the logical address is limited to 16 bits, a segment can have an extent of at most 65,536 bytes. The Intel Pentium processor, fifth-generation successor to the original 8086, retains the segmentation mechanism as an option and includes limit and access fields for protection and access control.

Memory Management by Paging.   The paging method of memory management is complementary to segmentation. Instead of employing variable-size segments, the paging technique employs fixed-size pages, usually ranging in size from 512 bytes to 8 K bytes, as the unit of commerce between physical memory and secondary memory. With *demand paging*, pages are brought into physical memory only as they are needed. Most paging schemes employ demand paging.

demand paging

Once again, it is the task of the MMU to translate logical addresses to physical ones, but the mapping is simpler; rather than adding the segment base to the offset in the segment, paged memory management maps virtual pages to physical pages by concatenating the page number with the word field of the memory reference. Figure 7.42 depicts the arrangement of pages in virtual, physical, and secondary memory. Notice that the virtual pages in a program unit are in linear ascending order, as they must be if a virtual address is formed by concatenating page number with word field. The MMU maps these pages to pages in physical memory or, if they are not present in physical memory, to secondary memory. As the figure shows, some pages in virtual memory may not exist in physical memory, but only in secondary memory. This might be because there is no room in physical memory, or because the virtual page has not been accessed by the running program, and so there has been no request to bring the page from secondary memory to physical memory.

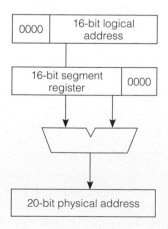

Fig. 7.41 The Intel 8086 Segmentation Scheme

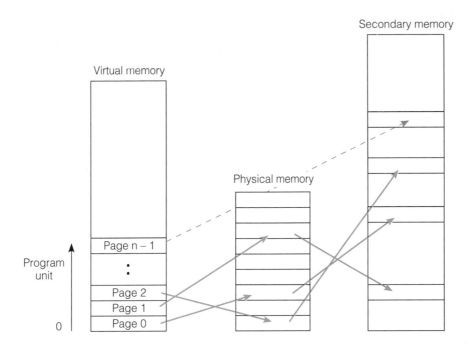

Fig. 7.42 Page References as Seen by the CPU, and as They Actually Exist in Physical Memory and on the Disk

The mapping process is more complex in paging than in segmentation, since there are likely to be a greater number of pages present than there would have been segments because of the smaller average size of the former. There is only one segment for each program unit in segmented memories, but there will be $\lceil$ProgramUnitSize/PageSize$\rceil$ pages in a paged system. The operating system must therefore maintain a *page table* that maps virtual pages to physical pages or else to locations in secondary memory. Typically there will be a separate page table for each program in a multiprogramming system, or for each user in a multiuser system.

page table

Figure 7.43 shows a simplified mechanism for virtual address translation in a paged MMU. The process begins in a manner similar to the segmentation process. The virtual address, composed of a high-order page number and a low-order word number, is applied to the MMU. The virtual page number is limit-checked to be certain that the page is within the page table, and if it is, it is added to the page table base to yield the page table entry. (If the limit check fails, a bounds exception is raised. This is usually the cause of the too-often-seen messages, "Segmentation fault" and "Bus error.") The page table entry contains several control fields in addition to the page field. The control fields may include *access-control bits*, a presence bit, a dirty bit, and one or more use bits. Typically, the access-control field will include bits specifying read, write, and perhaps execute permission. The *presence bit* indicates whether the page is currently in main memory. The *use bit* is set upon a read or write to the specified page, as an indication to the replacement algorithm in case a page must be replaced.

access-control bits

presence bit

use bit

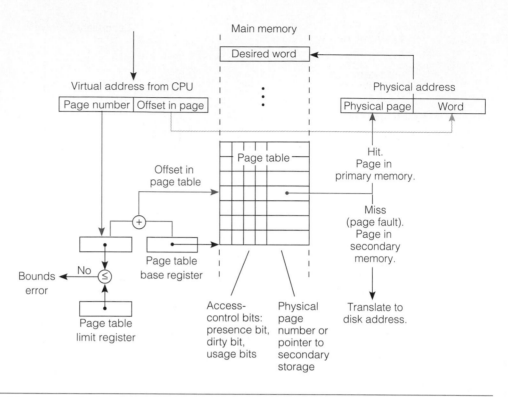

Fig. 7.43 Virtual Address Translation in a Paged MMU

If the presence bit indicates a hit, then the page field of the page table entry will contain the physical page number. That page number is concatenated with the word field of the virtual address to yield the physical address where the desired value will be found. If the presence bit signals a miss, that is, a page fault, then the page field of the page table entry will contain an address in secondary memory where the page is stored. This miss condition also generates an interrupt. The interrupt service routine will initiate the page fetch from secondary memory, and will also suspend the requesting process until the page has been brought into main memory. If the CPU operation is a write hit, then the *dirty bit* is set. If the CPU operation is a write miss, then the MMU will begin a write-allocate process.

dirty bit

There will be unavoidable *internal fragmentation* in paged systems. It is unlikely that the last page of any program unit will be exactly full. In fact, one can surmise that, on average, half of the last page in the program unit will be unused. This can amount to a significant amount of wasted storage in systems that contain many small program units. Such waste is unavoidable, and can be minimized only by the use of smaller page sizes. Generally small pages are not used in system design, however, because they increase traffic between primary and secondary storage, as well as increasing page table size.

internal
fragmentation

In practical systems there may be multiple page tables arranged in a hierarchical fashion. In a *multilevel page table* the entries in the highest-level page table, often referred to as the *root page table*, point not to pages in memory, but to other page tables. Entries in these second-level page tables may point to either pages in memory or to other page tables.

mult-level page
tables

Multilevel page table organization can reduce the total number of page table entries present in memory. Separate page tables can be devoted to each CPU process, or to each user.

Processor Dispatch—Multiprogramming.   We noted on page 344 the extreme penalty incurred upon a page fault—often several hundred thousand clock cycles. If there are other tasks, processes, or programs waiting for their turn at the processor, then rather than wait for the page to be brought in, the CPU is dispatched to other tasks. First, however, the processor's attention is turned to servicing the page fault. The first activity is to save the state of the suspended process. This may not be a simple job, since the processor may have been in the midst of an instruction when the page fault occurred. In machines such as the Intel 80X86 series, the problem can be particularly acute, because a single string-move instruction may touch thousands of words. In any case, provision must be made to save all of the relevant processor state before proceeding with the interrupt service activity. The processor may save sufficient state to resume execution where it halted, or it may undo the side effects caused by the partial instruction execution and then restart the instruction.

After preserving the processor state, the operating system turns to the task of requesting the proper page from secondary storage. It then service any pending requests from other processes, tasks, or programs. When the page has been retrieved by the secondary storage system, another interrupt is generated, signaling the availability of the page. The page is transferred to main memory, either by the operating system or by a DMA transfer, and the page table is updated to indicate the presence and location of the page. The suspended process is then put back into the queue of processes that are ready for execution.

Page Placement and Replacement.   Page tables can be considered to be direct-mapped, since the location of the physical page in the page table is computed directly from the virtual page number. On the other hand, physical pages can be located anywhere in physical memory; they are not restricted to a certain location as direct-mapped caches restrict the placement of cache blocks. Page table structures like those of Figure 7.42 result in large page tables, since there must be a page table entry for every page in the program unit. Often hashed page tables are used instead. In this technique only the pages actually resident in physical memory have page table entries, and the hashing function is used to compute the mapping between virtual page and physical page. The replacement policy generally employs the use bits to guide replacement.

Regaining Lost Ground: Fast Address Translation.   You will notice in Figure 7.43 that two memory references are required to accomplish each actual memory reference: the first to retrieve the page table entry and the second to access the memory location. Multilevel page tables will result in even more memory accesses per actual memory access. Furthermore, since most caches are designed to store physical addresses, the translation from virtual address to physical address must take place before the cache can be accessed. This is an expensive proposition, and many techniques have been employed to speed up the process. The most frequently used is the *translation lookaside buffer* (*TLB*). The TLB is a small cache, normally inside the CPU, that stores the most recent page table entry references that were made in the MMU. It contains not only the mapping from virtual to physical address, but also the valid, dirty, and protection bits, so a TLB hit allows the processor to go directly from the TLB to memory. The TLB is usually implemented as a fully associative cache, because of the greater flexibility in placement that it affords.

translation
lookaside
buffer (TLB)

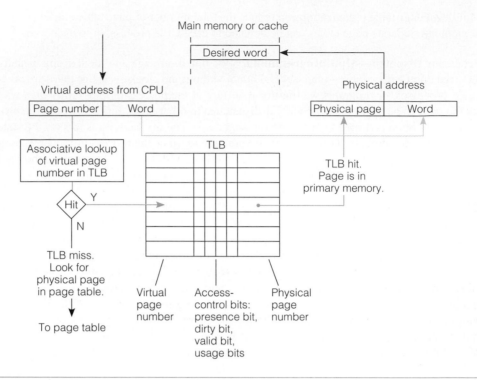

Fig. 7.44 Translation Lookaside Buffer Structure and Operation

Figure 7.44 shows the operation of the TLB. The TLB is searched associatively for a match between the virtual page number of the memory reference and the virtual page numbers in the TLB. If a match is found (TLB hit) and the valid bit is set, then the access-control bits are checked, and if there is no access violation, the physical page that is mapped to the virtual page is concatenated with the word field, and the resulting physical address is used to access memory. If there is a TLB miss, then the page tables are searched for a match. A page table fault indicates that the page is not in physical memory, as before.

7.6.2   PUTTING IT ALL TOGETHER: TLB, CACHE, PRIMARY AND SECONDARY MEMORY

So far we have discussed cache, virtual memory, and the TLB independently. In fact, they interact in an intimate fashion. The interaction may take a number of forms, but they all follow the general scenario shown in Figure 7.45. The figure shows a memory hierarchy with a TLB, page table, cache, main memory, and secondary memory. The CPU issues a virtual address. If there is a TLB hit, then the physical address is applied to the cache. If there is then a cache hit, the cache is accessed. If there is a cache miss at this point, it is handled as described in the section on cache operation. If there is a TLB miss, then the page table is searched. (There is a good chance that the page table, or a portion of the page table, may be present in the cache.) A page table hit results in the generation of a physical address, an update of the TLB, and a cache search. A page table miss results in an access

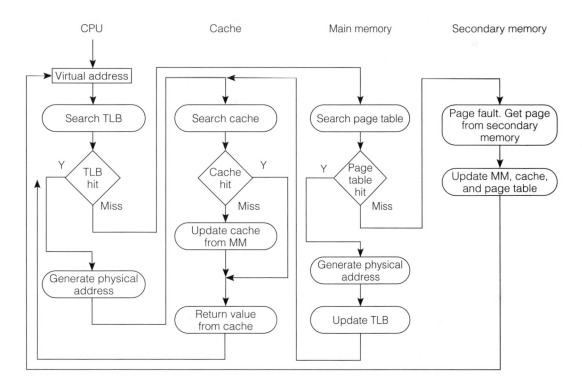

Fig. 7.45 Operation of the Memory Hierarchy

of secondary memory, followed by an update of main memory, the cache, and the page table. The next attempt to access that virtual address will result in an update of the TLB, and a normal (cache) access.

GETTING SPECIFIC: THE POWERPC 601 MEMORY SYSTEM The PowerPC 601's memory management facilities are fairly sophisticated. The memory management and cache hardware are integrated on-chip, rather than in a separate component. The processor supports 32-bit logical and physical addresses, and 52-bit virtual addresses. Logical memory is divided into 16 segments, each 256 MB in size. These segment sizes are fixed, and more similar to what we have referred to as blocks rather than segments. There are three ways to access physical memory, under the control of the operating system:

1. Paged address translation in segments. Addressing is by 4 K pages in one of the 16 256 MB segments. This is the normal addressing mechanism used in the 601, and the one that we will elaborate upon below.

2. Block address translation. This addressing mode is more like the segmentation method discussed. Block sizes can range from 128 KB to 8 MB in powers of 2. This mode is generally used when contiguous logical addresses must map to contiguous physical addresses, as would be the case in video frame buffers or other large I/O buffers, for example. This translation mechanism will not be further discussed here.

3. Direct address translation. Memory management is disabled, and logical addresses map directly to physical addresses. Memory protection mechanisms are disabled. This mode is used to gain direct access to physical addresses without the intervention of the MMU.

There are two TLBs: a 128×2, block-set-associative, unified TLB (UTLB) that contains translations of both instructions and data references, and a fully associative, four-entry instruction TLB (ITLB) that contains the four most recent instruction translations. The ITLB allows more rapid translations of instruction references, since an ITLB hit only requires 1 clock cycle for translation. Instruction accesses that miss in the ITLB and all data accesses are looked up in the UTLB. A hit in either TLB results in a cache search. A miss in both results in a page table search.

Figure 7.46 shows the operation of the UTLB portion of the PowerPC 601 MMU. The 32-bit logical address issued by the CPU is input to the MMU. The most significant 4 bits are used to select one of the 16 24-bit virtual segment identifiers, VSIDs. The 24-bit VSID

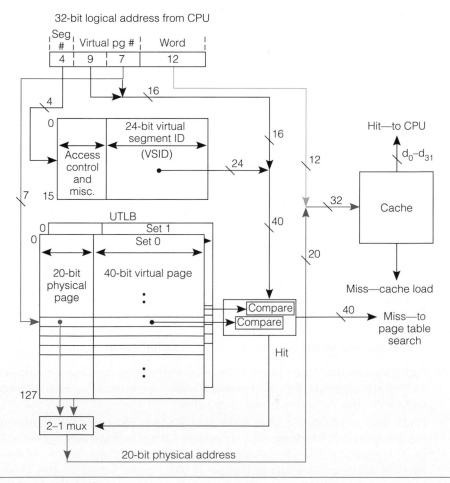

Fig. 7.46 Power PC 601 MMU Operation

is concatenated with the next 16 most significant bits of the logical address to form a 40-bit virtual page number. This 40-bit value, when concatenated with the 12-bit word field, forms the 52-bit virtual address. The 7 least significant bits of the logical page number are used to select one set of 128 sets in the 2×128 block-set-associative UTLB. The two entries in the set are compared in parallel. A hit selects the matching 20-bit physical page number, which, when concatenated with the 12-bit word field, becomes the 32-bit physical address. The page number is looked up in the cache. A UTLB miss results in a page table search. A UTLB hit but cache miss results in a cache line load.

The page table is a variable-size data structure whose size is a power of 2. Page table entries, PTEs, are 8 bytes each, and are grouped into page table entry groups, PTEG, each containing 8 PTEs. Rather than adding a page table base to a virtual page number to get the entry, the 601 uses a hashing technique that computes the PTEG that a PTE must reside in from the virtual address. The computed PTEG is searched linearly for the proper PTE. If the PTE is not found, indicating that the page is not in physical memory, then a data or instruction access exception is raised, indicating that the page is to be retrieved from secondary storage.   ■

7.7   The Memory Subsystem in the Computer

The complete computer memory system can be fairly complex. There may be cache on the processor chip, a secondary SRAM cache, a DRAM main memory, and a disk for virtual memory. These must be designed to work efficiently together and with the rest of the computer system. Many of the components perform cooperatively in a way that depends strongly on the memory access pattern. We have mentioned that programs exhibit locality, that blocks are transferred between cache and main memory, and between main memory and disk, and that I/O does long sequential transfers to and from files. To choose the right components and their parameters, a designer must study the workload that will be handled. The important topic of workload characterization is beyond the scope of this book, but we will mention a few issues related to the overall structure and integration of the memory into the computer.

For one thing, instruction accesses and data accesses have different patterns. Instructions are normally only read, and the kind of locality exhibited by program references can be quite different from that of data. Thus a separate cache for instructions, a special TLB mechanism for instruction fetch, or other hardware to support program reading may be a good idea. The ITLB of the PowerPC 601, described in Section 7.6.2, is one example of a way to enhance instruction fetch performance. The Intel Pentium processor, described in Section 7.5, includes a separate *instruction cache*.

instruction cache

Block size may be determined for a given pair of hierarchy levels from their relative speeds, but a level will typically have different block sizes to communicate with levels nearer to and farther from the processor. To make these block sizes consistent, the larger should be a multiple (usually a power of 2) of the smaller. Blocks throughout the hierarchy will be sub-blocks of disk pages. Since disks are I/O devices, page size is related to disk block size for efficient I/O transfer. A rule of thumb is that the time to locate the data, seek, and rotational delay, should not be too much larger than the time to transfer the block. Disk access times are 10 ms or more, and transfer rates are at least 1 MByte/second, so

8 KByte or more block transfers are indicated for efficiency. This is a large block for most virtual memory and I/O purposes, so efforts are made to reduce the average disk access time to be consistent with a smaller block size.

One way to do this is to apply memory hierarchy concepts to the disk itself by using a disk cache, in the form of a semiconductor memory buffer, for blocks moving to and from the disk. The management algorithm should be adjusted for the different demands on disk, a combination of page requests and file accesses. The disk cache can be optimized for block transfers and need not be very fast to reduce the average access time below tens of milliseconds. Since the objective is to improve disk performance and not to match semiconductor memory speeds, the required miss ratio is also not extremely small. Thus memory system ideas can be used to help I/O.

I/O to cache or main memory

I/O that does not involve virtual memory pages also makes heavy use of the memory. How should I/O interact with the hierarchy between main memory and the processor? Figure 7.47 shows that a DMA device can either issue read and write requests to the cache, as the CPU does, or it can issue them directly to main memory. For the DMA associated with pages, a direct transfer to main memory seems the obvious choice. However, the state of the cache cannot be ignored when a page is replaced. Some line in the page may have been modified and, if this is a write-back cache, may not yet have been written to the main memory's copy of the page. Thus, unless cache is write-through, all lines of a page to be replaced must be purged from the cache.

For I/O not associated with gs, access through the cache gives I/O the same view of memory state that the CPU has, but it has a heavy performance penalty. It competes with the CPU for the address translation mechanism used for every word accessed. Going directly to main memory competes with the CPU only on a cache miss, but now I/O has an inconsistent view of memory. Not only is there the problem mentioned above of outputting old information with a write-back cache, but if an input operation uses main memory which is cached, the cache copy must be invalidated. A possible solution, short of doing I/O through the cache, is for the I/O controller to do its own address translation using a copy of the cache address map, which only needs to be updated on a miss. Another solution is to make areas of main memory noncacheable while they are being used for I/O. For example, the PowerPC 601 allows individual blocks to be marked as "cache inhibited." To prevent memory and I/O inconsistency, the mark can be set for each block of an I/O buffer, the I/O completed, and the marks cleared.

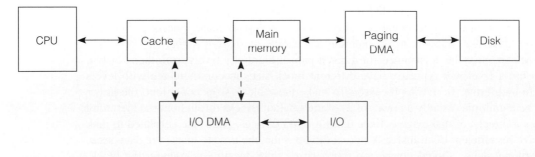

Fig. 7.47 I/O Connection to a Memory with Cache

Both the parameters, such as block sizes and replacement policies, and the components and interconnections used are a sensitive function of technology. At one time, memory systems were optimized around magnetic core memory. Currently, they are optimized around DRAM chips. The ideas described in this chapter are useful with components of the size and speed ranges shown in Table 7.3 to build computers ranging from PCs to supercomputers. Any new technology, and even the normal evolution of old technology, can cause the best choices to change. Some effects are tricky. As main memory sizes grow, larger and more powerful programs are written and come to dominate the workload. The larger programs may have different memory access patterns that change the cache management policy. Students and computer architects cannot be content to learn only what structures are currently used, because they will change. The principles for evaluating the cost and performance of components in systems will endure even though the components themselves change.

Current trends indicate that semiconductor memory densities and speeds will continue to increase. Bits per chip and accesses per second tend to double at constant rates, though it takes more years to halve the access time than to double the density. In recent history, DRAM density has increased by a factor of 4 every three years, while DRAM access time has decreased by a factor of 2 over 10 years. Disk recording densities, and hence the number of bits per second transferred after a block is reached, have also steadily increased. Disk access time, however, has not improved much for many years. Perhaps the most promising niche for a new type of memory is in the huge access-time gap between DRAM and disk. Ways of using lasers to access stored information without mechanical movement to the right position are currently being studied. The elimination of mechanical movement is what is needed to fill the access-time gap, but it must be done with a low enough cost per bit of memory to compete with other system components. Any promising new memory device must be evaluated in light of the entire hierarchy of subsystems making up the computer memory. If it has lower cost per performance, it will eventually replace current devices, even though they are well established.

Summary

- We have discussed all the components of a multilevel storage system in a modern computer: cache, main memory, disk, and tape.

- Semiconductor RAM, both static and dynamic, forms the fastest levels of the memory hierarchy, so its speed has the strongest influence on memory system performance.

- Assembling memory chips into larger structures, such as memory boards and modules, also has performance and cost implications.

- To supply fast access to a large amount of memory, large and slow memories are attached to small fast ones in a hierarchical structure.

- Cache and main memory form the pair of levels closest to the CPU and require address translation, block placement, and replacement to be done by hardware.

- Virtual memory is the main memory and disk pair. Slow disk access requires CPU reallocation on a page fault, and the use of software favors different placement, replacement, and block transfer than used with cache.

- All levels of the memory hierarchy must be engineered to work well together and with the CPU, and with the I/O system, which is discussed in the next chapter.

Bibliography

A similar textbook treatment of computer memory can be found in:

J. B. Peatman, *Digital Hardware Design*, McGraw-Hill, New York, 1980.

Information on memory chip organization is primarily found in the product literature. One source is:

The TTL Data Book, vol. 4, Texas Instruments, Dallas, TX, 1984.

Good textbook treatments of cache memories can be found in:

J. Hennessy, D. Patterson, D. Goldberg, *Computer Architecture: A Quantitative Approach*, 2nd ed. Morgan Kaufmann, San Mateo, CA, 2002.

H. G. Cragon, *The Cache Memory book*, Academic Press, San Diego, CA, 1998.

The following are survey journal articles on cache memories and associative memory systems:

A. J. Smith, "Cache memories," *ACM Computing Surveys*, vol. 14, no. 3 (1982), pp. 473–530.

J. Bell, D. Casasent, and C. G. Bell, "An investigation of alternative cache organizations," *IEEE Transactions on Computers*, vol. C-23 (April 1974), pp. 346–51.

A. G. Hanlon, "Content addressable and associative memory systems: A survey," *IEEE Transactions on Electronic Computers*, vol. EC-15 (Aug. 1966), pp. 509–21.

Virtual memory is described in two classic papers:

T. Kilburn, D. B. G. Edwards, M. J. Lanigan, and F. H. Sumner, "One level storage system," *IRE Transactions on Electronic Computers*, vol. EC-11, no. 2 (April 1962), pp. 223–35.

P. J. Denning, "Virtual memory," *Computing Surveys* (Sept. 1970), pp. 153–87.

Exercises

7.1 What is the maximum number of 64-bit words that can be stored in the physical memories of each of the processors shown in Table 7.1? **(§7.1)**

7.2 a. What is the memory layout of the 16-bit value, 0x7654 in a big-endian 16-bit machine, and a little-endian 16-bit machine?

   b. What would the layouts be in 32-bit machines? **(§7.1)**

7.3 What would the layout of the following data structure be in little-endian and big-endian machines with 32-bit words? **(§7.1)**

```
char    d[7];    /*'7','1','2','6','5','4','8'byte array*/
```

7.4 Compute t_{AA} and t_W, defined in Figure 7.10 and Figure 7.11, respectively, for the RAM cell of Figure 7.3, if the gate propagation time for all gates is 0.5 ns. Assume all external information is applied to the cell simultaneously. **(§7.2)**

7.5 Show a plausible gate-level design for the control box at the bottom of Figure 7.6. You may show the multiplexers and demultiplexers as black boxes. Assume you are driving a tri-state data bus. **(§7.2)**

7.6 Repeat the problem above for the control box at the bottom of Figure 7.7. **(§7.2)**

7.7 a. Design a 5–32 tree decoder from 2–4 decoders and 2-input AND gates. **(§7.2)**

   b. Design a 6-64 matrix decoder from 2-4 decoders and 2-input AND gates. **(§7.2)**

7.8   Derive an expression for the number of 2-input AND gates required to implement an m-to-2^m line tree decoder.   **(§7.2)**

7.9   Derive an expression for the number k-input AND gates required to implement an m-to-2^m line tree decoder.   **(§7.2)**

7.10 A 256 M $\times$ 1 dynamic RAM, organized as a 16,384 $\times$ 16,384 cell array, must be refreshed every 13 ms. If RAS-only refresh is employed, and $t_C = 50$ ns, what is the minimum percentage of time that must be devoted to refreshing the chip?   **(§7.2)**

7.11 A 64 M $\times$ 1 dynamic RAM, organized as a 8,192 $\times$ 8,192 cell array, has a t_A of 50 ns. When used in page mode, the cycle time for subsequent (CAS CA) cycles, referred to as page mode cycle time, t_{PM}, is only 20 ns. How long will it take to read 8,192 values in page mode?   **(§7.2)**

7.12 To expand the address space by connecting dynamic RAMs strobed with a negative-going $\overline{CAS}$ input, an overall $\overline{CAS}$ signal must be passed through a decoder with a complemented enable input and complemented outputs. Show that if we are willing to renumber the outputs, such a decoder is identical to an ordinary decoder, but with ANDs replaced by ORs. What happens if the decoder is built as a tree decoder or a matrix decoder?   **(§7.2)**

7.13 Draw a timing diagram for the memory system using 70 ns static RAMs discussed in the first Illustrative Example on page 337.   **(§7.3)**

7.14 Combine the word size expansion of Figure 7.18 with the expansion in number of words of Figure 7.19. Diagram a 2^{24} word, 16-bits-per-word memory built from static RAM chips that contain 2^{20} words of 4 bits.   **(§7.3)**

7.15 You are designing a memory with static RAM chips having three chip select inputs and a capacity of 2^{20} words of 8 bits. Extend the matrix idea of Figure 7.20 to three dimensions to design a 2^{23} byte memory.   **(§7.3)**

7.16 A static RAM memory module is interleaved on a bus that is 4 times faster. The Control signal generator of Figure 7.22 must generate control signals to the memory chip, a strobe to load the Data register, and a Ready signal. Show a timing diagram with the signals coming in to the module during a length t_b bus cycle starting a read, and the signals coming out of the Control signal generator during the length t_c memory cycle following the read request.   **(§7.3)**

7.17 Using AND, OR, and NOT gates and edge-triggered D flip-flops, design the Refresh clock and control, the Refresh Counter, and the Address multiplexer of Figure 7.23. The DRAMs are 1,024 $\times$ 1,024 arrays requiring a RAS-only refresh cycle of 20 ns for each row every 12 ms. Assume a clock source of a convenient cycle time and any clock rate divider needed.   **(§7.3)**

7.18 In the memory module interleaving scheme of Table 7.5, a specific system is to be delivered with six memory modules of 2^{28} words each. What is the maximum amount of interleaving that can be used in this system?   **(§7.3)**

7.19 A certain two-way set-associative cache has an access time of 4 ns, compared to a miss time of 60 ns. Without the cache, main memory access time was 50 ns. Running a set of benchmarks with and without the cache indicated a speedup of 90%. What is the approximate hit ratio?   **(§7.5)**

7.20 A 128 MB main memory has a 64 KB direct-mapped cache with 16 bytes per line.   **(§7.5)**

   a.   How many lines are there in the cache?

   b.   Show how the main memory address is partitioned.

7.21 A certain memory system has a 128 MB main memory and a 2 MB cache. Blocks are 32 bytes in size. Show the fields in a memory address if the cache is

   a.   associative

   b.   direct-mapped

   c.   8-way set-associative   **(§7.5)**

7.22 Design an associative memory that can search all of the tag fields in Figure 7.33 and indicate a match. Hint: Use XOR gates for the bit comparisons. Assume all gates have sufficient fan-in and fan-out. **(§7.5)**

7.23 Design the 5-bit comparator and the selector of Figure 7.35. **(§7.5)**

7.24 List the specific design decisions from the list for a two-level hierarchy on page 345 that apply to the PowerPC G4 cache example on page 354. **(§7.5)**

7.25 A disk has an average seek time of 7 ms and an average rotational latency of 8.3 ms. Its transfer rate is 54 MB/s. What size block is necessary so that delay in locating the data is only 50% of the total time to read or write a block? Discuss whether all of a virtual memory page of this size would be likely to be accessed in main memory before it is replaced. See the discussion of disk organization on page 411 for a description of disk properties. **(§7.6)**

7.26 List the specific design decisions from the list for a two-level hierarchy on page 345 that apply to the PowerPC 601 virtual memory described on page 363. **(§7.6)**

Input and Output

Chapter Outline

We briefly covered several aspects of computer input and output in previous chapters. In Chapter 3 we touched on programmed I/O and interrupts in connection with the MC68000, and in Chapter 4 we discussed the details of the interrupt process at the abstract RTN level. In this chapter we both extend our focus outward to encompass the I/O subsystem as a component of the computer, and then cover some of the detailed aspects of the I/O hardware and software. We begin by defining the role and purpose of the I/O subsystem, and then cover the hardware and software design aspects of both programmed and interrupt-driven I/O. In these sections we concentrate on the hardware/software interface as the focal point of I/O performance. As part of that coverage we discuss the software drivers, that is, the software routines that control the I/O process. Following that, we discuss DMA, direct memory access. DMA provides the highest I/O rates by allowing external devices to read and write data directly into main memory without passing it through the CPU. We conclude with an examination of the data stream itself. The data stream may require changes in data format, and error detection and correction. We discuss both of these topics in detail.

This chapter forms an important link between processor and memory design, as discussed in Chapters 4–7, and peripheral devices, communications, and networking, which are covered in Chapters 9 and 10. Both of these chapters treat the details of the devices and systems external to the computer. This chapter provides an understanding of the interface between the computer and the outside world.

8.1   The I/O Subsystem

What constitutes input/output in a computer system? It is clear that a keyboard is an input device and a printer is an output device, but what about an internal disk drive? The answer is that a disk is an I/O device, not because information comes from or goes to the world outside the computer, but because it moves through an I/O subsystem that connects the processor and memory to devices having very different physical characteristics, especially when it comes to speed and timing. The *I/O subsystem* provides the mechanism for communications between the CPU and the outside world. It must manage communications that are not only asynchronous with respect to the CPU, but also have widely ranging data rates, from a few bits to dozens of megabytes per second. Processor and memory live in an artificial world regulated entirely by a master clock. Even things like waits for dynamic RAM refresh are limited to a few whole clock cycles. On the other hand, print timing may be governed by the mechanical movement of print hammers; keyboard input depends on human muscles and thought, and internal disk timing is bound to the real world through both read/write head movement and rotational delay. Data arriving from a network connection will likewise arrive unexpectedly. Furthermore, in this latter case, the data must be captured by the computer as it arrives. This chapter deals with the I/O interfaces that support the general data transmission requirements of the range of I/O or peripheral devices that are discussed in the next chapters.

Three factors must be considered in designing an I/O subsystem:

1. Data location: device selection, address of data within device
2. Data transfer: amount, rate, to or from device
3. Synchronization: output only when device ready; input only when data available

All of these items differ in fundamental ways from the corresponding features of processor-memory data transmission. A location in memory is always identified by a single unsigned integer address, whereas data location in the I/O world first specifies a device and then, depending on the type of device, a location that may be as complex as the triple (platter, track, sector) for a disk. The amount of data transmitted may range from 1 bit for a mouse pushbutton to 4,096 bytes for a large disk block—many more possibilities than a memory that can transfer bytes, half words, words, and double words. It is in synchronization, or mutual timing, that I/O is really different from processor-memory data transmission. For example, as sketched in Figure 8.1, a disk request might delay 20 milliseconds, about a million processor cycles, before returning 4,096 bytes at a rate of a byte every few cycles. Both the delay, or *latency,* and the data rate, or *bandwidth,* are completely independent of the processor clock, being determined by the motion of mechanical parts. The bandwidth is usually specified as *peak,* or *burst, bandwidth,* the number of bytes per second transferred after transmission starts. The average bandwidth, which includes the latency time, is much lower.

I/O latency
I/O bandwidth

peak, or burst, bandwidth

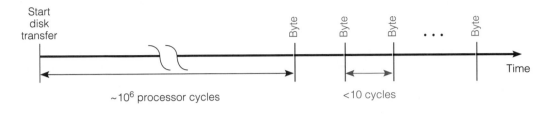

Fig. 8.1 Disk Data Transfer Timing

Standardizing I/O Interfaces. All of the three things needed to carry out an I/O data transfer are dependent on the type of I/O device involved, and it is important to move toward some standardization—a *contract* between CPU and I/O device defining the data structure(s) at the device interface. An easy step is for the device interface to handle the (messy) details such as assembling bits into words, doing low-level error detection and correction, and accepting or providing words in word-sized registers located at defined addresses within the I/O space. This places the responsibility for low-level data formatting on the I/O device, thus presenting a uniform interface to the CPU. Thus to the CPU and the I/O device, the device interface consists of a set of data and control registers within the I/O address space. The contract between CPU and I/O device is specific to the device, and is generally spelled out in a written document. In a given I/O device specification, some registers, such as those holding data provided by the device, will be read-only. Others, such as those that are designed to receive data from the CPU, will be write-only. Some, such as device status registers, will be read/write.

I/O interface as contract

Even synchronization can sometimes be cast in the form of data transmitted and received. A bit in an output register may tell a device to start a specific operation, and a bit in an input register may signal the completion of the operation to the processor. This synchronization method is known as *programmed I/O*. If the speed of an I/O device is in the right range, neither too fast for the processor to read and write the signaling bits nor too slow for the processor to wait for its activity, this form of signaling may be sufficient. Different forms of synchronization are appropriate for different device speed ranges. Long and variable latencies, or response times, bring a need for *I/O interrupts* to support synchronization, and high-bandwidth bursts of data transmission are synchronized using *direct memory access,* or DMA. We will treat these forms of synchronization in Sections 8.2 through 8.4.

programmed I/O

interrupt-driven I/O

DMA

I/O Bus Structures. Reducing all three requirements of location, data transfer, and synchronization to moving control or data information to and from I/O registers puts the focus on the data transmission path, or bus, between processor and I/O device registers. Only two I/O operations are needed, input from and output to a specified I/O register. One parameter of these operations is an I/O register address, and a second might identify a processor register as source or destination for the information. Input looks very much like a load instruction and output like a store. An I/O bus thus behaves much like a memory bus. It could differ in timing and synchronization, or it could leave those differences to the individual I/O device interfaces making up the I/O subsystem. Different computer systems use different degrees of separation between I/O data transmission and memory data

isolated I/O

shared I/O

memory-
mapped I/O

transmission, as shown in Figure 8.2. The system of Figure 8.2a, sometimes referred to as *isolated I/O*, has one set of address, data, and control wires for an I/O bus and another set for a memory bus. The system of Figure 8.2b shares address and data wires between I/O and memory buses but has different control signals for read, write, input, and output. This is sometimes called *shared I/O*. Since there are usually many fewer device I/O registers in a system than memory addresses, not all address signals may be used in connection with input and output operations.

Finally, in *memory-mapped I/O,* shown in Figure 8.2c, a single bus is used for both I/O and memory. The diagram is obtained by simply combining I/O and memory control connections. A range of memory addresses is reserved for I/O registers, and these registers are read and written using standard load and store instructions. Memory-mapped I/O is common in modern processors. It has two primary motivations: Data transfer to and from the processor is standardized, and the number of connections to the processor chip or board is reduced.

The early minicomputers and microcomputers, with their 16- and 24- bit address spaces, generally used isolated or shared I/O to increase the total address space, so that I/O did not encroach upon the limited memory address space. Nearly all of today's machines, with their 32-bit and larger memory address spaces, have sufficient extra room to apportion some of the memory space to I/O and still have plenty of space for system memory. Therefore we take memory-mapped I/O as the norm in this chapter.

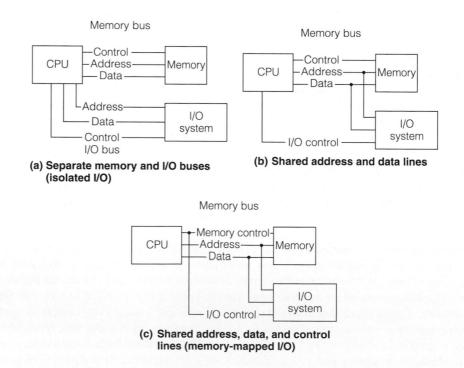

Fig. 8.2 Independent and Shared Memory and I/O Buses

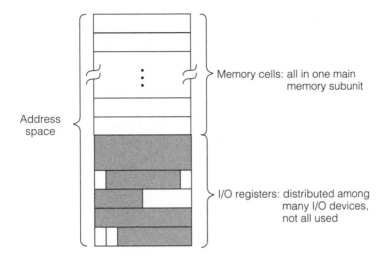

Fig. 8.3 Address Space of a Computer Using Memory-Mapped I/O

The total address space of a computer system with memory-mapped I/O is shown in Figure 8.3. While main memory cells are contained in one or a few memory modules, I/O registers are physically distributed among different I/O device interfaces. Only a fraction of the possible I/O register addresses will be used in a given system. In addition, it may be that not all bits of a memory word are used in a particular device register. In memory-mapped I/O, unused bits are ignored on a write and return unspecified values on a read.

8.2   Programmed I/O

Programmed I/O is used with devices that perform operations that take many instruction execution times and do not deliver or demand quantities of data larger than 1 word in a high-speed burst. Printers would fall into this category, for example. Under these conditions, the processor has time to execute instructions that read and test control bits from the device, write control bits to the device, and read or write data. In this chapter we are not concerned with the structure of specific peripheral devices; we confine our attention to the *I/O interface*. The primary function of an I/O device interface is to match the speed and protocol of the processor bus to what is required by the device. The left side of Figure 8.4 shows the relationship between the CPU, the device interfaces, and the devices. The right side of the figure shows the details of a general I/O interface for a programmed I/O device. Control bits going from processor to device are grouped into one or more *command registers,* and control signals from the device to the processor are recorded in one or more *status registers*. Data from and to the device passes through the in and out registers, respectively. The interface also decodes addresses for just the registers of this device.

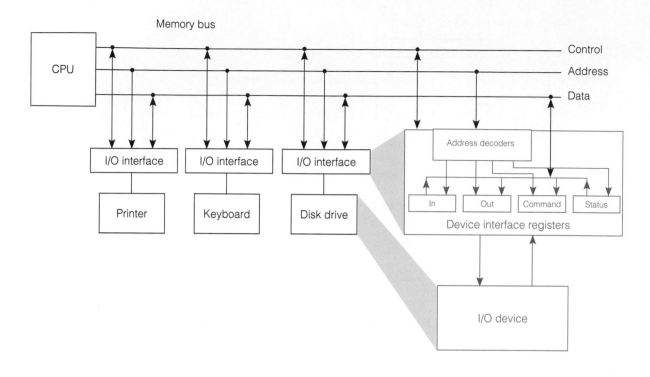

Fig. 8.4 Programmed I/O Device Interface Structure

8.2.1   PROGRAMMED I/O HARDWARE

As an example of I/O addressing, consider the 32-bit address space of the SRC computer. Reserving addresses above 0xFFFFF000 for I/O registers would allow for up to 1,024 full 32-bit word registers. This set of addresses also falls within the range 0xFFFF0000 to 0xFFFFFFFF of negative address displacement values, so an I/O address could be specified directly by a 17-bit displacement in a load or store instruction. It is important that the address decode and registers be independent of other interfaces, so that a self-contained interface can be packaged with each I/O device. This becomes more challenging in connection with interfaces having interrupt and DMA capability. Switches or jumpers are often used for the variable part of an address, as the example decoder of Figure 8.5 shows, so that an interface can be adapted to different devices or different systems. The leftmost AND gate selects all addresses in the top 2^{12} bytes (2^{10} words) of memory—the I/O space. The middle AND gate has 9 inputs, which are jumper-selectable between 0 and 1. This allows selection of a specific device in the I/O space. The rightmost AND gates select either the status word or the data word.

Table of SRC I/O Addresses.   Table 8.1 lists the I/O addresses used in the SRC examples of this chapter. These are arbitrarily chosen within the I/O space, but they do correspond to those I/O addresses used in the SRC Simulator.

Table 8.1 SRC I/O Ports

Port Name	Decimal address for assembly language equates	Hex address	Name
CICTL	equ -3328	0xFFFFF300	Keyboard Control Port
CIN	equ -3324	0xFFFFF304	Keyboard Data Port
COSTAT	equ -3824	0xFFFFF110	Printer Status Port
COUT	equ -3820	0xFFFFF114	Printer Data Port
LSTAT	equ -3792	0xFFFFF130	Line Printer Status
LOUT	equ -3788	0xFFFFF134	Line Printer Data Port
LCMD	equ -3784	0xFFFFF138	Line Printer Command Port

Hardware for Character Output. As a concrete example of an I/O interface with a minimum of complexity, consider a character output device such as a printer or CRT terminal attached to the SRC example computer. Figure 8.6 shows a complete logic design for this simple interface, using the address decoder of Figure 8.5. The character output operation is initiated by writing a character to the data register, Char. Performing this write strobes the character into Char, ①, clears the 1-bit Ready register, ②, and sends a Start signal to the printer, ③. The 8-bit Char register must not be changed until the device returns a Done signal. Arrival of the Done signal from the printer, ④, sets the Ready register. The device is then ready for a new character and start signal. The CPU can test the

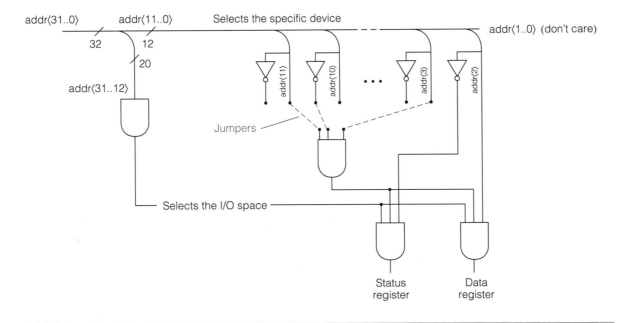

Fig. 8.5 SRC I/O Register Address Decoder

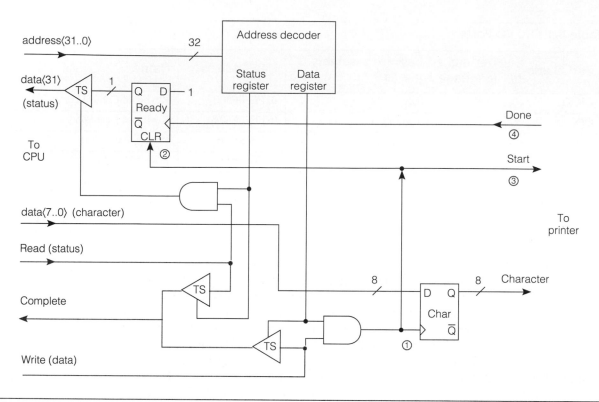

Fig. 8.6 Interface Design for SRC Character Output

Ready bit by reading Status. Since the Ready bit is the msb of the SRC word, SRC can test for Ready in a busy-wait loop by the branch-on-plus instruction, brpl.

The processor bus has separate read and write signals and returns a complete signal to the processor. The data register can only be written, and the status register can only be read. Either operation returns a Complete signal to the processor after a round trip time on the bus. A read of the data register or write of the status register has no effect on the interface and does not produce a Complete signal. Bits 31..8 are lost on writing the data register, and bits 30..0 have meaningless information when the status register is read. Note that these I/O "registers" only contain the few bits mentioned. When they are loaded into or stored from 32-bit general registers, the other bits are ignored on write and set to unknown values on read.

Synchronization of Data Transfer.   The synchronization of I/O data transmission deserves some attention. There are three principal types of data transfer timing: synchronous, semisynchronous, and asynchronous. The timing of these three types is shown in parts a, b, and c of Figure 8.7, respectively. The figure shows the source of each signal, Master (M) or Slave (S). It also shows the strobe signal used to latch the input data.

synchronous
transmission

Synchronous transmission, shown in Figure 8.7a, assumes that the slave device can respond to the signals sent by the master at full speed, so no handshaking signals are needed.

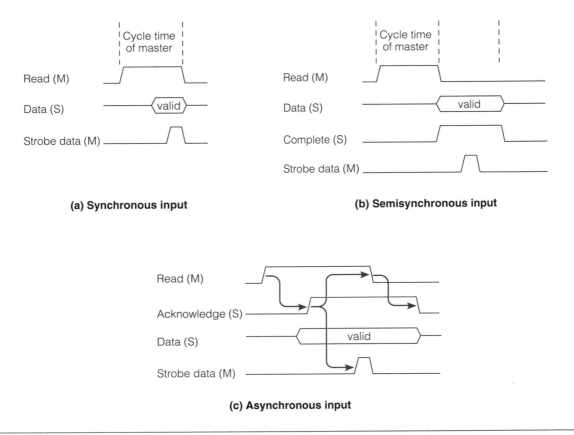

Fig. 8.7 Synchronous, Semisynchronous, and Asynchronous Data Transfer

Synchronous timing is used for register-to-register transfer in the CPU, for example. Data are strobed toward the end of the cycle in which it is gated, as shown in Figure 4.11 on page 161.

Semisynchronous transmission, shown in Figure 8.6b, is the protocol that was assumed for the CPU-to-memory interface in Chapter 4. There the Complete signal shown above was called Done. The signal is synchronized with the master clock of the CPU to produce a delay of 1 or more clock cycles while a memory operation completes. Figure 8.7b shows the slave delaying the data transfer by 1 bus cycle. Semisynchronous transmission was employed in the interface to the printer, shown on the right side of Figure 8.6.

Asynchronous transmission, shown for input in Figure 8.7c, takes into account that the slave may take time to even recognize the data transfer command signals, not just to respond to them. This is especially true with I/O, where bus transmission delays and logic designed separately from that of the CPU may contribute to speed differences. Asynchronous transmission protocol could be called "polite" data transmission because it distinguishes four interaction points. The first is the 0-to-1 transition of Ready, which asks, "May I have your data?" The second is the 0-to-1 transition of Acknowledge, which says, "Yes, you may (data are now valid)." At the third interaction point, the master says, "Thank you (data has been received)," by setting Ready to 0, and the last interaction

semisynchronous
transmission

asynchronous
transmission

comes when the slave sets Acknowledge to 0, in effect saying, "You are welcome." The master strobes the input data and then immediately sets Ready to 0. An asynchronous output transfer is similar, except that the master places data on the bus before raising Ready and holds it there until Acknowledge is seen as 1. Signal pairs like Ready and Acknowledge and the protocol governing their use go under the name *hardware handshaking*.

hardware handshaking

To summarize, synchronous and semisynchronous data transmission are used when there is little or no delay between a request for service and the completion of the transaction. Asynchronous data transmission is used when the delay between request and completion is long and variable.

8.2.2   SOFTWARE FOR PROGRAMMED I/O

The software that manages the data transfer to and from I/O devices is of critical importance. It manages the communications of data and control information between the device and the CPU. This includes initiating, controlling, and terminating the data transmission, and the handling of exceptional events such as "out of paper" or "device not ready." This software module is known as a *device driver,* or *device handler*.

device driver, device handler

In this section we cover three increasingly complex device driver fragments. The first is a fragment that handles the output of a single character. After describing that fragment, we show a more complex routine that prints an 80-character line. We conclude with a discussion of a device driver that handles input from 32 different character input devices, such as keyboards, at once. In all these discussions we assume a nonpipelined SRC, with no branch or load delay.

Output Device Programming.   The first two fragments assume the device interface described in Figure 8.6. Figure 8.8 shows the SRC instructions needed to do synchronized output of one character using this interface. For readability, I/O addresses are represented by symbols with all capital letters, program locations have an initial capital letter, and instruction mnemonics are in lowercase. The first instruction loads the branch target, and the second loads a character into the lower 8 bits of register r2 in preparation for output. The two-instruction loop that follows reads the status register and tests the sign, thereby

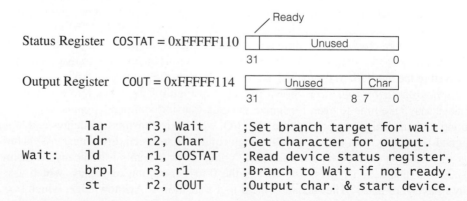

Fig. 8.8 Program Fragment for Character Output

testing Ready. The loop repeats until Ready becomes 1. On loop exit the character is written to the device data register by the st instruction.

The short loop that waits for the ready state may be executed many times if the device is slow. Even a relatively fast 1,000-character-per-second printer will have Ready equal to 0 for 1 millisecond for every character printed, which equals 10,000 instructions for a 10 MIPS processor. This is idle time during which the processor could be doing other useful tasks.

A slightly more complicated interface that illustrates the use of a command register is that for a line printer, which prints an 80-character line at one time. Characters are sent to the line printer exactly as for the character interface of Figure 8.6, but a separate control signal is needed to print the line after all of its 80 characters have been sent. Adding code to that of Figure 8.8 to output 80 characters from a buffer storing 1 character per word and to start the line print operation gives the program fragment of Figure 8.9. The instructions preceding the label initialize registers to a pointer to the character buffer area, Buff, a character count of 80, and branch target Wait. There are two nested loops starting at the label Wait. The two-instruction inner loop waits for Ready, and the outer, seven-instruction loop outputs a character, advances the buffer pointer, decrements the register containing the number of characters left to print, and repeats if there are more characters left to send. The last two instructions issue the command to print the line.

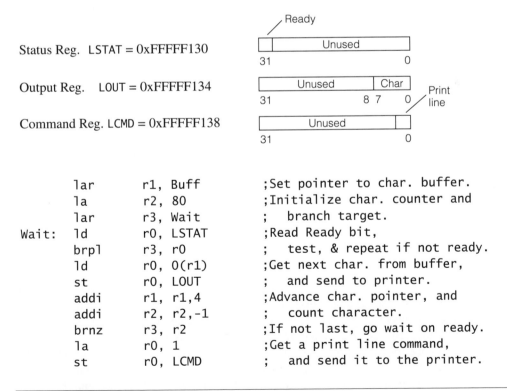

Fig. 8.9 Program Fragment to Print 80-Character Line

The line printer device must have an 80-character buffer, so it is likely to be able to accept the 80 characters of the line rapidly, with Ready going false only briefly for each character. The total instruction count to print the line is $3 + (80 \times 7) + 2 = 565$ instructions required to send the 80 characters and start the print. If there is no wait, this is equivalent to an output bandwidth of 80 bytes in 56.5 μs, or 1.42 MB/s for a 10 MIPS processor. This high-rate burst, however, is followed by a line printing operation that will take roughly 80 ms for a 1,000-character-per-second printer, so the average rate would be only a little less than 1,000 B/s.

An Input Device Driver That Handles Multiple Input Devices. The device driver of Figure 8.9 is simple compared to many drivers, which accounts for the fairly high speed at which it can transfer characters. As an example of a more complex driver, we consider a device driver that can handle input from 32 different character input devices, such as keyboards, at once. Each input device is assumed to have its own control and data registers. The control register for each device has a Ready status bit in position 31. The data register can only be read, and it returns the character in bits 7..0. The control and data register addresses for each input device are located at contiguous I/O word addresses beginning at 0xFFFFF300. Thus the control and data registers for device 0 have addresses 0xFFFFF300 and 0xFFFFF304, respectively. Those for device 1 have addresses 0xFFFFF308 and 0xFFFFF30C, respectively, and so on for each of the 32 devices. Thus the 32 devices occupy word addresses from 0xFFFFF300 to 0xFFFFF3FC. The hardware interface for each device is quite simple, differing only from the character output interface of Figure 8.6 by reversing the direction of the data register, so a character is read from the interface rather than being written to it.

Consider a device driver that will input and store a line of characters from each device, each line terminated by a carriage return. The driver is capable of handling input from all 32 devices by polling each to see if it has a character ready. *Polling* is the process by which the device driver tests each device in some predetermined order of priority, to see if it has a character ready. Polling each device takes only a small amount of time compared to the input data rate from devices such as keyboards. As with the character output device, accessing the data register enables the next input operation. Input from each device is controlled by 2 words. The first contains a pointer into a line buffer that stores 1 character per word, and the second is a Done flag that is 0 when the device is actively receiving characters and is set to –1 for an inactive device or when its line is complete. The driver, shown in Figure 8.10, terminates when all devices are inactive. The driver assumes that a buffer pointer has been initialized and Done flag set to 0 for each active device.

On entry to the driver, branch target registers are initialized for the three labels in the code. All 32 devices are scanned in turn, beginning with the label Start and ending at the last instruction in the routine. A flag indicating that all devices are inactive is set, and will be reset if any active device is encountered. The 17-instruction loop beginning at Check is executed once for each of the 32 devices. Parts of the loop will be skipped if the buffer is inactive or the device is not ready, or if the input character is not a carriage return. If the buffer is active for the device, the "all inactive" flag in register r3 is reset, and the Ready flag is tested. If the device is not ready, the program goes on to the next device, and will

polling

```
;Driver for 32 char. input devices. Register usage:
;r0 - working register. r1 - stores a char. into
;Selected buffer. r2 -indexes (CIN, CICTL) pairs
;of I/O registers & (Bufp, Done) pairs controlling
;input lines. r3 - =1 at the end of a pass only if
;no device is active.

CICTL   .equ    0◊FFFFF300      ;First char.-in control reg.
CIN     .equ    0◊FFFFF304      ;First input data register.
CR      .equ    13              ;ASCII carriage return.
Bufp:   .dcw    1               ;First pointer into a buffer.
Done:   .dcw    63              ;1st done & rest of pointers.
Driver: lar     r4, Next        ;Branch targets: move to next
        lar     r5, Check       ;  char., check device active,
        lar     r6, Start       ;  & start a new polling pass.
Start:  la      r2, 0           ;Point to first device, &
        la      r3, 1           ;  set all inactive flag.
Check:  ld      r0, Done(r2)    ;If device not still active,
        brmi    r4, r0          ;  go advance to next.
        la      r3, 0           ;Clear the all inactive flag.
        ld      r0, CICTL(r2)   ;Get device ready flag, & go
        brpl    r4, r0          ;  move to next if not ready.
        ld      r0, CIN(r2)     ;Get character and
        ld      r1, Bufp(r2)    ;  correct bufer pointer, &
        st      r0, 0(r1)       ;  store character in buffer.
        addi    r1, r1, 4       ;Advance character pointer,
        st      r1, Bufp(r2)    ;  and return it to memory.
        addi    r0, r0,-CR      ;If not carriage return,
        brnz    r4, r0          ;  go advance to next device.
        la      r0, -1          ;Set done flag to -1 on
        st      r0, Done(r2)    ;  detecting carriage return.
Next:   addi    r2, r2,8        ;Advance device pointer, and
        addi    r0, r2,-256     ;  if not last device,
        brnz    r5, r0          ;  go check next one.
        brzr    r6, r3          ;If any active, make new pass.
```

Fig. 8.10 Programmed I/O Driver for 32 Character Input Devices

test this device's Ready flag again only after all 31 other devices have been checked. If Ready is true for a device, then a character is input and stored in the character buffer, the buffer pointer is advanced, and the character tested to see if it is a carriage return. Receipt of a carriage return inactivates that device's buffer. At the bottom of the loop, the device pointer is advanced, and when it reaches 256, indicating that the last device has been serviced, a test is done to see if any are active. If some are, then another pass is made through all 32 devices. The driver exits when all 32 devices are inactive.

Let us now estimate the speed at which this driver can service input devices. If all the devices are active and a character is always ready when a device is tested, 32 bytes will be input at an instruction count consisting of 2 at the start, 32 executions of the 17-instruction loop, and a final branch, for a total of $3 + (32 \times 17) = 547$ instructions. This is about 585 KB/s in a 10 MIPS processor. If the processor just misses the ready bit for some device, it will execute the Check loop 31 more times, the Start loop once, and a few instructions to reach the Ready test again, for a total of about 538 instructions before it again polls the device. With a 10 MIPS processor, a single input device running faster than

18.6 Kchar/s would risk losing characters. For character-by-character input, this 53.8 μs delay is probably not significant, but there are more serious problems with the driver. One that is correctable with more code is that all input lines must finish before any new ones are started. The major problem, however, is that the processor is completely occupied with doing input from devices that are slow enough to leave it plenty of time to do other work. We will see how to improve the driver by using I/O interrupts in Section 8.3.

GETTING SPECIFIC: THE CENTRONICS PARALLEL INTERFACE   Before leaving programmed I/O, we give an example of a real interface to show some of the complexity encountered with a practical device. The specification was developed for Centronics printers and has been adopted by many printers and other devices that can use a one-directional, byte-wide parallel interface. The Centronics Interface signals are listed in Table 8.2. The interface standard lists pins of a 36-pin connector for each signal and its individual ground in a twisted-pair configuration. We suppress these for simplicity. In addition to the eight data lines and handshake signals, STROBE and ACKNLG, there are three status inputs from the printer and three command outputs to it. These could be assigned to different

Table 8.2 Signal Names and Functions for the Centronics Printer Interface

Interface Signal Name	Direction	Description
STROBE	Out	Data out strobe
D0	Out	Least significant data bit
D1	Out	Data bit
D2	Out	"
D3	Out	"
D4	Out	"
D5	Out	"
D6	Out	"
D7	Out	Most significant data bit
ACKNLG	In	Pulse when done with character
BUSY	In	Not ready
PE	In	No paper when high
SLCT	In	Pulled high
AUTO FEED XT	Out	Auto line feed
INIT	Out	Initialize printer
ERROR	In	Can't print when low
SLCT IN	Out	Deselect protocol

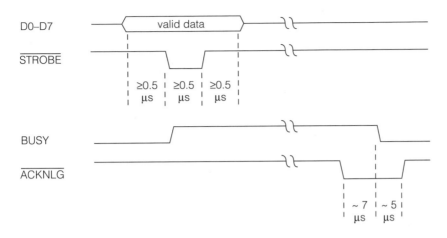

Fig. 8.11 Centronics Printer Data Transfer Timing

bits of a printer control register, which would output commands when written and return status bits when read. The $\overline{\text{SLCT IN}}$ signal is a good example of real-world complexity. When it is high, sending an ASCII control character called DC3 the printer deselects it. It is only reselected by sending the ASCII control character DC1, also while $\overline{\text{SLCT IN}}$ is high.

The Centronics Interface could be used to connect the SRC I/O interface of Figure 8.6 to a printer. Start would be inverted and connected to $\overline{\text{STROBE}}$, Done would be inverted and connected to $\overline{\text{ACKNLG}}$, and D0–D7 would be connected to Char.

The details of the device synchronization handshake are shown in Figure 8.11. Signal timing is specified so that the printer will not quit working as processor speeds improve. In addition to the BUSY signal, which behaves like the complement of the Complete signal of Figure 8.6, there is also an acknowledge pulse after every character transmission. The pulse can be used to strobe a status bit in the interface. The 0.5 µs minimum times specified in the diagram require the device interface designer to time data and strobe signals so as to satisfy the setup and hold times of the flip-flops in the printer.

Key Concepts: Programmed I/O

Programmed I/O is the simplest of the I/O techniques, both conceptually and physically.

- Programmed I/O is appropriate when the speed of the device does not overwhelm the CPU's processing ability.
- The processor is likely to spend considerable time in busy-wait loops while doing programmed I/O.
- The hardware interface for programmed I/O usually consists of a buffer register to store the data item being transferred and 1 or more bits of status information.
- The interface most often employs an asynchronous handshaking protocol.
- The device driver is of great importance, as it must mediate communications of data, control, and status between processor and device.

8.3   I/O Interrupts

The main problem with programmed I/O that we saw in the last section is that a processor may waste many instructions polling a device to see if it is ready for the next operation. What is needed is for the device to initiate the operation when it is ready. One way to do this is by using the processor's exception handling mechanism. An I/O interrupt can cause the processor to stop what it is doing and execute code associated with a particular I/O device. I/O is still done by the processor, but the waiting is eliminated because the interrupt occurs only when the device is ready to transfer data.

8.3.1   INTERRUPT HARDWARE

An interrupt request is synchronized by handshake signals, called ireq and iack in the SRC machine. An I/O device asserts ireq, and when the processor completes the current instruction, it responds by asserting iack, provided that interrupts are enabled. Since several devices may request interrupts, ireq is usually a wired OR signal, and its bus wire is usually active low. On receiving an acknowledge, a device must identify itself to the processor, so that the correct software routine, called an *interrupt handler*, or *interrupt service routine (ISR)* can be executed. The next section presents the details of the interrupt handler.

**interrupt handler,
or interrupt service
routine (ISR)**

type code

Processors vary in the way in which the interrupt handler's address is communicated to the CPU. In most systems a small integer called a *type code* is put on the processor's data lines and converted to an address by the processor. The address of the interrupt handler will be found at the location pointed to by the converted type code. In SRC this is done by having the I/O device send the processor 8 bits from which an interrupt vector address can be formed. SRC also allows for different interrupts to be served by the same handler by having the device send 16 additional information bits that are placed in the II register. You may wish to refer to Section 4.8.3, "Exception Processing in the SRC," or to Appendix B, to refresh your memory about the details of SRC's interrupt mechanism. The 24 bits of interrupt information can be returned to the processor on the data bus in response to iack. A device with interrupt capability will have an interrupt request flip-flop that is often set by the same condition that sets the ready status flag. It will also have an interrupt enable flip-flop that can be cleared to disable interrupts from this one device.

**interrupt request
line**

**interrupt
acknowledge line**

Figure 8.12 shows a partial diagram of the interface hardware associated with an I/O interrupt. SRC, and for that matter most processors, have only a single $\overline{\text{ireq}}$, *interrupt request*, line shared by all devices in the interrupt system. This line is driven by an open collector NAND gate, marked o.c., so that a single pull-up resistor can hold this line high, and thus inactive, if no device is requesting an interrupt. The iack, *interrupt acknowledge*, signal is for this one device, so tri-state gates can be used to drive the data lines with interrupt response information from only one device. The data bus is used by the device to return interrupt information and vector bits. The address bus plays no role because the processor does not know the address of the interrupting device.

priority chain

Priority Chain.   The wired OR interrupt request signal allows several devices to request interrupts simultaneously, but for proper operation, one and only one requesting device must receive an acknowledge signal. Otherwise, more than one device will drive the data bus with interrupt information simultaneously. The usual solution is called a *priority chain*. Assume the jth device has request req_j and enable enb_j. Device 0 always receives the

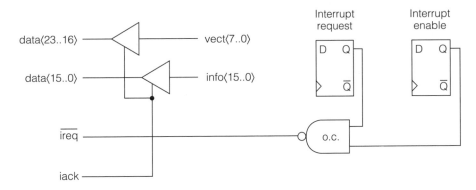

Fig. 8.12 Simplified Interrupt Circuit for an I/O Interface

acknowledge signal, $iack_0 = iack$, but device j only receives an acknowledge if device $j - 1$ does, and $j - 1$ does not have an enabled interrupt request,

$$iack_j = iack_{j-1} \wedge \overline{(req_{j-1} \wedge enb_{j-1})}$$

Thus the only requesting and enabled device to receive an acknowledge signal is the lowest-numbered one. While the ireq signal is a single, continuous bus wire to all devices, iack is logically different at every device, with each device producing iack for the next one in a linear chain, as shown in Figure 8.13. Such a signal is said to be *daisy-chained* through the I/O devices.

daisy chain

Interface Logic for Interrupts. An I/O interface with interrupt capability makes the interrupt request and enables flip-flop values available to the processor along with Ready when device status is read. It also allows the processor to set the value of enable. Figure 8.14 shows the complete I/O interface logic associated with SRC interrupts. The interface has a control register, (parts of) which can be both read and written. On receiving an acknowledge to its interrupt request, the interface becomes the source for the 8 interrupt vector bits and the 16 information bits. These bits should uniquely identify the device and, if necessary, one of several possible causes of the interrupt. The value of these bits can be fixed or set by jumpers or switches. Especially for the vector bits, it can be useful to have these bits written to the device under program control during initialization, so that vector addresses can be flexibly assigned to devices.

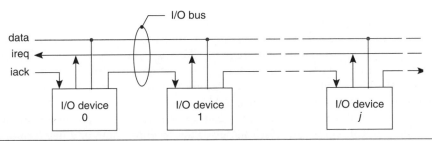

Fig. 8.13 Daisy-Chained Interrupt Acknowledge Signal

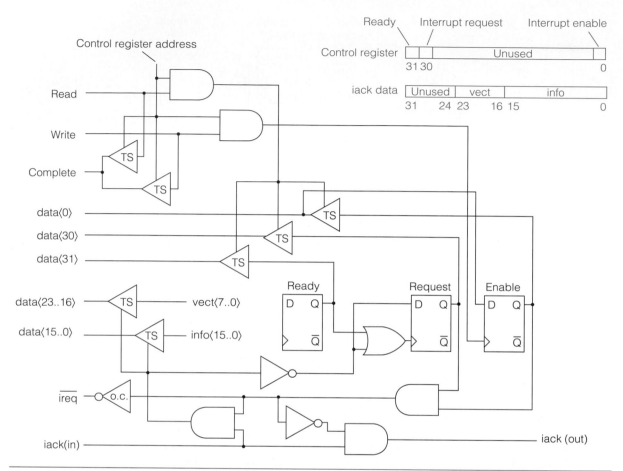

Fig. 8.14 Interrupt Logic in an I/O Interface

The diagram does not show the hardware required for the programmed setup of the interrupt vector and information bits. It also suppresses the address decoding, all circuitry associated with data transfer, and the device signals that set Ready.

8.3.2 INTERRUPT HANDLER SOFTWARE

As an example of interrupt-driven I/O, consider a character input device, such as a keyboard. If enabled, the device generates an interrupt every time a new character is available to be read from the data register. We take the programmed I/O portion of the interface to be the same as that for 1 of the 32 devices driven by the software of Figure 8.10. The inclusion of interrupt capability modifies the control register by the addition of interrupt request and enable bits. We also assign bits 11..4 of the control register to interrupt vector bits, which can be written by the processor. Figure 8.15 shows the control register structure and gives the code for input of a line terminated by a carriage return into a 1-character-per-word buffer under interrupt control.

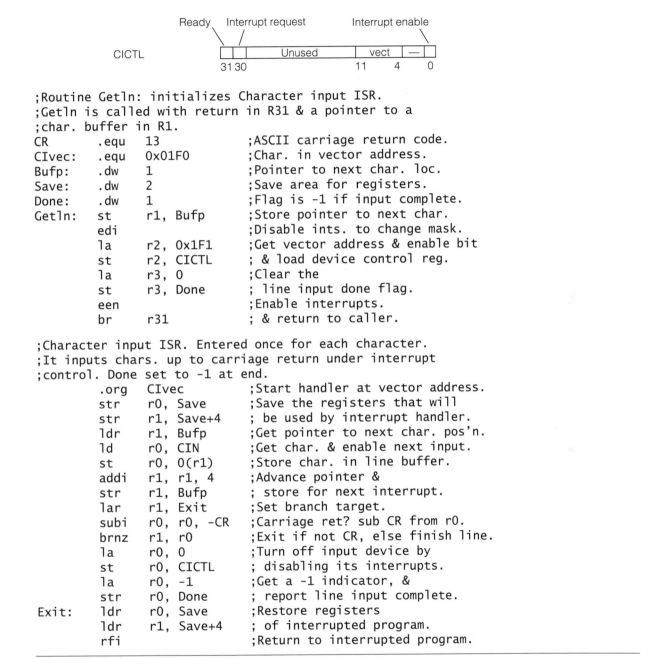

```
;Routine Getln: initializes Character input ISR.
;Getln is called with return in R31 & a pointer to a
;char. buffer in R1.
CR       .equ   13            ;ASCII carriage return code.
CIvec:   .equ   0x01F0        ;Char. in vector address.
Bufp:    .dw    1             ;Pointer to next char. loc.
Save:    .dw    2             ;Save area for registers.
Done:    .dw    1             ;Flag is -1 if input complete.
Getln:   st     r1, Bufp      ;Store pointer to next char.
         edi                  ;Disable ints. to change mask.
         la     r2, 0x1F1     ;Get vector address & enable bit
         st     r2, CICTL     ; & load device control reg.
         la     r3, 0         ;Clear the
         st     r3, Done      ; line input done flag.
         een                  ;Enable interrupts.
         br     r31           ; & return to caller.

;Character input ISR. Entered once for each character.
;It inputs chars. up to carriage return under interrupt
;control. Done set to -1 at end.
         .org   CIvec         ;Start handler at vector address.
         str    r0, Save      ;Save the registers that will
         str    r1, Save+4    ; be used by interrupt handler.
         ldr    r1, Bufp      ;Get pointer to next char. pos'n.
         ld     r0, CIN       ;Get char. & enable next input.
         st     r0, 0(r1)     ;Store char. in line buffer.
         addi   r1, r1, 4     ;Advance pointer &
         str    r1, Bufp      ; store for next interrupt.
         lar    r1, Exit      ;Set branch target.
         subi   r0, r0, -CR   ;Carriage ret? sub CR from r0.
         brnz   r1, r0        ;Exit if not CR, else finish line.
         la     r0, 0         ;Turn off input device by
         st     r0, CICTL     ; disabling its interrupts.
         la     r0, -1        ;Get a -1 indicator, &
         str    r0, Done      ; report line input complete.
Exit:    ldr    r0, Save      ;Restore registers
         ldr    r1, Save+4    ; of interrupted program.
         rfi                  ;Return to interrupted program.
```

Fig. 8.15 Initialization and Handler to Input a Line Using Interrupts

The program is in two parts. The first part is an initialization subroutine, Getln, that is called to initialize the device, line done flag, and pointer to the buffer. On return from this subroutine, interrupts from the device are enabled. Upon the press of a key, an interrupt is generated, and the interrupt service routine, ISR, is entered. The ISR is entered once for each character of the line. Input of the carriage return character sets the Done flag, which can be tested by the main program to determine whether the line is complete. The interrupt handler code is located at the vector address for simplicity, but in a real program the 4 words separating interrupt vector addresses would contain code to save a register and branch to handler code elsewhere in memory.

The general functions of an interrupt handler are

1. Save the state of the interrupted program.
2. Do programmed I/O operations to satisfy the interrupt request.
3. Restart or disable the interrupting device.
4. Restore the state and return to the interrupted program.

In the example, only two registers must be saved and restored, r0 and r1. The program counter of the interrupted program has already been saved by the interrupt response sequence and is restored by the rfi instruction at the end of the handler. Interrupts are disabled for the duration of the handler execution. The call to Getln is made with the return address in r31 and a pointer to an 80-word buffer in r1. The subroutine stores the buffer pointer where it can be accessed by the interrupt handler and disables exceptions so it can make changes in the device's interrupt control. The vector address, CIvec = 0x01F0, and an interrupt enable bit, =1, are stored in the I/O device's control register, and the Done flag for the input buffer is cleared. For the sake of clarity in the example, Getln uses een and br at the end of the routine to enable interrupts and return to the caller. In reality, these would probably be replaced by ri and rfi to prevent an incoming interrupt from occurring between the een and br instructions. The ri instruction is used to clear II and place the return address that is in r31 into IPC. Then the rfi instruction is used to return from the subroutine and simultaneously enable interrupts.

The interrupt handler, or ISR, starting at CIvec, is invoked each time a key is pressed. The ISR saves registers, gets the buffer pointer, reads the character from the device data register, and stores it in the buffer. The handler then advances the buffer pointer, stores it away, and tests the character for carriage return. If it is a carriage return, then further device interrupts from the device are disabled by clearing the enable bit in the control register. In either case, the handler exits by restoring the saved registers and executing an rfi.

Only one interrupting device is explicitly considered, but there is no reason not to have several enabled devices, each of which invokes its own handler on interrupt. Response to another interrupt that occurs while the handler is executing is just delayed until interrupts are reenabled by the rfi instruction. The code of Figure 8.15 shows that interrupts will be disabled for a maximum of one passage through the handler: 17 instruction times plus the time for the processor's interrupt response sequence. Suppose that the processor clock is 20 MHz, that it takes 10 cycles to respond to an interrupt, and that the average execution rate is 8 CPI. Then a second interrupt could be delayed as long as $(17 \times 8 + 10)/20 = 7.3\ \mu s$. A direct comparison of interrupt-driven I/O with programmed I/O is difficult; suffice it to say that polling can occupy the processor for the duration of the I/O activity. For keyboard entry, this will be the entire time period from when the processor is ready to accept keyboard input until it no longer accepts keyboard input. If the same activity is interrupt-driven, then the processor will only spend 7 or 8 μs per keystroke. If a typist is operating at 120 words per minute, 10 characters per second, then the processor is busy accepting input from a keyboard only $7.3/10^5$, or .007% of the time.

An interrupt handler synchronizes with two other independent entities, the I/O device and the main program. In the example, synchronization with the main program is based on Done, which is cleared by the main program and set by the handler. It is needed because the rate of progress of the main program depends entirely on the work it has to do, while the duration of the interrupt handler task depends on the I/O device, the line length, and typing speed. Synchronization with the I/O device is through the interrupt's invocation of the handler and the I/O operation through which the handler restarts the device.

The example did not use the bits sent to the processor's II register by the interrupting device. A simple extension to the example where information in the II register would be useful is an interrupt version of the 32-input-device driver of Figure 8.10. If each device sent the processor a unique identifier in the II bits, a single vector address and handler could serve all of them. Details of this extension are left for exercises.

8.3.3 INTERRUPT PRIORITY AND NESTED INTERRUPTS

Speed has several different meanings with respect to I/O operation. We have already discussed the bandwidth of a data transmission and the latency from a request to the start of transmission. A third speed concern is immediacy, or *response deadline*. The response deadline is the maximum time that a handler can take between when a request is issued and when the device must be serviced. Deadlines arise in connection with devices that have limited buffering. For example, if characters come into a 1-character buffer from a moving tape, the buffer must be read by the processor before the next character passes the read head, or either it or the character in the buffer will be lost. Estimating response deadlines is not a trivial activity, because the data rate from a given input device can vary widely. The designer must estimate the maximum sustained data rate of the device and design an I/O subsystem that can handle that rate under all conditions if data are not to be lost. If the device I/O is "bursty," that is, the data come in bursts, with periods of latency in between, then a buffer of sufficient length to hold the burst of data may be required. Data rates of I/O devices can vary from a few bits per second for a keyboard to 100 megabits per second for the highest-speed network interconnections.

In an interrupt I/O system, such deadlines put restrictions on how long interrupts may remain disabled. The deadlines also establish a priority among interrupt requests. Devices with shorter deadlines should be acknowledged first. The priority established by a daisy-chained acknowledge signal only partially addresses the problem. If devices with shorter deadlines are placed closer to the processor in the chain, they will be acknowledged first in case of simultaneous requests, but if a slower device interrupts just before one with a short deadline, interrupts may be disabled to handle the slow device for longer than the deadline allows. The solution is to allow high-priority devices to interrupt lower-priority handlers. An interrupt handler is just a program, and its state can be saved and restored to allow it to resume where it left off. It is only necessary that interrupts be enabled at some time during interrupt handler execution. A system of interrupts that allows an interrupt handler to be interrupted is known as *nested interrupts*.

Interrupts must remain disabled during critical sections of the interrupt handler. A *critical section* is a code sequence in the handler during which a second interrupt would interfere. In SRC, for example, interrupts must be disabled until the IPC and II registers have been saved with an svi instruction. Devices of lower priority than the one being

response deadline

bursty data

nested interrupts
critical section

handled would also be disabled before enabling interrupts. The general structure of a nested interrupt handler involves the following steps:

1. Save state that is changed by interrupt response (IPC and II).
2. Disable lower-priority interrupts.
3. Reenable exception processing.
4. Service the interrupting device.
5. Disable exception processing.
6. Reenable lower-priority devices.
7. Restore state involved in interrupt response (IPC and II).
8. Return to interrupted program and reenable exceptions.

Much of implementing a nested interrupt system is a matter of software design, but there are places where hardware support is needed. Steps 2 and 6 could be time consuming if the only way to disable lower-priority devices is to clear their individual enable bits. Hardware support for priority disabling is indicated. To understand what needs to be done, consider the collection of all I/O device interrupt enable bits as a bit vector, usually called an *interrupt mask*. Order them so that enables for higher-priority devices come first (right end) and those for lower-priority devices come last (left end). Then, if device j interrupts, the correct configuration of the mask while executing device j's handler is as shown in Figure 8.16. Device j and lower-priority devices are disabled, and higher-priority devices are enabled.

interrupt mask

The priority mask should actually be distinct from the individual enables because some devices may be disabled for reasons having nothing to do with priority (e.g., device off or in error). The value of a mask of the preceding priority form is entirely determined by the *interrupt-level j* of the current handler. The interrupt-level mask should also differ from a simple collection of enable bits in another regard. Many devices should really be equivalent with respect to priority level. All disk drives of a given type should have one priority, which is higher than that of all keyboards. Within groups of devices of the same priority, a daisy-chained acknowledge is still needed to arbitrate simultaneous requests, but the order of devices on the chain is not important within the group.

Figure 8.17 shows a possible organization of a priority interrupt system. There are $m = 2^k$ groups of devices, each group having its own wired OR request and acknowledge daisy chain. The priority system has a register to store the current interrupt level. The priority encoder outputs the binary index j of the lowest-numbered request that is asserted. This index is compared with the current level, and if it is smaller, an interrupt request is sent on to the processor. When the processor acknowledges the request, the current level is set to the level of the new request, and an acknowledge is sent out on daisy chain ack_j. Not shown in the figure is the mechanism for saving the previous interrupt level and restoring it when the interrupt handler returns. This can be done using a push-down stack. The stack depth is limited by the number m of priority levels.

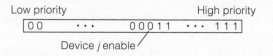

Fig. 8.16 Interrupt Mask for Executing Device *j* Handler

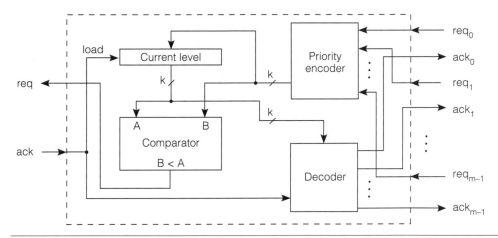

Fig. 8.17 Priority Interrupt System with $m = 2^k$ Levels

Figure 8.17 shows the priority interrupt mechanism as a separate subsystem, but many commercial processors have a priority mechanism built into their exception response. The Motorola MC68000, for example, provides seven levels of priority interrupt. It also saves the program counter and other processor status on a stack in memory instead of in processor registers. The combination of state saving and level change in the interrupt response sequence means that the exception mechanism does not need to be disabled at all during handler execution. Of course, exception response takes longer when items are stored in memory. The PowerPC has more of a RISC-style architecture. It stores program counter and other processor status in special processor registers and starts the handler code with exceptions disabled. All I/O interrupts in the PowerPC have one priority level. A priority system for I/O interrupts would require a separate chip.

Key Concepts: Interrupt-Driven I/O

Interrupt-driven I/O is a major improvement on programmed I/O for many input and output tasks.

- The processor need not concern itself with I/O until the device is actually ready for service, as opposed to having to poll the device repeatedly.

- The interrupt handler, sometimes known as the interrupt service routine, is invoked by a request for service from the device.

- Individual device interrupts can be enabled or disabled by software. This provides a mechanism for prioritizing interrupts and preventing unwanted interference by an interrupting device.

- Interrupt nesting allows higher-priority interrupts to interrupt lower-priority interrupt handlers.

8.4   Direct Memory Access (DMA)

Let us return to the problem of disk transfer timing illustrated by Figure 8.1. The problem posed by the long latency from the start of the operation to the burst of data transmissions is adequately handled by the interrupt mechanism, but the high-bandwidth burst remains a concern. We calculated in connection with the code of Figure 8.9 that a 10 MIPS processor could only output about 1.4 MB/s using programmed I/O. Some disk drives, however, can read and write at speeds exceeding 10 MB/s. Even if a program can keep up with a disk, the processor cycles are wasted on the simple task of moving bytes between disk and memory. In the program of Figure 8.9, a loop of 7 instructions and 10 memory accesses, including instruction fetch, transfers only 1 byte from memory to the output device. The solution is *direct memory access* (DMA), or allowing an I/O device to read from or write to memory directly, without using the processor.

bus master

multiple master bus

With memory-mapped I/O, the memory signals are available on the combined bus. For an I/O device to access memory, it only needs to drive the address, read, and write signals without conflicting with the processor. Taking control of these signals is known as becoming *bus master,* and a bus attached to one or more DMA devices and one or more processors is called a *multiple master bus*. Only one device can be bus master at a time, so the processor or other DMA devices may be delayed for the duration of a read or write.

The job of a DMA device is to transfer a block of data to or from memory. To do this, it must accomplish essentially the same operations done by the software of Figure 8.9. The steps follow:

1. Become bus master.
2. Send the memory address and read or write signal.
3. Synchronize the sending or receiving of data using the Complete signal.
4. Release the bus for use by the processor or other DMA device.
5. Advance the memory address.
6. Count the read or write and test for end of data.
7. Repeat from step 1 if there is more data.

The only situation in which the DMA device would not release the bus between memory accesses is when only one very high-speed device could be active at a time.

bus request

bus grant

cycle stealing

The architecture of an interface that can perform these steps is shown in Figure 8.18. A device becomes bus master by asserting the *bus request* signal and waiting for *bus grant*. The protocol is essentially the same as that of the asynchronous two-wire handshake shown in Figure 8.7c. Bus grant is a daisy-chained signal, so that multiple requests can be arbitrated, just as with interrupt acknowledge. Bus request is dropped after every memory read or write, so that the processor or another DMA device can have access to the bus. There is usually no deadline associated with program execution, so DMA requests take precedence over the processor and use the bus by *cycle stealing*. The DMA device takes the memory bus from the processor and "steals" the one cycle required for read or write.

Two speed requirements apply to large systems with multiple DMA devices. First, the deadlines must be satisfied for all DMA devices. The worst-case delay between a bus request and bus grant depends on the number of other DMA devices closer to the processor on the bus grant chain. It must be small enough to satisfy the device deadline requirements. Further, the total number of memory cycles per second required by all DMA devices and

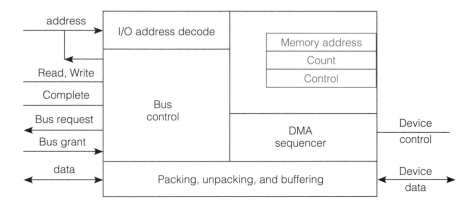

Fig. 8.18 I/O Interface Architecture for a DMA Device

the processor when all are operating simultaneously must be no more than the bandwidth of the memory. If B_m is the memory bandwidth, B_p is the memory bandwidth that must be left over for the processor, and B_j is the maximum bandwidth of DMA device j, then

$$B_m \geq B_p + \sum_j B_j$$

I/O driver software associated with DMA devices, in addition to doing control operations such as disk seeks, must perform the following steps to control the DMA:

1. Load the memory address register.
2. Load the word or byte count.
3. Load the command (read or write).
4. Start the operation.
5. Detect completion of the block transfer (interrupt or device ready flag).

For an input device, it is possible that fewer bytes may be input than the count specifies before the device runs out of data. In this case, the processor should be able to read the count register as well as write it to determine the actual number of bytes transferred.

DMA logic can be organized in a system in several ways. Each I/O device can have its own interface with DMA capability, or a DMA controller can be separate from one or more devices for which it performs block transfers. This separate DMA controller is often called a *channel,* a term used especially with IBM computers. If it can do block transfers for several devices, but only one at a time, it is a *selector channel.* If it can control several block transfers at once, it is a *multiplexer channel.* The two types are shown in Figure 8.19.

channels

selector channels
multiplexer
channels

Channels can be made more complex and capable. Instead of doing just one input or output block transfer and stopping, information for one or more subsequent transfers can be programmed into the channel, to be done when the current one is complete. In the limit, the channel becomes a special purpose *I/O processor* that can fetch operations from memory and execute them in sequence. It is possible to use a general purpose processor chip with I/O software in a ROM as an I/O processor, but processors designed for I/O usually have distinct block- transfer instructions to serve the purpose of DMA.

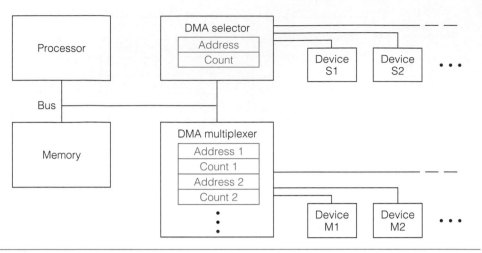

Fig. 8.19 Multiplexer and Selector DMA Channels

8.5   I/O Data Format Change and Error Control

Data often undergo a change of format in going between the processor/memory system and I/O devices. We are not concerned with changes in the physical format, such as voltage levels to ink on paper, but with the logical form of the data. Data in main memory are usually organized into bytes and words. External data may be organized as a serial bit stream on devices such as disk drives, or as a byte stream on devices such as tape drives. Multibyte words may have big-endian organization internally, and need to be changed to little-endian format externally. Depending on the data rate, the responsibility for this reformatting may fall upon the processor as part of the I/O task, or it may be encoded in the hardware of the I/O interface.

Data integrity also varies between main memory and the external world. Inside main memory the probability of error in a bit read is extremely low; processors usually run for months or years without a bit error. Raw bit-error rates in external devices and systems, on the other hand, are considerably higher; so much so that the error rate would be unacceptably high if not corrected. These relatively high error rates are due to factors such as imperfections in disk surfaces and noise on communications lines. As a result of these high bit-error rates, external data are often encoded with redundant bits that are used to detect and correct errors.

This section deals with both of these matters. We begin with a short discussion of the reformatting of data during I/O. Following that, we discuss several methods of error detection and correction.

8.5.1   REFORMATTING DATA: PARALLEL/SERIAL CONVERSION

Parallel-to-serial and serial-to-parallel conversion are common activities in the I/O interface. They are almost always handled by hardware in the interface except in the simplest of processors. The most common hardware technique uses shift registers. An example of the use of a shift register for parallel-to-serial data conversion is in the serialization of bytes to a serial bit stream representing pixels in alphanumeric video display terminals.

This is presented in Chapter 9, beginning on page 425. In addition to undergoing a parallel-to-serial conversion, external serial data may need to be encoded in a way other than the simple high = 1, low = 0 method used to encode bits in the processor, for signaling or timing purposes. This will be discussed in Chapter 10, Section 10.1.1. The EIA RS-232 serial data communications protocol is discussed in Section 10.2.1.

Illustrative Example: I/O to a Tape System.   Consider the interface between a 32-bit CPU and a magnetic tape system that stores information as 1 K byte blocks. When the tape is read, the incoming byte stream must be assembled into 32-bit words before they are written to main memory. This can be accomplished by eight 4-bit shift registers with parallel output. One bit of each byte is shifted into each of the eight shift registers. When 4 bytes have arrived, the 32-bit word is ready for transfer to a buffer, where it can be read by the CPU, or transferred directly to main memory by a DMA controller. The buffer frees up the shift registers to receive additional bytes while the 32-bit word transfer is occurring. Output conversion of words to bytes can be by means of the same shift registers if they have parallel input as well as output capability. The shift register is loaded in parallel from the word buffer, and the bytes shifted out one by one. All conversion between serial↔parallel uses shift registers in a similar way.

We will see in the next section that error detection and correction bits are applied during this serial-to-parallel conversion process. A parity check bit, defined in the next section, may be added as a ninth bit to each byte of the outgoing byte stream, and additional check bytes may be added at the end of each block of bytes. When the block is read from the tape, logic in the interface uses the parity bits and check bytes to detect and possibly correct errors that have been introduced by the tape machine. The CRC codes treated in the next section are examples of bit-serially computed error control codes that are used in applications such as the one in this example.

8.5.2   ERROR CONTROL CODES

In this section we consider the detection and correction of data errors. The fundamental parameter to be considered in discussing errors is the bit-error rate. The *bit-error rate, BER,* is the probability that when read, a given bit will be in error. It is a statistical parameter that may be determined by experimental measurement or by calculation.

bit-error rate, BER

Error control is important in all parts of a computer system, but it is particularly critical in I/O, where signals leave the carefully controlled electronic environment of the main chassis. Error rates inside processors are very low, usually in the 10^{-18} range. The comparatively higher error rates associated with I/O are still fairly low, in the range of 10^{-8} to 10^{-12}, and can be controlled by adding redundant information to data as it leaves the processor environment. At the receiving end, a check can be made to see that the same form of redundancy exists when it returns. We distinguish between the *raw bit-error rate,* which is the bit error rate without error correction, and the *corrected bit-error rate*, which is the error rate after the bit stream has passed through the error correction circuitry. Given the low level of bit-error rates in the computer itself, error detection and correction circuitry is less often found there, although single-error-correct, double-error-detect (SECDED) memories are employed in circumstances where ultra-high reliability is required. On the other hand, raw bit-error rates in many I/O systems are often unacceptably high unless error detection and correction systems are employed. We will discuss three different schemes for detecting and

raw bit-error rate
corrected bit-error rate

correcting errors, beginning with the simple parity check, proceeding with the Hamming Code and its variant, SECDED coding, and ending with the cyclic redundancy check (CRC) technique.

parity checking
parity bits
even and odd parity

Parity Checks.   The simplest form of redundancy for checking errors is called *parity* and is most often used with data represented in a parallel format. One extra *parity bit* is added to the data, and its value is chosen so as to make the number of 1-bits in the augmented data odd for *odd parity* encoding or even for *even parity* encoding. An even parity bit, P, can be generated from the exclusive OR of the bits in the word to be transmitted. For example the even parity bit for a byte to be transmitted would be $P = b_7 \oplus b_6 \oplus \ldots \oplus b_0$. The parity bit is generated and added to the data before it is transmitted into a less reliable part of the system. If any single bit of the data, including the added parity bit, changes during transmission, the parity will be incorrect when the data are received. A parity checker at the receiving end evaluates the parity by computing the exclusive OR over both data and parity bit and signals an error if it is wrong.

For example, if odd parity is used with the 8-bit byte 01101010, which has an even number of 1-bits, a 1 is appended on the left to give 101101010 and make the number of ones in the 9-bit word odd. Suppose that during data transmission a bit error occurred, so that the receiving hardware received 101101011. This word contains an even number of bits, and the parity error detection hardware would detect that error. Such a simple scheme cannot detect which bit is in error. In fact, if two bits were received in error, then no error would be detected.

The utility of parity checks is based on the assumption that a change in 1 bit is much more probable than a change in several bits. One parity bit will not detect a change of 2 bits, or any other even number of bit changes. The assumption is justified if the probabilities of change of different bits are independent and small. Then, if the probability of a single error is p, the probability of two errors is p^2. A single bit-error rate of 10^{-8} would mean a probability of two errors of 10^{-16}. Since parallel representations use separate hardware for different bits, independence of errors can be expected, explaining the applicability of parity to parallel data.

Hamming codes

Hamming Codes.   Combinations of parity checks can be used both to check multiple bit errors and to correct errors. One important scheme is *Hamming coding,* which is used to detect and correct errors in data that is stored in RAM or transmitted from one computer to another. Although memory generally resides on the computer's motherboard and is considered quite reliable, high-density memory chips are subject to independent, single bit errors resulting from microscopic processes such as alpha particle decay. The Hamming code can be used to correct single bit errors in memory words and is often used in computer systems that require a high degree of reliability, such as the process-control systems used in power plants.

The Hamming code adds a group of parity check bits to the original data. The scheme is most easily described if the parity bits, P, are interspersed with the data bits, D. Out of a set of bits numbered 1 through $2^k - 1$, bits whose numbers are powers of 2 are reserved for parity bits, where parity bit P_j is in bit position $j = 2^i$, for some integer $i = 0, 1, \ldots .$ A Hamming code generator accepts the data bits, places them in bit positions with indices that are not a power of 2, and computes the parity bits by the following scheme. Let the binary representation of the position number j of a bit be $j_{k-1} \ldots j_1 j_0$. Then the value of

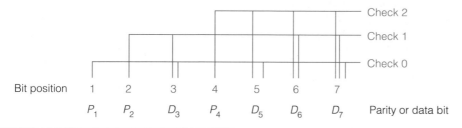

Fig. 8.20 Multiple Parity Checks Making Up a Hamming Code

parity bit P_{2^i} is chosen to give odd (or even) parity over all bit positions j such that $j_i = 1$. For example, bit position 4, having binary index 0100, will contain a parity bit, P_4, that makes parity odd when it is computed over all the data bits, D_j, that have a binary index of 1 in that bit position. So data bits D_5 and D_6, having indices 0101 and 0110 respectively, will participate in the computation of P_4, as will D_{14}, since it has the binary index 1110.

Thus each bit takes part in a different combination of parity checks. The working of the Hamming code is illustrated for 4 data bits in Figure 8.20. Notice that we start bit numbering from 1 rather than from 0. The 0 bit position is reserved for later use in SECDED coding, which is discussed next. The parity bit P_1 in position 1 checks bits with a 1 in the binary representation of their index, that is, all odd-numbered bits; the parity bit in position 2 checks all bits with a 2 in the binary representation of their index, that is, bits 2, 3, 6, and 7; the parity bit in position 4 is used for the parity check on bits 5, 6 and 7.

After the parity bits are inserted, the data-plus-parity bits are sent into the unreliable subsystem. When they return to the reliable environment, the $\log_2 k$ parity checks are reevaluated. If one and only one bit is in error, then all the parity bits that include that bit in their check will be in error. An error in one and only one bit will cause failures in a unique set of parity bits, thus allowing the position of the erroneous bit to be determined. Let c_i be true if check i fails and false otherwise. Then, in the case of a 1-bit error, $c_{k-1} \cdots c_1 c_0$ is the binary index of the bit in error. For example, if only the data bit at position 3 is in error, then check 2 will pass, and checks 1 and 0 will fail. Thus the bit in error has the index $c_2 c_1 c_0 = 011_2 = 3$. If only the data bit at position 5 is in error, then check 1 will pass, and checks 2 and 0 will fail. Thus the error will be in position $c_2 c_1 c_0 = 101_2 = 5$. An error correction circuit will receive the data and parity bits, evaluate the checks, and if any are wrong, correct the specific bit indicated to be in error. The parity bits would then be removed and the data returned. This collection of checks that fail, $c_{k-1} \cdots c_1 c_0$, is referred to as the *syndrome* of the error.

Error syndrome

Motivating Example—Using the Venn Diagram to Explain Error Correction. Figure 8.21 provides an illustration of the use of Hamming encoding using even parity checks, to detect and correct a single-bit error in the word 1011. Figure 8.21a shows the classic Venn diagram, which is a visual representation of the universe of values that can be assumed by 3-bit binary variables, A, B, and C. Each variable is represented by a circle. The top circle represents the area where C is true, the bottom left circle is where B is true, and the bottom right circle is where A is true. Each distinct area enclosed by the three intersecting circles has an "address" that represents the variables that are true in the particular area. So the area where only C is true has the address 001, B, 010, and A, 100; thus the area where the bottom two circles intersect has the address 110, as it is the intersection, or OR, of A and B.

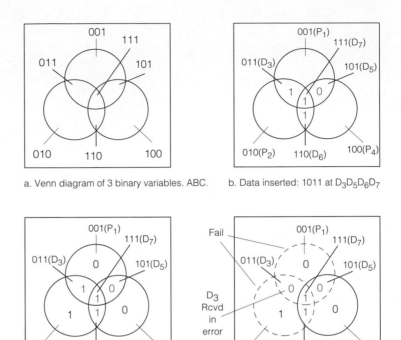

a. Venn diagram of 3 binary variables. ABC.   b. Data inserted: 1011 at $D_3D_5D_6D_7$

c. Even parity bits inserted: 010 at $P_1P_2P_4$ d. D_3 Rcvd in error: P_1 & P_2 fail

Fig. 8.21 Error Detection and Correction Using the Hamming Code

Following the discussion in the previous section, areas 001, 010, and 100 are reserved for the parity bits, P. The data bits, D, occupy the remaining areas. We use the address of the area to identify it. Figure 8.21b shows the identities of the 7 areas, $P_1P_2D_3P_4D_5D_6$ and D_7, with the four data bits, 1011, inserted into their appropriate areas, D_3 D_5D_6 and D_7. Into the remaining 3 areas we insert the appropriate bit, 1 or 0, to make the parity of the entire circle even, as shown in Figure 8.21c. Thus P_1 is 0, P_2 is 1, and P_4 is 0. The entire 7-bit code word $P_1P_2D_3P_4D_5D_6D_7$ before transmission is thus 0110011.

Now suppose the code word is transmitted over a noisy channel to a receiving entity, and that bit D_3 has flipped from a 1 to a 0 during transmission. That is, the word is received as 0100011. In Figure 8.21d we see that when the receiving entity recomputes the three parity checks, both P_1 and P_2 fail, both showing odd parity instead of the even parity expected. Since 001 and 010 failed, the bit received in error must have the address 011, 3, and thus bit D_3 must have been received in error, as a 0 instead of the correct value, 1.

Of course, it is equally probable that a parity bit itself may flip and be received in error. Notice that in this case, only a single parity check will fail.

We now turn to the more conventional way of computing the Hamming code, which will be much more useful when larger words are encoded.

Example 8.1   Encode 1011 Using the Hamming Code and Odd Parity

- Inserting the data bits: $P_1 P_2 1 P_4 011$.
- P_1 is computed from $P_1 \oplus D_3 \oplus D_5 \oplus D_7 = 1$, so $P_1 = 1$.
- P_2 is computed from $P_2 \oplus D_3 \oplus D_6 \oplus D_7 = 1$, so $P_2 = 0$.
- P_4 is computed from $P_4 \oplus D_5 \oplus D_6 \oplus D_7 = 1$, so $P_4 = 1$, and the final Hamming code is 1011011. ■

Note that the ability of a Hamming code to correct an error depends on the assumption that only 1 bit has changed. Changes in 2 or more bits will give a check pattern indicating a false, single bit error or no error. A common extension to this scheme is called *SECDED coding* (single-error-correct, double-error-detect), which allows the correction of single errors and the detection, but not correction, of double errors. Its correct working depends on the probability of the occurrence of three or more errors being so small as to make it effectively impossible. The Hamming code is extended to SECDED by adding a parity bit chosen to make the parity over all bits, parity and data, odd (or even). The overall parity bit is conventionally added in the leftmost position that is unused by the Hamming code and is called P_0. Now if 1 bit is in error, a unique set of Hamming checks will fail, and the overall parity will also be wrong. The failure of one or more Hamming checks with correct overall parity signals that 2 or more bits are in error, but does not allow them to be corrected.

SECDED coding

Example 8.2   Compute the Odd-Parity SECDED Encoding of the 8-Bit Value 01101011

The 8 data bits 01101011 would have 5 parity bits added to them to make the 13-bit string $P_0 P_1 P_2 0 P_4 110 P_8 1011$. Now $P_1 = 0$, $P_2 = 1$, $P_4 = 0$, and $P_8 = 0$. From this we can compute the overall parity $P_0 = 1$. Thus the encoded value is 1010011001011. ■

Example 8.3   Extract the Correct Data Value from the Odd-Parity SECDED String 0110101101101

The value 0110101101101 shows even overall parity instead of odd, indicating a single bit error. Checks c_2 and c_4 fail, giving the binary index of the erroneous bit as $0110_2 = 6$, so D_6 is in error. It should be 0 instead of 1. The corrected value of the data is $P_0 P_1 P_2 0 P_4 001 P_8 1101$. Note that the 5 check bits could have checked up to 11 data bits with a 16-bit code. ■

SECDED is efficient for large words. The number of extra bits needed for checks increases roughly as $\log_2$ of the number of data bits. A 64-bit word requires 8 SECDED bits. In main memory, SECDED could be applied to a full cache line, making it even more efficient.

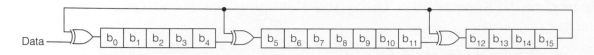

Fig. 8.22 CRC Generator Based on the Polynomial $x^{16} + x^{12} + x^5 + 1$

Cyclic Redundancy Checks (CRC). With serial transmission of data, the assumption of independent errors in individual bits breaks down. At high bandwidths, a momentary disturbance in a single serial channel can easily cause several successive bits to be wrong. Parity codes are not as useful in this situation; thus *cyclic redundancy check* (*CRC*) codes are used instead. The theory behind their effectiveness is beyond the scope of this book, but they are easy to implement in practice. A CRC is generated serially from all the bits of a string of any given length. The number of bits in the CRC is specified by the particular CRC scheme chosen. A *CRC generator* is shown in Figure 8.22. The generator consists of a shift register and some XOR gates. Each new data bit is applied to the input, followed by a shift. The number of bits in the CRC and the positions of the XOR gates is determined by a *generating polynomial* associated with the particular CRC used. Commonly used CRCs are represented by the polynomials of Table 8.3. The powers of x in the generating polynomial identify bit positions connected to the outputs of the XOR gates.

The utility of CRCs is confined to error detection; they do not support correction. Erroneous data must be reported by the receiver to the transmitter, which must send it again. The length of the string of bits checked by a CRC is arbitrary, but the longer the string, the more bits must be retransmitted in case of an error. The probability that the check will succeed even though some bits are in error depends on the number of bits checked and the generating polynomial. We will not treat it here.

To use a CRC, a number of data units, say words in a memory are reformatted into a serial stream of bits. As the bits are sent out, the transmitter computes the CRC by applying all bits to the shift register CRC generator. When all bits have been transmitted, the transmitter appends the CRC bits to the data and sends them too, as shown in Figure 8.23. The receiver independently generates its own CRC over the data bits and compares it to the transmitted CRC. The receiver reports errors to the transmitter, so that it can retransmit the data.

Key Concepts: Data Formatting and Error Control

■ Data representations are different inside main memory and outside in the I/O system. Reformatting is part of the duties of the I/O interface.

Table 8.3 Generating Polynomials for Commonly Used CRCs

Name	Code Length	Generating Polynomial
CRC-12	12 bits	$x^{12} + x^3 + x + 1$
CRC-16	16 bits	$x^{16} + x^{15} + x^2 + 1$
CCITT-CRC	16 bits	$x^{16} + x^{12} + x^5 + 1$

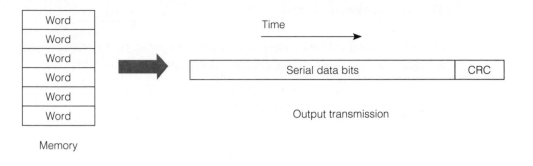

Fig. 8.23 Serial Data Transmission with Appended CRC Code

- Error detection and correction are often necessary in the I/O subsystem because of the relatively high bit-error rates associated with peripheral devices.

- A simple parity check may suffice when error rates are not too high or when additional error checking and correction takes place elsewhere.

- Hamming codes and SECDED coding allow error detection and correction.

- CRC checks are easy to implement and can detect multiple bit errors, but error correction must be implemented by retransmission of data.

Summary

- Even though the I/O subsystem may appear to the programmer as part of the memory address space, it has a number of characteristics that make it differ from memory. Data location, data transfer, and synchronization all have special characteristics associated with the broad range of characteristics that different I/O devices can have. Speed variation, both in latency and bandwidth, is very important and gives rise to three different ways of handling I/O data transmission: programmed I/O, interrupt driven I/O, and DMA.

- In all three types of I/O data transmission, a combination of hardware and software protocols guarantee correct delivery of information. In programmed I/O, an instruction starts the input or output, and a several-instruction loop tests for completion. In interrupt-driven I/O, hardware protocols for arbitration of and response to interrupt requests combine with software protocols in an interrupt handler program to accomplish data transfers initiated by the I/O device instead of the CPU. Finally, in DMA the concept of a multiple master bus allows an all-hardware solution to the problem of communicating with memory for individual data item transfer. The only problem left to software is starting and finishing large block transfers and doing device-dependent control functions.

- The characteristics of interconnections outside the CPU/memory chassis lead to data format changes. In addition to the use of a more serial transmission to use cables with fewer wires, error control also becomes important. By adding check bits or multiple-bit codes to the data, errors can be detected, so that data can be retransmitted, or the data can actually be corrected automatically at the receiver.

Bibliography

A somewhat dated but excellent treatment of I/O interfaces can be found in:

J. B. Peatman, *The Design of Digital Systems*, McGraw-Hill, New York, 1972.

A more recent book by the same author is

J. B. Peatman, *Digital Hardware Design*, McGraw-Hill, New York, 1980.

Another comprehensive treatment of I/O is given in:

Ronald L. Krutz, *Interfacing Techniques in Digital Design*, John Wiley & Sons, New York, 1988.

Treatments of I/O at a level of coverage similar to that in this text can be found in the following texts:

M. Mano, *Computer Engineering: Hardware Design*, Prentice-Hall, Englewood Cliffs, NJ, 1988.

V. C. Hamacher, Z. G. Vranesic, and S. G. Zaki, *Computer Organization*, 5th ed., McGraw-Hill, New York, 2001.

A good historical perspective on the evolution of DMA and I/O processors in computer systems is found in:

C. Gordon Bell and A. Newell, *Computer Structures: Readings and Examples*, McGraw-Hill, New York, 1971.

The following is a tutorial article surveying I/O system architecture:

J. Buzen, "I/O subsystem architecture," *Proceedings of the IEEE,* June 1995.

Error detecting and correcting codes are thoroughly treated in:

R. W. Hamming, *Coding and Information Theory*, 2nd ed., Prentice-Hall, Englewood Cliffs, NJ, 1986.

Exercises

8.1 Discuss the advantages and disadvantages of isolated versus memory-mapped I/-O. **(§8.1)**

8.2 Show the additions required for the I/O interface hardware of Figure 8.5 and Figure 8.6 to support the line printer used by the program fragment of Figure 8.9. **(§8.2)**

8.3 a. The printer driver of Figure 8.9 uses a software buffer that stores only 1 character per word. Modify the driver program for a buffer that packs 4 characters per word.
b. With the new program, what is the maximum burst bandwidth from a 10MIPS processor for the 80 characters of a line if there is no wait between characters? **(§8.2)**

8.4 Write a routine similar to that given in Figure 8.9 that reads characters from a keyboard and stores them, up to a carriage return character, in an 80-character buffer. **(§8.2)**

8.5 If a routine such as that in Exercise 8.4 accepts all characters as typed, it is known as *raw* input. If the routine interprets certain input characters, such as tab and backspace, as modifying the characters in the character buffer, that is known as *cooked* input. Write a routine similar to the one in Exercise 8.4 that partially cooks the input by accepting the backspace character, 0x08, as a signal to back up 1 character in the buffer and overwrite it with the next nonbackspace character input. **(§8.2)**

8.6 Draw timing diagrams like those of Figure 8.7 for synchronous, semisynchronous, and asynchronous output, rather than input. Where is the data strobe located in each case? **(§8.2)**

8.7 Design an input device interface for one of the 32 character input devices handled by the device driver of Figure 8.10. The logic diagram should be similar to that of Figure 8.5 and Figure 8.6 for the character output interface.   **(§8.2)**

8.8 What percentage of time will the processor in the 80-character line printer example of Figure 8.9 spend in the busy-wait loop?   **(§8.2)**

8.9 Assume there are many character input devices attached to a 10 MIPS processor, each running at 1,000 characters per second. They are all handled under interrupt control, using the handler code of Figure 8.15. If hardware interrupt response takes 1 μs, what is the maximum number of devices that could be handled simultaneously?

8.10 Modify the Get1n and interrupt handler code of Figure 8.15 to pack input characters into the buffer, 4 per word. With a 10 MIPS processor and a 1 μs interrupt response, what is the maximum time that interrupts can be disabled for one execution of the new handler?   **(§8.3)**

8.11 Modify the input device interface hardware of Exercise 8.7 for interrupt-driven handling of 32 input devices, as suggested on page 391. Control and data register addresses are as in Figure 8.10. The control register includes program-writable interrupt vector bits, and the interface puts its 5-bit number (equal to bits 7–3 of its CTL register address) into the least significant bits of info in response to iack.   **(§8.3)**

8.12 Modify the Get1n routine and handler of Figure 8.15 to use the hardware of Exercise 8.11. The new Get1n subroutine takes an input device number from 0 to 31 as a second input parameter in register r2, initializes buffer and interface, and starts a line input for that device. The new handler should process interrupts from any of the 32 devices that is active. Assume that if the SRC interrupt information register II = k, then device k caused the interrupt.   **(§8.3)**

8.13 Design a two-level AND, OR, NOT circuit for the following I/O priority circuit. When the ack input is true, ack$_j$ will be made true for the smallest j for which req$_j$ is true. The req output is true if any req$_j$ is true. All ack$_j$ outputs are false when ack is false and when all req$_j$ are false.   **(§8.3)**

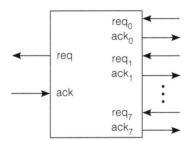

8.14 A certain disk interface accepts requests to read a 32 KB block of data. It has a 32 KB buffer on board its I/O interface, in which it stores the data as it comes off the drive. The interface is interrupt-driven and has DMA capability. Describe the likely sequence of events from the time the processor requests a block of data until the data have been transferred to main memory.   **(§8.4)**

8.15 Add even parity bits to each of the 7-bit ASCII characters in the string, "D'Oh!" Consult the chart on page 456 for the 7-bit ASCII codes.   **(§8.5)**

8.16 Design a circuit to convert an incoming parallel 32-bit word from little-endian form to big-endian form.   **(§8.5)**

8.17 Design the hardware to signal a parity error if the 8-bit value in a register is not even parity.   **(§8.5)**

8.18 Use even parity Hamming code to encode the following 4-bit values: 1101, 0101, 0010, 1101.   **(§8.5)**

8.19 Use odd parity SECDED coding to encode the following 4-bit values: 1001, 1110, 0111. **(§8.5)**

8.20 What is the percentage increase in the size of main memory necessary to include SECDED coding in the following two cases?

   a. Errors are checked on each 32-bit word.

   b. Errors are checked on a 4-word cache line.   **(§8.5)**

8.21 In the following SECDED-coded data, what is the number of data bits, how many bit errors are there, and what is the corrected value? Bit positions are numbered from zero at the left, and parity checks are odd.   **(§8.5)**

   a. 1011 0101 1110 1011

   b. 0001 1010 1110 1100

   c. 0110 1010 1010 0111

CHAPTER 9
Peripheral Devices

In the last chapter we discussed the common ways of interfacing the processor to external peripheral devices. In this chapter we cover the operation and behavior of the most common peripheral devices—hard disk drives, video displays, printers, input devices, and analog devices. The primary focus is on the logical behavior of peripheral devices, but we also discuss their physical operation. Chapter 8 pointed out that device I/O speeds could range from so slow that the processor spends negligible time servicing the device to speeds beyond the capacity the processor to keep up without assists from DMA or dedicated I/O processors. We present examples of both kinds of peripheral devices in this chapter.

The term *peripherals* seems pejorative, implying that they are somehow superficial or unimportant aspects of the computer system. Of course, they are in fact essential components of system operation; without them we could neither input information to the processor nor observe its output.

One of the most interesting aspects of peripheral devices is the wide range of I/O bandwidth they span, from the keyboard and printer at a few bytes to a few hundred bytes per second to disk drives and video interfaces, some of which can operate in the tens of megabytes per second. Some devices place such extreme demands on the computer system that special purpose processors may be designed into the peripheral to off-load much of the I/O service.

Thus a computer designer might be employed in designing the processor and memory portion of the peripheral device itself, or a general purpose computer designer might need to match the interface specifications determined by the peripheral designer. In either case, the character of the interface will be determined to some extent by the data capacity and transfer rate of the peripheral, and it is on this interface that the two designers must agree. Only the largest manufacturers will expect to supply all the peripherals for their own systems and thus specify this interface independently. Others will use one of the standard bus interfaces so that any peripheral meeting the standard can be used with their system. More computer designers are probably employed in designing complex peripherals than in designing general purpose computers.

Standard buses have detailed specifications, such as those we discussed for the Centronics interface in Chapter 8. Some bus standards and their speeds are listed in Table 9.1. The SCSI bus is widely used to connect disk drives to small computers. The Ethernet and EIA RS232/422 buses are used to interconnect computers as well as computers and peripherals, and they are treated in more detail in Chapter 10.

The design or selection of the peripheral device interface must be made from a systems perspective, considering cost and performance in the broadest sense. For example, an inexpensive, low-speed printer can be interfaced using an inexpensive serial interface. A modern disk drive, however, will require the highest-speed parallel interface and will probably employ the services of a DMA controller if one is available. In this chapter, we will consider several of the most widely used peripherals, which span the range of I/O bandwidths. We will begin by discussing the hard disk drive, the device that probably places the most severe demands on the processor and I/O system.

9.1 Magnetic Disk Drives

Having some of the aspects of both serial and parallel I/O, and some of the aspects of both random and sequential access memories, the modern hard disk drive system is one of the most complex and interesting of the peripheral devices. In this section we first discuss the general organization of the typical disk system. Then we discuss the factors that influence its static (capacity) and dynamic (bandwidth and latency) attributes.

9.1.1 HARD DISK DRIVE ORGANIZATION

The modern hard disk drive is a system in itself. It contains not only the disks that are used as the storage medium and the read/write heads that access the raw data encoded on them, but also the signal conditioning circuitry and the interface electronics that separate the system user from the details of getting bits on and off of the magnetic surface. Figure 9.1 is a photograph of a $2\frac{1}{2}" \times 4" \times \frac{1}{2}"$ Maxtor Laramie disk drive of 1.3 GB capacity. The drive has four platters with read/write heads on the top and bottom of each platter. The drive rotates at a constant 3,600 rpm.

Table 9.1 Some Common Peripheral Interface Standards

Bus Standard	Data Rate	Bus Width
Centronics	≈50 KB/s	8-bit parallel
EIA RS232/422	30–20 KB/s	Bit-serial
SCSI	Few MB/s	16-bit parallel
Ethernet	10 Mb/s	Bit-serial

Fig. 9.1 Photograph of a 1.3 GB Maxtor Disk Drive   (Photo courtesy of Vincent P. Heuring)

Typical drive dimensions range from $5\frac{1}{4}$" wide × 7" deep × 3" high to $2\frac{1}{2}$" wide × 4" deep × $\frac{1}{2}$" high, the latter being a popular dimension for laptop and notebook computers. In 2002, high-end drive capacities ranged from 100 to 200 GB, with these capacities expected to increase by 50% each year until at least 2006. The raw data rate of bits streaming from the head can be over 1 Gb/s, and high-speed drives can output data at rates exceeding 160 MB/s.

Drive capacities and sizes have changed dramatically in the last 30 years. Figure 9.2 shows a photograph of a disk platter built in the 1960s by CDC that is presently being used as a coffee table. The platter is 4 feet in diameter and had a capacity of 2.5 MB. For reference, the drive of Figure 9.1 is shown atop the platter, along with a 700 MB CD ROM.

Fig. 9.2 A 2.5 MB Disk Platter from the 1960s, Now Used as a Coffee Table
(Photo courtesy of Vincent P. Heuring)

Platters and Read/Write Heads.   The heart of the disk drive is the stack of rotating platters that contain the encoded data, and the read and write heads that access that data. Figure 9.3 shows a cutaway view of such a drive. The drive shown contains five platters, although this varies. There are read/write heads on the top and bottom of each platter, so information can be recorded on both surfaces. All heads move together across the platters. The platters rotate at a constant speed, usually 3,600 rpm or higher—1 revolution in 17 ms.

disk surface

There is one read/write head for each *surface*, which rides a few microns above the platter surface, buoyed up by a small cushion of air. A servomechanism is responsible for moving the heads across the platter surface to the correct data track. The read/write heads can traverse the active area of the disk in approximately the same 17 ms required for the disk to complete a single revolution. This makes for a system that is of interest to the mechanical engineer as well as the computer engineer.

Regardless of how many heads, tracks, or surfaces there are, only one head is active at a time: The data stream is always bit-serial to and from the surface.

Drive Electronics.   The disk drive electronics are located on a printed circuit board attached to the disk drive, as shown in Figure 9.3. The drive electronics perform an impressive task. To the processor, the drive electronics provide an interface to a standard bus such as the SCSI (small computer systems interface) bus along with a relatively simple logical interface that allows the processor to treat the disk as if it were just another (admittedly slow) memory device. At the business end of the drive, after a read request, the electronics must seek out and find the block requested, stream it off the surface, error-check and possibly error-correct

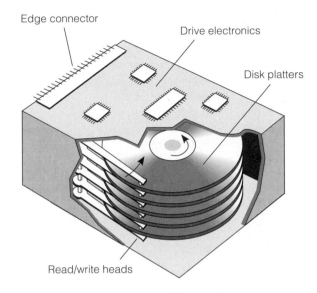

Edge connector

Drive electronics

Disk platters

Read/write heads

Fig. 9.3 Cutaway View of Multiplatter Hard Disk Drive

it on the fly, assemble it into bytes, store it in an on-board buffer, and signal the processor that the task is complete. Complex error correction might be computed after information is stored in the buffer.

To assist in the task, the drive electronics include a *disk controller:* a special purpose processor in its own right. The drive electronics are contained on a small printed circuit board attached to the drive, and I/O is by means of the edge connector shown on the left side of the board.

disk controller

Data Organization on the Disk. The drive needs to know where the data to be accessed are located on the disk. To provide that location information, data are organized on the disk platters by tracks and sectors. Figure 9.4 shows a simplified view of the organization of tracks and sectors on a disk. The figure shows a disk with 1,024 *tracks*, each of which has 64 *sectors*. The head can determine which track it is on by counting tracks from a known location, and sector identities are encoded in a header written on the disk at the front of each sector.

tracks
sectors

The number of bytes per sector is fixed for a given disk drive, varying in size from 512 bytes to 2 KB, with the former figure being the most popular at the present time. All tracks with the same number, but on different surfaces, form a *cylinder*. For the platter layout of Figure 9.4 and five platters, there would be 1,024 cylinders, each of which has 10 tracks. Modern drives divide the disk surface into concentric zones, with the number of sectors per track varying by zone, fewer toward the center, more toward the outside.

cylinder

The information is recorded on the disk surface 1 bit at a time by magnetizing a small area on the track with the write head. That bit is detected by sensing the direction of that magnetization as the magnetized area passes under the read head, as shown in Figure 9.5. Magnetization is shown as pointing left, L, or right, R, looking in the direction of head motion along the track. There are several points to be made about this figure:

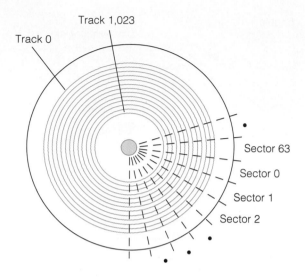

Fig. 9.4 Simplified View of Disk Track and Sector Organization

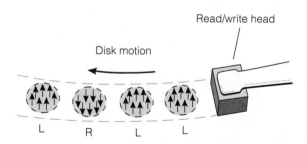

Fig. 9.5 Individual Bits Encoded on a Disk Track

1. The track is not a physical groove or mark on the platter; it is defined by the path of the magnetized bits.

2. The L R L L pattern shown in the figure does not represent the bit pattern 0 1 0 0 or 1 0 1 1. The bit pattern as seen by the outside world must be encoded to facilitate detection by the low-level head electronics before writing it on the disk; there are several encoding schemes, but they all encode the data in such a way as to avoid long strings of Ls or Rs, which can confuse the drive electronics.

3. The individual bit areas are so small and the unavoidable surface defect rate is so high that additional data must be included for error correction using an error correcting code, ECC. There are several ECCs in use, the most common being the Reed-Solomon ECC.

4. Every sector, regardless of what track it is on, has the same byte capacity.
5. The platters rotate at a constant angular velocity. If the numbers of sectors per track and bytes per sector do not change from inner track to outer track, the bits are spaced closest together on the innermost track and farthest apart on the outermost track. Constant angular velocity and a constant number of sectors per track capacity mean that the data rate at the heads is constant regardless of track.

Figure 9.6 shows how a typical sector might be organized. The header usually contains both synchronization and location information. The synchronization information allows the head positioning circuitry to keep the heads centered on the track, and the location information allows the disk controller to determine the sector's identity as the header passes, so that the data can be captured if it is a read, or stored if it is a write. The 12 bytes of ECC information are used to detect and correct errors in the 512-byte data field.

Generally the disk drive manufacturer *initializes*, or *formats*, the drive by writing its original track and sector information on the surfaces, and checks to determine whether data can be written and read from each sector. If any sectors are found to be bad, that is, incapable of being used even with ECC, then they are marked as being defective so their use can be avoided by the operating system.

disk formatting

The Operating System Interface.   The operating system (OS) insulates users and application programs from the need to understand the details of how a given file is actually stored on the disk. Details vary OS by OS, but typically the OS specifies the track, sector, and surface of the desired block. The disk controller translates that request to a series of low-level disk operations. Figure 9.7 shows a portion of the PC AT disk interface *logical block address* (LBA) used to communicate requests to the drive controller. Head #, Cylinder #, and Sector # refer to the starting address of the information, and Sector Count specifies the number of sectors requested. The LBA consists of 5 bytes written to designated I/O ports in the AT drive interface. Five additional byte-wide registers are devoted to drive command and status information. (The term *logical* is used because, as we will see, the LBA may not correspond to the actual physical address of the block on the disk; the controller takes care of the mapping from LBA to physical block address.)

logical block address

The Disk Access Process.   Let us follow the process of reading a sector from the disk:

1. The OS communicates the LBA to the disk drive and issues the read command.
2. The drive *seeks* the correct track by moving the heads to the correct position and enabling the one on the specified surface. The read head reads sector numbers as they travel by until the requested one is found.
3. Sector data and ECC stream into a buffer on the drive interface. ECC is done on the fly.
4. The drive communicates "data ready" to the OS.
5. The OS reads data, either byte by byte or by issuing a DMA command.

disk seek

Having presented this introductory material, we now turn our attention to the calculation of actual static and dynamic disk drive properties.

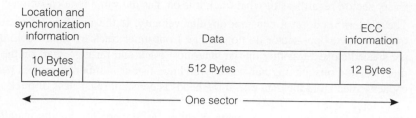

Fig. 9.6 Typical Hard Disk Sector Organization

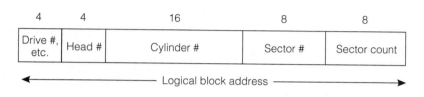

Fig. 9.7 The PC AT Block Address for Disk Access

9.1.2 DISK DRIVE STATIC PROPERTIES

By static properties, we mean the properties related to drive capacity and unrelated to access speed. There are a number of ways to specify drive capacity. These range from areal density, which is a measure of the ultimate drive capacity, never realized in practice, to formatted capacity, which represents the actual storage capacity of the drive. Here we present the terms and formulas needed to compute drive capacity.

areal density

Areal density is the bit density in bits per unit area. Areal density at a specific spot on the disk is computed from

$$\frac{1}{(\text{bit spacing} \times \text{track spacing})} \qquad \text{[Eq. 9.1]}$$

maximum areal density

Maximum areal density is the areal density at the innermost track. It represents the maximum bit density per unit area that the drive can support. The maximum areal density is a function of the magnetic storage density, head size, head positioning accuracy, and many other factors.

maximum linear bit density

Maximum linear bit density is the bit density in bits per unit length on the innermost track.

average bit density

Average bit density is the total bit capacity of a surface divided by the total surface area where data are stored.

unformatted capacity

Unformatted capacity is the product of the total number of bits per sector multiplied by the number of sectors on the disk. This figure is less useful to the end user than formatted capacity, since it includes the sync, location, and ECC bits as well as the data bits.

Formatted capacity is the product of the number of data bytes per sector times the number of sectors on the drive. Here is an example of a simple drive capacity calculation:

$$\text{formatted capacity} \;=\; \frac{\text{bytes}}{\text{sector}} \;\times\; \frac{\text{sectors}}{\text{track}} \;\times\; \frac{\text{tracks}}{\text{surface}} \;\times\; \text{no. of surfaces} \qquad \text{[Eq. 3.2]}$$

formatted
capacity

There are a number of easily derived variations of this equation that involve unformatted capacity, cylinders, bit capacity, or other factors. Rather than slavishly memorizing this equation, you are advised to understand the underlying principles well enough so that the appropriate equation can be derived as needed. The student is also advised to employ dimensional analysis to check the correctness of the form of the derived equation.

9.1.3   Disk Drive Dynamic Properties

Dynamic properties are those that deal with the access time for the reading and writing of data. The calculation of data access time is not simple. It depends not only on the rotational speed of the disk, but also the location of the read/write head when it begins the access. There are several measures of data access times.

Seek time is the average time required to move the read/write head to the desired track. Actual seek time will depend on where the head is when the request is received, and how far it has to travel, but since there is no way to know what these values will be when an access request is made, the average figure is used. Average seek time must be determined by measurement. It will depend on the physical size of the drive components and how fast the heads can be accelerated and decelerated. Seek times are generally in the range of 8–20 ms, and have not changed much in recent years.

seek time

Track-to-track access time is the time required to move the head from one track to an adjoining one. This time is in the range of 1–2 ms.

track-to-track time

Rotational latency is the average time required for the needed sector to pass under the head once the head has been positioned at the correct track. Since on average the desired sector will be half way around the track from where the head is when the head first arrives at the track, rotational latency is taken to be $\frac{1}{2}$ the rotation time. Current rotation rates are from 3,600 to 7,200 rpm, which yield rotational latencies in the 4–8 ms range.

rotational latency

Average access time is equal to seek time plus rotational latency.

access time

Burst rate is the maximum rate at which the drive produces or accepts data once the head reaches the desired sector. It is equal to the rate at which data bits stream by the head, provided that the rest of the system can produce or accept data at that rate:

burst rate

$$\text{burst rate (bytes/sec)} \;=\; \frac{\text{revs}}{\text{sec}} \;\times\; \frac{\text{sectors}}{\text{rev}} \;\times\; \frac{\text{bytes}}{\text{sector}} \qquad \text{[Eq. 9.3]}$$

Sustained data rate is the rate at which data can be accessed over a sustained period of time. This parameter is of great interest when designing systems that must access large files in real time, such as video or audio data. The rate can be estimated from the drive specifications, as previously described, but must be verified by actual testing. Unexpected factors can influence the sustained data rate. For example, many drives periodically undergo a *head recalibration* activity, during which time the heads are moved over the

sustained rate

head recalibration

surface for recalibration. During this time the drive is unavailable for read/write activity. If head recalibration occurs during a sustained file transfer there may be an unacceptable pause in data access. Some manufacturers are producing "multimedia" drives that suspend head recalibration during sustained data access.

CLASSIC EXAMPLE: CALCULATING THE CAPACITY AND SPEED OF A DISK DRIVE

A hard drive has eight surfaces, with 512 tracks per surface and a constant 64 sectors per track. Sector size is 1K bytes. The average seek time is 8 ms, the track-to-track access time is 1.5 ms, and the drive runs at 3,600 rpm. Successive tracks in a cylinder can be read without head movement.

a. What is the drive capacity?

Capacity = $8 \times 512 \times 6\,4 \times 1\,K = 256$ MB.

b. What is the average access time for the drive?

$$\text{Rotational latency} = \text{Rotation time}/2 = \frac{60}{3,600 \times 2} = 8.3 \text{ ms}$$

Average access time = Seek time + Rotational latency = $8 + 8.3 = 16.3$ ms.

c. Estimate the time required to transfer a 5-MB file.

Assume this file is stored in successive sectors and tracks, starting at sector #0, track #0 of cylinder #i. A 5 MB file will need 1,000 blocks and will occupy from cylinder #i, track #0, sector #0, to, cylinder #(i+9), track #6, sector #7. We also assume the size of disk buffer is unlimited.

The disk will need 8 ms, which is the seek time, to find the cylinder #i, 8.3 ms to find sector #0, and $8 \times (60 / 3,600)$ seconds to read all 8 tracks' data of this cylinder. Then, the time needed for the head to move to the next adjoining track will be only 1.5 ms, which is the track-to-track access time. Assume a rotational latency before each new track.

Access time =

$$8 + 9 \times (8.3 + 8 \times 16.6 + 1.5) + 8.3 + 6 \times 16.6 + \frac{8}{64} \times 16.6 = 1406.9 \text{ ms}$$

d. What is the burst transfer rate?

$$\text{Burst rate} = \frac{\text{revs}}{\text{sec}} \times \frac{\text{sectors}}{\text{rev}} \times \frac{\text{bytes}}{\text{sector}} = \frac{3600}{60} \times 64 \times 1\,K = 3.84 \text{ MB/s} \qquad \blacksquare$$

Performance and Design: Disk Access.   We can see from these relationships that a disk with a burst rate of 20 MB/s could transfer the data from a 512-byte sector in about 25 μs. Seek time and rotational latency are both on the order of 10 ms, so that during the combined access time about 200 KB could have been transferred. Thus it is important for the system designer to keep in mind that for transfers of a few blocks, almost all the time is spent in seek and rotational delay.

Sequential Sector Storage.   Access to a file that spans multiple sectors will be optimized when the sectors are stored sequentially on a given track, and when that track is full, continuing on the track that is the nearest from a seek-time standpoint. In drives made in earlier days, track-to-track spacing was large compared to the head-to-head misalignment of heads on different surfaces, and so it was advantageous to store contiguous sectors on all the tracks in a cylinder. This way there was no track-to-track seek until all the sectors in a cylinder had been read. The current generation of drives, with their small track-to-track spacing, have a head-to-head misalignment that is of the same order as track-to-track spacing, so heads on other surfaces cannot be guaranteed to be centered over tracks. Even the concept of a cylinder is not very useful with such drives, so data are read from adjoining tracks on the same surface, at least across a single zone, as defined in the following section.

Zone-Bit Recording.   The sectoring shown in Figure 9.4 is wasteful. The maximum bit recording density is achieved only on the innermost track, and the bit spacing on the outermost tracks may be 3 to 4 times as large as on the innermost track. To counteract this waste, nearly all drive manufacturers now employ a technique known as *zone-bit recording*. With this technique the disk surface is divided into from 4 to 30 or more *zones*. Progressing out disk zones from the innermost zone, each zone contains on *its* innermost track the maximum number of sectors permitted by the maximum areal density of the drive. This means that the number of sectors per track changes from zone to zone; it might range from 40 on the innermost track to 80 on the outermost track, for example. Note also that since the rotational speed does not change as the heads move from zone to zone, the data rate will change as the head moves from zone to zone. This complicates the job of the drive electronics, since the bit clock must be changed each time the head crosses zones.

This variation in the number of sectors per track across zones also complicates the sectoring of the drive. The current trend is to separate synchronization information from sector information. That way at least the clock that is checking sync information can run at a constant rate. In this technique there are synchronization "spokes" running from the innermost track of the disk to the outermost, similar in appearance to the dashed lines in Figure 9.4. When a portion of a sector falls on top of a synchronization spoke in a given zone, the sector is split in two, with part stored before the synchronization information and part after. In its most sophisticated form, the drive does not encode sector IDs at each individual sector, relying instead on the information embedded at each spoke to identify upcoming sectors.

Zone-bit recording plays havoc with any attempt by the operating system to specify access to a specific physical sector and track, because any attempt to do so would require the operating system to know about zones and sectors per track in each zone. As a consequence, the contemporary disk controller transparently maps LBAs to physical blocks whose block addresses bear no relationship to those specified by the operating system. Newer disk controllers even allow the operating system to specify all requests by sector number only, starting with 0 and increasing up to the maximum number of sectors on the drive, without specifying tracks, heads, or cylinders.

GETTING SPECIFIC: THE IBM 75GXP The IBM 75GXP is a 4"w × 6"l × 1"d drive that is suitable for a personal computer. It has a capacity of 76 GB, a rotational speed of 7200 rpm, 5 platters, and 10 read-write heads. It has 15 physical zones, with 370 to 792 sectors per track, resulting in data rates of from 174 to 374 Mbps. The drive has 34,327 tracks, and 512 byte sectors. It has an average seek time of 9.2 ms. It has a track density of 28,350 tracks per inch and a maximum areal density of 11 Gb/in^2. ■

9.2 Improving Disk System Performance and Reliability

There have been in recent years new ways developed of increasing both disk system performance and disk system security. With the increased capacity of today's disk drives comes the desire to record and play back multimedia materials such as movies and home video. Digital camcorders and other multimedia devices such as DVDs place considerable stress on disk system throughput. And it has become increasingly difficult to back up these large-capacity disk drives. No other storage technology, be it tape, DVD-ROM, or other removable media, has kept up with the increase in storage capacity of the disk drive. Prior to the early 1990s it was possible to back up a hard drive with one tape drive or a few Zip disks. With today's 100 GB disk drives, it would take roughly 20 tapes, 200 CDROM disks, or 500 Zip disks to back up the drive!

This section describes two technologies that address these problems: RAID, Redundant Array of Inexpensive Disk, technology uses multiple disk drives in various configurations to improve disk system performance and/or reliability. The SMART, Self Monitoring and Reporting Technology has been adopted by the disk drive industry as a means of automatically monitoring disk drive performance and reporting possible potential future failures to the user.

9.2.1 RAID: REDUNDANT ARRAYS OF INEXPENSIVE DISKS

The concept of configuring an array of disk drives to improve the performance and/or reliability of disk systems originated at the University of California at Berkeley's Computer Science Department, in research by Patterson, Gibson, and Katz. They described six ways in which disk arrays could be used: RAID Levels 0 through 5. We describe them below:

RAID Level 0. Level 0 actually does nothing to improve reliability, only speed. Level 0 employs an array of disks and distributes the contents of each file across each disk, in "stripes." When a portion of a file is requested by the operating systems, all disks that contain some of that portion go into action simultaneously, which can result in a great increase in disk read and write performance. Most disk controllers and operating systems support RAID level 0.

RAID Level 1. Level 1 is sometimes referred to as "mirroring." A mirrored system contains exactly two disks, each of which has exactly the same contents: All reads and writes are made to each drive simultaneously. If one drive fails, the single remaining good drive can be used with no loss of data or throughput. Nearly all disk controllers and operating systems support Level 1 as well.

RAID Level 2. Level 2 implements striping at the bit level, along with additional bits that are used to detect and correct errors. Each bit from each byte is stored in a separate drive, with additional drives to store the error checking and correction (ECC) bits. ECC uses Hamming encoding to encode the ECC bits. See Section 8.5.2 for details of Hamming encoding. Because of the high cost and complexity of Level 2, it is seldom used.

RAID Level 3.   Level 3 stripes data across multiple disks, like Level 0, but the striping is at the byte level. An additional disk is used to store ECC information during each disk write. Level 3 has the advantage of high data-read rates, but data writes are slow because of the need to compute the ECC information as the data are written to the other drives.

RAID Level 4.   As with Level 3, Level 4 combines disk striping with parity. The major difference is each disk acts independently, and thus it does not have to be synchronized. Each disk can work concurrently on different application I/O requests. Parity is still stored on a single disk. It is like Level 3 except that it uses blocks instead of bytes for striping. It is slightly slower at large file reads, but can act on independent tasks simultaneously. This is of great advantage when operating in a "transaction" environment, such as an airline reservation system, where multiple independent transactions must be handled simultaneously. When there is a disk failure, data reconstruction slows the system considerably.

RAID Level 5.   Level 5 is similar to Level 4 except that it stripes both data and parity across three or more drives. Thus it writes data and parity blocks across all the drives in the array. This removes the "bottleneck" that the dedicated parity drive represents, improving write performance slightly and allowing somewhat better parallelism in a multiple-transaction environment, although the overhead necessary in dealing with the parity once again slows down writes. The parity information for any given block of data are placed on a drive separate from those used to store the data itself. The performance of a RAID 5 array can be "adjusted" by trying different stripe sizes until one is found that is well-matched to the application being used.

Several additional levels have been developed that expand the trade-off between data rates and immunity to hardware failure. RAID systems are used extensively in large systems that must maintain reliability. Often the drives are "hot pluggable." See the further discussion on the hot-plugability of USB and FireWire devices in Section 10.4.1.

9.2.2   SMART DISK DRIVES

Disk drives seldom go suddenly from perfect operation to complete failure, though it may seem so to the hapless owners of such drives. Most total failures are preceded by increasing levels of errors that are silently corrected by the disk's microprocessor. In 1994 the disk drive industry adopted a standardized specification for issuing failure warnings called SMART, Self Monitoring and Reporting Technology. The SMART drive monitors error rates, and when they exceed a certain level, the drive produces a warning that is transmitted by the drive's interface.

Virtually all disk drive manufacturers implement the SMART technology, but most operating systems have not been upgraded to process these warnings. There are, however, a number of shareware programs that enable the SMART technology.

9.3   Other Mass Storage Devices

There are many variations on the magnetic hard disk described above. They are all based on moving some physical medium by a stationary or near-stationary head.

Magnetic Tape.   The use of magnetic tape as a computer storage medium predates the use of the disk drive, probably due to its previous development as a storage medium for analog audio applications. Magnetic tape drives are still used in computer applications, chiefly for backup or for archival storage, which can write and read long blocks of contiguous information. The main reason they are not used for other purposes is the long latency that results from having to move serially through the tape, a process which can take several minutes in the worst case. There are still significant developments taking place in the industry, however; for example, a postage-stamp-sized tape and drive with 1 GB capacity is presently under development.

The CD and CD ROM.   The compact disk (CD) and CD ROM store data in a manner slightly different from that of the magnetic hard disk. Rather than being divided and stored into concentric tracks, data are laid down in one continuous spiral track that begins at the center of the disk and proceeds to the outside. Bits are encoded as small pits in the reflective surface of the disk. An infrared laser in the playback head is used to bounce light off the surface, and a detector in the head senses the reflections from the pits as they pass under the head. When used for its originally designed purpose of audio playback, the CD guarantees a constant sustained data rate of $44,100 \times 2$ 16-bit words per second, 1 word for each stereo channel. Each 16-bit word represents the amplitude of the audio signal during the sampling period. The word stream is run through a digital-to-analog converter (DAC) that converts each 16-bit word to an analog signal. After filtering to remove high-frequency noise caused by the conversion process, the original analog waveform is restored to an accuracy of one part in 65,536, with a frequency response of 5 Hz to 20 KHz.

The pits are recorded on the disk a constant distance apart, so the speed of the disk must be changed as the head moves from center to outside to keep the data rate constant. Varying the drive speed is not as much of a problem with the CD player as with the hard disk, because rotation speed is only about 300 rpm, which results in an average rotational latency of approximately 100 ms. This 100 ms latency is abysmally long for computer data storage, and as a result, CD ROM drives have been developed that run at 4 to 10 times the speed of the audio player. In both the audio and CD ROM formats, additional ECC bits are added.

Key Concepts: Mass Storage Devices

- Disk, tape, and CD ROM are at present the primary devices for storing large volumes of data in current computer systems.
- All require physical movement to reach the position where data are to be read or written.
- Data can be transferred at rates of tens of megabytes per second. Thus blocks of 1 KB can be accessed in tens of microseconds, but it takes on the order of 10 ms to reach the data.
- The physical characteristics of disks require data location by surface, track, and sector. This complex addressing must be dealt with either by the computer designer or the disk controller designer.

9.4 Display Devices

The video monitor is the most common output device in general purpose computers today, although flat-panel displays of various kinds are becoming increasingly popular, especially in laptop and portable computers. The video display system, like the hard disk drive, places considerable demands on the processor. Many modern computer systems are touted as being "multimedia ready." This is usually taken to mean that the system is capable of playing back movies and animations in real time, which means that the video display system must be capable of displaying 10 to 30 frames of animation or video per second.

We begin by describing the video monitor and how it is employed in various kinds of video display systems. Then we discuss the details of the interface between the video display system and the computer.

9.4.1 VIDEO MONITORS

The video monitors used in today's computers descended from the television set, which first came into common use nearly 50 years ago. In fact, the television set contains a video monitor within it. The "front end" of the television set contains a tuner and frequency converter that allows the selection of one channel from the dozens or hundreds of channels coming from the cable or antenna. The selected channel is converted to a video signal, which is input to a video monitor within the TV set. The video monitor used in computer applications has a higher spatial resolution than the monitor in the TV set, but is otherwise the same. *Spatial resolution* is the number of dots per inch that can be distinguished on the screen.

spatial resolution

Principles of Operation. The video monitor used for computer applications may be color or black and white. If it is a color monitor, it may receive its input from the computer as a single signal, called composite video, or as three separate signals, one for each of the three primary video colors, red, green, and blue (the RGB monitor). Monitors also vary in their bandwidth, measured in Mbps and expressed in MHz. A monitor's bandwidth translates directly into spatial resolution, since the bandwidth determines how many pixels can be written to the screen per unit time. However, all monitors operate on essentially the same principles. A pixel-serial analog signal is presented to the monitor, which paints it onto the screen at a fixed rate, usually 60 frames per second.

Figure 9.8 shows a simplified view of the operation of a black-and-white video monitor. The input signals contain pixel intensity and vertical and horizontal synchronization (sync) information. Circuitry within the monitor extracts the pixel intensity information and presents it to the electron gun of the cathode ray tube (CRT). The electron gun emits a stream of electrons proportional to that intensity. The electrons are accelerated toward the screen by the applied high-voltage power supply shown at the bottom of the figure. When the electrons strike the screen, they cause the phosphor coating to glow, or phosphoresce, for 1 to 10 ms, lending a slight persistence to the image, thereby reducing flicker.

The beam is deflected, or swept, from left to right and top to bottom by the horizontal and vertical sweep, or deflection, currents applied to the deflection yoke shown at the neck

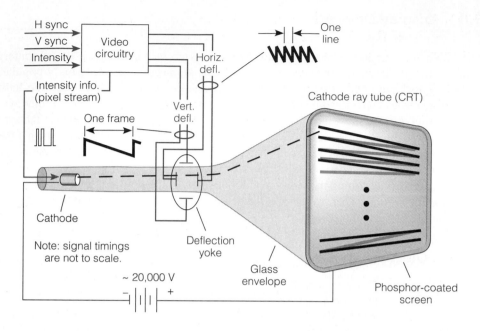

Fig. 9.8 Schematic View of a Black-and-White Video Monitor

of the tube. In reality, the deflection yoke employs inductors, rather than the plates shown in the figure. Oscillators within the monitor generate the sawtooth-shaped horizontal and vertical sweep signals. The sweep signals are synchronized with the video information by vertical and horizontal synchronization pulses generated by the computer. The sync pulses may be on separate signal lines, as shown, or they may be combined with the video (pixel) information and separated out by the monitor circuitry.

raster

The left-to-right, top-to-bottom scanning pattern is known as a *raster*, and such a screen is said to be raster-scanned. The horizontal and vertical scan frequencies that the monitor expects must be reasonably near the scan frequencies of the video input signal to allow the sync signals to adjust the sweeps to the exact data rate. Horizontal scan frequency is given by the number of lines per frame times the number of frames per second, and vertical scan frequency is just the number of frames per second. Vertical scan frequency is usually 60 Hz, for two reasons: It is close to the AC line frequency, which is good for technical reasons, and it is faster than the eye can follow, so no flicker is observed.

Color Monitors. Color monitors have three separate electron guns, one for each of the primary video colors, red, green, and blue. At each pixel location on the screen, there are three small phosphor dots, one that emits red light, one that emits green light, and one that emits blue light. Each electron gun is focused on its own color phosphor dot. In the less-expensive *composite video color monitors*, a single video input contains all information about color, intensity, and sync, and the video circuitry must extract the three color signals from it, along with the sync signals. The more expensive *RGB monitors* have three separate input signals, one each for red, green, and blue, with the horizontal

composite video
color monitors

RGB monitors

and vertical sync pulses usually riding on the green signal. RGB monitors tend to have better resolution, since there is no opportunity for "smearing" of one color's information into another.

Bandwidth and Resolution.   Monitors differ widely in their ability to resolve, that is to faithfully display the signals presented to them. Resolution can be expressed as the number of lines that can be distinguished on the screen, or as the number of pixels or characters that can be distinguished horizontally and vertically. *Dot pitch* relates resolution to screen size: It is the number of pixels per inch of screen. A common dot pitch is 72 dpi (dots per inch), giving a dot spacing of 0.28 mm. A dot pitch of 72 dpi is common and convenient, because newspaper and book publishers and font and printer manufacturers all specify character fonts in points, with 72 points per inch. This means that fonts displayed on a 72 dpi monitor will be displayed at the same size on the monitor as they will when printed, the so-called WYSIWYG mode—"What you see is what you get."

    dot pitch

Bandwidth refers to the number of pixels per second that the monitor can display faithfully. For example, a monitor with a resolution of 640×480 (h $\times$ v) black-and-white pixels having a refresh rate of 60 Hz would have a bandwidth of 18.4 MHz.

Broadcast and cable television signals in North America are transmitted as 60 interlaced half-frames of 262 lines each second, for an effective maximum resolution of 525 lines at a full-frame rate of 30 Hz. The 60 Hz interlaced half-frames are used to avoid the flicker that the eye would perceive at 30 Hz. In actuality, the FCC limits the bandwidth of over-the-air broadcast signals to 3 MHz to conserve space in the frequency spectrum, so the theoretical bandwidth of the television set of approximately $525 \times 525 \times 30 = 8$ MHz is impossible to achieve in practice.

If a video monitor with a 60 Hz refresh rate is displaying text at the common display resolution of 80×24 characters, and each character is composed of an 8×10 pixel array, then the bandwidth required to read the characters is

$$80 \times 8 \times 24 \times 10 \times 60 = 9 \text{ MHz}$$

Thus the television set has insufficient bandwidth to serve as a monitor for most computer applications.

9.4.2   MEMORY-MAPPED VIDEO AND VIDEO DISPLAY TERMINALS

The most common way of using the video monitor as a computer peripheral is by means of memory-mapped video, used when the monitor is located no more than a few feet from the rest of the computer. Not as frequently seen today, but still in use, is the video display terminal, normally only used when the monitor is located at a distance from the rest of the computer or when the computer is infrequently accessed, as is the case in computers used as servers, for example.

The two approaches have in common the concept of a block of memory, variously referred to as the *display memory*, screen buffer, or video RAM, which is mapped or swept onto the screen once each frame-display time, approximately 60 times per second, by the video drive circuitry. Thus characters that are copied into the frame buffer get mapped onto the screen within 1/60th of a second.

    display memory

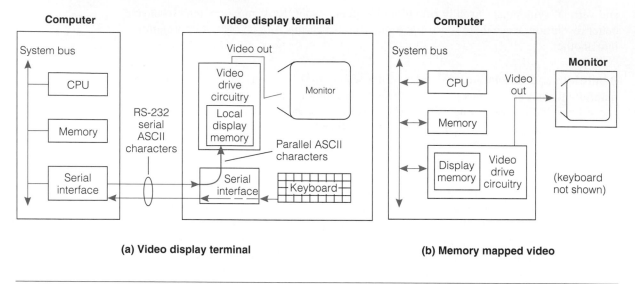

Fig. 9.9 Two Video Display Methods: The Video Display Terminal and Memory-Mapped Video

Memory-mapped video and the video display terminal are shown schematically in Figure 9.9 and described in more detail in the sections that follow.

Video Display Terminals.   The *video display terminal*, or VDT, packages the monitor and display memory with an RS-232 serial interface. It is used when the distance between the computer and monitor is more than a few feet. RS-232 signals can be propagated for over 1,000 ft. using ordinary twisted-pair wire, or for many miles using modems, whereas video signals cannot be transmitted more than a few dozen feet without observable degradation. The VDT has the disadvantage that only ASCII characters can be transmitted, and usually at rates of no more than 28.8 Kbps. This can be a serious limitation. Essentially only text can be transmitted, both because of the small bandwidth and because of the limitation to ASCII characters.

Being designed for use at considerable distance from the computer, the VDT nearly always includes a keyboard for input, except for simple information displays like those in airports. Notice that the VDT has its own local screen buffer. Each character only needs to be transmitted once, as it is stored in the local buffer. On the other hand, this means that the computer must transmit and the VDT must process the ASCII control characters to perform screen operations such as backspace, carriage return, clear screen, tab, and so on, as well as scrolling text up the screen when the screen is full. Because of this complexity, there is always a processor within the VDT to assist with these actions. In fact, Datapoint Corporation's request to Intel in the early 1970s to develop a small processor for use as a VDT controller resulted in the development of the Intel 8008, an 8-bit microprocessor that can be said to have ushered in the microprocessor era.

Memory-Mapped Video.   *Memory-mapped video* is much preferred when the monitor and keyboard are located near the computer because of the cost savings due to avoiding the serial interface, and the greatly increased bandwidth: tens of MHz instead of a maximum of

28 KHz. The display memory is located on the system bus, so the processor can transfer characters or graphic information to it at the full bandwidth of the bus. This makes graphics and even real-time video possible, although for the highest-speed graphics and video applications a special purpose video or graphics processor may be required. DMA can also be pressed into service to speed the copying of large blocks of memory into the display buffer.

Video Drive Circuitry.   The video drive circuitry cycles through the display RAM once each frame period, converting the RAM's contents to an analog bit stream and at the same time generating the sync signals. We first discuss the video circuitry that would be used in alphanumeric-only displays, that is, displays that are capable of displaying only alphanumeric (ASCII) characters. Then we discuss more complex, bit-mapped graphic displays.

Alphanumeric displays are only capable of displaying the printable ASCII characters. (Actually, since the ASCII code is a 7-bit code, some terminal vendors use the eighth, undefined bit, originally introduced as a parity check bit, to specify 128 additional characters. These characters may be from another alphabet, such as the Greek characters, or may represent primitive graphic objects such as line segments, etc.)

alphanumeric displays

Since the set of displayable objects is limited, it is possible to store their display patterns in a separate character memory. The character display pattern is a pattern of dots in a fixed rectangular array, 5×7, for example. When stored in a ROM, the memory is often referred to as a *character generator ROM*. Character generator ROMs containing various fonts and array sizes can be purchased from a number of vendors. Character generators for video display terminals accept two inputs: the ASCII value and the row or line desired. They output the bit pattern for the specified line. Figure 9.10 shows the character "A" on a 5×7 dot matrix, with an additional blank row and column on each side for spacing. The character generator is shown outputting the dot pattern for the second line of the input character, an "A" in this case.

character generator

The video controller is shown in Figure 9.11. The circuit displays 80 characters horizontally by 64 characters vertically. It uses the character generator of Figure 9.10, which

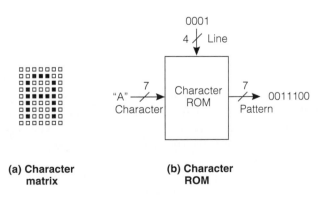

(a) Character matrix

(b) Character ROM

Fig. 9.10 Dot Matrix Characters and Character Generator

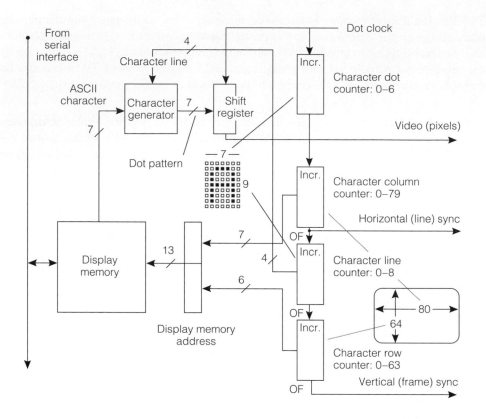

Fig. 9.11 Video Controller for an Alphanumeric Display

generates 7×9 dot matrix characters. The controller cycles through each row of 80 characters 9 times, once for each line making up the character, and then moves on to the next row, until all 64 rows have been displayed, and then it repeats. The ASCII values are accessed in the display memory by the 13-bit address formed by concatenating the character column number obtained from a modulo 80 counter with the character row number obtained from a modulo 64 counter. The purpose of the counter between them, a modulo 9 counter, is to allow the column counter to cycle through its count 9 times before the character row is incremented. As each character is fetched from the character memory, the proper line is selected by the character line counter and shifted out dot by dot, becoming the video signal. When 80 characters have been displayed, the mod-80 counter overflows, incrementing the character row counter and sending a horizontal sync pulse to the monitor. Likewise, when all rows have been displayed, the row counter overflows, sending a vertical sync pulse to the monitor.

Let us calculate the dot clock rate if the display is to run at 60Hz:

$$\text{Dot Rate} = \frac{60 \text{ frames}}{\text{sec.}} \times \frac{80 \text{ char}}{\text{row}} \times \frac{64 \text{ rows}}{\text{frame}} \times \frac{7 \text{ dots}}{\text{line}} \times \frac{9 \text{ lines}}{\text{char}} = 19.35 \text{ MHz}$$

Thus the display memory needs to supply somewhat less than 3 MB/s to the character generator. In like manner we can calculate the horizontal and vertical scan frequencies.

This use of two memories, the display memory accessing the character memory, is reminiscent of nanocoding as a means of minimizing memory usage, which we saw in Chapter 5. It suffers from the limitation that the only objects that can be displayed are those that are in the character ROM. Furthermore the video output is binary: Each pixel is either on or off. The memory-mapped video display, which we consider next, sheds both of these limitations: It can display arbitrary patterns and can be designed with more than 1 bit per pixel, allowing color or gray-scale images.

The *memory-mapped video display controller* does not suffer the limitation of having a slow serial interface between it and the processor's memory bus; thus, more complex information can be displayed at reasonable data rates. The basic structure of the controller is the same as that of Figure 9.11, except that the character memory is eliminated. The display memory contains pixel-by-pixel display information instead of character-by-character information. Additionally, instead of assigning just 1 bit per pixel, resulting in a binary image, 1 to 3 or more bytes can be devoted to each pixel, resulting in a gray-scale or colored image.

memory-mapped display controller

Figure 9.12 shows how a video controller for a 24-bit color monitor might be implemented. The display memory is 24 bits wide—that is, 24 bits per pixel. The CPU now must assume the task of writing the dot pattern representing the character, line, and so on, into the display memory, devoting 8 bits of each 24-bit pixel to each of the colors red,

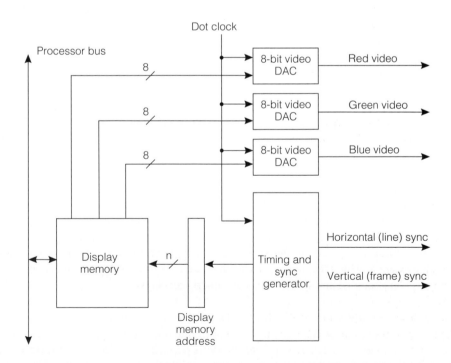

Fig. 9.12 Memory-Mapped Video Controller for 24-Bit Color Display

green, and blue. The 8 bits representing each color are sent to a separate video DAC (digital-to-analog converter). The DACs are referred to as *video DACs* because of the extremely high rates they must work at. Notice that they are clocked at the dot rate, which can be over 20 megapixels per second. Given the high bandwidth required for the display memory, page-mode and nibble-mode RAM, or VRAM, are often used. They have the advantage that once a given row is addressed in the RAM chip, the entire column can be shifted out without further addressing.

The processor overhead can be considerable in such a system. Separate video controllers have been designed that relieve the processor of much of the overhead. These controllers may incorporate DMA-like block-transfer capabilities and may also accept high-level commands such as the following:

draw_line(color, start point, end point, pensize, pattern), or
draw_char(color, font, point size, rotation, location).

This off-loading of the overhead of controlling a peripheral device to a controller that accepts high-level abstract commands is reminiscent of the disk controllers that were discussed earlier in the chapter.

9.4.3   FLAT-PANEL DISPLAYS

After years of being "next year's technology," flat-panel displays are becoming available in sizes and speeds appropriate to computer usage. There are many kinds of flat-panel displays available; we will describe just two, the passive matrix and active matrix liquid crystal displays. Both employ liquid crystals as the display medium. Liquid crystals are viscous, organic liquids that change their light transmittance and reflectivity in response to an applied electric field. The liquid crystal material is sandwiched between glass plates, with pixel drive circuitry deposited on the surfaces of the glass plates. Both kinds of displays operate by scanning the pixels row by row and column by column, as with video monitors. Most also employ backlighting, with each pixel being made more or less transparent by activating the pixel drive circuitry.

Passive-Matrix Liquid Crystal Displays.   The lower-cost passive-matrix displays employ horizontal and vertical electrodes, one for each pixel row and one for each pixel column. There is a driver transistor at the edge of each row and each column, so only $m + n$ drivers and $m + n$ drive lines are required for an $m \times n$ pixel display. Both scanning and pixel display occur by "addressing" each pixel in turn. A single row electrode is turned on, and then the column electrodes are cycled through one by one, with the applied electrode voltage determining the extent to which the pixel is activated. Passive-matrix displays are inexpensive, but tend to have less contrast and speed than active matrix displays.

Active-Matrix Liquid Crystal Displays.   The active matrix differs from the passive in having a drive transistor at each pixel, resulting in much more complex deposition on the front and back glass surfaces. A single electrode is deposited on one of the surfaces, and $m \times n$ drive transistors are deposited on the other surface for an $m \times n$ display. There must also be $m \times n$ drive lines. The controller IC to manage the display is generally included with it, so the $m \times n$ drive lines do not need to leave the display panel. Color is three times more complex: there are three drive transistors located at each pixel, one for each color. Precisely aligned *color filters* filter out all but the appropriate color at each pixel location.

color filters

Key Concepts: Visual Displays

- Maintaining a visual display requires refreshing a large amount of data at a rate fast enough so the eye detects no flicker.
- The high data rate applies to reading the display memory. Information may be written into the display memory at a lower rate.
- Video display terminals combine the monitor and display memory into a single remote unit, connected to the computer by a moderate-speed interface.
- Memory-mapped video drives the monitor directly from a display memory connected to the processor bus. The monitor must be located near the computer for this to be possible.
- High-speed character generator ROMs and video DACs are required to achieve high video data rates.
- Flat-panel displays use different technology, but place the same requirements for high data rates on the systems to which they are connected.

9.5 Printers

As with disk drives and video systems, there are many different kinds of printers that use many different print technologies. Furthermore there are several different kinds of "languages" that printers "understand." The slowest, simplest, and least expensive printers are of the dot-matrix and ink-jet variety; the fastest and most expensive are laser printers. As with video systems, the quest by printer manufacturers has been for higher speed and better image quality. In this section we briefly describe the operation of these printers and the three common languages that they understand.

9.5.1 PRINTER CHARACTERISTICS

If the disk drive and the video system are at the top end in terms of I/O bandwidth, and the keyboard and mouse at the bottom, printers are somewhere in the middle at the present time. In the past, printers printed only ASCII characters and had to rely on relatively cumbersome mechanisms. As a result, their bandwidth was in the range of several hundred characters per second—slow enough so that the slowest serial interface could more than keep up with the printer's I/O activity. This has changed. Even inexpensive printers are capable of printing color bit-mapped graphics at 300 dpi resolution, and data rates are in the Kbps to Mbps range for the modern printer.

printer bandwidth

The least expensive printers still use the standard RS-232 and parallel Centronics interfaces, which can both support the relatively small I/O demands of these printers. The more expensive printers require higher bandwidths than these interfaces can support. Many users of this class of printers want them to be shared among the computers on the local area network. Therefore, many of the more expensive printers are "network ready."

printer interfaces

The two most common network printer interfaces are the Ethernet and LocalTalk networks. We cover networks and networking in the next chapter; suffice it to say here that these interfaces allow any computer on the network to select and print to any printer on the network.

PostScript

In the past, printers behaved very much like the alphanumeric display terminals described in Section 9.4.2. They accepted an ASCII character stream and printed it in the font that was stored in the character ROM on board the printer.[1] The quest for "letter-quality" (≥ 300 dpi) output led to the development of the PostScript page description language by John Warnock, founder of Adobe Systems. PostScript printers have on-board PostScript processors that allow them to accept high-level PostScript print commands similar to the draw_line and draw_char commands mentioned previously. Fonts can be downloaded from the computer to the printer, and the printer can render the fonts at any specified point size. (Image rendering is the process of converting an image from some input format to the pixel stream or array that is to be painted on the output device.) There are also a number of proprietary high-level printer languages: Microsoft's PCL, Hewlett-Packard's HPGL, and Apple Computer's QuickDraw are three. PostScript is the dominant language at the present time. Printers that recognize a page-description language such as Postscript also have a proprietary low-level language that can receive a pixel-serial stream for printing.

9.5.2 Kinds of Printers

dot matrix printer

The *dot matrix printer* employs a print head that has a number of solenoid-activated pins that strike an inked ribbon, transferring a column at a time of "pixels" of ink to the paper as the head moves from one side of the paper to the other. The number of pins is usually equal to the number of dots in a column of the character matrix. Thus, unlike the video display, the dot matrix printer prints a column of dots at a time instead of the single dot from the same row. Thus the character ROM must read out a column of pixels at a time instead of a row, as it does for video displays.

Figure 9.13 shows the character generator outputting the second column of the character "A" to the print head. The print head has activated the "on" solenoids, indicated in black. The solenoids of the dot matrix printer cannot be made close enough together to provide true letter-quality output, so there has been relatively little effort by dot matrix printer manufacturers to provide more sophisticated pixel-level control of the printer. As in the alphanumeric VDT, ASCII control characters such as return, tab, and so on, are used to control the location of the characters on the page.

laser printer

The *laser printer* operates by raster-scanning the image onto a rotating drum using a low-powered laser beam. The drum is initially positively charged, and that charge is neutralized wherever the beam strikes. The drum then passes through a bath of finely divided, negatively charged powder known as *toner.* Toner adheres to the drum where the positive charge remains and is transferred to the paper by heat and pressure. Much higher resolution is possible with this technology than with the dot matrix printer. Laser printers are available in resolutions of from 300 dpi to 1200 dpi.

---

1. The person of middle years will recall wryly that printers actually predated video display terminals by nearly 25 years.

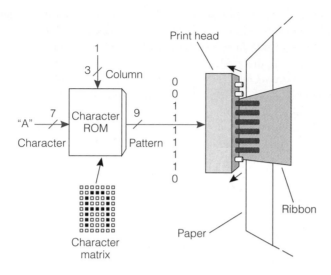

Fig. 9.13 Character Generation in Dot Matrix Printers

In the *ink-jet printer* the print head contains a cartridge or cartridges containing viscous inks. An extremely small jet of ink is squirted onto the paper by an ultrasonic transducer as the head moves across the paper, thereby forming the image. Ink-jet printers are intermediate in price and resolution between dot matrix printers and laser printers.

ink-jet printer

9.6   Input Devices

Most devices that rely on the human muscles and human reaction time to produce input data for the computer have very low data rate requirements. The lowest speed interface used with programmed I/O is sufficient for these devices. Interrupt control is used to manage what, from the point of view of program execution rates, is a very long delay between input operations. The most common computer input devices are the keyboard and the mouse. These two devices are among the least demanding in terms of I/O bandwidth, and are likely to remain so, given the low signaling rate of the human hand.

The *keyboard* predates the computer, having been used in telegraphy since the development of the Teletype in the 1920s. The maximum typing speed for the most skilled typist is 10 to 15 characters per second, for a maximum data rate of 120 bps, slower than the slowest serial communications channels. In Western countries the computer keyboard encodes the key pressed as an ASCII character. Most keyboards contain a buffer that holds 2 or more characters, so that if two keys are pressed in rapid succession the second keystroke will not be lost if the computer interface is tardy in accepting the character.

keyboard

The mouse is a common input device that allows the user to move the cursor rapidly over the screen for selecting or pointing. There are several kinds of mice available. The optical mouse relies on transmitting two pairs of low-powered optical signals from its bottom, one pair for the *x*-direction and one pair for the *y*. The mouse rests on a pad that has

mouse

horizontal and vertical lines drawn on it. The light reflected from these lines is sensed by two photodetectors, one for each dimension. The pulses from these photodetectors are transmitted to the mouse interface. The individual members of each pair of optical transmitters are set at a spacing that is slightly different from the line spacing on the pad, so the order in which signals are received from the two members of each pair tells the interface in which direction the mouse is moving—left to right, or right to left, for example.

Most mechanical mice rely on a hard rubber ball that rolls as the mouse is moved to drive two pairs of toothed wheels. Optical sensors on either side of each wheel are offset slightly so that once again the order in which the pair of signals arrives at the interface signals which direction the mouse movement had taken.

9.7 Interfacing to the Analog World

analog to digital converter, ADC

digital to analog converter, DAC

The computer is digital; the world is analog. Examples of interfaces between the two abound. There is an *analog-to-digital converter, ADC,* at the output of the microphones used in recording compact disks, and as mentioned previously, there is a DAC in the CD player to convert the digital signal back to analog form for amplification. We also mentioned that video DACs are required to drive gray-scale and color monitors. Figure 9.14 shows the typical interfaces encountered with the ADC and the DAC. The DAC simply takes a binary number as input and puts out an analog voltage. The ADC does a multistep process that may require a significant time for conversion. It therefore must synchronize using the handshaking signals, Clear, Clock, and Begin as input, outputting Done when conversion is complete.

9.7.1 DIGITAL-TO-ANALOG CONVERSION

The conversion of a digital signal to an analog signal is accomplished by summing the contribution of each bit to the overall analog voltage. For an unsigned integer that relationship will be given by

$$V_0 = \left(x_{n-1} + \frac{1}{2}x_{n-2} + \frac{1}{4}x_{n-3} + \ldots + \frac{1}{2^{n-1}}x_0 \right) k V_R \qquad \text{[Eq. 9.4]}$$

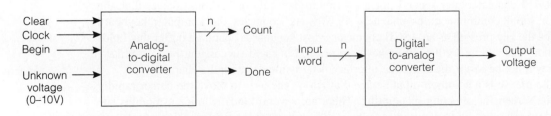

Fig. 9.14 ADC and DAC Interfaces

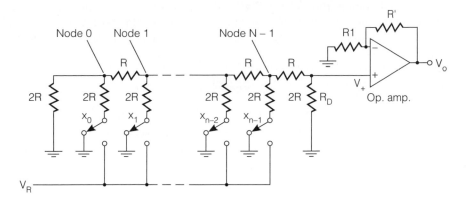

Fig. 9.15 The R-2R Ladder DAC

where V_o is the output voltage, x_i is the bit value of the ith bit, V_R is the reference voltage, and k is some constant. This conversion can be accomplished by summing the appropriately weighted current contributions from each bit at the input to an operational amplifier. Figure 9.15 shows such a circuit. It is called an *R-2R ladder DAC*, because the only resistance values used in the summing operation have values of R and 2R. Having all resistances in the ladder with values of R or 2R is a big advantage when integrating the circuit, since resistors of similar value are easier to make with precision than resistors of widely differing values. The switches in the figure are actuated by the individual bits $x_0 \ldots x_{N-1}$. Each switch connects its associated resistor to ground if the bit value is 0, or to V_R, the reference voltage, if the bit value is 1. The sum of currents flowing from V_P through each closed switch and thence through each node to R_D develop a voltage v_+, at the input to the operational amplifier. The operational amplifier amplifies that voltage to V_o, the output voltage.

R-2R ladder DAC

Observe that for all nodes in the ladder, the resistance is 2R to the left of the node, 2R to the right of the node, and 2R looking toward the switch. Thus when a given switch is connected to V_R, the current flowing through it due to V_R is $V_R/3R$, and that current is split equally at the node, with $\frac{1}{2}$ flowing to the left and $\frac{1}{2}$ to the right. Each node that is connected to V_R makes its own contribution to the current flowing through R_D, but that contribution is halved at each intervening node: Half of the current flowing into a node from the right flows downward to the switch and half flows to the right toward R_D. The voltage developed at the output from the msb, x_{N-1}, will be

$$V_{o(N-1)} = \frac{V_R}{3} \frac{R_1 + R'}{R_1} \qquad \text{[Eq. 9.5]}$$

and the contribution from x_{N-2} will be half that, and so on. The total voltage developed will therefore be:

$$V_o = \left(x_{n-1} + \frac{1}{2} x_{n-2} + \frac{1}{4} x_{n-3} + \cdots + \frac{1}{2^{n-1}} x_0 \right) V_R \frac{R_1 + R'}{3R_1} \qquad \text{[Eq. 9.6]}$$

thus achieving the desired behavior.

The conversion time from the time when the bits settle to their correct values until the time when the analog voltage has settled to its correct value will be determined by the stray capacitances in the network, and will be in the range of microseconds to nanoseconds.

9.7.2 ANALOG-TO-DIGITAL CONVERSION

There are many designs for ADCs that provide a wide range of precision and conversion time to meet applications requirements. The conversion time needed may vary from microseconds to seconds, and the requirements for measurement precision may vary from 4 bits to 16 or more. Here we will describe two kinds of ADC: the counting converter and the successive-approximation converter.

The Counting ADC. In the counting ADC a counter drives a DAC (!) whose output is sent to an analog comparator that stops the counter when the DAC output is equal to the voltage of the unknown analog input signal. Figure 9.16 shows how this is accomplished. The interface circuitry begins the counting operation by issuing a Clear signal, then a Begin signal to the converter. Next the counter begins counting, with the counter output driving the DAC. As long as the output voltage from the DAC is less than the voltage being measured, the output of the comparator is 0 and the counter continues counting. When the reference voltage from the DAC becomes greater than the input voltage being measured, the comparator's output goes from 0 to 1, stopping the counter and issuing a Done signal. The completion time will depend on the value of the voltage being measured, and the maximum measurement time will be $\tau \times 2^n$ where τ is the clock period. The successive-approximation converter avoids this long conversion time.

Successive-Approximation ADC. The successive-approximation converter avoids the 2^n dependence of count time by replacing the counter with a digital circuit that "homes in" on the correct value by testing each bit in turn from msb to lsb to see whether the approximation is less than or greater than the unknown voltage. Figure 9.17 shows the circuitry involved. The successive approximation performs, in effect, a binary search, as shown by the example of a 3-bit successive-approximation conversion in Figure 9.18. The conversion now takes place in n clock cycles, resulting in a conversion time of $\tau \times n$.

binary search

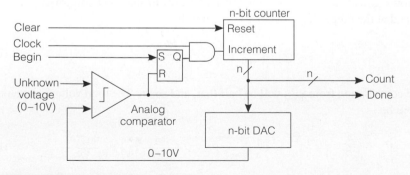

Fig. 9.16 Counting Analog-to-Digital Converter

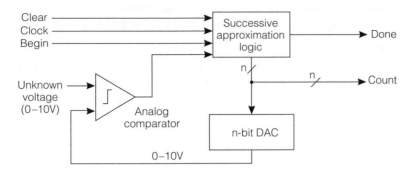

Fig. 9.17 Successive-Approximation ADC

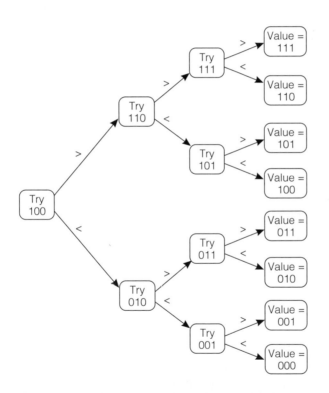

Fig. 9.18 Successive-Approximation Search Tree

9.7.3 ACCURACY AND ERRORS IN DACS AND ADCS

There is always error in any measurement. Even if the ADC or DAC is error-free, there must be an error in the digital representation of an analog value. In the ideal case it will be $\frac{1}{2}$ of a lsb. In digital-analog interfacing and conversion, this is referred to as *quantization*

quantization error

error. In production converters there will be additional errors due to "missing codes" in the converter, and gain and offset errors as well. This section presents a brief discussion of errors in converters.

Quantization Error.   Even the ideal ADC or DAC has a quantization error that varies from 0 to $\pm\frac{1}{2}$ lsb, depending upon the exact analog value being measured. Figure 9.19 shows the magnitude of the unavoidable quantization error introduced by a 3-bit converter with full-scale voltage input *Vf*. For an *n*-bit word the number of quantization intervals will be 2^n, and the error in the ideal case will range from 0 to $\pm\frac{1}{2}$ the quantization interval, which is $(Vf/2^n)/2 = Vf/2^{n+1}$. The *resolution* of a DAC or ADC is $Vf/2^n$.

Other Sources of Errors.   In addition to the quantization error, the converter may change its digital value earlier or later than it "should" in the ideal case. The maximum deviation from the ideal case is referred to as *differential nonlinearity*, and is usually expressed as fractions of a lsb or as a percentage of full-scale voltage.

Gain error, or *full-scale error*, is the difference between the ideal full-scale voltage, that is the voltage that should produce all 1's in an ADC or that is produced by all 1's in a DAC, and the actual voltage. It is expressed as fractional bits or as a percentage of full scale voltage.

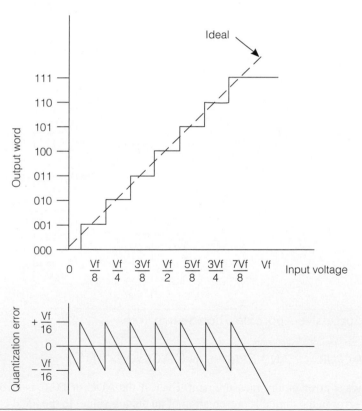

Fig. 9.19 Signal Quantization and Quantization Error by an ADC

Offset error in a DAC is the output voltage that exists when the input word is all 0's. The entire output voltage range is offset by this value.

offset error

Missing codes refers to a situation where an ADC has so much differential nonlinearity that the digital output skips a step—that is, there are one or more digital values that never occur.

missing codes

Monotonicity in a DAC is the (desirable) situation where the voltage never decreases with an increasing input word value, and *vice versa*.

monotonicity

Summary

Without peripheral devices the computing system would be of no value. The CPU can process only information it has collected from the outside world, and that information is of no use if it is not output to us, in a convenient and desirable form.

- At present, the disk drive provides the highest storage capacity at the lowest per-bit cost for random access data. In most virtual memory systems it is at the end of the hierarchy. Its high latency and bandwidth present a significant challenge to the computer architect. The modern disk drive may have an on-board processor that is more powerful in terms of sheer throughput than the CPU of the system to which it is interfaced.

- The video monitor is the primary real-time output device for most computing systems. Like the disk drive, its bandwidth requirements stress most computers, and as a result, it also may have a special purpose processor that accepts high-level graphics commands, relieving the CPU of the details of converting the graphical information to pixels.

- Printers provide us with paper copies of processed information. There is a wide range of cost and capability in printers also. The most powerful printers can also stress the ability of the CPU to keep up with their bandwidth. As with video monitors, most printers contain processors that manage the details of converting high-level printer control languages such as PostScript to the low-level, bit-mapped data that is written onto the paper.

- The world is analog, the computer digital; thus the need for ADCs and DACs. These devices are present in every CD player and other audio device, and are available in a wide range of conversion accuracy and speed.

Bibliography

Because of the proprietary nature of the technological advances in disk drives and printers, there is not much published literature about them. Manufacturer's literature and industry publications are the best source of up-to-date information. See, for example, the following:

Seagate Product Guide, Seagate Technology, 920 Disk Drive, Scotts Valley, CA 95066.

Electronic Design, Penton Publishing, Cleveland, OH.

The original paper describing the RAID concept is:

D. A. Patterson and G. Gibson and R. H. Katz, *A Case for Redundant Arrays of Inexpensive Disks (RAID)*, Proc ACM SIGMOD Conf, Chicago, IL, Jun 1988.

A good source of information about video monitors and flat-panel displays is:

J. A. Castellano, *Video Display Engineering*, McGraw-Hill Professional Publishing, New York NY, 2000.

There is a good discussion of analog interfacing techniques in the following texts:

Stuart Ball, *Analog Interfacing to Embedded Microprocessors: Real World Design*, Elsevier Science, St. Louis, MO, 2001.

P. Horowitz and W. Hill, *The Art of Electronics*, 2nd ed., Cambridge University Press, New York, 1989.

Exercises

9.1 A 128 K byte block of data are read from a disk drive. What is the overall data transmission rate if the disk drive has a latency of 4 ms, and a burst bandwidth of 16 MB per second?   **(§9.1)**

9.2 A hard drive has eight surfaces, with 4192 tracks per surface and a constant 2048 sectors per track. Sector size is 1 K bytes. The average seek time is 8 ms, the track-to-track access time is 1.5 ms, and the drive runs at 7200 rpm. Successive tracks in a cylinder can be read without head movement.

   a. What is the drive capacity?

   b. What is the average access time for the drive?

   c. Estimate the time required to transfer a 5 MB file.

   d. What is the burst transfer rate?   **(§9.1)**

9.3 A floppy disk drive has a maximum areal bit density of 1024 bits per mm^2. Its innermost track is at a radius of 2.5 cm, and its outermost track is at a radius of 5 cm. It rotates at 300 rpm.

   a. What is the total capacity of the drive?

   b. What is its burst data rate in bytes per second?   **(§9.1)**

9.4 An advanced hard disk uses zone-bit recording. Its innermost track is at an inside diameter of 0.5". There are 2048 sectors on the innermost track, each of which holds 512 bytes. Track-to-track spacing is 0.1 mm, and the disk rotates at 7,200 rpm. The designer has decided to create a new zone each time an additional, complete sector can be added. What will be the inside diameter of the second zone?   **(§9.1)**

9.5 It is said that A. Morita, when he was president of Sony Corporation, insisted during the development of the compact disk that it be able to hold the longest version of Beethoven's Ninth Symphony, which is the longest symphony in the common classical music repertory. Sony engineers scoured the used record bins, and the longest version of the symphony they could find played for 74 minutes. Assume a 10% overhead for ECC bits, and so on, and assume that the bits are spaced equally in the radial and tangential directions. The active area has an inside diameter of 42 mm and an outside diameter of 112 mm.

   a. What must the total bit capacity of the drive be to meet Mr. Morita's specification?

   b. What is the areal density of the disk?   **(§9.1)**

9.6 A VDT has a 70 Hz refresh rate and displays 80×64 dot matrix characters. Each character is on a 9×12 dot matrix, including intercharacter spacing.

   a. What must the size of the display memory be?

   b. What is the dot clock frequency?   **(§9.2)**

9.7 VDTs receive their characters as a serial stream from the host computer, as shown in Figure 9.11. The figure is incomplete, however, as it does not show how the display controller handles scrolling and the screen control characters such as return, delete, tab, and so on. Modify the figure to show how this character control is achieved by including the hardware to handle scrolling and the return character. Assume scrolling is line by line. That is, when the screen is full of lines, the next arriving character causes the display to scroll up one line, so that the top line scrolls off the screen.   **(§9.2)**

9.8 An advanced color monitor has a $1{,}280 \times 1{,}024$ pixel display, at 90 dpi. It can display 24 bits per pixel. The refresh rate is 70 Hz.

    a. What is the active display area, $h \times v$?

    b. What is the rate at which the 24-bit wide memory must be accessed in bytes/second?

    c. What is the monitor frequency?   **(§9.2)**

9.9 Estimate the data rate between a computer and printer if the printer is printing a 72 dpi, full-page graphic. Pick a specific printer for your calculations, and attach a copy of its specifications. State any assumptions you have to make.   **(§9.3)**

9.10 A 5" × 7", 24-bit color image with a resolution of 300 dpi is to be printed on a 300 dpi color laser printer. How many bytes will be transmitted to the printer, and how long will it take to transmit them over a 9600 bps serial line, assuming a 10-bit serial frame? (See Figure 10.6 for the definition of a serial frame.)   **(§9.3)**

9.11 A 16-bit, 0–10 volt ADC is being clocked at 10 MHz.

    a. What is the maximum conversion time?

    b. What would the conversion time be if the converter were a successive approximation type?   **(§9.5)**

9.12 A laboratory instrument requires 5 mV accuracy on a 12 V, full-scale measurement, and must be able to acquire 100 samples per second. Specify the ADC that will meet these requirements.   **(§9.5)**

9.13 A data logging device in a chemical plant needs to acquire voltages from each of 150 devices at least once per second with an accuracy of 5 mV. Full-scale voltage of the sensors is 10 volts. Design a data acquisition system that employs one ADC and analog multiplexers (multiplexers with digital select but analog data inputs and outputs) to sample the data. Your data logger should have a 16-bit parallel interface. Upon receipt of the sensor number, ranging from 0 to 149, the logger should respond with the digital value after conversion.   **(§9.5)**

Communications, Networking, and the Internet

The first widely used computer communications standard, the EIA RS-232 point-to-point communications protocol, was introduced in 1962. Not long thereafter a number of researchers began the serious study of the issues involved in interconnecting not just two computers, but many. Much of this early research was funded by the Department of Defense's Advanced Research Projects Agency, ARPA, later known as DARPA, D for defense. The first experiments were conducted in 1969, and by 1974–75 the ARPANET, as it was known at the time, supported a few dozen hosts running telnet (a remote login capability), ftp (file transfer protocol, the ability to send and receive arbitrary files from host to host), and e-mail. During this period, DARPA program manager R. E. Kahn began funding research into "internetting"; that is, forming an *internet* by connecting many networks of computers.

Thus the ARPANET evolved into *the* Internet, by far the largest and most complex information system on the planet. When the first edition of this book was being written, in 1995, there were about 4 million host computers "on the net." By 2003 this number had grown to over 170 million. Large organizations may have their own internets, but *the* Internet is unique. Over the last 25 years networking has evolved from a research curiosity to an integral and taken-for-granted part of the computer system, and anyone involved with the design and architecture of computers should understand the principles of operation of networks and the Internet. This chapter is intended to provide this knowledge.

During these discussions we will often use bottom-up descriptions, where we describe the low-level hardware and data-link details before getting on to the higher levels of the communications process. We justify this approach as moving from the already-known, the transfer of bits from one place to another, to the less-known, more abstract details of network communications protocols.

Thus we begin the chapter with a discussion of network-level issues: what physical media are used, and how a number of computers share the same data link. This will lead to a discussion of network topologies—that is, the interconnection strategies that are used in various networks. The focus is on the wires, or links, over which data passes because they are long, expensive, and have limited capacity. Thus their importance begins to exceed that of computation and switching.

Above the network hardware are the layers of abstraction that create the appearance of a seamless interface between an application program running on one machine and an application program running on another machine. We discuss several of the most common layer models.

We then present examples of three representative network implementations. The example for serial data communications protocols in Section 10.2 is the EIA RS-232 and similar protocols that allow point-to-point communications. The Ethernet protocol serves as an example in Section 10.3 for local area networks, or LANs, with extents of a mile or less. The final example in Section 10.5 is the Internet, the 900-pound gorilla of contemporary internetworking.

10.1 Computer to Computer Data Communications

The issues involved in designing a data communications system for communication between and among computers begin with deciding how many computers should be interconnected, and by what means they should communicate. The higher-level issues are those such as which applications will use the network, their data rates, reliability requirements, and so on. At the lowest level are issues dealing with the data link: signaling protocols, hardware interfaces, and physical wiring.

communications
protocols

Communication between any two entities implies that they "speak the same language"; that is, they rely on common *communications protocols*. These protocols settle issues at all layers of the system, from machine names to wire types. As might be expected, standards committees oversee and approve communications protocols. They range in size and formality from the International Standards Organization (ISO), whose representatives are appointed by member nations, to the Internet Society, which develops and modifies the standards that apply to the Internet, and whose membership is open to all. Both of these bodies have developed standards for the protocols used by various layers in the communications process. These layered protocols are sometimes referred to informally as *protocol*

protocol stacks

stacks, with the applications layer being on the top and the physical layer on the bottom.

10.1.1 NETWORK STRUCTURES AND COMMUNICATIONS CHANNELS

entity or station

When referring to networks and communications, we use the term *entity* or *station* to refer to any device that transmits or receives information on the network—not only computers in the normally accepted sense, but also devices such as VDTs (video display terminals), special purpose processors, and bridges and routers used to interconnect networks. We use the term *data link* to refer to the path connecting two or more entities, and *physical link* to refer to the physical characteristics of that path.

data link

physical link

Network Communications Mechanisms.   Among the more interesting questions to be resolved in network communications is "Who talks when?" When two communicating entities use the communications link, there are three possibilities:

1. *Simplex* communications links allow data transmission in one direction only. This communications method is seldom used, as it does not allow for transmission of link status back to the transmitting station. An example of simplex communications would be a remote sensor that communicates temperature or some other measurement to a computer for data logging.

   simplex

2. *Half-duplex* communications allow transmission in either direction, but only one entity may transmit at a time. Taxicab and police radio communications are examples of half-duplex communications. A tri-state bus is also half-duplex, since only one source can send at a time.

   half-duplex

3. *Full-duplex* communications allow both entities to transmit simultaneously. The telephone system operates in full duplex mode, allowing callers at both ends of the link to talk at once—unfortunately, some would say.

   full-duplex

Time-Division and Frequency-Division Multiplexing.   When more than one entity is using the same data link at the same time, it must be *multiplexed* among the entities. There are two common kinds of multiplexing: *frequency-division multiplexing (FDM)* and *time-division multiplexing (TDM)*. FDM divides the communications link into frequency bands, normally allocating one band for each communicating entity. TDM divides the communications link into time slots, one for each entity currently sharing the channel.

FDM devotes a modulator-demodulator pair to each frequency channel on the data link, allowing each communicating pair to use the link as if they were the only entities using it. The cable TV system is an example of an (analog) FDM system. The cable company modulates each cable channel to a different frequency, and the cable box at the TV set demodulates the desired channel. (More precisely it remodulates it to channel 3 and sends it on to the TV set, which is tuned to receive channel 3.) In FDM each of the n communication channels has $1/n$th of the total bandwidth of the link reserved to it, and with FDM only that $1/n$th fraction of the total bandwidth will be available to it no matter how many or few other entities are using the link. FDM is not used as often as TDM because of this limitation and also the greater cost of the hardware. We will not discuss FDM further. The rest of this chapter will discuss TDM data links, by far the most popular for computer communications.

Time-division multiplexing shares the communications channel by slicing it into time slots and dynamically allocating a time slot for each station that wishes to use the channel. The time slots may be as fine-grained as 1 bit per slot, or as coarse-grained as 8 K bytes or more per slot. On the average, the bandwidth when n entities are communicating using TDM is $1/n$ or less of the total bandwidth of the link. Because the allocation is dynamic, there is no limit to the number of entities that can use a TDM data link provided adequate bandwidth is available, and this is a major advantage of TDM. The total bandwidth of the link is divided among those entities using it at a given time, so, for example if only a single station is using the link, the entire bandwidth of the link is available to it, and if 100 stations are using the network, the average bandwidth will be reduced to 1/100th or less of the full bandwidth if they are all attempting to "talk at once." (The phrase "or less" is used because some networks do not handle contention for bandwidth gracefully, and a heavy load may cause the bandwidth to be reduced to levels much lower than the simple estimate above.)

baseband versus broadband

TDM systems use the entire frequency spectrum to form the digital signal, and are referred to as *baseband* systems. FDM systems that split the frequency spectrum into channels are called *broadband* systems.

Baseband Digital Signal-Encoding Methods.   There are many ways to encode baseband serial bit streams besides the ways we normally consider. Figure 10.1 shows four of the common ones.

RZ encoding

■ *RZ (return to zero) encoding,* sometimes referred to as pulse encoding, encodes one of the binary bit values as a high signal value, the other binary bit value as a low signal value, and the signal returns to zero in between each bit. RZ encoding provides a well-defined start to the beginning of each high bit, and is used where the transitions cause a specific action. The 1 bits act as clock pulses, and so encode information about the transmission rate.

NRZ encoding

■ *NRZ (non-return-to-zero) encoding* encodes the data exactly as RZ encoding does, but the bit value stays at its level, high or low, until the next bit change. Most of the signals inside the computer can be thought of as being encoded in NRZ form.

NRZI encoding

■ *NRZI (non-return-to-zero inverted)* encoding encodes 1s as transitions at the beginning of the period, and 0s as no transition at the beginning of the period.

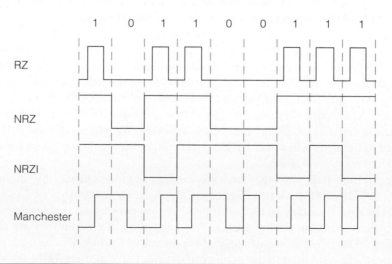

Fig. 10.1 Baseband Bit-Encoding Schemes

■ *Manchester encoding* encodes each bit as a transition in the middle of the period. The figure shows a high-to-low transition for a 0 and low-to-high transition for a 1, however this is an arbitrary choice made by the particular system designer. This encodes the clock in each period, and also ensures that there is no DC component to the signal, which is an advantage when using certain kinds of detectors.

Manchester encoding

There are many other bit-encoding methods, but these are the most popular.

Packet-Switching and Circuit-Switching.   In most local area networks (LANs) and internets, the time slots are capable of holding from 512 bytes to 8 KB or more, and messages that will not fit in the maximum allowable slot size are broken into *packets* for transmission. The internal structure of the packet is known as its *frame*. The frame may include header information for packet recognition as well as address and other fields.

packets
frame

Packet-switched networks route each packet independently, without knowledge of the possibility that the packet may be one of many comprising a message between two stations. Independently routed packets are called *datagrams*. Routing information in a packet-switched network must be computed for each packet of a message independently. The Internet is a packet-switched network. These networks are referred to as *connectionless*. That means that an origination point may issue a packet bound for any destination without prior arrangement and without any assurance that the packet arrived, or if it did arrive, that it arrived error-free. In packet-switched networks it is up to higher layers in the communications protocol stack to establish and maintain reliable communications, so these higher layers deal with lost and mangled packets.

packet-switched networks

datagrams

connectionless networks

Circuit-switched networks, on the other hand, establish a route between the two stations before any data is transmitted, and that route remains in place until the communications session is complete, as in the original relay-switched telephone networks. Circuit switching has the advantage that the routing computation needs to be done only once for a given message. The circuit may be a dedicated path, implemented with actual switches, in which case the packets may be of arbitrary size. Alternatively, it may be a *virtual circuit*, where the routers use the circuit information to route packets for the duration of a message, but time-share the same physical circuit among several entities, devoting the physical circuit to several virtual circuits in turn as needed. A problem arises if several packets arrive at a node in a short time interval and the node is incapable of establishing virtual circuits for all of them, perhaps because the establishment of one virtual circuit blocks the establishment of another. In this case packets must be stored at the node until the physical circuit becomes available. Networks of such nodes are known as *store-and-forward networks*.

circuit-switched networks

virtual circuit

store-and-forward networks

Network Topologies.   When more than two entities share a physical link, there are a number of ways they can be interconnected. The term *network topology* refers to the logical interconnection pattern of the entities. Figure 10.2 shows three common network topologies: the bus, the star, and the ring.

The *bus* topology shown in Figure 10.2a has the advantage that there is no central controller; control resides in each station, so if one station becomes inoperative, the others can continue communicating. Also, in most situations less interconnecting wire is required than with the other topologies. On the other hand, without central control it is possible that more than one station may attempt transmission simultaneously. This is referred to as a

bus network topology

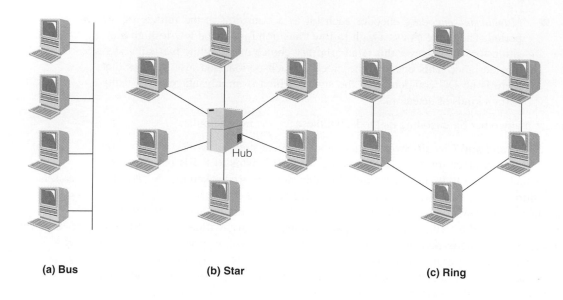

(a) Bus   (b) Star   (c) Ring

Fig. 10.2 Three Network Topologies

collision or contention, and it must be accounted for in the data link design. Ethernet implementations use the bus topology.

star network topology

There are actually three ways in which the *star* topology shown in Figure 10.2b may use the central station, or hub. The hub may act as a switch to connect any two stations in point-to-point fashion. The telephone system has this topology: One telephone is connected to another telephone through the services of the switch at the central office. The second way the hub can be used is as a broadcaster; when the hub receives a signal from one station it retransmits it to all the other stations. In this configuration the star acts logically as a bus: All stations are connected over a common path, and only one station may transmit at a time. This is referred to as a *star-bus*. When used in this way, the hub serves as a repeater, providing signal amplitude restoration, and often allowing a longer distance between stations. The third way is known as a star-ring, which we describe in the next paragraph.

star-bus topology

The ring topology, shown in Figure 10.2c, avoids the collisions that are possible in the bus topology. Each pair of stations has a point-to-point connection. The most common communications method used in the ring topology is the IBM-designed token ring protocol. Here a data packet, called a token, is passed in one direction around the ring. When a station receives a token that does not contain a data packet, it may attach a packet of data to the token and send it on to the next station. The token continues around the ring until reaching its destination, where the data are removed, the token marked as empty, and the empty token sent on its way. The token ring is usually implemented as a star-ring. The *star-ring* has the physical topology of a star, but uses a ring protocol. The hub, now called a media access unit (MAU), implements the ring by routing the token from one station to the next in ringlike fashion.

star-ring topology

Internetworking.   The three topologies in Figure 10.2 are used to implement LANs, whose extents are usually limited to a few hundred to a few thousand feet. It is often desirable to interconnect a number of LANs into an internetwork. Bridges and routers are used for this purpose.

Figure 10.3 shows four LANs interconnected into an internetwork. The *bridges* used to interconnect LANs 1 and 2, and LANs 3 and 4 have little intelligence beyond knowing which stations are on the LANs that they are directly connected to. The main purpose of a bridge is to isolate local LAN traffic from the rest of the network. It accomplishes this by transmitting only packets that it knows have nonlocal destinations. The bridge also restores signal amplitude during retransmission, thereby possibly increasing the maximum length of the network. *Routers* examine the destination addresses of packets they receive and are capable of making routing decisions based on route tables that they maintain. We will cover internetworking in more detail later.

bridges

routers

The Communications Medium.   Up until now we have been discussing network structures and communications without reference to the communications media over which the signals travel. Commonly used media include copper wire, optical fiber, and free space. Specific kinds of wire have their own characteristics that influence the behavior of the data link. A simple twisted pair has the lowest cost, the lowest bandwidth, and the highest signal attenuation. Coaxial cable is intermediate in these properties, while optical fiber is emerging as the medium of choice in high-bandwidth, long distance communications. Point-to-point free space communications have seen little use except in cases where the signals can be spatially focused, as for example in satellite communications, because of the limited capacity of the radio frequency spectrum to support a large number of users. Free space communications is rapidly gaining in application, however, because of extension of the spectrum into the microwave and infrared regions, and the increasing use of cell communications, where small geographical regions are served by individual transmitting and receiving cells.

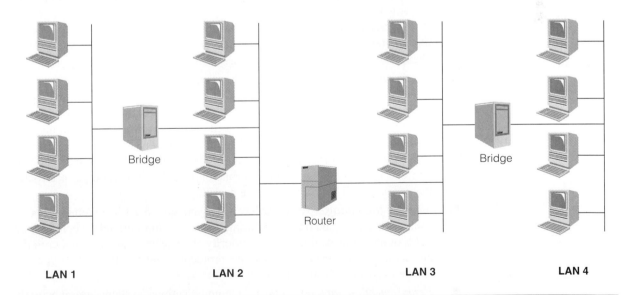

Fig. 10.3 Several LANs Interconnected with Bridges and Routers

Bit-Error Rate. The usual measure of errors in communications channels is the bit-error rate (BER). The BER is the probability that a given bit in the bit stream is erroneous; it is normally 10^{-12} or less. The BER is a statistical property of the channel. It can be calculated from a knowledge of the signal-to-noise ratio if the noise on the channel is white noise, that is, noise whose frequency components are equally distributed across the frequency spectrum. Often communications channel noise is impulse noise—noise that occurs in bursts or pulses, rather than white noise. In any event, BER is measured by injecting a very long bit stream into the channel and measuring the resulting errors at the receiving end of the channel.

10.1.2 TASKS, ROLES, AND LEVELS IN THE COMMUNICATIONS SYSTEM

According to the well-established principles of abstraction and separation of concerns, an application running on one computer should be able to communicate with an application on a computer over a network without any knowledge of the intervening, lower-level details. Yet these details are an indispensable part of providing reliable communications. Here are some of the tasks that the communications system must perform.

- *Provide a high-level interface to the application.* Ideally, the application should only have to communicate where the data is and where it should go. The lower layers should handle all of the lower-level details.

- *Establish, maintain, and terminate the session gracefully.* The communications system must provide fairly elaborate handshaking between entities that wish to communicate. These will include tasks such as establishing that an entity is alive and ready to enter into a transaction, keeping the communications channel open until all messages have passed, and then ending the session.

- *Addressing and routing.* An entity may have both a text name and a numerical network address. The name is purely a convention to aid human memory. If an entity is identified by name during a communications session, then a lookup must be performed to translate the name to the address. We have already discussed routing as a necessary function of internetworks.

- *Synchronization and flow control.* An entity's transmission must be synchronized with the reception status of the receiving entity. In particular, a receiving entity must be able to exert *flow control*, that is, to communicate its ability or inability to receive information. The need for flow control arises from the possibility that data can be sent faster than it can be received and processed. Flow control messages may originate from any layer in the system, from an application that is unable to write the information to a disk fast enough, to a router that is temporarily unable to receive packets.

flow control

- *Message formatting.* At lower levels, the message must be assembled into a packet or packets, and the packet frame formatted appropriately. There may be fields in the frame dealing with its priority, the packet sequence number in the current message, the communications protocol being employed, the type and size of the data in the data field, and so on.

- *Error detection and correction.* Communications systems are inherently noisy and unreliable. Packets may be dropped and never delivered, they may be delivered out of sequence, or they may arrive garbled. Thus the packet frame includes either error correcting codes (ECC) or cyclic redundancy check (CRC) fields that allow the recipient to determine whether the arriving packet is error-free. ECC allows a certain number of errors in the packet to be detected and corrected; CRC allows error detection only. It may seem that ECC would be the desirable choice, but ECC requires more bits to implement, and it is usually advantageous to just detect an error and request that the packet be retransmitted.

- ■   *Signal generation and detection.*   These tasks are performed at the lowest levels in the communications system. The transmitter in the hardware interface is responsible for actually placing the bit stream on the communications channel. It may also be responsible for appending additional fields to the outgoing frame, such as a preamble for timing purposes, or error check information. The receiver is responsible for receiving packets addressed to it, and possibly for stripping off preamble bits and doing a certain amount of error checking before handing the received data up to the next level.

10.1.3 COMMUNICATION LAYER MODELS

Given the range of tasks that the communications system must perform, it is natural to define a layered system, and to assign those tasks to the various layers. There are a number of layer models in use, from the seven-layer OSI, Open Systems Interconnection model developed by the ISO in 1974 to the TCP/IP, Transmission Control Protocol/Internet Protocol model used by the Internet. In this section we will present the seven-layer OSI model, and later the TCP/IP model.

Layer Models and Protocols.   From these layer models come protocol definitions. A communications entity that adheres to the protocols is assured that it can participate in any communications system that uses them. At the lowest level, a manufacturer who wishes to develop an Ethernet interface card can consult the Ethernet hardware protocols to obtain the specifications that will allow it to design an Ethernet card that can be plugged into an Ethernet and run correctly. At the highest level, a software company that wants to design a new email system for the Internet can consult the TCP/IP protocol suite, as it is called, to obtain information about how to make its software compatible with existing Internet mail systems.[1]

The OSI Layer Model.   We should stress that the OSI model represents an architectural model and does not provide any explicit protocols. We will present the seven layers top-down, since that mirrors the flow of data.

Application layer. The application layer is the originator of transmitted data. It specifies the data in unpacketized form and often specifies destination addresses in symbolic form. Typical applications with a network access component include email, file transfer, remote login, and various distributed applications such as distributed databases. *application layer*

Presentation layer. The presentation layer is concerned with translating between the syntaxes of the two communicating entities. It would include such matters as encryption/ *presentation layer*

---

1.   Battle-scarred veterans of such attempts will point out that the specifications are often vague or contradictory, and much experimentation may be required to understand and successfully implement them.

decryption and translation between terminal protocols. The presentation layer is often missing from network protocol suites.

session layer

Session layer. The session layer provides for the establishment, maintenance, and termination of the connection.

transport layer

Transport layer. The transport layer packetizes the data and ensures that all packets are received, in the order in which they were sent, error-free. This is accomplished by requesting retransmission of all dropped or erroneous packets and perhaps by reordering correctly received packets that were received out of order.

network layer

Network layer. The network layer manages the lower-level network details. These include formatting the packet for transmission over the LAN, including the appropriate LAN addressing information. For example, a packet destined for an Ethernet LAN would be formatted to the Ethernet packet specifications by "wrapping" the Ethernet-specific fields around the packet.

data-link layer

Data-link layer. This layer is concerned with the final preparation for transmission over the physical link. This layer performs the final framing, low-level synchronization, flow control, and error control.

physical layer

Physical layer. This layer is concerned with the physical means used to transmit and receive data on the network. It consists of the wiring, transmitting and receiving hardware, and the signaling involved in packet transmission and reception.

Figure 10.4 shows data flow in the OSI model, from application down to the LAN and into an internet, to the LAN at the other station, and up through the layers to the application.

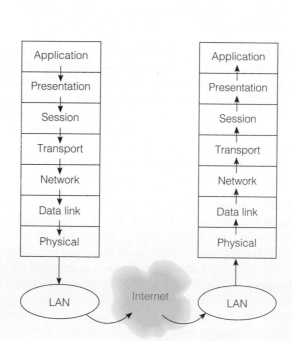

Fig. 10.4 The OSI Layer Model

We know of no widespread use of the OSI model per se, but every network access model is based on it in some way. Many models don't encompass all seven levels, or compress several OSI levels into one of their own, or skip a level, or allow access to a very low level from a much higher level. For example, the Ethernet specification encompasses only the lowest two levels, and TCP/IP only specifies the middle three levels of the OSI layer model.

10.2 Serial Data Communications Protocols

As the first of our three examples of communications protocols, we take the EIA RS-232 communications protocol and its variants. The standard was issued in 1962 by the Electronic Industries Association, long before computer networks were contemplated seriously. The standard deals with communications between two entities only, which are referred to as *data terminal equipment*, or *DTE*. The DTE is typically a computer or a terminal. The standard was devised so that the two stations could use the telephone system in an era before the pushbutton tone dialing common today.

data terminal equipment, DTE

Unfortunately the bandwidth of the telephone system is only 50 to 3,500 Hz, and so it does not support the DC pulses that are issued by a serial interface. Thus the RS-232 protocol includes the signals needed to interface with *data communications equipment*, or *DCE*. The DCE generates tones that can be transmitted across a telephone circuit. The DCE that converts bits into tones and tones into bits is known as a *modem*, for *mo*dulator-*dem*odulator. In the United States the latest standard is EIA RS-232-D, known outside the United States as CCITT Recommendation V.24. (CCITT stands for Consultative Committee for International Telephony and Telegraphy, an international standards-setting organization.)

data communication equipment, DCE

modem

In the following discussion, we consider the DTE to be a computer, and the DCE to be a modem, and remind the reader that these are just two specific examples, and that the DTE could be, for example, a VDT. We first describe some of the details of the RS-232 interface, and then discuss modems and some of the higher-level protocols that use the interface.

10.2.1 THE EIA RS-232 PROTOCOL

From the perspective of the layering model, we would say that the RS-232 protocol employs TDM, with 1-byte data packets. Most of the RS-232 protocol deals with the physical and data-link layers, although, as we will see, there are session-level components to the specification as well.

Synchronous and Asynchronous Communications. The RS-232 protocol supports both synchronous and asynchronous data communications. In synchronous communications the clock signal is transmitted to the modem along with the data, and the modem encodes the clock signal in the data. In asynchronous communications there is no common clock. A variable time can exist between character frames, so the receiving DCE must either infer or be told the transmitting clock rate. Asynchronous communications are much more frequently used, so we will limit our discussion to that mode.

Figure 10.5 shows the communications path between two DTE-DCE pairs that use the telephone system. The RS-232 interface provides the various signaling lines, which are connected to the telephone modem. The meanings of the signal names can be found in Table 10.1. Notice that the transmit and receive lines are crossed in the telephone system. This makes sense, since during normal telephone operation the mouthpiece at one end must be connected to the earpiece at the other end. It also explains why, when two computers or a computer or a terminal are connected via direct RS-232 serial lines without modems and an intervening telephone system, the transmit and receive lines must be switched somewhere in the connecting cable. A special cable is made for the purpose, the *null modem*. The modem's interface to the telephone system is not part of this standard. The next three sections describe the physical, data-link, and session layers of the RS-232

null modem

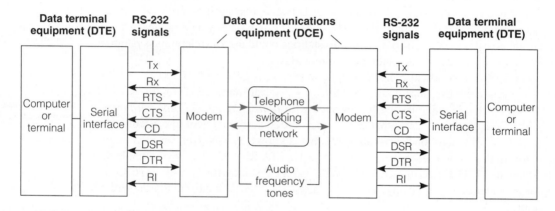

Fig. 10.5 Telecommunications by Modem

Table 10.1 EIA RS-232 Signal Identities and Pin Assignments

DB-25 Pin No.	Signal Name	Signal Identity	Signal Direction
2	Tx	Transmitted data	To modem
3	Rx	Received data	To computer
7	Gnd	Signal ground	Common reference
22	RI	Ring indicator	To computer
8	CD	Carrier detect	To computer
20	DTR	Data terminal ready	To modem
6	DSR	Data set ready	To computer
4	RTS	Request to send	To modem
5	CTS	Clear to send	To computer

communications protocol. Following that, we discuss the modem-telephone interface and the various telephone interface protocols.

Physical Layer. The RS-232-C specification allows various connectors; RS-232-D calls for a specific 25-pin connector, the DB-25, with each pin's functionality specified by the standard. Discussion of some of these signals follows. The electrical specification for the computer-modem interface says that received voltages from –3 to –12 volts will be interpreted as a binary 1, also called a MARK, and received voltages from +3 to +12 volts will be interpreted as a binary 0, also called a SPACE. This allows the interface to distinguish between 1s, 0s, and dead lines. The specifications say that the interface should allow reliable communications at up to 20 K bps at distances of up to 15 meters.

MARK
SPACE

Asynchronous Data Communications Frames. The RS-232 data-link layer accepts bytes from the DTE and formats them into frames for transmission, and accepts received frames from the DCE, which it then disassembles into bytes. Since no clock is transmitted in asynchronous data transmission, the frame must "stand alone," with respect to the receiver. Thus the frame must have a means for signalling its start and its stop. A parity bit is often included as well. Figure 10.6 shows the setup of the frame. A single start bit signals the beginning of the frame. The receiving interface, which must by this time know the signaling rate and the frame configuration by prior arrangement, samples the incoming stream $\frac{1}{2}$ of a bit time from the leading edge of the start bit, and one bit time thereafter until the frame is complete. An optional parity bit, which may be even or odd, is appended to the end of the data bits, and the frame concludes with 1, $1\frac{1}{2}$, or 2 stop bits. An arbitrary amount of time may pass before the beginning of the next frame.

Data-Link Layer. There are eight signals commonly used between the computer and modem, shown in Table 10.1. Tx and Rx and Gnd stand for transmit, receive, and signal ground. The RI signal is sent from modem to computer when it detects the ring signal indicating an incoming call. CD is sent to the computer after the modem has gone off hook and detected a carrier signal from the modem on the other end. *Off hook* is the state of a telephone when the handset is removed from its cradle. The next four signals are for handshaking between computer and modem, and their proper use is often not understood. DTR and DSR are signals from the computer and the modem, respectively, indicating that they are operative and ready for use. These signals are only used at the beginning and end of the call, to establish and terminate the session. RTS and CTS are used during the call to control the circuit between the two ends of the communications channel. The particular ways these signals are used is part of the RS-232 procedural specification, which in the OSI model is part of the session layer.

off hook

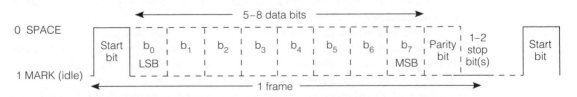

Fig. 10.6 Asynchronous Data Frame

The Session Layer.   A portion of the RS-232 specification deals with what we would today refer to as the session-level protocol—the establishment, maintenance, and termination of a communications session. The last six signals in Table 10.1 (RI, CD, DTR, DSR, RTS, and CTS) are used for this purpose. We will not cover the specification in that much detail, but only indicate the general procedure. The approximate sequence follows:

1.   Both computers assert DTR.
2.   Modem #1 dials number. (This is outside the RS-232 specification.)
3.   Modem #2 detects ring, asserts RI, goes off hook.
4.   Modem #2 asserts DSR.
5.   Modem #2 sends a 2,100 Hz answer tone for 3.3 s.
6.   Modem #1 detects tone, asserts CD.
7.   Computer #1 asserts RTS, signaling modem #1 to send a tone in reply.
8.   The modems now begin an elaborate communications sequence during which they establish the communications protocols under which they will communicate. These protocols specify the baud rate (defined in Section 10.2.2), the bit rate, and any error correction and data compression capabilities. (This is also outside the RS-232 specification.)
9.   On a full-duplex channel, both modems assert CTS.
10.   Data transmission and reception proceeds. The computers exert hardware flow control through RTS and CTS.
11.   The process is essentially reversed when one computer wishes to terminate the session.

Steps 5 through 8 are not part of the RS-232 specification. The original "telephone" specification was the Bell 103 300-baud specification, developed by Bell Telephone Laboratories. It and the 1,200-baud Bell 212A specification have largely been superseded by CCITT specifications. The V.90 CCITT specification allows for bit rates up to 56,000 bps, as negotiated by the modems.

10.2.2   MODEMS

modem data rates

Modem data rates vary and have increased significantly over time. Earlier fixed-bit-rate modems required the users to set the transmit and receive bit rate in the RS-232 interface to the bit rate that both modems and the telephone line could accept. In the more advanced variable-bit-rate modems, described in the preceding 11-step sequence, the accepted practice is to program the interface to run at the maximum bit rate possible and let the hardware handshaking of CTS/RTS exert flow control. This allows the modems to run at their maximum data rates.

Modem data rates hark back to the work of the French engineer Jean-Maurice-Emile Baudot. In 1859, he received a patent for a new 5-bit telegraphy code, called the Baudot code. By the middle part of this century the Baudot code had supplanted the Morse code for printing telegraphy because of its fixed, 5-bit frame size. The *baud rate*, which is the number of signal changes per second, was named after him. If the transmitted signal can assume only one of two binary states, then the bit rate will be equal to the baud rate,

baud rate

because 1 bit is transmitted per baud, but if the signal value can have more than two different states, more than 1 bit can be sent per signal change. Thus the *bit rate* can be greater
than the baud rate.

bit rate

It is true that the maximum number of *signal changes* per second that can be sent
through a communications channel is equal to its bandwidth. We observed earlier that the
bandwidth of the telephone system was limited to approximately 50 to 3500 Hz, which
means that the baud rate through the telephone system is limited to 3,500 baud. In practice, modems using the telephone system are limited to 2,400 baud. How then, can modem
data rates be as high as 56,000 bps? The answer is that they send multiple bits per baud.
The modem sends one of 2^n different signals each baud, which is encoded back to an n-bit
value at the receiving end. If this class of modem has a baud rate of b, then the bit rate is
$b \times n$. Consider a 2,400-baud modem that can send any one of four tones during each
baud. One tone would represent 00, the next 01, the third 10, and the fourth 11. This
modem could send 2,400 signals per second, each one of which carried 2 bits, for a data
rate of $2,400 \times 2 = 4,800$ bps, so this modem is a 2,400-baud, 4,800-bps modem.

bit rate versus baud rate

There are both dumb modems and smart modems. Dumb modems are dumb in the
sense that they do not understand the codes that are sent through them. The modem transmits and receives bits, neither recognizing nor altering them. The *smart modem* can be
configured by using the *modem configuration codes*, sometimes called the Hayes, or AT
codes. Dennis Hayes originated the AT codes in modems that he began manufacturing in
the 1970s. AT stands for "attention." When a "Hayes-compatible" modem is idle, that is,
not communicating with another modem, and it receives the ASCII characters AT, it
accepts the characters following the AT up to the next return character as command
codes, which allow the modem to be configured in various ways. For example, sending
the string "ATDT555-1212" to a Hayes-compatible modem would result in the modem
tone-dialing the telephone number 5551212. The Hayes modem allowed a direct connection to the telephone wall plug; prior to that, the number had to be dialed from the telephone instrument and then the receiver mashed down into two foam-padded acoustic
couplers attached to the modem.

dumb modem

smart modem
modem
configuration codes

10.2.3 ASCII Data-Link Control

The ASCII code, or American Standard Code for Information Interchange, became a standard in 1967, replacing the Baudot code that had been in use for many decades in telegraphy. Originally intended mainly as a code to control printers and tape punches, it quickly
became the standard code for representing characters and paper control in computers as
well. Table 10.2 shows the ASCII code, arranged with the least significant 4 bits running
vertically down and the most significant 3 bits running horizontally left to right. For our
discussion, the most important information is found in the two left columns. These contain
the so-called control characters, indicated by a caret, ^, before the character; so the carriage return character, CR, is ^M, with an ASCII value of 000 1101. The names of the control characters are given at the bottom of the table.

While the printing characters of the rightmost six columns communicate information,
the control characters determine how that information is transmitted or presented. Some,
such as CR or VT, determine how printed characters are to be positioned on the page,
while others, such as ETX and ACK, are used to control the transmission protocols.

Table 10.2 The ASCII Code

Lsb's, 3210	Most Significant Bits, 654							
	000	001	010	011	100	101	110	111
0000	NUL, ^@	DLE, ^P	space	0	@	P	`	p
0001	SOH, ^A	DC1, ^Q	!	1	A	Q	a	q
0010	STX, ^B	DC2, ^R	"	2	B	R	b	r
0011	ETX, ^C	DC3, ^S	#	3	C	S	c	s
0100	EOT, ^D	DC4, ^T	$	4	D	T	d	t
0101	ENQ, ^E	NAK, ^U	%	5	E	U	e	u
0110	ACK, ^F	SYN, ^V	&	6	F	V	f	v
0111	BEL, ^G	ETB, ^W	'	7	G	W	g	w
1000	BS, ^H	CAN, ^X	(	8	H	X	h	x
1001	HT, ^I	EM, ^Y	)	9	I	Y	i	y
1010	LF, ^J	SUB, ^Z	*	:	J	Z	j	z
1011	VT, ^K	ESC, ^[	+	;	K	[	k	{
1100	FF, ^L	FS, ^\	,	<	L	\	l		
1101	CR, ^M	GS, ^]	-	=	M	]	m	}
1110	SO, ^N	RS, ^^	.	>	N	^	n	~
1111	SI, ^O	US, ^_	/	?	O	_	o	DEL

NUL	Null, idle		SI	Shift in
SOH	Start of heading		DLE	Data link escape
STX	Start of text		DC1–4	Device control
ETX	End of text		NAK	Negative acknowledgment
EOT	End of transmission		SYN	Sync character
ENQ	Enquiry		ETB	End of transmitted block
ACK	Acknowledge		CAN	Cancel preceding message or block
BEL	Audible bell		EM	End of medium (paper or tape)
BS	Backspace		SUB	Substitute for invalid character
HT	Horizontal tab		ESC	Escape (give alternate meaning to following)
LF	Line feed		FS	File separator
VT	Vertical tab		GS	Group separator
FF	Form feed		RS	Record separator
CR	Carriage return		US	Unit separator
SO	Shift out		DEL	Delete

An examination of the table reveals the teletype and paper tape punch origins of the code. For example the ENQ code was used as a "Who are you?" request for a station to identify itself, and the EM code signaled that the tape had run out. By now the control characters have lost much of their meaning, or the meaning has been extended to the computer environment. ^D, end of transmission, is often used as a log-out character, and ^C, end of text, is sometimes used to terminate a keyboard entry. Software flow control is sometimes implemented with ^S as "stop transmission" and ^Q as "continue transmission."

The ASCII code contains several clever features:

- Ordinary uppercase characters are converted to the equivalent control characters by flipping bit 6, the msb, from 1 to 0. For example, "X" is 101 1000, and "^X" is 001 1000.

- Uppercase alphabetical characters are converted to lowercase by flipping bit 5 from 0 to 1. "X" is 101 1000; "x" is 111 1000.

- The ASCII integers are converted to binary integers by flipping bits 5 and 4 to 0 (and ensuring that bit 7, not part of the ASCII code, is also 0); "5" is 011 0101, and 5 B is 000 0101.

10.3 Local Area Networks

Having looked at point-to-point transmission, we now consider *local area networks* consisting of several interconnected computers. The term *LAN* is not precisely defined, but it is generally taken to mean a computer network that is wholly contained within a building or campus. LANs are defined more by their intended use than by their physical characteristics. Most LANs are used to exploit the resource-sharing capability and internetwork access. This includes the sharing of files and programs as well as physical resources such as printers. LAN types vary from Apple Computer's 230 Kbps LocalTalk LAN network, which has been built into every computer they produced since 1984, to the newest 100 Mbps Ethernet variants.

To be useful, a LAN must provide network access not just at the physical and data-link layers, but at all protocol levels from the application level to the physical level. In this section we cover the physical and data-link levels with only a brief mention of the higher-level protocols. Details of higher-level protocols are covered in Section 10.5, where we describe the Internet.

LAN: local area network

10.3.1 THE ETHERNET LAN

Ethernet was developed by Bob Metcalf of Xerox in the late 1970s, and now represents perhaps the most popular LAN. Because of its popularity, Ethernet interfaces are available for virtually every brand of computer. The computer on which these words are being written has a built-in 100 Mbps Ethernet interface, and gigabit Ethernet is being seen on high-end desktop computers. Ethernet's popularity has led to a number of implementations of the physical layer.

Physical Layer. The original Ethernet physical layer implementation, which used expensive, thick, coaxial cable, has been supplanted with several higher-speed, lower-cost

UTP: Unshielded
Twisted Pair

versions. The most commonly used for the slower speeds is Unshielded Twisted Pair, UTP. In the early 1990s, ANSI (American National Standards Institute) defined a series of telecommunication wiring standards for different frequency application requirements. The UTP cables are referred to by category number, Category 3, 4, and 5, often referred to as Cat 3, 4, or 5. Cat 3 cable is suitable only for telephone or 10MHz usage, whereas Cat 5 cable can be used for 100MHz and 1000 MHz applications.

Ethernet hub

Table 10.3 shows the kinds of cable and the speeds supported. They support from 10 MHz to 1GHz bit rates and up to 1,024 devices on the network. They trade cost against maximum network length. The twisted pair employs a star-bus design, with a hub providing signal amplitude and pulse-shape restoration between each pair of stations. The hub, sometimes called a concentrator, in effect just acts as a bus driver. In the IEEE standards column, the initial number, 10-1000, refers to the data transmission rate supported in Mbps; the word BASE refers to the signaling method, baseband; and the last character, if a number, refers to the maximum segment length in hundreds of meters. "T" refers to twisted pair. The three 10 MHz standards use Manchester bit encoding. More sophisticated signaling techniques are used with 100 and 1000 MHz systems. Gigabit Ethernet, as it is commonly referred to, may be implemented with a full-duplex rather than half-duplex communications, with a subsequent reduction in collisions. These higher-speed implementations often use switches instead of hubs. The switches further reduce collisions by routing packets only to the destination rather than broadcasting them to the entire network.

velocity factor

The complete physical layer specifications also include wire impedances, connector types, voltage levels, pulse rise and fall times, and so on. The two coaxial cables have *velocity factors* of 0.66, meaning that the signal propagation speed is 0.66 times the speed of light in a vacuum.

One point that you should derive from this discussion is that a given data-link layer specification may spawn a number of physical layer specifications that adhere to it. This reflects the entrepreneurship of firms that believe they can design a physical layer that is

Table 10.3 Ethernet Cabling

Cable	IEEE Standard	Maximum Cable Length (m)	Maximum Total Length (m)	Topology
RG-8U (thicknet)	10BASE-5	500	2,500	Bus
RG-58U (thinnet)	10BASE-2	185	1,000	Bus
UTP, Cat 3 minimum	10BASE-T	100	2,500 with thick backbone	Star-bus (requires hub)
UTP, Cat 5 minimum, or optical fiber	100BASE-T	100	412 with fiber optic cables	Star-bus (requires hub)
Shielded copper, UTP, (cat 5 minimum), or Optical Fiber,	1000BASE-X	Shielded copper - 25 Cat 5 - 100 Optical Fiber, 550-3,000	3000	Various

superior to the current market offerings in price/performance. There are a number of current efforts aimed at the development of fiber-optic and free-space infrared implementations of the Ethernet physical layer.

Data-Link Layer.   At the data-link layer, Ethernet transmits packets with allowable sizes from 64 to 1,518 bytes in total length. It is a connectionless protocol: Any entity can transmit packets to any other entity, and the originating entity is indifferent to the fate of the packet once it has been successfully transmitted. The slower-speed Ethernet implementations employ the CSMA/CD method of accessing the bus. CSMA/CD stands for carrier sense multiple access with collision detection, and it means, informally, that when a station wishes to transmit, it may do so if it does not sense anyone transmitting. During its transmission period, if it senses another station transmitting (a collision), then it stops packet transmission and transmits a jamming signal to ensure that all other stations realize that there has been a collision. It then waits a random period, and tries again. Figure 10.7 shows this in flowchart form. The possibility of collision is one of the main factors limiting the network's maximum physical length. The longer the maximum line length, the greater the chance that two stations on opposite ends of the network will begin transmitting without sensing each other's signals. Packet collisions become more frequent as network traffic increases and are the reason that the network can never reach its theoretical maximum packet transmission rate. "Intelligent hubs" that monitor and mediate collisions are used in the higher-speed implementations, resulting in fewer collisions and longer maximum cable lengths.

carrier sense multiple access: CSMA
collision detection: CD

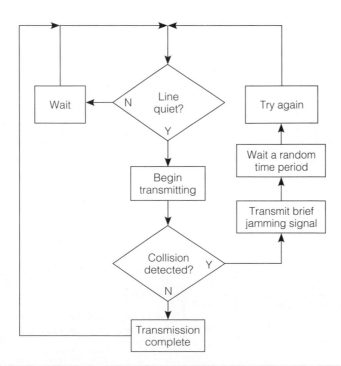

Fig. 10.7 Ethernet CSMA/CD Media Access Control Mechanism

Packet Reception.   Ethernet is a broadcast medium: The controller at every station receives every packet that is transmitted and must compare the packet's destination Ethernet address with its address. If the destination address matches the controller address, then the packet is accepted. If it does not match, it is discarded. If there is a match, the controller does a CRC check for errors and a check to see that the packet size is within limits. If the packet is found to be valid, then it is handed up to the next layer for further processing.

address octets

Ethernet Addressing.   Ethernet addresses are 48 bits long, organized as 6 8-bit *address octets*, as they are called. The Ethernet address is guaranteed to be globally unique, as is one's telephone number. In the past Xerox handed out Ethernet addresses, but this task has been assumed by the IEEE. Each vendor of Ethernet interface cards must register with the IEEE, who will assign the vendor the first 3 octets. The vendor is free to assign the last 3 octets as they see fit. For example, Sun Microsystems was assigned the hexadecimal value 08-00-20, and is free to allocate addresses from 08-00-20-00-00-00 to 08-00-20-FF-FF-FF. Usually these addresses are encoded in a ROM on board the Ethernet interface card or chip.

preamble

MAC addresses

Ethernet Packets.   Ethernet packet structure is shown in Figure 10.8. The field sizes are given in bytes. Notice that the 8-byte *preamble* is not included in the packet size; it is used only to provide a clock reference. The Destination and Source addresses are the 48-bit Ethernet addresses of the respective stations. These LAN hardware addresses are referred to as *MAC addresses*, standing for media access control. The MAC addresses are physical and data-link layer addresses. The Type field identifies the kind of information to be found in the Data field. For example, a type value of 0x0800 indicates that the type of data is an IP (Internet Protocol) packet; 0x8137 indicates it is a Novell NetWare packet. Thus the Ethernet packet may be an Internet packet, a Novell packet, an AppleTalk packet, or the packet of some other higher-level network protocol.

The Ethernet Interface to Other Network Protocols.   The data in most Ethernet packets originates at higher levels in the protocol stack, and the Type field identifies the kind of higher-level network information that is in the Data packet. In these cases the Data field may contain router information, network information, session information, and transport information, all in addition to the actual data. If the packet destination is outside the LAN, then routers will alter the MAC address fields and other subfields in the Data field to reflect intermediate destinations and the progress of the packet to its final destination. In particular, it will set the destination MAC (physical) address to the address of the router to which the packet is to be sent.

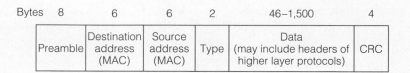

Bytes	8	6	6	2	46–1,500	4
	Preamble	Destination address (MAC)	Source address (MAC)	Type	Data (may include headers of higher layer protocols)	CRC

Fig. 10.8 Ethernet Packet Structure

10.4   Modern Serial Buses: USB and FireFire

In the preceding sections we discussed the decades-old RS-232 and Ethernet serial buses. In this section we cover two relative newcomers: the USB, Universal Serial Bus, and IEEE1394 serial bus, now more commonly known as FireWire. Both of these buses were developed to provide capabilities not present in the older two. The two buses have many characteristics in common.

10.4.1   SHARED CHARACTERISTICS OF USB AND FIREWIRE

Powered Bus Design.   These new buses convey electrical power as well as data signals, and are capable of supplying power to connected devices. The obvious advantage of this capability is that devices that require only a small amount of power for their operation can obtain it from the bus, and therefore do not require an external power source. This can be particularly important for devices that are designed for portability, since it frees the user from having to carry a power supply and cord along with the device. Maximum cable length is 5m for current implementations of both USB and FireWire.

Hot-plugability and Self-Configuration.   Both buses can accept and configure devices plugged in during active operation of the bus. This "plug-and-play" characteristic removes the need to set any switches to configure the device; further, devices can be plugged and unplugged during system operation without powering down the equipment. None of the older buses had this property. In fact, most systems using the older-type buses specifically warned that plugging or unplugging devices during operation could lead to damage to the bus interfaces, the device, or both. Many users can attest to the importance of these warnings. From an electrical standpoint, hot-plugability is based upon the "Make First/Break Last" rule for the power and ground pins. This is implemented by making the power-carrying pins approximately 1 mm longer than the data pins. This ensures that the electrical power supplied to the device is settled and stable prior to connecting the data lines to the bus.

Plug-and-Play

Make First/Break Last

Versatility.   These new buses were designed to be used with a wide variety of devices, including keyboards, mice, disk drives, scanners, video and still digital cameras, among others. They are even used as LANs capable of transmitting Internet packets.

Implement the Four Bottom Layers of the ISO Layer Model.   Unlike Ethernet, these buses implement the transaction, network, logical, and physical layers. In USB, the transaction and network layers are referred to as the Function Layer. In FireWire they are referred to as Transaction Layer. Having these layers defined in within the bus protocol considerably reduces the application's chores.

Fixed Bus Cycle, or Frame Time.   In both USB and FireWire each frame may contain packets with different sources and destinations. The two buses differ in how and where the packets are assembled. This will be discussed further below.

Both Asynchronous and Isochronous Data Transmissions.   In asynchronous data transmissions, each packet competes for bandwidth independently, without any bandwidth or data rate guarantees. The transmitting device must make separate requests for each packet of data it wishes to send. The connection is established at the transaction layer, using request and acknowledge packets. In the isochronous data transmission regime, once a device has been granted access, a certain portion of every packet is reserved for its use, thus providing a guaranteed bandwidth. Isochronous data transmission is necessary in applications such as audio or video, where data must arrive at a constant rate. In the isochronous mode, consistent data delivery is considered to be more important than data integrity. Thus once an isochoronous channel has been established, data transmissions are not acknowledged by the receiving entity.

10.4.2 DIFFERENCES BETWEEN USB AND FIREWIRE

The discussion above shows the many similarities between these two buses. Bus power, hot-plugability, an extensive layer model, fixed bus cycles, and both asynchronous and isochronous data transmission. There are many differences between these buses as well, mostly stemming from the differences in initial design goals. USB was primarily designed as a slow-speed bus for peripheral device interconnection. FireWire was designed primarily to support high-speed, independent transfer of multimedia content. Although much of the initial research and development took place at Apple Computer, the design efforts also had the involvement of companies such as Sony, which wished to have a high-speed serial interface for its upcoming generation of digital camcorders. In the sections below we describe the characteristics that are unique to each of these buses.

Characteristics that are Unique to USB.   USB was designed specifically as a low-cost, relatively low-speed bus, for use primarily in interfacing slow-speed devices such as keyboards, mice, and printers to personal computers. It has two data transmission rates, 1.5 and 12 Mbps. The USB relies on a host controller that mediates all communications through a root hub. It is designed to use low-cost 4-pin connectors having two power lines and a single twisted pair for data. It supports the attachment of up to 127 devices. The next generation, USB-2, is capable of 480 Mbps operation, but maximum cable length remains at 5m.

Characteristics that are Unique to FireWire.   FireWire was designed to function as a higher-speed bus, for interfacing with devices such as digital camcorders and disk drives. It has bus speeds of 100, 200, and 400 Mbps. It is designed to be self-configuring without a predefined host controller. The role of host or bus controller is negotiated each time a device is plugged or unplugged from the bus. For example, a digital camcorder with a FireWire interface can be plugged directly into a VCR, and data transferred from camera to or from the VCR without the intervention of a host computer.

IEEE 1394b

FireWire normally uses 6-pin connectors, with two lines for power and two twisted pairs for data transmission. There is also a specification for a smaller 4-pin connector that lacks power and ground pins. The FireWire bus supports up to 64 nodes. The newest generation, IEEE1394b, is capable of 800, 1600, or 3200 Mbps, and extends maximum cable length to 100m.

USB Packet Assembly and Data Transmission.   USB relies on the host controller to manage all transactions. USB devices that wish to transfer data make a request of the host controller, specifying the nature of the transaction. Upon receiving the request, the

Transfer
descriptor

host controller generates a transfer descriptor for that transfer and appends it to a list of pending transfers. The transfer descriptor contains all the information that the host controller needs to complete the transfer: source node, destination node, amount of data to be transferred, whether it is a read or a write, the speed of the transaction, and the location of the memory buffer from which or to which the data are to be transferred. At the start of each frame the host controller generates and transmits packets as specified by the list of transfer descriptors.

All USB transfers take place through the host controller. If device A requests that data be read from device B into a buffer belonging to device A, the host controller must make two transfers: device B to host, and then host to device A. USB devices can be thought of as being "second class citizens," since they only make requests for data transfer. The actual transfer is done by the host.

FireWire Packet Assembly and Data Transmission.   In contrast to USB, FireWire devices are all "first class citizens." By a process of negotiation, one device is selected as host and bus controller. The designated controller maintains a data structure containing information about the bus: speeds, bus topology, bus bandwidth available, power available and being consumed, and number and identities of isochronous channels available. Prior to the start of a given bus cycle, nodes wishing to make isochronous transfers query the host for channel availability. Available channels are reserved by channel number, and at the beginning of the next bus cycle they are transmitted in order by each host that has requested a channel. The first 80% of the frame is available for isochronous channels.

Table 10.4 USB and FireWire Characteristics

Characteristic	USB (USB2)	IEEE1394 (IEE1394B)
Powered Bus	Yes	Yes
Hot-pluggable, plug-and-play	Yes	Yes
Data rates	1.5, 12 Mbps (480 Mbps)	100, 200, 400 Mbps (800, 1600, 3200 Mbps)
Topology	Star-hub	Arbitrary acyclic graph.
Root node (host controller, bus manager) configuration	At system design time.	Negotiated by devices whenever a new device is connected
Maximum cable length	5m (5m)	5m (100m)
No. of wires in cable	4: 4.5 V, Ground, +Data, −Data	6: 8 - 40 V, Ground, 2 Twisted Pairs; Optional 4-pin mini-cable without power.
Bus cycle time (time per frame)	1ms.	125 µs
Asynchronous max payload size per packet.	64 bytes at 12 Mbps bus speed	2048 bytes at 400 Mbps bus speed.
Isochronous max payload size per packet.	1024 bytes at 12 Mbps bus speed	4096 bytes at 400 Mbps bus speed.
Percent total bus cycle time guaranteed to isochronous data transfers	90	80

When all isochronous data has been transmitted, which is signaled by a defined gap in data transmission, all nodes wishing to transit asynchronous data vie for the bus. Possible node starvation is avoided by means of a "fair arbitration" mechanism.

In FireWire, each device is responsible for acquiring the bus during a portion of the cycle. When it has acquired the bus, it is responsible for transmitting its packetized data.

Data Link Layers.   These bus designs are considerably more complex at the data link layer than those discussed previously. The bus specifications include protocols for connection and disconnection, asynchronous and isochronous packets, bus and device electrical current characteristics, self-configuration, and node configuration. Further details can be found in the Bibliography.

10.5 The Internet

In the preceding section on LANs, we stressed that the Ethernet protocol, and indeed most LAN protocols, such as token ring and LocalTalk, encompass only the physical and data-link layers. Several higher-level protocols employ these lower-level protocols to get their data from one place to another. These include AppleTalk,[2] formerly used mainly with Apple Macintosh computers and peripherals; Novell NetWare, a DOS/Windows-based network; Xerox's XNS; DEC's DECnet; and TCP/IP, the Internet protocol stack.

10.5.1 THE TCP/IP PROTOCOL SUITE

Figure 10.9 shows the correspondence between the OSI layer model and TCP/IP combined with applications at the top and various LAN protocols at the bottom layers. TCP subsumes the presentation, session, and transport layers, and IP corresponds to the network layer of the OSI protocol model. TCP depends on applications developed external to the protocol, and the IP layer depends on the services of other lower-level protocols to manage the actual physical packet delivery. Once again, vendors have developed a number of data-link and physical layer implementations that adhere to the IP layer specification. Applications-level services such as email, ftp, and telnet are not part of TCP/IP, but were developed to run on top of it and use its services.

Internet Names and Addresses: Domain Name Service.   The domain name service (DNS) facility is usually invoked by another application rather than directly by a user. It provides translation between a *domain name*, such as crusher.cs.colorado.edu and its Internet, or *IP address*, 128.138.244.11 in this case. In the current version 4 of the Internet Protocol, IPv4, the IP address is a 32-bit integer often expressed in *dotted decimal notation*: four decimal numbers, each representing an octet, separated by periods. DNS was developed because human beings find it much easier to remember names than integer strings. When the user invokes a domain name from within an application program, DNS handles the details of looking up the IP address by sending a request to a domain name server. The retrieved IP address is passed to the TCP layer along with the data for packetization.

domain name
IP address

dotted decimal
notation

---

2.   The reader should not confuse LocalTalk, the 230 Kbps physical and data-link layer protocol, with AppleTalk, the network-to-application level protocol suite. AppleTalk can run on Ethernet and token ring LANs, and LocalTalk can be used to transmit Internet packets.

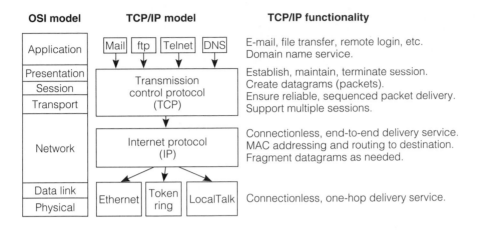

Fig. 10.9 The TCP/IP Protocol Stack Functionality

We cover IP addressing in detail later in this section; for now, we note that the IP address is actually composed of two parts: a network number and a host ID. One, two, or three of the most significant octets represent the network number, and the remainder represent the host ID within the given network:

IP address → Network # . Host ID

In the case of riker.cs.colorado.edu, 128.138 represents the network number of the colorado.edu domain conventionally expressed as 128.138.0.0. All hosts that are in the colorado.edu domain will have the network address 128.138.0.0, and no other domain will have this network address. The 244.11 part of the IP address represents the host ID, although it may be chopped up still further when inside the colorado.edu domain to provide LAN addressing within the domain. The dividing point between network number and host ID will be different for different IP addresses.

Exceptions to the Layer Rule.   In the OSI model, all communications must move up or down through all intervening layers of the protocol stack. In reality, most protocol stacks do not adhere strictly to this rule, and TCP/IP is a big violator of it. In TCP/IP there are instances where a layer is bypassed, or where the services of another module that is not directly part of the protocol are used for expediency or efficiency. These exceptions and special cases are beyond the scope of this text, but interested readers can consult the Bibliography at the end of this chapter.

Data Movement Through the Protocol Stack.   As data move through the TCP/IP stack, each layer modifies it in some way. Figure 10.10 shows the packet structure at each layer.

- *Applications level.* The application passes the data to be sent along with the destination IP address to the TCP layer. If necessary, it employs DNS to convert from domain address to IP address.

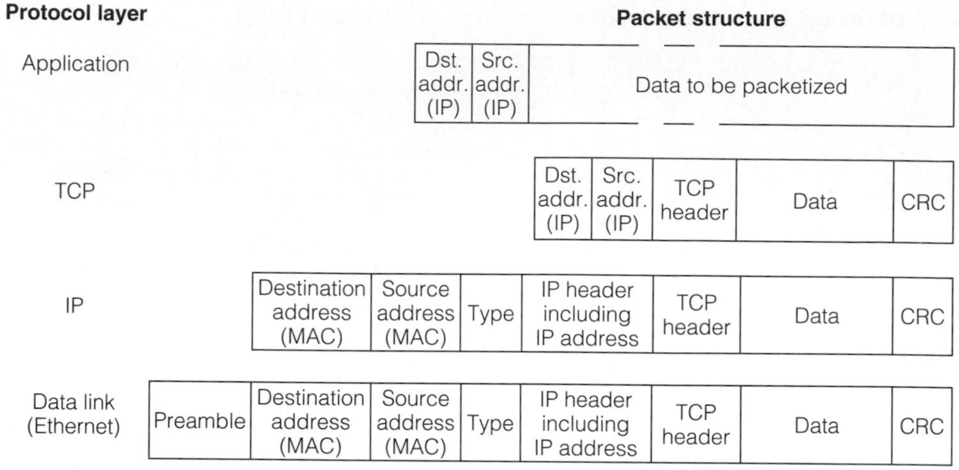

Protocol layer   **Packet structure**

Application

Dst. addr. (IP)	Src. addr. (IP)	Data to be packetized

TCP

		Dst. addr. (IP)	Src. addr. (IP)	TCP header	Data	CRC

IP

Destination address (MAC)	Source address (MAC)	Type	IP header including IP address	TCP header	Data	CRC

Data link (Ethernet)

Preamble	Destination address (MAC)	Source address (MAC)	Type	IP header including IP address	TCP header	Data	CRC

Fig. 10.10 Data Flow Through the Protocol Stack

- *TCP level.* The functions of the TCP level are to packetize the data, establish a session with the destination node, send data packets to that node, ensure that all packets are received in order and error-free, and terminate the session. These tasks may involve considerable two-way packet traffic between the TCP levels of source and destination. TCP will provide an initial packet size that it knows the LAN can accept. The TCP protocol attaches a TCP header that has information on which segment of the data is in the packet, and which session it represents. It then calculates the CRC, appends it to the packet, and passes the packet to the IP level. TCP can establish multiple sessions if the applications request it. For example, a user may be running several telnet remote login sessions with the same host simultaneously, while also using ftp to transfer files with the same host.

- *IP level.* IP is at the network level in the OSI model. The IP layer is responsible for formatting the IP header, which contains the IP addresses of source and destination hosts, and attaching the source and destination MAC addresses as well. Another round of address translation, this time from IP address to hardware (MAC) address, occurs at this level. IP will first consult its routing tables to see if the mapping is there. Of course the table will contain the mapping of the source IP address to source MAC address, but if it does not have the destination MAC address, it will first query the LAN, and if it receives no reply, it will attach the MAC address of a router attached to the LAN (see Figure 10.3). IP then adds the type field and preamble (not shown at this level), recomputes the CRC and passes the now Ethernet packet to the data-link layer for transmission. Again we stress that the IP is a connectionless protocol. It sends packets to the data-link layer, but it neither knows nor cares about their fate. That is a function of the TCP layer.

■ *Data-link and physical link level*. The packet is transmitted on the LAN with the MAC destination address set to either the final destination, if the final destination is on the same LAN, or with its MAC address set to a router, if the final destination is not on the same LAN.

10.5.2 PACKET ROUTING

If an Internet packet is headed for a LAN different from the one in which it originated, it wends its way from router to router until it reaches its final destination.

IP Routing.   Routers are special purpose computers that contain the TCP/IP protocol stack in addition to Internet routing protocols. Many hosts also act as routers. The routers use several protocols to keep their routing tables up-to-date. These protocols do not require human intervention; the Internet routers are in effect their own autonomous system. They dynamically adapt to changes in the network, adding or deleting from the routing tables as the network changes. The subject of how routers maintain their routing tables is quite complex in practice. The interested reader is referred to the Bibliography at the end of the chapter.

Figure 10.11 illustrates IP routing in flowchart form. First, the router accepts a packet addressed to its MAC address. It extracts the destination IP address from the packet and checks to see if that address matches its IP address. If so, it passes the packet to its TCP layer for processing. Otherwise, it masks off the host ID part of the IP address using a *network mask*, a bit pattern designed to separate host ID from network, and examines the remaining network number for a match with an entry in its routing table. If it cannot find an entry, it looks for a default route entry.

The default route is a "punt" by the router to a default router that will also attempt to route the packet. If neither entry exists, the packet is discarded. This might be the case if, for example, a user typed in a nonexistent IP address. In that case, the originating TCP level would not receive any reply packet and would inform the application of its lack of success in delivering the message. If either entry does exist, then the router looks up the corresponding destination MAC address, which will be either the final destination MAC address or the MAC address of the next router. In either case, the router then determines if the packet size is too large for the next network, and if so, it fragments it. It then replaces the old destination MAC address with the new destination MAC address, and the source MAC address with *its* MAC address. Finally, it computes and appends a new checksum and passes the packet to the data-link layer for transmission out the correct port. (A router will have connections, or ports, to several networks, and each port will have separate IP and MAC addresses.)

In summary, routers do not change the IP addresses in the IP header, but they do change both MAC addresses in the arriving packet before routing, putting their own address in the source field and the address of the next station in the destination field. The router takes this opportunity to see if it has the *source* IP address of the arriving packet in its routing table, and if not, it updates its table. Then when (and if) the destination machine sends reply packets back to the source machine, this entry will be available. One could say that the router receives on-the-job training.

Ultimately the packet should arrive at a router connected to the destination LAN, at which point the router will attach the destination's MAC address, and the packet will be

network mask

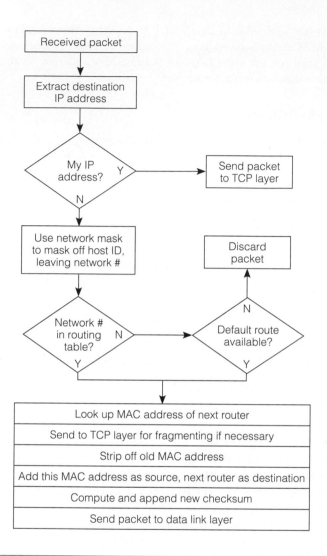

Fig. 10.11 The Internet Routing Process (Simplified)

accepted by the destination host and passed up the protocol chain. Again we emphasize that the preceding is a simplified description of routing. Interested readers can consult the Bibliography at the end of this chapter for more details.

Packet Reception at the Final Destination. At some point the packet (we hope) arrives at its destination node; that is, the destination IP address in the packet matches the destination IP address of the receiving machine. When the IP layer detects this match it sends the packet to the TCP layer for further processing. At the TCP level, the packet's arrival generates a reply packet that is sent back to the originating station, acknowledging receipt of the packet. The first packets to arrive establish a session, and the later ones convey the data that are to be transmitted. The TCP level begins the task of accumulating the packets' data fields and reconstructing the original data, which it passes to the application when it is complete. Retransmission requests are made back to the originating station for lost or damaged packets. Final packets confirm the successful reception of the data and terminate the session.

10.5.3 IP ADDRESSES—IPv4

IPv4, Internet Protocol version 4, has been essentially unchanged since 1981. An IPv4 IP address is a 32-bit integer, composed of 4 octets. From 1 to 3 of the leading octets specify the network address; the remaining one(s) specify the host ID within that network. In this section we discuss the assignment of network numbers and host IDs, and how the two fields are distinguished by the network routers and hosts.

Assignment of IP Addresses. Assigned IP addresses are globally unique, with the exception of several ranges of private, permanently unassigned IP addresses discussed below. The Internet Corporation for Assigned Names and Numbers (ICANN) is the non-profit corporation that was formed to assume responsibility for the IP address space allocation, protocol parameter assignment, domain name system management, and root server system management functions. It has delegated some of that authority to other organizations, each one of which is responsible for a top-level domain. Some example domains include EDU for educational institutions, COM for commercial enterprises, GOV and MIL for governmental and military organizations, NET for network organizations, and ORG for other miscellaneous organizations. There are separate domains for countries, such as UK for the United Kingdom and CA for Canada. Occasionally in this discussion we will refer to the network administrator. The *network administrator* is an individual within the local organization who makes local decisions about the network: assigning local IP addresses, deciding on network topology, and so on.

network administrator

IP Address Classes. One of the only mistakes that the original designers of the Internet made was to vastly underestimate the popularity of the Internet, with the corresponding demand for IP addresses. Prior to 1995, the network address part of the IP address consisted of the first 1, 2, or 3 octets, depending on the assigned address class, class A, B, or C. These classes were designed to meet the needs of large, medium, and small subnetworks of the Internet. A state university might have a class B address and a small company a class C address. The remaining unassigned octets of the 4 are assigned locally by the network administrator. Table 10.5 shows the split between network number and host ID for the three classes, where N stands for an octet that is part of the network number and H for an octet that is part of the host ID.

Table 10.5 Class A, B, and C IP Addresses

IP Address Class	Network #/Host ID Split	Network #
A	N.H.H.H	N.0.0.0
B	N.N.H.H	N.N.0.0
C	N.N.N.H	N.N.N.0

The third column shows the network number corresponding to the IP address of each class. It is derived from the IP number by setting the host ID octets to 0. For example the colorado.edu domain network address is 128.138.0.0.

IP Class Identification.   The three classes are distinguished by the values of their most significant bits, as shown in Figure 10.12. To the left of the figure are two number ranges associated with each class: the network number range of the class and the IP address range of the class.

class A address

If the msb of the address is 0 it is a *class A address*, and only the most significant octet is interpreted as the network address. The remaining 3 specify the host ID as assigned by the network administrator. There are only 126 networks in this class, because network numbers of 0 and 127 are reserved for special purposes. Thus the network numbers in this class range from 1.0.0.0 to 126.0.0.0, because the first octet, which specifies the network number, must have an msb of 0, so the octet ranges from 0000 0001 to 0111 1110, which are the decimal values 1 and 126. The IP addresses range from 1.0.0.1 to 126.255.255.254, obtained by allowing the host ID octets to range from 0 to 255, with the exception that no network number or host ID may be all 0s or all 1s.

class B address

If the most significant 2 bits are 10, then it is a *class B address*, and the most significant 2 octets are interpreted as the network address. The least significant 2 are available to be assigned to hosts by the network administrator. Because the 2 msbs of a class B address are fixed, the network numbers in this class range from 128.0.0.0 to 191.255.0.0. Thus the first octet will range from 1000 0000 to 1011 1111, yielding decimal values of 128 and 191, and the second octet can range from 0000 0000 to 1111 1111, that is, from 0 to 255 decimal. The IP address range is therefore from 128.0.0.1 to 191.255.255.254.

class C address

If the most significant 3 bits are 110, then it is a *class C address,* and the most significant 3 octets are interpreted as the network address. The remaining octet is locally assigned as the host ID. The first octet can therefore range from 1100 0000 to 1101 1111, which is 192 and 223 decimal, resulting in network addresses from 192.0.0.0 to 223.255.255.0, and IP addresses from 192.0.0.1 to 223.255.255.254.

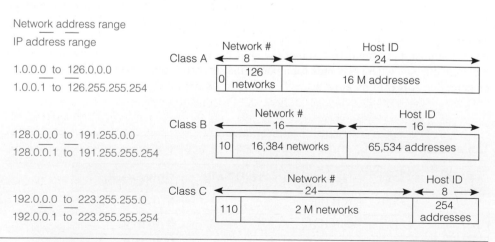

Fig. 10.12 Class A, B, and C Network Addresses

As an example of how to decipher an IP address, consider the network node with IP address 185.121.9.12. It is a class B address, because its first octet is 1011 1001, which contains a leading 10, the signature of a class B address. Its network address is 185.121.0.0, and the host ID is 9.12.

IP Address Restrictions.   There are some restrictions on IP address assignment. We mentioned above that no network number (or subnet, see the following section) or host ID may be all 0s or all 1s. In addition, the class A network 127.X is used as a *loop-back* function for processes residing on the same host that need to communicate with TCP, and addresses with 0s for the host ID portion are taken to refer to "this network." Likewise, addresses with 1110 and 11110 for their most significant bits are reserved for special purposes.

loop back

Wasted IP Address Space.   A bit of observation of the class A, B, C system will reveal that there are many wasted IP addresses. There are two ways that addresses are wasted. The first way is due to the fixing of the first 1, 2, or 3 significant digits of the first octet. For example, from Figure 10.12 we can see that restricting the msb of class A addresses to a 0 results in there being only 126 possible class A networks instead of the 254 networks that could be allocated if that msb could be either a 0 or a 1. This alone results in the loss of $(254 - 126) \times 16 \times 10^6$, or approximately 2 billion addresses! The second way is by restricting the number of classes to only three, A, B, and C. For example, although a class C network address can contain 254 hosts, a typical small businesses that applies for a class C address might only use a few of these host Ids, with the resulting waste of many IP addresses.

Reclaiming Address Space: CIDR, Classless Internet Domain Routing.   In 1995 the CIDR system, pronounced "cider," was adopted as an Internet standard, and now all ISPs are expected to use this system in their routers. In the class A, B, and C system, there are only three network classes identified by the first 1-3 msbs of the first octet. CIDR, in contrast, uses the first n bits to identify the network number, where n can be between 1 and 31. A CIDR address is represented as A.B.C.D/n with the n representing the number of msbs associated with the network number. So, for example, our class B address, 128.138.244.11, would be represented in the CIDR system as 128.138.244.11/24. Address 192.143.16.95/15 would mean that the first 15 bits represent the network number and the last 17 represent the host ID within the network.

Reclaiming More Address Space: Private IP Addresses, NAT, and DHCP.   The IPv4 specification allocates several IP address ranges as permanently unassigned: 10.0.0.0/8, 172.16.0.0/12, and 192.168.0.0/16. These can be used for any purpose inside a local site, provided they are not referenced outside of that site. Typically they are used to assign local IP addresses that are translated by hardware or software to public IP addresses before they are routed outside the local site. Hardware or software routers accomplish this by means of Network Address Translation, or NAT. NAT routers can be used to assign multiple internal hosts to a single external IP address. In this way a single assigned IP address can be used by many hosts within an internal network.

NAT: Network Address Translation

DHCP, Dynamic Host Configuration Protocol, can be used alone or in combination with NAT to further extend the number of host IDs within a local network. Prior to DHCP, each host had to be assigned a *static IP address*, which remained permanently with the

DHCP: Dynamic Host Confiiguration Protocol

host, whether or not the host was in service. Under the DHCP protocol, each time a host comes on line it requests an IP address, which is assigned dynamically by the DHCP server. This is referred to as a "lease" of the IP address, and when the host goes off-line, that address is freed up to be used by another host.

10.5.4 SUBNETS

An Internet site may have many hosts on its network. For example, the colorado.edu domain, which includes only the University of Colorado at Boulder campus, has over 36,000 hosts listed as having IP addresses on the 128.138.0.0 network. This is far too many hosts to have on a single LAN. Experience shows that an average LAN can support 6 to 12 hosts before users begin to notice a slowdown in LAN performance. So network administrators with many hosts will be motivated to have the hosts on their network distributed over many LANs within the domain, interconnecting the LANs by routers. In effect, this creates many internets within the domain. The Boulder campus has over 100 LANs within the colorado.edu domain.

This partitioning of the domain reduces overall network traffic within it, because routers isolate local LAN traffic within the local LAN. Experience has shown that much LAN traffic is local to the LAN—printer access and file transfer often involve only local LAN access, for example. In order for this to work, the routers *inside* the network must have a way of resolving addresses into *sub*networks, or LANs, within the larger network. The routers inside the domain must be fooled into thinking that part of the host ID field is part of the network address. Subnetting does just this. The administrator divides the host ID field into two parts. The most significant part becomes a subnet field, and the least significant part stays as the host ID field. The dividing line between the subnet bits and the host ID bits can be anywhere. It is not constrained to be at a dot. For example, a class B network administrator may decide to have 64 subnetwork LANs, and so devote the most significant 6 bits of the 16-bit (2-octet) host ID field to specifying the subnet, leaving 10 bits of the original 16 for host IDs.

Network and Subnetwork Masks.   In the routing section, we mentioned that routers used a network mask to isolate the network number from the host ID. That mask will be 255.0.0.0 for a class A address, 255.255.0.0 for class B, and 255.255.255.0 for class C. With *subnetting*, the network administrator creates a subnet mask for use within the LAN routers of the administered network that includes both the network mask bits and the subnet mask bits. This creates more networks within the domain and allows the routers to route to the subnetworks within the main network.

subnetting

Let us use the preceding network description as an example: a class B network whose administrator decides to devote 6 bits of the host ID field to a subnet field. Follow Figure 10.13 from top to bottom. The world outside the network sees a class B network. Inside the network, the leading 6 bits of the host ID field are to be devoted to subnets. The 6-bit subnet field will thus support up to 62 subnets. The remaining 10 bits are devoted to the subnet host ID. This means that every subnet can have up to 1,022 hosts residing on it. (Remember that no network or host field may have all 0s or all 1s.) The normal class B network mask, 255.255.0.0, must be altered for use inside the local routers to include the 6 bits of the subnet. The resulting subnet mask to be used by internal routers will then be 255.255.252.0, and will cause the routers to use the 6 msbs of the host ID field as part of the network field.

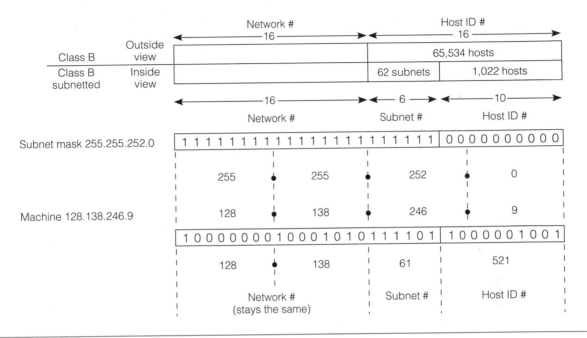

Fig. 10.13 Example of a Class B Network with a 6-Bit Subnet

Consider as an example a machine with IP address 128.138.246.9, shown at the bottom of the figure. What is its subnet and host ID inside the network? To compute those numbers we lay out the host's IP address as a 32-bit pattern, leaving the 16-bit network number part strictly alone, but dividing up the original 16-bit host ID field into subnet part and host ID part as specified by the network administrator: 6 bits and 10 bits. We compute the subnet number and host ID using these new fields, learning that machine 128.138.246.9 has a subnet number of 61 and a host ID of 521. Notice the following points:

- The IP address does not change! It remains 128.138.246.9 regardless of the subnetting scheme. This is because in dotted decimal notation the dots separate octets, and the bit pattern of the assigned address does not change.

- What changes is the subnet mask. It enlarges to include the subnet bits, and in so doing, it generates a subnet number and a new host ID number.

- To a router inside the 128.138 domain, the machine resides on subnet 61 and has a host ID of 521, but this is normally of concern only to the network system administration personnel.

Figure 10.14 shows two more ways of subnetting a class B network: with an 8-bit subnet address and with a 10-bit subnet address. Observe again that to the outside world, that is, the Internet world outside of the network, the IP address is an ordinary class B address, with the first 2 octets devoted to the network number, and the last 2 devoted to host IDs inside that network. Also observe that in Figure 10.13, the dots separating the octets in the subnet mask do not move.

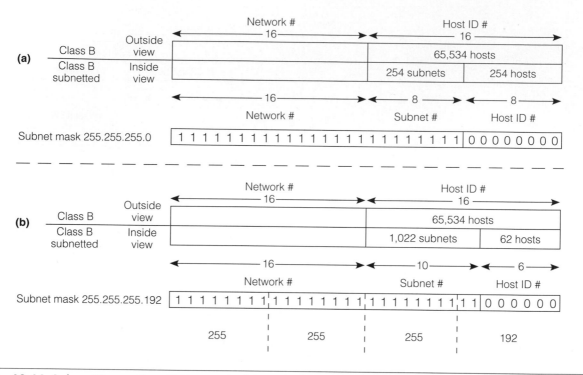

Fig. 10.14 Subnetting a Class B Network: (a) an 8-Bit Subnet Address; (b) a 10-Bit Subnet Address

10.5.5 TRENDS AND RESEARCH: INTERNET FUTURES

We observed earlier that electronic mail, remote login by use of the telnet command, and file transfer by use of the ftp file transfer protocol were developed many years ago to support Internet users. At that time, nearly all Internet hosts ran the Bell Laboratory's Unix operating system. With the increasing popularity and importance of the Internet, nearly every operating system supports TCP/IP and access to variants of the applications above. Many of the variants support graphical user interfaces that allow point-and-click email, and remote login and file transfer. The advent of the World Wide Web allows web browsers to roam at will over web sites worldwide. Some web sites report tens of thousands of accesses daily.

TCP/IP applications under development include Internet Phone, a means of sending voice communications over the Internet, and video conferencing, which allows two-way video communications over the Internet. All of the on-line services such as Compuserve and America Online now provide Internet access.

This extraordinary boom in Internet popularity threatens to bog it down due to bandwidth requirements. Firms such as Sprint and Level 3, which provide long-haul Internet bandwidth, find it difficult to keep pace with demand. This may become a serious problem as bandwidth hogs such as real-time video become more popular and finally the norm. Some people predict that the Internet will lose traffic to private networks that provide similar services.

In 1969, Internet designers estimated that 256 networks would be more than adequate to serve the national network needs. This is reminiscent of the (reputed) statement by an

IBM executive in the 1940s that five computers would be adequate to handle the nation's computing requirements or the (reputed) statement by an Intel executive in 1973 that the microprocessor market would probably top out at 5,000 units per year. We intend no disrespect toward IBM or Intel with these statements, which just reflect human nature.

Even with the CIDR system described above we will soon run out of IP addresses. A new protocol, IPv6, Internet Protocol version 6, extends IP addresses from 32 to 128 bits. This protocol is only slowly being adopted, however, because of the need to reprogram or replace routers to handle the new protocol. With the possibility that in the future every single wall plug, every appliance, every *wristwatch* will have an IP address, one hopes that IPv6 is adopted in a timely fashion.

Summary

- More and more computer I/O is going not to peripheral devices, but over networks to other computers. Network protocols are the key to allowing machines to correctly interpret each other's data.

- At the lowest level, data-link signaling standards and interconnection topologies must be agreed on and supported.

- Communications layer models, such as the OSI model, partition the overall problem of communication between two applications programs running on different machines into a chain of interacting protocols.

- The EIA RS-232 protocol is an important example of a point-to-point communications protocol. Combined with modems and data link control, it applies to connecting home computers as well as to long-distance connections between routers.

- Ethernet is an important example of a local area network. Many computers can communicate at high speeds on a LAN because they are physically near each other. Machines that attach to an Ethernet must obey the signaling and addressing standards it specifies.

- The Internet is a global interconnection of subnetworks. Communication uses the TCP/IP protocol supported by one of several LAN protocols for the data-link and physical levels.

- Important aspects of Internet communication include the way addresses are interpreted to identify subnetworks and machines, and how messages are routed through the individual networks to reach their final destinations.

Bibliography

Two good general references covering the topics found in this chapter follow:

D.Comer, *Internetworking with TCP/IP Vol.1: Principles, Protocols, and Architecture*, 4th ed. Prentice-Hall, Englewood Cliffs, NJ, 2000.

W. Stallings, *Data and Computer Communications*, 6th ed., Prentice-Hall, Englewood Cliffs, NJ, 1999.

A good analysis of digital data signaling and encoding schemes can be found in the following texts:

B. Sklar, *Digital Communications: Fundamentals & Applications*, 2nd ed., Prentice-Hall, Englewood Cliffs, NJ, 2001.

R. Freeman, *Telecommunications Transmission Handbook*, 4th ed., John Wiley & Sons, New York, 1998.

A discussion of error detection and correction techniques in communications can be found in:

S. B. Wicker, *Error Control Systems for Digital Communication and Storage*, Prentice-Hall, Englewood Cliffs, NJ, 1995.

The RS-232 standard is well covered in:

J. Axelson, *Serial Port Complete*, Lakewood Research, Madison, WI, 1998.

In-depth coverage of local area networks appears in:

W. Stallings, *Local and Metropolitan Area Networks*, 6th ed., Prentice-Hall, Englewood Cliffs, NJ, 2000.

For a more thorough discussion of network protocols, see:

M. G. Naugle, *Network Protocol Handbook*, McGraw-Hill, New York, 1994.

USB and FireWire are well covered in the Mindshare series:

Mindshare, Inc., Don Anderson, *Universal Serial Bus System Architecture*, 2nd ed., Addison-Wesley, Reading, MA, 2001.

Mindshare, Inc., Don Anderson, *FireWire System Architecture: IEEE 1394*, 2nd ed., Addison-Wesley, Reading, MA, 1998.

The TCP/IP protocol suite is covered in detail in these texts:

R. Stevens, *The Protocols (TCP/IP Illustrated, Volume 1)*, Addison-Wesley, Reading, MA, 1994.

U. Black, *IP Routing Protocols: RIP, OSPF, BGP, PNNI and Cisco Routing Protocols*, Prentice-Hall, Englewood Cliffs, NJ, 2000.

Interconnection issues are well covered in:

R. Perlman, *Interconnections: Bridges, Routers, Switches, and Internetworking Protocols*, 2nd ed., Addison-Wesley, Reading, MA, 1999.

In-depth coverage of ATM can be found in:

D. E. McDysan, D. L. Spohn, *ATM Theory and Applications*, Osborne McGraw-Hill, Berkeley, CA, 1998.

Exercises

10.1 A packet-switched network has a bit-error rate of 10^{-14}. Assume that each 1 K packet will contain either a 4-byte CRC field or a 16-byte ECC field. If you were designing the error detection and correction strategy, which approach would you choose to maximize throughput if each erroneous packet must be retransmitted? Show your calculations, and state any assumptions you make.   **(§10.1)**

10.2 a. How many distinguishable signals must be capable of being sent per signal change in a 57,600 bps modem?

   b. How many bits are effectively transmitted per signal change in this modem?   **(§10.2)**

10.3 Design the 2^n-to-n encoder that a modem might use to convert the 2^n different possible signals detected by a modem during one baud time into the n bits that are part of the received message.   **(§10.2)**

10.4 A 14,400 bps modem is transmitting frames with 1 start bit, 8 data bits, no parity bits, and 1 stop bit. What is the maximum number of characters per second that can be transmitted?   **(§10.2)**

10.5   Write a C program fragment to convert a string of text to uppercase.   (**§10.2**)

10.6   Write a C program fragment to convert a string of ASCII digits to BCD digits, stored 2 to a byte.   (**§10.2**)

10.7   Both RG-8 and RG-58 coaxial cables and twisted pair wiring have a velocity factor of approximately 0.66.

   a. What is the worst-case time interval between when a thicknet Ethernet station begins transmitting and when it detects a collision?

   b. What is the physical length of a bit in the 100BASE-T Ethernet?

   c. How many bits may be on the cable simultaneously in this 100BASE Ethernet?

   d. Suggest an average back-off time for this net after a collision. Justify your answer with a brief discussion.   (**§10.3**)

10.8   What is the *maximum* data transmission rate for the data portion of a 100BASE-T Ethernet if one station is transmitting a large file, and it is the only station transmitting? Assume the maximum allowable packet size is used, and that the packet's entire data field is used for the transmitted data.   (**§10.3**)

10.9   a. What is the raw data rate of a digital video signal with 1260×1024 24-bit pixels at 30 frames per second? Express your answer in bps.

   b. How many packets per second would be required to transmit the signal over a 100BASE-5 Ethernet link?

   c. What percentage of the total bandwidth of the Ethernet LAN is consumed by this transmission, assuming no collisions, use of the entire data field, and a connectionless protocol?   (**§10.3**)

10.10   a. How long would it take to transmit the contents of a 1-hour-long CD over a 100BASE-T Ethernet link, assuming that the full network bandwidth were available. Assume no collisions, use of the entire data field, and a connectionless protocol.

   b. How many people could be listening to their own CD selection over this network simultaneously?   (**§10.3**)

10.11   How many networks can the current class A, B, and C 32-bit IP addresses support?   (**§10.4**)

10.12   Approximately how many IP addresses cannot be used in class B?   (**§10.4**)

10.13   The IP address of a certain machine is 63.251.176.141.

   a. What class network does this machine belong to?

   b. What is its network address?

   c. What is the network mask?

   d. What is the host ID?   (**§10.4**)

10.14   Suppose that network 216.241.34.0 is subnetted using a 4-bit subnet mask.

   a. How many host IDs can each subnet support?

   b. How many subnets can it support?

   c. What is the subnet address of machine 216.241.34.243?

   d. What is its host ID?

   e. What is its subnet mask?   (**§10.4**)

10.15   Internet routers need network masks for class A, B, and C networks. Assume that the router stores the incoming IP address in a 32-bit register.

   a. Design a combinational circuit that will generate the proper mask to extract the network address from the received IP address.

   b. Further assume that the router's IP network address is stored in a 32-bit register. Design the circuitry to generate the 1-bit "match" signal if the two addresses match.   (**§10.4**)

APPENDIX A
Digital Logic

by Miles Murdocca
Internet Institute USA

Appendix Outline

In this appendix, we take a look at a few basic principles of digital logic that we can apply to the design of a digital computer. We start by studying *combinational logic*, in which logical decisions are based only on

479

combinations of the inputs. We then look at *sequential logic*, in which decisions are based on combinations of the current inputs as well as the past history of inputs. With an understanding of these underlying principles, we can design digital logic circuits from which an entire computer can be constructed. We begin with the fundamental building block of a digital computer, the *combinational logic unit (CLU)*.

A.1 Combinational Logic

A combinational logic unit translates a set of inputs into a set of outputs according to one or more mapping functions. The outputs of a CLU are strictly functions of the inputs, and the outputs are updated immediately after the inputs change. A basic model of a CLU is shown in Figure A.1. A set of inputs $i_0 - i_n$ is presented to the CLU, which produces a set of outputs according to mapping functions $f_0 - f_m$.

Inputs and outputs for a CLU normally have two distinct values: high and low. When signals (values) are taken from a finite set, the circuits that use them are referred to as being *digital*. A digital electronic circuit receives inputs and produces outputs in which 0 volts (0 V) is typically considered to be a low value and +5 V is considered to be a high value. This convention is not used everywhere: High-speed circuits tend to use lower voltages; some computer circuits work in the *analog* domain, in which a continuum of values is allowed; and digital optical circuits might use phase or polarization in which high or low values are no longer meaningful. An application in which analog circuitry is appropriate is in flight simulation, since the analog circuits more closely approximate the mechanics of an aircraft than do digital circuits.

Although the vast majority of digital computers are binary, multivalued circuits also exist. A wire that is capable of carrying more than two values can be more efficient at transmitting information than a wire that carries only two values. A digital *multivalued* circuit is different from an analog circuit in that a multivalued circuit deals with signals that take on one of a finite number of values, whereas an analog signal can take on a continuum of values. The use of multivalued circuits is theoretically valuable, but in practice it is difficult to create reliable circuitry that distinguishes between more than two values. For this reason, multivalued logic is currently in limited use. In this text, we are primarily concerned with digital binary circuits, in which exactly two values are allowed for any input or output. Thus, we will consider only binary signals.

A.2 Truth Tables

In 1854 George Boole published his seminal work on an algebra for representing logic. Boole was interested in capturing the mathematics of thought, and developed a representation for statements of factual information such as "The door is open" or "The door is not open." Boole's algebra was further developed by Shannon into the form we use today.

In Boolean algebra, we assume the existence of a basic postulate, that a binary variable takes on a single value of 0 or 1. These values correspond to the 0 and +5 voltages mentioned in the previous section. The assignment can also be done in reverse order for 1 and 0, respectively. For purposes of understanding the behavior of digital circuits, we can abstract away the physical correspondence to voltages and consider only the symbolic values 0 and 1.

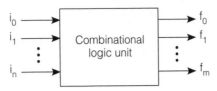

Fig. A.1   External View of a Combinational Logic Unit

truth table

One of Boole's key contributions was the development of the *truth table,* which captures logical relationships in a tabular form. Consider a room with two three-way switches A and B that control a light Z. Either switch can be up or down, or both switches can be up or down. When exactly one switch is up, the light is on. When both switches are up or down, the light is off. A truth table can be constructed that enumerates all possible settings of the switches as shown in Figure A.2. In the table, a switch is assigned the value 0 if it is down, otherwise it is assigned the value 1. The light is on when $Z = 1$.

In a truth table, all possible input combinations of binary variables are enumerated, and a corresponding output value of 0 or 1 is assigned for each input combination. For the truth table shown in Figure A.2, the output function Z depends upon input variables A and B. For each combination of input variables, there are two values that can be assigned to Z: 0 or 1. We can choose a different assignment for Figure A.2, in which the light is on only when both switches are up or both switches are down, in which case the truth table shown in Figure A.3 enumerates all possible states of the light for each switch setting. The wiring pattern would also need to be changed to correspond. For two input variables, there are $2^2 = 4$ input combinations, and $2^4 = 16$ possible assignments of outputs to input combinations. In general, since there are 2^n input combinations for n inputs, there are $2^{(2^n)}$ possible assignments of output values to input combinations.

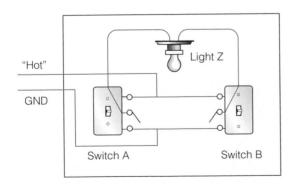

Inputs		Output
A	B	Z
0	0	0
0	1	1
1	0	1
1	1	0

Fig. A.2   A Truth Table Relates the State of 3-Way Switches *A* and *B* to Light *Z*

Inputs		Output
A	B	Z
0	0	1
0	1	0
1	0	0
1	1	1

Fig. A.3   Alternate Assignment of Outputs to Switch Settings

A.3   Logic Gates

Boolean logic functions

If we enumerate all possible assignments of switch settings for two input variables, then we will obtain the 16 assignments shown in Figure A.4. We refer to these functions as *Boolean logic functions*. A number of assignments have special names. The *AND* function is true (produces a 1) only when A and B are 1, whereas the *OR* function is true when either A or B is 1, or when both A and B are 1. A function is false when its output is 0, and so the *False* function is always 0, whereas the *True* function is always 1. The plus signs in the Boolean expressions denote logical *OR*; they do not imply arithmetic addition. The juxtaposition of two variables, as in *AB*, denotes logical *AND* among the variables.

Inputs		Output							
A	B	False	AND	$A\bar{B}$	A	$\bar{A}B$	B	XOR	OR
0	0	0	0	0	0	0	0	0	0
0	1	0	0	0	0	1	1	1	1
1	0	0	0	1	1	0	0	1	1
1	1	0	1	0	1	0	1	0	1

Inputs		Output							
A	B	NOR	XNOR	$\bar{B}$	$A+\bar{B}$	$\bar{A}$	$\bar{A}+B$	NAND	True
0	0	1	1	1	1	1	1	1	1
0	1	0	0	0	0	1	1	1	1
1	0	0	0	1	1	0	0	1	1
1	1	0	1	0	1	0	1	0	1

Fig. A.4   Truth Table Showing All Possible Functions of Two Binary Variables

The *A* and *B* functions simply repeat the *A* and *B* inputs, respectively, whereas the $\overline{A}$ and $\overline{B}$ functions *complement A* and *B*, by producing a 0 where the uncomplemented function is a 1 and by producing a 1 where the uncomplemented function is a 0. In general, a bar over a term denotes the complement operation, and so the *NAND* and *NOR* functions are complements to *AND* and *OR*, respectively. The *XOR* function is true when either of its inputs, but not both, is true. The *XNOR* function is the complement to *XOR*. The remaining functions are interpreted similarly.

A *logic gate* is a physical device that implements a simple Boolean function. The functions that are listed in Figure A.4 have representations as logic gate symbols, a few of which are shown in Figure A.5 and Figure A.6. For each of the functions, *A* and *B* are binary inputs and *F* is the output.

In Figure A.5, the AND and OR gates behave as previously described. The output of the AND gate is true when both of its inputs are true, and is false otherwise. The output of the OR gate is true when either or both of its inputs are true, and is false otherwise. The buffer simply copies its input to its output. Although the buffer has no logical significance, it serves an important practical role as an amplifier, allowing a number of logic gates to be driven by a single signal. The NOT gate (also called an *inverter*) produces a 1 at its output for a 0 at its input, and produces a 0 at its output for a 1 at its input. Again, the inverted output signal is referred to as the complement of the input. The circle at the output of the NOT gate denotes the complement operation.

complement

logic gate

inverter

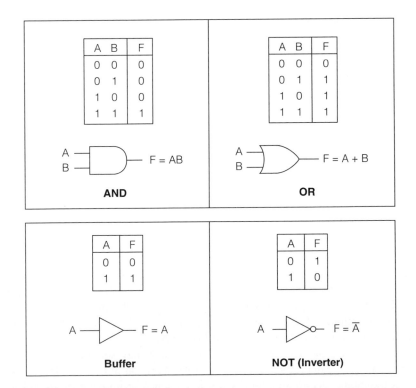

Fig. A.5   Logic Gate Symbols for *AND*, *OR*, Buffer, and *NOT* Boolean Functions

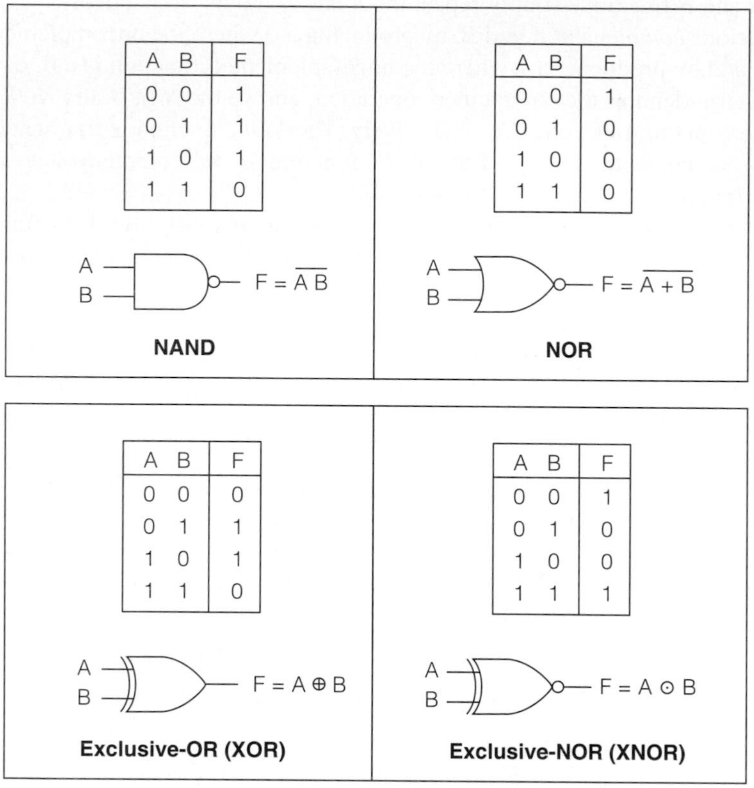

NAND

A	B	F
0	0	1
0	1	1
1	0	1
1	1	0

NOR

A	B	F
0	0	1
0	1	0
1	0	0
1	1	0

Exclusive-OR (XOR)

A	B	F
0	0	0
0	1	1
1	0	1
1	1	0

Exclusive-NOR (XNOR)

A	B	F
0	0	1
0	1	0
1	0	0
1	1	1

Fig. A.6 Logic Gate Symbols for *NAND, NOR, XOR,* and *XNOR* Boolean Functions

In Figure A.6, the NAND and NOR gates produce complementary outputs to the AND and OR gates, respectively. The exclusive-OR (XOR) gate produces a 1 when either of its inputs, but not both, are 1. In general, XOR produces a 1 at its output whenever the number of 1's at its inputs is odd. This generalization is important in understanding how an XOR gate with more than two inputs behaves. The exclusive-NOR (XNOR) gate produces a complementary output to the XOR gate.

The logic symbols shown in Figure A.5 and Figure A.6 are only the basic forms; several variations are often used. For example, there can be more inputs, as for the three-input AND gate shown in Figure A.7a. The circles at the outputs of the NOT, NOR, and XNOR gates denote the complement operation, and can be placed at the inputs of logic gates to indicate that the inputs are inverted upon entering the gate, as shown in Figure A.7b. Depending on the technology used, some logic gates produce complementary outputs. The corresponding logic symbol for a complementary logic gate indicates both outputs, as illustrated in Figure A.7c.

Physically, logic gates are not magical, although it may seem that they are when a device like an inverter can produce a logical 1 (+5 V) at its output when a logical 0 (0 V) is provided at the input. Electrically, logic gates have power terminals that are not normally shown. Figure A.8a illustrates an inverter in which the +5 V and 0 V (GND) terminals are

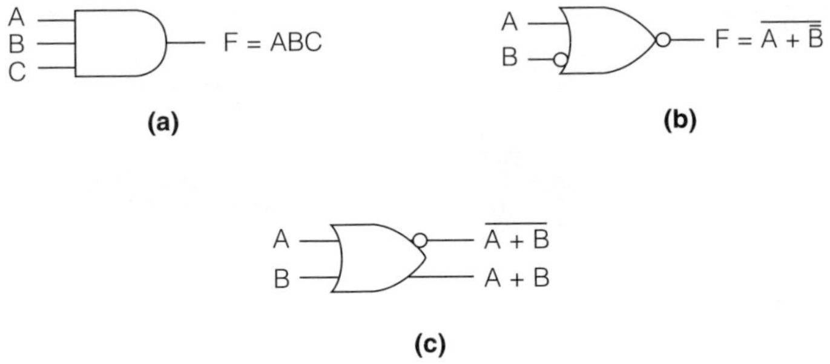

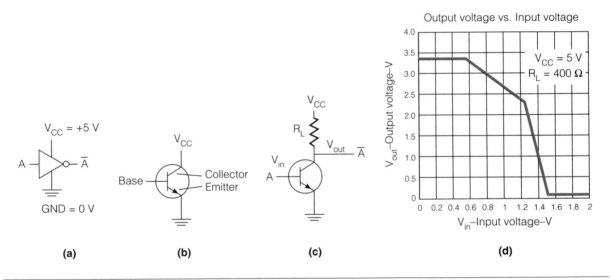

Fig. A.7   Variations of the Basic Logic Gate Symbols for (a) Three Inputs; (b) a Negated Input; (c) Complementary Outputs

Fig. A.8   (a) Power Terminals for an Inverter Made Visible; (b) Schematic Symbol for a Transistor; (c) Transistor Circuit for an Inverter; (d) Static Transfer Function for Inverter

made visible. The +5 V signal is commonly referred to as V_{CC} for "voltage collector-collector." In a physical circuit, all of the V_{CC} and GND terminals are connected to the corresponding terminals of a power supply.

Logic gates are composed of electrical devices called *transistors,* which have a funda-   transistor
mental switching property that allows them to control a strong electrical signal with a weak signal. This supports the process of amplification, which is crucial for cascading logic gates. Without amplification, we would only be able to send a signal through a few logic gates before it deteriorated to the point that it was overcome by noise, which exists at every point in an electrical circuit to some degree.

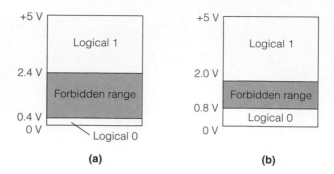

Fig. A.9   Assignments of Logical 0 and 1 to Voltage Ranges (a) at the Output of a Logic Gate;
(b) at the Input to a Logic Gate

The schematic symbol for a transistor is shown in Figure A.8b. When there is no positive voltage on the base, then a current will not flow from V_{CC} to GND. Thus, for an inverter, a logical 0 (0 V) on the base will produce a logical 1 (+5 V) at the collector terminal, as illustrated in Figure A.8c. If, however, a positive voltage is applied to V_{in}, then a current will flow from V_{CC} to GND, which prevents V_{out} from producing enough signal for the inverter output to be a logical 1. In effect, when +5 V is applied to V_{in}, a logical 0 appears at V_{out}. The input-output relationship of a logic gate follows a nonlinear curve, as shown in Figure A.8d for transistor-transistor logic (TTL). The nonlinearity is an important gain property that makes cascadable operation possible.

A useful paradigm is to think of current flowing through wires as water flowing through pipes. If we open a connection on a pipe from V_{CC} to GND, then the water flowing to V_{out} will be reduced to a great extent, although some water will still make it out. By choosing an appropriate value for the resistor R_L, we can restrict the flow to minimize this effect.

Since there will always be some current that flows even when we have a logical 0 at V_{out}, we need to assign logical 0 and 1 to voltages using safe margins. If we assign logical 0 to 0 V and logical 1 to +5 V, then our circuits may not work properly if .1 V appears at the output of an inverter instead of 0 V, which can happen in practice. For this reason, we design circuits in which assignments of logical 0 and 1 are made using *thresholds*. In Figure A.9a, logical 0 is assigned to the voltage range 0 V to 0.4 V and logical 1 is assigned to the voltage range 2.4 V to +5 V. The ranges shown in Figure A.9a are for the output of a logic gate. There may be some attenuation (a reduction in voltage) introduced in the connection between the output of one logic gate and the input to another, and for that reason the thresholds arc relaxed by 0.4 V at the input to a logic gate, as shown in Figure A.9b. These ranges can differ depending on the logic family. The output ranges only make sense, however, if the gate inputs settle into the logical 0 or 1 ranges at the input. For this reason, inputs to a logic gate should never be left "floating," that is, disconnected from a gate output, V_{CC}, or GND.

Figure A.10 shows transistor circuits for two-input NAND and NOR gates. For the NAND case, both of the V_1 and V_2 inputs must be in the logical 1 region to produce a voltage in the logical 0 region at V_{out}. For the NOR case, if either or both of the V_1 and V_2 inputs are in the logical 1 region, then a voltage in the logical 0 region will be produced at V_{out}.

threshold

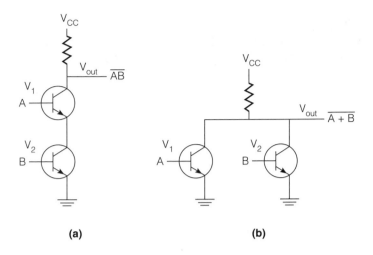

Fig. A.10 Transistor Circuits for (a) Two-Input NAND Gate; (b) Two-Input NOR Gate

A.4 Properties of Boolean Algebra

Table A.1 a summarizes a few basic properties of Boolean algebra that can be applied to Boolean logic expressions. The postulates (known as Huntington's postulates) are basic axioms of Boolean algebra and therefore need no proofs. The theorems can be proven from the postulates. Each relationship shown in the table has both an AND and an OR form as a result of the *principle of duality*. The dual form is obtained by changing ANDs to ORs, changing ORs to ANDs, and exchanging 1 and 0.

principle of duality

The *commutative* property states that the order in which two variables appear in an AND or OR function is not significant. By the principle of duality, the commutative property has an AND form ($AB = BA$) and an OR form ($A + B = B + A$). The *distributive* property shows how a variable is distributed over an expression with which it is ANDed. By the principle of duality, the dual form of the distributive property is obtained as shown.

commutative and distributive properties

The *identity* property states that a variable that is ANDed with 1 or is ORed with 0 produces the original variable. The *complement* property states that a variable that is ANDed with its complement is logically false (produces a 0, since at least one input is 0), and a variable that is ORed with its complement is logically true (produces a 1, since at least one input is 1).

identity and complement properties

The *zero* and *one* theorems state that a variable that is ANDed with 0 produces a 0, and a variable that is ORed with 1 produces a 1. The *idempotence* theorem states that a variable that is ANDed or ORed with itself produces the original variable. For instance, if the inputs to an AND gate have the same value or the inputs to an OR gate have the same value, then the output for each gate is the same as the input. The *associative* theorem states that the order of ANDing or ORing is logically of no consequence. The *involution* theorem states that the complement of a complement leaves the original variable (or expression) unchanged.

zero, one, idempotence, and involution theorems

Table A.1 Basic Properties of Boolean Algebra

Relationship	Dual	Property
Postulates		
$A\,B = B\,A$	$A + B = B + A$	Commutative
$A\,(B + C) = A\,B + A\,C$	$A + B\,C = (A + B)\,(A + C)$	Distributive
$1\,A = A$	$0 + A = A$	Identity
$A\,\bar{A} = 0$	$A + \bar{A} = 1$	Complement
Theorems		
$0\,A = 0$	$1 + A = 1$	Zero and one theorems
$AA = A$	$A + A = A$	Idempotence
$A\,(B\,C) = (A\,B)\,C$	$A + (B + C) = (A + B) + C$	Associative
$\bar{\bar{A}} = A$		Involution
$\overline{A\,B} = \bar{A} + \bar{B}$	$\overline{A + B} = \bar{A}\,\bar{B}$	DeMorgan's theorem
$AB + \bar{A}\,C + BC$ $= AB + \bar{A}\,C$	$(A + B)(\bar{A} + C)(B + C)$ $= (A + B)(\bar{A} + C)$	Consensus theorem
$A\,(A + B) = A$	$A + A\,B = A$	Absorption theorem

DeMorgan's theorem, consensus and absorption theorems

DeMorgan's theorem, the *consensus theorem,* and the *absorption theorem* may not be obvious, and so we prove DeMorgan's theorem for the two-variable case using perfect induction (enumerating all cases), and leave the proofs of the consensus theorem and the absorption theorem as exercises (see Exercises 25 and 26 at the end of this Appendix. Figure A.11 shows a truth table for each expression that appears in either form of DeMorgan's theorem. The expressions that appear on the left and right sides of each form of DeMorgan's theorem produce equivalent outputs, which proves the theorem for two variables.

computational completeness

Not all of the logic gates discussed so far are necessary to achieve *computational completeness,* which means that any digital logic circuit can be created from these gates. Three sets of logic gates that are computationally complete are {AND, OR, NOT}, {NAND}, and {NOR}; there are others as well.

As an example of how a computationally complete set of logic gates can implement other logic gates that are not part of the set, consider implementing the OR function with the {NAND} set. DeMorgan's theorem can be used to map an OR gate onto a NAND gate, as shown in Figure A.12. The original OR function $(A + B)$ is complemented twice,

A	B	$\overline{AB} = \bar{A} + \bar{B}$		$\overline{A + B} = \bar{A}\bar{B}$	
0	0	1	1	1	1
0	1	1	1	0	0
1	0	1	1	0	0
1	1	0	0	0	0

Fig. A.11 DeMorgan's Theorem Is Proven for the Two-Variable Case

DeMorgan's theorem: $A + B = \overline{\overline{A + B}} = \overline{\overline{A}\,\overline{B}}$

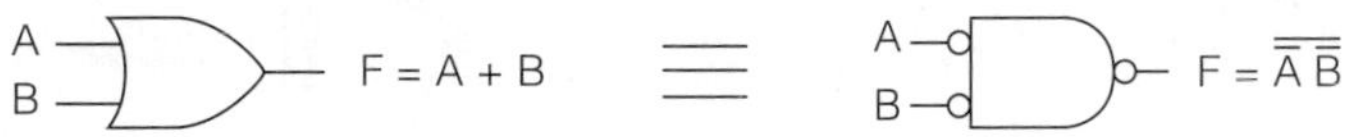

$F = A + B$ ≡ $F = \overline{\overline{A}\,\overline{B}}$

Fig. A.12 DeMorgan's Theorem Is Used in Mapping an OR Gate onto a NAND Gate

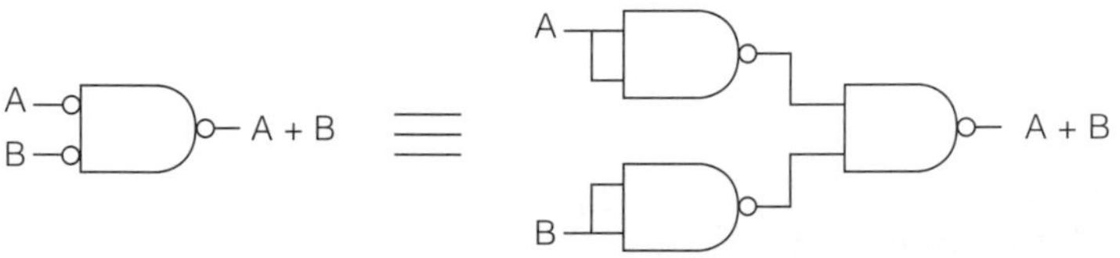

$A + B$ ≡ $A + B$

Fig. A.13 Inverted Inputs to a NAND Gate Implemented with NAND Gates

which leaves the function unchanged by the involution property. DeMorgan's theorem then changes OR to AND, and distributes the innermost overbar over the terms A and B. The inverted inputs can also be implemented with NAND gates by the property of idempotence, as shown in Figure A.13. The OR function is thus implemented with NANDs. Functional equivalence among logic gates is important for practical considerations, because one type of logic gate may have better operating characteristics than another for a given technology.

A.5 The Sum-of-Products Form and Logic Diagrams

Suppose now that we need to implement a more complex function than just a simple logic gate, such as the three-input *majority* function described by the truth table shown in Figure A.14. The majority function is true whenever more than half of its inputs are true; it can be thought of as a balance that tips to the left or right depending on whether there are more 0's or 1's at the input. This is a common operation used in fault recovery, in which the outputs of identical circuits operating on the same data are compared, and the greatest number of similar values determines the output (also referred to as "voting" or "odd one out").

majority function

Since no single logic gate discussed up to this point implements the majority function directly, we transform the function into a two-level AND-OR equation, and then implement the function with an arrangement of logic gates from the set {AND, OR, NOT}, for instance. The two levels come about because exactly one level of ANDed variables is followed by exactly one OR level. The Boolean equation that describes the majority function is true whenever F is true in the truth table. Thus, F is true when $A = 0$, $B = 1$, and $C = 1$, or when $A = 1$, $B = 0$, and $C = 1$, and so on for the remaining cases.

One way to represent logic equations is to use the *sum-of-products (SOP) form,* in which a collection of ANDed variables are ORed together. The Boolean logic equation that describes the majority function is shown in SOP form in Equation A.1. Again, the plus signs denote logical OR and do not imply arithmetic addition.

sum-of-products

Minterm Index	A	B	C	F
0	0	0	0	0
1	0	0	1	0
2	0	1	0	0
3	0	1	1	1
4	1	0	0	0
5	1	0	1	1
6	1	1	0	1
7	1	1	1	1

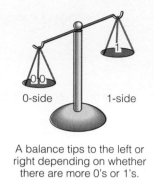

0-side   1-side

A balance tips to the left or right depending on whether there are more 0's or 1's.

Fig. A.14 Truth Table for the Majority Function

$$F = \overline{A}BC + A\overline{B}C + AB\overline{C} + ABC \qquad \text{[Eq. A.1]}$$

By inspecting the equation, we can determine that four three-input AND gates will implement the four *product terms* $\overline{A}BC$, *x*, $AB\overline{C}$, and ABC, and then the outputs of these four AND gates can be connected to the inputs of a four-input OR gate, as shown in Figure A.15. This circuit performs the majority function, which we can verify by enumerating all eight input combinations and observing the output for each case.

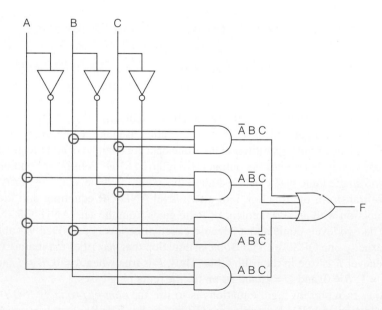

Fig. A.15 A Two-Level AND-OR Circuit Implements the Majority Function (Inverters at the Inputs Are Not Included in the Two-Level Count)

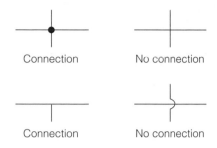

Fig. A.16 Four Notations Used at Circuit Intersections

The circuit diagram shows a commonly used notation that indicates the presence or absence of a connection, which is summarized in Figure A.16. Two lines that pass through each other do not connect unless a darkened circle is placed at the intersection point. Two lines that meet in a ⊤ are connected, as indicated by the six highlighted intersections in Figure A.15, and so darkened circles do not need to be placed over those intersection points.

When a product term contains exactly one instance of every variable, either in true or complemented form, it is called a *minterm*. A minterm has a value of 1 for exactly one of the entries in the truth table. That is, a *minimum* number of terms (one) will make the function true. As an alternative, the function is sometimes written as the logical sum over the true entries. Equation A.1 can be rewritten as shown in Equation A.2, in which the indices correspond to the minterm indices shown at the left in Figure A.14.

minterm

$$F = \sum \langle 3, 5, 6, 7 \rangle \qquad \text{[Eq. A.2]}$$

This notation is appropriate for the *canonical form* of a Boolean equation, which contains only minterms. Equation A.1 and A.2 are both said to be in "canonical sum-of-products form."

canonical form

A.6   The Product-of-Sums Form

As a dual to the sum-of-products form, a Boolean equation can be represented in the *product-of-sums (POS) form*. An equation that is in POS form contains a collection of ORed variables that are ANDed together. One method of obtaining the POS form is to start with the complement of the SOP form and then apply DeMorgan's theorem. For example, referring again to the truth table for the majority function shown in Figure A.14, the complement is obtained by selecting input terms that produce 0's at the output, as shown in Equation A.3:

product-of-sums (POS) form

$$F = \overline{\overline{ABC} + \overline{A}B\overline{C} + \overline{A}B\overline{C} + A\overline{BC}} \qquad \text{[Eq. A.3]}$$

Complementing both sides yields Equation A.4:

$$\overline{F} = \overline{ABC} + \overline{A}B\overline{C} + \overline{A}B\overline{C} + A\overline{BC} \qquad \text{[Eq. A.4]}$$

Applying DeMorgan's theorem in the form $\overline{W + X + Y + Z} = \overline{W}\,\overline{X}\,\overline{Y}\,\overline{Z}$ at the outermost level produces Equation A.5:

$$F = (\overline{\overline{A}BC})(\overline{\overline{A}\overline{B}C})(\overline{\overline{A}B\overline{C}})(\overline{A\overline{B}\overline{C}}) \qquad \text{[Eq. A.5]}$$

Applying DeMorgan's theorem in the form $\overline{WXYZ} = \overline{W} + \overline{X} + \overline{Y} + \overline{Z}$ to the parenthesized terms produces Equation A.6:

$$F = (A + B + C)(A + B + \overline{C})(A + \overline{B} + C)(\overline{A} + B + C) \qquad \text{[Eq. A.6]}$$

maxterms

Equation A.6 is in POS form, and contains four *maxterms*, in which every variable appears exactly once in either true or complemented form. A maxterm, such as *(A + B + C)*, has a value of 0 for only one entry in the truth table. That is, it is true for the *maximum* number of truth table entries without reducing to the trivial function of being always true. An equation that consists of only maxterms in POS form is said to be in "canonical product-of-sums form." An OR-AND circuit that implements Equation A.6 is shown in Figure A.17. The OR-AND form is logically equivalent to the AND-OR form shown in Figure A.15.

One motivation for using the POS form over the SOP form is that it may result in a smaller Boolean equation. A smaller Boolean equation may result in a simpler circuit, although this does not always hold true since there are a number of considerations that do not directly depend on the size of the Boolean equation, such as the complexity of the wiring topology.

gate count,
gate input count

The *gate count* is a measure of circuit complexity that is obtained by counting all of the logic gates. The *gate input count* is another measure of circuit complexity that is obtained by

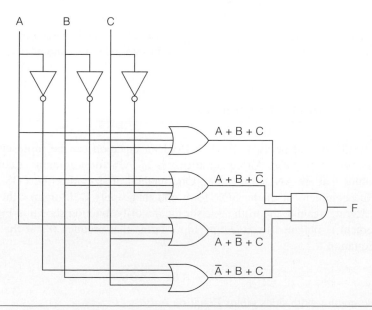

Fig. A.17 A Two-Level OR-AND Circuit that Implements the Majority Function (Inverters Are Not Included in the Two-Level Count)

counting the number of inputs to all of the logic gates. For the circuits shown in Figure A.15 and Figure A.17, a gate count of eight and a gate input count of 19 are obtained for both the SOP and POS forms. For this case, there is no difference in circuit complexity between the SOP and POS forms, but for other cases the differences can be significant. There is a variety of methods for reducing the complexity of digital circuits, a few of which are presented in Section A.10.

A.7   Positive versus Negative Logic

Up to this point we have assumed that high and low voltage levels correspond to logical 1 and 0 respectively, which is known as *active-high* or *positive logic*. We can make the reverse assignment instead: low voltage for logical 1 and high voltage for logical 0, which is known as *active-low* or *negative logic*. The use of negative logic is sometimes preferred to positive logic for applications in which the logic inhibits an event rather than enabling an event.

active-high, or positive logic

active-low, or negative logic

Figure A.18 illustrates the behavior of AND-OR and NAND-NOR gate pairs for both positive and negative logic. The positive logic AND gate behaves as a negative logic OR gate. The physical logic gate is the same regardless of the positive or negative sense of the logic—only the interpretation of the signals is changed.

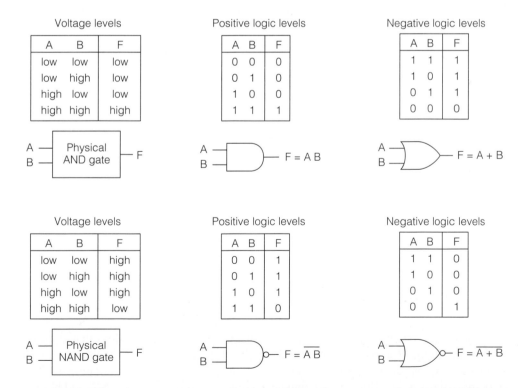

Fig. A.18   Positive and Negative Logic Assignments for AND-OR and NAND-NOR Duals

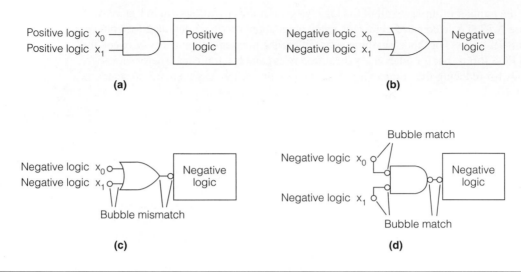

Fig. A.19   The Process of Bubble Matching

bubble matching

The mixing of positive and negative logic in the same system should be avoided to prevent confusion, but sometimes it cannot be avoided. For these cases, a technique known as *bubble matching* helps keep the proper logic sense correct. The idea is to assume that all logic is asserted high (positive logic) and to place a bubble (denoting logical inversion) at the inputs or outputs of any negative logic circuits. Note that these bubbles are the same in function as the bubbles that appear at the complemented outputs of logic gates such as NOR and NAND; that is, the signal that leaves a bubble is the complement of the signal that enters it.

Consider the circuit shown in Figure A.19a, in which the outputs of two positive logic circuits are combined through an AND gate that is connected to a positive logic system. A logically equivalent system for negative logic is shown in Figure A.19b. In the process of bubble matching, a bubble is placed on each active-low input or output, as shown in Figure A.19c.

To simplify the process of analyzing the circuit, active-low input bubbles need to be matched with active-low output bubbles. In Figure A.19c there are bubble mismatches because there is only one bubble on each line. DeMorgan's theorem is used in converting the OR gate in Figure A.19c to the NAND gate with complemented inputs in Figure A.19d, in which the bubble mismatches have been fixed.

A.8   The Data Sheet

data sheet

Logic gates and other logic components have many technical specifications that are relevant to the design and analysis of digital circuits. The *data sheet,* or "spec sheet," lists technical characteristics of a logic component, as shown, for example, in Figure A.20. The data sheet starts with a title of the component, which for this case is the SN7400 NAND gate. The description gives a functional description of the component in textual form.

SN7400 QUADRUPLE 2-INPUT POSITIVE-NAND GATES

description

These devices contain four independent 2-input NAND gates.

schematic (each gate)

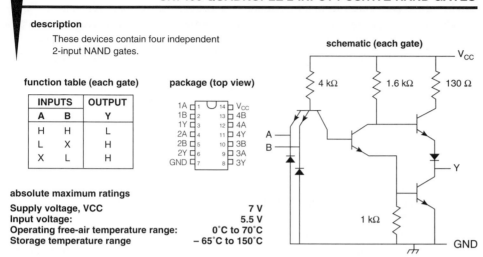

function table (each gate)

INPUTS		OUTPUT
A	B	Y
H	H	L
L	X	H
X	L	H

package (top view)

1A	1	14	V_{CC}
1B	2	13	4B
1Y	3	12	4A
2A	4	11	4Y
2B	5	10	3B
2Y	6	9	3A
GND	7	8	3Y

absolute maximum ratings

Supply voltage, VCC	7 V
Input voltage:	5.5 V
Operating free-air temperature range:	0°C to 70°C
Storage temperature range	−65°C to 150°C

logic diagram (positive logic)

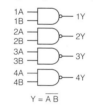

$Y = \overline{A\,B}$

recommended operating conditions

		MIN	NOM	MAX	UNIT
V_{CC}	Supply voltage	4.75	5	5.25	V
V_{IH}	High-level input voltage	2			V
V_{IL}	Low-level input voltage			0.8	V
I_{OH}	High-level output current			−0.4	mA
I_{OL}	Low-level output current			16	mA
T_A	Operating free-air temperature	0		70	°C

electrical characteristics over recommended operating free-air temperature range

VALUE	OPERATING CONDITIONS	MIN	TYP	MAX	UNIT
V_{OH}	V_{CC} = MIN, V_{IL} = 0.8 V, I_{OH} = −0.4 mA	2.4	3.4		V
V_{OL}	V_{CC} = MIN, V_{IH} = 2 V, I_{OL} = 16 mA		0.2	0.4	V
I_{IH}	V_{CC} = MAX, V_I = 2.4 V			40	μA
I_{IL}	V_{CC} = MAX, V_I = 0.4 V			−1.6	mA
I_{CCH}	V_{CC} = MAX, V_I = 0 V		4	8	mA
I_{CCL}	V_{CC} = MAX, V_I = 4.5 V		12	22	mA

switching characteristics, V_{CC} = 5 V, T_A = 25° C

PARAMETER	FROM (input)	TO (output)	TEST CONDITIONS	MIN	TYP	MAX	UNIT
t_{PLH}	A or B	Y	R_L = 400 Ω C_L = 15 pF		11	22	ns
t_{PHL}					7	15	ns

Fig. A.20 Simplified Data Sheet for SN7400 NAND Gate, Adapted from Texas Instruments *TTL Databook,* Texas Instruments, 1988 (Reprinted by permission of Texas Instruments, Inc.)

The package section shows the pin layout and the pin assignments. There can be several package types for the same component. The function table enumerates the input-output behavior of the component from a functional perspective. The symbols "H" and "L" stand for high and low voltages, respectively, to avoid confusion with the sense of positive or negative logic. The symbol "X" indicates that the value at an input does not influence the output. The logic diagram describes the logical behavior of the component, using positive logic for this case. All four NAND gates are shown with their pin assignments.

The schematic shows the transistor-level circuitry for each gate. In the text, we treat this low-level circuitry as an abstraction that is embodied in the logic gate symbols.

The absolute maximum ratings section lists the range of environmental conditions in which the component will safely operate. The supply voltage can go as high as 7 V, and the input voltage can go up to 5.5 V. The ambient temperature should be between 0°C and 70°C during operation, but can vary between –65°C and 150°C when the component is not being used.

Despite the absolute maximum rating specifications, the recommended operating conditions should be used during operation. The recommended operating conditions are characterized by minimum (MIN), nominal (NOM), and maximum (MAX) ratings.

The electrical characteristics describe the behavior of the component under certain operating conditions. V_{OH} and V_{OL} are the minimum output high voltage and the maximum output low voltage, respectively. I_{IH} and I_{IL} are the maximum currents into an input pin when the input is high or low, respectively. I_{CCH} and I_{CCL} are the package's power supply currents when all outputs are high or low, respectively.

This data can be used in determining maximum fan-outs under the given conditions. *Fan-out* is a measure of the number of inputs that a single output can drive for logic gates implemented in the same technology. That is, a logic gate with a fan-out of 10 can drive the inputs of 10 other logic gates of the same type. Similarly, *fan-in* is a measure of the number of inputs that a logic gate can accept (simply, the number of input lines to that gate). The absolute value of I_{OH} must be greater than or equal to the sum of all I_{IH} currents that are being driven, and I_{OL} must be greater than or equal to the sum of all I_{IL} currents (absolute values) that are being driven. The absolute value of I_{OH} for the SN7400 gate is .4 mA (or 400 μA); thus the SN7400 gate output can drive 10 SN7400 inputs (I_{IH} = 40 μA per input).

The switching characteristics show the propagation delay to switch the output from a low to a high voltage (t_{PLH}) and the propagation delay to switch the output from a high to a low voltage (t_{PHL}). The maximum ratings show the worst cases. A circuit can be safely designed using the typical case as the worst case, but only if a test-and-select-the-best approach is used. That is, since t_{PLH} varies between 11 ns and 22 ns and t_{PHL} varies between 7 ns and 15 ns from one packaged component to the next, components can be individually tested to determine their true characteristics. Not all components of the same type behave identically, even under the most stringent fabrication controls, and the differences can be reduced by testing and selecting the best components.

A.9   Digital Components

High-level digital circuit designs are normally made using collections of logic gates referred to as *components,* rather than using individual logic gates. This allows a degree of

fan-out

fan-in

component

circuit complexity to be abstracted away, and also simplifies the process of modeling the behavior of circuits and characterizing their performance. A few of the more common components are described in the sections that follow.

A.9.1   LEVELS OF INTEGRATION

Up to this point, we have focused on the design of combinational logic units. Since we have been working with individual logic gates, we have been working at the level of *small-scale integration* (SSI), in which there are 10 to 100 components per chip. (*Components* has a different meaning in this context, referring to transistors and other discrete elements.) Although we sometimes need to work at this low level in practice, typically for high-performance circuits, the advent of microelectronics usually allows us to work at higher levels of integration. In *medium-scale integration* (MSI), approximately 100 to 1,000 components appear in a single chip. *Large-scale integration* (LSI) deals with circuits that contain 1000 to 10,000 components per chip, and *very large-scale integration* (VLSI) goes higher still. There are no sharp breaks between the classes of integration, but the distinctions are useful in comparing the relative complexity of circuits. In this section we deal primarily with MSI components.

small-scale integration (SSI)

medium-scale integration (MSI)

large-scale integration (LSI)

very large-scale integration (VLSI)

A.9.2   MULTIPLEXERS

A *multiplexer (MUX)* is a component that connects a number of inputs to a single output. A block diagram and the corresponding truth table for a 4-to-1 MUX are shown in Figure A.21. The output F takes on the value of the data input that is selected by control lines A and B. For example, if $AB = 00$, then the value on line D_0 (a 0 or a 1) will appear at F. The corresponding AND-OR circuit is shown in Figure A.22. When we design circuits with MUXes, we normally use the "black box" form shown in Figure A.21, rather than the more detailed form shown in Figure A.22. In this way, we can abstract away detail when designing complex circuits.

multiplexer (MUX)

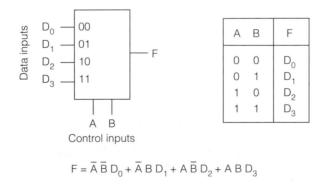

$$F = \overline{A}\,\overline{B}\,D_0 + \overline{A}\,B\,D_1 + A\,\overline{B}\,D_2 + A\,B\,D_3$$

Fig. A.21   Block Diagram and Truth Table for a 4-to-1 MUX

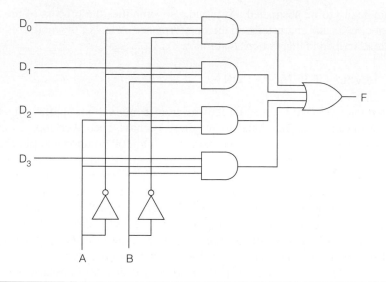

Fig. A.22 An AND-OR Circuit Implements a 4-to-1 MUX

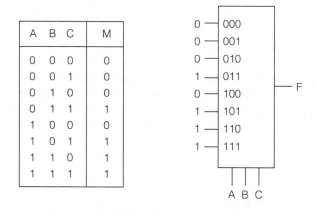

Fig. A.23 An 8-to-1 Multiplexer Implements the Majority Function

Multiplexers can be used to implement Boolean functions. In Figure A.23, an 8-to-1 MUX implements the majority function. The data inputs are taken directly from the truth table for the majority function, and the control inputs are assigned to the variables A, B, and C. The MUX implements the function by passing a 1 from the input of each true minterm to the output. The 0 inputs mark portions of the MUX that are not needed in implementing the function, and as a result, a number of logic gates are underutilized. Although portions of them are almost always unused in implementing Boolean functions, multiplexers are widely used because their generality simplifies the design process, and their modularity simplifies the implementation.

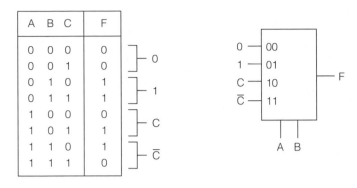

Fig. A.24   A 4-to-1 MUX Implements a Three-Variable Function

As another case, consider implementing a function of three variables using a 4-to-1 MUX. Figure A.24 shows a three-variable truth table and a 4-to-1 MUX that implements function F. We allow data inputs to be taken from the set $\{0, 1, C, \overline{C}\}$, and the groupings are obtained as shown in the truth table. When $AB = 00$, then $F = 0$ regardless of whether $C = 0$ or $C = 1$, and so a 0 is placed at the corresponding 00 data input line on the MUX. When $AB = 01$, then $F = 1$ regardless of whether $C = 0$ or $C = 1$, and so a 1 is placed at the 01 data input. When $AB = 10$, then $F = C$, since F is 0 when C is 0 and F is 1 when C is 1; thus C is placed at the 10 input. Finally, when $AB = 11$, then $F = \overline{C}$, and so $\overline{C}$ is placed at the 11 input. In this way, we can implement a three-variable function using a two-variable MUX.

A.9.3   DEMULTIPLEXERS

A *demultiplexer* (DEMUX) is the converse of a MUX. A block diagram of a 1-to-4 DEMUX with control inputs A and B and the corresponding truth table are shown in Figure A.25. A DEMUX sends its single data input D to one of its outputs F_i according to the settings of the control inputs. A circuit for a 1-to-4 DEMUX is shown in Figure A.26. An application for a DEMUX is to send data from a single source to one of a number of destinations, such as from a call request button for an elevator to the closest elevator car.

demultiplexer (DEMUX)

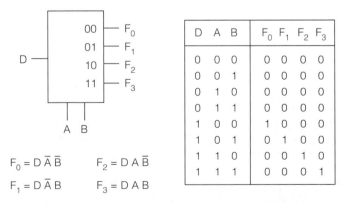

$$F_0 = D\,\overline{A}\,\overline{B} \qquad F_2 = D\,A\,\overline{B}$$
$$F_1 = D\,\overline{A}\,B \qquad F_3 = D\,A\,B$$

D	A	B	F_0	F_1	F_2	F_3
0	0	0	0	0	0	0
0	0	1	0	0	0	0
0	1	0	0	0	0	0
0	1	1	0	0	0	0
1	0	0	1	0	0	0
1	0	1	0	1	0	0
1	1	0	0	0	1	0
1	1	1	0	0	0	1

Fig. A.25   Block Diagram and Truth Table for a 1-to-4 DEMUX

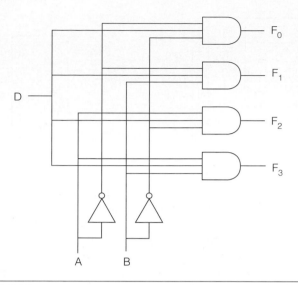

Fig. A.26 A Circuit for a 1-to-4 DEMUX

The DEMUX is not normally used in implementing ordinary Boolean functions, although there are ways to do it (see Exercise 18 at the end of this Appendix).

A.9.4 DECODERS

decoder

A *decoder* translates a logical encoding into a spatial location. Exactly one output of a decoder is high (logical 1) at any time, which is determined by the settings on the control inputs. A block diagram and a truth table for a 2-to-4 decoder with control inputs A and B are shown in Figure A.27. A corresponding logic diagram that implements the decoder is shown in Figure A.28. A decoder may be used to control other circuits, and at times it may be inappropriate to enable any of the other circuits. For that reason, we add an enable line to the decoder, which forces all outputs to 0 if a 0 is applied at its input. (Notice the logical equivalence between the DEMUX with an input of 1 and the decoder.)

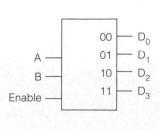

Enable = 1		
A B	D_0 D_1 D_2 D_3	
0 0	1 0 0 0	
0 1	0 1 0 0	
1 0	0 0 1 0	
1 1	0 0 0 1	

Enable = 0		
A B	D_0 D_1 D_2 D_3	
0 0	0 0 0 0	
0 1	0 0 0 0	
1 0	0 0 0 0	
1 1	0 0 0 0	

$$D_0 = \overline{A}\,\overline{B} \qquad D_1 = \overline{A}\,B \qquad D_2 = A\,\overline{B} \qquad D_3 = A\,B$$

Fig. A.27 Block Diagram and Truth Table for a 2-to-4 Decoder

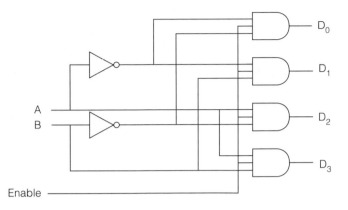

Fig. A.28 An AND Circuit for a 2-to-4 Decoder

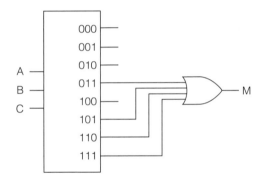

Fig. A.29 A 3-to-8 Decoder Implements the Majority Function

One application for a decoder is in translating memory addresses into physical locations. Decoders can also be used in implementing Boolean functions. Since each output line corresponds to a different minterm, a function can be implemented by logically ORing the outputs that correspond to the true minterms in the function. For example, in Figure A.29, a 3-to-8 decoder implements the majority function. Unused outputs remain disconnected.

A.9.5 PRIORITY ENCODERS

An *encoder* translates a set of inputs into a binary encoding and can be thought of as the converse of a decoder. A *priority encoder* is one type of an encoder, in which an ordering is imposed on the inputs. A block diagram and a corresponding truth table for a 4-to-2 priority encoder are shown in Figure A.30. A priority scheme is imposed on the inputs, in which A_i has higher priority than A_{i+1}. The 2-bit output takes on the value 00, 01, 10, or 11, depending on which inputs are active (in the 1 state) and their relative priorities. When no inputs are active, the default output gives priority to A_0 ($F_0F_1 = 00$).

encoder; priority encoder

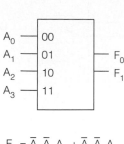

A_0	A_1	A_2	A_3	F_0	F_1
0	0	0	0	0	0
0	0	0	1	1	1
0	0	1	0	1	0
0	0	1	1	1	0
0	1	0	0	0	1
0	1	0	1	0	1
0	1	1	0	0	1
0	1	1	1	0	1
1	0	0	0	0	0
1	0	0	1	0	0
1	0	1	0	0	0
1	0	1	1	0	0
1	1	0	0	0	0
1	1	0	1	0	0
1	1	1	0	0	0
1	1	1	1	0	0

$$F_0 = \overline{A}_0\overline{A}_1 A_3 + \overline{A}_0\overline{A}_1 A_2$$
$$F_1 = \overline{A}_0\overline{A}_2 A_3 + \overline{A}_0 A_1$$

Fig. A.30 Block Diagram and Truth Table for a 4-to-2 Priority Encoder

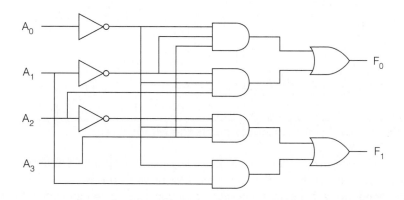

Fig. A.31 Logic Diagram for a 4-to-2 Priority Encoder

Priority encoders are used for arbitrating among a number of devices that compete for the same resource, as when a number of users simultaneously attempt to log on to a computer system. A circuit diagram for a 4-to-2 priority encoder is shown in Figure A.31. (The circuit has been reduced using methods described in Section A.10, but the input/output behavior can be verified without needing to know the reduction method.)

A.9.6   PROGRAMMABLE LOGIC ARRAYS

programmable logic array (PLA)

A *programmable logic array* (PLA) is a component that consists of a customizable AND matrix followed by a customizable OR matrix. Figure A.32 shows a PLA with three inputs

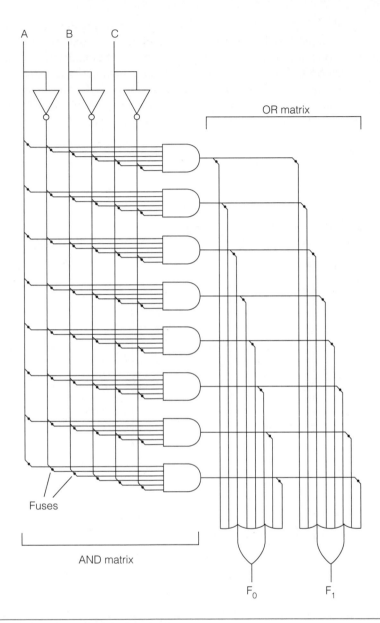

Fig. A.32 A Programmable Logic Array

and two outputs. The three inputs A, B, and C and their complements are available at the inputs of each of eight AND gates that generate eight product terms. The outputs of the AND gates are available at the inputs of each of the OR gates that generate functions F_0 and F_1. A programmable fuse is placed at each crosspoint in the AND and OR matrices. The matrices are customized for specific functions by disabling fuses. When a fuse is disabled at an input to an AND gate, then the AND gate behaves as if the input is tied to a 1. Similarly, a disabled input to an OR gate in a PLA behaves as if the input is tied to a 0.

As an example of how a PLA is used, consider implementing the majority function on a 3×2 PLA (three input variables × two output functions). In order To simplify the illustrations, the form shown in Figure A.33 is used, in which it is understood that the single input line into each AND gate represents six input lines, and the single input line into each OR gate represents eight input lines. Darkened circles are placed at the crosspoints to indicate where connections are made. In Figure A.33, the majority function is implemented using just half of the PLA, which leaves the rest of the PLA available for another function.

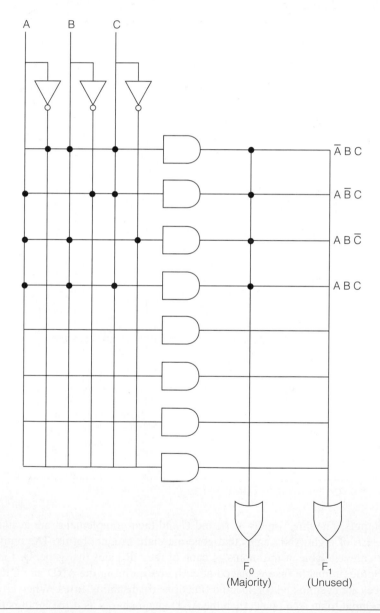

Fig. A.33 Simplified Representation of a PLA

Fig. A.34 Black Box Representation of a PLA

PLAs are workhorse components that are used throughout digital circuits. An advantage of using PLAs is that there are only a few inputs and a few outputs, while there is a large number of logic gates between the inputs and outputs. It is important to minimize the number of connections at the circuit edges to modularize a system into discrete components that are designed and implemented separately. A PLA is ideal for this purpose, and a number of automated programs exist for designing PLAs from functional descriptions. In keeping with this concept of modularity, we will sometimes represent a PLA as a black box, as shown in Figure A.34, and assume that we can leave the design of the internals of the PLA to an automated program.

Example A.1   A Ripple-Carry Adder

As an example of how PLAs are used in the design of a digital circuit, consider designing a circuit that adds two binary numbers. Binary addition is performed in much the same way as we perform decimal addition by hand, as illustrated in Figure A.35. Two binary numbers A and B are added from right to left, creating a sum and a carry in each bit position. Two input bits and a carry-in must be summed at each bit position, so that a total of eight input combinations must be considered, as shown in the truth table in Figure A.36.

The truth table in Figure A.36 describes an element known as a *full adder*, which is shown schematically in the figure. A *half adder*, which could be used for the rightmost bit position, adds 2 bits and produces a sum and a carry, whereas a full adder adds 2 bits and a carry and produces a sum and a carry. The half adder is not used here to keep the number of different components to a minimum. Four full adders can be cascaded to form an adder large enough to add the 4-bit numbers used in the example of Figure A.35, as shown in Figure A.37. The rightmost full adder has a carry-in (c_0) of 0.

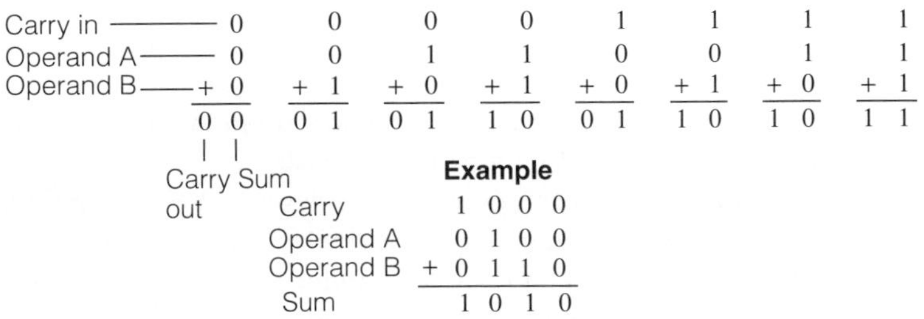

full adder
half adder

```
Carry in ──────── 0      0      0      0      1      1      1      1
Operand A ─────── 0      0      1      1      0      0      1      1
Operand B ─────+ 0    + 1    + 0    + 1    + 0    + 1    + 0    + 1
                ───    ───    ───    ───    ───    ───    ───    ───
                0 0    0 1    0 1    1 0    0 1    1 0    1 0    1 1
                │ │
            Carry Sum              Example
            out      Carry           1  0  0  0
                     Operand A       0  1  0  0
                     Operand B  +    0  1  1  0
                                    ────────────
                     Sum            1  0  1  0
```

Fig. A.35 Example of Addition for Two Unsigned Binary Numbers

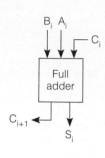

A_i	B_i	C_i	S_i	C_{i+1}
0	0	0	0	0
0	0	1	1	0
0	1	0	1	0
0	1	1	0	1
1	0	0	1	0
1	0	1	0	1
1	1	0	0	1
1	1	1	1	1

Fig. A.36 Truth Table for a Full Adder

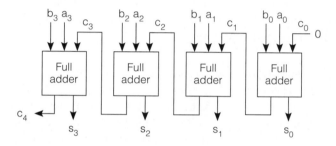

Fig. A.37 A 4-Bit Adder Implemented with a Cascade of Full Adders

An approach to designing a full adder is to use a PLA, as shown in Figure A.38. The PLA approach is very general, and computer-aided design (CAD) tools for VLSI typically favor the use of PLAs over random logic or MUXes because of their generality. CAD tools typically reduce the sizes of the PLAs (we will see a few reduction techniques in the next section), and so the seemingly high gate count for the PLA is not actually so high in practice. ∎

A.10 Reduction of Two-Level Expressions

It may be the case that a logically equivalent but smaller Boolean equation can be obtained than is represented by the canonical SOP or POS forms. A smaller Boolean equation translates to a lower gate input count in the target circuit, and so reduction is an important consideration when circuit complexity is an issue.

algebraic reduction
Karnaugh-map
reduction

Two methods of reducing Boolean equations are described in the sections that follow: *algebraic reduction* and *Karnaugh-map reduction*. The algebraic method is the more powerful of the two because it can be used to reduce equations in three-level, four-level, and deeper forms. It is also a less algorithmic approach. Karnaugh-map reduction is a visually easier process for performing reductions manually and is generally preferred for equations with small numbers of variables.

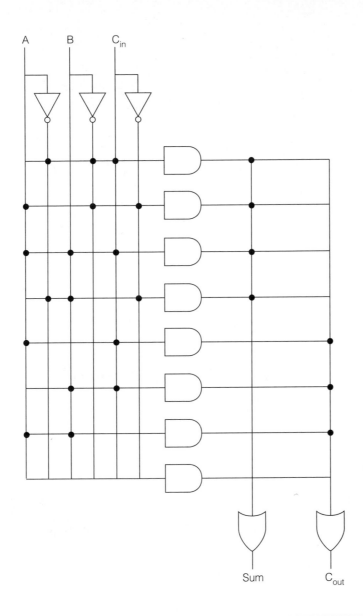

Fig. A.38 PLA Realization of a Full Adder

A.10.1 THE ALGEBRAIC METHOD

One method of reducing the size of a Boolean equation is to apply the properties of Boolean algebra that were introduced in Section A.4. Consider the Boolean equation for the majority function, which is repeated here:

$$F = \overline{A}BC + A\overline{B}C + AB\overline{C} + ABC \qquad \text{[Eq. A.1]}$$

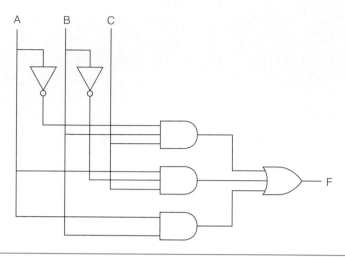

Fig. A.39 Reduced Circuit for the Majority Function

The properties of Boolean algebra can be applied to reduce the equation to a simpler form, as shown in Equation A.7 through A.9:

$$F = \overline{A}BC + A\overline{B}C + AB(\overline{C} + C) \qquad \text{Distributive property} \qquad \text{[Eq. A.7]}$$

$$F = \overline{A}BC + A\overline{B}C + AB(1) \qquad \text{Complement property} \qquad \text{[Eq. A.8]}$$

$$F = \overline{A}BC + A\overline{B}C + AB \qquad \text{Identity property} \qquad \text{[Eq. A.9]}$$

The corresponding circuit for Equation A.9 is shown in Figure A.39. In comparison with the majority circuit shown in Figure A.15, the gate count is reduced from 8 to 6 and the gate input count is reduced from 19 to 13.

We can reduce Equation A.9 further. By applying the property of idempotence, we obtain Equation A.10, in which we have reintroduced the minterm ABC:

$$F = \overline{A}BC + A\overline{B}C + AB + ABC \qquad \text{Idempotence property} \qquad \text{[Eq. A.10]}$$

We can then apply the distributive, complement, and identity properties again and obtain a simpler equation as shown in the following series:

$$F = \overline{A}BC + AC(\overline{B} + B) + AB \qquad \text{Distributive property} \qquad \text{[Eq. A.11]}$$

$$F = \overline{A}BC + AC(1) + AB \qquad \text{Complement property} \qquad \text{[Eq. A.12]}$$

$$F = \overline{A}BC + AC + AB \qquad \text{Identity property} \qquad \text{[Eq. A.13]}$$

Equation A.13 has a smaller gate input count of 11. We can iterate this method one more time and reduce the equation further:

$$F = \overline{A}BC + AC + AB + ABC \qquad \text{Idempotence property} \qquad \text{[Eq. A.14]}$$

$$F = BC(\overline{A} + A) + AC + AB \qquad \text{Distributive property} \qquad \text{[Eq. A.15]}$$

$$F = BC(1) + AC + AB \qquad \text{Complement property} \qquad \text{[Eq. A.16]}$$

$$F = BC + AC + AB \qquad \text{Identity property} \qquad \text{[Eq. A.17]}$$

Equation A.17 is now in its minimal two-level form and can be reduced no further.

A.10.2 THE MAP METHOD

The process of simplifying Boolean expressions algebraically is tedious and can be difficult without having a better way to visualize where reductions can be made. A Venn diagram is a mechanism that helps visualize the relationship among binary variables. A *Venn diagram* for binary variables consists of a large rectangle that represents the binary universe, which contains overlapping circles for each variable. A Venn diagram for three variables *A, B,* and *C* is shown in Figure A.40. Within a circle, a variable has the value 1, and outside a circle, a variable has the value 0.

Venn diagram

   Adjacent shaded regions are candidates for reduction since they vary in exactly one variable. In the figure, region *ABC* can be combined with each of the three adjacent regions to produce a reduced form of the majority function. The spatial layout of the Venn diagram and the irregularly shaped regions can sometimes be confusing, and a more structured layout is commonly used that is based on *Karnaugh maps (K-maps)*. In a K-map, minterms that differ in exactly one variable are placed next to each other to take advantage of the complement property of Boolean algebra. A K-map for the majority function is shown in Figure A.41. Each cell in the K-map corresponds to an entry in the truth table for the function, and since there are eight entries in the truth table, there are eight cells in the corresponding K-map. A 1 is placed in each cell that corresponds to a true entry. A 0 is entered in each remaining cell, but can be omitted from the K-map for clarity, as it is here. The labeling along the top and left sides is arranged in a *Gray code,* in which exactly one variable changes between adjacent cells along each dimension.

Gray code

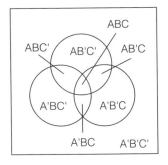 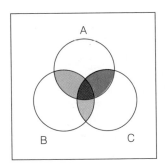

Fig. A.40 A Venn Diagram Representation for 3 Binary Variables (left) and for the Majority Function (right)

	AB			
C	00	01	11	10
0			1	
1		1	1	1

Fig. A.41 A K-Map for the Majority Function

prime implicants

Adjacent 1s in the K-map satisfy the condition needed to apply the complement property of Boolean algebra. Since there are adjacent 1s in the K-map shown in Figure A.41, a reduction is possible. Groupings of adjacent cells are made into rectangles in sizes that correspond to powers of 2, such as 1, 2, 4, and 8. These groups are referred to as *prime implicants*. As groups increase in size above a 1-group (a group with one member), more variables are eliminated from a Boolean expression, and so the largest groups that can be obtained are used. To maintain the adjacency property, the shapes of groups must always be rectangular, and each group must contain a number of cells that corresponds to an integral power of 2.

We start the reduction process by creating groups for 1's *that can be contained in no larger group* and progress to larger groups until all cells with a 1 are covered at least once. The adjacency criterion is crucial, since we are looking for groups of minterms that differ in such a way that a reduction can be applied by using the complement and identity properties of Boolean algebra, as in Equation A.18:

$$ABC + AB\overline{C} = AB(C + \overline{C}) = AB(1) = AB \qquad \text{[Eq. A.18]}$$

For the majority function, three groups of size 2 are made as shown in Figure A.42. Every cell with a 1 has at least one neighboring cell with a 1, and so there are no 1-groups. We look next at 2-groups, and find that all of the 1-cells are covered by 2-groups. One of the cells is included in all three groups, which is allowed in the reduction process by the property of idempotence. The complement property eliminates the variable that differs between cells, and the resulting minimized equation is obtained:

$$M = BC + AC + AB \qquad \text{[Eq. A.19]}$$

The BC term is derived from the 2-group $(ABC + \overline{A}BC)$, which reduces to $BC(A + \overline{A})$ and then to BC. The AC term is similarly derived from the 2-group $(ABC + A\overline{B}C)$, and the AB term is similarly derived from the 2-group $(ABC + AB\overline{C})$. The corresponding circuit is shown in Figure A.43. The gate count is reduced from 8 to 4, as compared with the circuit shown in Figure A.15, and the gate input count is reduced from 19 to 9.

Looking more closely at the method of starting with 1-cells that can be included in no larger subgroups, consider what would happen if we started with the largest groups first. Figure A.44 shows both approaches applied to the same K-map. The reduction on the left is obtained by working with 1's that can be included in no larger subgroup, which is the method we have been using. Groupings are made in the order indicated by the numbers. A total of four groups are obtained, each of size 2. The reduction on the right is obtained by starting with the largest groups first. Five groups are thus obtained, one of size 4 and four of

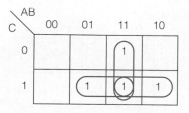

Fig. A.42 Adjacency Groupings for the Majority Function

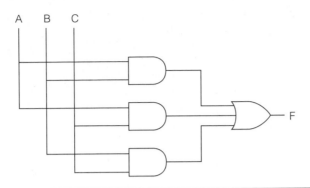

Fig. A.43 Minimized AND-OR Circuit for the Majority Function

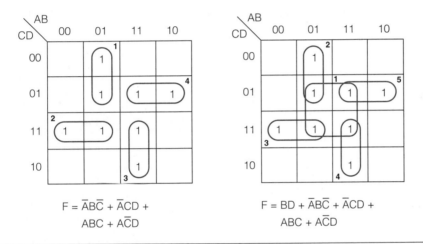

$$F = \overline{A}B\overline{C} + \overline{A}CD +$$
$$ABC + A\overline{C}D$$

$$F = BD + \overline{A}B\overline{C} + \overline{A}CD +$$
$$ABC + A\overline{C}D$$

Fig. A.44 Minimal K-Map Grouping (left) and K-Map Grouping That Is Not Minimal (right) of a K-Map

size 2. Thus, the minimal equation is not obtained if we start with the largest groups first. Both equations shown in Figure A.44 describe the same function, and a logically correct circuit will be obtained in either case; however, one circuit will not be produced from a minimized equation.

As another example, consider the K-map shown in Figure A.45. The edges of the K-map wrap around horizontally and vertically, and the four corners are logically adjacent. The corresponding minimized equation is shown in the figure.

Don't Cares. Now consider the K-maps shown in Figure A.46. The d entries denote don't cares, which can be treated as 0's or as 1's, at our convenience. A *don't care* represents a condition that cannot arise during operation. For example, if variable X represents the condition in which an elevator is on the ground floor, and variable Y represents the condition in which the elevator is on the top floor, then X and Y will not both be 1 at the same time, although they may both be 0 at the same time. Thus, a truth table entry for an elevator function that corresponds to $X = Y = 1$ would be marked as a don't care.

don't cares

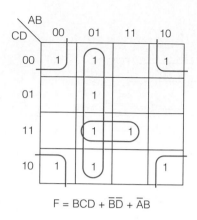

$$F = BCD + \overline{B}\overline{D} + \overline{A}B$$

Fig. A.45 The Corners of a K-Map Are Logically Adjacent

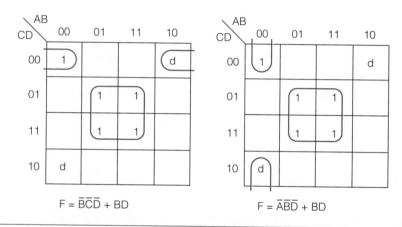

$$F = \overline{B}\overline{C}\overline{D} + BD \qquad\qquad F = \overline{A}\overline{B}\overline{D} + BD$$

Fig. A.46 Two Different Minimized Equations Are Produced from the Same K-Map

Figure A.46 shows a more complex function in which two different results are obtained from applying the same minimization process. The K-map on the left treats the top right don't care as a 1 and the bottom left don't care as a 0. The K-map on the right treats the top right don't care as a 0 and the bottom left don't care as a 1. Both K-maps result in minimized Boolean equations of the same size, and so it is possible to have more than one minimal expression for a Boolean function. In practice, one equation may be preferred over another, possibly to reduce the fan-out for one of the variables or to take advantage of sharing minterms with other functions.

A.11 Speed and Performance

Up to this point, we have largely ignored the physical characteristics that affect performance and have focused entirely on organizational issues such as circuit depth and gate count. In this section, we explore a few practical considerations of digital logic.

A.11.1   SWITCHING SPEED

The propagation delay (latency) between the inputs and output of a logic gate is a continuous effect, even though we considered propagation delay to be negligible in Section A.2. A change at an input to a logic gate is also a continuous effect. In Figure A.47, an input to a NOT gate has a finite transition time, which is measured as the time between the 10% and 90% points on the waveform. This is referred to as the *rise time* for a rising signal and the *fall time* for a falling signal.

rise time, fall time

The propagation delay is the time between the 50% transitions on the input and output waveforms. The propagation delay is influenced by a number of parameters, and power is one parameter over which we have a good deal of control. As power consumption increases, propagation delay decreases, up to a limit. A rule of thumb is that the product of power consumption and the propagation delay for a gate stays roughly the same. Although we generally want fast logic, we do not want to operate with a high power dissipation, because the consumed power manifests itself as heat that must be removed to maintain a safe and reliable operating condition.

In the complementary metal-oxide semiconductor (CMOS) logic family, power dissipation scales with speed. At a switching rate of 1 MHz, the power dissipation of a CMOS gate is about 1 mW. At this rate of power dissipation, 10,000 CMOS logic gates dissipate 10,000 gates × 1mW/gate = 10 W, which is at the limit of heat removal for a single integrated circuit using conventional approaches (for a 1 cm^2 chip).

Single CMOS chips can have more than 10^6 logic gates, however, and operate at rates in the GHz range. This gate count and speed are achieved partially by increasing the chip size, although this accounts for little more than a factor of 10. The key to achieving such a high component count and switching speed while managing power dissipation is to switch only a fraction of the logic gates at any time, which luckily is the most typical operating mode for an integrated circuit.

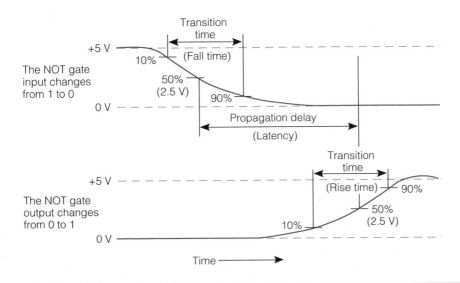

Fig. A.47 Propagation Delay for a NOT Gate (Adapted from Hamacher et al, 1990)

A.11.2 CIRCUIT DEPTH

circuit depth

The latency between the inputs and outputs of a circuit is governed by the number of logic gates on the longest path from any input to any output. This is known as *circuit depth*. In general, a circuit with a small circuit depth operates more quickly than a circuit with a large circuit depth. There are a number of ways to reduce circuit depth that involve increasing the complexity of some other parameter. We look at one way of making this trade-off here.

In Section A.9.2, we used a MUX to implement the majority function. Now consider using a four-variable MUX to implement Equation A.20, which follows. Equation A.20 is in two-level form, because only two levels of logic are used in its representation: six AND terms that are ORed together. A single MUX can implement this function, which is shown on the left side of Figure A.48. The corresponding circuit depth is 2. If we factor out A and B, then we obtain the four-level Equation A.21, and the corresponding four-level circuit shown on the right side of Figure A.48. The gate input count of a 4-to-1 MUX is 18, as taken from Figure A.22 (including inverters), so the gate input count of the decomposed MUX circuit is $3 \times 18 = 54$. A single 16-to-1 MUX has a gate input count of 100. The 4-to-1 MUX implementation has a circuit depth of 4 (not including inverters), while the 16-to-1 MUX implementation has a circuit depth of 2. This illustrates the trade-off of circuit complexity against an increase in the circuit depth.

$$F(A, B, C, D) = \overline{A}\,\overline{B}\,\overline{C}\,\overline{D} + \overline{A}\,\overline{B}CD + \overline{A}B\overline{C}D + \overline{A}BC\overline{D} + A\overline{B}\,\overline{C}D + ABCD \quad \text{[Eq. A.20]}$$

$$F(A, B, C, D) = \overline{A}\,\overline{B}(\overline{C}\,\overline{D} + CD) + \overline{A}B(\overline{C}D + C\overline{D}) + A\overline{B}(\overline{C}D) + AB(CD) \quad \text{[Eq. A.21]}$$

Although there are techniques that aid the circuit designer in discovering trade-offs between circuit complexity and circuit depth, the development of algorithms that cover the space of possible alternatives in reasonable time is only a partially solved problem. In the next section, we will see another aspect of how circuit complexity and circuit depth interact.

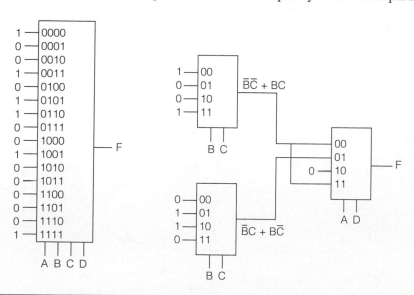

Fig. A.48 A Four-Variable Function Implemented with a 16-to-1 MUX (left)

A.11.3 FAN-IN VERSUS CIRCUIT DEPTH

Suppose that we need a four-input OR gate, as used in Figure A.15, but only two-input OR gates are available. What should we do? This is a common practical problem that is encountered in a variety of design situations. The associative property of Boolean algebra can be used to decompose the OR gate that has a fan-in of 4 into a configuration of OR gates that each have a fan-in of 2 as shown in Figure A.49.

In general, the decomposition of the four-input OR gate should be performed in balanced tree fashion to reduce circuit depth. A degenerate tree can also be used, as shown in Figure A.49, which produces a functionally equivalent circuit with the same number of logic gates as the balanced tree, but results in a maximum circuit depth.

Although it is important to reduce circuit depth to decrease the latency between the inputs and the outputs, one reason for preferring the degenerate tree to the balanced tree is that the degenerate tree has a minimum cross-sectional diameter at each stage, which makes it easy to split the tree into pieces that are spread over a number of separate circuits. This mirrors a practical situation encountered in packaging digital circuits. The depth of the balanced tree is $\lceil \log_F(N) \rceil$ logic gates for an N-input gate mapped to logic gates with a fan-in of F, and the depth of the degenerate tree is

$$\left\lceil \frac{N-1}{F-1} \right\rceil$$

logic gates for an N-input gate mapped to logic gates with a fan-in of F.

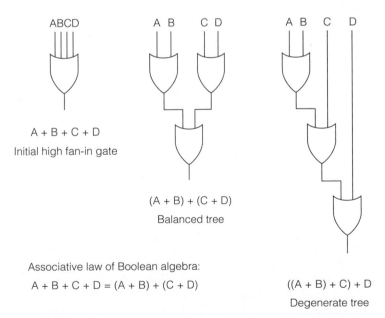

A + B + C + D

Initial high fan-in gate

Associative law of Boolean algebra:

A + B + C + D = (A + B) + (C + D)

(A + B) + (C + D)

Balanced tree

((A + B) + C) + D

Degenerate tree

Fig. A.49 A Logic Gate with a Fan-In of 4 Is Decomposed into Logically Equivalent Configurations of Logic Gates with Fan-Ins of 2

In theory, any binary function can be realized in two levels of logic gates, given an arbitrarily large stage of AND gates followed by an arbitrarily large stage of OR gates, both having arbitrarily large fan-in and fan-out. For example, an entire computer program can be compiled in just two gate levels if it is presented in parallel to a Boolean circuit that has an AND stage followed by an OR stage that is designed to implement this function. Such a circuit would be prohibitively large, however, since every possible combination of inputs must be considered.

Fan-outs larger than about 10 are too costly to implement in many logic families due to the sacrifice in performance; it is similar in form to filling 10 or more leaky buckets from a single faucet. Boolean algebra for two-level expressions is still used to describe complex digital circuits with high fan-outs, however, and then the two-level Boolean expressions are transformed into multilevel expressions that conform to the fan-in and fan-out limitations of the technology. Optimal fan-in and fan-out are argued to be $e \cong 2.7$ (see Mead and Conway, 1980) in terms of transistor-stepping size for bringing a signal from an integrated circuit (IC) to a pin of the IC package. The derivation of that result is based on capacitance of bonding pads, signal rise times, and other considerations. The result cannot be applied to all aspects of computing, since it does not take into account overall performance, which may create local variations that violate the e rule dramatically. Electronic digital circuits typically use fan-ins and fan-outs of between 2 and 10.

A.12 Sequential Logic

finite state machine (FSM)

In the earlier part of this appendix we explored combinational logic units, in which the outputs are completely determined by functions of the inputs. A sequential logic unit, commonly referred to as a *finite state machine* (*FSM*), takes an input and a current state and produces an output and a new state. An FSM is distinguished from a CLU in that the past history of the inputs to the FSM influences its state and output. This is important for implementing memory circuits as well as control units in a computer.

The classical model of a finite state machine is shown in Figure A.50. A CLU takes inputs from lines i_0–i_k, which are external to the FSM, and also takes inputs from state bits s_0–s_n, which are internal to the FSM. The CLU produces output bits f_0–f_m and new state bits. Delay elements maintain the current state of the FSM until a synchronization signal causes the D_i values to be loaded into the s_i, which appear at Q_i as the new state bits.

A.12.1 THE S-R FLIP-FLOP

flip-flop

A *flip-flop* is an arrangement of logic gates that maintains a stable output even after the inputs are made inactive. The output of a flip-flop is determined by both the current inputs and the past history of inputs, and thus a combinational logic unit is not powerful enough to capture this behavior. A flip-flop can be used to store a single bit of information, and it serves as a building block for computer memory.

If either or both inputs of a two-input NOR gate is 1, then the output of the NOR gate is 0; otherwise the output is 1. As we saw in the previous section, the time that it takes for a signal to propagate from the inputs of a logic gate to the output is not instantaneous, and there is some delay $\Delta\tau$ that represents the propagation delay through the gate. The delay is

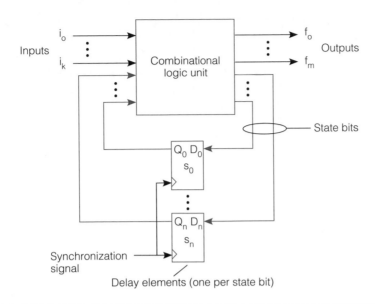

Fig. A.50 Classical Model of a Finite State Machine

sometimes considered lumped at the output of the gate for purposes of analysis, as illustrated in Figure A.51. The lumped delay is not normally indicated in circuit diagrams, but its presence is implied.

The propagation time through the NOR gate affects the operation of a flip-flop. Consider the *set-reset (S-R) flip-flop* shown in Figure A.52, which consists of two cross-coupled NOR gates. If we apply a 1 to S, then $\overline{Q}$ goes to 0 after a delay $\Delta\tau$, which causes Q to go to 1 (assuming R is initially 0) after a delay $2\Delta\tau$. As a result of the finite propagation time, there is a brief period of time $\Delta\tau$ when both the Q and $\overline{Q}$ outputs assume a value of 0, which is logically incorrect, but we will see how this condition is fixed when the master-slave configuration is discussed later. If we now apply a 0 to S, then Q retains its state until some later time, when R goes to 1. The S-R flip-flop thus holds a single bit of information and serves as an elementary memory element.

set-reset (S-R) flip-flop

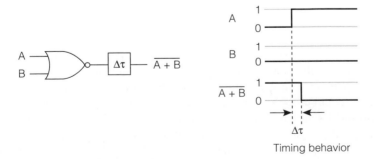

Fig. A.51 A NOR Gate with a Lumped Delay at Its Output

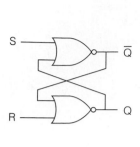

Q_t	S_t	R_t	Q_{t+1}
0	0	0	0
0	0	1	0
0	1	0	1
0	1	1	(disallowed)
1	0	0	1
1	0	1	0
1	1	0	1
1	1	1	(disallowed)

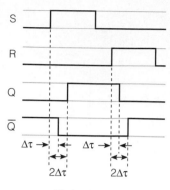

Timing behavior

Fig. A.52   An S-R Flip-Flop

Fig. A.53   A NOR Implementation of an S-R Flip-Flop Is Converted into a NAND Implementation

There is more than one way to make an S-R flip-flop, and the use of cross-coupled NOR gates is just one configuration. Two cross-coupled NAND gates can also implement an S-R flip-flop, with $S = R = 1$ being the quiescent state. Making use of DeMorgan's theorem, we can convert the NOR gates of an *S-R* flip-flop into AND gates, as shown in Figure A.53. By "bubble pushing," we change the AND gates into NAND gates, and then reverse the sense of *S* and *R* to remove the remaining input bubbles.

A.12.2   THE CLOCKED S-R FLIP-FLOP

Now consider that the inputs to the S-R flip-flop may originate from the outputs of some other circuits, whose inputs may originate from the outputs of other circuits, forming a cascade of logic circuits. This mirrors the form of conventional digital circuits. A problem with cascading circuits is that transitions may occur at times that are not desired.

Consider the circuit shown in Figure A.54. If signals *A*, *B*, and *C* all change from the 0 state to the 1 state, then signal *C* may reach the XOR gate before *A* and *B* propagate through the AND gate, which will momentarily produce a 1 output at *S*, which will revert to 0 when the output of the AND gate settles and is XORed with *C*. At this point it may be too late, however, since *S* may be in the 1 state long enough to set the flip-flop, destroying the integrity of the stored bit.

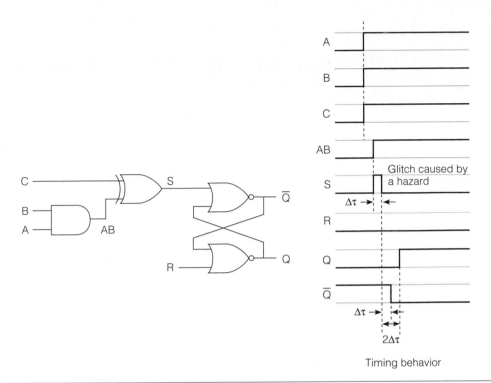

Fig. A.54 A Circuit with a Hazard

When the final state of a flip-flop is sensitive to the relative arrival times of signals, the result may be a *glitch*, which is an unwanted state or output. A circuit that can produce a glitch is said to have a *hazard*. The hazard may or may not manifest itself as a glitch, depending on the operating conditions of the circuit at a particular time.

glitch
hazard

To achieve synchronization in a controlled fashion, a *clock* signal is provided, to which every state-dependent circuit (such as a flip-flop) synchronizes itself by accepting inputs only at discrete times. A clock circuit produces a continuous stream of 1s and 0s, as indicated by the waveform shown in Figure A.55. The time required for the clock to rise, then fall, then begin to rise again is called the *cycle time*. The square edges that are shown in the waveform represent an ideal square wave. In practice, the edges are rounded because instantaneous rise and fall times do not occur.

clock

cycle time

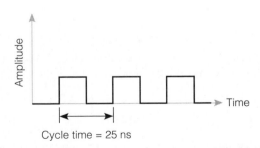

Fig. A.55 A Clock Waveform

Table A.2 Standard Scientific Prefixes for Cycle Times and Clock Rates

Prefix	Abbreviation	Quantity	Prefix	Abbreviation	Quantity
milli	m	10^{-3}	Kilo	K	10^{3}
micro	μ	10^{-6}	Mega	M	10^{6}
nano	n	10^{-9}	Giga	G	10^{9}
pico	p	10^{-12}	Tera	T	10^{12}
femto	f	10^{-15}	Peta	P	10^{15}
atto	a	10^{-18}	Exa	E	10^{18}

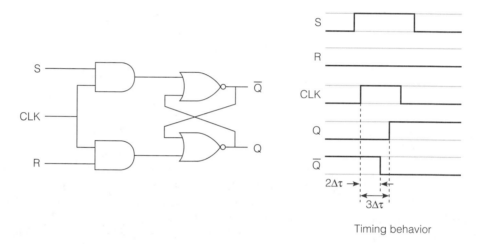

Timing behavior

Fig. A.56 A Clocked S-R Flip-Flop

The *clock rate* is taken as the inverse of the cycle time. For a cycle time of 25 ns/cycle, the corresponding clock rate is 1/25 cycles/ns, which corresponds to 40,000,000 cycles per second, or 40 MHz (for 40 megahertz). A list of other abbreviations that are commonly used to specify cycle times and clock rates is shown in Table A.2.

clocked S-R
flip-flop

We can make use of the clock signal to eliminate the hazard by creating a *clocked S-R flip-flop*, which is shown in Figure A.56. The symbol *CLK* labels the clock input. Now, *S* and *R* cannot change the state of the flip-flop until the clock is high. Thus, as long as *S* and *R* settle into stable states while the clock is low, when the clock makes a transition to 1, the stable value will be stored in the flip-flop.

A.12.3 THE D FLIP-FLOP AND THE MASTER-SLAVE CONFIGURATION

A disadvantage of the S-R flip-flop is that to store a 1 or a 0, we need to apply a 1 to a different input (*S* or *R*) depending on the value that we want to store. An alternative configuration

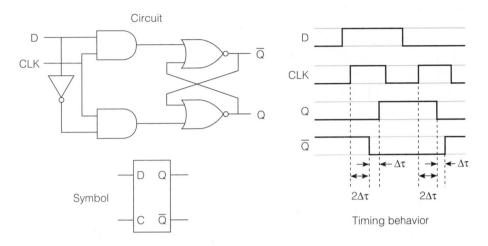

Fig. A.57 A Clocked D Flip-Flop (The Letter *C* Denotes the Clock Input in the Symbol Form)

that allows either a 0 or a 1 to be applied at the input is the *D flip-flop* which is shown in Figure A.57. The D flip-flop is constructed by placing an inverter across the *S* and *R* inputs of an S-R flip-flop. Now, when the clock goes high, the value on the *D* line is stored in the flip-flop.

    The D flip-flop is commonly used in situations where there is feedback from the output back to the input through some other circuitry, and this feedback can sometimes cause the flip-flop to change states more than once per clock cycle. To ensure that the flip-flop changes state just once per clock pulse, we break the feedback loop by con-structing a master-slave flip-flop, as shown in Figure A.58. The *master-slave flip-flop* consists of two flip-flops arranged in tandem, with an inverted clock used for the second

D flip-flop

master-slave flip-flop

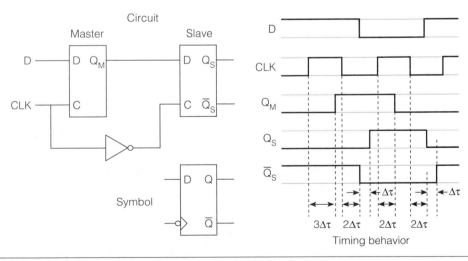

Fig. A.58 A Master-Slave Flip-Flop

flip-flop. The master flip-flop changes when the clock is high, but the slave flip-flop does not change until the clock is low; thus the clock must first go high and then go low before the input at D in the master is clocked through to Q_S in the slave. The triangle shown in the symbol for the master-slave flip-flop indicates that transitions at the output occur only on a rising (0-to-1 transition) or falling (1-to-0 transition) edge of the clock. Transitions at the output do not occur continuously during a high level of the clock as for the clocked S-R flip-flop. For the configuration shown in Figure A.58, the transition at the output occurs on the falling edge of the clock.

level-triggered
edge-triggered

A *level-triggered* flip-flop changes state continuously while the clock is high (or low, depending on how the flip-flop is designed). An *edge-triggered* flip-flop changes only on a high-to-low or low-to-high clock transition. Some textbooks do not place a triangle at the clock input to distinguish between level-triggered and edge-triggered flip-flops; they indicate one form or the other on the basis of their usage or in some other way. In practice, the notation is used somewhat loosely. Here, we will use the triangle symbol and also make the flip-flop type clear from the way it is used.

A.13 J-K and T Flip-Flops

J-K flip-flop
T flip-flop

In addition to the S-R and D flip-flops, the J-K and T flip-flops are very common. The *J-K flip-flop* behaves similarly to an S-R flip-flop, except that it flips its state when both inputs are set to 1. The *T flip-flop* (for "toggle") alternates states, as when the inputs to a J-K flip-flop are set to 1. Logic diagrams and symbols for the clocked J-K and T flip-flops are shown in Figure A.59 and Figure A.60, respectively. Notice that the T flip-flop is created by tying the J and K inputs together.

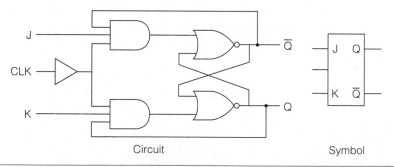

Fig. A.59 Logic Diagram and Symbol for a Basic J-K Flip-Flop

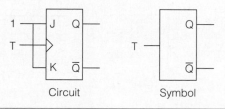

Fig. A.60 Logic Diagram and Symbol for a T Flip-Flop

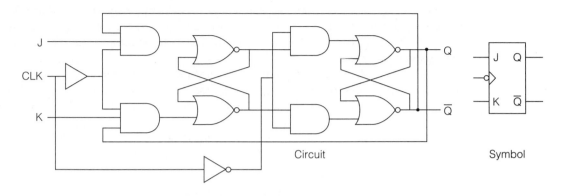

Fig. A.61 Logic Diagram and Symbol for a Master-Slave J-K Flip-Flop

A problem with the toggle mode operation for the J-K flip-flop is that when J and K are both high when the clock is also high, the flip-flop may toggle more than once before the clock goes low. This is another situation in which a master-slave configuration is appropriate. A schematic diagram for a master-slave J-K flip-flop is shown in Figure A.61. The "endless toggle" problem is now fixed with this configuration, but there is a new problem of "1s catching." If an input is high for any time while the clock is high, and if the input is simply in a transition mode before settling, the flip-flop will "see" the 1 as if it was meant to be a valid input. The situation can be avoided if hazards are eliminated in the circuit that provides the inputs.

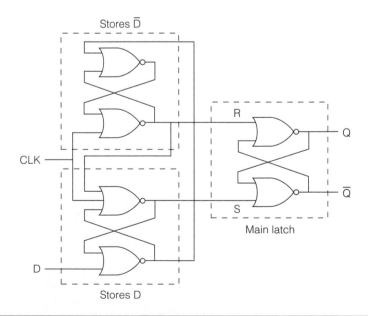

Fig. A.62 Negative Edge-Triggered D Flip-Flop

We can solve the 1s catching problem by constructing edge-triggered flip-flops in which only the transition of the clock (low to high for positive edge-triggered and high to low for negative edge-triggered) causes the inputs to be sampled, at which point the inputs should be stable.

Figure A.62 shows a configuration for a negative edge-triggered D flip-flop. When the clock is high, the top and bottom latches output 0s to the main (output) S-R latch. The D input can change an arbitrary number of times while the clock is high without affecting the state of the main latch. When the clock goes low, only the settled values of the top and bottom latches will affect the state of the main latch. While the clock is low, if the D input changes, the main flip-flop will not be affected.

A.14 Design of Finite State Machines

Refer again to the classical model of an FSM shown in Figure A.50. The delay elements can be implemented with master-slave flip-flops, and the synchronization signal can be provided by the clock. In general, there should be a flip-flop on each feedback line. Notice that we can label the flip-flops in any convenient way as long as the meaning is clear. In Figure A.50, the positions of the inputs D_i and the outputs Q_i have been interchanged with respect to the figures in Section A.12.

Consider a modulo(4) synchronous counter FSM, which counts from 00 to 11 and then repeats. Figure A.63 shows a block diagram of a synchronous counter FSM. The RESET (positive logic) function operates synchronously with respect to the clock. The outputs appear as a sequence of values on lines q_0 and q_1 at time steps corresponding to the clock. As the outputs are generated, a new state, $s_1 s_0$, is generated that is fed back to the input.

We can consider designing the counter by enumerating all possible input conditions and then creating four functions for the output $q_1 q_0$ and the state $s_1 s_0$. The corresponding functions can then be used to create a combinational logic circuit that implements the counter. Two flip-flops are used for the 2 state bits.

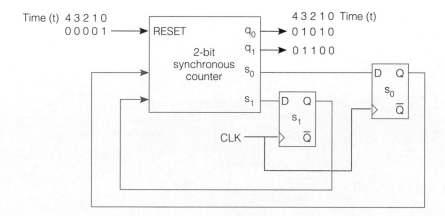

Fig. A.63 A Modulo(4) Counter

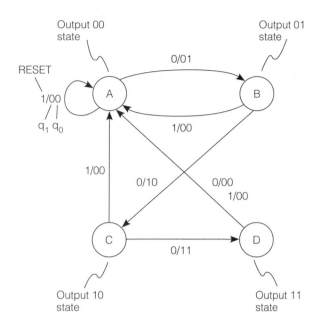

Fig. A.64 State Transition Diagram for a Modulo(4) Counter

How did we know that 2 state bits were needed on the feedback path? The fact is, we may not know in advance how many state bits are needed, and so we would like to have a more general approach to designing a finite state machine. For the counter, we can start by constructing a *state transition diagram*, as shown in Figure A.64, in which each state represents a count from 00 to 11, and the directed arcs represent transitions between states. State *A* represents the case in which the count is 00, and states *B*, *C*, and *D* represent counts 01, 10, and 11, respectively.

state transition diagram

Assume the FSM is initially in state *A*. There are two possible input conditions: 0 or 1. If the input (RESET) line is 0, then the FSM advances to state *B* and outputs 01. If the RESET line is 1, then the FSM remains in state A and outputs 00. Similarly, when the FSM is in state *B*, the FSM advances to state *C* and outputs 10 if the RESET line is 0; otherwise the FSM returns to state *A* and outputs 00. Transitions from the remaining states are interpreted similarly.

Once we have created the state transition diagram, we can rewrite it in tabular form as a *state table*, as shown in Figure A.65. The present states are shown at the left, and the input conditions are shown at the top. The entries in the table correspond to next state/output pairs, which are taken directly from the state transition diagram in Figure A.64. The highlighted entry corresponds to the case in which the present state is *B* and the input is 0. For this case, the next state is *C*, and the next output is 10.

state table

After we have created the state table, we encode the states in binary. Since there are four states, we need at least 2 bits to uniquely encode the states. We arbitrarily choose the following encoding: $A = 00$, $B = 01$, $C = 10$, and $D = 11$, and replace every occurrence of *A*, *B*, *C*, and *D* with their respective encodings, as shown in Figure A.66. In practice, the

Input Present state	RESET	
	0	1
A	B/01	A/00
B	C/10	A/00
C	D/11	A/00
D	A/00	A/00

Next state   Output

Fig. A.65 State Table for a Modulo(4) Counter

Input Present state (S_t)	RESET	
	0	1
A:00	01/01	00/00
B:01	10/10	00/00
C:10	11/11	00/00
D:11	00/00	00/00

Fig. A.66 State Table with State Assignments for a Modulo(4) Counter

RESET r(t)	$s_1(t)$	$s_0(t)$	$s_1s_0(t+1)$	$q_1q_0(t+1)$
0	0	0	01	01
0	0	1	10	10
0	1	0	11	11
0	1	1	00	00
1	0	0	00	00
1	0	1	00	00
1	1	0	00	00
1	1	1	00	00

$$s_0(t+1) = \overline{r(t)}\,\overline{s_1(t)}\,\overline{s_0(t)} + \overline{r(t)}\,s_1(t)\,s_0(t)$$

$$s_1(t+1) = \overline{r(t)}\,\overline{s_1(t)}\,s_0(t) + \overline{r(t)}\,s_1(t)\,\overline{s_0(t)}$$

$$q_0(t+1) = \overline{r(t)}\,\overline{s_1(t)}\,\overline{s_0(t)} + \overline{r(t)}\,s_1(t)\,\overline{s_0(t)}$$

$$q_1(t+1) = \overline{r(t)}\,\overline{s_1(t)}\,s_0(t) + \overline{r(t)}\,s_1(t)\,\overline{s_0(t)}$$

Fig. A.67 Truth Table for the Next State and Output Functions for a Modulo(4) Counter

state encoding may affect the form of the resulting circuit, but the circuit will be logically correct regardless of the encoding.

From the state table, we can extract truth tables for the next state and output functions as shown in Figure A.67. The subscripts for the state variables indicate timing relationships.

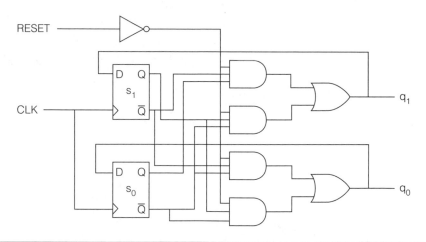

Fig. A.68 Logic Design for a Modulo(4) Counter

The present state is s_t, and s_{t+1} is the next state. The subscripts are commonly omitted since it is understood that the present signals appear on the right side of the equation and the next signals appear on the left side of the equation. Notice that $s_0(t+1) = q_0(t+1)$, and $s_1(t+1) = q_1(t+1)$, so we only need to implement $s_0(t+1)$ and $s_1(t+1)$ and tap the outputs for $q_0(t+1)$ and $q_1(t+1)$.

Finally, we implement the next state and output functions, using logic gates and master-slave D flip-flops for the state variables, as shown in Figure A.68.

Example A.2   A Sequence Detector

As another example, suppose we wish to design a machine that outputs a 1 when exactly two of the last three inputs are 1. For example, an input sequence of 011011100 produces an output sequence of 001111010. There is a 1-bit serial input line, and we can assume that initially no inputs have been seen. For this problem, we will use D flip-flops and 8-to-1 MUXes.

We start by constructing a state transition diagram, as shown in Figure A.69. There are eight possible 3-bit sequences that our machine will observe: 000, 001, 010, 011, 100, 101, 110, and 111. State A is the initial state, in which we assume that no inputs have yet been seen. In states B and C, we have seen only one input, so we cannot output a 1 yet. In states D, E, F, and G we have only seen two inputs, so we cannot output a 1 yet, even though we have seen two 1's at the input when we enter state G. The machine makes all subsequent transitions among states D, E, F, and G. State D is visited when the last two inputs are 00. States E, F, and G are visited when the last two inputs are 01, 10, or 11, respectively.

The next step is to create a state table, as shown in Figure A.70, which is taken directly from the state transition diagram. Next, we make a state assignment, as shown in Figure A.71a. We then use the state assignment to create a truth table for the next state and output functions, as shown in Figure A.71b. The last two entries in the table correspond to state 111, which cannot arise in practice, according to the state table in Figure A.71a. Therefore, the next state and output entries do not matter, and are labeled as 'd' for *don't care*.

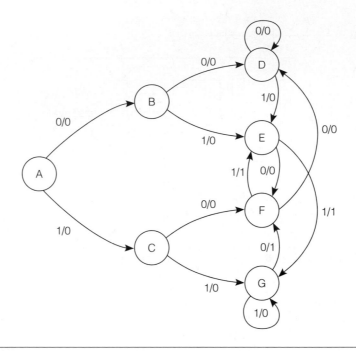

Fig. A.69 State Transition Diagram for Sequence Detector

	Input	X	
Present state		0	1
A		B/0	C/0
B		D/0	E/0
C		F/0	G/0
D		D/0	E/0
E		F/0	G/1
F		D/0	E/1
G		F/1	G/0

Fig. A.70 State Table for Sequence Detector

Finally, we create the circuit, which is shown in Figure A.72. There is one flip-flop for each state variable, so there are a total of three flip-flops. There are three next-state functions and one output function, so there are four MUXes. Notice that the choice of s_2, s_1, and s_0 for the MUX control inputs is arbitrary. Any other grouping or ordering will also work. ∎

Input	X	
Present state	0	1
$s_2s_1s_0$	$s_2s_1s_0z$	$s_2s_1s_0z$
A: 000	001/0	010/0
B: 001	011/0	100/0
C: 010	101/0	110/0
D: 011	011/0	100/0
E: 100	101/0	110/1
F: 101	011/0	100/1
G: 110	101/1	110/0

(a)

Input and state at time t				Next state and output at time $t + 1$			
s_2	s_1	s_0	x	s_2	s_1	s_0	z
0	0	0	0	0	0	1	0
0	0	0	1	0	1	0	0
0	0	1	0	0	1	1	0
0	0	1	1	1	0	0	0
0	1	0	0	1	0	1	0
0	1	0	1	1	1	0	0
0	1	1	0	0	1	1	0
0	1	1	1	1	0	0	0
1	0	0	0	1	0	1	0
1	0	0	1	1	1	0	1
1	0	1	0	0	1	1	0
1	0	1	1	1	0	0	1
1	1	0	0	1	0	1	1
1	1	0	1	1	1	0	0
1	1	1	0	d	d	d	d
1	1	1	1	d	d	d	d

(b)

Fig. A.71 State Assignment and Truth Table for Sequence Detector

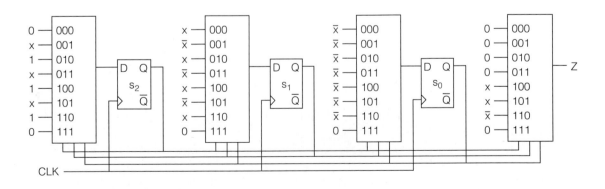

Fig. A.72 Logic Diagram for Sequence Detector

Example A.3   A Vending Machine Controller

For this problem, we will design a vending machine controller using D flip-flops and a black box representation of a PLA (as in Figure A.34). The vending machine accepts three U.S. coins: the nickel (5¢), the dime (10¢), and the quarter (25¢). When the value of the inserted coins equals or exceeds 20¢, the machine dispenses the merchandise, returns any excess money, and waits for the next transaction.

We begin by constructing a state transition diagram, as shown in Figure A.73. In state A, no coins have yet been inserted, and so the money credited is 0¢. If a nickel or dime is inserted when the machine is in state A, then the FSM makes a transition to state B or state C, respectively. If a quarter is inserted, then the money credited to the customer is 25¢. The controller dispenses the merchandise, returns a nickel in change, and remains in state A. This is indicated by the label "$Q/110$" on the state A self-loop. States B and C are then expanded, producing state D, which is also expanded, producing the complete FSM for the vending machine controller. (Notice the behavior when a quarter is inserted when the FSM is in state D.)

From the FSM we construct the state table shown in Figure A.74a. We then make an arbitrary state assignment and encode the symbols N, D, and Q in binary as shown in Figure A.74b. Finally, we create a circuit diagram, which is shown in Figure A.75a. There are 2 state bits, so there are two D flip-flops. The PLA takes four inputs for the present-state bits and the x_1x_0 coin bits. The PLA produces five outputs for the next-state bits and the dispense and return-nickel/return-dime bits. (We can assume that the clock input is asserted only on an event such as an inserted coin.)

Notice that we have not explicitly specified the design of the PLA itself in obtaining the FSM circuit in Figure A.75a. At this level of complexity, it is common to use a computer program to generate a truth table, and then feed the truth table to a PLA design program. We could generate the truth table and PLA design by hand, of course, as shown in Figure A.75b and Figure A.75c.   ∎

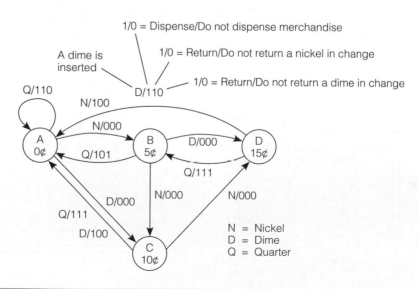

Fig. A.73   State Transition Diagram for Vending Machine Controller

Input \ P.S.	N 00	D 01	Q 10
A	B/000	C/000	A/110
B	C/000	D/000	A/101
C	D/000	A/100	A/111
D	A/100	A/110	B/111

(a)

Input \ P.S.	N x_1x_0 00	D x_1x_0 01	Q x_1x_0 10
s_1s_0		$s_1s_0 / z_2z_1z_0$	
A:00	01/000	10/000	00/110
B:01	10/000	11/000	00/101
C:10	11/000	00/100	00/111
D:11	00/100	00/110	01/111

(b)

Fig. A.74 (a) State Table for Vending Machine Controller; (b) State Assignment for Vending Machine Controller

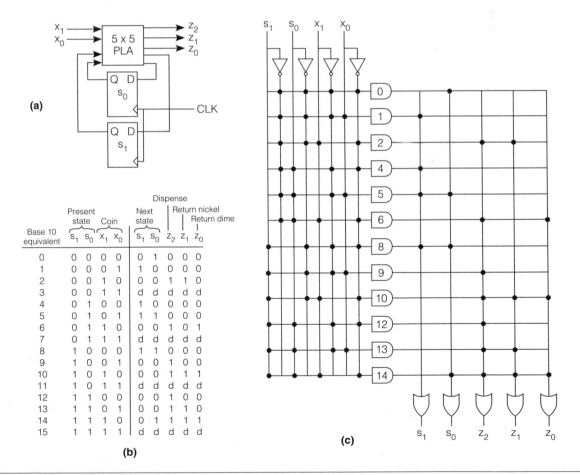

Fig. A.75 (a) FSM Circuit; (b) Truth Table; (c) PLA Realization for Vending Machine Controller

A.15 Mealy versus Moore Machines

The outputs of the FSM circuits we have studied so far are determined by the present states and the inputs. The states are maintained in falling edge-triggered flip-flops, and so a state change can only occur on the falling edge of the clock. Any changes that occur at the inputs have no effect on the state as long as the clock is low. The inputs are fed directly through the output circuits, however, with no intervening flip-flops. Thus a change to an input at any time can cause a change in the output, regardless of whether the clock is high or low. In Figure A.75, a change at either the x_1 or x_0 inputs will propagate through to the $z_2 z_1 z_0$ outputs regardless of the level of the clock. This organization is referred to as the Mealy model of an FSM.

Mealy model
Moore model

In the *Mealy* model, the outputs change as soon as the inputs change, and so there is no delay introduced by the clock. In the *Moore* model of an FSM, the outputs are embedded in the state bits, and so a change at the outputs occurs on the clock pulse *after* a change at the inputs. Both models are used by circuit designers, and either model may be encountered outside this textbook. In this section we simply highlight the differences through an example.

An example of a Moore FSM is shown in Figure A.76. The FSM counts from 0 to 3 in binary and then repeats, similar to the modulo(4) counter shown in Figure A.68. The machine only counts when $x = 1$; otherwise the FSM maintains its current state. Notice that the outputs are embedded in the state variables, and so there is no direct path from the input to the outputs without an intervening flip-flop.

The Mealy model might be considered to be more powerful than the Moore model because in a single clock cycle, a change in the output of one FSM can ripple to the input of another FSM, whose output then changes and ripples to the next FSM, and so on. In the Moore model, lock-step synchronization is strictly maintained, and so this ripple scenario does not occur. Spurious changes in the output of an FSM thus have less influence on the rest of the circuit in the Moore model. This simplifies circuit analysis and hardware debugging, and for these situations, the Moore model may be preferred. In practice, both models are used.

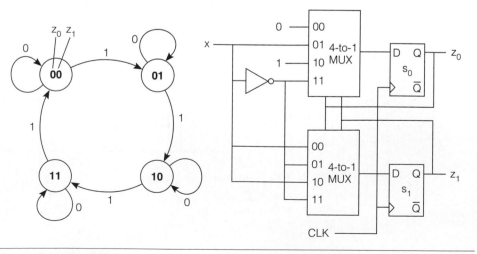

Fig. A.76 A Moore Binary Counter FSM

A.16 Registers

A *tri-state buffer* behaves in a manner similar to the ordinary buffer that was introduced earlier in this appendix, except that a control input determines the value at the output. Depending on the value of the control input, the output is either 0, 1, or *disabled*, thus providing
three output states. In Figure A.77, when the control input C is 1, the tri-state buffer behaves
like an ordinary buffer. When C is 0, then the output is electrically disconnected and no output is produced. The ϕ's in the corresponding truth table entries mark the disabled (disconnected) states. The inverted control tri-state buffer is similar to the tri-state buffer, except
that the control input C is complemented as indicated by the bubble at the control input.

An electrically disconnected output is different from an output that produces a 0, in
that an electrically disconnected output behaves as if no output connection exists, whereas
a logical 0 at the output is still electrically connected to the circuit. The tri-state buffer
allows the outputs from a number of logic gates to drive a common line without risking
electrical shorts, provided that only one buffer is enabled at a time. The use of tri-state
buffers is important in implementing registers, which are described next.

A single bit of information is stored in a D flip-flop. A group of N bits, making up an
N-bit word, can be stored in N D flip-flops organized as shown in Figure A.78 for a 4-bit

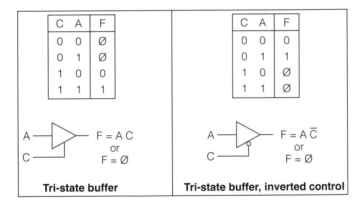

Fig. A.77 Tri-State Buffers

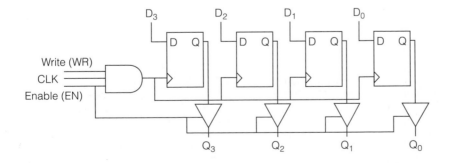

Fig. A.78 A 4-Bit Register

register

word. We refer to such an arrangement of flip-flops as a *register*. In this particular configuration, the data at inputs D_i are loaded into the register when the Write and Enable lines are high, synchronous with the clock. The contents of the register can be read at outputs Q_i only if the Enable line is high, since the tri-state buffers are in the electrically disconnected state when the Enable line is low. We can simplify the illustration by just marking the inputs and outputs as shown in Figure A.79.

A shift register copies the contents of each of its flip-flops to the next, while accepting a new input at one end and "spilling" the contents at the other end, which makes cascading possible. Consider the shift register shown in Figure A.80. The register can shift to the left,

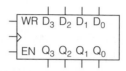

Fig. A.79 Abstract Representation of a 4-Bit Register

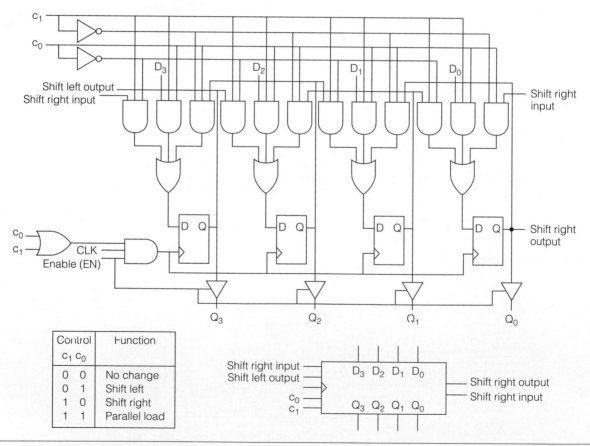

Control $c_1\ c_0$	Function
0 0	No change
0 1	Shift left
1 0	Shift right
1 1	Parallel load

Fig. A.80 Internal Layout and Block Diagram for a Left/Right Shifter with Parallel Read/Write Capabilities

shift to the right, accept a parallel load, or remain unchanged, all synchronous with the clock. The parallel load and parallel read capabilities allow the shift register to function as either a serial-to-parallel converter or as a parallel-to-serial converter.

A.17 Counters

A counter is a different form of a register in which the output pattern sequences through a range of binary numbers. Figure A.81 shows a configuration for a modulo(8) counter that steps through the following binary patterns: 000, 001, 010, 011, 100, 101, 110, 111, and then repeats. Three J-K flip-flops are placed in toggle mode, and each clock input is ANDed with the Q outputs from the previous stages, which successively halves the clock frequency. The result is a progression of toggle flip-flops operating at rates that differ in powers of 2, corresponding to the sequence of binary patterns from 000 to 111.

Notice that we have added an active-low asynchronous RESET line to the counter, which resets it to 000, regardless of the states of the clock or enable lines. Except for the flip-flop in the least significant position, the remaining flip-flops change state according to changes in states from their neighbors to the right rather than synchronously with respect to the clock. It is similar in function to the modulo(4) counter in Figure A.68, but is more easily extended to large sizes because it is not treated like an ordinary FSM for design purposes, in which all states are enumerated. It is, nevertheless, an FSM.

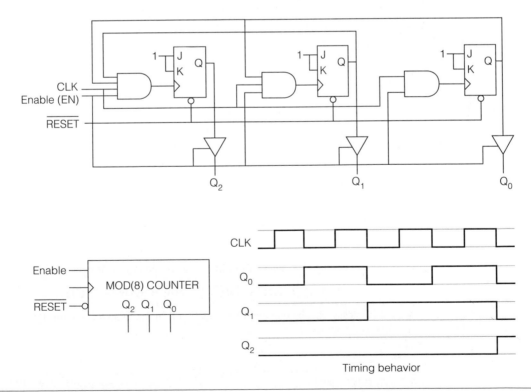

Fig. A.81 A Modulo(8) Counter

Bibliography

Hamacher, V. C., Z. G. Vranesic, and S. G. Zaky, *Computer Organization*, 3rd ed., McGraw-Hill, 1990.

Katz, R. H., *Contemporary Logic Design*, Benjamin/Cummings, Redwood City, CA, 1994.

Kohavi, Z., *Switching and Finite Automata Theory*, 2nd ed., McGraw-Hill, New York, 1978.

Mead, C., and L. Conway, *Introduction to VLSI Systems*, Addison-Wesley, 1980.

Texas Instruments, *TTL Logic Data Book*, Dallas, Texas, 1988.

Exercises

A.1 Figure A.12 shows an OR gate implemented with a NAND gate and inverters, and Figure A.13 shows inverters implemented with NAND gates. Show the logic diagram for an AND gate implemented entirely with NAND gates.

A.2 Draw logic diagrams for each member of the computationally complete set {AND, OR, NOT}, using only the computationally complete set {NOR}.

A.3 Given the following logic circuit, construct a truth table that describes its behavior.

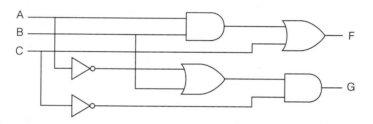

A.4 Construct a truth table for a three-input XOR gate.

A.5 Compute the gate input count of the 4-to-2 priority encoder shown in Figure A.31. Include the inverters in your count.

A.6 Design a circuit that implements function f, using AND, OR, and NOT gates.

$$f(A, B, C) = \overline{A}BC + \overline{A}\,\overline{B}C + AB\overline{C}$$

A.7 Design a circuit that implements function g, using AND, OR, and NOT gates. Do not attempt to change the form of the equation.

$$g(A, B, C, D, E) = \overline{A}(BC + \overline{B}\,\overline{C}) + B(CD + E)$$

A.8 Are functions f and g equivalent? Show how you arrived at your answer.

$$f(A, B, C) = ABC + \overline{A}B\overline{C} \qquad g(A, B, C) = (A \oplus C)B$$

A.9 Write a Boolean equation that describes function F in the following circuit. Put your answer in SOP form (without parentheses).

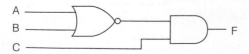

A.10 A four-bit *comparator* is a component that takes two four-bit words as inputs and produces a single bit of output. The output is a 0 if the words are identical, and is a 1 otherwise. Design a four-bit comparator with any of the logic gates you have seen in this appendix. Hint: Think of the four-bit comparator as four one-bit comparators combined in some fashion.

A.11 Redraw the circuit shown here so that the bubble matching is correct. The overbars on the variable and function names indicate active-low logic.

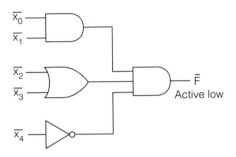

A.12 Use two 4-to-1 MUXes to implement the following functions:

A	B	F_0	F_1
0	0	0	0
0	1	1	0
1	0	1	0
1	1	0	1

A.13 Use one 4-to-1 MUX to implement the majority function.

A.14 Use function decomposition to implement function f with two 4-to-1 MUXes. Parenthesize the equation so that C and D are in the innermost level, as in Equation A.21. Make sure that every input to each MUX is assigned to a value (0 or 1), to a variable, or to a function.

$$f(A, B, C, D) = ABCD + AB\overline{C}D + ABC\overline{D} + \overline{A}B$$

A.15 Use a 2-to-4 decoder and an OR gate to implement the XOR of two inputs A and B.

A.16 Draw a logic diagram that uses a decoder and two OR gates to implement functions F and G. Be sure to label all lines in your diagram.

$$F(A, B, C) = \overline{A}B\overline{C} + \overline{A}\overline{B}C + A\overline{B}C + \overline{A}BC$$

$$G(A, B, C) = \overline{A}B\overline{C} + ABC$$

A.17 Design a circuit using only 2-to-1 MUXes that implements the function of an 8-to-1 MUX. Show your design in the form of a logic diagram, and label all of the lines.

A.18 Since any combinational circuit can be constructed using only two-input NAND gates, the two-input NAND is called a universal logic gate. The two-input NOR is also a universal logic gate; however, AND and OR are not. Since a two-input NAND can be constructed using only

4-to-1 MUXes (it can be done with one 4-to-1 MUX), any combinational circuit can be constructed using only 4-to-1 MUXes. Consequently, the 4-to-1 MUX is also a universal device. Show that the 1-to-2 DEMUX is a universal device by constructing a two-input NAND using only 1-to-2 DEMUXes. Draw a logic diagram. Hint: Compose the NAND from an AND and an inverter, each made from 1-to-2 DEMUXes.

A.19   The outputs of a seven-segment display, like one you might find in a calculator, are shown here. The seven segments are labeled a through g. Design a circuit that takes as input a 4-bit binary number and produces as output the control signal for just the b segment (not the letter *b*, which has the 1011 code). A 0 at the output turns the segment off, and a 1 turns the segment on. Show the truth table and an implementation using a single MUX and no other logic components. Label all of the lines of the MUX.

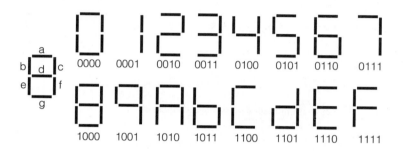

A.20   Implement function *F* shown in the following truth table, using the 16-to-1 MUX shown. Label all of the lines, including the unmarked control line.

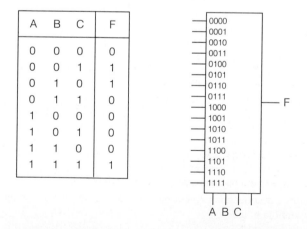

A	B	C	F
0	0	0	0
0	0	1	1
0	1	0	1
0	1	1	0
1	0	0	0
1	0	1	0
1	1	0	0
1	1	1	1

strict encoder

A.21   A *strict encoder* takes 2^N binary inputs, of which exactly one input is 1 at any time and the remaining inputs are 0, and produces an *N*-bit, coded binary output that indicates which of the *N* inputs is high. For this problem, create a truth table for a 4-to-2 strict encoder in which there are four inputs: *A, B, C,* and *D,* and two outputs: *X* and *Y. A* and *X* are the most significant bits.

A.22   Consider a combinational logic circuit with three inputs *a, b,* and *c,* and six outputs *u, v, w, x, y,* and *z.* The input is an unsigned number between 0 and 7, and the output is the square of the input. The most significant bit of the input is *a,* and the most significant bit of the output is *u.* Create a truth table for the six functions.

A.23 Consider the function $f(a, b, c, d)$ that takes on the value 1 if and only if the number of 1's in b and c is greater than or equal to the number of 1's in a and d.

    a. Write the truth table for function f.

    b. Use an 8-to-1 multiplexer to implement function f.

A.24 Create a truth table for a single digit ternary (base 3) comparator. The ternary inputs are A and B, which are each a single ternary digit wide. The output Z is 0 for $A < B$, 1 for $A = B$, and 2 for $A > B$. Using this truth table as a guide, rewrite the truth table in binary, using the assignment $(0)_3 \rightarrow (00)_2$, $(1)_3 \rightarrow (01)_2$, and $(2)_3 \rightarrow (10)_2$.

A.25 Prove the consensus theorem for three variables, using perfect induction.

A.26 Use the properties of Boolean algebra to prove the absorption theorem algebraically.

A.27 Given the following functions, construct K-maps, and find minimal sum-of-products expressions for f and g.

$$f(A,B,C,D) = 1$$

when two or more inputs are 1; otherwise,

$$f(A,B,C,D) = 0$$

$$g(A,B,C,D) = 1$$

when the number of inputs that are 1 is even (including the case when no inputs are 1); otherwise,

$$g(A,B,C,D) = \overline{f(A, B, C, D)}$$

A.28 Use K-maps to simplify function f and its don't-care condition below. Perform the reduction for

    a. the sum-of-products form

    b. the product-of-sums form

$$f(A, B, C, D) = \sum(2, 8, 10, 11) + \sum{}_d(0, 9)$$

A.29 Given a logic circuit, is it possible to generate a truth table that contains don't cares? Explain your answer.

A.30 The following K-map is formed incorrectly. Show the reduced equation that is produced by the incorrect map, and then form the K-map correctly, and derive the reduced equation from the correct map. Note that both K-maps will produce functionally correct equations, but only the properly formed K-map will produce a minimized two-level equation.

ABC D	000	001	011	010	110	111	101	100
0	1			1	1			1
1	1			1	1			1

A.31 Can an S-R flip-flop be constructed with two cross-coupled XOR gates? Explain your answer.

A.32 Create a state transition diagram for an FSM that sorts two binary words A and B, input serially with most significant bit first, onto two binary outputs GE and LT. If A is greater than or equal to B, then A appears on the GE line, and B appears on the LT line. If B is greater than A, then B appears on the GE line, and A appears on the LT line.

A.33   Design a circuit that produces a 1 at the Z output when the input X changes from 0 to 1 or from 1 to 0, and produces a 0 at all other times. For the initial state, assume a 0 was last seen at the input. For example, if the input sequence is 00110 (from left to right), then the output sequence is 00101. Show the state transition diagram, the state table, state assignment, and the final circuit, using MUXes.

A.34   Design an FSM that outputs a 1 when the last three inputs are 011 or 110. Just show the state table. Do not draw a circuit.

A.35   Design a finite state machine that takes two binary words X and Y in serial form, least signifi-cant bit (LSB) first, and produces a 1-bit output Z that is true when $X > Y$ and is 0 for $X \le Y$. When the machine starts, assume that $X = Y$. That is, Z produces 0's until $X > Y$. The diagram shows a sample input sequence and the corresponding output sequence.

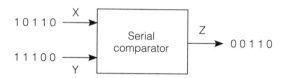

A.36   Create a state transition diagram for an FSM that sorts two ternary inputs, most significant digit first, onto two ternary outputs GE and LT. If A is greater than or equal to B, then A appears on the GE line, and B appears on the LT line; otherwise B appears on the GE line and A appears on the LT line. A sample input/output sequence follows. Use the ternary symbols 0, 1, and 2 when you label the arcs.

   Input A: 02112012
   Input B   02120211
   Output GE 02120211
   Output LT: 02112012
   Time: 01234567

A.37   Create a state transition diagram for a machine that computes an even parity bit z for its 2-bit input $x_1 x_0$. The machine outputs a 0 when all of the previous 2-bit inputs collectively have an even number of 1's, and outputs a 1 otherwise. For the initial state, assume that the machine starts with even parity.

A.38   Given the state transition diagram shown on the next page, do the following:

   a.   Create a state table.

   b.   Design a circuit for the state machine described by your state table, using D flip-flop(s), a single decoder, and OR gates. For the state assignment, use the bit pattern that corresponds to the position of each letter in the alphabet, starting from 0. For example, A is at position 0, so the state assignment is 000; B is at position 1, so the state assignment is 001, and so on.

A.39   Redraw the circuit shown in Figure A.15 using AND and OR gates that have a fan-in of 2.

A.40   Suppose that you need to implement an N-input AND gate using only three-input AND gates. What is the minimum number of gate delays required to implement the N-input AND gate? A single AND gate has a gate delay of 1; two cascaded AND gates have a combined gate delay of 2, and so on.

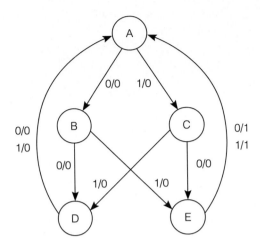

RTN Description of SRC

This appendix collects the entire RTN definition of the SRC in one place. The definition proceeds as it did in the text. That is, reset and exception processing are added after the main definition.

The RTN symbols are defined at the end of the appendix.

B.1   SRC Without Reset or Exceptions

Memory

Processor State

PC$\langle 31..0 \rangle$:	Program counter (address of next instruction)
IR$\langle 31..0 \rangle$:	Instruction register
Run:	1-bit run/halt indicator
Strt:	Start signal
R[0..31]$\langle 31..0 \rangle$:	General purpose registers

Main Memory State

Mem[0..2^{32} − 1]$\langle 7..0 \rangle$: 2^{32} addressable bytes of memory

M[x]$\langle 31..0 \rangle$:= Mem[x]#Mem[x+1]#Mem[x+2]#Mem[x+3]:

Formats

Instruction Formats

$op\langle 4..0\rangle := IR\langle 31..27\rangle$:   Operation code field
$ra\langle 4..0\rangle := IR\langle 26..22\rangle$:   Target register field
$rb\langle 4..0\rangle := IR\langle 21..17\rangle$:   Operand, address index, or branch target
$rc\langle 4..0\rangle := IR\langle 16..12\rangle$:   Second operand, condition, or shift count
$c1\langle 21..0\rangle := IR\langle 21..0\rangle$:   Long displacement field
$c2\langle 16..0\rangle := IR\langle 16..0\rangle$:   Short displacement or immediate field
$c3\langle 11..0\rangle := IR\langle 11..0\rangle$:   Count or modifier field

Effective Address Calculations

$disp\langle 31..0\rangle := ((rb=0) \rightarrow c2\langle 16..0\rangle$ {sign extend}:
Displacement
          $(rb \neq 0) \rightarrow R[rb] + c2\langle 16..0\rangle$ {sign ext., 2's comp.}):   address
$rel\langle 31..0\rangle := PC\langle 31..0\rangle + c1\langle 21..0\rangle$ {sign ext., 2's comp.}:   Rel. address

Instruction Interpretation

(instruction_interpretation := (
$\neg Run \wedge Strt \rightarrow Run \leftarrow 1$; instruction_interpretation):
$Run \rightarrow (IR \leftarrow M[PC]$: $PC \leftarrow PC + 4$; instruction_execution):

Instruction Execution

instruction_execution := (
ld (:= op= 1) $\rightarrow R[ra] \leftarrow M[disp]$:   ld ra, offset(rb)   Load register
ldr (:= op= 2) $\rightarrow R[ra] \leftarrow M[rel]$:   ldr ra, offset   Load reg. rel.
st (:= op= 3) $\rightarrow M[disp] \leftarrow R[ra]$:   st ra, offset(rb)   Store register
str (:= op= 4) $\rightarrow M[rel] \leftarrow R[ra]$:   str ra, offset(rb)   Store reg. rel.
la (:= op= 5) $\rightarrow R[ra] \leftarrow disp$:   la ra, offset(rb)   Load disp. adr.
lar (:= op= 6) $\rightarrow R[ra] \leftarrow rel$:   lar ra, offset   Load rel. adr.

Branch Instructions

cond := ($c3\langle 2..0\rangle=0 \rightarrow 0$:   br(l)nv (ra)   Never
     $c3\langle 2..0\rangle=1 \rightarrow 1$:   br(l) (ra,) rb   Always
     $c3\langle 2..0\rangle=2 \rightarrow R[rc]=0$:   brzr(l) (ra,) rb, rc $R[rc] = 0$
     $c3\langle 2..0\rangle=3 \rightarrow R[rc]\neq 0$:   brnz(l) (ra,) rb, rc $R[rc] \neq 0$
     $c3\langle 2..0\rangle=4 \rightarrow R[rc]\langle 31\rangle=0$:   brpl(l) (ra,) rb, rc $R[rc] \geq 0$
     $c3\langle 2..0\rangle=5 \rightarrow R[rc]\langle 31\rangle=1$):   brmi(l) (ra,) rb, rc $R[rc] < 0$
br (:= op= 8) $\rightarrow$ (cond $\rightarrow PC \leftarrow R[rb]$):   Conditional branch
brl (:= op= 9) $\rightarrow$ ($R[ra] \leftarrow PC$: cond $\rightarrow$ ($PC \leftarrow R[rb]$)):   Branch and link

Arithmetic Instructions (Assumed to Be 2's Complement Arithmetic)

add (:= op= 12) → R[ra] ← R[rb] + R[rc]:   add ra, rb, rc
addi (:= op= 13) → R[ra] ← R[rb] + c2⟨16..0⟩
        {2's comp. sign ext.}:   addi ra, rb, imm
sub (:= op= 14) → R[ra] ← R[rb] – R[rc]:
neg (:= op= 15) → R[ra] ← – R[rc]:   neg ra, rc
and (:= op= 20) → R[ra] ← R[rb] ∧ R[rc]:
andi (:= op= 21) → R[ra] ← R[rb] ∧ c2⟨16..0⟩ {sign-extend}:
or (:= op= 22) → R[ra] ← R[rb] ∨ R[rc]:
ori (:= op= 23) → R[ra] ← R[rb] ∨ c2⟨16..0⟩ {sign-extend}:
not (:= op= 24) → R[ra] ← ¬R[rc]:

Shift Instructions

n := ((c3⟨4..0⟩=0) → R[rc]⟨4..0⟩:   Shift count in a register or
        (c3⟨4..0⟩≠0) → c3⟨4..0⟩   ):   constant field of the inst.
shr (:= op= 26)→R[ra]⟨31..0⟩ ← (n @ 0) # R[rb]⟨31..n⟩:
                                            shr ra, rb, cnt; shr ra, rb, rc
shra (:= op= 27) → R[ra]⟨31..0⟩ ← (n @ R[rb]⟨31⟩) # R[rb]⟨31..n⟩:
shl (:= op= 28) → R[ra]⟨31..0⟩ ← R[rb]⟨31–n..0⟩ # (n @ 0):
shc (:= op= 29) → R[ra]⟨31..0⟩ ← R[rb]⟨31–n..0⟩ # R[rb]⟨31..32 – n⟩:

Miscellaneous Instructions

nop (:= op= 0) → :   No operation
stop (:= op= 31) → Run ← 0   Stop instruction
        );   End of instruction_execution
instruction_interpretation):

B.2   Additions to SRC for Reset and Interrupts

Adding a Reset to SRC

instruction_interpretation := (¬Run∧Strt → (Run ← 1: PC, R[0..31] ← 0);
Run∧¬Rst → (IR ← M[PC]: PC ← PC + 4; instruction_execution):
Run∧Rst → (Rst ← 0: PC ← 0); instruction_interpretation):

Adding Interrupt Processing to SRC

Processor Interrupt Mechanism

ireq: Interrupt request signal
iack: Interrupt acknowledge signal
IE: 1-bit interrupt enable flag
IPC⟨31..0⟩:   Storage for program counter saved upon interrupt
II⟨31..0⟩:   Interrupt information: info. on source of last interrupt
Isrc_info⟨15..0⟩:   Information from interrupt source
Isrc_vect⟨7..0⟩:   Type code from interrupt source
Ivect⟨31..0⟩ := 20@0 # Isrc_vect⟨7..0⟩ # 4@0:

The modified instruction interpretation sequence follows:

instruction_interpretation :=
$(\neg\text{Run}\wedge\text{Strt} \to \text{Run} \leftarrow 1:$
$\text{Run}\wedge\neg(\text{ireq}\wedge\text{IE}) \to (\text{I} \leftarrow \text{M[PC]}: \text{PC} \leftarrow \text{PC} + 4; \text{instruction\_execution}):$
$\text{Run}\wedge(\text{ireq}\wedge\text{IE}) \to (\text{IPC} \leftarrow \text{PC}\langle31..0\rangle:$
$\qquad\qquad\qquad\text{II}\langle15..0\rangle \leftarrow \text{Isrc\_info}\langle15..0\rangle : \text{iack} \leftarrow 1:$
$\qquad\qquad\qquad\text{IE} \leftarrow 0: \text{PC} \leftarrow \text{Ivect}\langle31..0\rangle;$
$\qquad\qquad\qquad\text{iack} \leftarrow 0);$
$\qquad\qquad\qquad\text{instruction\_interpretation});$

Additional Instructions to Support Interrupts

The svi and ri instructions provide a means for saving and restoring II and IPC: svi saves II and IPC to general registers ra and rb, respectively, and ri reverses the process, restoring II and IPC from registers ra and rb:

$\text{svi (:= op= 16)} \to (\text{R[ra]}\langle15..0\rangle \leftarrow \text{II}\langle15..0\rangle: \text{R[rb]} \leftarrow \text{IPC}\langle31..0\rangle):$
$\text{ri (:= op= 17)} \to (\text{II}\langle15..0\rangle \leftarrow \text{R[ra]}\langle15..0\rangle : \text{IPC}\langle31..0\rangle \leftarrow \text{R[rb]}):$

There are two instructions that allow the programmer to control interrupt recognition, een and edi: exception enable and exception disable:

$\text{een (:= op= 10)} \to (\text{IE} \leftarrow 1):$
$\text{edi (:= op= 11)} \to (\text{IE} \leftarrow 0):$

The rfi, return from interrupt instruction returns control to the interrupted process:

$\text{rfi (:= op= 30)} \to (\text{PC} \leftarrow \text{IPC}: \text{IE} \leftarrow 1):$

B.3 Unified RTN for SRC

Below is the entire RTN description for SRC with reset and exception handling integrated into it.

Memory

Processor State

$\text{PC}\langle31..0\rangle$:	Program counter (address of the next instruction)
$\text{IR}\langle31..0\rangle$:	Instruction register
Run:	1-bit run/halt indicator
Strt:	Start and hard reset signal
Rst:	Soft reset signal
$\text{R[0..31]}\langle31..0\rangle$:	General purpose registers

Processor Interrupt Mechanism

ireq: Interrupt request signal
iack: Interrupt acknowledge signal
IE: 1-bit interrupt enable flag
IPC$\langle 31..0 \rangle$: Storage for PC saved upon interrupt
II$\langle 31..0 \rangle$: Interrupt info. about source of last interrupt
Isrc_info$\langle 15..0 \rangle$: Information from interrupt source
Isrc_vect$\langle 7..0 \rangle$: Type code from interrupt source
Ivect$\langle 31..0 \rangle$:= 20@0 # Isrc_vect$\langle 7..0 \rangle$ # 4@0:

Main Memory State

Mem[0..2^{32} – 1]$\langle 7..0 \rangle$: 2^{32} addressable bytes of memory
M[x]$\langle 31..0 \rangle$:= Mem[x]#Mem[x+1]#Mem[x+2]#Mem[x+3]:

Formats

Instruction Formats

op$\langle 4..0 \rangle$:= IR$\langle 31..27 \rangle$: Operation code field
ra$\langle 4..0 \rangle$:= IR$\langle 26..22 \rangle$: Target register field
rb$\langle 4..0 \rangle$:= IR$\langle 21..17 \rangle$: Operand, address index, or branch target
rc$\langle 4..0 \rangle$:= IR$\langle 16..12 \rangle$: Second operand, conditional test, or shift count
c1$\langle 21..0 \rangle$:= IR$\langle 21..0 \rangle$: Long displacement field
c2$\langle 16..0 \rangle$:= IR$\langle 16..0 \rangle$: Short displacement or immediate field
c3$\langle 11..0 \rangle$:= IR$\langle 11..0 \rangle$: Count or modifier field

Branch Condition Format

cond := (c3$\langle 2..0 \rangle$=0 → 0:Never
   c3$\langle 2..0 \rangle$=1 → 1:   Always
   c3$\langle 2..0 \rangle$=2 → R[rc]=0: If register is zero
   c3$\langle 2..0 \rangle$=3 → R[rc]≠0: If register is nonzero
   c3$\langle 2..0 \rangle$=4 → R[rc]$\langle 31 \rangle$=0:If register is positive or zero
   c3$\langle 2..0 \rangle$=5 → R[rc]$\langle 31 \rangle$=1):If register is negative

Shift Count Format

n := ((c3$\langle 4..0 \rangle$=0) → R[rc]$\langle 4..0 \rangle$:Shift count is register or
   (c3$\langle 4..0 \rangle$≠0) → c3$\langle 4..0 \rangle$):   constant field of instruction

Effective Address Calculations

disp$\langle 31..0 \rangle$:= ((rb=0) → c2$\langle 16..0 \rangle$ {sign-extend}:Disp.
   (rb≠0) → R[rb] + c2$\langle 16..0 \rangle$ {sign-extend, 2's complement}):Addr.
rel$\langle 31..0 \rangle$:= PC$\langle 31..0 \rangle$ + c1$\langle 21..0 \rangle$ {sign-extend, 2's comp.}: Rel. addr.

Instruction Interpretation

instruction_interpretation :=

$(\neg \text{Run} \wedge \text{Strt} \rightarrow (\text{Run} \leftarrow 1: \text{PC}, \text{R}[0..31] \leftarrow 0;$ Hard reset
     instruction_interpretation):

$\text{Run} \wedge \text{Rst} \rightarrow (\text{Rst} \leftarrow 0: \text{IE} \leftarrow 0: \text{PC} \leftarrow 0;$ Soft reset
     instruction_interpretation):

$\text{Run} \wedge \neg \text{Rst} \wedge (\text{ireq} \wedge \text{IE}) \rightarrow (\text{IPC} \leftarrow \text{PC}\langle 31..0\rangle:$ Interrupt
     $\text{II}\langle 15..0\rangle \leftarrow \text{Isrc\_info}\langle 15..0\rangle:$
     $\text{IE} \leftarrow 0: \text{PC} \leftarrow \text{Ivect}\langle 31..0\rangle:$
     $\text{iack} \leftarrow 1; \text{iack} \leftarrow 0;$
     instruction_interpretation):

$\text{Run} \wedge \neg \text{Rst} \wedge \neg (\text{ireq} \wedge \text{IE}) \rightarrow (\text{IR} \leftarrow \text{M}[\text{PC}]:$ Normal fetch
     $\text{PC} \leftarrow \text{PC} + 4;$ instruction_execution)):

Instruction Execution

instruction_execution := (

Load and Store Instructions

$\text{ld} (:= \text{op} = 1) \rightarrow \text{R}[\text{ra}] \leftarrow \text{M}[\text{disp}]:$ Load register
$\text{ldr} (:= \text{op} = 2) \rightarrow \text{R}[\text{ra}] \leftarrow \text{M}[\text{rel}]:$ Load register relative
$\text{st} (:= \text{op} = 3) \rightarrow \text{M}[\text{disp}] \leftarrow \text{R}[\text{ra}]:$ Store register
$\text{str} (:= \text{op} = 4) \rightarrow \text{M}[\text{rel}] \leftarrow \text{R}[\text{ra}]:$ Store register relative
$\text{la} (:= \text{op} = 5) \rightarrow \text{R}[\text{ra}] \leftarrow \text{disp}:$ Load displacement address
$\text{lar} (:= \text{op} = 6) \rightarrow \text{R}[\text{ra}] \leftarrow \text{rel}:$ Load relative address

Branch Instructions

$\text{br} (:= \text{op} = 8) \rightarrow (\text{cond} \rightarrow \text{PC} \leftarrow \text{R}[\text{rb}]):$ Cond. branch
$\text{brl} (:= \text{op} = 9) \rightarrow (\text{R}[\text{ra}] \leftarrow \text{PC}: \text{cond} \rightarrow (\text{PC} \leftarrow \text{R}[\text{rb}])):$ Branch and link

Arithmetic Instructions (Assumed to Be 2's Complement Arithmetic)

$\text{add} (:= \text{op} = 12) \rightarrow \text{R}[\text{ra}] \leftarrow \text{R}[\text{rb}] + \text{R}[\text{rc}]:$
$\text{addi} (:= \text{op} = 13) \rightarrow \text{R}[\text{ra}] \leftarrow \text{R}[\text{rb}] + \text{c2}\langle 16..0\rangle \{2\text{'s comp. sign-ext.}\}:$
$\text{sub} (:= \text{op} = 14) \rightarrow \text{R}[\text{ra}] \leftarrow \text{R}[\text{rb}] - \text{R}[\text{rc}]:$
$\text{neg} (:= \text{op} = 15) \rightarrow \text{R}[\text{ra}] \leftarrow - \text{R}[\text{rc}]:$
$\text{and} (:= \text{op} = 20) \rightarrow \text{R}[\text{ra}] \leftarrow \text{R}[\text{rb}] \wedge \text{R}[\text{rc}]:$
$\text{andi} (:= \text{op} = 21) \rightarrow \text{R}[\text{ra}] \leftarrow \text{R}[\text{rb}] \wedge \text{c2}\langle 16..0\rangle \{\text{sign-extend}\}:$
$\text{or} (:= \text{op} = 22) \rightarrow \text{R}[\text{ra}] \leftarrow \text{R}[\text{rb}] \vee \text{R}[\text{rc}]:$
$\text{ori} (:= \text{op} = 23) \rightarrow \text{R}[\text{ra}] \leftarrow \text{R}[\text{rb}] \vee \text{c2}\langle 16..0\rangle \{\text{sign-extend}\}:$
$\text{not} (:= \text{op} = 24) \rightarrow \text{R}[\text{ra}] \leftarrow \neg \text{R}[\text{rc}]:$

Shift Instructions

$\text{shr} (:= \text{op} = 26) \rightarrow \text{R}[\text{ra}]\langle 31..0\rangle \leftarrow (n @ 0) \# \text{R}[\text{rb}]\langle 31..n\rangle:$ Right
$\text{shra} (:= \text{op} = 27) \rightarrow \text{R}[\text{ra}]\langle 31..0\rangle \leftarrow (n @ \text{R}[\text{rb}]\langle 31\rangle) \# \text{R}[\text{rb}]\langle 31..n\rangle:$ Arithmetic
$\text{shl} (:= \text{op} = 28) \rightarrow \text{R}[\text{ra}]\langle 31..0\rangle \leftarrow \text{R}[\text{rb}]\langle 31 - n .. 0\rangle \# (n @ 0):$ Left
$\text{shc} (:= \text{op} = 29) \rightarrow \text{R}[\text{ra}]\langle 31..0\rangle \leftarrow \text{R}[\text{rb}]\langle 31 - n .. 0\rangle \# \text{R}[\text{rb}]\langle 31 .. 32 - n\rangle:$ Circular

Interrupt Instructions

een (:= op= 10) → (IE ← 1):   Exception enable
edi (:= op= 11) → (IE ← 0):   Exception disable
rfi (:= op= 30) → (PC ← IPC: IE ← 1):   Return from interrupt
svi (:= op= 16) →
       (R[ra]⟨15..0⟩ ← II⟨15..0⟩: R[rb] ← IPC⟨31..0⟩):   Save interrupt state
ri (:= op= 17) →
       (II⟨15..0⟩ ← R[ra]⟨15..0⟩ : IPC⟨31..0⟩ ← R[rb]):   Restore interrupt state

Miscellaneous Instructions

   nop (:= op= 0) → :   No operation
   stop (:= op= 31) → Run ← 0   Stop instruction
   );   End of instruction_execution
   instruction_interpretation.

B.4   Register Transfer Notation—RTN

←	Register transfer: register on LHS stores value from RHS
[ ]	Word index: selects word or range from a named memory
⟨ ⟩	Bit index: selects bit or bit range from named register
n..m	Index range: from left index n to right index m; can be decreasing
→	If-then: true condition on left yields value and/or action on right
:=	Definition: text substitution with dummy variables
#	Concatenation: bits on right appended to bits on left
:	Parallel separator: actions or evaluations carried out simultaneously
;	Sequential separator: RHS evaluated and/or performed after LHS
@	Replication: LHS repetitions of RHS are concatenated
{ }	Operation modifier: information about preceding operation, e.g., arithmetic type
( )	Operation or value grouping: arbitrary nesting; used with operators or separators
$= \neq < \leq > \geq$	Comparison operators: produce 0 or 1 (true or false) logical value
$+ - \times \div$	Arithmetic operators: also $\lceil \rceil, \lfloor \rfloor$, and mod
$\wedge \vee \neg \oplus \equiv$	Logical operators: and, or, not, exclusive or, equivalence

Notes: Expressions can be values and/or actions. Actions can be considered side effects if a value is present. A list of conditional expressions need not have disjoint conditions. Right-hand sides (RHS) of conditionals are evaluated for all conditions that are true. No sequencing is implied unless there are sequential separators between conditional expressions. There is no *else* equivalent. LHS means left-hand side.

B.5   SRC Assembly Language Conventions

Certain SRC assembly language conventions have been assumed in presenting examples of SRC code. They are listed in Tables B.1 and B.2 along with a summary of SRC instructions and their assembly language forms.

A line of SRC assembly code has the following form:

Label: opcode   operands   ;comments.

The label and its associated colon may be missing. The opcode field contains either a machine instruction mnemonic of a few lowercase letters or an assembler pseudo-operation that begins with a period. The pseudo-operations used are summarized in Table B.1.

Values are assumed to be decimal unless terminated by B (binary) or preceded by 0x (hexadecimal).

Instruction operands contain register specifiers and constants. Registers are listed separated by commas in the order in which their specifier fields appear from left to right in the machine language instruction. Constants appear last, with the exception of those in displacement addresses. The displacement address r3+12 is written in assembly language as 12(r3). Displacement addresses only occur in loads and stores. A label appearing as an operand of a load or store assumes that the assembler will be able to compute a displacement or relative address for the label from its symbol table, and that the constant field will fit in the instruction field it must occupy.

SRC instruction mnemonics are summarized in Table B.1.

Table B.1 SRC Assembly Language Pseudo-Operations

.org	Value	Load the program starting at address Value.
.equ	Value	Define the Label symbol to be the constant Value.
.dc	Value [,Value]	Allocate memory words and set to the 32-bit Values.
.dcb	Value [,Value]	Allocate bytes and load them with the 8-bit Values.
.dch	Value [,Value]	Allocate halfwords and load with the 16-bit Values.
.db	Count	Allocate storage for Count bytes.
.dh	Count	Allocate storage for Count 16-bit halfwords.
.dw	Count	Allocate storage for Count 32-bit words.

Table B.2 SRC Instructions—Assembly Language Form

ld	ra, c2	Load from absolute address; rb is register 0.
ld	ra, c2(rb)	Load from displacement address.
ldr	ra, c1	Load from relative address.
st	ra, c2	Store into absolute address; rb is register 0.

Table B.2 SRC Instructions—Assembly Language Form (Continued)

st	ra, c2(rb)	Store into displacement address.
str	ra, c1	Store into relative address.
la	ra, c2	Load value of absolute address into ra; rb is register 0.
la	ra, c2(rb)	Load value of displacement address into ra.
lar	ra, c1	Load value of relative address into ra.
add	ra, rb, rc	Add rb to rc, and put result in ra.
addi	ra, rb, c2	Add rb to immediate constant, and put result in ra.
sub	ra, rb, rc	Subtract rc from rb, and put result in ra.
neg	ra, rc	Place 2's complement negative of rc into ra.
or	ra, rb, rc	OR rb and rc, and put result in ra.
ori	ra, rb, c2	OR rb and immediate constant, and put result in ra.
and	ra, rb, rc	AND rb and rc, and put result in ra.
andi	ra, rb, c2	AND rb and immediate constant, and put result in ra.
not	ra, rc	Place logical NOT of rc into ra.
shr	ra, rb, c3	Shift rb right into ra by constant shift count $c3 \le 31$.
shr	ra, rb, rc	Shift rb right into ra by count in rc; c3 is 0.
shra	ra, rb, c3	Shift rb right with sign-extend into ra by constant c3.
shra	ra, rb, rc	Shift rb right with sign-extend into ra by count in rc.
shl	ra, rb, c3	Shift rb left into ra by constant c3.
shl	ra, rb, rc	Shift rb left into ra by count in rc; c3 is 0.
shc	ra, rb, c3	Shift rb left circularly into ra by constant c3.
shc	ra, rb, rc	Shift rb left circularly into ra by count in rc; c3 is 0.
br	rb, rc, c3	Branch to target in rb if rc satisfies condition c3.
brl	ra,rb,rc,c3	Branch to rb if rc satisfies c3, and save PC in ra.
br	rb	Branch unconditionally to rb.
brl	ra, rb	Branch unconditionally to rb, and save PC in ra.
brlnv	ra	Do not branch, but save PC in ra.
brzr	rb, rc	Branch to rb if rc is zero.
brlzr	ra, rb, rc	Branch to rb if rc is zero, and save PC in ra.
brnz	rb, rc	Branch to rb if rc is nonzero.
brlnz	ra, rb, rc	Branch to rb if rc is nonzero, and save PC in ra.
brpl	rb, rc	Branch to rb if rc is positive or zero (sign is plus).
brlpl	ra, rb, rc	Branch to rb if rc is positive, and save PC in ra.
brmi	rb, rc	Branch to rb if rc is negative (sign is minus).
brlmi	ra, rb, rc	Branch to rb if rc is negative, and save PC in ra.

Table B.2 SRC Instructions—Assembly Language Form (Continued)

nop		No operation. Used to insert pipeline bubble.
stop		Set Run to zero, halting the machine.
een		Exception enable. Set overall exception enable bit.
edi		Exception disable. Clear overall exception enable.
rfi		Return from interrupt. PC ←IPC; enable exceptions.
svi	ra, rb	Save II and IPC in ra and rb, respectively.
ri	ra, rb	Restore II and IPC from ra and rb, respectively.

Assembly and Assemblers

This appendix begins by defining assemblers and their capabilities. We first examine these capabilities in detail and then discuss the structure of assembly language. We then explore the assembly process, considering the more-or-less standard "two-pass assembler," that is, an assembler that makes two passes over the assembly program text.

C.1   What Is an Assembler?

Let us first consider what the assembler is, and how it fits into the overall program development picture. To put it briefly, an assembler is a program that accepts assembly language as input and provides binary machine language as output. Assemblers were among the first "software tools" developed, shortly after the stored program computer itself was invented. The development of the assembler at such an early stage in the history of computing shows, if nothing else, a strong motivation on the part of machine language programmers to be rid of the sheer drudgery of programming in binary.

C.1.1   ASSEMBLY AS PART OF PROGRAM DEVELOPMENT AND EXECUTION

To expand on the preceding definition, the assembler is one component used in the program development process. Modern software engineering encompasses not just programming, but requirements analysis, user interface design, design for testability and maintainability, and much more. In this Appendix, however, we will only discuss assembly language programming and briefly describe how the assembler fits into the programming effort. We begin with a slight digression to consider the stepwise phases of assembly language program development and execution. Figure C.1 shows these steps. The left side of the figure shows the *epoch,* or time period, at which each step in the overall process takes place. We use the term *epoch* in the sense of its definition as "a particular period of time marked by distinctive features," rather than its definition as marking a geological time period, though the programmer stuck on a particularly hard-to-find bug may relate to the second definition as well.

assemble time

machine language
module

start symbol

public symbols
external symbols

The first step in the process is to develop the assembly program text. At *assemble time,* this text is input to the assembler, which passes over it, emitting a program listing and, if there are no errors, a binary machine language module. The module must contain information about where the program or module is to be loaded in memory, and if it contains the starting address of the program, this *start symbol* must also be made known. If the module is to be linked with other separately assembled modules, then it must also contain additional linkage information. This would include the addresses of any labels that must be visible to other separately assembled modules, *public symbols,* and the locations of symbols that are defined in other modules, *external symbols.*

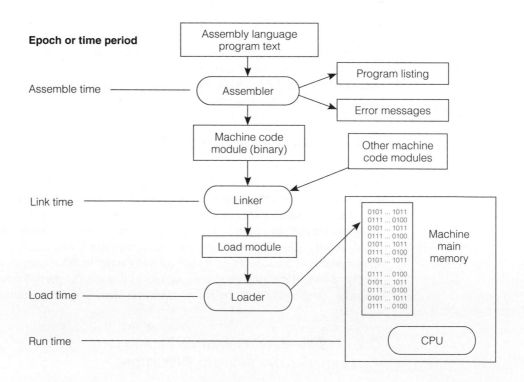

Fig. C.1 Time Periods of the Various Processes in Program Development

At *link time,* separately assembled modules are combined into one single *load module* by the *linker.* The linker will also add any required initialization or finalization code to allow the operating system to start the program running and to return control to the operating system after the program has completed. Most linkers allow assembly language modules to be linked with machine code modules compiled from high-level languages as well. This allows the programmer to insert a time-critical assembly language routine into a program written in a higher-level language.

At *load time,* the program *loader* copies the program into the computer's main memory, and at *run time,* program execution begins. These latter two operations, loading and initiation of program execution, are normally done by the operating system in response to a user request, typically by invoking the program's name.

The rest of the Appendix focuses on assembly, the first of these processes.

link time
load module

linker

load time
loader
run time

C.1.2   CAPABILITIES OF THE ASSEMBLER

Assemblers provide most of the following capabilities:[1]

1. Access to all the machine's resources by the assembled program. This includes access to the entire instruction set of the machine.
2. A means for specifying run-time locations of program and data in memory.
3. Provide symbolic labels for the representation of constants and addresses.
4. Perform assemble-time arithmetic.
5. Provide for the use of any synthetic instructions.
6. Emit machine code in a form that can be loaded and executed.
7. Report syntax errors and provide program listings.
8. Provide an interface to the module linkers and program loader.
9. Expand programmer-defined macro routines.

C.2   Assembly Language Structure

In this section we discuss the structure of assembly language statements and the use of *pseudo-operations*—that is, operations that are not machine instructions, but instructions to the assembler.

pseudo-operations

C.2.1   ASSEMBLY LANGUAGE SYNTAX

Although each assembler has its own unique syntactical structure, such as requiring uppercase or lowercase, or requiring colons after label definitions, there are some common features that assemblers share.

When preparing an assembly language program, the assembly text is usually divided into fields, separated by spaces or tabs. Here is the format of a typical line from an assembly language program:

---

1   One occasionally encounters "stripped-down" assemblers that provide only the first three capabilities. These are usually referred to as "mini-assemblers."

Label   OPCODE   Op1, Op2, . . .   ;Comment field

label field

opcode field
operand field

comment field

The first field, which is optional, is the *label field,* used to specify symbolic labels and constants. Some assemblers require labels to end with a colon, as in the SRC assembler, for example. The second field is the *opcode field,* and the third and following fields are *operand fields,* usually comma-separated. Some assembly languages mandate uppercase for opcodes and operands, as in the MC68000, and others use lowercase, as in the SRC. The *comment field* begins with a delimiter such as the semicolon and continues to the end of the line.

C.2.2   PSEUDO-OPERATIONS

assembler
directives

Some assembler capabilities, such as allowing the specification of memory locations for data and programs, are not part of the instruction set; rather, they are instructions to the assembler, linker, and loader. They are sometimes referred to as pseudo-operations or as *assembler directives,* because they are instructions to the assembler, and they do not result in any code being directly generated.

There are many specialized assembler directives; the most common are those that allow the definition of a symbolic constant, fix a memory location, reserve memory, and reserve and initialize memory. Table C.1 shows examples of these directives as implemented in the SRC assembler. Note that equ is an abbreviation for "equate," org for "origin," dw, dh, and db for define word, define halfword, and define byte, respectively, and dc, dch, and dcb for define constant word, halfword, and byte, respectively. Other assemblers provide equivalent capability, but may have slightly different syntax. The VAX11, for example, uses .equ, .org, .byte. word, and .long, and the MC68000 uses EQU, ORG, DS.B, DS.W, and DS.L. Many assemblers distinguish pseudo-ops from normal opcodes by beginning all pseudo-ops with a leading dot, "." as both SRC and the VAX do.

We next discuss an SRC assembly language program that computes the Fibonacci series as an example of assemblers and assembly.

An Example Assembly Language Program and Program Listing.   Consider the example program, Fib.asm, shown in Figure C.2. Fib.asm is a less optimized version of the Fibonacci program shown in Chapter 2. We will first go through the assembly source text, line by line, and then we will examine the listing produced by the SRC assembler.

- Lines 1–4 are comments that describe what the program does. It is considered essential to document programs in this way.
- Lines 5–9 contain not assembly language statements, but assembler directives:
- Line 5, cnt: .equ 8, sets the symbol cnt to the value 8 for the duration of the assembly process. This value 8 represents the number of additional series members to compute after the first two and will be used both to reserve storage and to specify the number to compute. Thus if the programmer wishes to change the number of members to compute, that number need be changed in only one place. Note that equates do not reserve storage, and disappear after assembly.
- Lines 6–8 are pseudo-ops that reserve and initialize storage for the series.
- Line 6, .org 0, specifies that assembly should begin at location 0.

Table C.1 Typical Assembler Directives

Directive Type	Example			Action
Define a symbolic constant	NOV	.equ	11	Set the symbol NOV equal to the constant 11.
	MAY	.equ	"May"	Set the symbol MAY equal to the string "May".
	Size	.equ	10	Set the symbol Size equal to the constant 10.
Fix a memory location	Start	.org	0x2000	Fix the location at which the following program or data word will load to 2000_{16}.
	main:	ld r0, Size		Begin program execution at this location.
Reserve a block of storage	Array:	.dcb	20	Reserve space for 20 bytes. Base address is Array.
	Harray:	.dch	Size	Reserve space for 10 halfwords. Base address is Harray.
	Warray	.dc	20	Reserve space for 20 words. Base address is Warray.
Initialize memory location(s)	Minus1:	.dch	0xffff	Reserve a halfword at location Minus1; initialize it to the hexadecimal value ffff.
	Colors:	.dc 0, 1, 2, 3		Reserve space at location Colors for 4 words, and initialize them to 0, 1, 2, and 3.
	Hi	.dcb	"Hello"	Reserve space at location Hi for 5 bytes; init. to 'Hello'
Describe[†] module linkage	Out:	...	PUBLIC	Make the value of Out available to the linker for linkage to other assembled modules.
	... Val EXTERN			The value of Val is defined externally in another module.

†Not available in SRC, but available in production assemblers.

```
; fib.asm. Compute Fibonacci numbers.
; The Fibonacci sequence is defined as follows:
; fib(1) = 1, fib(2) = 1,
; fib(n) = fib(n-1) + fib(n-2) n > 2.
cnt:    .equ 8           ; No. to compute after first two
        .org 0           ; Store sequence at addr. 0
seq:    .dc 1, 1         ; Init. the first two Fib. Nos.
        .dw cnt          ; Storage for the next 8 Fib. Nos.
        .org 0x1000      ; Begin ass'y. at hex. addr. 1000
main:   lar r31, loop    ; Pgm start. Init. branch address
        la r0, cnt       ; Init. count
        la r1, 0         ; Init r1 to index of seq[0]
        la r2, 4         ; Init r2 to index of seq[1]
loop:   ld r3, seq(r1)   ; Get fib(n-2)
        addi r1, r1, 4   ; Increment index
        ld r4, seq(r1)   ; Get fib(n-1)
        add r3, r3, r4   ; compute fib(n)
        addi r2, r2, 4   ; fib(n) = fib(n-1) + fib(n-2)
        st r3, seq(r2)   ; Store fib(n)
        addi r0, r0, -1; Decrement count
        brnz r31, r0     ; loop untill done
        stop
```

Fig. C.2 An Example Assembly Language Program

■ Line 7, `.dc 1, 1`, reserves two words of storage for the first two members of the series, beginning at the symbolic location seq, and initializes them both to 1.

■ Line 8, `.dw cnt`, reserves cnt additional words for members of the series, but does not initialze them. The assembler will substitute the value of cnt, 8, in the assembled program. The program will compute the 8 additional series members and store them in these locations.

■ Line 9, `.org 0x1000`, specifies that assembly of the program itself should begin at hexadecimal address 1000.

■ On line 10, the keyword label `main` is an instruction to the assembler to generate code in the binary file to initialize the PC to location 1000 at program loading time.

■ Lines 11–22 contain the assembly language code that computes the series members and stores them in the array seq. It begins by initializing r31 to the branch address, loop. It then loads cnt and the starting indices of the two elements to be summed into r0, r1, and r2 respectively.

■ Line 14 begins the main program loop. This loop steps through the array, summing the two preceding elements and storing the result as the current element. The program ends the stop instruction.

The listing file generated by the assembler, fib.lst, shown in Figure C.3, is similar to most assembly language listing files. It repeats the original program text, but also adds the address and value of all objects to be loaded into memory at load time. This includes both

```
*****SRC Assembler***** (SRCTools Version 2.1.0)

HexLoc      DecLoc      MachWord   Label     Source Code          Comments
00000000    0000000000  00000000             ; fib.asm. Compute Fibonacci numbers.
00000000    0000000000  00000000             ; The Fibonacci sequence is defined as follows:
00000000    0000000000  00000000             ; fib(1) = 1, fib(2) = 1,
00000000    0000000000  00000000             ; fib(n) = fib(n-1) + fib(n-2) n > 2.
00000000    0000000000  00000000   cnt:      .equ 8          ; No. to compute after first two
00000000    0000000000  00000000             .org 0          ; Store sequence at addr. 0
00000000    0000000000  00000001   seq:      .dc 1           ; Init the first two numbers
00000004    0000000004  00000001             .dc 1           ;
00000008    0000000008  00000000             .dw cnt         ; Storage for the next 8 Fib. Nos.
00000028    0000000040  00000000             .org 0x1000     ; Begin ass'y. at hex. addr. 1000
00001000    0000004096  37c0000c   main:     lar r31, loop   ; Pgm start: init branch address
00001004    0000004100  28000008             la r0, cnt      ; Init. count
00001008    0000004104  28400000             la r1, 0        ; Init r1 to index of seq[0]
0000100c    0000004108  28800004             la r2, 4        ; Init r2 to index of seq[1]
00001010    0000004112  08c20000   loop:     ld r3, seq(r1)  ; Get fib(n-2)
00001014    0000004116  68420004             addi r1, r1, 4  ; Increment index
00001018    0000004120  09020000             ld r4, seq(r1)  ; Get fib(n-
1)
0000101c    0000004124  60c64000             add r3, r3, r4  ; compute fib(n)
00001020    0000004128  68840004             addi r2, r2, 4  ; fib(n) = fib(n-1) + fib(n-2)
00001024    0000004132  18c40000             st r3, seq(r2)  ; Store fib(n)
00001028    0000004136  6801ffff             addi r0, r0, -1 ; Decrement count
0000102c    0000004140  403e0003             brnz r31, r0    ; loop untill done
00001030    0000004144  f8000000             stop
```

Fig. C.3 Assembler Listing File, fib.lst, Generated from the Program fib.asm data values and machine code. The first two columns specify, in hexadecimal and decimal representations, the address at which each data item or instruction will be loaded. The MachWord column shows the assembled code that will be loaded at the address specified by the first column. The Addr column shows the actual address of any branch targets. There follows the original assembly language source text and any comment. Any error or warning messages are also included in the listing.

C.3   Tasks of the Assembler

During the process of assembling a program, the assembler must pass over the text, resolve all symbols to their numeric values, and convert the assembly language text to binary machine code.

The Symbol Table.   As the assembler is passing over the assembly language text, it will encounter programmer-defined symbols. These symbols may represent labels or defined constants, or other entities. The assembler manipulates these symbols by means of its *symbol table*. At its simplest, the symbol table maps symbols to their defined values, records the state of the definition, and perhaps records the type of symbol—float or int, for example. In the preceding program, for example, the symbol cnt is mapped to the value 8 in the symbol table.

symbol table

  The modern production assembler may encounter many thousands of symbols during the assembly process, especially in machine-generated programs. In this case the symbol table must be implemented so that access operations are fast and not so dependent on program size. Generally this involves providing an access key when the symbol is first encountered, by which it can be retrieved later. Consider the state of the symbol table describing the fib program shown in Figure C.3 just as the assembler encounters the instruction at address 0x1008. The defining occurrences of the strings "cnt," "seq," and "main" have been encountered, and their definitions entered into the table. On the other hand, the string string "loop" was encountered as an applied occurrence without a defining occurrence.

Table C.2 Snapshot of the Symbol Table of Figure C.3 During Pass 1 at Address 0x1008

Key	Symbol	Type	Value	Defined
0	"cnt"	constant	8	defined
1	"seq"	label	00000000	defined
2	"main"	label	00001000	defined
3	"loop"	unknown		undefined

The elements of the **Type** field will depend upon the particular assembler, but most assemblers will have at least the following types:

Type {Integer, Float, Label, External, Public, Unknown}

The **Defined** field is used to record the status of symbol definitions. Its values may include

Defined {undefined, defined, multiply_defined}.

During the assembler's second pass, discussed in the following paragraphs, it will check for undefined or multiply defined symbols, and flag them as errors.

The assembler converts the assembly language instructions to machine language by a process similar to pattern matching. It maintains a table of instructions and their corresponding binary encoding, and as each instruction is encountered, it is matched against the instruction patterns in its instruction tables. This matching may occur when the line is originally parsed, or later as the line is being processed. Once a match is encountered, the assembler is able to assemble the instruction to its corresponding machine code.

Examining the preceding list, you can see that each instruction and data value is matched to an address at which it will be assembled. This means that as the assembler marches down the program text, it must associate every instruction and data value with an address. It does so by maintaining a counter called the *location counter,* which is the assemble-time equivalent of the program counter. You should understand clearly the difference between the location counter and the program counter—the location counter exists only at assemble time, and the program counter exists only during run time.

location counter

The assembler initializes the location counter to 0 before it begins the assembly process. Then, as it encounters instructions or data reservation directives, it increments the location counter appropriately. When it encounters an ORG directive, it sets the location counter to the value specified by the ORG directive.

A complication occurs in the use of symbolic addresses, however, and it arises due to forward branches. When a forward branch is encountered, the branch target label is not yet in the assembler's symbol table, since the defining occurrence of the label is farther down in the program text. Thus the assembler has no way of computing the value to be stored as the branch target offset. The best it can do is to enter the label in its symbol table as having an unknown value. When the label definition is encountered later in the program text, its value is entered in the symbol table. This means that the assembler must go back and "fix up" any unknown branch targets after it has passed over the text the first time.

A further complication occurs in instruction sets that have short and long versions of instructions. The MC68000 has several kinds of branches and immediate instructions, depending on the value of the branch target or immediate value. For example, the BSR instruction can occupy one or two words depending on whether the branch target can be represented as a byte or whether it must be represented by a word. In the case of a forward branch, the assembler will not know the value of the target offset, which means it cannot know whether to generate the long form or the short form of the branch. In this case, the assembler generally takes a pessimistic view and leaves space for the long branch. If it turns out the branch is a short one, the assembler may either take the lazy approach and insert a NOP instruction in place of the branch target word, or it may again "fix up" the assembly code by adjusting the addresses of the instructions following it.

The Two-Pass Assembler—First Pass. One way of dealing with the complications introduced by forward branches and instructions that can have several sizes is to use a *two-pass assembler,* which makes a first pass over the program text to define the values of all symbols and the identities and lengths of all instructions. When the assembler encounters a symbol that is not in its symbol table, it enters the symbol into the table. If the symbol is associated with a value, as in the case of an EQU, then the value is stored in the table. Likewise, if the symbol is a label definition, that is, a label to the left of an instruction, then the value of the location counter is stored in the symbol table as the value of the label. Since assemblers do not require definition before use, the assembler may encounter a label used as a branch target or operand prior to its definition. In this case, the assembler enters the symbol in the symbol table with the value "undefined." The assembler also examines opcodes and operands for a match to patterns stored in its instruction table. At the end of the first pass, if any instruction patterns are unrecognized, or if its symbol table contains multiply defined or undefined symbols, the assembler signals a syntax error, generates a listing with errors reported, and exits.

two-pass assembler

The Two-Pass Assembler—Second Pass. If there are no errors, the assembler passes over the program text a second time, line by line. If the line contains an instruction, then the binary pattern corresponding to the instruction encoding is inserted in the growing machine language program. At each line the assembler "resolves" symbolic references by replacing them with their associated values. At this time the assembler may need to perform arithmetic on branch target references to compute the branch offset. It is at this point that the "fix-ups" described earlier are performed. If the line contains a data initialization directive such as DC.W, then the assembler must insert the proper value as a constant to be loaded at that address. The assembler completes the process by inserting linkage information such as the values of public and external symbols, and the value of the program start symbol.

Key Concepts: The Assembler

- Assemblers were one of the first "software tools" developed, in response to the error-prone and laborious process of converting an algorithm to a series of 1s and 0s for entry into the computer.

- The assembler allows the programmer to use easily remembered mnemonics for machine instructions in place of binary patterns.

- The assembler provides a means to reserve memory locations for data storage, to initialize these locations at program loading time, and to specify where the program should begin execution at run time.

- Nearly all assemblers allow the use of symbolic labels to refer to specified locations in the assembly code and to represent constants.

- Most assemblers and linkers allow small, separately assembled modules to be linked together, and to be linked with modules compiled from a high-level language.

Bibliography

The assembler and the assembly process, including symbolic addresses and subroutines, was developed by C. W. Adams and his research group at MIT, as described in:

C. W. Adams and J. H. Laning, Jr., *The M. I. T. Systems of Automatic Coding: Comprehensive Summer Session*, Office of Naval Research, Washington, DC, 1954.

A good description of early work in assemblers is also given in:

M. V. Wilkes, D. J. Wheeler, and S. Gill, *The Preparation of Programs for an Electronic Digital Computer*, Addison-Wesley, Reading, MA, 1951, 1957.

The history of assemblers and assembly languages is described in:

Jean E. Sammat, *Programming Languages: History and Fundamentals*, Prentice-Hall, Englewood Cliffs, NJ, 1969.

More recent treatments of assemblers and assembly language programming can be found in the following texts. The Gorsline text has several helpful flowcharts describing the two-pass assembly process.

John F. Wakerly, *Microcomputer Architecture and Programming. The 68000 Family,* John Wiley & Sons, New York, 1989.

G. W. Gorsline, *Assembly and Assemblers: the Motorola MC68000 Family,* Prentice-Hall, Englewood Cliffs, NJ, 1988.

A good short introduction to the assembly and loading process is also given in:

D. W. Barron, *Assemblers and Loaders*, 3rd ed., Elsevier Publishing, New York, 1978.

APPENDIX D
Selected Problems and Solutions

This Appendix contains a selection of typical, or classic problems that are encountered in the practice of computer design and architecture. We advise the student to not examine the solution to each problem until a solid attempt has been made to solve the problem.

CHAPTER 1

These first two exercises deal with conversion of memory capacity. Note that when dealing with memory capacity one uses powers of 2 rather than powers of 10.

1.1 The Intel 8086 processor addresses a maximum of 2^{20} bytes of memory. What is the maximum number of 16-bit words that can be stored in this memory? **(§1.2)**

SOLUTION: One byte = 8 bits, so a 16-bit word = 2 bytes. 2^{20} bytes of memory is equivalent to 2^{19} 16-bit words. In decimal this is about a half million words.

1.2 If a certain Motorola PPC601 has a system clock frequency of 100 MHz, what is the clock period? **(§1.2)**

SOLUTION: 100MHz is 100×10^6 clock cycles per second, so the period is 10^{-8}s = 10ns.

1.3 a) How many 100MB tapes will be required to back up a 9GB hard drive? b) How long will the backup process require if one tape can be filled in 5 minutes? (No coffee breaks allowed.) **(§1.2)**

This exercise requires an estimate of the time required to perform a certain operation. The dimensional analysis for part a) should yield a number of tapes, N, which is dimensionless, and for part b) it should yield time in the appropriate units:

$$N = \frac{GBytesInHardDrive}{MBytesInOneTape}$$

$$TimeInHours = \frac{N \times TimeInMinutes}{\frac{60 Minutes}{Hour}}$$

SOLUTION: There are 9×2^{30} B/disk and 100×2^{20} B/tape. Thus one needs about $9 \times 2^{30}/100 \times 2^{20}$ tapes/disk. This works out to 93 tapes. 93 tapes $\times$ 5 minutes/tape = 465 minutes = 7 hours 45 minutes.

1.4   If one printed character can be stored in 1 byte, approximately how many bytes will be required to store the text of this chapter? Do not include the graphics, and do not count the characters one by one. Show your work and state your assumptions.   **(§1.2)**

This exercise involves an activity which should be a commonplace not only in this field but in life in general: making an estimate from inherently inaccurate parameters. It recalls the famous Enrico Fermi question, "How many piano tuners are there in Chicago," the real meaning of which was that one can make a reasonable estimate of almost anything using reasonable guesses about the parameters of the problem.

SOLUTION: In manuscript form there are about 96 characters (including spaces and punctuation) in a full line of text. About 3/4 of a page is full lines on the average, and there are 29 pages in the chapter. A full page could contain 50 lines.

50 lines/page $\times$ 29 pages/chap $\times$ 75% $\times$ 96 char/line $\approx$ 34,800 char/chapter $\approx$ 35 KB.

CHAPTER 2

2.1   In the last two instructions of Table 2.2, which of the five items on page 40 are explicitly specified and which are implicit?   **(§2.2)**

It is important to recognize that every instruction must specify these five things, either explicitly or implicitly.

SOLUTION:

	DEC R2	SHL AX, 4
Operation to be performed	Explicit: DEC	Explicit: SHL
Location of first operand	Explicit: R2	Explicit: AX
Location of second operand	Implicit: minus 1	Explicit: 4
Place to store the result	Explicit: R2	Explicit: AX
Location of next instruction	Implicit: program counter	Implicit: program counter

2.2 Write the code to implement the expression A = (B + C)*(D + E) on 3-, 2-, 1-, and 0-address and general-register machines. In accordance with programming language practice, computing the expression should not change the values of its operands. **(§2.2)**

This exercise gives the student experience in coding arithmetic expressions using the various classes of machines. The student should note that all these examples use direct addressing to access the operands in stored memory at symbolic addresses A, B, C, D, and E. It may seem that the general register

SOLUTION: T is a memory location used as a temporary.

3-address	2-address	1-address	0-address	General register
ADD A, B, C	LOAD A, B	LDA A	PUSH D	load r1, B
ADD T, D, E	ADD A, C	ADD E	PUSH E	load r2, C
MPY A, A, T	LOAD T, D	STA T	ADD	load r3, D
	ADD T, E	LDA B	PUSH C	load r4, E
	MPY A, T	ADD C	PUSH B	add r0, r1, r2
		MPY T	ADD	add r5, r3, r4
		STA A	MPY	mpy r0, r0, r5
			POP A	stoe r0, A

2.3 Write an SRC program, squeeze.asm, that implements the "squeeze" function on the value stored at mem loc X:

```
if (X < 0) X = X + 1; else if (X > 0) X = X - 1;
```

SOLUTION:

```
; squeeze.asm
; Implements the "squeeze" function on the value stored at
    mem loc X:
; if (X < 0) X = X + 1; else if (X > 0) X = X - 1;
; vph 1/15/03
;
            .org 4096 ; Begin execution at 0x1000.
    Main:   lar r30, Minus ; Init label registers.
            lar r31,Done
            ld r0, X ; pick up a copy of the value to squeeze.
            brmi r30,r0 ; It's < 0. br to Minus
            brzr r31,r0 ; It's = 0. br to Done
            addi r0,r0,-1 ; It's > 0 so decr.
            br r31      ; Hop over to Done
    Minus:  addi r0,r0,1 ; <0 so incr.
    Done:   st r0, X ; Stash it away.
            stop
    space:  .dw 1      ; Leave some space between program and data.
    X:      .dc -9     ; The value to squeeze.
```

CHAPTER 3

3.1 A program contains the following instruction mix:
- 60% load/store instructions with execution time of 1.2 µs each
- 10% ALU instructions with execution time of 0.8 µs each
- 30% branch instructions with execution time of 1.0 µs each.   **(§3.1)**

a. If the clock period is 0.2 µs, calculate the average CPI for the program.

b. What is the average MIPS rate of the program?

These types of calculations permit the designer to estimate performance of a system by making estimates prior to actual construction of the system.

SOLUTION: a. CPI   = Average execution time of one instruction / clock period

$$= (0.6 \times 1.2 + 0.1 \times 0.8 + 0.3 \times 1.0) / 0.2$$

$$= 5.5 \text{ clock periods per instruction}$$

b. Average MIPS rate $= 1 / (\text{CPI} \times \text{clock period} \times 10^6)$

$$= 1 / (5.5 \times 0.2 \times 10^{-6} \times 10^6) = 0.909 \text{ MIPS}$$

3.2 In each of the following lines of MC68000 code, what value will be in the destination after execution of each instruction? Also what addressing modes were used? The following conditions apply:

A0 = 0x2000, M[0x2000] = 0xAAAA, M[0x1FFE] = 0x5555.   **(§3.3)**

a.	MOVE.W	#'BE', D0
b.	MOVE.L	#0xFFE07DCA, (A0)
c.	MOVE.W	A0, D0
d.	MOVE.W	-(A0), D0

SOLUTION:

	Value of destination	**Addressing modes**
a.	D0 = 0x4245	Immediate, Data register direct
b.	Ml[0x2000] = 0x0FFE07DCA	Immediate, Address register indirect
c.	D0 = 0x2000	Address register direct, Data register indirect
d.	D0 = 0x5555	Autodecrement, Data register direct

3.3 Generate hexadecimal machine code for the following MC68000 instructions. **(§3.3)**

a.	MOVE.L	(A2), D4
b.	MOVE.W	2AH(A3, D6), D1
c.	ADD.L	A5, D6
d.	ROL	#3, D4
e.	BGT	-24

SOLUTION: a. 0x2812 b. 0x3233, 0x682A   c. 0x0DC8D

d. 0x0E75C   e. 0x6EE8

CHAPTER 4

4.1 Write concrete RTN steps for the SRC instructions ldr and lar using the 1-bus SRC microarchitecture of Section 4.2.   **(§4.2)**

SOLUTION: a. ldr

Step	RTN
T0.	$MA \leftarrow PC: C \leftarrow PC+4;$
T1.	$MD \leftarrow M[MA]: PC \leftarrow C;$
T2.	$IR \leftarrow MD;$
T3.	$A \leftarrow PC;$
T4.	$C \leftarrow A + c1 \ \{sign\ extend\};$
T5.	$MA \leftarrow C;$
T6.	$MD \leftarrow M[MA];$
T7.	$R[ra] \leftarrow MD;$

b. lar

Step	RTN
T0-T4.	same as ldr
T5.	$R[ra] \leftarrow C;$

4.2 Using Tables 4.6 to 4.11, develop as much as you can of the control signals MA_{in}, C_{out}, and INC4. Show both the Boolean equations and the gate-level designs.   **(§4.5)**

SOLUTION: $MA_{in} = T0 + T5 \cdot ld + \dots$

$C_{out} = T0 + T4 \cdot (add + addi + ld) + T5 \cdot shr + T6 \cdot shr \ (n \neq 0) + \dots$

$INC4 = T0 + \dots$

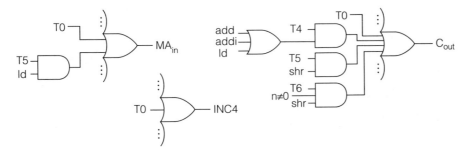

4.3 Write concrete RTN steps and control sequences for the brl instruction implemented in the 1-bus microarchitecture.   **(§4.4)**

SOLUTION:

Step	RTN	Control sequence
T0.	$MA \leftarrow PC: C \leftarrow PC+4;$	PC_{out}, MA_{in}, INC4, C_{in}
T1.	$MD \leftarrow M[MA]: PC \leftarrow C;$	C_{out}, PC_{in}, Read, Wait
T2.	$IR \leftarrow MD;$	MD_{out}, IR_{in}
T3.	$R[ra] \leftarrow PC;$	PC_{out}, Gra, R_{in}
T4.	$CON \leftarrow cond(R[rc]);$	Grc, R_{out}, CON_{in}
T5.	$CON \rightarrow PC \leftarrow R[rb];$	Grb, R_{out}, $CON \rightarrow PC_{in}$, End

CHAPTER 5

5.1 For the following pairs of SRC instructions:

Indicate how many bubbles must be placed between them in the presence of and in the absence of data forwarding to resolve the dependence. **(§5.1)**

1. ld   r2, (r4)
   add r6, r4, r2
	2. add r0, r2, r4
	   sub r6, r0, r0
		3. lar r31, -12
		   br r31

4. add r0, r2, r4
   st r0, 12(r2)
	5. add r0, r2, r4
	   st r2, 12(r0)
		6. br r31
		   addi r31,r31,-20

SOLUTION:

Condition	1.	2.	3.	4.	5.	6.
Staller	ld	add	lar	add	None	None
Stallee	add	sub	br	st	None	None
Hazard register	r2	r0	r31	r0	None	None
Bubbles without/with forwarding	3/1	3/0	3/1	3/0	0/0	0/0

5.2 The RTN in fragments 5.1 to 5.3 on pages 221–222 describes the hazard detection with bubble insertion for the 2-operand ALU-ALU instructions. Modify these equations to account for the 1-operand ALU instructions. **(§5.1)**

SOLUTION: The object is to detect 1-operand alu instructions in stage 2, and not to test for hazards on rb in those cases, since rb is undefined for 1-operand alu instructions. Provide a new name for 1-operand instructions, aluI:

$$\text{aluI} := \text{neg} \lor \text{not:} \qquad \qquad \text{;1-operand alu instructions.}$$

Modify the tests to detect when 1-operand instructions are in stage 2, and to not test for hazards to rb in that case:

$$\text{alu3} \land \text{alu2} \land (((\text{ra3} = \text{rb2}) \land \neg\text{aluI2}) \lor ((\text{ra3} = \text{rc2}) \land \neg\text{imm2}))$$
$$\rightarrow (\text{pause2: pause1: op3} \leftarrow 0):$$
$$\text{alu4} \land \text{alu2} \land (((\text{ra4} = \text{rb2}) \land \neg\text{aluI2}) \lor ((\text{ra4} = \text{rc2}) \land \neg\text{imm2}))$$
$$\rightarrow (\text{pause2: pause1: op3} \leftarrow 0):$$
$$\text{alu5} \land \text{alu2} \land (((\text{ra5} = \text{rb2}) \land \neg\text{aluI2}) \lor ((\text{ra5} = \text{rc2}) \land \neg\text{imm2}))$$
$$\rightarrow (\text{pause2: pause1: op3} \leftarrow 0):$$

CHAPTER 6

6.1 Convert the following decimal values to 8-bit sign-magnitude, 1's complement, 2's complement, and excess 127 representations:

a. 54   b. 127   c. −1   d. −12   e. −127   f. 0   **(§6.1)**

SOLUTION:

	Sign-magnitude	1's complement	2's complement	Excess 127
a. 54	00110110	00110110	00110110	10110101
b. 127	01111111	01111111	01111111	11111110
c. −1	10000001	11111110	11111111	01111110
d. −12	10001100	11110011	11110100	01110011
e. −127	11111111	10000000	10000001	00000000
f. 0	00000000	00000000	00000000	01111111

6.2 Convert the following hexadecimal values to 16-bit binary and octal representations:
   a. F0F0   b. 0A1B   c. 0123   d. A0B0   e. 88FF   (§6.1)

SOLUTION:

a. F0F0	1111000011110000_2	170360_8
b. 0A1B	0000101000011011_2	005033_8
c. 0123	0000000100100011_2	000443_8
d. A0B0	1010000010110000_2	120260_8
e. 88FF	1000100011111111_2	104377_8

What decimal value does the binary word 1010 1111 0101 0100 have when it represents an
   a. unsigned integer b. 1's complement integer c. 2's complement integer d. sign-magnitude integer   (§6.1)

SOLUTION: a. 44884_{10} b. -20651_{10} c. -20652_{10} d. -12116_{10}

6.3 Repeat Exercise 6.3 assuming the binary point is
   a. at the far left   b. in the middle.   (§6.1)

SOLUTION:

	a. Point at the far left	b. Point at the middle
Unsigned	0.6848754_{10}	175.32813_{10}
1's complement	-0.6302185_{10}	-80.667969_{10}
2's complement	-0.6302490_{10}	-80.671875_{10}
Sign-magnitude	-0.3697509_{10}	-47.328125_{10}

6.4 Perform the following additions assuming the values are unsigned, 1's complement, 2's complement, and excess 31. In each instance report overflow if it occurs.   (§6.2)

a.	b.	c.	d.
100 111 111 110	010 110 100 001	001 100 010 101	111 010 100 101

SOLUTION:

	Unsigned	1's complement	2's complement	Excess 31
a.	100 101 (ov)	100 110	100 101	000 110 (ov)
b.	110 111	110 111	110 111	011 000
c.	100 001	100 001 (ov)	100 001 (ov)	000 010
d.	011 111 (ov)	100 000	011 111 (ov)	000 000 (ov)

6.5 Repeat Exercise 6.4 but perform a. Unsigned multiplications. b. 2's complement multiplications. c. Divisions instead of additions.   (§6.2)

SOLUTION: a. and b.

a.   Unsigned multiplication

```
            1 0 0 1 1 1
            1 1 1 1 1 0
            _____
                      0
          1 0 0 1 1 1
        1 0 0 1 1 1
      1 0 0 1 1 1
    1 0 0 1 1 1
  1 0 0 1 1 1
  _____
  1 0 0 1 0 1 1 1 0 0 1 0
```

b.   2's complement multiplication

```
                    1 0 0 1 1 1
                    1 1 1 1 1 0
                    _____
                              0
      1 1 1 1 1 1 0 0 1 1 1
      1 1 1 1 1 0 0 1 1 1
      1 1 1 1 0 0 1 1 1
      1 1 1 0 0 1 1 1
      0 0 1 1 0 0 1
      _____
      0 0 0 0 0 0 1 1 0 0 1 0
```

Unsigned multiplication

b.	001 011 010 110
c.	000 011 111 100
d.	100 001 100 010

2's complement multiplication

110 101 010 110
000 011 111 100
000 010 111 101

c. Division

	Quotient	Remainder
a.	000 000	100 111
b.	000 000	010 110
c.	000 000	001 100
d.	000 001	010 101

6.6 Repeat Exercise 6.4 but perform multiplications using the following:

   a. Booth recoding. b. Bit-pair recoding   **(§6.2)**

SOLUTION:

	Booth recoding	**Bit-pair recoding**
a.	100111 0000$\bar1$0 ――――― 0 011001 ――――― 000000110010	10 01 11 00 00 $\bar1$0 ――――― 0110010 000000110010
b.	010110 $\bar1$0001$\bar1$ ――――― $\bar1$10101010110	01 01 10 $\bar1$0 00 01 ――――― 110101010110
c.	001100 1$\bar1$1$\bar1$11 ――――― 000011111100	00 11 00 01 0$\bar1$ 00 ――――― 000011111100
d.	111010 $\bar1$01$\bar1$1$\bar1$ ――――― 000010111101	11 10 10 $\bar1$0 01 01 ――――― 000010111101

6.7 You are stranded on a desert island with nothing but an SRC computer. Write the code fragment to run on SRC that implements "branch less than" on comparison of two signed 2's complement integers.   **(§6.3)**

SOLUTION: Table 6.6 gives the condition for "less than" as $N\bar V + \bar N V$, where N is the msb of the result, s_{m-1}. V is given as $x_{m-1}y_{m-1}\bar s_{m-1} + \bar x_{m-1}\bar y_{m-1}s_{m-1}$, but this is for an addition. For subtraction the y argument is complemented, giving
$V = x_{m-1}\bar y_{m-1}\bar s_{m-1} + \bar x_{m-1}y_{m-1}s_{m-1}$. So "x < y" $= N\bar V + \bar N V = x_{31}\bar y_{31} + $
$+ x_{31}s_{31} + y_{31}s_{31}$.
Assuming that x is in r1 and y is in r2:

	lar r30, lt	;the "true" jump target
	lar r31, done	;the exit jump target
	not r3, r2	;r3 msb has $\bar y_{31}$
	and r0, r1, r3	;r0 msb has $x_{31}\bar y_{31}$
	brmi r30, r0	;$x_{31}\bar y_{31}$ is true
	sub r6, r1, r2	;r6 msb is s_{31}
	and r0, r1, r6	;r0 msb has $x_{31}s_{31}$
	brmi r30, r0	;$x_{31}s_{31}$ is true
	and r0, r3, r6	;r0 msb has $\bar y_{31}s_{31}$
	brmi r30, r0	;$\bar y_{31}s_{31}$ is true
ge:	...	;code for not less than
	br r31	;exit the code
lt:	...	;code for less than
done:	...	;continue

6.8 Convert the following decimal numbers to IEEE single-precision floating-point numbers. Report the results as hexadecimal values. You need not extend the calculation of the significand value beyond its most significant 8 bits.   (§6.4)   a. −65   b. 7.3125   c. 0.8

SOLUTION: a. 0xC2820000   b. 0x40EA0000   c. 0x3F4C0000

6.9 Convert the following IEEE single-precision floating-point numbers to their decimal values. Report the answers to three significant figures. Use scientific notation if needed to maintain precision: (§6.4) a. 0x3FF0 0000   b. 0xC698 0000   c. 0xBD90 0000   d. 0x806A 0000

SOLUTION: a. $1.875 \times 2^0 = 1.875$ b. $-1.1875 \times 2^{14} = -1.9456 \times 10^4$
c. $-1.125 \times 2^{-4} = -7.03125 \times 10^{-2}$ d. $-0.828125 \times 2^{-126} = -9.73456 \times 10^{-39}$

CHAPTER 7

7.1 a. What is the memory layout of the 16-bit value, 0xABCD, in a big-endian 16-bit machine, and a little-endian 16-bit machine?

b. What would the layouts be in 32-bit machines?   (§7.1)

SOLUTION: a. 16-bit big-endian byte address contents, starting at address 0: 0xAB CD.
16-bit little-endian byte address contents, starting at address 0: 0xCD AB.
b. 32-bit big-endian byte address contents, starting at address 0: 0x00 00 AB CD.
32-bit little-endian byte address contents, starting at address 0: 0xCD AB 00 00.

7.2 What would the layout of the following data structure be in little-endian and big-endian machines?   (§7.1)

char   d[7];   /*'1','2','3','4','5','6','7'   byte array*/

SOLUTION: The storage will be the same in both cases, since the objects being stored are byte-sized. Thus the layout starting at the lowest address will be: 31 32 33 34 35 36 37.

7.3 A certain two-way set associative cache has an access time of 40 ns, compared to a miss time of 90 ns. Without the cache, main memory access time was 70 ns. Running a set of benchmarks with and without the cache indicated a speedup of 1.4. What is the approximate hit ratio?   (§7.5)

SOLUTION: Hit: $t_h = 40$ ns; miss: $t_m = 90$ ns; no cache: $t_n = 70$ ns. Access time with cache $t_a = h \cdot t_h + (1 - h)\, t_m = t_m - h(t_m - t_h)$. So speedup $S = \dfrac{t_n}{t_a} = \dfrac{70}{90 - 50h} = 1.4$, which gives $h = 80\%$.

7.4 A 16 MB main memory has a 32 KB direct-mapped cache with 8 bytes per line.   (§7.5)

a. How many lines are there in the cache?

b. Show how the main memory address is partitioned.

SOLUTION: a. Number of cache lines = $2^{15} / 2^3 = 2^{12}$ lines.

b.

23		15 14		3 2		0
	Tag		Group		Byte	

7.5 A certain memory system has a 32 MB main memory, and a 64 KB cache. Blocks are 16 bytes in size. Show the fields in a memory address if the cache is
   a. associative   b. direct-mapped   c. 8-way set-associative   (§7.5)

SOLUTION: A 32 MB memory requires a 25-bit address. A byte in the 64 KB cache is located by a 16-bit address. 4 bits select one byte from a 16-byte block.

   a. For an associative cache, a main memory address appears as:

24		4 3		0
	Tag		Byte	

   b. For a direct-mapped cache, a main memory address appears as:

24		16 15		4 3		0
	Tag		Group		Byte	

   c. For an 8-way set-associative cache, a main memory address appears as:

24		13 12		4 3		0
	Tag		Group		Byte	

CHAPTER 8

8.1 Add odd parity bits to each of the 7-bit ASCII characters in the string, "Pay attention!" Consult the chart on page 460 for the 7-bit ASCII codes.   (§8.5)

SOLUTION: The ASCII value of this character string is
   1010000 1100001 1111001 0100000 1100001 1110100 1110100 1100101
   1101110 1110100 1101001 1101111 1101110.
   Assume the parity bit is added to the left most:
   11010000 01100001 01111001 00100000 01100001 11110100 11110100
   11100101 01101110 11110100 11101001 11101111 01101110.
   So each number has odd number of "1" bits.

8.2 An 8 KByte block of data is read from a disk drive. What is the overall data transmission rate and time to transfer the block if the disk drive has a latency of 7 ms and a burst bandwidth of 32 MB/s?   (§8.1)

SOLUTION: Total time = 8K / 32M × 10^3 ms + 7 ms = 7.2 ms
   Overall transmission rate = 8KB / 7.2ms = 1.1 MB/s
   Note that in this case latency is the dominant factor in transmission time.

8.3 Use odd parity Hamming code to encode the following 4-bit values: 0110, 1001, 0000, 1111.   (**§8.5**)

SOLUTION: The encoding scheme is: $P_1P_2D_3P_4D_5D_6D_7$. Using odd parity,

$0110 \rightarrow 0001110$ $1001 \rightarrow 1110001$

$0000 \rightarrow 1101000$ $1111 \rightarrow 0010111$

8.4 Use SECDED coding to encode the following 4-bit values: 1011, 1100, 0101.   (**§8.5**)

SOLUTION: The encoding scheme is: $P_0P_1P_2D_3P_4D_5D_6D_7$. Using odd parity,

$1011 \rightarrow 01011011$

$1100 \rightarrow 01010100$

$0101 \rightarrow 11001101$

8.5 In the following SECDED-coded data, what is the number of data bits, how many bit errors are there, and what is the corrected value? Bit positions are numbered from zero at the left, and parity checks are odd.   (**§8.5**)

a. 1011 0101 1110 1011

b. 0001 1010 1110 1100

c. 0110 1010 1010 0111

SOLUTION: The encoding scheme is shown below. Note there are 11 data bits.

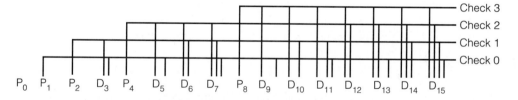

a. $c_3c_2c_1c_0$ is 1010, but P_0, the DED bit, is odd parity, so there must more than one error. This number cannot be corrected.

b. $c_3c_2c_1c_0$ is 0100, and P_0, the DED bit, is odd parity. There is an error in P_4. So the corrected value is 0001 1010 1110 1100, and the original value is 1001101100.

c. $c_3c_2c_1c_0$ is 0000, and P_0, the DED bit, is odd parity. So there is no error.

CHAPTER 9

9.1 A disk drive has eight surfaces, with 512 tracks per surface and a constant 64 sectors per track. Sector size is 1 K bytes. The average seek time is 8 ms, the track-to-track access time is 1.5 ms, and the drive runs at 3,600 rpm. Successive tracks in a cylinder can be read without head movement.

a. What is the drive capacity?

b. What is the average access time for the drive?

c. Estimate the time required to transfer a 5 MB file.

d. What is the burst transfer rate?   (**§9.1**)

SOLUTION: a. Capacity $= 8 \times 512 \times 64 \times 1\,K = 256\,MB$

b. Rotational latency = Rotation time/2 $= \dfrac{60}{3600 \times 2} = 8.3\,ms$

Average access time = Seek time + Rotational latency $= 8 + 8.3 = 16.3\,ms$

c. Assume this file is stored in successive sectors and tracks, starting at sector #0, track #0 of cylinder #i. A 5 MB file will need 1,000 blocks and will occupy from cylinder #i, track #0, sector #0, to, cylinder #($i+9$), track #6, sector #7. We also assume the size of disk buffer is unlimited.

The disk will need 8 ms, which is the seek time, to find the cylinder #i, 8.3 ms to find sector #0, and $8 \times (60 / 3600)$ seconds to read all 8 tracks' data of this cylinder. Then, the time needed for the head to move to next adjoining track will be only 1.5 ms, which is the track-to-track access time. Assume a rotational latency before each new track.

Access time =

$$8 + 9 \times (8.3 + 8 \times 16.6 + 1.5) + 8.3 + 6 \times 16.6 + \frac{8}{64} \times 16.6 = 1406.9\,ms$$

d. Burst rate =

$$\frac{revs}{sec} \times \frac{sectors}{rev} \times \frac{bytes}{sector} = \frac{3600}{60} \times 64 \times 1\,K = 3.84\,MB/s$$

9.2 An old floppy disk drive has a maximum areal bit density of 500 bits per mm^2. Its innermost track is at a radius of 2 cm, and its outermost track is at a radius of 5 cm. It rotates at 300 rpm.

a. What is the total capacity of the drive?

b. What is its burst data rate in bytes per second?   **(§9.1)**

SOLUTION: a. At the maximum areal density the bit spacing equals the track spacing, t, so $500 = 1/t^2$, or $t = 0.045$ mm. The number of tracks $= \dfrac{(50 - 20)}{0.045} = 666$. The number of bits / track $= \dfrac{40\pi}{0.045} = 2791$. Thus the unformatted, or raw, capacity is $666 \times 2791 = 1,841,400$ bits, or 232,360 bytes. Not exactly today's technology.

b. Given 5 revs per second, the burst rate is $\dfrac{revs}{second} \times \dfrac{bytes}{rev} = 5 \times \dfrac{2791}{8} = 1744$ bytes/sec.

9.3 A certain monitor has a 60 Hz refresh rate, and displays 132×64 dot matrix characters. Each character is on a 14×20 dot matrix, including intercharacter spacing.

a. What must the size of the display memory be?

b. What is the dot clock frequency?   **(§9.2)**

SOLUTION: a. Display memory is $132 \times 64 = 8448$ bytes. (It is a VDT. Data are stored as characters.)

b. Dot clock frequency $= 132 \times 64 \times 14 \times 20 \times 60 = 141.9264\,MHz$.

9.4 Estimate the data rate between a scanner and computer if the scanner is scanning a 300 dpi, full-page graphic. Assume the area scanned = 6.5×9 in^2, 24-bit color scan (3 bytes per pixel), with a scan time of 5 minutes per page. State any assumptions you have to make.   (**§9.3**)

SOLUTION: Example solution: active scan area = 6.5×9 in^2, 3 bytes per pixel, with a scan time of 5 minutes per page. (This is not unrealistic for inexpensive color scanners.)

$$\text{Data rate in Bytes/second } = \frac{6.5 \times 9 \times 300^2 \times 3}{5 \times 60 \times 1024} = 51.4 \text{ KB per second}$$

9.5 A certain digital automobile speed detector requires 5 mV accuracy on a 12 V, full-scale reading, and must be able to acquire 100 samples per second. Specify the ADC that will meet these requirements.   (**§9.5**)

SOLUTION: The ADC will need to resolve to .001/10 or 1 part in 10,000. This means at least 14 bits of precision. If a successive approximation converter is used, it will take 14 clocks to provide a sample. To provide at least 10 samples per second, the ADC will need to be clocked at 140 Hz.

CHAPTER 10

10.1 a. How many distinguishable signals must be capable of being sent per signal change in a 28,800 bps modem?

b. How many bits are effectively transmitted per signal change in this modem?   (**§10.2**)

SOLUTION: a. If we assume that the 28,800 bps modem is clocked at 2,400 baud, there must be 28,800/2,400 = 12 bits per baud. This means there must be 2^{12} or 4,096 distinguishable signals sent per baud.   b. 12 bits are sent per signal change.

10.2 A 28,800 bps modem is transmitting frames with 1 start bit, 7 data bits, a parity bit, and 1 stop bit. What is the maximum number of characters per second that can be transmitted?   (**§10.2**)

SOLUTION: There are 10 bits per frame, and one character per frame. 28,800/10 = 2,880 cps, assuming no data compression.

10.3 a. What is the raw data rate of a digital video signal with 512×512 1-bit pixels at 30 frames per second?

b. How many packets per second would be required to transmit the signal over a 10BASE-5 Ethernet link?

c. What percentage of the total bandwidth of the Ethernet LAN is consumed by this transmission, assuming no collisions, use of the entire data field, and a connectionless protocol?   (**§10.3**)

SOLUTION: a. $512 \times 512 \times 1 \times 30 = 7.862 \times 10^6$ bits per second

b. Number of packets $= \left\lceil \dfrac{7.862 \times 10^6}{1500 \times 8} \right\rceil = 655$ packets

c. % of the total bandwidth = $7.862 \times 10^6 / 9.83 \times 10^6 \times 100\% = 80\%$

10.4 a. How long would it take to transmit the contents of a 1-hour-long CD over a 10BASE-T Ethernet link, assuming that the full network bandwidth were available. Assume no collisions, use of the entire data field, and a connectionless protocol.

b. How many people could be listening to their own CD selection over this network simultaneously?   **(§10.3)**

SOLUTION: a. The CD's capacity is $44{,}100 \times 2 \times 16 \times 3{,}600 = 5.08 \times 10^9$. That will be $5.08 \times 10^9 / 9.83 \times 10^6 = 517$ seconds $= 8.6$ minutes   .

b. Each listener will require

$44{,}100 \times 2 \times 16 / 0.983 = 1.44$ Mb/s. $10/1.44 = 6.94$, or about six listeners could be listening to their CD selection over this net work simultaneously. Digital audio eats up the bandwidth.

10.5 The IP address of a certain machine is 112.123.241.195.

a. What class network does this machine belong to?

b. What is its network address?

c. What is the network mask?

d. What is the host ID?   **(§10.4)**

SOLUTION: a. 112 means it is a class A address.

b. Network address is thus 112.0.0.0.

c. The network mask is 255.0.0.0.

d. This host ID is 123.241.195.

10.6 Suppose that network 204.123.216.0 is subnetted using a 4-bit subnet mask.

a. How many host IDs can each subnet support?

b. How many subnets can it support?

c. What is the subnet address of machine 204.123.216.23?

d. What is its host ID?

e. What is its subnet mask?   **(§10.4)**

SOLUTION: a. This class C network has one octet available for host ID, and with a 4-bit subnet mask, this leaves 4 bits for identifying host IDs on each subnet. But all 0s and all 1s are reserved and cannot be used as host IDs, so there are 14 host IDs possible on each subnet.

b. The same holds for the number of subnets, $16 - 2 = 14$ subnets.

c. The final octet of machine 204.123.216.23 is 23, which is 00010111. With a 4-bit subnet mask, the machine's subnet address is 0001, or 1.

d. The host ID is 0111, or 7.

e. The subnet mask for this machine, and the entire network, is 255.255.255.(1111 0000b), which is 255.255.255.240.

Index

Numerics

A